Exploring Fiction

Writing and Thinking About Fiction

Frank Madden
SUNY Westchester Community College

Longman

New York   San Francisco   Boston
London   Toronto   Sydney   Tokyo   Singapore   Madrid
Mexico City   Munich   Paris   Cape Town   Hong Kong   Montreal

Senior Vice President and Editor-in-Chief: Joseph Terry
Acquisitions Editor: Erika Berg
Development Editor: Adam Beroud
Marketing Manager: Melanie Craig
Production Manager: Donna DeBenedictis
Project Coordination, Text Design, Art, and Electronic
    Page Makeup: Elm Street Publishing Services, Inc.
Cover Designer/Manager: John Callahan
Cover Illustration: "Flying People Holding Up Book" by Janet Atkinson,
    courtesy of the Stock Illustration Source, Inc.
Photo Researcher: Photosearch, Inc.
Senior Manufacturing Buyer: Dennis J. Para
Printer and Binder: Quebecor World–Taunton
Cover Printer: Phoenix Color Corp.

For permission to use copyrighted material, grateful acknowledgement is
made to the copyright holders on pp. 488–490, which are hereby made part of
this copyright page.

Library of Congress Cataloging-in-Publication Data

Madden, Frank
    Exploring fiction: writing and thinking about fiction / Frank Madden.
        p. cm.
    Includes index.
    ISBN 0-321-09051-9 (alk. paper)
    1. English language—Rhetoric—Problems, exercises, etc. 2. Fiction—
History and criticism—Problems, exercises, etc. 3. Criticism—Authorship—
Problems, exercises, etc. 4. College readers. I. Title.

PE1479.C7 M34 2002
808.3—dc21

                                                            2001038639

Please visit our website at http://www.ablongman.com/madden

ISBN 0-321-09051-9

1 2 3 4 5 6 7 8 9 10—WCT—04 03 02 01

*For my mother, Marguerite,
and in memory of
my father, John (1912–1974)*

છ

CONTENTS

PREFACE

We can ask of every assignment or method or text, no matter what its short-term effectiveness: Does it get in the way of the live sense of literature? Does it make literature something to be regurgitated, analyzed, categorized, or is it a means toward making literature a more personally meaningful and self-disciplined activity?

—*Louise Rosenblatt*, Literature as Exploration

At the heart of *Exploring Fiction* is a belief that literature can have an important impact on students' lives, but that this impact will be felt only when students experience the "live sense of literature"—the joy, the sorrow, the comfort, and the wisdom that fiction offers. Coupled with this belief is an acknowledgment that most students taking literature courses at colleges and universities in this country are not English majors. If asked why they are taking a literature course, they are likely to respond, "Because it's required." Or, "It fit my schedule." It is not evident to many students why literature is important. Other than completing the requirements for a course or curriculum, they don't know *why* they are reading it. Instruction in textual analysis and literary theory alone does not solve this problem. Students must have a stake in the process—a reason to care about literature. And they need the kind of support that will help them read with more confidence. It is the intention of this text to provide this support.

By encouraging students to see their reading in the light of their own experiences, the commentary, questions, and prompts in this book acknowledge the importance of their personal responses and authorize the "meaning making" role students play in the literary experience. The case study in this text expands this role further by helping students understand the relationship between the stories they read and the larger historical and cultural contexts from which the stories spring. Realizing their active role in this process gets students personally involved and gives them a reason to care about literature. Chapters on writing about fiction, critical thinking, and argumentation complete this experience by helping students understand that the construction of a coherent response is a process that changes with rereading and reflection—and that the quality of their interpretations is measured by the strength of the evidence they bring to support their interpretations.

Exploring Fiction is designed for instructors who believe, as I do, that a successful experience with fiction requires students' engagement as well as their analysis—not only as motivation to complete the requirements of a course but as a prelude to a lifelong relationship with literature.

KEY FEATURES

The key features of this text are intended to support an expansive process of engaging students in the literary experience. By exploring fiction as an "experience" within a world of personal responses and contextual influences, these features encourage students to invest their emotions, to build on their knowledge and experience, and to think critically—to be fully involved with the live sense of literature.

Making Connections

Confident, experienced readers tap their storehouse of emotional and intellectual knowledge naturally, and, when they draw a blank, feel confident that other elements of the sentence, paragraph, or entire work will allow them to make sense of it. Less experienced readers, however, need support and guidance to become confident readers. Questions and exercises in Part I, "Making Connections," are designed to "sensitize" students to the emotional context of fiction by encouraging them to recall their own experiences and to read stories "impressionistically" and with more confidence. This process does not guarantee a masterful analysis, but it does help students acknowledge and build on what they know and feel when they read, enabling them to connect with stories more easily. Acknowledging, reviewing, and thinking critically about the responses students make as they read may provide them with valuable insights into literature and themselves. These early chapters focus on the process of personal response as a starting point in a recursive sequence leading from engagement and reflection to formal critical tasks and literary interpretation—a journey from participating to observing responses.

Writing About Fiction

From journals to formal critical and research essays, students use writing to learn about fiction. The use of writing as the most important instructional tool in literature classes is well documented. Students who examine their own practices in reading and writing become more self-aware and more independent, stronger readers and writers.

Critical Thinking

Whether they are reviewing their own judgments or citing evidence to support a critical essay, students are encouraged to think critically about their responses throughout this book. Of special note is Chapter 4, "Argumentation: Interpreting and Evaluating Fiction," which focuses directly on the processes of critical thinking and argumentation. Explanations, examples, and exercises guide students through the processes of inductive reasoning and substantiation, interpretation and evaluation, and planning and supporting an argument. Issues of purpose, audience, and evidence are central to this discussion that culminates in the writing of a critical essay.

Two Readers, Two Choices

Two stories in Chapter 4, Alice Walker's "Everyday Use" and John Updike's "A & P," are highlighted and followed by two student essays written from different perspectives. These essays illustrate diversity of opinion, exemplify ways in which the stories might be read, and demonstrate how students' own experiences, behaviors, values, and opinions are tools for deepening their understanding and appreciation of fiction.

Samples of Student Writing

There are six student essays and many other samples of students' writing throughout the text.

The Stories

The stories in this book, a broad selection of both classic and contemporary pieces, have been chosen for their quality, diversity, and appeal to students.

A Case Study on Culture and Research

A case study, **"Thinking About Interpretation, Culture, and Research,"** invites students to see how literature, culture, and their own experiences may provide a rich context for research. A student writer describes his identification with the pull of family in James Joyce's short story "Eveline," and investigates conditions in Ireland that prompted the vast migration of the Irish. A narrative of the student's process precedes the final draft of his research essay.

Questions and Prompts

Questions throughout this book tap students' responses without implying right or wrong answers. They encourage students to reflect and evaluate. Prompts in this book help students flesh out, clarify, and support their responses and encourage students to ask their own questions—questions that open up, not shut down, additional possibilities. They respect the reader's role and encourage divergent responses but emphasize that the value of an assertion lies not in itself but in the nature of its supporting evidence.

Voice

The narrative "voice" of *Exploring Fiction* is informal and conversational. This textbook is intended to be read by students—to be accessible, friendly, and informative.

ORGANIZATION: USING THIS TEXT

Exploring Fiction can be used in many different ways. Its explanations, prompts, and stories are resources to be chosen by instructors and students as needed, in or out of sequence, with maximum flexibility. Although the reading and writing activities in this book are organized in a sequence of increasing complexity, the recursive nature of both writing and responding to fiction is emphasized throughout.

For instructors who want to emphasize a reader-response approach or have their students keep journals or write response essays about the stories they read, **Part I, "Making Connections,"** provides a rich source of material. These chapters are more than an exploration of fiction. They are an exploration of the students who read and write about it. Students are encouraged to think about the ways that their own backgrounds and personalities, their understanding of others, their knowledge of texts and contexts—their "meaning making" processes—influence their responses to stories. Questions that accompany the literature help students clarify their responses and develop them into text-supportable hypotheses and essays. **Chapter 1, "Participation: Personal Response and Critical Thinking,"** helps students develop connections to fiction through their own backgrounds and experiences. **Chapter 2, "Communication: Writing About Fiction,"** introduces students to aspects of literary craft through the chapter's discussions of voice, description, and comparison—fostering the sensitivity to language necessary for a complete experience with literature. The chapter concludes with a discussion of the writing process, samples of drafts, and a final response essay.

Instructors who favor a more text-based approach may choose to skip Part I and move directly to **Part II, "Analysis and Argumentation." Chapter 3, "Exploration and Analysis: The Elements of Fiction"** emphasizes the importance of close reading and analysis. A general introduction to fiction is followed by a comprehensive explanation of the elements that make fiction a distinct form. Carefully chosen literary selections illustrate and support these explanations. Wherever possible, explanations of the elements are illustrated with reference to students' experiences and are accompanied by specific examples from stories in the text.

Chapter 4, "Argumentation: Interpreting and Evaluating Fiction," guides students through the processes of critical thinking, reading, writing, and research. Students are reminded of the ways in which they use critical thinking in their own lives, and how similar methods of analysis and support can be used to interpret and evaluate fiction. Inductive thinking, substantiation, interpretation, and evaluation are explained and discussed. The use of argumentation to develop critical essays is presented and supported by student entries, giving students insights into how to develop their own ideas. Based on the elements discussed in Chapter 3, students are provided with questions, prompts, and checklists to help them develop standards. A comprehensive discussion of argumentation helps students see the difference between response and critical essays and suggests specific questions to ask when constructing an effective argument. The chapter concludes with a short story and two different student essays in response to the story.

Part III, "An Anthology of Fiction," offers students a broad range of alpha-betically-organized stories. The fiction has been chosen for its quality, diversity, and appeal to students. These stories represent both classic and contemporary literature.

Appendix A, "Critical Approaches to Literature," is a succinct discussion of major critical theories.

Appendix B, "Research and Documentation—Some Basics," explains what must be documented, discusses Internet sources and plagiarism, shows the physi-cal layout of a research essay, and gives the correct format for MLA documentation.

The **Glossary of Literary Terms** provides a useful reference tool.

SUPPLEMENTS

Exploring Literature **Website**   The *Exploring Literature* website can be found at http://www.ablongman.com/madden. This site includes in-depth informa-tion about featured authors, activities for writing about literature and helpful links to literature and research sites.

Audio- and Videotapes   For qualified adopters, an impressive selection of videotapes and Longman audiotapes is available to enrich students' experience of literature.

Penguin Program   In cooperation with Penguin Putnam Inc., one of Longman's sibling companies, we are proud to offer a variety of Penguin paperbacks at a significant discount when packaged with any Longman title. Excellent additions to any literature course, Penguin titles give students the opportunity to explore contemporary and classic fiction and drama. Available titles include works by authors as diverse as Julia Alvarez, Mary Shelley, Shakespeare, and Toni Morrison.

English Pages (http://www.ablongman.com/englishpages)   This website provides professors and students with continuously updated resources for reading, writing, and research practice in four areas: composition, literature, technical writing, and basic skills. Features include simulated searches, where students simulate the process of finding and evaluating information on the World Wide Web, and first-person essays that show students how everyday men and women have applied what they have learned in composition to a wide variety of writing issues and research topics.

The Longman Guide to Columbia Online Style   This 32-page booklet includes an overview of Columbia Online Style (COS), guidelines for finding and evaluating electronic sources, and examples for citing electronic sources. COS is a documentation style developed specifically for citing electronic sources.

The Longman Guide to Columbia Online Style is free when packaged with any Longman text. ISBN 0-321-06745-2

Analyzing Literature   This brief supplement provides critical reading strategies, writing advice, and sample student papers to help students interpret and discuss literary works in a variety of genres. Suggestions for collaborative activities and online research on literary topics are also featured, as are numerous exercises and writing assignments. ISBN 0-321-05504-7

Responding to Literature: A Writer's Journal   This free journal provides students with their own personal space for writing. Helpful writing prompts for responding to fiction, poetry, and drama are also included. ISBN 0-321-09542-1

Course Compass   **Course Compass** combines the strength of Longman content with state-of-the-art learning tools! **Course Compass** is a nationally hosted, dynamic, interactive online course management system powered by Blackboard, leaders in the development of Internet-based learning tools. This easy-to-use and customizable program enables professors to tailor content and functionality to meet individual needs! Every **Course Compass** course includes a range of pre-loaded content such as testing and assessment question tools, chapter-level objectives, chapter summaries, photos, illustrations, videos, animations, and Web activities—all designed to help students master core course objectives. For more information, or to see a demo, visit www.coursecompass.com, or contact your local Longman sales representative.

The Longman Journal for Creative Writing   This FREE journal is designed to help students explore and discover their own writing habits and styles. Various features are provided that will incite students to practice many forms of writing such as: freewriting, concrete and abstract description, exploring the past, and exploring dreams. In addition, there are numerous exercises and activities on a variety of topics including: poetic and prose forms, image, voice, character, plot, setting, sound and rhythm, and theme. A great deal of space is also provided for students to record their thoughts and ideas whenever the urge strikes. ISBN 0-321-09540-5

A Workshop Guide for Creative Writing   This laminated reference offers suggestions for students to keep in mind in a workshop situation—both as a participant and presenter. Blank space is provided for students to record additional guidelines provided by their instructor. ISBN 0-321-09539-1.

Researching On-line, Fifth Edition   This supplement shows students how to do research on the Internet in an easy-to-follow, step-by-step format. Internet resources, such as the Internet, e-mail, and "real time discussion," are explained with straightforward language and clear examples. ISBN 0-321-09277-5.

ACKNOWLEDGMENTS

I am indebted to many people over the years who have had a direct and indirect influence on my teaching philosophy—and on the writing of this book. Most notable among these teacher-scholars is Louise Rosenblatt, my teacher at NYU nearly 30 years ago. In addition, John Clifford, Alan Purves, Peter Elbow, Wayne Booth, Robert Scholes, Ann Berthoff, Toby Fulwiler, Robert Berlin, Carl Schmidt, Cindy Onore, John Mayher, Dawn Rodrigues, Judith Stanford, Kathi Blake Yancey, and others have influenced and inspired my work. I am grateful to my generous and caring colleagues at WCC: Bill Costanzo, Joanne Falinski, Richard Courage, Mira Sakrajda, and others who read the manuscript, tried out the materials, contributed ideas, and/or submitted student samples—and to Alan Devenish and Tahira Naqvi who contributed their work to this volume. I am grateful to my students who have taught me so much about teaching and this book, especially those students who contributed their work to this text: Debra Monserrate, Michelle McAuliffe, Julie Fitzmaurice, Alejandro Ramos, Debora Van Coughnett, Kevin Chamberlain, and others. I am indebted to President Joseph Hankin for fostering an atmosphere at WCC that made this work possible. And I am especially grateful to my brother John, who early in my life gave me a reason to care about literature, and to my wife, Sharon, my most discerning reader and loving supporter.

For their thoughtful and insightful comments to many drafts of manuscript, I am very grateful to the following reviewers: Maryam Barrie, Washtenaw Community College; Kristi Larken Havens, University of Tennessee, Knoxville; Dan Holt, Lansing Community College; Dan Kline, University of Alaska at Anchorage; Kristine Miller, Utah State University; D. K. Peterson, Wayne State University; Justin Pittas-Giroux, College of Charleston; Tison Pugh, University of California at Irvine; and Jeffrey White, Bellevue Community College.

At Longman, I am grateful to Erika Berg and Joe Terry whose vision, support, and friendship made this book possible, and to Adam Beroud whose skill, patience, and advice were much appreciated during the process. I am indebted to Katharine Glynn whose guidance on a previous text continued to inform my work on this one. I wish to thank Melanie Craig for getting the word out so effectively, and Donna DeBenedictis, Abby Westapher, and Phyllis Padula for their dedication, fine work, and patience while turning a manuscript into a book.

Frank Madden
SUNY Westchester Community College

FRANK MADDEN

Frank Madden is Professor and Chair of the English Department at SUNY Westchester Community College. His undergraduate degree is from St. John's University, where he played baseball, and his Ph.D. is from New York University. He has taught in graduate programs at CCNY, Iona College, and the New School for Social Research, and in 1998 was Chair of the NCTE College Section Institute on the Teaching of Literature. He is a recipient of the SUNY Chancellor's Award for Excellence in Teaching, the Foundation for Westchester Community College Faculty Award for Excellence in Scholarship, and the Phi Delta Kappan Educator of the Year Award from Iona College. He was Chair of the College Section of the NCTE from 1995–1998 and has served on the Executive Committees of the NCTE, the MLA-ADE, the SUNY Council on Writing, and as Chair of the MLA ad hoc Committee on Teaching. He is currently Chair of TYCA and serves on the CCCC and NCTE Executive Committees. His articles and chapters about the teaching of lit-erature have appeared in a variety of books and journals, including College English, College Literature, English Journal, Computers and Composition, Computers and the Humanities, *and the* ADE Bulletin. *He is the author of* Exploring Literature *(Longman, 2001) and* Exploring Poetry *(Longman, 2002). He lives in Brewster, New York, with his wife, Sharon, and they have two daughters, Michelle and Suzanne.*

PART I

Making
Connections

CHAPTER 1

Participation
Personal Response and Critical Thinking

We begin our exploration of fiction with you, the reader. Your engagement creates the literary experience. By themselves, the stories in this book, as brilliantly crafted or as famous or critically acclaimed as they may be, are just words on a page. It is your reading of these words through the lenses of your own experiences and beliefs that brings them to life and gives them meaning, a meaning ultimately as unique as you are.

Literature reveals a possible world to us. Our engagement and involvement are the keys to enter this world and to imagine its possibilities. Our backgrounds and personalities, our understanding of others, our prior experience with literature, our knowledge of the world—our sources for making meaning—are important factors in this process. And unlike our busy lives, which sometimes race forward with little time for reflection, literature awaits our examination. We can participate in it as we experience it, and analyze it as we step back and observe it.

THE PERSONAL DIMENSION OF READING FICTION

Most fiction does not intend to convey a moral or lesson. At its best, it reveals as life reveals. But like life, our *reading* of fiction evokes our emotion and judgment. Narrators and literary characters express their beliefs in what they say or do, and as we read, we respond to their words and actions through our own beliefs—comparing their choices with our own, and approving or disapproving as they meet or fail to meet our expectations. While most good fiction does not teach or preach, it does explore and reveal what it means to be human and provides us with a substantial opportunity for learning and self-understanding.

Later on in this chapter, and throughout the book, you are asked to think about your responses and to consider how your own experiences and beliefs influence them. Acknowledging, reviewing, and thinking critically about the judgments you make as you read may provide you with valuable insights into the stories and yourself.

PERSONAL RESPONSE AND CRITICAL THINKING

Thinking critically about stories is an outgrowth of our personal responses. It is natural for us to want to comprehend what moves us or has meaning to us. As children, we may have tried to make sense of what we read by making connections with other things we had read or experienced. We might have remembered reading something similar in another story or believed that a particular author would keep us in suspense. We knew which stories we liked, and even if we didn't analyze our reading systematically, we may have wondered what made those stories appealing to us.

When we think critically about fiction we build on our personal responses—recording them, reviewing them, discussing them, and supporting them. Being engaged is a crucial initial component of a complete literary experience. But once we experience this engagement and believe that a story has something to offer us, it follows that we want to know more about it, to see how it triggers our responses and judgments, to understand the skill with which it was created, and to articulate what it means to us.

Critical thinking does not mean searching for one right answer. There may be as many answers as there are readers. *Your* best answers are those that analyze and articulate your responses in the light of supporting evidence. This is critical thinking, a process that can make your opinions about literature well-informed ones.

WRITING TO LEARN

Writing is an excellent way to learn about literature. Whether you are jotting down notes, writing in a journal, or constructing a formal essay, you're learning. You're learning when you struggle to choose the right words to describe your impressions, and when you revise those words because they are not quite what you mean. And you are learning when you "get it just right" and see your words match what you want to say. In short, writing your responses down helps you learn and articulate what you think and feel more clearly.

Keeping a Journal or Reading Log

One of the best tools for exploring and thinking about your experiences in writing is a journal or reading log, and you may find it helpful to keep one in which to record your responses to the stories in this book. Journals and reading logs can help you view and review your ideas. Writing and reading your words on paper may help you articulate, clarify, and expand your ideas. Use your journal to identify and express your reactions, what moves or bothers you, or what seems intriguing or confusing. Write in your most natural voice and don't worry about sounding wise. Take chances and try out ideas. Unless you decide to share them, you are the only one who will see these entries.

If you use your journal to keep a record of your responses, you can look back for connections later on. These responses, along with subsequent reading and the comments of classmates, can help you develop ideas as you write the essays required by your instructor. If you are conscientious about keeping your journal, your entries will evolve naturally into a statement of the meaning you've constructed from the work. In the long run, the most important ingredient in your essays will not be the position you take, but the support you derive from the literature and your experience with it. Recording these observations in your journal now may provide you with some of this support later.

What you write in your journal or log is your choice. It should be as unique as your experience with the story itself. You may or may not like what you read. You may find it engaging or filled with meaning. You may find it confusing or boring. Whatever your response, you'll benefit most from keeping a journal or log if your entries honestly reflect your experience.

A variation of the journal is a **literature response sheet**. Like the journal, each response sheet accounts for your first impressions during and after your reading. Your instructor may collect them and use them to initiate class discussion.

There is no one correct way of keeping a journal or log. The student samples that follow are all different, but each is a start and might be built upon to develop a more formal essay. ("Araby" appears on p. 51.) Even if you are not familiar with this story, these responses reflect the kinds of issues that might be addressed in response to any story.

From confusion:

I found the story of "Araby" to be a little confusing. I couldn't really fathom what the actual point of the story was. There is a boy whose name is not mentioned, and he apparently has some sort of infatuation with a nun. He spies on her, peering through a tiny crack in his shades. He ends up talking to her and telling her that if he goes to Araby, the bazaar, he will buy her a present because she cannot go.

I realize this is a very well written and powerful piece of writing not written in modern (today's) terms. The last line of the story intrigued me. "Gazing up into the darkness I saw myself as a creature driven and derided by vanity; and my eyes burned with anguish and anger."

I guess he said this because he did not buy her anything at Araby. I don't exactly know why. Maybe because he got there too late or maybe in the back of his mind he expected her to be there.

To an appreciation of the author's artistry:

The beginning of "Araby" was written with a lot of descriptive words. As soon as I began to read sentence by sentence, the words formed pictures in my mind. I got the feeling of a painting being painted stroke by stroke. The description of the street being blind and quiet except when the school set the boys free gave me a feeling of quiet and then sudden noise, as the boys came rushing through the streets. Describing the air as cold, the space of the sky ever-changing violet allowed me to feel the cold and see the colors.

From identification:

I liked this story for several reasons. The main reason was that it brought back many fond memories of my childhood. The story reminded me of the very first crush I had on a girl. I was just as uncomfortable about speaking to the girl as was the boy in the story. Unlike the boy in the story, I did get to speak with her on various occasions because our families were friendly. In the fourth paragraph the writer explains how the boy would carefully watch the girl from his window and follow her every day. Since I went to the same school as the girl (she was a year older) and our houses were within sight of each other, I did the same thing the boy in the story did. I knew exactly when she would leave for school, and I would be exactly a half a block behind her.

The line "her image accompanied me even in places the most hostile to romance" is very true. I would always think of her at times that were inappropriate. I would think of her during my baseball games, during school exams, and even during Church services.

To complete frustration:

I will be totally honest and say that "Araby," by far, is the worst piece of material I have ever read. The story is so confusing and there are a lot of questions that I would like answered. But maybe that is why I feel the way I do about the story. How am I supposed to identify with this story if I don't know anything about the characters? He doesn't say how old either one of them is and he doesn't mention any background information. If there is a point to this story, then it is very well hidden, and I'll never be able to find it.

Double-Entry Journals and Logs

Because you may be asked to read and write comments about your journal or log entries from time to time, an especially effective format is the double-entry journal. By writing on only the front side of each page (or on the right half of each page), you will leave the back of the previous page (or the left half of each page) free for subsequent commentary (new ideas, revisions, summation, etc.) while rereading and reflecting. Leaving this space, you may go back later, read through your comments, circle and make notes about entries you've made, or add additional comments based on subsequent readings or class discussion.

I liked this story. I could tell by the way the author wrote that this was long ago in the early 1900s. It sounded like my grandfather's young life, but it's still timeless. I could relate what Joyce was saying to nowadays. I myself have felt that way. All your words and feelings are jumbled around one person. A crush. It's very stressful and exhilarating at the same time. I do have one question, though. Was the object of Joyce's desire and affection a nun? I thought maybe she was because she was always "clad in brown" and she couldn't go to Araby because her convent was having a meeting. I didn't feel that aspect was presented too clearly. Maybe I'm misreading. Overall, I enjoyed this story very much.

She's not a nun. I found out in class that parochial schools were sometimes called convent schools back then. You didn't have to be a nun to go there. That part of the story makes much more sense to me now.

The Social Nature of Learning: Collaboration

Writing ideas down is one effective way to learn, but so much of what we learn is also learned through conversation. Sharing our responses with others, and listening to their feedback and ideas, helps us build and clarify our own ideas.

By articulating what you think you know and what you need to know through conversation, you may develop a clearer understanding of the story. Throughout this text you'll be encouraged to share and exchange your ideas and collaborate with your classmates in pairs and small groups.

Personal, Not Private

Many of the questions that follow in this chapter prompt you to write about personal issues. These questions are not an attempt to invade your privacy or encourage you to write about aspects of your life or experience that may embarrass you or make you feel uncomfortable. What is personal or private is very different for each of us. You may choose to write some responses for your eyes only, some to share, or some not at all. That choice is always yours.

OURSELVES AS READERS

Our early experiences with books may have a significant influence on how we feel about reading. For many of us who enjoy reading, this joy was discovered outside the classroom. We felt free to experience the stories we read without fear of having our responses judged as right or wrong. For many who do not like to read, however, reading was often a painful chore, usually an assignment for the classroom with all the accompanying pressures of being evaluated. How often we read now and whether we see ourselves as good readers may have much to do with these earlier experiences.

You might find it worthwhile to write about some of these reading experiences in your journal or share them with others. It may be illuminating to see how much you have in common as a reader with other members of the class.

Different Kinds of Reading

Unfortunately, for many of us, the different types of reading we were given in school were often treated the same way. Reading assignments that primarily dealt with content or factual information were often not distinguished from imaginative literature. We know, however, that different types of reading material require very different kinds of involvement. Reading a science text, for example, requires that we focus on acquiring information for future use, whereas a story, while requiring our understanding of the facts, seeks to involve us personally in the moment—to have us share an experience, to evoke our feelings.

Read the following paragraph:

CAUTION—NOT FOR PERSONAL USE—If splashed on skin or in eyes, rinse immediately. If accidentally taken internally give large amounts of milk or water. Call a physician. Point mouth of container away from you when removing cap. AVOID TRANSFER TO FOOD OR BEVERAGE CONTAINERS—KEEP CONTAINER UPRIGHT IN A COOL PLACE TIGHTLY CAPPED.

► *GETTING STARTED—YOUR FIRST RESPONSE*

1. What is your response to this paragraph?
2. Of what use is the information in this statement?
3. Did you learn anything from this paragraph?

Read the following brief story.

W. SOMERSET MAUGHAM (1874–1965)

THE APPOINTMENT IN SAMARRA   [1933]

Death speaks: There was a merchant in Bagdad who sent his servant to market to
buy provisions and in a little while the servant came back, white and trembling, and
said, Master, just now when I was in the marketplace I was jostled by a woman in
the crowd and when I turned I saw it was Death that jostled me. She looked at me
and made a threatening gesture; now, lend me your horse, and I will ride away from
this city and avoid my fate. I will go to Samarra and there death will not find me.
The merchant lent him his horse, and the servant mounted it, and he dug his spurs
in its flanks and as fast as the horse could gallop he went. Then the merchant went
down to the marketplace and he saw me standing in the crowd and he came to me
and said, Why did you make a threatening gesture to my servant when you saw him
this morning? That was not a threatening gesture, I said, it was only a start of surprise. I was astonished to see him in Bagdad, for I had an appointment with him
tonight in Samarra.

► *GETTING STARTED—YOUR FIRST RESPONSE*

1. What is your reaction to this story?
2. What information is being conveyed?
3. Of what use is the information in this story?
4. What did you learn from this story?
5. How did your reading experience with this story differ from your experience with the warning label on page 7?

Different Kinds of Fiction

One basic difference between the caution label on page 7 and "The Appointment
at Samarra" is its intention. The caution label is trying to convey vital information
as clearly as possible to alert us to the dangers of handling bleach—not, as the
story does, to engage us in the moment, surprise us with an ironic ending, or
interpret human nature.

Stories, too, though sharing the designation "fiction," do not always share
the same intentions. "The Appointment at Samarra" has a tight plot structure
and an ending that seems to "wrap things up." But most modern fiction does
not intend to end conflict so neatly. Life doesn't work that way, and stories
that intend to capture life as it is don't "wrap up" so neatly either. Many of these

stories conclude when the central character sees beyond a comforting illusion and confronts a painful reality.

Read the following brief story.

JOHN CHEEVER (1912–1982)

REUNION   [1962]

The last time I saw my father was in Grand Central Station. I was going from my grandmother's in the Adirondacks to a cottage on the Cape that my mother had rented,—and I wrote my father that I would be in New York between trains for an hour and a half, and asked if we could have lunch together. His secretary wrote to say that he would meet me at the information booth at noon, and at twelve o'clock sharp I saw him coming through the crowd. He was a stranger to me—my mother divorced him three years ago and I hadn't been with him since—but as soon as I saw him I felt that he was my father, my flesh and blood, my future and my doom. I knew that when I was grown I would be something like him; I would have to plan my campaigns within his limitations. He was a big, good-looking man, and I was terribly happy to see him again. He struck me on the back and shook my hand. "Hi, Charlie," he said. "Hi, boy. I'd like to take you up to my club, but it's in the Sixties, and if you have to catch an early train I guess we'd better get something to eat around here." He put his arm around me, and I smelled my father the way my mother sniffs a rose. It was a rich compound of whiskey, after-shave lotion, shoe polish, woolens, and the rankness of a mature male. I hoped that someone would see us together. I wished that we could be photographed. I wanted some record of our having been together.

We went out of the station and up a side street to a restaurant. It was still early, and the place was empty. The bartender was quarreling with a delivery boy, and there was one very old waiter in a red coat down by the kitchen door. We sat down, and my father hailed the waiter in a loud voice. "*Kellner!*" he shouted. "*Garçon! Cameriere! You!*" His boisterousness in the empty restaurant seemed out of place. "Could we have a little service here!" he shouted. "Chop-chop." Then he clapped his hands. This caught the waiter's attention, and he shuffled over to our table.

"Were you clapping your hands at me?" he asked.

"Calm down, calm down, *sommelier*," my father said. "If it isn't too much to ask of you—if it wouldn't be too much above and beyond the call of duty, we would like a couple of Beefeater Gibsons."

5   "I don't like to be clapped at," the waiter said.

"I should have brought my whistle," my father said. "I have a whistle that is audible only to the ears of old waiters. Now, take out your little pad and your little pencil and see if you can get this straight: two Beefeater Gibsons. Repeat after me: two Beefeater Gibsons."

"I think you'd better go somewhere else," the waiter said quietly.

"That," said my father, "is one of the most brilliant suggestions I have ever heard. Come on, Charlie, let's get the hell out of here."

I followed my father out of that restaurant into another. He was not so boisterous this time. Our drinks came, and he cross-questioned me about the baseball season. He then struck the edge of his empty glass with his knife and began shouting again. "Garcon! Kellner! Cameriere! *You!* Could we trouble you to bring us two more of the same."

"How old is the boy?" the waiter asked.

"That," my father said, "is none of your God-damned business."

"I'm sorry, sir," the waiter said, "but I won't serve the boy another drink."

"Well, I have some news for you," my father said. "I have some very interesting news for you. This doesn't happen to be the only restaurant in New York. They've opened another on the corner. Come on, Charlie."

He paid the bill, and I followed him out of that restaurant into another. Here the waiters wore pink jackets like hunting coats and there was a lot of horse tack on the walls. We sat down, and my father began to shout again. "Master of the hounds! Tallyhoo and all that sort of thing. We'd like a little something in the way of a stirrup cup. Namely, two Bibson Geefeaters."

"Two Bibson Geefeaters?" the waiter asked, smiling.

"You know damned well what I want," my father said angrily. "I want two Beefeater Gibsons, and make it snappy. Things have changed in jolly old England. So my friend the duke tells me. Let's see what England can produce in the way of a cocktail."

"This isn't England," the waiter said.

"Don't argue with me," my father said. "Just do as you're told."

"I just thought you might like to know where you are," the waiter said.

"If there is one thing I cannot tolerate," my father said, "it is an impudent domestic. Come on, Charlie."

The fourth place we went to was Italian. "*Buon giorno,*" my father said. "*Per favore, possiamo avere due cocktail americani, forti, forti. Molto gin, poco vermut.*"

"I don't understand Italian," the waiter said.

"Oh, come off it," my father said. "You understand Italian, and you know damned well you do. *Vogliamo due cocktail americani. Subito.*"

The waiter left us and spoke with the captain, who came over to our table and said, "I'm sorry, sir, but this table is reserved."

"All right," my father said. "Get us another table."

"All the tables are reserved," the captain said.

"I get it," my father said, "You don't desire our patronage. Is that it? Well, the hell with you. *Vada all'inferno.* Let's go, Charlie."

"I have to get my train," I said.

"I'm sorry, sonny," my father said. "I'm terribly sorry." He put his arm around me and pressed me against him. "I'll walk you back to the station. If there had only been time to go up to my club."

"That's all right, Daddy," I said.

"I'll get you a paper," he said. "I'll get you a paper to read on the train."

Then he went up to a newsstand and said, "Kind sir, will you be good enough to favor me with one of your God-damned, no-good, ten-cent afternoon papers?" The clerk turned away from him and stared at a magazine cover. "Is it asking too much, kind sir," my father said, "is it asking too much for you to sell me one of your disgusting specimens of yellow journalism?"

"I have to go, Daddy," I said. "It's late."

"Now, just wait a second, sonny," he said. "Just wait a second. I want to get a rise out of this chap."

35   "Goodbye, Daddy," I said, and I went down the stairs and got my train, and that was the last time I saw my father.

► GETTING STARTED—YOUR FIRST RESPONSE

1. What is your reaction to this story?
2. What information is being conveyed?
3. Of what use is the information in this story?
4. What did you learn from this story?
5. What is your response to the unresolved ending of this story? What do you think has happened here?

► QUESTIONS FOR READING AND WRITING

Compare your response to the warning label paragraph with your response to the stories "The Appointment in Samarra" and "Reunion."

1. The two stories and the warning label all convey information. In what way was your reading experience with each different?
2. Did the physical appearance of each influence *how* you read it? If the warning label were written like a story, would you have read it with different expectations?
3. To what extent can you connect the information in either of the stories to your own background or experience? To what extent can you connect the information in the warning label?
4. Did you learn anything from the stories? From the warning label? If so, did the *nature* of what you learned differ in each case? Explain.

The process of reading often raises more questions than it answers. After reading, some of the most important questions to address are the ones you have raised yourself. So before you answer the questions that follow each selection in this chapter, you may want to write down your first impressions and any questions that came to mind during and after your reading.

MAKING CONNECTIONS

Among the many factors that influence our response to a story is identification with characters, circumstances, and issues. Our personalities, backgrounds, and experiences can have a strong impact on these connections.

We may identify with characters because we see aspects of our own personalities in them or admire aspects of their personalities and wish we had them ourselves. We might respond negatively to characters because aspects of their personalities are different than ours or similar to ones we don't like in ourselves. We may agree or disagree with what the characters say or do, or ask ourselves if we would have behaved the same way.

Conversely, by showing us a view of life that is different from our own, a story might influence our beliefs and behavior. We may learn from fiction as we learn from life itself.

Images of Ourselves

How we view ourselves in relation to the world around us is very complex. We probably have an image of who we are that we carry within ourselves most of the time, but we are likely to project a different personality according to the situations (home, work, school, etc.) in which we find ourselves. Depending on our relationships with them, the people we know are also likely to describe us very differently. Our families, friends, casual acquaintances, employers, and teachers may experience who we are in very different ways.

➤ *MAKING CONNECTIONS—"Girl"*

How we see ourselves is often influenced by the expectations placed on us by our parents or other authority figures in our lives when we were growing up. Can you recall the kinds of things that your parents, teachers, or other authority figures said to you about who they thought you were or should be? If so, try to remember how it made you feel to hear those comments or experience that pressure.

JAMAICA KINCAID (b. 1949)

GIRL   [1978]

Wash the white clothes on Monday and put them on the stone heap; wash the color clothes on Tuesday and put them on the clothes-line to dry; don't walk barehead in the hot sun; cook pumpkin fritters in very hot sweet oil; soak your little clothes right after you take them off; when buying cotton to make yourself a nice blouse, be sure that it doesn't have gum on it, because that way it won't hold up well after a wash; soak salt fish overnight before you cook it; is it true that you sing benna in Sunday school? always eat your food in such a way that it won't turn someone else's stomach; on Sundays try to walk like a lady and not like the slut you are so bent on becoming; don't sing benna in Sunday school; you mustn't speak to wharf-rat boys, not even to give directions; don't eat fruits on the street—flies will follow you; *but I don't sing benna on Sundays at all and never in Sunday school;* this is how to sew on a button; this is how to make a buttonhole for the button you have just sewed on; this is how to hem a dress when you see the hem coming down and so to prevent yourself from looking like the slut I know you are so bent on becoming; this is how you iron your father's khaki shirt so that it doesn't have a crease; this is how you iron your father's khaki pants so that they don't have a crease; this is how you grow okra—far from the house, because okra tree harbors red ants; when you are growing dasheen, make sure it gets plenty of water or else it makes your throat itch when you are eating it; this is how you sweep a corner; this is how you sweep a whole house; this is how you sweep a yard; this is how you smile to someone you don't like too much; this is how you smile at someone you don't like at all; this is how you smile to someone you like completely; this is how you set a table for tea; this is how you set a table for dinner; this is how you set a table for dinner with an important guest; this is how you set a table for lunch; this is how you set a table for breakfast; this is how to behave in the presence of men who don't know you very well, and this way they won't recognize immediately the slut I have warned you against becoming; be sure to wash every day, even if it is with your own spit; don't squat down to play marbles—you are not a boy, you know; don't pick people's flowers—you might catch something; don't throw stones at blackbirds, because it might not be a blackbird at all; this is how to make a bread pudding; this is how to make doukona; this is how to make pepper pot; this is how to make a good medicine for a cold; this is how to make a good medicine to throw away a child before it even becomes a child; this is how to catch a fish; this is how to throw back a fish you don't like, and that way something bad won't fall on you; this is how to bully a man; this is how a man bullies you; this is how to love a man, and if this doesn't work there are other ways, and if they don't work don't feel too bad about giving up; this is how to spit up in the air if you feel like it, and this is how to move quick so that it doesn't fall on you; this is how to make ends meet; always squeeze bread to make sure it's fresh; *but what if the baker won't let me feel the bread?* you mean to say that after all you are really going to be the kind of woman who the baker won't let near the bread?

▶ QUESTIONS FOR READING AND WRITING

1. If you could remember what it was like to hear advice or comments of this kind, to what extent did that influence your response to "Girl"?
2. What effect does the nonstop advice—in a nonstop paragraph—have on you?
3. Who is making the italicized comments? What difference do they make to you?
4. How would you describe this relationship?

Culture, Experience, and Values

Who we are and how we respond to stories is also influenced by many other factors. Family, religion, race, gender, friends, other influential people in our lives, and our experiences shape our views in significant ways.

We may come from a family that is strongly connected to its ethnic roots, religious or not religious at all, closely knit or disconnected, warm and welcoming, suffocating, or cold and impersonal. Or we may not have a family at all. Our friends, too, may affect who we are, what we believe, and how we act.

We may be strongly influenced by our race, ethnic background, or gender. If we have never experienced or witnessed discrimination, we might not be able to understand its significance. If we have witnessed prejudice or had it directed against us, we know how devastating it can be. Our gender may affect the expectations others have for us, the encouragement we receive for education and career goals, marriage and family, even our involvement in sports. And it certainly influences our view of the opposite sex.

If we are deeply religious, it might be at the heart of everything we value. If we are not, our religious backgrounds may still exert a strong influence on our lives. What we do for a living, how old we are, our sexual orientation, our disabilities, or other factors may also affect how we see the world—and the literature we read.

▶ MAKING CONNECTIONS—"Snow"

Most of us at some time have found ourselves struggling to adjust to new and strange circumstances, for which our own backgrounds had not prepared us. See if you can recall a time in your life when you were in a situation like this and how it made you feel.

JULIA ALVAREZ (b. 1954)

SNOW
[1991]

Our first year in New York we rented a small apartment with a Catholic school nearby, taught by the Sisters of Charity, hefty women in long black gowns and bonnets that made them look peculiar, like dolls in mourning. I liked them a lot, especially my grandmotherly fourth grade teacher, Sister Zoe. I had a lovely name, she said, and she had me teach the whole class how to pronounce it. *Yo-lan-da.* As the only immigrant in my class, I was put in a special seat in the first row by the window, apart from the other children so that Sister Zoe could tutor me without disturbing them. Slowly, she enunciated the new words I was to repeat: *laundromat, cornflakes, subway, snow.*

Soon I picked up enough English to understand holocaust was in the air. Sister Zoe explained to a wide-eyed classroom what was happening in Cuba. Russian missiles were being assembled, trained supposedly on New York City. President Kennedy, looking worried too, was on the television at home, explaining we might have to go to war against the Communists. At school, we had air-raid drills: an ominous bell would go off and we'd file into the hall, fall to the floor, cover our heads with our coats, and imagine our hair falling out, the bones in our arms going soft. At home, Mami and my sisters and I said a rosary for world peace. I heard new vocabulary: *nuclear bomb, radioactive fallout, bomb shelter.* Sister Zoe explained how it would happen. She drew a picture of a mushroom on the blackboard and dotted a flurry of chalkmarks for the dusty fallout that would kill us all.

The months grew cold, November, December. It was dark when I got up in the morning, frosty when I followed my breath to school. One morning as I sat at my desk daydreaming out the window, I saw dots in the air like the ones Sister Zoe had drawn—random at first, then lots and lots. I shrieked, "Bomb! Bomb!" Sister Zoe jerked around, her full black skirt ballooning as she hurried to my side. A few girls began to cry.

But then Sister Zoe's shocked look faded. "Why, Yolanda dear, that's snow!" She laughed. "Snow."

5   "Snow," I repeated. I looked out the window warily. All my life I had heard about the white crystals that fell out of American skies in the winter. From my desk I watched the fine powder dust the sidewalk and parked cars below. Each flake was different, Sister Zoe said, like a person, irreplaceable and beautiful.

► QUESTIONS FOR READING AND WRITING

1. If you could recall a time when you struggled with a new and strange situation, how did that affect your response to this story?
2. Why is the snowfall such a shocking experience for the narrator?
3. At the end of this brief story, Sister Zoe tries to calm Yolanda by describing the "fallout" that frightened her. Do you think her explanation of snow is effective? Why?
4. Think about the stories "Reunion," "Girl," and"Snow" and how your response to them was influenced by your background (your self-image, family, culture, experience, or values).

THE WHOLE AND ITS PARTS

You've probably come across the statement "The whole is equal to the sum of its parts." Seems to make sense, doesn't it? Well, in some areas of study it does, but it cannot account for our response to fiction. In literature and other artistic expressions, there is a whole that is greater than the sum of its parts, a whole that blossoms as the parts come together in our imaginations.

We don't like our favorite music because we identify the parts and add them up to a whole experience; we like it because we experience the sound of the instruments, the rhythms, the voices, the lyrics, all together and all at once. For all of us that means more than the sum of the notes or words we hear, and to each of us that means something different.

Like a piece of music, a story cannot be reduced to its parts to account for its meaning. But fiction, like music, has parts, and as we become more experienced readers we want to know how those parts work together. Later on in this book, we will try to comprehend the craft with which the parts are assembled. However, not until we believe the experience of fiction has something to offer us will we care about the skill with which it was created, so for now, let's continue to explore how and what it means to us.

Participating, Not Solving

It's essential that we are *active* participants when we read fiction. But if we look for the parts of a story before we have experienced the whole, we may shut down the emotions we need to experience it—and miss the *life* of the work. Placing ourselves *emotionally* inside the story, rather than examining it *rationally* from the outside, enables us to feel and sense the words and images and lets these impressions wash over us.

Stories are not math problems—they don't have one "correct" answer. They might not even "add up." The right answer is the one that makes the most sense to you, a "sense" supported by your own imagination and the text of the story itself. Being confused and making mistakes along the way is part of the process of finding your own right answer.

Being in the Moment

We can't get at the heart of our experience with a story by summarizing it. We might account for all that matters on the "Caution" label on the bleach bottle (p. 7) by saying, "This is a very caustic liquid and you could hurt yourself by coming in contact with it." But we couldn't get at the essence of the story "Reunion" by saying, "A kid finds out his father is a jerk." We read the warning label for the information we take away with us; the label seeks to inform us. Fiction seeks to involve us.

A magazine article, for example, might relate the "who, what, when, where, and why" of an event, but literature must do much more than that. It may even move us to question events in our own lives and influence us as we make our own decisions. The following article appeared in *Life* magazine after the arrest of a man in Tucson, Arizona, for the kidnap and murder of teenage girls.

Don Moser

The Pied Piper of Tucson: He Cruised in a Golden Car, Looking for the Action

[1966]

> *Hey, c'mon babe, follow me,*
> *I'm the Pied Piper, follow me,*
> *I'm the Pied Piper,*
> *And I'll show you where it's at.*
> —Popular song, Tucson, winter 1965

At dusk in Tucson, as the stark, yellow-flared mountains begin to blur against the sky, the golden car slowly cruises Speedway. Smoothly it rolls down the long, divided avenue, past the supermarkets, the gas stations and the motels; past the twist joints, the sprawling drive-in restaurants. The car slows for an intersection, stops, then pulls away again. The exhaust mutters against the pavement as the young man driving takes the machine swiftly, expertly through the gears. A car pulls even with him; the teenage girls in the front seat laugh, wave and call his name. The young man glances toward the rearview mirror, turned always so that he can look at his own reflection, and he appraises himself.

The face is his own creation: the hair dyed a raven black, the skin darkened to a deep tan with pancake make-up, the lips whitened, the whole effect heightened by a mole he has painted on one cheek. But the deep-set blue eyes are all his own. Beautiful eyes, the girls say.

Approaching the Hi-Ho, the teenagers' nightclub, he backs off on the accelerator, then slowly cruises on past Johnie's Drive-in. There the cars are beginning to

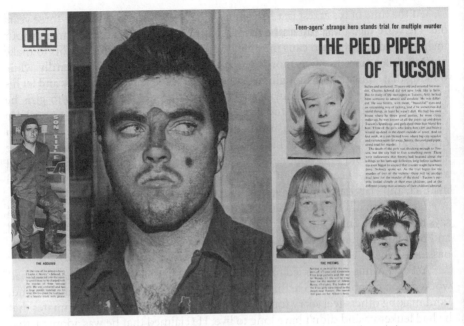

These are the first pages of *Life's* article on the murderer Charles Schmid Jr. and his three victims.

orbit and accumulate in the parking lot—neat sharp cars with deep throated mufflers and Maltese-cross decals on the windows. But it's early yet. Not much going on. The driver shifts up again through the gears, and the golden car slides away along the glitter and gimcrack of Speedway. Smitty keeps looking for the action.

Whether the juries in the two trials decide that Charles Howard Schmid Jr. did or did not brutally murder Alleen Rowe, Gretchen Fritz, and Wendy Fritz has from the beginning seemed of almost secondary importance to the people of Tucson. They are not indifferent. But what disturbs them far beyond the question of Smitty's guilt or innocence are the revelations about Tucson itself that have followed on the disclosure of the crimes. Starting with the bizarre circumstances of the killings and on through the ugly fragments of the plot—which in turn hint at other murders as yet undiscovered, at teenage sex, blackmail, even connections with the *Cosa Nostra*—they have had to view their city in a new and unpleasant light. The fact is that Charles Schmid—who cannot be dismissed as a freak, an aberrant of no consequence—had for years functioned successfully as a member, even a leader of the yeastiest stratum of Tucson's teenage society.

5   As a high school student Smitty had been, as classmates remember, an outsider—but not that far outside. He was small but he was a fine athlete, and in his last year—1960—he was a state gymnastics champion. His grades were poor, but he was in no trouble to speak of until his senior year, when he was suspended for stealing tools from a welding class.

But Smitty never really left the school. After his suspension he hung around waiting to pick up kids in a succession of sharp cars which he drove fast and well. He haunted all the teenage hangouts along Speedway, including the bowling alleys and the public swimming pool—and he put on spectacular diving exhibitions for girls far younger than he.

At the time of his arrest last November, Charles Schmid was twenty-three years old. He wore face make-up and dyed his hair. He habitually stuffed three or four inches of old rags and tin cans into the bottoms of his high-topped boots to make himself taller than his five-foot-three and stumbled about so awkwardly while walking that some people thought he had wooden feet. He pursed his lips and let his eyelids droop in order to emulate his idol, Elvis Presley. He bragged to girls he knew a hundred ways to make love, that he ran dope, that he was a Hell's Angel. He talked about being a rough customer in a fight (he was, though he was rarely in one), and he always carried in his pocket tiny bottles of salt and pepper, which he said he used to blind his opponents. He liked to use highfalutin language and had a favorite saying, "I can manifest my neurotical emotions, emancipate an epicureal instinct, and elaborate on my heterosexual tendencies."

He occasionally shocked even those who thought they knew him well. A friend says he once saw Smitty tie a string to a tail of his pet cat, swing it around his head and beat it bloody against a wall. Then he turned calmly and asked, "You feel compassion—why?"

Yet even while Smitty tried to create an exalted, heroic image of himself, he had worked on a pitiable one. "He thrived on feeling sorry for himself," recalls a friend, "and making others feel sorry for him." At various times Smitty told intimates that he had leukemia and didn't have long to live. He claimed that he was adopted, that his real name was Angel Rodriguez, that his father was a "bean" (local slang for Mexican, an inferior race in Smitty's view), and that his mother was a famous lawyer who would have nothing to do with him.

. . .

He had a nice car. He had plenty of money from his parents, who ran a nursing home, and he was always glad to spend it on anyone who'd listen to him. He had a pad of his own where he threw parties and he had impeccable manners. He was always willing to help a friend and he would send flowers to girls who were ill. He was older and more mature than most of his friends. He knew where the action was, and if he wore make-up—well, at least he was *different*.

Some of the older kids—those who worked, who had something else to do—thought Smitty was a creep. But to the youngsters—to the bored and the lonely, to the dropout and the delinquent, to the young girls with beehive hairdos and tight pants they didn't quite fill out, and to the boys with acne and no jobs—to these people, Smitty was a kind of folk hero. Nutty maybe, but at least more dramatic, more theatrical, more *interesting* than anyone else in their lives: a semi-ludicrous, sexy-eyed pied-piper who, stumbling along in his rag-stuffed boots, led them up and down Speedway.

On the evening of May 31, 1964, Alleen Rowe prepared to go to bed early. She had to be in class by six a.m. and she had an examination the next day. Alleen was a pretty girl of fifteen, a better-than-average student who talked about going to college and becoming an oceanographer. She was also a sensitive child—given to reading romantic novels and taking long walks in the desert at night. Recently she had been going through a period of adolescent melancholia, often talking with her mother, a nurse, about death. She would, she hoped, be some day reincarnated as a cat.

On this evening, dressed in a black bathing suit and thongs, her usual costume around the house, she had watched the Beatles on TV and had tried to teach her mother to dance the Frug. Then she took her bath, washed her hair, and came out to kiss her mother good night. Norma Rowe, an attractive, womanly divorcée, was somehow moved by the girl's clean fragrance and said, "You smell so good—are you wearing perfume?"

"No, Mom," the girl answered, laughing, "it's just me."

15   A little later Mrs. Rowe looked in on her daughter, found her apparently sleeping peacefully, and then left for her job as a night nurse in a Tucson hospital. She had no premonition of danger, but she had lately been concerned about Alleen's friendship with a neighbor girl named Mary French.

Mary and Alleen had been spending a good deal of time together, smoking and giggling and talking girl talk in the Rowe backyard. Norma Rowe did not approve. She particularly did not approve of Mary French's friends, a tall, gangling boy of nineteen named John Saunders and another named Charles Schmid. She had seen Smitty racing up and down the street in his car and once, when he came to call on Alleen and found her not at home, he had looked at Norma so menacingly with his "pinpoint eyes" that she had been frightened.

Her daughter, on the other hand, seemed to have mixed feelings about Smitty. "He's creepy," she once told her mother, "he just makes me crawl. But he can be nice when he wants to."

At any rate, later that night—according to Mary French's sworn testimony—three friends arrived at Alleen Rowe's house: Smitty, Mary French, and Saunders. Smitty had frequently talked with Mary French about killing the Rowe girl by hitting her over the head with a rock. Mary French tapped on Alleen's window and asked her to come out and drink beer with them. Wearing a shift over her bathing suit, she came willingly enough.

Schmid's two accomplices were strange and pitiable creatures. Each of them was afraid of Smitty, yet each was drawn to him. As a baby, John Saunders had been so afflicted with allergies that scabs encrusted his entire body. To keep him from scratching himself his parents had tied his hands and feet to the crib each night, and when eventually he was cured he was so conditioned that he could not go to sleep without being bound hand and foot.

20   Later, a scrawny boy with poor eyesight ("Just a skinny little body with a big head on it"), he was taunted and bullied by larger children; in turn he bullied those who were smaller. He also suffered badly from asthma and he had few friends. In high school he was a poor student and constantly in minor trouble.

Mary French, nineteen, was—to put it straight—a frump. Her face, which might have been pretty, seemed somehow lumpy, her body shapeless. She was not dull but she was always a poor student, and she finally had simply stopped going to high school. She was, a friend remembers, "fantastically in love with Smitty. She just sat home and waited while he went out with other girls."

Now, with Smitty at the wheel, the four teen-agers headed for the desert, which begins out Golf Links Road. It is spooky country, dry and empty, the yellow sand clotted with cholla and mesquite and stunted, strangely green palo verde trees, and the great humanoid saguaro that hulk against the sky. Out there at night you can hear the yip and ki-yi of coyotes, the piercing screams of wild creatures—cats, perhaps.

According to Mary French, they got out of the car and walked down into a wash, where they sat on the sand and talked for a while, the four of them. Schmid and Mary then started back to the car. Before they got there, they heard a cry and Schmid turned back toward the wash. Mary went on to the car and sat in it alone. After forty-five minutes, Saunders appeared and said Smitty wanted her to come back down. She refused, and Saunders went away. Five or ten minutes later, Smitty showed up. "He got into the car," says Mary, "and he said, 'We killed her. I love you very much.' He kissed me. He was breathing real hard and seemed excited." Then Schmid got a shovel from the trunk of the car and they returned to the wash. "She was lying on her back and there was blood on her face and head," Mary French testified. Then the three of them dug a shallow grave and put the body in it and covered it up. Afterwards, they wiped Schmid's car clean of Alleen's fingerprints.

More than a year passed. Norma Rowe had reported her daughter missing and the police searched for her—after a fashion. At Mrs. Rowe's insistence they picked up Schmid, but they had no reason to hold him. The police, in fact, assumed that Alleen was just one more of Tucson's runaways.

25   Norma Rowe, however, had become convinced that Alleen had been killed by Schmid, although she left her kitchen light on every night in case Alleen did come home. She badgered the police and she badgered the sheriff until the authorities began to dismiss her as a crank. She began to imagine a high-level conspiracy against her. She wrote the state attorney general, the FBI, the U.S. Department of Health, Education and Welfare. She even contacted a New Jersey mystic, who said she could see Alleen's body out in the desert under a big tree.

Ultimately Norma Rowe started her own investigation, questioning Alleen's friends, poking around, dictating her findings to a tape recorder; she even tailed Smitty at night, following him in her car, scared stiff that he might spot her.

Schmid, during this time, acquired a little house of his own. There he held frequent parties, where people sat around amid his stacks of *Playboy* magazines, playing Elvis Presley records and drinking beer.

He read Jules Feiffer's novel, *Harry, the Rat with Women*, and said that his ambition was to be like Harry and have a girl commit suicide over him. Once, according to a friend, he went to see a minister, who gave him a Bible and told him to read the first three chapters of John. Instead Schmid tore the pages out and burned them in the street. "Religion is a farce," he announced. He started an upholstery business with some friends, called himself "founder and president," but then failed to put up the money he promised and the venture was short-lived.

He decided he liked blondes best, and took to dyeing the hair of various teenage girls he went around with. He went out and bought two imitation diamonds for about $13 apiece and then engaged himself, on the same day, both to Mary French and to a fifteen-year-old girl named Kathy Morath. His plan, he confided to a friend, was to put each of the girls to work and have them deposit their salaries in a bank account held jointly with him. Mary French did indeed go to work in the convalescent home Smitty's parents operated. When their bank account was fat enough, Smitty withdrew the money and bought a tape recorder.

By this time Smitty also had a girl from a higher social stratum than he usually was involved with. She was Gretchen Fritz, daughter of a prominent Tucson heart surgeon. Gretchen was a pretty, thin, nervous girl of seventeen with a knack for trouble. A teacher described her as "erratic, subversive, a psychopathic liar."

At the horsy private school she attended for a time she was a misfit. She not only didn't care about horses, but she shocked her classmates by telling them they were foolish for going out with boys without getting paid for it. Once she even committed the unpardonable social sin of turning up at a formal dance party accompanied by boys wearing what was described as beatnik dress. She cut classes, she was suspected of stealing and when, in the summer before her senior year, she got into trouble with juvenile authorities for her role in an attempted theft at a liquor store, the headmaster suggested she not return and then recommended she get psychiatric treatment.

Charles Schmid saw Gretchen for the first time at a public swimming pool in the summer of 1964. He met her by the simple expedient of following her home, knocking on the door and, when she answered, saying, "Don't I know you?" They talked for an hour. Thus began a fierce and stormy relationship. A good deal of what authorities know of the development of this relationship comes from the statements of a spindly scarecrow of a young man who wears pipestem trousers and Beatle boots: Richard Bruns. At the time Smitty was becoming involved with Gretchen, Bruns was eighteen years old. He had served two terms in the reformatory at Fort Grant. He had been in and out of trouble all his life, had never fit in anywhere. Yet, although he never went beyond the tenth grade in school and his credibility on many counts is suspect, he is clearly intelligent and even sensitive. He was, for a time, Smitty's closest friend and confidant, and he is today one of the mainstays of the state's case against Smitty. His story:

"He and Gretchen were always fighting," says Bruns. "She didn't want him to drink or go out with the guys or go out with other girls. She wanted him to stay home, call her on the phone, be punctual. First she would get suspicious of him, then he'd get suspicious of her. They were made for each other."

Their mutual jealousy led to sharp and continual arguments. Once she infuriated him by throwing a bottle of shoe polish on his car. Another time she was driving past Smitty's house and saw him there with some other girls. She jumped out of her car and began screaming. Smitty took off into the house, out the back, and climbed a tree in his backyard.

35   His feelings for her were an odd mixture of hate and adoration. He said he was madly in love with her, but he called her a whore. She would let Smitty in her bedroom window at night. Yet he wrote an anonymous letter to the Tucson Health Department accusing her of having venereal disease and spreading it about town. But Smitty also went to enormous lengths to impress Gretchen, once shooting holes through the windows of his car and telling her that thugs, from whom he was protecting her, had fired at him. So Bruns described the relationship.

On the evening of August 16, 1965, Gretchen Fritz left the house with her little sister Wendy, a friendly, lively thirteen-year-old, to go to a drive-in movie. Neither girl ever came home again. Gretchen's father, like Alleen Rowe's mother, felt sure that Charles Schmid had something to do with his daughters' disappearance, and eventually he hired Bill Heilig, a private detective, to handle the case. One of Heilig's men soon found Gretchen's red compact car parked behind a motel, but the police continued to assume that the girls had joined the ranks of Tucson's runaways.

About a week after Gretchen disappeared, Bruns was at Smitty's home. "We were sitting in the living room," Bruns recalls. "He was sitting on the sofa and I was in the chair by the window and we got on the subject of Gretchen. He said, 'You know I killed her?' I said I didn't, and he said, 'You know where?' I said no. He said, 'I did it here in the living room. First I killed Gretchen, then Wendy was still going "*huh, huh, huh*," so I . . . [here Bruns showed how Smitty made a garroting gesture.] Then I took the bodies and put them in the trunk of the car. I put the bodies in the most obvious place I could think of because I just didn't care any more. Then I ditched the car and wiped it clean."

Bruns was not particularly upset by Smitty's story. Months before, Smitty had told him of the murder of Alleen Rowe, and nothing had come of that. So he was not certain Smitty was telling the truth about the Fritz girls. Besides, Bruns detested Gretchen himself. But what happened next, still according to Bruns's story, did shake him up.

One night not long after, a couple of tough-looking characters, wearing sharp suits and smoking cigars, came by with Smitty and picked up Bruns. Smitty said they were Mafia, and that someone had hired them to look for Gretchen. Smitty and Bruns were taken to an apartment where several men were present whom Smitty later claimed to have recognized as local *Cosa Nostra* figures.

They wanted to know what had happened to the girls. They made no threats, but the message, Bruns remembers, came across loud and clear. These were no street-corner punks: these were the real boys. In spite of the intimidating company, Schmid lost none of his insouciance. He said he didn't know where Gretchen was, but if she turned up hurt he wanted these men to help him get whoever was responsible. He added that he thought she might have gone to California.

By the time Smitty and Bruns got back to Smitty's house, they were both a little shaky. Later that night, says Bruns, Smitty did the most unlikely thing imaginable: he called the FBI. First he tried the Tucson office and couldn't raise anyone. Then he called Phoenix and couldn't get an agent there either. Finally he put in a person-to-person call to J. Edgar Hoover in Washington. He didn't get Hoover, of course, but he got someone and told him that the Mafia was harassing him over the disappearance of a girl. The FBI promised to have someone in touch with him soon.

Bruns was scared and said so. It occurred to him now that if Smitty really had killed the Fritz girls and left their bodies in an obvious place, they were in very bad trouble indeed—with the Mafia on one hand and the FBI on the other. "Let's go bury them," Bruns said.

"Smitty stole the keys to his old man's station wagon," says Bruns, "and then we got a flat shovel—the only one we could find. We went to Johnie's and got a hamburger, and then we drove out to the old drinking spot [in the desert]—that's what Smitty meant when he said the most obvious place. It's where we used to drink beer and make out with girls.

"So we parked the car and got the shovel and walked down there, and we couldn't find anything. Then Smitty said, 'Wait, I smell something.' We went in opposite directions looking, and then I heard Smitty say, 'Come here.' I found him kneeling over Gretchen. There was a white rag tied around her legs. Her blouse was pulled up and she was wearing a white bra and Capris.

"Then he said, 'Wendy's up this way.' I sat there for a minute. Then I followed Smitty to where Wendy was. He'd had the decency to cover her—except for one leg, which was sticking up out of the ground."

"We tried to dig with the flat shovel. We each took turns. He'd dig for a while and then I'd dig for a while, but the ground was hard and we couldn't get anywhere with that flat shovel. We dug for twenty minutes and finally Smitty said we'd better do something because it's going to get light. So he grabbed the rag that was around Gretchen's legs and dragged her down in the wash. It made a noise like dragging a hollow shell. It stunk like hell. Then Smitty said wipe off her shoes, there might be fingerprints, so I wiped them off with my handkerchief and threw it away.

"We went back to Wendy. Her leg was sticking up with a shoe on it. He said take off her tennis shoe and throw it over there. I did, I threw it. Then he said, 'Now you're in this as deep as I am.'" By then, the sisters had been missing for about two weeks.

Early next morning Smitty did see the FBI. Nevertheless—here Bruns's story grows even wilder—that same day Smitty left for California, accompanied by a couple of Mafia types, to look for Gretchen Fritz. While there, he was picked up by the San Diego police on a complaint that he was impersonating an FBI officer. He was detained briefly, released and then returned to Tucson.

But now, it seemed to Richard Bruns, Smitty began acting very strangely. He startled Bruns by saying, "I've killed—not three times, but four. Now it's your turn, Richie." He went berserk in his little house, smashing his fist through a wall, slamming doors, then rushing out into the backyard in nothing but his undershorts, when he ran through the night screaming, "God is going to punish me!" He also decided, suddenly, to get married—to a fifteen-year-old girl who was a stranger to most of his friends.

• • •

50   Bruns went to Ohio to stay with his grandmother and to try to get a job. It was hopeless. He couldn't sleep at night, and if he did doze off he had his old nightmare again.

One night he blurted out the whole story to his grandmother in their kitchen. She thought he had had too many beers and didn't believe him. "I hear beer does strange things to a person," she said comfortingly. At her words Bruns exploded, knocked over a chair and shouted, "The one time in my life when I need advice what do I get?" A few minutes later he was on the phone to the Tucson police.

Things happened swiftly. At Bruns's frantic insistence, the police picked up Kathy Morath and put her in protective custody. They went into the desert and discovered—precisely as Bruns had described them—the grisly, skeletal remains of Gretchen and Wendy Fritz. They started the machinery that resulted in the arrest a week later of John Saunders and Mary French. They found Charles Schmid working in the yard of his little house, his face layered with make-up, his nose covered by a patch of adhesive plaster which he had worn for five months, boasting that his nose was broken in a fight, and his boots packed full of old rags and tin cans. He put up no resistance.

John Saunders and Mary French confessed immediately to their roles in the slaying of Alleen Rowe and were quickly sentenced, Mary French to four to five years, Saunders to life. When Smitty goes on trial for this crime, on March 15, they will be principal witnesses against him.

Meanwhile Richie Bruns, the perpetual misfit, waits apprehensively for the end of the Fritz trial, desperately afraid that Schmid will go free. "If he does," Bruns says glumly, "I'll be the first one he'll kill."

55   As for Charles Schmid, he has adjusted well to his period of waiting. He is polite and agreeable with all, though at the preliminary hearings he glared menacingly at Richie Bruns. Dressed tastefully, tie neatly knotted, hair carefully combed, his face scrubbed clean of make-up, he is a short, compact, darkly handsome young man with a wide, engaging smile and those deepset eyes.

Life, March 4, 1966

➤ *GETTING STARTED—YOUR FIRST RESPONSE*

1. What is your response to this magazine article?
2. Of what use is the information in this article?

Read the following story (inspired by the same event).

JOYCE CAROL OATES (b. 1938)

WHERE ARE YOU GOING, WHERE HAVE YOU BEEN?   [1970]

For Bob Dylan

Her name was Connie. She was fifteen and she had a quick nervous giggling habit of craning her neck to glance into mirrors, or checking other people's faces to make sure her own was all right. Her mother, who noticed everything and knew everything and who hadn't much reason any longer to look at her own face, always scolded Connie about it. "Stop gawking at yourself, who are you? You think you're so pretty?" she would say. Connie would raise her eyebrows at these familiar complaints and look right through her mother, into a shadowy vision of herself as she was right at that moment: she knew she was pretty and that was everything. Her mother had been pretty once too, if you could believe those old snapshots in the album, but now her looks were gone and that was why she was always after Connie.

"Why don't you keep your room clean like your sister? How've you got your hair fixed—what the hell stinks? Hair spray? You don't see your sister using that junk."

Her sister June was twenty-four and still lived at home. She was a secretary in the high school Connie attended, and if that wasn't bad enough—with her in the same building—she was so plain and chunky and steady that Connie had to hear her praised all the time by her mother and her mother's sisters. June did this, June did that, she saved money and helped clean the house and cooked and Connie couldn't do a thing, her mind was all filled with trashy daydreams. Their father was away at work most of the time and when he came home he wanted supper and he read the newspaper at supper and after supper he went to bed. He didn't bother talking much to them, but around his bent head Connie's mother kept picking at her until Connie wished her mother was dead and she herself was dead and it was all over. "She makes me want to throw up sometimes," she complained to her friends. She had a high, breathless, amused voice which made everything she said sound a little forced, whether it was sincere or not.

There was one good thing: June went places with girl friends of hers, girls who were just as plain and steady as she, and so when Connie wanted to do that her mother had no objections. The father of Connie's best girl friend drove the girls the three miles to town and left them off at a shopping plaza, so that they could walk through the stores or go to a movie, and when he came to pick them up again at eleven he never bothered to ask what they had done.

5   They must have been familiar sights, walking around that shopping plaza in their shorts and flat ballerina slippers that always scuffed the sidewalk, with charm bracelets jingling on their thin wrists; they would lean together to whisper and laugh secretly if someone passed by who amused or interested them. Connie had long dark blond hair that drew anyone's eye to it, and she wore part of it pulled up on her head and puffed out and the rest of it she let fall down her back. She wore a pull-over jersey blouse that looked one way when she was at home and another way when she was away from home. Everything about her had two sides to it, one for home and one for anywhere that was not home: her walk that could be childlike and bobbing, or languid enough to make anyone think she was hearing music in her head, her mouth which was pale and smirking most of the time, but bright and pink on these evenings out, her laugh which was cynical and drawling at home—"Ha, ha, very funny"—but high-pitched and nervous anywhere else, like the jingling of the charms on her bracelet.

Sometimes they did go shopping or to a movie, but sometimes they went across the highway, ducking fast across the busy road, to a drive-in restaurant where older kids hung out. The restaurant was shaped like a big bottle, though squatter than a real bottle, and on its cap was a revolving figure of a grinning boy who held a hamburger aloft. One night in mid-summer they ran across, breathless with daring, and right away someone leaned out a car window and invited them over, but it was just a boy from high school they didn't like. It made them feel good to be able to ignore him. They went up through the maze of parked and cruising cars to the bright-lit, fly-infested restaurant, their faces pleased and expectant as if they were entering a sacred building that loomed out of the night to give them what haven and what blessing they yearned for. They sat at the counter and crossed their legs at the ankles, their thin shoulders rigid with excitement, and listened to the music that made everything so good: the music was always in the background like music at a church service, it was something to depend upon.

A boy named Eddie came in to talk with them. He sat backwards on his stool, turning himself jerkily around in semi-circles and then stopping and turning again, and after a while he asked Connie if she would like something to eat. She said she did and so she tapped her friend's arm on her way out—her friend pulled her face up into a brave droll look—and Connie said she would meet her at eleven, across the way. "I just hate to leave her like that," Connie said earnestly, but the boy said that she would-n't be alone for long. So they went out to his car and on the way Connie couldn't help but let her eyes wander over the windshields and faces all around her, her face gleaming with a joy that had nothing to do with Eddie or even this place; it might have been the music. She drew her shoulders up and sucked in her breath with the pure pleasure of being alive, and just at that moment she happened to glance at a face just a few feet from hers. It was a boy with shaggy black hair, in a convertible jalopy painted gold. He stared at her and then his lips widened into a grin. Connie slit her eyes at him and turned away, but she couldn't help glancing back and there he was still watching her. He wagged a finger and laughed and said, "Gonna get you, baby," and Connie turned away again without Eddie noticing anything.

She spent three hours with him, at the restaurant where they ate hamburgers and drank Cokes in wax cups that were always sweating, and then down an alley a mile or so away, and when he left her off at five to eleven only the movie house was still open at the plaza. Her girl friend was there, talking with a boy. When Connie came up the two girls smiled at each other and Connie said, "How was the movie?" and the girl said, "*You* should know." They rode off with the girl's father, sleepy and pleased, and Connie couldn't help but look at the darkened shopping plaza with its big empty parking lot and its signs that were faded and ghostly now, and over at the drive-in restaurant where cars were still circling tirelessly. She couldn't hear the music at this distance.

Next morning June asked her how the movie was and Connie said, "So-so."

10   She and that girl and occasionally another girl went out several times a week that way, and the rest of the time Connie spent around the house—it was summer vacation—getting in her mother's way and thinking, dreaming, about the boys she met. But all the boys fell back and dissolved into a single face that was not even a face, but an idea, a feeling, mixed up with the urgent insistent pounding of the music and the humid night air of July. Connie's mother kept dragging her back to the daylight by finding things for her to do or saying, suddenly, "What's this about the Pettinger girl?"

And Connie would say nervously, "Oh, her. That dope." She always drew thick clear lines between herself and such girls, and her mother was simple and kindly enough to believe her. Her mother was so simple, Connie thought, that it was maybe cruel to fool her so much. Her mother went scuffling around the house in old bedroom slippers and complained over the telephone to one sister about the other, then the other called up and the two of them complained about the third one. If June's name was mentioned her mother's tone was approving, and if Connie's name was mentioned it was disapproving. This did not really mean she disliked Connie and actually Connie thought that her mother preferred her to June because she was prettier, but the two of them kept up a pretense of exasperation, a sense that they were tugging and struggling over something of little value to either of them. Sometimes, over coffee, they were almost friends, but something would come up—some vexation that was like a fly buzzing suddenly around their heads—and their faces went hard with contempt.

One Sunday Connie got up at eleven—none of them bothered with church—and washed her hair so that it could dry all day long, in the sun. Her parents and sister were going to a barbecue at an aunt's house and Connie said no, she wasn't interested, rolling her eyes to let her mother know just what she thought of it. "Stay home alone then," her mother said sharply. Connie sat out back in a lawn chair and watched them drive away, her father quiet and bald, hunched around so that he could back the car out, her mother with a look that was still angry and not at all softened through the windshield, and in the back seat poor old June all dressed up as if she didn't know what a barbecue was, with all the running yelling kids and the flies. Connie sat with her eyes closed in the sun, dreaming and dazed with the warmth about her as if this were a kind of love, the caresses of love, and her mind slipped over onto thoughts of the boy she had been with the night before and how nice he had been, how sweet it always was, not the way someone like June would suppose but sweet, gentle, the way it was in movies and promised in songs; and when she opened her eyes she hardly knew where she was, the back yard ran off into weeds and a fence-line of trees and behind it the sky was perfectly blue and still. The asbestos "ranch house" that was now three years old startled her—it looked small. She shook her head as if to get awake.

It was too hot. She went inside the house and turned on the radio to drown out the quiet. She sat on the edge of her bed, barefoot, and listened for an hour and a half to a program called XYZ Sunday Jamboree, record after record of hard, fast, shrieking songs she sang along with, interspersed by exclamations from "Bobby King": "An' look here you girls at Napoleon's—Son and Charley want you to pay real close attention to this song coming up!"

And Connie paid close attention herself, bathed in a glow of slow-pulsed joy that seemed to rise mysteriously out of the music itself and lay languidly about the airless little room, breathed in and breathed out with each gentle rise and fall of her chest.

15   After a while she heard a car coming up the drive. She sat up at once, startled, because it couldn't be her father so soon. The gravel kept crunching all the way in from the road—the driveway was long—and Connie ran to the window. It was a car she didn't know. It was an open jalopy, painted a bright gold that caught the sunlight opaquely. Her heart began to pound and her fingers snatched at her hair, checking it, and she whispered "Christ. Christ," wondering how bad she looked. The car came to a stop at the side door and the horn sounded four short taps as if this were a signal Connie knew.

She went into the kitchen and approached the door slowly, then hung out the screen door, her bare toes curling down off the step. There were two boys in the car and now she recognized the driver: he had shaggy, shabby black hair that looked crazy as a wig and he was grinning at her.

"I ain't late, am I?" he said.

"Who the hell do you think you are?" Connie said.

"Toldja I'd be out, didn't I?"

20   "I don't even know who you are."

She spoke sullenly, careful to show no interest or pleasure, and he spoke in a fast bright monotone. Connie looked past him to the other boy, taking her time. He had fair brown hair, with a lock that fell onto his forehead. His sideburns gave him a fierce, embarrassed look, but so far he hadn't even bothered to glance at her. Both boys wore sunglasses. The driver's glasses were metallic and mirrored everything in miniature.

"You wanta come for a ride?" he said.

Connie smirked and let her hair fall loose over one shoulder.

"Don'tcha like my car? New paint job," he said. "Hey."

25   "What?"

"You're cute."

She pretended to fidget, chasing flies away from the door.

"Don'tcha believe me, or what?" he said.

"Look, I don't even know who you are," Connie said in disgust.

30   "Hey, Ellie's got a radio, see. Mine's broke down." He lifted his friend's arm and showed her the little transistor the boy was holding, and now Connie began to hear the music. It was the same program that was playing inside the house.

"Bobby King?" she said.

"I listen to him all the time. I think he's great."

"He's kind of great," Connie said reluctantly.

"Listen, that guy's *great*. He knows where the action is."

35   Connie blushed a little, because the glasses made it impossible for her to see just what this boy was looking at. She couldn't decide if she liked him or if he was just a jerk, and so she dawdled in the doorway and wouldn't come down or go back inside. She said, "What's all that stuff painted on your car?"

"Can'tcha read it?" He opened the door very carefully, as if he was afraid it might fall off. He slid out just as carefully, planting his feet firmly on the ground, the tiny metallic world in his glasses slowing down like gelatin hardening and in the midst of it Connie's bright green blouse. "This here is my name, to begin with," he said. ARNOLD FRIEND was written in tarlike black letters on the side, with a drawing of a round grinning face that reminded Connie of a pumpkin, except it wore sunglasses. "I wanta introduce myself, I'm Arnold Friend and that's my real name and I'm gonna be your friend, honey, and inside the car's Ellie Oscar, he's kinda shy." Ellie brought his transistor radio up to his shoulder and balanced it there. "Now these numbers are a secret code, honey," Arnold Friend explained. He read off the numbers 33, 19, 17 and raised his eyebrows at her to see what she thought of that, but she didn't think much of it. The left rear fender had been smashed and around it was written, on the gleaming gold background: DONE BY CRAZY WOMAN DRIVER. Connie had to laugh at that. Arnold Friend was pleased at her laughter and looked up at her. "Around the other side's a lot more—you wanta come and see them?"

"No."

"Why not?"

"Why should I?"

40   "Don'tcha wanta see what's on the car? Don'tcha wanta go for a ride?"

"I don't know."

"Why not?"

"I got things to do."

"Like what?"

45   "Things."

He laughed as if she had said something funny. He slapped his thighs. He was standing in a strange way, leaning back against the car as if he were balancing himself. He wasn't tall, only an inch or so taller than she would be if she came down to him. Connie liked the way he was dressed, which was the way all of them dressed: tight faded jeans stuffed into black, scuffed boots, a belt that pulled his waist in and showed how lean he was, and a white pull-over shirt that was a little soiled and showed the hard small muscles of his arms and shoulders. He looked as if he probably did hard work, lifting and carrying things. Even his neck looked muscular. And his face was a familiar face, somehow: the jaw and chin and cheeks slightly darkened, because he hadn't shaved for a day or two, and the nose long and hawk-like, sniffing as if she were a treat he was going to gobble up and it was all a joke.

"Connie, you ain't telling the truth. This is your day set aside for a ride with me and you know it," he said, still laughing. The way he straightened and recovered from his fit of laughing showed that it had been all fake.

"How do you know what my name is?" she said suspiciously.

"It's Connie."

50 "Maybe and maybe not."

"I know my Connie," he said, wagging his finger. Now she remembered him even better, back at the restaurant, and her cheeks warmed at the thought of how she sucked in her breath just at the moment she passed him—how she must have looked to him. And he had remembered her. "Ellie and I come out here especially for you," he said. "Ellie can sit in back. How about it?"

"Where?"

"Where what?"

"Where're we going?"

55 He looked at her. He took off the sunglasses and she saw how pale the skin around his eyes was, like holes that were not in shadow but instead in light. His eyes were chips of broken glass that catch the light in an amiable way. He smiled. It was as if the idea of going for a ride somewhere, to some place, was a new idea to him.

"Just for a ride, Connie sweetheart."

"I never said my name was Connie," she said.

"But I know what it is. I know your name and all about you, lots of things," Arnold Friend said. He had not moved yet but stood still leaning back against the side of his jalopy. "I took a special interest in you, such a pretty girl, and found out all about you like I know your parents and sister are gone somewheres and I know where and how long they're going to be gone, and I know who you were with last night, and your best girl friend's name is Betty. Right?"

He spoke in a simple lilting voice, exactly as if he were reciting the words to a song. His smile assured her that everything was fine. In the car Ellie turned up the volume on his radio and did not bother to look around at them.

60 "Ellie can sit in the back seat," Arnold Friend said. He indicated his friend with a casual jerk of his chin, as if Ellie did not count and she should not bother with him.

"How'd you find out all that stuff?" Connie said.

"Listen: Betty Schultz and Tony Fitch and Jimmy Pettinger and Nancy Pettinger," he said, in a chant. "Raymond Stanley and Bob Hutter—"

"Do you know all those kids?"

"I know everybody."

65 "Look, you're kidding. You're not from around here."

"Sure."

"But—how come we never saw you before?"

"Sure you saw me before," he said. He looked down at his boots, as if he were a little offended. "You just don't remember."

"I guess I'd remember you," Connie said.

70 "Yeah?" He looked up at this, beaming. He was pleased. He began to mark time with the music from Ellie's radio, tapping his fists lightly together. Connie looked away from his smile to the car, which was painted so bright it almost hurt her eyes to look at it. She looked at that name, ARNOLD FRIEND. And up at the front fender was an expression that was familiar—MAN THE FLYING SAUCERS. It was an expression kids had used the year before, but didn't use this year. She looked at it for a while as if the words meant something to her that she did not yet know.

"What're you thinking about? Huh?" Arnold Friend demanded. "Not worried about your hair blowing around in the car, are you?"

"No."

"Think I maybe can't drive good?"

"How do I know?"

75 "You're a hard girl to handle. How come?" he said. "Don't you know I'm your friend? Didn't you see me put my sign in the air when you walked by?"

"What sign?"

"My sign." And he drew an X in the air, leaning out toward her. They were maybe ten feet apart. After his hand fell back to his side the X was still in the air, almost visible. Connie let the screen door close and stood perfectly still inside it, listening to the music from her radio and the boy's blend together. She stared at Arnold Friend. He stood there so stiffly relaxed, pretending to be relaxed, with one hand idly on the door handle as if he were keeping himself up that way and had no intention of ever moving again. She recognized most things about him, the tight jeans that showed his thighs and buttocks and the greasy leather boots and the tight shirt, and even that slippery friendly smile of his, that sleepy dreamy smile that all the boys used to get across ideas they didn't want to put into words. She recognized all this and also the singsong way he talked, slightly mocking, kidding, but serious and a little melancholy, and she recognized the way he tapped one fist against the other in homage to the perpetual music behind him. But all these things did not come together.

She said suddenly, "Hey, how old are you?"

His smile faded. She could see then that he wasn't a kid, he was much older—thirty, maybe more. At this knowledge her heart began to pound faster.

80 "That's a crazy thing to ask. Can'tcha see I'm your own age?"

"Like hell you are."

"Or maybe a coupla years older, I'm eighteen."

"Eighteen?" she said doubtfully.

He grinned to reassure her and lines appeared at the corners of his mouth. His teeth were big and white. He grinned so broadly his eyes became slits and she saw how thick the lashes were, thick and black as if painted with a black tarlike material. Then he seemed to become embarrassed, abruptly, and looked over his shoulder at Ellie. "*Him*, he's crazy," he said. "Ain't he a riot, he's a nut, a real character." Ellie was still listening to the music. His sunglasses told nothing about what he was thinking. He wore a bright orange shirt unbuttoned halfway to show his chest, which was a pale, bluish chest and not muscular like Arnold Friend's. His shirt collar was turned up all around and the very tips of the collar pointed out past his chin as if they were protecting him. He was pressing the transistor radio up against his ear and sat there in a kind of daze, right in the sun.

5 "He's kinda strange," Connie said.

"Hey, she says you're kinda strange! Kinda strange!" Arnold Friend cried. He pounded on the car to get Ellie's attention. Ellie turned for the first time and Connie saw with shock that he wasn't a kid either—he had a fair, hairless face, cheeks reddened slightly as if the veins grew too close to the surface of his skin, the face of a forty-year-old baby. Connie felt a wave of dizziness rise in her at this sight and she stared at him as if waiting for something to change the shock of the moment, make it all right again. Ellie's lips kept shaping words, mumbling along, with the words blasting in his ear.

"Maybe you two better go away," Connie said faintly.

"What? How come?" Arnold Friend cried. "We come out here to take you for a ride. It's Sunday." He had the voice of the man on the radio now. It was the same voice, Connie thought. "Don'tcha know it's Sunday all day and honey, no matter who you were with last night today you're with Arnold Friend and don't you forget it!—Maybe you better step out here," he said, and this last was in a different voice. It was a little flatter, as if the heat was finally getting to him.

"No. I got things to do."

90   "Hey."

"You two better leave."

"We ain't leaving until you come with us."

"Like hell I am—"

"Connie, don't fool around with me. I mean, I mean, don't fool *around*," he said, shaking his head. He laughed incredulously. He placed his sunglasses on top of his head, carefully, as if he were indeed wearing a wig, and brought the stems down behind his ears. Connie stared at him, another wave of dizziness and fear rising in her so that for a moment he wasn't even in focus but was just a blur, standing there against his gold car, and she had the idea that he had driven up the driveway all right but had come from nowhere before that and belonged nowhere and that everything about him and even about the music that was so familiar to her was only half real.

95   "If my father comes and sees you—"

"He ain't coming. He's at the barbecue."

"How do you know that?"

"Aunt Tillie's. Right now they're—uh—they're drinking. Sitting around," he said vaguely, squinting as if he were staring all the way to town and over to Aunt Tillie's backyard. Then the vision seemed to get clear and he nodded energetically. "Yeah. Sitting around. There's your sister in a blue dress, huh? And high heels, the poor sad bitch—nothing like you, sweetheart! And your mother's helping some fat woman with the corn, they're cleaning the corn—husking the corn—"

"What fat woman?" Connie cried.

100   "How do I know what fat woman. I don't know every goddam fat woman in the world!" Arnold Friend laughed.

"Oh, that's Mrs. Hornby. . . . Who invited her?" Connie said. She felt a little light-headed. Her breath was coming quickly.

"She's too fat. I don't like them fat. I like them the way you are, honey," he said, smiling sleepily at her. They stared at each other for a while, through the screen door. He said softly, "Now what you're going to do is this: you're going to come out that door. You're going to sit up front with me and Ellie's going to sit in the back, the hell with Ellie, right? This isn't Ellie's date. You're my date. I'm your lover, honey."

"What? You're crazy—"

"Yes, I'm your lover. You don't know what that is but you will," he said. "I know that too. I know all about you. But look: it's real nice and you couldn't ask for nobody better than me, or more polite. I always keep my word. I'll tell you how it is, I'm always nice at first, the first time. I'll hold you so tight you won't think you have to try to get away or pretend anything because you'll know you can't. And I'll come inside you where it's all secret and you'll give in to me and you'll love me—"

05 "Shut up! You're crazy!" Connie said. She backed away from the door. She put her hands against her ears as if she'd heard something terrible, something not meant for her. "People don't talk like that, you're crazy," she muttered. Her heart was almost too big now for her chest and its pumping made sweat break out all over her. She looked out to see Arnold Friend pause and then take a step toward the porch lurching. He almost fell. But, like a clever drunken man, he managed to catch his balance. He wobbled in his high boots and grabbed hold of one of the porch posts.

"Honey?" he said. "You still listening?"

"Get the hell out of here!"

"Be nice, honey. Listen."

"I'm going to call the police—"

10 He wobbled again and out of the side of his mouth came a fast spat curse, an aside not meant for her to hear. But even this "Christ!" sounded forced. Then he began to smile again. She watched this smile come, awkward as if he were smiling from inside a mask. His whole face was a mask, she thought wildly, tanned down onto his throat but then running out as if he had plastered make-up on his face but had forgotten about his throat.

"Honey—? Listen, here's how it is. I always tell the truth and I promise you this: I ain't coming in that house after you."

"You better not! I'm going to call the police if you—if you don't—"

"Honey," he said, talking right through her voice, "honey, I'm not coming in there but you are coming out here. You know why?"

She was panting. The kitchen looked like a place she had never seen before, some room she had run inside but which wasn't good enough, wasn't going to help her. The kitchen window had never had a curtain, after three years, and there were dishes in the sink for her to do—probably—and if you ran your hand across the table you'd probably feel something sticky there.

15 "You listening, honey? Hey?"

"—going to call the police—"

"Soon as you touch the phone I don't need to keep my promise and can come inside. You won't want that."

She rushed forward and tried to lock the door. Her fingers were shaking. "But why lock it," Arnold Friend said gently, talking right into her face. "It's just a screen door. It's just nothing." One of his boots was at a strange angle, as if his foot wasn't in it. It pointed out to the left, bent at the ankle. "I mean, anybody can break through a screen door and glass and wood and iron or anything else if he needs to, anybody at all and specially Arnold Friend. If the place got lit up with a fire honey you'd come running out into my arms, right into my arms and safe at home—like you knew I was your lover and'd stopped fooling around. I don't mind a nice shy girl but I don't like no fooling around." Part of those words were spoken with a slight rhythmic lilt, and Connie somehow recognized them—the echo of a song from last year, about a girl rushing into her boy friend's arms and coming home again—

Connie stood barefoot on the linoleum floor, staring at him. "What do you want?" she whispered.

120   "I want you," he said.

"What?"

"Seen you that night and thought, that's the one, yes sir. I never needed to look any more."

"But my father's coming back. He's coming to get me. I had to wash my hair first—" She spoke in a dry, rapid voice, hardly raising it for him to hear.

"No, your daddy is not coming and yes, you had to wash your hair and you washed it for me. It's nice and shining and all for me, I thank you, sweetheart," he said, with a mock bow, but again he almost lost his balance. He had to bend and adjust his boots. Evidently his feet did not go all the way down; the boots must have been stuffed with something so that he would seem taller. Connie stared out at him and behind him Ellie in the car, who seemed to be looking off toward Connie's right, into nothing. This Ellie said, pulling the words out of the air one after another as if he were just discovering them, "You want me to pull out the phone?"

125   "Shut your mouth and keep it shut," Arnold Friend said, his face red from bending over or maybe from embarrassment because Connie had seen his boots. "This ain't none of your business."

"What—what are you doing? What do you want?" Connie said. "If I call the police they'll get you, they'll arrest you—"

"Promise was not to come in unless you touch that phone, and I'll keep that promise," he said. He resumed his erect position and tried to force his shoulders back. He sounded like a hero in a movie, declaring something important. He spoke too loudly and it was as if he were speaking to someone behind Connie. "I ain't made plans for coming in that house where I don't belong but just for you to come out to me, the way you should. Don't you know who I am?"

"You're crazy," she whispered. She backed away from the door but did not want to go into another part of the house, as if this would give him permission to come through the door. "What do you . . . You're crazy, you . . . "

"Huh? What're you saying, honey?"

130   Her eyes darted everywhere in the kitchen. She could not remember what it was, this room.

"This is how it is, honey: you come out and we'll drive away, have a nice ride. But if you don't come out we're gonna wait till your people come home and then they're all going to get it."

"You want that telephone pulled out?" Ellie said. He held the radio away from his ear and grimaced, as if without the radio the air was too much for him.

"I toldja shut up, Ellie," Arnold Friend said, "you're deaf, get a hearing aid, right? Fix yourself up. This little girl's no trouble and's gonna be nice to me, so Ellie keep to yourself, this ain't your date—right? Don't hem in on me. Don't hog. Don't crush. Don't bird dog. Don't trail me," he said in a rapid meaningless voice, as if he were running through all the expressions he'd learned but was no longer sure which one of them was in style, then rushing on to new ones, making them up with his eyes closed, "Don't crawl under my fence, don't squeeze in my chipmunk hole, don't sniff my glue, suck my popsicle, keep your own greasy fingers on yourself!" He shaded his eyes and peered in at Connie, who was backed against the kitchen table. "Don't mind him honey he's just a creep. He's a dope. Right? I'm the boy for you and like I said you come out here nice like a lady and give me your hand, and nobody else gets hurt, I mean, your nice old bald-headed daddy and your mummy and your sister in her high heels. Because listen: why bring them in this?"

"Leave me alone," Connie whispered.

35 "Hey, you know that old woman down the road, the one with the chickens and stuff—you know her?"

"She's dead!"

"Dead? What? You know her?" Arnold Friend said.

"She's dead—"

"Don't you like her?"

40 "She's dead—she's—she isn't here any more—"

"But don't you like her, I mean, you got something against her? Some grudge or something?" Then his voice dipped as if he were conscious of a rudeness. He touched the sunglasses perched on top of his head as if to make sure they were still there. "Now you be a good girl."

"What are you going to do?"

"Just two things, or maybe three," Arnold Friend said. "But I promise it won't last long and you'll like me that way you get to like people you're close to. You will. It's all over for you here, so come on out. You don't want your people in any trouble, do you?"

She turned and bumped against a chair or something, hurting her leg, but she ran into the back room and picked up the telephone. Something roared in her ear, a tiny roaring, and she was so sick with fear that she could do nothing but listen to it—the telephone was clammy and very heavy and her fingers groped down to the dial but were too weak to touch it. She began to scream into the phone, into the roaring. She cried out, she cried for her mother, she felt her breath start jerking back and forth in her lungs as if it were something Arnold Friend were stabbing her with again and again with no tenderness. A noisy sorrowful wailing rose all about her and she was locked inside it the way she was locked inside the house.

45 After a while she could hear again. She was sitting on the floor with her wet back against the wall.

Arnold Friend was saying from the door, "That's a good girl. Put the phone back."

She kicked the phone away from her.

"No, honey. Pick it up. Put it back right."

She picked it up and put it back. The dial tone stopped.

50 "That's a good girl. Now come outside."

She was hollow with what had been fear, but what was now just an emptiness. All that screaming had blasted it out of her. She sat, one leg cramped under her, and deep inside her brain was something like a pinpoint of light that kept going and would not let her relax. She thought, I'm not going to see my mother again. She thought, I'm not going to sleep in my bed again. Her bright green blouse was all wet.

Arnold Friend said, in a gentle-loud voice that was like a stage voice, "The place where you came from ain't there any more, and where you had in mind to go is cancelled out. This place you are now—inside your daddy's house—is nothing but a cardboard box I can knock down any time. You know that and always did know it. You hear me?"

She thought, I have got to think. I have to know what to do.

"We'll go out to a nice field, out in the country here where it smells so nice and it's sunny," Arnold Friend said. "I'll have my arms around you so you won't need to try to get away and I'll show you what love is like, what it does. The hell with this house! It looks solid all right," he said. He ran a fingernail down the screen and the noise did not make Connie shiver, as it would have the day before. "Now put your hand on your heart, honey. Feel that? That feels solid too but we know better, be nice to me, be sweet like you can because what else is there for a girl like you but to be sweet and pretty and give in?—and get away before her people come back?"

155   She felt her pounding heart. Her hand seemed to enclose it. She thought for the first time in her life that it was nothing that was hers, that belonged to her, but just a pounding, living thing inside this body that wasn't really hers either.

"You don't want them to get hurt," Arnold Friend went on. "Now get up, honey. Get up all by yourself."

She stood up.

"Now turn this way. That's right. Come over here to me—Ellie, put that away, didn't I tell you? You dope. You miserable creepy dope," Arnold Friend said. His words were not angry but only part of an incantation. The incantation was kindly. "Now come out through the kitchen to me honey and let's see a smile, try it, you're a brave sweet little girl and now they're eating corn and hotdogs cooked to bursting over an outdoor fire, and they don't know one thing about you and never did and honey you're better than them because not a one of them would have done this for you."

Connie felt the linoleum under her feet; it was cool. She brushed her hair back out of her eyes. Arnold Friend let go of the post tentatively and opened his arms for her, his elbows pointing in toward each other and his wrists limp, to show that this was an embarrassed embrace and a little mocking, he didn't want to make her self-conscious.

160   She put out her hand against the screen. She watched herself push the door slowly open as if she were safe back somewhere in the other doorway, watching this body and this head of long hair moving out into the sunlight where Arnold Friend waited.

"My sweet little blue-eyed girl," he said, in a half-sung sigh that had nothing to do with her brown eyes but was taken up just the same by the vast sunlit reaches of the land behind him and on all sides of him, so much land that Connie had never seen before and did not recognize except to know that she was going to it.

➤ GETTING STARTED—YOUR FIRST RESPONSE

1. What is your response to this story?
2. Of what use is the information in the story?
3. Describe Connie. Why is she so irked by her mother's criticism and comparisons to her older sister? What is her social life like?
4. Describe Arnold Friend. What is your reaction to him? If he called on you, would you go with him? Explain.
5. Why does Connie go with him? Did you find her "giving in" believable? What do you suppose will happen to her?

6. Arnold says, "What else is there for a girl like you but to be sweet and pretty and give in?" Do you think he's right? Explain.

► QUESTIONS FOR READING AND WRITING

1. Both the magazine article and the story recount an event. What makes the story different from the magazine article?
2. What did you learn from the magazine article? What did you learn from the story? How was the *nature* of what you learned different?
3. To what extent is your response to "Where Are You Going, Where Have You Been?" influenced by your own experience?

Imagining Is Believing

When we read, the strength of our emotional involvement is based on our ability to experience scenes as if we were there. If we "surrender" ourselves, we not only imagine the details provided, we create ones that are not. We may occasionally say, or hear people say, "I liked the book better than the movie" or "I can't believe so and so was cast in that role." We probably mean, "I liked the movie of the book in my mind better than the movie on the screen" or "That actor is nothing like the character I created in my mind." Unless we complete the picture in our minds by filling in the details, we won't have a satisfying experience with literature.

Where do we get these details? Some of what we imagine is shared and comes from our cultural backgrounds. And some of what we imagine is personal and familiar and is fueled by our own experiences—the people, places, or events in our own lives. For example, it doesn't have to be summer for us to imagine the sun and heat on the beach—or winter for us to imagine snow. Through our "sense" memories, we can "recall" now what we felt and saw then. What we see in our "mind's eye" may also derive from music, television, film and other forms of media, and other things we have read.

► QUESTIONS FOR READING AND WRITING

1. How did you picture the waiters and the restaurants in John Cheever's "Reunion"? What image did you have of the primary speaker in "Girl"? Think about the pictures in your mind from other stories you have read.
2. Where do your pictures come from?
3. How much of what you picture in each of these stories comes from detail that the author provided and how much is completely from your experience and your imagination?

► RESPONSE REVIEW

If you've been keeping a journal or writing down other initial reactions, take a look back at your entries up to this point. Identify the factors that seem most important in your responses. Add any insights that may have occurred since writing or reading these entries.

CHAPTER 2

Communication
Writing About Fiction

T he goal in this chapter is to develop your initial responses into an essay about fiction. We begin by emphasizing the response essay, but the habits of thinking and writing stressed in this chapter apply equally well to the critical essay explored in later chapters. Finding our writing voices; developing a clear thesis statement; showing what we mean through detail, illustration, and comparison; and citing evidence from the text are also core principles for writing a critical essay. Our emphasis on analysis and argumentation in Chapters 3 and 4 will complement and build on our discussion in this chapter.

THE RESPONSE ESSAY

In many ways, writing a response essay is like the journal writing described earlier. You can write in a conversational tone and explore personal connections and associations. You don't have to prove anything, but you do want to say something important enough to share with others.

Why would we want to share our experiences with literature? Perhaps the most compelling reason is the same one we have for communicating any other important event. Why do we discuss our experiences of movies, games, concerts, exhibits, or parties? Why do we chat about dates, meaningful events in our lives, or interesting people we have met?

Although some people need to impress others with their knowledge, accomplishments, or "important" acquaintances, many of us share because we have a need to "review" or "reexperience" with others, to have them say, "I see what you mean" or "I understand why you were affected that way." We don't want advice; we want caring listeners. This kind of sharing has a give-and-take to it. We give a rendering of our experience, and we receive other people's understanding, affirmation, and appreciation—their participation. It's not "scoring points" or *proving* we are right; it's an experience in itself.

The purpose of a response essay is to invite readers into our experience with literature—not to win an argument. If the voice in our writing, the reader's sense of who we are, is that of a "sharer," not a prosecuting attorney, the essay will feel like a welcome invitation, not a summons. Readers are better able to see when we *show*, not *show off*. The strength of their involvement is based on how much they care about what we share. Our voice in presenting that experience strongly influences their level of interest. For readers who accept our invitation, "I see what you mean" takes on a literal dimension. The clarity and thoughtfulness with which we write will determine how glad they are that they came.

Voice and Writing

Finding Our Voices   Few would question the importance of voice in the realm of speaking and listening. Accurately or not, we often make judgments about people's personalities by the sounds of their voices. It would not be unusual to hear someone say, "She sounds like someone I can trust" or "He sounds like a phony." On the other hand, when we speak to a friend, we know that our own voices will usually sound (and feel) more comfortable and confident than when we inquire about a job, ask someone for a date, or speak to a large audience. The sound of our voices and the style with which we speak are bound to be influenced by our level of comfort, to whom we are speaking, and what we want from the communication. It is not surprising, then, that we give so much attention to how we sound and the words we use when we are concerned about making an impression.

For example, leaving a message for incoming calls on a phone answering machine seems like a very simple procedure. But if you have ever recorded or witnessed someone recording a message of this kind, you know that it usually takes more than one try to "get it right." Getting it right, of course, has a lot to do with our situations and who we think will be calling. The kind of message we might leave to amuse our friends is likely to be very different from the one we would want a prospective employer to hear as we await the results of a job interview.

Voice in Writing   We know that the tone of voice we use when speaking is likely to make an impression—that *how* we say the words out loud can convey as much meaning as the words themselves. But speech and writing are different. We can think about and revise most writing, but speech is usually spontaneous, and we don't revise what we say in normal conversation. Spontaneous speech contains lots of stops and false starts and sound fillers that would look silly in writing. Unless we say something especially memorable or inflammatory, we're confident these words won't be heard (or read) over and over again. So, what does voice have to do with writing?

Virtually all of us learned to speak before we learned to read. Throughout our lives, we've been conditioned to hear the words we read. As children, many of us said the words out loud as we read to ourselves. Even if we don't move our lips or say the words out loud now, it's difficult to read them without triggering the nerves that activate speech and help us to "sub-vocalize" and hear the words voiced in our minds.

So, too, readers of our writing want to hear our voices—to get a sense of who we are. As writers we are conscious of this. For example, when writing a letter or an e-mail message our voices may change according to whom we send it, what we want, and how we want to be perceived. In a personal letter to an old friend we are probably free "to be ourselves." Our friends know us, and usually we're not anxious about the impression we will make. We are confident they will recognize our voices in the words. However, when writing a letter "To the Editor," flirting with a new romantic interest, or applying for a job, our voices are likely to be quite different. We may want to convey a sense of responsibility, wisdom, wit, or whatever else we can demonstrate to make a positive impression.

What we write about may also have a strong influence on how we are heard. As you might imagine, we write with more feeling and a clearer, stronger voice about issues that move us. Here too, we write with more confidence when we are sure of our audience. Those entries that are private (and for our eyes only) are likely to be different from those we know will be read by others. Those entries written for our friends or agreeable classmates will probably be different from those written for an unknown audience.

Voice and Response to Literature

Showing and Telling Most of us are best convinced when we see for ourselves. It would certainly seem risky to buy a car "sight unseen." We would probably insist on seeing it, trying it out, getting the "feel" of it before we decided to buy. When we talk with friends about a concert, game, or party, we probably wouldn't settle for "It was great." Again, we would like to get the "feel" of it, to hear the details, to imagine ourselves there, to share the experience.

As readers, we have a similar need. We are not likely to settle for being told an issue is compelling or trivial; an event exciting, suspenseful, or sad; a character fascinating, dull, or manipulative. We want to be moved by the issue, to be present at the event, to know the character for ourselves. Writers' voices are believable when we experience characters and events with them—when the conclusions ("exciting," "sad," "dull") are ours—when we are shown, not simply told.

The following four short stories are about children "coming of age." All of the stories have strong but different narrative voices. Sandra Cisneros's story "Eleven" is told by an eleven-year-old child who is the story's main character. Tahira Naqvi's "Brave We Are" is also told by the story's main character, but the voice is that of a child's mother. Liliana Heker's short story "The Stolen Party" is a story about a child but through the voice and point of view of a narrator outside the story. James Joyce's "Araby" is told from the point of view of a child—who is now an adult.

Before you answer the questions that follow the next four selections, you may want to write down your first impressions and any questions that come to mind during and after your reading.

▶ MAKING CONNECTIONS—"Eleven"

From our perspectives as adults, many of the problems of childhood may seem relatively unimportant. However, what may seem unimportant to us now may have affected us very differently when we were growing up.

Can you remember what it was like to be an eleven-year-old? See if you can recall an event that you found especially humiliating or embarrassing at that age. Try to remember what you were feeling and what you found especially difficult about the experience.

SANDRA CISNEROS (b. 1954)

ELEVEN   [1983]

What they don't understand about birthdays and what they never tell you is that when you're eleven, you're also ten, and nine, and eight, and seven, and six, and five, and four, and three, and two, and one. And when you wake up on your eleventh birthday you expect to feel eleven, but you don't. You open your eyes and everything's just like yesterday, only it's today. And you don't feel eleven at all. You feel like you're still ten. And you are—underneath the year that makes you eleven.

Like some days you might say something stupid, and that's the part of you that's still ten. Or maybe some days you might need to sit on your mama's lap because you're scared, and that's the part of you that's five. And maybe one day when you're all grown up maybe you will need to cry like if you're three, and that's okay. That's what I tell Mama when she's sad and needs to cry. Maybe she's feeling three.

Because the way you grow old is kind of like an onion or like the rings inside a tree trunk or like my little wooden dolls that fit one inside the other, each year inside the next one. That's how being eleven years old is.

You don't feel eleven. Not right away. It takes a few days, weeks even, sometimes even months before you say Eleven when they ask you. And you don't feel smart eleven, not until you're almost twelve. That's the way it is.

5   Only today I wish I didn't have only eleven years rattling inside me like pennies in a tin Band-Aid box. Today I wish I was one hundred and two instead of eleven because if I was one hundred and two I'd have known what to say when Mrs. Price put the red sweater on my desk. I would've known how to tell her it wasn't mine instead of just sitting there with that look on my face and nothing coming out of my mouth.

"Whose is this?" Mrs. Price says, and she holds the red sweater up in the air for all the class to see. "Whose? It's been sitting in the coatroom for a month."

"Not mine," says everybody. "Not me."

"It has to belong to somebody," Mrs. Price keeps saying, but nobody can remember. It's an ugly sweater with red plastic buttons and a collar and sleeves all stretched out like you could use them for a jump rope. It's maybe a thousand years old and even if it belonged to me I wouldn't say so.

Maybe because I'm skinny, maybe because she doesn't like me, that stupid Sylvia Saldivar says, "I think it belongs to Rachel." An ugly sweater like that, all raggedy and old, but Mrs. Price believes her; Mrs. Price takes the sweater and puts it right on my desk, but when I open my mouth nothing comes out.

10   "That's not, I don't, you're not . . . Not mine," I finally say in a little voice that was maybe me when I was four.

"Of course it's yours," Mrs. Price says. "I remember you wearing it once." Because she's older and the teacher, she's right and I'm not.

Not mine, not mine, not mine, but Mrs. Price is already turning to page thirty-two and math problem number four. I don't know why but all of a sudden I'm feeling sick inside, like the part of me that's three wants to come out of my eyes, only I squeeze them shut tight and bite down on my teeth real hard and try to remember today I am eleven, eleven.

Mama is making a cake for me for tonight, and when Papa comes home everybody will sing Happy birthday, happy birthday to you.

But when the sick feeling goes away and I open my eyes, the red sweater's still sitting there like a big red mountain. I move the red sweater to the corner of my desk with my ruler. I move my pencil and books and eraser as far from it as possible. I even move my chair a little to the right. Not mine, not mine, not mine.

15   In my head I'm thinking how long till lunchtime, how long till I can take the red sweater and throw it over the schoolyard fence, or leave it hanging on a parking meter, or bunch it up into a little ball and toss it in the alley. Except when math period ends Mrs. Price says loud and in front of everybody, "Now, Rachel, that's enough," because she sees I've shoved the red sweater to the tippy-tip corner of my desk and it's hanging all over the edge like a waterfall, but I don't care.

"Rachel," Mrs. Price says. She says it like she's getting mad. "You put that sweater on right now and no more nonsense."

"But it's not—"

"Now!" Mrs. Price says.

This is when I wish I wasn't eleven, because all the years inside of me—ten, nine, eight, seven, six, five, four, three, two, and one—are pushing at the back of my eyes when I put one arm through one sleeve of the sweater that smells like cottage cheese, and then the other arm through the other and stand there with my arms apart like if the sweater hurts me and it does, all itchy and full of germs that aren't even mine.

20   That's when everything I've been holding in since this morning, since when Mrs. Price put the sweater on my desk, finally lets go, and all of a sudden I'm crying in front of everybody. I wish I was invisible but I'm not. I'm eleven and it's my birthday today and I'm crying like I'm three in front of everybody. I put my head down on the desk and bury my face in my stupid clown-sweater arms. My face all hot and spit coming out of my mouth because I can't stop the little animal noises from coming out of me, until there aren't any more tears left in my eyes, and it's just my body shaking like when you have the hiccups, and my whole head hurts like when you drink milk too fast.

But the worst part is right before the bell rings for lunch. That stupid Phyllis Lopez, who is even dumber than Sylvia Saldivar, says she remembers the red sweater is hers! I take it off right away and give it to her, only Mrs. Price pretends like everything's okay.

Today I'm eleven. There's a cake Mama's making for tonight, and when Papa comes home from work we'll eat it. There'll be candles and presents and everybody will sing Happy birthday, happy birthday to you, Rachel, only it's too late.

I'm eleven today. I'm eleven, ten, nine, eight, seven, six, five, four, three, two, and one, but I wish I was one hundred and two. I wish I was anything but eleven, because I want today to be far away already, far away like a runaway balloon, like a tiny *o* in the sky, so tiny-tiny you have to close your eyes to see it.

➤ QUESTIONS FOR READING AND WRITING

1. If you could recall a childhood event that you found humiliating or embarrassing, how did that memory influence your response to this story?
2. How does the voice of the narrator affect your response?
3. What does the speaker mean when she says, "The way you grow old is kind of like an onion or like the rings inside a tree trunk or like my little wooden dolls that fit one inside the other"?
4. What other passages in the story had an impact on you? How so?
5. If you find the voice of the story convincing, what features of the writing seem to make it effective? To what extent does the story "show" what is told?

➤ MAKING CONNECTIONS—"Brave We Are"

If you have ever tried to explain a complex concept to a young child, you know how difficult that can sometimes be—for a variety of reasons. See if you can recall a time in your life when you were in this situation—or when you were the child who was trying to find out what something meant. Try to remember what that experience was like.

TAHIRA NAQVI (b. 1945)

BRAVE WE ARE   [2001]

"Mom, Ammi," he asks, the little boy Kasim who is my son, who has near-black eyes and whose buck teeth give him a Bugs Bunny look when his mouth is open, as it is now, in query. "What does hybrid mean?"

"Hybrid?" I'm watching the water in the pot very closely; the tiny bubbles quivering restlessly on its surface indicate it's about to come to boil. Poised over the pot, clutching a batch of straw-colored Prince spaghetti, is my hand, suspended, warm from the steam and waiting for the moment when the bubbles will suddenly and turbulently come to life.

I'm not fussy about brands, especially where spaghetti is concerned (it's all pasta, after all), but I wish there was one which would fit snugly at the outset into my largest pot. As things stand now, the strands bend uncomfortably, contort, embroiling themselves in something of a struggle within the confines of the pot once they've been dropped into the boiling water. Some day of course, I will have a pot large enough to accommodate all possible lengths and varieties.

"Yeah, hybrid. Do you know what it means?"

5   The note of restive insistence in his voice compels me to tear my gaze away from the water. Kasim's face looks darker now than when he left for school this morning. Perhaps running up the steep driveway with the March wind lashing against his lean nine-year-old frame has forced the blood to rush to his face. Flushed, his face reminds me he's still only a child, 'only ten, just a baby,' as my mother often says when I sometimes take him to task in her presence, arguing with him as if he were a man behaving like a child.

A new spelling word? Such a difficult word for a fourth-grader. "Are you studying plants?"

"No, but can you tell me what it means?" Impatient, so impatient, so like the water that's hissing and tumbling in the pot, demanding immediate attention. He slides against the kitchen counter and hums, his fingers beating an indecipherable rhythm on the Formica, his eyes raised above mine, below mine, behind me, to the window outside which white, lavender and gray have mingled to become a muddied brown. Just as he reaches for the cookie jar I quickly throw in the spaghetti.

"Well, that's a hard word. Let me see." Helplessly I watch as he breaks off a Stella Doro biscuit in his mouth and crumbs disperse in a steady fall-out, over the counter, on the kitchen tile, some getting caught in his blue-and-green striped sweater, like flies in a spider's web. "It's a sort of mixture, a combination of different sorts of things," I say wisely, with the absolute knowledge that 'things' is susceptible to misinterpretation. I rack my brain for a good example. If I don't hurry up with one he's going to move away with the notion that his mother doesn't know what hybrid means.

"You mean if you mix orange juice with lemonade it's going to become hybrid juice?" The idea has proved ticklish, he smiles, crumbs from the Stella Doro dangling on the sides of his face; they obviously don't bother him as much as they bother me. I lean forward and rub a hand around his mouth just as he lunges toward the cookie jar again. He squirms and recoils at the touch of my ministering hand. Another biscuit is retrieved. I turn down the heat under the spaghetti to medium and start chopping onions.

10   Today I'm making spaghetti the way my mother makes it in Lahore, like pulao, the way I used to make it after I got married and was just learning to cook for a husband who had selective tastes in food. That was about the only thing I could make then so I worked hard to embellish and innovate. There, we call it noodles, although it's unmistakably spaghetti, with no tomato sauce or meatballs in or anywhere near it, no cheese either, and no one has heard of mozzarella or romano. The idea of cheese with our recipe would surprise the people in Lahore; even the ones with the most adventurous palates will cringe.

"Well, that too." And why not? My eyes smart from the sharpness of the onions, tears fill my eyes and spill over my cheeks. I turn away from the chopping board. "The word is used when you breed two different kinds of plants or animals, it's called cross-breeding." I snaffle. This gets harder. I know his knowledge of breeding is limited and 'cross' isn't going to help at all.

"What's *cross-whatyoumaycallit?*"

An example. One that will put the seal on hybrid forever. So he can boast his mother knows everything.

I wipe my watering eyes with a paper napkin and turn to the onions again. These, chopped thinly, are for the ground beef which will be cooked with small green peas, cubed potatoes and cut-leaf spinach and will be spiced with coriander, garlic, cumin, a touch of turmeric and half-inch long bristly strands of fresh ginger root. I'll throw the beef into the spaghetti when it's done and my husband and I alone will eat what I make. My children like spaghetti the way it should be, the way it is, in America.

15   Moisture runs down my cheeks and my eyes smart. I place the knife down on the chopping board, tear out another sheet from the roll of Bounty towels on my right and rub my eyes and nose with it, my attention driven to the stark, brown limbs of trees outside as I wipe my face. The kitchen window that I now face as I do innumerable times during the day, faithfully reflects the movements of time and seasons of the small town in Connecticut where we live, compelling the spirit to buoyancy or, when the tones on its canvas are achromatous and dark, to melancholy, to sadness. Today, the sun is visible again and the white of the snow is distinguishable from the lavender of the bare, thin, stalky birches, unhealthy because we haven't tended them well. Sharply the sun cuts shadows on the clean, uncluttered snow.

Why does snow in February always remind me of February in Lahore? Incongruent, disparate, the seasons have so little in common. March is spring, grass so thick your foot settles into it, roses that bloom firm, their curves fleshy, the colors like undisturbed paint on an artist's palette, the air timberous, weaving in and out of swishing tree branches with the *sar, sar, sar* of a string instrument. Why do I turn to Eileen, my cleaning lady, and say, "Eileen, do you know it's spring in Lahore?" She looks up from the pot she's scrubbing in the kitchen sink with a good-humored smile. "No kidding? Really?" she asks, as if she didn't already know, as if she hadn't already heard it from me before.

An example, yes. "Now take an apple. A farmer can cross-breed a Macintosh apple with a Golden Yellow and get something which is a little bit like both. That will be a hybrid apple." I look closely at the boy's face for some signs of comprehension.

"You mean the apple's going to have a new name, like Macintosh Yellow?" he asks, his forehead creased thoughtfully.

"Yes." Relieved, I return to the onions, making a mental note to check the spaghetti soon, which, languorously swelled now, will have to be taken off from the stove and drained.

20   "But what about animals? You said there's *crosswhatyoumaycallit* in animals too." He sprawls against the counter, up and down, right and left, like a gymnast.

"Yes there is. A cow from one family may be bred with a steer from another family and they'll end up with a calf that's a bit like the two of them." I wash my hands and he skips on the floor, dance-like steps, his arms raised.

"But man's an animal too, teacher says. Do people also cross . . . *umm* . . . breed?"

He's humming again. I know the tune now: *"Suzie Q/ Suzie Q/ I love you/ 0 Suzie Q!"* It's from a song on his older brother Haider's tape, a catchy tune, sort of stays with you and you can't stop humming it. Both Haider and my younger son, Asghar, were amused when I showed an interest in the song. What do I know about music, their kind of music? Once, nearly two years ago, I tried to bribe Haider to memorize a ghazal by the poet Ghalib. The greatest Urdu poet of the subcontinent, I said passionately, the most complex. Egged on by the fifty dollars I was offering, he mastered the first verse by listening to a tape of ghazals sung by Mehdi Hasan.

Yeh naa thi hamari qismet ke visal-e-yaar ho
Agar aurjeete rehte yehi intizar hota

It was not fated that I should meet my beloved,
Life will merely prolong the waiting

25   Then, unable to sustain his interest, despite the now thirty-dollar a verse rate, Haider abandoned the project.

"The word's are too hard," he complained when I protested, somewhat angrily. "The music's easy, but I can't keep up with the lyrics."

And I would have given him the money too. Actually I had decided to give him all of it after he had moved on to the second verse.

"Does that mean Mary is also hybrid?" Kasim's voice crashes into my thoughts of Suzie Q with a loud boom.

I lower the heat under the spaghetti—so what if it's a bit overdone. The yellow-white strands jump at each other in frantic embraces, hurried, as if there's no time to be lost.

30   "Mary? What are you talking about?" I know exactly what he's talking about. His vagueness passes through the sieve in my head and comes out as clarity. I fill in any blanks, uncannily, never ceasing to be surprised at the way this peculiar magic works.

"You know, Mary Khan, Dr. Khan's daughter? She's in my class Mom, you know her."

Yes, I know Mary well. Her full name is Marium. Her father, Amjad Khan and my husband, Ali, were together in the same medical school in Lahore, they graduated the same year, they completed residencies together at the same hospital in New York, where Amjad met and married Helen, a nurse. Helen is English. She's a few years older than I, very tall, almost a half-inch taller than Amjad, and has sleek, golden hair. We're good friends, Helen and I, and at least once a week we meet for lunch at a restaurant, an activity we decided to call 'sampling restaurants for later.' Over salmon lasagna or papadi chat and dosa or tandoori chicken she'll tell me how difficult Amjad is when it comes to their children, how upset he is that their son has taken it upon himself to date without his father's consent or approval. I'll shake my head and try to explain that Amjad might have dated *her*, but like a good Muslim father, he can't accept that his son can have girlfriends. "Wait till Mary is older," I say with my hand on Helen's arm, "the Muslim father in him will drop all his masks."

Together we do what most women do quite unabashedly: spend a great deal of time talking about husbands.

When Mary was born Amjad said, "We're going to call her Marium, it's a name everyone knows." Familiar and convenient is what he meant, since it's tri-religious. That doesn't sound right, but if we can say bisexual, surely we can say tri-religious too. Why not? After all Islam, Christianity and Judaism all profess a claim to this name. However, before the child was quite one 'Marium' was shortened permanently to Mary.

Kasim is at the breakfast table now, some of his earlier energy dissipated. A small piece of biscuit lies forlornly before him on the table and he fusses with it slowly, obviously unwilling to pop the last bit in his mouth, content just to play with it.

35 "You know, her mother's English and her father's Pakistani like Dad, and she's got blue eyes and black hair."

"Yes, she does have lovely blue eyes and they look so pretty with her dark hair." I grapple with something to blunt the sharpness of his next question which I anticipate and I know I cannot repel.

"Well, then she's hybrid too, isn't she?" He's looking straight at me. His eyes are bright with the defiance of someone who knows he's scored a point.

Brave we are, we who answer questions that spill forth artlessly from the mouths of nine-year-old purists, questions that can neither be waved nor dismissed with flippant ambiguity. Vigilant and alert, we must be ready with our answers.

"Technically speaking she is, I mean, wait, you can say she is." I lift a hand and stop him before he says more. "But we don't use the word for people." The firmness in my voice sounds forced. "Beta, don't say anything to her, okay?"

40 "Why? Is it a swear?"

"No!" I hasten with denial. "Of course not. It's just a word we don't use for people, that's all. Understand?"

"But what do you call them then?" He persists. "Mary's like the apple, isn't she? Isn't she? Her name's Mary Khan, isn't it?"

"Yes, Kas, it is. But there's nothing wrong with that name, a name's a name." Kasim looks contemplative. I know he's saying to himself, *Mom doesn't really know, but Mary's a hybrid, she's got blue eyes and black hair.*

"She's a person, Kasim, not an apple. Anyway, you didn't tell me where you heard that word. Is it on your spelling list for this week?"

45 "No, Mrs. Davis was reading us something about plants in the *Weekly Reader*. It's not homework." He shrugs, abandons the Stella Doro and humming, leaves the kitchen.

"Get to homework now," I call after him, wondering if there's an equivalent of 'hybrid' in Urdu, a whole word, not one or two strung together in a phrase to mean the same thing. Offhand I can't think of one.

Without meaning to I throw in some oregano into the boiling spaghetti. I shouldn't have done that. How's oregano going to taste in the company of coriander and cumin? Well, no matter, it's too late anyway.

After I've drained the spaghetti I will take some out for the meat mixture, saving the rest for my children. Then I'll add to our portion, my husband's and mine, the beef and vegetable mixture and turn everything over ever so gently, making sure that the spaghetti isn't squelched. The strands must remain smooth, elusive, separate.

➤ QUESTIONS FOR READING AND WRITING

1. To what extent did your own experience influence your response to this story?
2. Why is the mother so concerned about explaining the word *hybrid*?
3. Describe the voice of the narrator. How has she "shown" what is told? What details give you a clear picture of the setting and the situation?

➤ MAKING CONNECTIONS—"The Stolen Party"

Before you read the story that follows, see if you can remember a time when you wanted to be a part of a group and felt unfairly rejected. Try to recall those emotions and what made you the most frustrated and angry about not being allowed to "belong."

LILIANA HEKER (b. 1943)

THE STOLEN PARTY   [1982]

As soon as she arrived she went straight to the kitchen to see if the monkey was there. It was: what a relief! She wouldn't have liked to admit that her mother had been right. *Monkeys at a birthday?* her mother had sneered. *Get away with you, believing any nonsense you're told!* She was cross, but not because of the monkey, the girl thought; it's just because of the party.

"I don't like you going," she told her. "It's a rich people's party."

"Rich people go to Heaven too," said the girl, who studied religion at school.

"Get away with Heaven," said the mother. "The problem with you, young lady, is that you like to fart higher than your ass."

5   The girl didn't approve of the way her mother spoke. She was barely nine, and one of the best in her class.

"I'm going because I've been invited," she said. "And I've been invited because Luciana is my friend. So there."

"Ah yes, your friend," her mother grumbled. She paused. "Listen, Rosaura," she said at last. "That one's not your friend. You know what you are to them? The maid's daughter, that's what."

Rosaura blinked hard: she wasn't going to cry. Then she yelled: "Shut up! You know nothing about being friends!"

Every afternoon she used to go to Luciana's house and they would both finish their homework while Rosaura's mother did the cleaning. They had their tea in the kitchen and they told each other secrets. Rosaura loved everything in the big house, and she also loved the people who lived there.

10 "I'm going because it will be the most lovely party in the whole world, Luciana told me it would. There will be a magician, and he will bring a monkey and everything."

The mother swung around to take a good look at her child, and pompously put her hands on her hips.

"Monkeys at a birthday?" she said. "Get away with you, believing any nonsense you're told!"

Rosaura was deeply offended. She thought it unfair of her mother to accuse other people of being liars simply because they were rich. Rosaura too wanted to be rich, of course. If one day she managed to live in a beautiful palace, would her mother stop loving her? She felt very sad. She wanted to go to that party more than anything else in the world.

"I'll die if I don't go," she whispered, almost without moving her lips.

15 And she wasn't sure whether she had been heard, but on the morning of the party she discovered that her mother had starched her Christmas dress. And in the afternoon, after washing her hair, her mother rinsed it in apple vinegar so that it would be all nice and shiny. Before going out, Rosaura admired herself in the mirror, with her white dress and glossy hair, and thought she looked terribly pretty.

Señora Ines also seemed to notice. As soon as she saw her, she said:

"How lovely you look today, Rosaura."

Rosaura gave her starched skirt a slight toss with her hands and walked into the party with a firm step. She said hello to Luciana and asked about the monkey. Luciana put on a secretive look and whispered into Rosaura's ear: "He's in the kitchen. But don't tell anyone, because it's a surprise."

Rosaura wanted to make sure. Carefully she entered the kitchen and there she saw it: deep in thought, inside its cage. It looked so funny that the girl stood there for a while, watching it, and later, every so often, she would slip out of the party unseen and go and admire it. Rosaura was the only one allowed into the kitchen. Señora Ines had said: "You yes, but not the others, they're much too boisterous, they might break something." Rosaura had never broken anything. She even managed the jug of orange juice, carrying it from the kitchen into the dining room. She held it carefully and didn't spill a single drop. And Señora Ines had said: "Are you sure you can manage a jug as big as that?" Of course she could manage. She wasn't a butterfingers, like the others. Like that blonde girl with the bow in her hair. As soon as she saw Rosaura, the girl with the bow had said:

20 "And you? Who are you?"

"I'm a friend of Luciana," said Rosaura.

"No," said the girl with the bow, "you are not a friend of Luciana because I'm her cousin and I know all her friends. And I don't know you."

"So what," said Rosaura. "I come here every afternoon with my mother and we do our homework together."

"You and your mother do your homework together?" asked the girl, laughing.

25 "I and Luciana do our homework together," said Rosaura, very seriously.

The girl with the bow shrugged her shoulders.

"That's not being friends," she said. "Do you go to school together?"

"No."

"So where do you know her from?" said the girl, getting impatient.

30   Rosaura remembered her mother's words perfectly. She took a deep breath. "I'm the daughter of the employee," she said.

Her mother had said very clearly: "If someone asks, you say you're the daughter of the employee; that's all." She also told her to add: "And proud of it." But Rosaura thought that never in her life would she dare say something of the sort.

"What employee?" said the girl with the bow. "Employee in a shop?"

"No," said Rosaura angrily. "My mother doesn't sell anything in any shop, so there."

35   "So how come she's an employee?" said the girl with the bow.

Just then Señora Ines arrived saying *shh shh*, and asked Rosaura if she wouldn't mind helping serve out the hotdogs, as she knew the house so much better than the others.

"See?" said Rosaura to the girl with the bow, and when no one was looking she kicked her in the shin.

Apart from the girl with the bow, all the others were delightful. The one she liked best was Luciana, with her golden birthday crown; and then the boys. Rosaura won the sack race, and nobody managed to catch her when they played tag. When they split into two teams to play charades, all the boys wanted her for their side. Rosaura felt she had never been so happy in all her life.

But the best was still to come. The best came after Luciana blew out the candles. First the cake. Señora Ines had asked her to help pass the cake around, and Rosaura had enjoyed the task immensely, because everyone called out to her, shouting "Me, me!" Rosaura remembered a story in which there was a queen who had the power of life or death over her subjects. She had always loved that, having the power of life or death. To Luciana and the boys she gave the largest pieces, and to the girl with the bow she gave a slice so thin one could see through it.

40   After the cake came the magician, tall and bony, with a fine red cape. A true magician: he could untie handkerchiefs by blowing on them and make a chain with links that had no openings. He could guess what cards were pulled out from a pack, and the monkey was his assistant. He called the monkey "partner." "Let's see here, partner," he would say, "turn over a card." And, "Don't run away, partner: time to work now."

The final trick was wonderful. One of the children had to hold the monkey in his arms and the magician said he would make him disappear.

"What, the boy?" they all shouted.

"No, the monkey!" shouted back the magician.

Rosaura thought that this was truly the most amusing party in the whole world.

45   The magician asked a small fat boy to come and help, but the small fat boy got frightened almost at once and dropped the monkey on the floor. The magician picked him up carefully, whispered something in his ear, and the monkey nodded almost as if he understood.

"You mustn't be so unmanly, my friend," the magician said to the fat boy.

"What's unmanly?" said the fat boy.

The magician turned around as if to look for spies.

"A sissy," said the magician. "Go sit down."

50   Then he stared at all the faces, one by one. Rosaura felt her heart tremble.

"You, with the Spanish eyes," said the magician. And everyone saw that he was pointing at her.

She wasn't afraid. Neither holding the monkey, nor when the magician made him vanish; not even when, at the end, the magician flung his red cape over Rosaura's head and uttered a few magic words . . . and the monkey reappeared, chattering happily, in her arms. The children clapped furiously. And before Rosaura returned to her seat, the magician said:

"Thank you very much, my little countess."

She was so pleased with the compliment that a while later, when her mother came to fetch her, that was the first thing she told her.

55   "I helped the magician and he said to me, 'Thank you very much, my little countess.'"

It was strange because up to then Rosaura had thought that she was angry with her mother. All along Rosaura had imagined that she would say to her: "See that the monkey wasn't a lie?" But instead she was so thrilled that she told her mother all about the wonderful magician.

Her mother tapped her on the head and said: "So now we're a countess!"

But one could see that she was beaming.

And now they both stood in the entrance, because a moment ago Señora Ines, smiling, had said: "Please wait here a second."

60   Her mother suddenly seemed worried.

"What is it?" she asked Rosaura.

"What is what?" said Rosaura. "It's nothing; she just wants to get the presents for those who are leaving, see?"

She pointed at the fat boy and at a girl with pigtails who were also waiting there, next to their mothers. And she explained about the presents. She knew, because she had been watching those who left before her. When one of the girls was about to leave, Señora Ines would give her a bracelet. When a boy left, Señora Ines gave him a yo-yo. Rosaura preferred the yo-yo because it sparkled, but she didn't mention that to her mother. Her mother might have said: "So why don't you ask for one, you blockhead?" That's what her mother was like. Rosaura didn't feel like explaining that she'd be horribly ashamed to be the odd one out. Instead she said:

"I was the best-behaved at the party."

65   And she said no more because Señora Ines came out into the hall with two bags, one pink and one blue.

First she went up to the fat boy, gave him a yo-yo out of the blue bag, and the fat boy left with his mother. Then she went up to the girl and gave her a bracelet out of the pink bag, and the girl with the pigtails left as well.

Finally she came up to Rosaura and her mother. She had a big smile on her face and Rosaura liked that. Señora Ines looked down at her, then looked up at her mother, and then said something that made Rosaura proud:

"What a marvelous daughter you have, Herminia."

For an instant, Rosaura thought that she'd give her two presents: the bracelet and the yo-yo. Señora Ines bent down as if about to look for something. Rosaura also leaned forward, stretching out her arm. But she never completed the movement.

70   Señora Ines didn't look in the pink bag. Nor did she look in the blue bag. Instead she rummaged in her purse. In her hand appeared two bills.

"You really and truly earned this," she said handing them over. "Thank you for all your help, my pet."

Rosaura felt her arms stiffen, stick close to her body, and then she noticed her mother's hand on her shoulder. Instinctively she pressed herself against her mother's body. That was all. Except her eyes. Rosaura's eyes had a cold, clear look that fixed itself on Señora Ines's face.

Señora Ines, motionless, stood there with her hand outstretched. As if she didn't dare draw it back. As if the slightest change might shatter an infinitely delicate balance.

➤ QUESTIONS FOR READING AND WRITING

1. To what extent is your response to this story affected by your experience?
2. Why do you think the story is called "The Stolen Party"? What has been "stolen"? Explain.
3. Who is the narrator (the voice) of this story? What impact does this narrative perspective have on the story? If the story were told by Rosaura or Señora Ines, how would it be different?
4. What details "show" you the story?

➤ MAKING CONNECTIONS—"Araby"

Before you read the story that follows, see if you can recall a time when you had a "crush" and what it felt like. Try to remember how obsessed, preoccupied, or overwhelmed you might have been—and even how silly it might have made you behave.

JAMES JOYCE (1882–1941)

ARABY   [1914]

North Richmond Street, being blind, was a quiet street except at the hour when the Christian Brothers' School set the boys free. An uninhabited house of two stories stood at the blind end, detached from its neighbors in a square ground. The other houses of the street, conscious of decent lives within them, gazed at one another with brown imperturbable faces.

The former tenant of our house, a priest, had died in the back drawing-room. Air, musty from having been long enclosed, hung in all the rooms, and the waste room behind the kitchen was littered with old useless papers. Among these I found a few paper-covered books, the pages of which were curled and damp: *The Abbot,*[1] by Walter Scott, *The Devout Communicant*[2] and *The Memoirs of Vidocq.*[3] I liked the

---

[1]**The Abbot**   an early-nineteenth-century romantic novel   [2]**The Devout Communicant**   a religious text   [3]**The Memoirs of Vidocq**   the memoirs of a French secret service agent

last best because its leaves were yellow. The wild garden behind the house contained a central apple-tree and a few straggling bushes under one of which I found the late tenant's rusty bicycle-pump. He had been a very charitable priest; in his will he had left all his money to institutions and the furniture of his house to his sister.

When the short days of winter came dusk fell before we had well eaten our dinners. When we met in the street the houses had grown sombre. The space of sky above us was the colour of ever-changing violet and towards it the lamps of the street lifted their feeble lanterns. The cold air stung us and we played till our bodies glowed. Our shouts echoed in the silent street. The career of our play brought us through the dark muddy lanes behind the houses where we ran the gauntlet of the rough tribes from the cottages, to the back doors of the dark dripping gardens where odours arose from the ashpits, to the dark odorous stables where a coachman smoothed and combed the horse or shook music from the buckled harness. When we returned to the street light from the kitchen windows had filled the areas. If my uncle was seen turning the corner we hid in the shadow until we had seen him safely housed. Or if Mangan's sister came out on the doorstep to call her brother in to his tea we watched her from our shadow peer up and down the street. We waited to see whether she would remain or go in and, if she remained, we left our shadow and walked up to Mangan's steps resignedly. She was waiting for us, her figure defined by the light from the half-opened door. Her brother always teased her before he obeyed and I stood by the railings looking at her. Her dress swung as she moved her body and the soft rope of her hair tossed from side to side.

Every morning I lay on the floor in the front parlour watching her door. The blind was pulled down to within an inch of the sash so that I could not be seen. When she came out on the doorstep my heart leaped. I ran to the hall, seized my books and followed her. I kept her brown figure always in my eye and, when we came near the point at which our ways diverged, I quickened my pace and passed her. This happened morning after morning. I had never spoken to her, except for a few casual words, and yet her name was like a summons to all my foolish blood.

5   Her image accompanied me even in places the most hostile to romance. On Saturday evenings when my aunt went marketing I had to go to carry some of the parcels. We walked through the flaring streets, jostled by drunken men and bargaining women, amid the curses of labourers, the shrill litanies of shop-boys who stood on guard by the barrels of pigs' cheeks, the nasal chanting of street-singers, who sang a *come-all-you* about O'Donovan Rossa, or a ballad about the troubles in our native land. These noises converged in a single sensation of life for me: I imagined that I bore my chalice safely through a throng of foes. Her name sprang to my lips at moments in strange prayers and praises which I myself did not understand. My eyes were often full of tears (I could not tell why) and at times a flood from my heart seemed to pour itself out into my bosom. I thought little of the future. I did not know whether I would ever speak to her or not or, if I spoke to her, how I could tell her of my confused adoration. But my body was like a harp and her words and gestures were like fingers running upon the wires.

One evening I went into the back drawing-room in which the priest had died. It was a dark rainy evening and there was no sound in the house. Through one of the broken panes I heard the rain impinge upon the earth, the fine incessant needles of water playing in the sodden beds. Some distant lamp or lighted window gleamed below me. I was thankful that I could see so little. All my senses seemed to desire to veil themselves and, feeling that I was about to slip from them, I pressed the palms of my hands together until they trembled, murmuring: "*O love! O love!*" many times.

At last she spoke to me. When she addressed the first words to me I was so confused that I did not know what to answer. She asked me was I going to Araby. I forget whether I answered yes or no. It would be a splendid bazaar, she said; she would love to go.

"And why can't you?" I asked.

While she spoke she turned a silver bracelet round and round her wrist. She could not go, she said, because there would be a retreat that week in her convent.[4] Her brother and two other boys were fighting for their caps and I was alone at the railings. She held one of the spikes, bowing her head towards me. The light from the lamp opposite our door caught the white curve of her neck, lit up her hair that rested there and, falling, lit up the hand upon the railing. It fell over one side of her dress and caught the white border of a petticoat, just visible as she stood at ease.

10   "It's well for you," she said.

"If I go," I said, "I will bring you something."

What innumerable follies laid waste my waking and sleeping thoughts after that evening! I wished to annihilate the tedious intervening days. I chafed against the work of school. At night in my bedroom and by day in the classroom her image came between me and the page I strove to read. The syllables of the word *Araby* were called to me through the silence in which my soul luxuriated and cast an Eastern enchantment over me. I asked for leave to go to the bazaar on Saturday night. My aunt was surprised and hoped it was not some Freemason affair. I answered few questions in class. I watched my master's face pass from amiability to sternness; he hoped I was not beginning to idle. I could not call my wandering thoughts together. I had hardly any patience with the serious work of life which, now that it stood between me and my desire, seemed to me child's play, ugly monotonous child's play.

On Saturday morning I reminded my uncle that I wished to go to the bazaar in the evening. He was fussing at the hall-stand, looking for the hat-brush, and answered me curtly:

"Yes, boy, I know."

15   As he was in the hall I could not go into the front parlour and lie at the window. I left the house in bad humour and walked slowly towards the school. The air was pitilessly raw and already my heart misgave me.

When I came home to dinner my uncle had not yet been home. Still it was early. I sat staring at the clock for some time and, when its ticking began to irritate me, I left the room. I mounted the staircase and gained the upper part of the house. The high cold empty gloomy rooms liberated me and I went from room to room singing. From the front window I saw my companions playing below in the street. Their cries reached me weakened and indistinct and, leaning my forehead against

---

[4]**convent** in this case a parochial school for girls

the cool glass, I looked over at the dark house where she lived. I may have stood there for an hour, seeing nothing but the brown-clad figure cast by my imagination, touched discreetly by the lamplight at the curved neck, at the hand upon the railings and at the border below the dress.

When I came downstairs again I found Mrs. Mercer sitting at the fire. She was an old garrulous woman, a pawnbroker's widow, who collected used stamps for some pious purpose. I had to endure the gossip of the tea-table. The meal was prolonged beyond an hour and still my uncle did not come. Mrs. Mercer stood up to go: she was sorry she couldn't wait any longer, but it was after eight o'clock and she did not like to be out late, as the night air was bad for her. When she had gone I began to walk up and down the room, clenching my fists. My aunt said:

"I'm afraid you may put off your bazaar for this night of Our Lord."

At nine o'clock I heard my uncle's latchkey in the halldoor. I heard him talking to himself and heard the hallstand rocking when it had received the weight of his overcoat. I could interpret these signs. When he was midway through his dinner I asked him to give me the money to go to the bazaar. He had forgotten.

20   "The people are in bed and after their first sleep now," he said.

I did not smile. My aunt said to him energetically:

"Can't you give him the money and let him go? You've kept him late enough as it is."

My uncle said he was very sorry he had forgotten. He said he believed in the old saying: "All work and no play makes Jack a dull boy." He asked me where I was going and, when I had told him a second time he asked me did I know *The Arab's Farewell to His Steed.* When I left the kitchen he was about to recite the opening lines of the piece to my aunt.

I held a florin tightly in my hand as I strode down Buckingham Street towards the station. The sight of the streets thronged with buyers and glaring with gas recalled to me the purpose of my journey. I took my seat in a third-class carriage of a deserted train. After an intolerable delay the train moved out of the station slowly. It crept onward among ruinous houses and over the twinkling river. At Westland Row Station a crowd of people pressed to the carriage doors; but the porters moved them back, saying that it was a special train for the bazaar. I remained alone in the bare carriage. In a few minutes the train drew up beside an improvised wooden platform. I passed out on to the road and saw by the lighted dial of a clock that it was ten minutes to ten. In front of me was a large building which displayed the magical name.

25   I could not find any sixpenny entrance and, fearing that the bazaar would be closed, I passed in quickly through a turnstile, handing a shilling to a weary-looking man. I found myself in a big hall girdled at half its height by a gallery. Nearly all the stalls were closed and the greater part of the hall was in darkness. I recognized a silence like that which pervades a church after a service. I walked into the center of the bazaar timidly. A few people were gathered about the stalls which were still open. Before a curtain, over which the words *Café Chantant* were written in coloured lamps, two men were counting money on a salver. I listened to the fall of the coins.

Remembering with difficulty why I had come I went over to one of the stalls and examined porcelain vases and flowered tea-sets. At the door of the stall a young lady was talking and laughing with two young gentlemen. I remarked their English accents and listened vaguely to their conversation.

"O, I never said such a thing!"

"O, but you did!"

"O, but I didn't!"

30 "Didn't she say that?"

"Yes. I heard her."

"O, there's a . . . fib!"

Observing me the young lady came over and asked me did I wish to buy anything. The tone of her voice was not encouraging; she seemed to have spoken to me out of a sense of duty. I looked humbly at the great jars that stood like eastern guards at either side of the dark entrance to the stall and murmured:

"No, thank you."

35 The young lady changed the position of one of the vases and went back to the two young men. They began to talk of the same subject. Once or twice the young lady glanced at me over her shoulder.

I lingered before her stall, though I knew my stay was useless, to make my interest in her wares seem the more real. Then I turned away slowly and walked down the middle of the bazaar. I allowed the two pennies to fall against the sixpence in my pocket. I heard a voice call from one end of the gallery that the light was out. The upper part of the hall was now completely dark.

Gazing up into the darkness I saw myself as a creature driven and derided by vanity; and my eyes burned with anguish and anger.

➤ QUESTIONS FOR READING AND WRITING

1. To what extent does your own experience influence your response to this story?
2. Describe the setting of the story. How are you affected by the personification in the first paragraph? Is North Richmond Street "blind" only because it's a dead-end street? Do you think the setting is an appropriate background for the boy's feelings? Explain.
3. Who is the narrator? How old is he at the time of the story? Is this the "voice" of a child or an adult? What difference does that make in the telling and in your response?
4. What aspects of the boy's reactions illustrate his feelings for Mangan's sister? Do you think the boy's crush is believable? Do people behave like this when they are "smitten"? Explain.
5. How does the narrator "show" the intensity of his feelings? What details or examples does he use?
6. At the end of the story, why do you think the boy sees himself "as a creature driven and derided by vanity"?

Responding from Experience

The entries that follow were written in response to Sandra Cisneros' "Eleven" (p. 40) earlier in this chapter. It's a very short story, so if you haven't read it you might want to do that now and write your own response before you read the entries below.

Peter's Response:

> I remember my fifth grade like it was yesterday. I remember the toughest times trying to understand what being at that age meant. When was I going to turn twelve? In fact, what does twelve mean? What does eleven mean? What do I have to do that I did not do at ten? Who should I try to impress and what should I impress them with? Am I ready to be eleven?
>
> And I remember those mean old teachers. I remember a Sunday school teacher who always bothered me about my homework not being done. Just like Rachel, I was an innocent kid trying to do what most kids were expected to do--learn about life and be like one of them, an adult.

Emily's Response:

> I feel so much sympathy for this girl. I love her voice, it sounds very 11 in all the examples. The only memories you have to think about are things like what happens when you drink cold milk too fast. I think she's a very deep child--she thinks through each experience and that's why she can see her past 1 to 10 in everything she does. The details and comparisons just make this whole story. It puts a picture in your mind, the same picture she has in hers--and you're there with her.

Matt's Response:

> I think everyone can relate to this. Everyone has been humiliated at one time or another, either by a classmate or a teacher. You have felt embarrassed to the point of tears. When Mrs. Price makes her put the sweater on even when she says it isn't hers that made something click with me. I have gotten in arguments with teachers. And they were wrong but won anyway because they were in charge. One great part was when the other child claims the sweater. The teacher acted like nothing happened and that really aggravated me. Even though she brought the child to tears--and was wrong--she

never apologizes. I can definitely relate to how she wants to be 102. At that age you might have all the answers.

However growing up and experiencing things is part of life. At age eleven you are trying to make an identity for yourself, and humiliation can put a real damper on that.

Rob's Response:

I definitely remember an event like this--only it was with a hat. The teacher and several classmates insisted that the hat belonged to my good friend Damon; only it didn't. It was a dirty, germ infested, dusty, Ninja Turtles winter hat. It had been floating around the room for a while before the teacher made Damon wear it. He cried and pleaded saying over and over "It's not mine, it's not mine, it's not mine!" And then after lunch, this kid Phillip got to school and wanted to beat Damon up for wearing his hat. The only thing was Mrs. Webb, the teacher, really believed it was Damon's hat. I hadn't really thought about this for a while but the story brought it back.

Jennifer's Response:

I can totally relate to this story. My Uncle John is known for singling people out. He's the kind of person that needs to impress people. He has singled me out so many times, especially at work, in front of everybody. No matter what you say, it's wrong--even if you're obviously right. He will never admit that he's wrong, and will never give up. If it happens that he does believe that he's wrong, which rarely happens, he'll just keep quiet, and that's OK, but all hell breaks loose when anybody else is wrong. Anyway, he really knows how to make someone feel small. This story reminds me of him.

John's Response:

I could picture second grade throughout the story--the desks, old weathered-through cubby holes and the protruding-poled coat hangers. My second-grade teacher wouldn't have had the same attitude as Mrs. Price, interrupting the class intentionally or not. Mrs. Price is a teacher who doesn't listen. She needs to get her way--the uncompromising scene--producing embarrassing way.

➤ *QUESTIONS FOR READING AND WRITING*

1. How were the responses of Peter, Emily, Matt, Rob, Jennifer, and John influenced by their experiences?
2. Consider your response to the story. How does it compare to theirs? Does reading their responses affect your own response to the story? If so, how?
3. To what extent have they "shown" what they've told?
4. Which entries seem most effective to you? What factors seem to make them effective?
5. Read your own response to the story. How does the voice in your response compare with those you've just read?
6. How would you describe the voice in Sandra Cisneros's "Eleven"? What factors make it effective?
7. In what way is "showing" a factor in both the story and the responses to it? What scenes, details, words, or phrases had the biggest impact on you?

WRITING TO DESCRIBE

An effective description is much more than a summary. A summary has no voice. An engaging description has our voice, impressions, and feelings, as well as relevant details. When someone asks us to describe a person we know very well (a friend, lover, spouse, parent) or a place with which we are very familiar (our home, bedroom, car, or a favorite hangout), we're not likely to respond with factual information alone. A summary of facts (dimensions, features, or colors) will not adequately convey what we feel is most important. Those details support our impression but do not replace it. Important details, however, do help the reader picture what we are describing and clarify *why* we feel the way we do.

Choosing Details

Which details we choose when describing and supporting our responses can make a big difference. Writing, "Tanya makes me feel very comfortable" by itself will not be as clear as combining it with examples or details of what she does that shows it is true: "She's very soft-spoken, smiles a lot, and is a good listener." We would not include every detail ("She's wants to graduate next year") unless it's relevant ("So she knows the kind of pressure I'm feeling"). Including details not important to our impression will not support, and may even dilute, the impact of ones that are.

Choosing Details from Stories

So, too, the details we choose to clarify and support our responses to stories have an important impact on readers. To describe the young girl's pain in "Eleven" without reference to the red sweater omits a crucial detail and contributing factor to her humiliation. When describing "The Stolen Party," leaving out the money offered by Señora Ines to Rosaura omits the real and symbolic trigger for her anger and hurt. Those details, those parts, capture the whole of the work in miniature.

➤ QUESTIONS FOR READING AND WRITING

1. How do you respond when someone asks you to describe a story that you've read? To what extent does a summary convey what you've experienced—what you feel is most important? To what extent does it seem inadequate? The following exercise may provide some insight:
   a. Choose a favorite story (either from these first two chapters or from past reading).
   b. Summarize it.
   c. Write down your strongest impressions of that story. Write down the details—from your experience and the literature—that support or clarify those impressions.
   d. What is the difference between the summary and your impressions?
   e. Which parts of the summary support your impression? Which do not?

WRITING TO COMPARE

How many times are we asked to describe something, and our first reaction is "Well, it's like . . ." or "It reminds me of. . . ." In fact it seems hard to describe anything without resorting to comparison somewhere along the way. When we think about our friends, we may compare and contrast them consciously and unconsciously with each other. When we take part in important events, we may compare them to similar events in our past: "This reminds me of the wedding I went to last year" or "My brother's graduation was done very differently."

Comparing and contrasting are also natural ways to describe our responses to literature. We might compare ourselves or others with literary characters, or our own experiences with those in a story. We may compare the choices made by various characters with the choices we would make. We might even be reminded of previous reading experiences and compare the story—or elements of the story—we are reading with one we've read before. We might also compare a story with another form of art, like painting.

Comparing and Contrasting Using a Venn Diagram

One effective technique for generating and organizing ideas when writing to compare is a Venn diagram (Fig 2.1). This technique works equally well when comparing personal experience with the work (Fig 2.2) or comparing works or characters with one another (Fig 2.3).

1. Draw two interconnecting circles. Identify each circle.
2. In the common, interconnecting area write down what the subjects have in common.
3. In the separate sections, write down what is different.

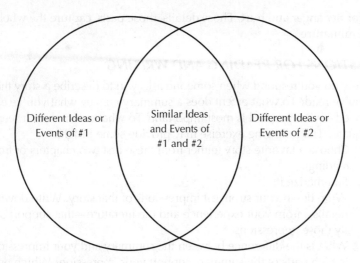

FIGURE 2.1   *Venn Diagram for Comparing*

FIGURE 2.2   *Comparing Experience with a Story*

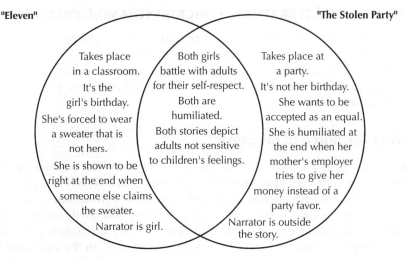

FIGURE 2.3   *Comparing Two Stories*

➤ *QUESTIONS FOR READING AND WRITING*

1. If you are jotting down responses to your reading, take a look back through your entries. How many times did a story remind you of someone or something in your own life? If none did at the time you wrote your response, are there entries that bring a comparison to mind now?

2. Can you compare any of the stories you've read in Chapters 1 and 2? Do any of these works remind you of other stories you've read in the past? If so, how are they alike? How different? Can you construct a Venn diagram to compare them?

Possible Worlds

The frequent comments and questions about "identifying with characters" or "connecting your experience" in the first two chapters of this text are not suggesting that it is necessary to have had similar experiences or to identify with characters to have a fulfilling experience with literature. In fact, connecting the characters and events in a story too closely with our own lives—so closely that we can't distinguish one from the other—can interfere with our ability to understand and appreciate the story.

When taking us where we have never been, literature has the power to increase the breadth and depth of our vision—to help us learn and grow in the way that all new experiences can. It is not necessary for us to have been embarrassed in school as an eleven-year-old, to have struggled to explain a sensitive concept to a young child, to have been "put in your place" by an unintended insult, or to have felt foolish and vain for having had a "crush" on someone to be moved by "Eleven," "Brave We Are," "The Stolen Party," or "Araby."

Ultimately, it is our intelligence and sensitivity to the human condition, not simply a shared experience, that helps us imagine the possibilities and become engaged with the story.

RESPONSE TO LITERATURE: DESCRIBING AND COMPARING

You are likely to write with more feeling and a clearer, stronger voice about issues that move you, so your strongest response or impression may provide the best topic to write about, but selecting relevant details to support that response is equally important. You are not only describing how you felt, but what prompted you to feel this way.

Staying Anchored in the Story

Remember, this is an essay in response to literature. When sharing personal responses, it can be very easy to see the story we've read simply as a prompt to tell our own stories. Seeing and sharing the parallels between our own experiences and those in a work may strengthen our voices and clarify our responses, but the work on the page must remain prominent in the presentation. To write an effective response essay, it is essential to stay "anchored" in the work and balance references to personal experience with references to the literature itself.

➤ *YOUR OWN RESPONSES*

In this exercise, you may find it illuminating to share your work with a partner or a small group.

1. Take a look back through your responses and select some of your strongest reactions or impressions.
2. If you wrote down details to support your response, do those details adequately convey it? Do those details include specific references to the text?
3. Are there places where you might have clarified your response through a comparison (with other characters, people you know, other students' responses)?
4. If you did not write down supporting details or if you did not cite the text for support, go back to the story and see if you can.

➤ *SUMMARY QUESTIONS FOR READING AND WRITING*

1. Take a look back at the responses to "Eleven" on pages 56–57. Which entries seem to convey the strongest impressions? How so?
2. Which responses seem more anchored in the literature and which seem to digress more to the reader's own experience?
3. Imagine the entry you like best as the opening of a response essay. Make some suggestions for how it might be supported from the text of "Eleven."
4. Consider your own response to the story. How do your responses compare to theirs?
5. Take a close look at your own response. What details, quotations, and examples have you used to support your response? To what extent have you anchored your response in the work itself?

✔CHECKLIST • *Developing a Response Essay*

❏ Write down your impressions.

❏ Write down whatever questions come to mind during and after your reading.

❏ What confuses you? What do you want to know more about? How can you find out?

❏ Do any of the characters remind you of yourself or people you know? Do any of the events remind you of ones in your own life?

❏ Do these associations with the story help or interfere with your response? If so, how?

❏ What do you find most interesting or compelling about the work? Why? How can you "show" what made this issue so compelling for you? What details or passages in the work illustrate support for your response?

FROM FIRST RESPONSE TO FINAL DRAFT

In the section that follows, we look at Debra Monserrate's response to James Joyce's "Araby" and follow its progress through to the final draft of her essay. Though her goal is to write a response essay, the strategies she illustrates work equally well when planning and generating ideas for a critical essay.

The purpose of the strategies that follow is not to move you step-by-step through a rigid sequence. Whether you are composing a response or a critical essay, writing is a continuous process of moving forward and returning and moving forward again. The best way to organize an essay may occur to you early or late in the process. You may get some of your best new ideas just when you thought you were almost finished. Try to let your ideas flow freely throughout the process. Don't close out ideas by imposing a structure that will keep you from expressing what you would really like to say.

Reading fiction encourages a variety of responses—and perhaps more questions than answers. Generate and explore as many of your questions and ideas as possible before you decide on one direction. Free your ideas and follow them where they go. You may be surprised by what you find on your journey.

Using First Responses

If you've been keeping a journal or writing other initial responses to your reading, chances are you have already generated some good ideas for writing an essay. After you read your entries and add any comments based on rereading and class discussion, go back and underline or circle what you believe are your strongest impressions.

Let's look at Debra's journal response as an example:

When I began to read this story I was confused. I think that the story jumped around too much. First, it describes a neighborhood, then it refers to a priest who dies, then it ends with the whole bazaar thing. I interpreted this story to be about a confused little boy. The story hints that he's in love with a nun(?), and his reason for going to the bazaar was to buy her a gift. In the end he gets there too late and never gets to buy her anything. I found the ending to be very dramatic and senseless. This was not a story I really enjoyed reading.

After discussing the story in class the meaning of the story comes through to me. I see now that the young boy has a crush on this older girl. It makes me think back to the first crush that I had. I was in the fourth grade, and his name was Joseph. He was adorable, and I don't think that I spoke a word to him. I recall watching him and getting butterflies whenever I heard his name. Now I see this story in a different light. <u>The more I read it, the more meaning it has</u>.

Making Choices When making a choice or choices about which idea(s) to pursue, you may want to answer two essential questions:

1. Do you care enough about this idea to pursue it further?
   You will write with your strongest voice about issues that have the most meaning to you and about which you believe you want to say something that is important for both you and your readers.
2. Is it "do-able"?
   Can you write an essay about this? No matter how compelling your idea is, you won't be able to write an essay about it unless you have enough to say, or you can support it from both your experience and the work (of literature). Remember, if the point you are trying to make is obvious, abstract, or very general, it may be impossible to develop it into an appealing essay in a reasonable amount of time.

Extending Ideas

Debra chose the sentence (underlined) from the entry above as the core of her response. It's obvious that she cares about this idea very much. And she feels confident that there are many quotations in the story that she can use to support the comparison between her relationship and that in the story. Her essay seems very "do-able," and her journal entry has given her a start.

Debra has already followed her core idea with some specific support from her own experience, but she has not provided much specific support from the text of the story itself. So if she wants to generate more ideas or extend or expand her support, there are a few other techniques she might use.

Directed Freewriting If you don't have a journal entry or other initial response, or you want to generate more ideas, directed freewriting can be a useful technique. The best time to do this exercise is immediately after you finish reading, while your thoughts and impressions are still fresh. The intention of this exercise is to release what you know without blocking it with pauses for reflection, punctuation, or editing.

1. Write down the name of the topic, phrase, or sentence you want to focus on.
2. Write down (nonstop) everything that comes into your mind for five or ten minutes. If punctuation or capitalization gets in the way, don't even use it.
3. Read what you have written and choose (circle or underline) your strongest responses.

Here is Debra's directed freewriting concerning James Joyce's "Araby," in response to these sentences from her journal entry:

> <u>I see now that the young boy has a crush on this older girl. It makes me</u> <u>think back to the first crush that I had.</u>
>
> When I realized what this was about it immediately reminded me of a crush I had on a kid in the fourth grade. Many of the things in the story reminded me of that especially the part where the young boy doesn't talk to his love. He just walks by her every day. He is so overwhelmed by his emotion that he can't bring himself to speak with her and hopes that somehow she feels the same way about him. All this is really silly when I think of it now as an adult. It makes no sense. Even if the girl felt something for him how would he ever find out without talking to her. But when you're young (and maybe when you're older too) these things don't matter. It's not about logic. It's about emotion and obsession and all your days are tied up in these thoughts. But you're bound to be let down. And while it seems so silly now, then it really hurt and there was no one to share it with because you feel so stupid and you don't want to make it worse by telling someone.

Debra's freewriting adds more detail to her earlier statement, and she is able to generate some ideas about her own "crush" and its connections to the story itself. By asking questions about and listing details of the selected statements, she may uncover even more specific material.

Asking Questions Having already narrowed her choice to a particular idea, she might ask as many questions (and subquestions) as she can about some aspect of that idea. Of course, it's useful to ask only questions that will provide new information (and cannot be answered yes or no).

1. Choose an important word, phrase, or sentence from your journal entry and write down as many related questions as you can.
2. Choose and answer the questions that will add to or clarify your support.

I see now that the young boy has a crush on this older girl.

Why doesn't he talk to her?

Does he really believe she feels the same way?

What's the point of his going to the bazaar?

Why is he so upset at his uncle?

What is he so angry with himself about at the end?

It makes me think back to the first crush that I had.

How silly did I feel?

Why didn't I talk to him?

What things in particular pulled me back?

How long did it take for me to get over it?

 Following up with detailed answers to these questions is likely to provide additional specific support for the original core idea.

Listing

1. Choose key words or sentences from your response (the name of a character, an event, an element of literature, etc.).
2. List as many related details under each as you can. By choosing some key phrases that apply to her identification with the speaker in the story, Debra is able to uncover other specific details.

The boy's neighborhood made me think of the house I grew up in.

The description of the houses.

He gave them personalities.

The personality of my own house.

The neighboring houses.

How I would describe them.

Being summoned in from play.

I really like James Joyce's descriptions.

The "faces" of the houses.

The boy's watching each morning.

His feelings being played like a harp.

Semantic Mapping, or Clustering

For some of us, it is easier to follow directions by looking at a map than following directions in a printed sequence. Sometimes we need to see the whole picture. When writing in response to literature, too, sometimes we can understand, see relationships, and generate and extend ideas better spatially than linearly. A technique called **semantic mapping** or **clustering** makes it possible to see ideas and relationships this way (Fig 2.4). This is how it works:

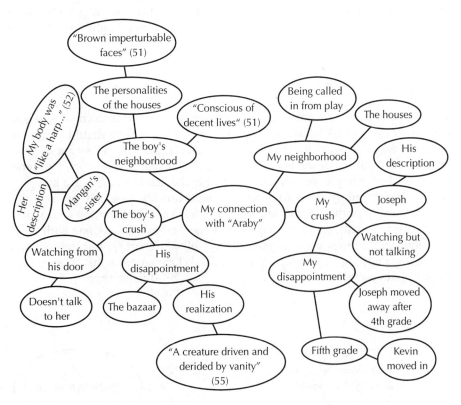

FIGURE 2.4 *Debra's Semantic Map*

1. Write down a question or statement in the center of a blank page in your journal or on another piece of paper. Put a circle around it.
2. Draw lines out from the circle and write a statement or idea related to that central idea.
3. Continue to draw lines out from the central circle and the subcircles. Those from the central circle are subsets of ideas; each circle farther along each line is a level of greater specificity.

One of the intriguing things about mapping is that once you get going, it's hard to stop. Seeing a picture of the ideas seems to make the relationships among them clearer.

Finding Connections With any of these strategies, an additional step that might be productive, and which emerges naturally from the mapping exercise, is finding and describing the relationships between and among the ideas (the circles) generated on different lines. When you finish your map, you might draw lines across circles and write statements identifying and examining the relationships. Such statements might go a long way toward answering the central question or identifying a unifying theme for the story. For example, writing a statement about the connection among the circles from Debra's map might provide some additional insights (Fig 2.5).

Mix and Match

The strategies above are not an end in themselves, but simply the means to generate and extend ideas, ask questions, and make choices. They should be used in whatever way they work for you. There is no one "right" way to ask questions or list ideas. If a particular method is working, keep using it. If it is not, try something else. For example, you may find that only the first few circles in a mapping exercise are useful. In order to generate details quickly, you may prefer to list them instead of putting circles around them. So you might want to start with a map, get a few ideas, and then make a list to get at the details. Along with keeping a journal, you may want to freewrite as well. Different ways, combinations, and paces of writing may bring different ideas. What matters in this "prewriting" stage is that you feel free to explore in your most productive way.

FIGURE 2.5   *Statements Connecting Ideas*

Collaboration

Sharing Responses If you are keeping a journal or jotting down responses to your reading, you may find it useful to exchange your writing with a classmate. In addition to sharing responses to the work of literature, you might comment on each other's entries. The biggest advantage to sharing this way is that it gives you an audience and immediate feedback.

Combining Questions After generating your own questions about a particular piece of literature, it might be worthwhile to share these questions in pairs or with a small group. Pool everyone's questions, discuss their strengths and weaknesses, and narrow the list down to the strongest ones.

Connecting Cluster Circles You might work collaboratively on a semantic map, or cluster sheet. In response to a question, topic, or character, each individual in a small group might take responsibility for a line of circles extending from the middle. Then your group might draw lines connecting one line of circles to another line of circles. By discussing these connections, new ideas, directions, and possibilities will emerge.

THE RESPONSE ESSAY: COMPOSING A DRAFT

Once you have settled on your topic and gathered supporting ideas and details, you can begin to write a draft of your essay. Even at this stage you may want to avoid forcing your writing into an inflexible outline. There may be possibilities you haven't thought of, so avoid putting walls around your work just yet.

As in earlier stages of the process, what works best for each of us may be different. Some students may work best by writing this first draft as quickly as possible without stopping and then going back to review and revise when finished. Many students (and probably most experienced writers) find that writing more reflectively at this stage works best for them. And if you have already narrowed your focus to a particular idea and generated lots of details to support it, you may want to proceed with more reflection and review what you have written while you write. You may want to read it out loud to hear how the wording sounds and if the ideas are complete and clear. Evaluating your writing may give you valuable insight into where you need to go.

Once you have narrowed your focus to a particular idea and generated lots of details in support of the idea, you are ready to create a thesis statement. Your thesis statement should incorporate all the evidence that you have, but also be specific enough for you to support. Your thesis statement should also reveal what you intend to show in your essay.

Debra's Draft

Earlier in this section, we saw Debra's journal entry, freewriting, listing, asking questions, and her semantic map in response to James Joyce's "Araby." Let's follow up by looking at a draft of her response essay.

Debra Monserrate

English 102

Dr. Madden

Oct. 24, 200X

Crushed Again

The first time I read the story of <u>Araby</u> I was slightly confused. I did not see any meaning to the story, and it just seemed to jump around from subject to subject. However, once we discussed <u>Araby</u> in class all that changed. Every time I reread this story I find that I enjoy it more and more. Each reading brings more meaning.

While reading <u>Araby</u> I found myself being drawn into the story with the verbiage used to describe the neighborhood in which the boy lives. In the first paragraph the houses are personified by being "conscious of decent lives within them" and described as "gaz[ing] at one another with brown imperturbable faces." Lines such as these make this story interesting and curious. Reading lines such as these triggers my imagination and takes me back to the house that I grew up in and the neighboring houses. I find myself reaching for words to describe their "personalities." However, the only word that comes to mind is unique.

Many times I found myself being brought back to memories of my own childhood. Early in the story, when the boy tells how he and Mangan "watched her from [their] shadow" as Mangan's sister called him to come in reminds me of the numerous times I was summoned and I too waited. I think all children wait to respond in hopes that if they ignore you long enough you'll eventually go away.

After reading less than half of the story it becomes apparent that the boy has a crush on Mangan's sister. He tells of how "her image accompanied [him] even in places the most hostile to romance" and how "her name sprang to [his] lips at moments in strange prayers and praises." These descriptions of the boy's feelings are truly warming to me. They make me feel good inside because I think of my own first crush and I know how he feels. I'm right there with him, feeling what he feels, back in the fourth grade again pining over a boy named Joseph. He was the cutest thing on the face of the earth. He had the greatest dimples and he was the toughest boy in the whole school as far as I was concerned. I was heartbroken when he didn't return in the fifth grade, but I recovered two weeks into the fifth grade thanks to a boy named Kevin.

There were many phrases in this story that had my heart soaring, but the one line that I found most beautiful was "my body was like a harp and her words and gestures were like fingers running upon the wires." Those words are very deep and intense and to a child that is exactly what a crush is. Looking back you can see the silliness of what you put yourself through-- the nervousness of being around the person, walking out of your way just to catch a glimpse of him--but not at that moment, not when you're young and innocent and full of dreams.

Toward the end of the story you feel bad for the boy. He wanted so badly to go to Araby to buy his love something and the only thing he gets is one problem after another. In the end he sees himself as a "creature driven and derided by vanity." I think that he finally realizes, as we all eventually do, that his crush will never be a reality. Also, I feel that he is angry for allowing himself to be driven so hard by his own desire. These are definitely emotions I can sympathize with.

REVISION

Rethinking, "re-visioning," and rewriting are just as important for a response essay about fiction as they are for any other kind of writing. Having discovered what you want to say, you can now focus on how well you have said it. How well is your draft organized? Does it have unnecessary or redundant information? Are there gaps that need to be filled in? Are there enough details? Is there enough support from the story? Have you expressed yourself as clearly as possible?

Organization and Unity

One of the most effective ways of checking the organization of a draft is by doing an **after-draft outline**. Go back to each paragraph and find the controlling idea. List the main ideas they represent, one after the other. This should give you an outline of your draft.

Let's look at an outline of Debra's draft:

1. I was confused by the story at first but now it has a lot of meaning to me.
2. I was drawn into the story by the language that reminded me of my own growing up.
3. It reminded me of my own childhood.

4. The lines that describe his response to Mangan's sister called up my emotions during my crush.
5. My favorite quote from the story and being young.
6. What happens to him at Araby.

When Debra looked at her list, she realized that her opening and closing could account better for all that she wanted to say. Paragraphs 2 and 3 seemed to be addressing the same issue, so she would have to make sure that 3 brought the reader to a different place than 2. Paragraph 4 continued the emphasis on remembering her own experience, and 5 addresses her favorite quotation from the story. The last paragraph does sum up a bit, but it doesn't really seem to account for all that has gone on in the story, or her experience of it.

Showing Support

The support Debra used in this essay came from two sources: the story and her personal experience. She supported her references to the text by quoting the story. She supported references to her experience by giving examples. But in both cases she believed that she might strengthen the essay if she got additional support, particularly for her own experience.

Clarity

Debra realized that she would have to tighten up her language by deleting unnecessary words, expressions, and sentences. The word you that she used occasionally did not really express what she meant. After cutting and combining, she could decide if some of the paragraphs or parts of paragraphs might be shifted around for better organization.

Voice

She believed that one of the strengths of this piece was its voice, a voice which "showed" through quotations and examples. Her biggest task was to maintain a strong voice throughout the essay while tightening up her prose overall.

✔ CHECKLIST • *Revision*

Organization and Unity

❑ Do all the paragraphs relate to the central thesis?

❑ Is the organization of those paragraphs within the essay clear?

❑ Do each of the sentences within the paragraphs relate to the central idea of the paragraph?

continued

Support

❏ Are there enough details to support or clarify your assertions? Have you "shown" what you've told?

❏ Are there enough quotations from the work of literature to support your assertions?

❏ Are the paragraphs fully developed?

❏ Is the essay fully developed? Have you accounted for all aspects of your thesis statement?

Clarity

❏ Is the central thesis of the essay clearly stated?

❏ Does the title of your essay account for your thesis?

❏ Is the language clear?

❏ Are there redundancies, digressions, or meaningless phrases that could be cut?

❏ Is the essay written in the format required by your instructor? Have you documented your references to the text and included a list of works cited?

Voice

❏ Does it sound like you? When you read it out loud, can you hear your voice and emotion?

Editing or proofreading is a crucial final step in the process of producing an essay. In addition to making any changes that did not occur to you earlier and fine-tuning your writing, it's essential to check your essays for correct grammar, spelling, punctuation, and typos.

✔ C H E C K L I S T • *Editing and Proofreading*

❏ Are all of your sentences complete sentences?

❏ Are all of your sentences punctuated appropriately?

❏ Are the words spelled correctly? Have you checked for easily confused words (then/than, your/you're, its/it's, etc.)?

❏ Are you sure of the meaning of all the words you've used?

❏ Are the titles of works underlined or in quotation marks as appropriate?

❏ Is the title and heading on the first page in the correct format?

❏ Have you followed your essay with a works cited list?

❏ Are there particular errors you have a tendency to make? Have you looked for those in this essay?

Remember, computer spell checkers do not make choices about word usage. Confused words (than/then, there/their/they're, etc.) will not be flagged by a spell checker. You will have to use your own eyes and judgment to correct those errors.

Debra's Revised Essay

After rewriting her introduction to include a thesis statement that would account for all that she was writing about, Debra shifted some of her examples.

Debra Monserrate

English 102

Dr. Madden

Oct. 24, 200X

Crushed Again

When I first read "Araby," I had trouble following the story because it seemed to jump around from subject to subject, and I did not see any meaning in it. However, once we discussed the story in class, I reread it more slowly and discovered language so descriptive and beautiful that it brought me back to my own experiences. I remembered my own crush in the fourth grade and how I felt just like the boy does in "Araby." Now, each reading of the story seems to bring me more meaning, and I find that I enjoy it more and more.

I was drawn into the story by the language used to describe the neighborhood in which the boy lives. In the first paragraph the houses are personified by being "conscious of decent lives within them" (51) and described as "gaz[ing] at one another with brown imperturbable faces (51)." When I read these lines I could picture the faces on the houses and their expressions. They seem to have nosey, but smug and "above it all" personalities. This description made me curious about what went on in this neighborhood and what might possibly "disturb" the houses. These lines also triggered my imagination and took me back to the neighborhood that I grew up in. I found myself reaching for words to describe those houses and their "personalities."

As I read on, I found myself being brought back to memories of my own childhood. Early in the story, when the boy tells how he and Mangan "watched her from [their] shadow" (52) as Mangan's sister called him to come in, reminded me of my childhood and the numerous times I was summoned to come in from play and I too waited. I think all children wait to respond in hopes that if they ignore whoever is calling long enough the caller will eventually go away.

Halfway through the story, it is apparent that the boy has a crush on Mangan's sister. He tells of how "her image accompanied me even in places the most hostile to romance" (52) and how "her name sprang to my lips at moments in strange prayers and praises" (52). These descriptions of the boy's feelings are truly heartwarming to me. They make me feel good inside because I think of my own first crush, and I know how he feels. I'm right there with him, feeling what he feels, back in the fourth grade again pining away over a boy named Joseph. I thought Joseph was the cutest thing on the face of the earth. He had the greatest dimples, and he was the toughest boy in the whole school, at least as far as I was concerned.

There were many phrases in this story that had my heart soaring, but the one line that I found most beautiful was "my body was like a harp and her words and gestures were like fingers running upon the wires" (52). Those words are very deep and intense and to a child that is exactly what a crush is. Looking back I can see the silliness of what I put myself through-- the nervousness of being near him, and walking out of the way just to catch a glimpse of him. But it didn't seem silly to me then.

Toward the end of the story I feel badly for the boy. He wanted so badly to go to Araby to buy his love something, and he runs into one problem after another. In the end he sees himself as a "creature driven and derided by vanity" (55). He finally realizes, as we all eventually do, that his crush will never be a reality. And he is angry for allowing himself to be driven so hard by his own desire. These are definitely emotions I can sympathize with. I was heartbroken, too, when Joseph didn't return in the fifth grade. But unlike the boy in the story who seems to be heartbroken without much hope, I recovered two weeks into the fifth grade thanks to my next romantic interest, a boy named Kevin.

Work Cited

Joyce, James. "Araby." Exploring Fiction. Ed. Frank Madden. New York:
    Longman, 2002, 51.

PART II

Analysis and Argumentation

৵

CHAPTER 3

Exploration and Analysis
The Elements of Fiction

To analyze anything is to look closely at how it works—to examine its parts. Our intention in this chapter, however, is not to reduce stories to parts. Our goal is to provide you with tools to articulate and develop your responses into effective critical essays. We know that the parts of a literary work alone cannot account for its meaning, a meaning that fully blossoms only as the parts work together. But reading a story carefully and analyzing its parts can tell you a great deal about it—and how it triggered your response. Analysis is an important step in interpreting or evaluating fiction, and it is through this process that you may gather the support to make your opinion an informed one.

YOUR FIRST RESPONSE

When you read a story for the first time, relax and give yourself enough time to experience it. Don't try too hard to figure it out. Get impressions. Notice words and phrases. Read them out loud. Listen to the rhythms. Follow the personal associations that come up. Let yourself feel the emotions connected to them. Don't be discouraged if you have difficulty understanding every word or line your first time through. Have a dictionary handy and look up unfamiliar words. Let your unanswered questions stick with you. Write them down if you think you won't remember them later.

Immediately after your first reading, jot down your impressions and the questions that came to mind during your reading. Capture your response while it's fresh. If you wait until later, you may forget. In fact, you may come away from your reading with more questions than answers. So a second or third reading with these questions in mind may clarify much that was confusing the first time through. If you were reminded of people or events in your life, try to think about the difference that those associations made in your response. Did they help? Did they interfere? Does the text of the work support your response?

Before you analyze the story, try to grab hold of what you found most provocative about it. You will write with a stronger voice and more conviction when you write about what interests you most.

✔**CHECKLIST** • *Your First Response*

- ❏ Write down your first impressions.
- ❏ Write down the questions that come to mind during and after your reading.
- ❏ What confuses you? What do you want to know more about? How can you find out?
- ❏ What words or phrases affect you most?
- ❏ Do any of the characters remind you of yourself or people you know?
- ❏ Do any of the events remind you of ones in your own life?
- ❏ Do these associations help or interfere with your response? If so, how?
- ❏ What do you find most interesting or compelling about the story?

CLOSE READING

Analysis requires close reading. In a way the term *close reading* means the opposite of what it sounds like. When we read closely, we don't get closer to the literature and our experience with it; rather, we step back. We move from being inside the work to looking at it from the outside, from participating to observing. This process requires a careful reading and a conscious examination of the elements of the work and how they contribute to its overall meaning.

A close reading is not a first reading, it is a rereading. When you return to read the work of literature or your notes again after discussion in class, you are doing a close reading. You have already stepped back from your own views to hear the responses of others. You are reading your notes and the literature informed by what you have learned from those discussions.

ANNOTATING THE TEXT

One effective way to do a close reading of a story is to mark up the text by underlining, circling, highlighting, or making notes in the margins. You may even find it useful to do these annotations in more than one stage. In the first stage you might want to concentrate on your understanding of the text by summarizing, noting words or passages you don't understand, and asking questions—exploring the text. Later on, as you narrow your focus, you may want to identify elements of the text, patterns, evidence, or quotations to support your thesis—analyzing the text. If you don't want to mark up the pages of your book, make a copy of the work and do your annotations on this copy. Or write your annotations on Post-it notes and attach them in the margins of the work.

First Annotation: Exploration

Luke (1st century A.D.)

Look up formal definition of "parable."

The Parable of the "Prodigal" Son

[CA. A.D. 80]

Look up "prodigal"

And he said, "A certain man had two sons: and the younger of them said to his father, 'Father, give me the portion of goods that <u>falleth</u> to me.' And he divided unto them his living. And not many days after, the younger son gathered all together, and took his journey into a far country, and there wasted his <u>substance</u> with riotous living.

That he deserves?

Substance? His portion?

"And when he had spent all, there arose a mighty famine in that land, and he began to be in want. And he went and joined himself to a citizen of that country, and he sent him into his fields to feed swine. And he would fain have filled his belly with the husks that the swine did eat: and no man gave unto him. And when he came to himself, he said, 'How many hired servants of my father's have bread enough and to spare, and I perish with hunger? I will arise and go to my father, and will say unto him, 'Father I have sinned against heaven, and before thee, and am no more worthy to be called thy son: make me as one of thy hired servants.'"

Was he working for this guy?

Is he really sorry? Or is this just a better deal?

"And he arose, and came to his father. But when he was yet a great way off, his father saw him, and had compassion, and ran, and fell on his neck, and kissed him. And the son said unto him, 'Father I have sinned against heaven, and in thy sight, and am no more worthy to be called thy son.' But the father said to his servants, 'Bring forth the best robe, and put it on him, and put a ring on his hand, and shoes on his feet. And bring hither the <u>fatted calf</u>, and kill it, and let us eat, and be merry. For this my son was dead, and is alive again; he was lost, and is found.' And they began to be merry.

What's a "fatted calf"?

"Now his elder son was in the field, and as he came and drew <u>nigh</u> to the house, he heard music and dancing. And he called one of the servants, and asked what these things meant. And he said unto him, 'Thy brother is come, and thy father hath killed the fatted calf, because he hath received him safe and sound.' And he was angry, and would not go in: therefore came his father out, and entreated him. And he answering said to his father, 'Lo, these many years do I serve thee, neither transgressed I at any time thy com-

Why is he angry? Is he jealous?

mandment, and yet thou never gavest me a kid, that I
might make merry with my friends: but as soon as
this thy son was come, which hath devoured thy living
with harlots, thou hast killed for him the fatted calf.'
And he said unto him, 'Son thou art ever with me,
and all that I have is thine. It was meet that we should
make merry, and be glad: for this thy brother was
dead, and is alive again; and was lost, and is found.'"

I think I would have been angry too!

Summary: The younger son goes off and blows his fortune—comes back and is forgiven by his father—but his older brother is angry and resentful because he has been loyal and is not rewarded.

Second Annotation: Analysis

LUKE (1st century a.d.)

THE PARABLE OF THE PRODIGAL SON

[CA. A.D. 80]

And he said, "A certain man had two sons: and the
younger of them said to his father, 'Father, give me the
portion of goods that falleth to me.' And he divided
unto them his living. And not many days after, the
younger son gathered all together, and took his journey into a far country, and there wasted his substance
with riotous living.

"And when he had spent all, there arose a mighty
famine in that land, and he began to be in want. And
he went and joined himself to a citizen of that country,
and he sent him into his fields to feed swine. And he
would fain have filled his belly with the husks that the
swine did eat: and no man gave unto him. And when
he came to himself, he said, 'How many hired servants
of my father's have bread enough and to spare, and I
perish with hunger? I will arise and go to my father,
and will say unto him, 'Father I have sinned against
heaven, and before thee, and am no more worthy to be
called thy son: make me as one of thy hired servants.'"

"And he arose, and came to his father. But when
he was yet a great way off, his father saw him, and had
compassion, and ran, and fell on his neck, and kissed
him. And the son said unto him, 'Father I have sinned
against heaven, and in thy sight, and am no more
worthy to be called thy son.' But the father said to his
servants, 'Bring forth the best robe, and put it on him,
and put a ring on his hand, and shoes on his feet. And
bring hither the fatted calf, and kill it, and let us eat,
and be merry. For this my son was dead, and is alive
again; he was lost, and is found.' And they began to be
merry.

Is this the type of tale typical of this era? Are all "parables" like this? How does it compare with the other writings of Luke?

The characterization and plot seem very flat. Who are these people?

He doesn't seem to expect forgiveness—I wonder how his father would have reacted if the son wasn't sorry.

Now this is unconditional love.

"Now his elder son was in the field, and as he came and drew nigh to the house, he heard music and dancing. And he called one of the servants, and asked what these things meant. And he said unto him, 'Thy brother is come, and thy father hath killed the fatted calf, because he hath received him safe and sound.' And he was angry, and would not go in: therefore came his father out, and entreated him. And he answering said to his father, 'Lo, these many years do I serve thee, neither transgressed I at any time thy commandment, and yet thou never gavest me a kid, that I might make merry with my friends: but as soon as this thy son was come, which hath devoured thy living with harlots, thou hast killed for him the fatted calf.' And he said unto him, 'Son thou art ever with me, and all that I have is thine. It was meet that we should make merry, and be glad: for this thy brother was dead, and is alive again; and was lost, and is found.'"

> *Is it fair to the loyal son? One conflict is resolved but another is introduced.*

> *I'm still a bit confused by the ending—what's the point? Is it better to forgive than be forgiven?*

The second annotation is a closer reading and more analytical. Here you might look for some of the elements of fiction we discuss in this chapter, try to find patterns, seek evidence to support your early conclusions, or even place the work within a larger historical, social, or biographical context.

FICTION IN ITS MANY CONTEXTS

Our focus on textual analysis in this chapter—on the elements of fiction—is not an attempt to limit the scope of your writing to parts of the story alone. Those parts and those stories exist in a larger world—a context framed by personal, cultural, historical, biographical, and other influences. Seeing beyond the work to the contexts that influenced its writing—and your reading—may enliven and enrich your experience of the story and help you produce a more interesting essay.

For example, the story that ends this chapter, Langston Hughes' "One Friday Morning" (p. 98), relies on our knowledge of what race relations were like in 1939 when the story was written. That historical and cultural setting has a major impact on the number of choices the protagonist, Nancy Lee, has open to her. If the same story were set in the twenty-first century, the situation, the character, and her response might not be believable.

Unconventional Fiction

While the elements of fiction, as described in this chapter, "fit" most of the stories you'll be reading, keep in mind that some stories are written with different intentions in mind. Notable among these other forms are **metafiction** and **magical**

realism. Metafiction explores the process of its own language and creation as it tells the story. Donald Barthelme's "At the Tolstoy Museum" (p. 200) and Italo Calvino's "If on a winter's night a traveler" (p. 220) are good examples of this approach. Magical realism is fiction that blends realistic or ordinary details and events with those that are magical or fantastic. Gabriel García Márquez's "A Very Old Man with Enormous Wings" (p. 369) exemplifies this form. So try to keep an open mind about the author's intentions before you do an analysis based on the elements that follow.

Your Critical Approach

What you value most about literature, your critical stance, can be an important factor in determining what you analyze and write about when interpreting and evaluating literature. Critical approaches are broadly classified as reader based (emphasizing the reader's response and the text), text based (emphasizing the text), context based (emphasizing the background of the story), and author based (emphasizing connections to the author's life or intentions). Whatever approach you take may determine the strategy and terms you use in your writing. For a more comprehensive explanation of these approaches, see Appendix A (p. 467). Keep in mind that critical approaches may easily overlap, and critics often combine them in their analyses. The difference between one critical stance and another may be more a matter of emphasis than kind, and drawing upon several approaches can yield a rich interpretation.

Interpretive Communities

Stanley Fish, a professor and literary critic, has suggested that groups of readers who value the same approach to analyzing literature belong to "an interpretive community." Although our interpretations are influenced by whatever collaborative group or class we are in at present, we also carry and apply our own individual values and those of the many other communities (family, friends, religion) to which we belong. In this respect, we are members of many interpretive communities, and we are continually refiguring and revising our interpretations and evaluations in the light of our personal beliefs and group discussions. You may find it worthwhile and productive to keep track of this complex mix of personal response and group discussion as you write about the stories you read and discuss.

READING AND ANALYZING FICTION

Telling stories and listening to stories seems to be a natural part of our lives. When we meet with friends to hear about an experience, "just the facts" won't do. We want to hear the stories that give meaning to those facts. Why do we read and listen to stories? What kind of experience do we expect to have when we sit down to read a short story or "curl up with a good book"? Many of us might say that we want to "escape" from the stress of everyday life. But in this highly complex world there are many other ways to escape. What is it about the experience of reading a good story that makes it unique and draws us to it?

Beyond an escape, reading a story brings us to a place in our imaginations where we can live through the experience of others. Prompted by the author's words, we imagine the scenes, characters, and conflicts. We take the chances, feel the emotions, and share the insights—but without suffering the risks or consequences that living through them ourselves might bring.

Stories and storytelling have been an important part of every culture since people first roamed the earth. Before there was written language to record them, people shared stories orally and passed them down to their descendants. Even today, these stories convey the "truths" of many cultures and religions and give meaning to the lives of millions of people.

Fiction and Truth

In many ways, the designation "fiction" is misleading. Most fiction tells a story that is "made up"—or at least the specific details of the story probably did not occur in exactly the way described, in this place, at this time, to characters with these names. The most important quality of good fiction, though, is the truth or truths it tells—about being human and struggling to make sense of a complex world. The truth of fiction transcends fact. In it we see a model of our own struggle, a model not limited by the daily news of specific time and place and fact.

NARRATION

The narrator is the storyteller, the intermediary who shapes and flavors the story for us. Try to distinguish between the author of the story and the narrator, or speaker. The narrator has been created by the author with a particular effect in mind. As you can imagine, *who* tells the story and *how* it is told can make a big difference. The same story told from a different point of view or with a different voice affects everything we experience as we read.

Point of View

Think about the last time you watched a concert or sports event on television. Can you recall how many different camera shots you were shown? When the camera gave you a distant shot, you could see a large part of the arena and most of the performers. You could see what no one performer could see. But you could not experience what it was like to be in the middle of the action. Only a close-up camera shot could help you feel the physical energy, the emotion, and give you the perspective of an individual performer. But, of course, by isolating your view to one performer, you lost the larger view of the entire event. Directors, camera operators, and announcers make choices about which perspectives work best at given times. From any of these distances and angles the event we witness is the same, but the point of view we have makes our experience of it quite different.

In similar fashion, our reading of fiction is strongly influenced by the narrator's point of view. Authors, like directors or camera operators, make choices about which point of view will convey the story most effectively. In Sandra Cisneros's short story "Eleven," for example, we experience the humiliation of the young girl from her perspective—so "close up" that we share what she thinks and feels. The author might have chosen to describe the event through a narrator who was looking on or from the viewpoint of the teacher or another student in her class. But because we see the event through the girl's eyes, we experience her pain as if it is happening to us. From any of these perspectives the event remains the same, but in each case our experience of it is quite different.

Point of view is the perspective from which the narrator tells the story. Generally, the pronoun that dominates the narration signals which point of view is represented. The terms most commonly used to identify point of view are *first person, third person, omniscient, objective,* and *shifting.*

First person uses the pronoun *I* and usually places the narrator in the story. We see through the view of that character (as an announcer and camera might isolate what we see to the view of one performer). The narrator sees through that character's eyes (as a camera sees through a performer's eyes). We see what he or she sees. As readers, we will know only what this one person experiences. The brief selections below from two short stories, "A & P" and "The Yellow Wallpaper," are examples of first-person point of view.

From "A & P," by John Updike (See the complete story on p. 146.)

In walks these three girls in nothing but bathing suits. I'm in the third checkout slot, with my back to the door, so I don't see them until they're over by the bread. The one that caught my eye first was the one in the plaid green two-piece. She was a chunky kid, with a good tan and a sweet broad soft-looking can with those two crescents of white just under it, where the sun never seems to hit, at the top of the backs of her legs. I stood there with my hand on a box of HiHo crackers trying to remember if I rang it up or not. I ring it up again and the customer starts giving me hell. She's one of these cash-register-watchers, a witch about fifty with rouge on her cheekbones and no eyebrows, and I know it made her day to trip me up. She'd been watching cash registers for fifty years and probably never seen a mistake before.

From "The Yellow Wallpaper," by Charlotte Perkins Gilman (See the complete story on p. 312.)

It is very seldom that mere ordinary people like John and myself secure ancestral halls for the summer.

A colonial mansion, a hereditary estate, I would say a haunted house and reach the height of romantic felicity—but that would be asking too much of fate!

Still I will proudly declare that there is something queer about it.

Else, why should it be let so cheaply? And why have stood so long untenanted?

John laughs at me, of course, but one expects that.

John is practical in the extreme. He has no patience with faith, an intense horror of superstition, and he scoffs openly at any talk of things not to be felt and seen and put down in figures.

John is a physician, and *perhaps*—(I would not say it to a living soul, of course, but this is dead paper and a great relief to my mind)—*perhaps* that is one reason I do not get well faster.

You see, he does not believe I am sick! And what can one do?

Third person uses the pronouns *he* or *she*, but still usually limits us to one character's view. The narrator does not see through the character's eyes but focuses on the character and what he or she sees and thinks. Specifically, this is called **limited third-person point of view**. The perspective below in Liliana Heker's "Stolen Party" is limited third person. The narrator describes the action and the characters from the distance of a third person, but limits us to the thoughts of one character, Rosaura.

From "The Stolen Party," by Liliana Heker (See the complete story on p. 47.)

Apart from the girl with the bow, all the others were delightful. The one she liked best was Luciana, with her golden birthday crown; and then the boys. Rosaura won the sack race, and nobody managed to catch her when they played tag. When they split into two teams to play charades, all the boys wanted her for their side. Rosaura felt she had never been so happy in her life.

But the best was still to come. The best came after Luciana blew out the candles. First the cake. Señora Ines had asked her to help pass the cake around, and Rosaura had enjoyed the task immensely, because everyone called out to her, shouting "Me, me!" Rosaura remembered a story in which there was a queen who had the power of life or death over her subjects. She had always loved that, having the power of life or death. To Luciana and the boys she gave the largest pieces, and to the girl with the bow she gave a slice so thin one could see through it.

Omniscient point of view also uses the pronouns *he, she,* and *they,* but the narrator is "all-knowing" and able to move in and out of the minds of all the characters, choosing what and when to share. The selection from "The Open Boat" below is written in an omniscient point of view. Only an omniscient narrator could know that "None of them knew the color of the sky."

From "The Open Boat," by Stephen Crane (See the complete story on p. 265.)

None of them knew the color of the sky. Their eyes glanced level, and were fastened upon the waves that swept toward them. These waves were of the hue of slate, save for the tops, which were of foaming white, and all of the men knew the colors of the sea. The horizon narrowed and widened, and dipped and rose, and at all times its edge was jagged with waves that seemed thrust up in points like rocks.

Objective point of view minimizes the intervention of the narrator. The setting and the action are described, and we "listen in" on the dialogue, but the narrator does not interpret for us. We must do that ourselves. The selection that follows from "Hills Like White Elephants" is written in objective point of view. The narrator describes the setting, the characters, and the action from a distance while we seem to overhear their conversation from a neighboring table.

From "Hills Like White Elephants," by Ernest Hemingway (See the complete story on p. 334.)

The hills across the valley of the Ebro were long and white. On this side there was no shade and no trees and the station was between two lines of rails in the sun. Close against the side of the station there was the warm shadow of the building and a curtain, made of strings of bamboo beads, hung across the open door into the bar, to keep out flies. The American and the girl with him sat at a table in the shade, outside the building. It was very hot and the express from Barcelona would come in forty minutes. It stopped at this junction for two minutes and went on to Madrid.

"What should we drink?" the girl asked. She had taken off her hat and put it on the table.

"It's pretty hot," the man said.

"Let's drink beer."

"Dos cervesas," the man said into the curtain.

"Big ones?" a woman asked from the doorway.

"Yes. Two big ones."

Shifting point of view gives us more than one point of view. It may shift from omniscient to first- or third-person point of view (like an overhead camera view of an arena that shifts focus to one performer). Or it may shift from first or third person to omniscient (like a camera that focuses on one performer, then opens up to show all of the action).

Voice

Voice refers to the narrator's persona, the personality that seems to come alive in the words. It is quite possible to have the same point of view but very different voices. The preceding selections from "A & P" and "The Yellow Wallpaper" both have a first-person point of view, but the voice (and personality) of Sammy in "A & P" is very different from that of the narrator in "The Yellow Wallpaper."

Reliability

Just as we make judgments about the credibility of characters, we should consider the stability and the motives of the narrator—especially if the narrator is a character in the story. If there are discrepancies between what you are being told and your own judgment of the same events or characters in the story, this may be an indication of the narrator's unreliability. For example, our response to a story like "The Yellow Wallpaper" is very dependent on our judgment of the narrator's stability.

✔CHECKLIST • *Narration*

❑ Who is the narrator?

❑ What is the point of view?

❑ How would you describe the narrator's voice?

❑ What is the narrator's relationship to the story? Is the narrator reliable? Does the narrator have any questionable motives? Is the narrator confused or emotionally unstable?

❑ Does the narration (point of view and voice) effectively convey the story's meaning?

SETTING

In our own lives, the places and company we seek have much to do with how we want to feel. When we want to relax, we go somewhere informal and familiar. When hungry but with little time to eat, we may go to a bare and efficient place where they serve fast food. On a dinner date, however, we are more likely to seek a restaurant with a sophisticated, romantic atmosphere.

If you were asked to describe the setting you are in right now, what factors would go into your description? Would you include more than its physical features? Setting is more than just physical surroundings. It includes the atmosphere, and atmosphere changes regularly. The weather, lighting, and time of day or night may change it. The people present may change it. Who are they? What is our relationship to them? Are we or they happy or sad? Can you "cut the tension with a knife"? Permanent factors, like physical qualities, are a "shell" for this atmosphere, but those factors that vary (people, time, weather, task) strongly influence a setting too.

In fiction, setting is the location *and* the atmosphere of the story. It has a direct and indirect impact on character and conflict; it supports and emphasizes the story's meaning. Its most important function is to make us feel present in the world that the characters inhabit. The more we can visualize, the more we participate, the more satisfying the experience.

Location

Location tells us where and when the story is taking place. John Updike's "A & P" (p. 146), set in the 1960s in suburban Massachusetts, has a very different feel to it than James Joyce's "Araby" (p. 51), set in Dublin in the 1890s, or John Steinbeck's "The Chrysanthemums" (p. 440), set in rural California in the 1930s. Both the *where* and the *when* will strongly influence the values and behavior of the characters and color the rest of the story.

Atmosphere

The **atmosphere** in a story arises from the mix of location and variable circumstances, such as the personalities present, the conflict, time of day, season, and even the weather. An effectively rendered atmosphere helps us see and experience concrete details of the setting as if we were present. It supports and complements the conflict and characters and helps to convey the story's meaning.

✔ **CHECKLIST** • *Setting*

- ❏ What physical location is this? What does it look like?
- ❏ When does the story take place? What difference does it make to the story?
- ❏ What details help us visualize the setting?
- ❏ Can you describe the atmosphere? How is the lighting? What are the dominant colors? How are the people behaving? How are they dressed? What is the weather like? What is the mood like?

CONFLICT

We spend a good portion of every day resolving conflicts. Most of them are so small we don't even think of them as conflicts. We solve them easily without much effort or anxiety. We get up in the morning when we don't feel like it. We wait patiently for the traffic light to change before we go forward. The solutions and consequences are clear. If we stay in bed, we'll lose pay or be late to class. If we go through the red light, we might kill someone. There is not much internal strife here. And these dilemmas are not likely to make compelling stories.

As the conflicts become more complex, however, our anxiety increases and the choices seem more difficult: "What classes will I take next semester?" "How will I get to school tomorrow?" "Should I ask that person for a date?" Increase the complexity to another level and we get: "Should I stay in school next semester?" "Will I have to buy a car?" "Should I get married?" As the stakes are raised, our internal conflict increases. As you might imagine, the internal nature of conflict also has a lot to do with the personalities of the people involved. For people who are sensitive and shy, asking for a date may be a major conflict. The possibility of being rejected may cause great anxiety. For someone very depressed, even getting out of bed may seem like a major accomplishment.

In literature, **conflict** is the struggle of opposing external or internal forces. Conflict is at the heart of every story. In fact, without it we don't have a story—at least not one most of us would want to hear or read. The impediments and complications of conflict keep us reading. The more important, challenging, believable, and coherent the conflict is, the more we are engaged by the story and want to follow it to its conclusion.

Internal and External Conflict

External conflict may be physical (characters against nature) or social (characters against each other or against society). Internal conflict is a struggle of opposing forces within a character. The best stories contain elements of both types of conflict, but the emphasis is usually on internal conflict.

Conflict and Characterization

Internal conflict has much to do with the makeup of the characters in the story. Consider the personality of each character. What provokes an internal conflict in one person may go unnoticed by another. A character who is insecure and self-conscious is likely to react very differently to some situations than a character who is confident and self-absorbed.

PLOT

When we share our own stories we structure them not only to convey the facts but also to have maximum impact. We might withhold information until later for the effect it will have on our listeners. We don't jump to answer the plea: So what happened!? We might say, "Hold on, I'm getting there, but you have to hear this part first to get a good sense of what happens later." We are naturally sensitive to the way that the arrangement of the details adds suspense or helps the listener "to be there" and feel the experience.

Plot is the structure of the story. It is the pattern of twists and turns the story takes. Most plots spring from conflict. To have a discernible plot, we must have impediments and complications for the work to take the twists and turns necessary to keep us reading.

One traditional arrangement of plot in a short story follows a pattern of exposition, rising action, crisis (sometimes called *climax*), falling action, and resolution (sometimes called *denouement* or *untying*).

CRISIS/CLIMAX
(The moment of truth, the turning point of the conflict.)

RISING ACTION
(The conflict builds, and our emotional involvement intensifies.)

FALLING ACTION
(The crisis is over, the conflict fades, the intensity subsides.)

EXPOSITION
(We learn about the circumstances, characters, and the conflict.)

RESOLUTION
(Things are wrapped up and we are returned to normalcy.)

The diagram of this structure is a bit misleading. Even stories that contain these elements in their plots are generally not balanced so evenly. The crisis, for example, rarely falls right in the middle of the story. The bulk of most stories is spent building (exposition and rising action) to the crisis. Once the crisis is reached, the story usually winds down (falling action and resolution) quickly.

Many television shows and crime stories are classic examples of this formula. In the early days of TV, Erle Stanley Gardner's *Perry Mason* mysteries were turned into a television series. As seen in the following excerpt, each episode fit this pattern especially well—so well it was easy to work in commercial breaks between stages of the plot as if they were part of the show.

Exposition: A desperate client appears at the office of famous defense attorney Perry Mason, reveals that a hideous crime has been committed (usually murder), indicates that he or she is a suspect, and proclaims innocence. Perry confers with his secretary and confidant Della Street and calls in private detective Paul Burke. In the course of these deliberations, we (the viewers or readers) find out about the circumstances, characters, and conflict of the story. (*Commercial break*)

Rising Action: The client is arrested and charged with the hideous crime. The conflict builds as a motive is established and overwhelming circumstantial evidence mounts. Meanwhile, Paul desperately seeks information and other suspects and the setting shifts to the courtroom. The conflict intensifies; the suspense increases. (*Commercial break*)

The Crisis or Climax: In the courtroom, the district attorney continues to build an ironclad case against the defendant. Occasionally private eye Paul enters the courtroom and passes notes to Perry. Perry occasionally sends Della on an errand. The crucial moment occurs when Perry calls the real killer (or an accomplice) to the stand and he or she breaks down under his scrutiny and the weight of the newly discovered evidence (gathered by the relentless Paul) and confesses to the crime. (*Commercial break*)

The Falling Action: The murderer reveals motive and method. (*Commercial break*)

The Resolution: Perry reveals how the good guys found out the truth and shares a joke with Della, Paul, and the grateful, relieved former defendant. Justice is done, and all return to normalcy. (*End of show*)

Consider some of your favorite television shows. Do they have predictable plot structures? Can you describe them? How well do they work?

A major impediment to finding a traditional plot structure is that it doesn't fit some of the best fiction. In many works of fiction, the crisis or climax occurs at the end of the story. Things are not wrapped up for us. There is no intention to provide us with a resolution. Life doesn't come in episodes that resolve conflict so neatly. Stories that intend to capture life as it is don't "wrap up" so neatly either. Joyce's "Araby," Steinbeck's "The Chrysanthemums" (p. 440), Updike's "A & P" (p. 146), Bobbie Ann Mason's "Shiloh" (p. 374), and many other stories don't fit this pattern. Most of these stories reach their crisis or climax and end when the protagonist or central character sees beyond a comforting illusion and confronts painful reality. After this climax there is no resolution—nor would we want one.

✔ CHECKLIST • *Conflict and Plot*

❑ What is the primary external conflict in the story?

❑ What is the primary internal conflict?

❑ Are there other conflicts? If so, what are they?

❑ How would you support your identification of conflict by what is in the text?

❑ To what extent do the traits of the characters lead to conflict?

❑ Can you identify the plot?

❑ Does it conform to the traditional structure? If so, how so? If not, what is the structure?

CHARACTER

Do you remember the first day of class? Surrounded by unfamiliar faces, you may have wondered, "Who are these people?" Even the instructor may have been unfamiliar to you. By the end of that class, though, you probably formed many impressions. You had some sense of what your classmates were like, perhaps even which ones you might like to know better. Some of those impressions may have come from *what* your classmates said about themselves and *how* they said it. But it's unlikely, even if they described themselves, that they told you what to think or feel about them. That was your decision. You probably decided what to think of them on the basis of their appearances, what they did, what they said, how they said it, and what others said about them. You wouldn't have settled for being told what to think; you wanted to see for yourself.

At its best, **characterization**, the development of characters in a story, gives us the same opportunity. The author brings characters to life and lets us "get to know them" as we know people in our own lives. While the narrator may tell us some things directly about the characters, we find out much of what we know indirectly through action and dialogue. We are not told what to think or feel about them. We observe the characters thinking, speaking, and doing. We hear what others say about them. They seem believable and motivated. And like our responses to people in our own lives, our reactions and judgments are based on our own observations.

The main character in a story is called the **protagonist**. When we find a character or characters who seem to be a major force in opposition to the protagonist, that character or characters is called the **antagonist** or **antagonists**. For example, the protagonist in Sandra Cisneros's short story "Eleven" is the young girl who narrates the story. The antagonist is Mrs. Price, who humiliates her in front of her classmates. In Ralph Ellison's "Battle Royal" (p. 286) the protagonist is the young man who narrates the story. The antagonists are "the town's leading white citizens," who degrade him at their brutally racist ceremony.

When characters lack the development that seems to bring them to life, lack the complexity that lets us know them as we know people in our own lives, and seem to represent "types" more than real personalities they are called **flat** or **stock characters**. When they seem fully developed, with all the complexities of real people, they are described as **round characters**.

✔ C H E C K L I S T • *Character*

- ❏ What is your impression of the characters?
- ❏ What do the characters do that makes you feel this way? What do they say that makes you feel this way? What is said about them by other characters that makes you feel this way?
- ❏ Are the characters motivated and consistent? Are they believable?
- ❏ Are there flat or stock characters in the story?
- ❏ Can you identify the protagonist? One or more antagonists?
- ❏ Can you support your responses from the text of the story?

LANGUAGE AND STYLE

It's not possible to separate language and style from other elements. Language is the vehicle that carries them to you. The formal or informal style of the language is an integral part of narration. The evocative nature of the language used to describe setting has so much to do with our visualization and response to it. The style of the language used by the characters tells us a great deal about who they are. And the symbolic nature of the language may complement and support the story's theme or meaning.

Denotation and Connotation

Faced with an unfamiliar word—dictionary in hand—you might look up its definition and be reasonably satisfied with what you find. But if you are already familiar with that word, a dictionary definition is not likely to account for everything the word means to you. While you might not disagree with the dictionary definition, or **denotation**, of the word, you probably won't be entirely satisfied with it, either. Your own definitions, or **connotations**, for familiar words are flavored with personal associations. Dictionary definitions alone cannot account for this complex response to language.

Writers are very conscious of the effect that connotations, or suggested meanings, have on readers. Synonyms for the word *thin,* for example, include *slim, slender, lean, skinny,* and *trim*—words that mean almost the same thing. But each of these words has a different connotation and slightly different meaning for each of us—and a different effect on us when we read it. Being conscious of word choices and patterns of language may tell us a great deal about what makes a story effective and how it triggers our responses.

Figurative Language

There is nothing unusual about figurative language. In fact, we would have a hard time communicating with each other without it. Comparison is at the core of "figures of speech," or figurative language. We use what is already familiar to describe something new, or we describe something familiar in a new way. Used in tandem with concrete language, similes and metaphors can lead to very striking images.

A **simile** is an announced comparison. We announce or introduce this comparison by using the words *like* or *as.* For example, "He's as quiet as a church mouse" or "She swims like a fish." Those things compared usually have only one characteristic in common. Some of the most evocative descriptions in literature are similes. James Joyce's description of a young boy's infatuation, "But my body was like a harp and her words and gestures were like fingers running upon the wires" (see "Araby," p. 51), is a vivid example of how simile can evoke lasting images in our minds.

A **metaphor** is a more direct and more complete comparison than a simile. A metaphor does not announce itself; it states that something *is* something else (My love is a red rose) or implies it (My love has red petals and sharp thorns). Our everyday language is filled with metaphors. We call attractive-looking people hunks and foxes. Businesses use implied metaphors to name their products. We buy an antiperspirant named Arrid, soap named Irish Spring, computers named Thinkpads, and cars named Jaguars. Sometimes, however, people get carried away and mix metaphors, with curious results. A baseball manager once remarked about a suspended player that "The ball was in his court now [tennis], so he better not step out of bounds [basketball], or he'd be down for the count [boxing]."

Symbol

A **symbol** is something that represents more than itself. Every word we speak is a symbol. Government flags, religious objects, and logos on college sweatshirts are all symbols. We have personal symbols (meaningful objects, special songs), public symbols (flags), and conventional symbols (a road as the journey of life, seasons to represent the stages of our lives). Symbols are subject to personal interpretation. A nation's flag may symbolize truth and justice to one person, but deceit and oppression to another.

Just about anything in a story might be symbolic. In fiction, symbols are most likely to be objects, names, or places, but they might be actions, sounds, or colors as well.

Diction

The type of language they use, their **diction**, tells us a lot about narrators and characters and establishes their voices. Their use of formal vocabulary tells us one thing, their use of informal or nonstandard words or phrases conveys something very different. The frequency of images and figurative language may also have an effect on our reading and response to a story.

✔ CHECKLIST • *Language and Style*

- ❑ Is the language formal or informal?
- ❑ What does the nature of the language tell you about the narrator or characters?
- ❑ Are there many instances of figurative language (imagery, simile, metaphor)?
- ❑ Is there a dominant symbol? Are there any symbols? If so, how do they connect to or support the story?

THEME

Theme is the central idea expressed by the story. It is a generalization, an insight about life derived from the work as a whole. Identifying and articulating this meaning is not easy. Although our experience of the theme may be holistic or impressionistic, the analysis and support required for its articulation demand a close look at the parts—the language, events, characters, and outcome of the story.

Theme or Moral?

When writing about a story, one temptation is to reduce what it means to a moral or lesson. Good literature reveals a complex world. Statements like

"Honesty is the best policy" may seem to reverberate with truth until we examine them closely. Is honesty always the best policy? Is it always the most ethical policy? Is it "moral" to tell people things that will hurt them? Didactic stories intend to deliver a moral. A moral preaches; it teaches a lesson or a code of conduct. A theme reveals; it gives us insight into human nature.

Consider the difference between revealing and preaching. If we read a story in which John loves Mary and Mary falls in love with Bill, we might state the simplified theme of the story as: People don't necessarily fall in love with those who are in love with them. To identify this theme, we examine the particulars of the story, come to a conclusion about them, and then expand this conclusion into a generalization about life itself.

A moral, however, is a simple lesson or rule of conduct. If we tried to find a moral in the previous John-Mary-Bill example, we might write, "Fall in love only with people who love you." But we know from our experience of the world that such a statement is much too simple to account for the complex nature of this situation. It would also seem silly to reduce John Steinbeck's story "The Chrysanthemums" to the moral "Don't trust strangers." It's clear that Elisa's unfulfilled desire for appreciation and love reveals a much more complex situation than such a moral could solve. Similarly, the frustration and humiliation of the protagonists in "Eleven" and "Battle Royal," or the intense emotional and ethical dilemma of the couple in "Hills Like White Elephants," cannot be reduced to clear lessons or morals. They reveal, as life reveals, complexity intact. In most modern literature, theme is not usually expressed as a moral, and it will probably take more than a few words to state the theme of a complex work.

✔ CHECKLIST • *Theme*

- ❏ What are the major details (characters, conflicts, outcome) of the story?
- ❏ What conclusion about the story did you draw from these details?
- ❏ What generalization about life does this conclusion lead to?
- ❏ What does the story mean? What is the theme of the story?
- ❏ Is the story didactic? Does it preach or give a lesson?

✔ SUMMARY CHECKLIST • *Analyzing Fiction*

Narration

- ❏ Who is the narrator?
- ❏ What is the point of view?
- ❏ How would you describe the narrator's voice?
- ❏ What is the narrator's relationship to the story? Is the narrator reliable?
- ❏ Does the narrator have any questionable motives? Is the narrator confused or emotionally unstable?

continued

❑   Does the narration (point of view and voice) effectively convey the story's meaning?

Setting
❑   What physical location is this? What does it look like?

❑   When does the story take place? What difference does it make to the story?

❑   What details help us visualize the setting?

❑   Can you describe the atmosphere?

❑   How is the lighting? What are the dominant colors?

❑   How are the people behaving? How are they dressed?

❑   What is the weather like? What is the mood like?

Conflict and Plot
❑   What is the primary external conflict in the story?

❑   What is the primary internal conflict?

❑   Are there other conflicts? If so, what are they?

❑   How would you support your identification of conflict by what is in the text?

❑   To what extent do the traits of the characters lead to conflict?

❑   Can you identify the plot?

❑   Does it conform to the traditional structure? If so, how so? If not, what is the structure?

Character
❑   What is your impression of the characters?

❑   What do the characters do that makes you feel this way?

❑   What do they say that makes you feel this way?

❑   What is said about them by other characters that makes you feel this way?

❑   Are the characters motivated and consistent? Are they believable?

❑   Are there flat or stock characters in the story?

❑   Can you identify the protagonist? One or more antagonists?

❑   Can you support your responses from the text of the story?

Language and Style
❑   Is the language formal or informal?

❑   What does the nature of the language tell you about the narrator or characters?

❑   Are there many instances of figurative language (imagery, simile, metaphor)?

continued

❑ Is there a dominant symbol? Are there any symbols? If so, how do they connect to or support the story?

Theme

❑ What are the major details (characters, conflicts, outcome) of the story?

❑ What conclusion about the story did you draw from these details?

❑ What generalization about life does this conclusion lead to?

❑ What does the story mean? What is the theme or story?

❑ Is the story didactic? Does it preach or give a lesson?

The Story in Context

❑ What historical, biographical, cultural factors are important to this story?

GETTING IDEAS FOR WRITING ABOUT FICTION

Following "One Friday Morning," many of the questions from the summary checklist above are applied to the story, and we consider some of the ways the elements on this list might be used to prompt ideas for a critical essay.

LANGSTON HUGHES (1902–1967)

One of the most important figures of the Harlem Renaissance,—a movement of African-American artists, writers, poets, and musicians in the 1920s and 1930s centered in the Harlem neighborhood of New York City— Langston Hughes was born in Joplin, Missouri, and graduated from Lincoln University in Pennsylvania. As a young man, he traveled the world as a merchant seaman, visiting Africa and living for a time in Paris and Rome. A poet, writer of fiction, playwright, lyricist, editor, critic and essayist, Hughes published two volumes of autobiography, The Big Sea (1940) and I Wonder as I Wander (1956). Hughes's work, which is filled with the sounds and music of the African-American experience, has influenced generations of American writers.

ONE FRIDAY MORNING [1939]

The thrilling news did not come directly to Nancy Lee, but it came in little indirections that finally added themselves up to one tremendous fact: she had won the prize! But being a calm and quiet young lady, she did not say anything, although the

whole high school buzzed with rumors, guesses, reportedly authentic announcements on the part of students who had no right to be making announcements at
all—since no student really knew yet who had won this year's art scholarship.

But Nancy Lee's drawing was so good, her lines so sure, her colors so bright and
harmonious, that certainly no other student in the senior art class at George
Washington High was thought to have very much of a chance. Yet you never could
tell. Last year nobody had expected Joe Williams to win the Artist Club scholarship
with that funny modernistic watercolor he had done of the high-level bridge. In
fact, it was hard to make out there was a bridge until you had looked at the picture
a long time. Still, Joe Williams got the prize, was feted by the community's leading
painters, club women, and society folks at a big banquet at the Park-Rose Hotel, and
was now an award student at the Art School—the city's only art school.

Nancy Lee Johnson was a colored girl, a few years out of the South. But seldom
did her high-school classmates think of her as colored. She was smart, pretty, and
brown, and fitted in well with the life of the school. She stood high in scholarship,
played a swell game of basketball, had taken part in the senior musical in a soft, vel-
vety voice, and had never seemed to intrude or stand out except in pleasant ways,
so it was seldom even mentioned—her color.

Nancy Lee sometimes forgot she was colored herself. She liked her classmates
and her school. Particularly she liked her art teacher, Miss Dietrich, the tall red-
haired woman who taught her law and order in doing things; and the beauty of
working step by step until a job is done; a picture finished; a design created; or a
block print carved out of nothing but an idea and a smooth square of linoleum,
inked, proofs made, and finally put down on paper—clean, sharp, beautiful, individual, unlike any other in the world, thus making the paper have a meaning
nobody else could give it except Nancy Lee. That was the wonderful thing about
true creation. You made something nobody else on earth could make—but you.

5   Miss Dietrich was the kind of teacher who brought out the best in her students—but their own best, not anybody else's copied best. For anybody else's best,
great though it might be, even Michelangelo's, wasn't enough to please Miss
Dietrich, dealing with the creative impulses of young men and women living in an
American city in the Middle West, and being American.

Nancy Lee was proud of being American, a Negro American with blood out of
Africa a long time ago, too many generations back to count. But her parents had
taught her the beauties of Africa, its strength, its song, its mighty rivers, its early
smelting of iron, its building of the pyramids, and its ancient and important civi-
lizations. And Miss Dietrich had discovered for her the sharp and humorous lines
of African sculpture, Benin, Congo, Makonde. Nancy Lee's father was a mail carrier,
her mother a social worker in a city settlement house. Both parents had been to
Negro colleges in the South. And her mother had gotten a further degree in social
work from a Northern university. Her parents were, like most Americans, simple
ordinary people who had worked hard and steadily for their education. Now they
were trying to make it easier for Nancy Lee to achieve learning than it had been for
them. They would be very happy when they heard of the award to their daughter—
yet Nancy did not tell them. To surprise them would be better. Besides, there had
been a promise.

Casually, one day, Miss Dietrich asked Nancy Lee what color frame she thought would be best on her picture. That had been the first inkling.

"Blue," Nancy Lee said. Although the picture had been entered in the Artist Club contest a month ago, Nancy Lee did not hesitate in her choice of a color for the possible frame since she could still see her picture clearly in her mind's eye—for that picture waiting for the blue frame had come out of her soul, her own life, and had bloomed into miraculous being with Miss Dietrich's help. It was, she knew, the best watercolor she had painted in her four years as a high-school art student, and she was glad she had made something Miss Dietrich liked well enough to permit her to enter in the contest before she graduated.

It was not a modernistic picture in the sense that you had to look at it a long time to understand what it meant. It was just a simple scene in the city park on a spring day with the trees still leaflessly lacy against the sky, the new grass fresh and green, a flag on a tall pole in the center, children playing, and an old Negro woman sitting on a bench with her head turned. A lot for one picture, to be sure, but it was not there in heavy and final detail like a calendar. Its charm was that everything was light and airy, happy like spring, with a lot of blue sky, paper-white clouds, and air showing through. You could tell that the old Negro woman was looking at the flag, and that the flag was proud in the spring breeze, and that the breeze helped to make the children's dresses billow as they played.

10   Miss Dietrich had taught Nancy Lee how to paint spring, people, and a breeze on what was only a plain white piece of paper from the supply closet. But Miss Dietrich had not said make it like any other spring-people-breeze ever seen before. She let it remain Nancy Lee's own. That is how the old Negro woman happened to be there looking at the flag—for in her mind the flag, the spring, and the woman formed a kind of triangle holding a dream Nancy Lee wanted to express. White stars on a blue field, spring, children, ever-growing life, and an old woman. Would the judges at the Artist Club like it?

One wet, rainy April afternoon Miss O'Shay, the girls' vice-principal, sent for Nancy Lee to stop by her office as school closed. Pupils without umbrellas or rain-coats were clustered in doorways, hoping to make it home between showers. Outside the skies were gray. Nancy Lee's thoughts were suddenly gray, too.

She did not think she had done anything wrong, yet that tight little knot came in her throat just the same as she approached Miss O'Shay's door. Perhaps she had banged her locker too often and too hard. Perhaps the note in French she had writ-ten to Sallie halfway across the study hall just for fun had never gotten to Sallie but into Miss O'Shay's hands instead. Or maybe she was failing in some subject and wouldn't be allowed to graduate. Chemistry! A pang went through the pit of her stomach. She knocked on Miss O'Shay's door. That familiarly solid and competent voice said, "Come in."

Miss O'Shay had a way of making you feel welcome, even if you came to be expelled.

"Sit down, Nancy Lee Johnson," said Miss O'Shay. "I have something to tell you." Nancy Lee sat down. "But I must ask you to promise not to tell anyone yet."

15   "I won't, Miss O'Shay," Nancy Lee said, wondering what on earth the vice-principal had to say to her.

"You are about to graduate," Miss O'Shay said. "And we shall miss you. You have been an excellent student, Nancy, and you will not be without honors on the senior list, as I am sure you know."

At that point there was a light knock on the door. Miss O'Shay called out, "Come in," and Miss Dietrich entered. "May I be a part of this, too?" she asked, tall and smiling.

"Of course," Miss O'Shay said. "I was just telling Nancy Lee what we thought of her. But I hadn't gotten around to giving her the news. Perhaps, Miss Dietrich, you'd like to tell her yourself."

Miss Dietrich was always direct. "Nancy Lee," she said, "your picture has won the Artist Club scholarship."

20   The slender brown girl's eyes widened, her heart thumped, then her throat tightened again. She tried to smile, but instead tears came to her eyes.

"Dear Nancy Lee," Miss O'Shay said, "we are so happy for you." The elderly white woman took her hand and shook it warmly while Miss Dietrich beamed with pride.

Nancy Lee must have danced all the way home. She never remembered quite how she got there through the rain. She hoped she had been dignified. But certainly she hadn't stopped to tell anybody her secret on the way. Raindrops, smiles, and tears mingled on her brown cheeks. She hoped her mother hadn't yet gotten home and that the house was empty. She wanted to have time to calm down and look natural before she had to see anyone. She didn't want to be bursting with excitement—having a secret to contain.

Miss O'Shay's calling her to the office had been in the nature of a preparation and a warning. The kind, elderly vice-principal said she did not believe in catching young ladies unawares, even with honors, so she wished her to know about the coming award. In making acceptance speeches she wanted her to be calm, prepared, not nervous, overcome, and frightened. So Nancy Lee was asked to think what she would say when the scholarship was conferred upon her a few days hence, both at the Friday morning high-school assembly hour, when the announcement would be made, and at the evening banquet of the Artist Club. Nancy Lee promised the vice-principal to think calmly about what she would say.

Miss Dietrich had then asked for some facts about her parents, her background, and her life, since such material would probably be desired for the papers. Nancy Lee had told her how, six years before, they had come up from the Deep South, her father having been successful in achieving a transfer from the one post office to another, a thing he had long sought in order to give Nancy Lee a chance to go to school in the North. Now they lived in a modest Negro neighborhood, went to see the best plays when they came to town, and had been saving to send Nancy Lee to art school, in case she were permitted to enter. But the scholarship would help a great deal, for they were not rich people.

25   "Now Mother can have a new coat next winter," Nancy Lee thought, "because my tuition will all be covered for the first year. And once in art school, there are other scholarships I can win."

Dreams began to dance through her head, plans and ambitions, beauties she would create for herself, her parents, and the Negro people—for Nancy Lee possessed a deep and reverent race pride. She could see the old woman in her picture (really her grandmother in the South) lifting her head to the bright stars on the flag in the distance. A Negro in America! Often hurt, discriminated against, sometimes lynched—but always there were the stars on the blue body of the flag. Was there any other flag in the world that had so many stars? Nancy Lee thought deeply, but she could remember none in all the encyclopedias or geographies she had ever looked into.

"Hitch your wagon to a star," Nancy Lee thought, dancing home in the rain. "Who were our flag makers?"

Friday morning came, the morning when the world would know—her high-school world, the newspaper world, her mother and dad. Dad could not be there at the assembly to hear the announcement, nor see her prize picture displayed on the stage, nor to listen to Nancy Lee's little speech of acceptance, but Mother would be able to come, although Mother was much puzzled as to why Nancy Lee was so insistent she be at school on that particular Friday morning.

When something is happening, something new and fine, something that will change your very life, it is hard to go to sleep at night for thinking about it, and hard to keep your heart from pounding, or a strange little knot of joy from gathering in your throat. Nancy Lee had taken her bath, brushed her hair until it glowed, and had gone to bed thinking about the next day, the big day when, before three thousand students, she would be the one student honored, her painting the one painting to be acclaimed as the best of the year from all the art classes of the city. Her short speech of gratitude was ready. She went over it in her mind, not word for word (because she didn't want it to sound as if she had learned it by heart), but she let the thoughts flow simply and sincerely through her consciousness many times.

30   When the president of the Artist Club presented her with the medal and scroll of the scholarship award, she would say:

"Judges and members of the Artist Club, I want to thank you for this award that means so much to me personally and through me to my people, the colored people of this city who, sometimes, are discouraged and bewildered, thinking that color and poverty are against them. I accept this award with gratitude and pride, not for myself alone, but for my race that believes in American opportunity and American fairness—and the bright stars in our flag. I thank Miss Dietrich and the teachers who made it possible for me to have the knowledge and training that lie behind this honor you have conferred upon my painting. When I came here from the South a few years ago, I was not sure how you would receive me. You received me well. You have given me a chance and helped me along the road I wanted to follow. I suppose the judges know that every week here at assembly the students of this school pledge allegiance to the flag. I shall try to be worthy of that pledge, and of the help and friendship and understanding of my fellow citizens of whatever race or creed, and of our American dream of 'Liberty and justice for all!'"

That would be her response before the students in the morning. How proud and happy the Negro pupils would be, perhaps almost as proud as they were of the one colored star on the football team. Her mother would probably cry with happiness. Thus Nancy Lee went to sleep dreaming of a wonderful tomorrow.

The bright sunlight of an April morning woke her. There was breakfast with her parents—their half-amused and puzzled faces across the table, wondering what could be this secret that made her eyes so bright. The swift walk to school; the clock in the tower almost nine; hundreds of pupils streaming into the long, rambling old building that was the city's largest high school; the sudden quiet of the homeroom after the bell rang; then the teacher opening her record book to call the roll. But just before she began, she looked across the room until her eyes located Nancy Lee.

"Nancy," she said, "Miss O'Shay would like to see you in her office, please."

35   Nancy Lee rose and went out while the names were being called and the word *present* added its period to each name. Perhaps, Nancy Lee thought, the reporters from the papers had already come. Maybe they wanted to take her picture before assembly, which wasn't until ten o'clock. (Last year they had had the photograph of the winner of the award in the morning papers as soon as the announcement had been made.)

Nancy Lee knocked at Miss O'Shay's door.

"Come in."

The vice-principal stood at her desk. There was no one else in the room. It was very quiet.

"Sit down, Nancy Lee," she said. Miss O'Shay did not smile. There was a long pause. The seconds went by slowly. "I do not know how to tell you what I have to say," the elderly woman began, her eyes on the papers on her desk. "I am indignant and ashamed for myself and for this city." Then she lifted her eyes and looked at Nancy Lee in the neat blue dress sitting there before her. "You are not to receive the scholarship this morning."

40   Outside in the hall the electric bells announcing the first period rang, loud and interminably long. Miss O'Shay remained silent. To the brown girl there in the chair, the room grew suddenly smaller, smaller, smaller, and there was no air. She could not speak.

Miss O'Shay said, "When the committee learned that you were colored, they changed their plans."

Still Nancy Lee said nothing, for there was no air to give breath to her lungs.

"Here is the letter from the committee, Nancy Lee." Miss O'Shay picked it up and read the final paragraph to her.

" 'It seems to us wiser to arbitrarily rotate the award among the various high schools of the city from now on. And especially in this case since the student chosen happens to be colored, a circumstance which unfortunately, had we known, might have prevented this embarrassment. But there have never been any Negro students in the local art school, and the presence of one there might create difficulties for all concerned. We have high regard for the quality of Nancy Lee Johnson's talent, but we do not feel it would be fair to honor it with the Artist Club award.' " Miss O'Shay paused. She put the letter down.

45   "Nancy Lee, I am very sorry to have to give you this message."

"But my speech," Nancy Lee said, "was about. . . ." The words stuck in her throat. " . . . about America. . . ."

Miss O'Shay had risen; she turned her back and stood looking out the window at the spring tulips in the school yard.

"I thought, since the award would be made at assembly right after our oath of allegiance," the words tumbled almost hysterically from Nancy Lee's throat now, "I would put part of the flag salute in my speech. You know, Miss O'Shay, that part about 'liberty and justice for all.' "

"I know," said Miss O'Shay, slowly facing the room again. "But America is only what we who believe in it, make it. I am Irish. You may not know, Nancy Lee, but years ago we were called the dirty Irish, and mobs rioted against us in the big cities, and we were invited to go back where we came from. But we didn't go. And we didn't give up, because we believed in the American dream, and in our power to make that dream come true. Difficulties, yes. Mountains to climb, yes. Discouragements to face, yes. Democracy to make, yes. That is it, Nancy Lee! We still have in this world of ours democracy to *make*. You and I, Nancy Lee. But the premise and the base are here, the lines of the Declaration of Independence and the words of Lincoln are here, and the stars in our flag. Those who deny you this scholarship do not know the meaning of those stars, but it's up to us to make them know. As a teacher in the public schools of this city, I myself will go before the school board and ask them to remove from our system the offer of any prizes or awards denied to any student because of race or color."

50   Suddenly Miss O'Shay stopped speaking. Her clear, clear blue eyes looked into those of the girl before her. The woman's eyes were full of strength and courage. "Lift up your head, Nancy Lee, and smile at me."

Miss O'Shay stood against the open window with the green lawn and the tulips beyond, the sunlight tangled in her gray hair, her voice an electric flow of strength to the hurt spirit of Nancy Lee. The Abolitionists who believed in freedom when there was slavery must have been like that. The first white teachers who went into the Deep South to teach the freed slaves must have been like that. All those who stand against ignorance, narrowness, hate, and mud on stars must be like that.

Nancy Lee lifted her head and smiled. The bell for assembly rang. She went through the long hall filled with students toward the auditorium.

"There will be other awards," Nancy Lee thought. "There're schools in other cities. This won't keep me down. But when I'm a woman, I'll fight to see that these things don't happen to other girls as this has happened to me. And men and women like Miss O'Shay will help me."

She took her seat among the seniors. The doors of the auditorium closed. As the principal came onto the platform, the students rose and turned their eyes to the flag on the stage.

55   One hand went to the heart, the other outstretched toward the flag. Three thousand voices spoke. Among them was the voice of a dark girl whose cheeks were suddenly wet with tears, ". . . one nation indivisible, with liberty and justice for all."

"That is the land we must make," she thought.

GENERATING IDEAS FOR WRITING

One of the best ways to get ideas for an essay is to ask and answer your own most compelling questions. Write down whatever questions come to mind during and after your reading. See if your answers to these questions provide topics for writing. Or choose a compelling idea from a journal entry, draw a Venn diagram to compare elements, characters, or stories (pp. 60–61), use directed freewriting (p. 65), ask questions (p. 66), list, or draw a cluster, or semantic map (pp. 67–68), to loosen up ideas.

Listed below is a much more structured approach based on the elements of fiction discussed earlier in this section. Applying these questions to "One Friday Morning" may demonstrate how the elements might be applied to any work of short fiction.

Getting Started—Your First Response

1. What questions came to mind as you read "One Friday Morning"?

2. To what extent can you connect "One Friday Morning" to your own background or experience?

3. What do you find most compelling or provocative about the story?

Narration

1. Unlike the first-person narrative of Sandra Cisneros's "Eleven" in Chapter 2, this story is told from the third-person point of view. How does this narrative perspective affect your experience of the story?

2. What is the tone of the narration? What is the attitude of the narrator toward Nancy Lee? To what extent is the narrator reliable?

3. If the story were told in the first person by Nancy Lee herself, how would it change the way you experience it? Would you know any more than you do now? If so, what?

4. If the story were told by Miss O'Shay or Miss Dietrich, how would it change the way you experience the story?

Setting

1. Describe the setting of "One Friday Morning." In what location does the story take place? When does it occur?

2. What effect does the setting have on your response to the story?

3. "Outside the skies were gray" is a description of the weather in one scene. In what way does the weather agree with or contrast the action in the story?

4. What other details in Langston Hughes's writing were most effective in conveying the setting? Quote them from the text.

5. This story was originally published in 1939. If the story were written and published recently, would you have responded differently? Explain.

Conflict and Plot

1. What events in "One Friday Morning" lead to the conflict?

2. How would you describe the conflict? Which elements of the conflict are external? Which ones are internal?

3. To what extent does the conflict derive from Nancy Lee, Miss Dietrich, Miss O'Shay, and their beliefs?

4. What is the climax of this story? What is the resolution? To what extent are you satisfied with the resolution?

Character
1. Describe Nancy Lee. How does what she says and does show you who she is? Do you learn about her directly or indirectly? Explain.
2. How would you describe Miss Dietrich? Miss O'Shay? What do they do or say that supports your description? Are they round or flat characters? Why?
3. What quotations from the text support your description of Nancy Lee? Of Miss Deitrich? Of Miss O'Shay?
4. To what extent do Nancy Lee, Miss Deitrich, or Miss O'Shay change or develop in the story?
5. If Nancy Lee is the protagonist, who is the antagonist?

Language and Style
1. Is the language of "One Friday Morning" formal or informal?
2. What does the nature of the language Nancy Lee uses tell you about her? The language of Miss Dietrich? Of Miss O'Shay? Cite examples.
3. How does the language of the narration affect you? For example, the sentence "Raindrops, smiles, and tears mingled on her brown cheeks" paints an especially touching picture. What other images appeal to you and why?
4. Do you see any symbols in "One Friday Morning"? If so, explain.

Theme
1. What conclusion do you draw from "One Friday Morning"?
2. What details and events lead to this conclusion?
3. What is the point of the story? What is the theme?

The Story in Context
1. What historical, biographical, or cultural factors are important to this story?

Topics for Writing
The following list is not exhaustive, but simply illustrative of the kinds of questions that might emerge from more specific analytical questions (and combinations of questions) like those above. Your responses to these questions might provide worthwhile topics for writing.

1. What is the effect of third-person narration on the characterization of Nancy Lee?
2. What would this story be like if told by Nancy Lee?

3. In what way is the school setting a factor in the outcome of "One Friday Morning"?

4. In what way is the larger setting of the Midwest a factor in the outcome?

5. To what extent are Miss Deitrich and Miss O'Shay helpful mentors for Nancy Lee?

6. To what extent are Miss Deitrich and Miss O'Shay cooperating with a racist system?

7. What were race relations like in this country in 1939? How does "One Friday Morning" fit within the time period and culture in which it was written? To what extent would the resolution of this story be acceptable today?

CHAPTER 4

Argumentation
Interpreting and Evaluating Fiction

The goal in this chapter is to develop your writing and analysis into a critical essay. Writing a critical essay is a natural extension of your earlier work. At their best, your essays should continue to express, in your strongest voice, what you believe is important. There is no need for you to become completely formal or use complicated terminology. But writing a critical essay does require reading and rereading a story carefully, gathering textual evidence, building observations into an interpretation or evaluation, and articulating a sound argument. Convincing others requires clear thinking and writing. We may write with a stronger voice when we feel passionate about an issue, but it is our ability to explain *why* with evidence, not just our passion, that gives clarity and credibility to our arguments.

THE CRITICAL ESSAY

The difference between a response essay and a critical essay is more a matter of emphasis than kind. A response essay describes our experience with literature—how we are personally affected by the story. The primary intention of a response essay is to share our personal experience, not to argue for a position.

A critical essay, while motivated by our experience with literature, shifts the emphasis toward the work itself and builds an argument for what the work or some aspect of it means (an interpretation), or its worth (an evaluation), or both. In addition to analyzing or explicating the text of a work, or making comparisons, a critical essay may address the beliefs or actions of the narrator or characters, or view a work or its elements within a variety of historical, cultural, biographical, or other contexts (see the Appendix for an explanation of these approaches).

Writing a critical essay builds on your earlier work. Beyond this work, you must be prepared to offer arguments in support of your views and state them clearly and persuasively. Reading the two excerpts below—taken from student essay samples later in this chapter—may give you an insight into the difference between a personal and a critical response.

Alejandro's Response to Alice Walker's "Everyday Use":

> This story reminds me of my own identity crisis. Like Dee's mother, my father believed that life is a certain way and one just accepted it. He was easygoing and believed in working hard and making sure that everything was in order. He was amused by my "identity crisis" and wondered what the fuss was all about.

Debora's Response to "Everyday Use":

> In the short story "Everyday Use," by Alice Walker, Dee accuses her mother of not understanding her heritage, yet Dee herself denies her own true roots. Not only does she change her name, trying to become someone she isn't, but she criticizes her mother and sister for living the way they do. Maggie and her mother, however, are the only ones in this family who can truly grasp their heritage.

Alejandro writes about how the story affected him—what emotions he felt and what he was reminded of as he saw the similarities between the events of the story and his own life. The emphasis in his *response essay* is on these parallels, and his intention is to share his personal experience of the story, not to argue an interpretation or evaluation.

Debora, on the other hand, writes about the beliefs and actions of the characters in the story. Her reaction to these characters may very well be motivated by her personal response, but the intention of her *critical essay* is to interpret and evaluate the characters in the story, not to share how her own background and/or experiences might have caused this reaction. Her emphasis is on characterization in the story, not on her personal identification with those characters.

CHOOSING A TOPIC: PROCESS AND PRODUCT

The explanations below identify a number of different approaches you might choose when writing a critical essay.

Writing to Analyze or Explicate

To analyze a story is to look closely at how it works—to examine its parts or elements (language, form, conflict, plot, characterization, theme) as they contribute to its meaning.

An **explication** is a detailed analysis, a line-by-line interpretation of *how* and *what* a short work (or brief section of a larger work) means. An explication is not just a summary or translation of the author's language into your own; it is a detailed explanation of *how* the work conveys meaning.

Writing to Compare

In what way are characters or other aspects of this work comparable to each other? To what extent is the work or some aspect of it comparable to other works or aspects of them? The objective of a comparison is not just to list similarities and differences but to reveal something important about whatever is being compared. Which details you choose as the basis of this comparison can make a difference. To give yourself a clear direction, and an overview of what you have, it may be helpful to make separate lists of similarities and differences before you start to write. Ask yourself what's worth comparing and what's not—and how this comparison might yield an effective essay. One useful method of lining up similarities and differences is the Venn diagram, described in Chapter 2 on pages 59–61.

Writing About the Beliefs or Actions of the Narrator or Characters

As we've discussed, narrators and literary characters often express their beliefs in what they say or do. It's natural for us to judge their words and actions through our own beliefs, compare their choices with our own, and approve or disapprove as they meet or fail to meet our expectations. This is the kind of topic that lends itself well to a response essay—an essay that describes our experience of the work and the emotions we felt—the outrage, frustration, pleasure, or pride we experienced in response to the beliefs expressed. But writing about the beliefs or actions of the narrator or characters can also be a good topic for a critical essay.

Remember, a critical essay shifts the emphasis toward the work and builds an argument for what the work or some aspect of it means (an interpretation) or its worth (an evaluation), or both. To write a critical essay about the beliefs or actions of the narrator or characters, you must clearly identify those beliefs or actions and cite evidence that exemplifies them. Based on your own clearly stated criteria, you might interpret what they mean or build an argument for or against them.

In her essay following "Everyday Use" (p. 121), Debora VanCoughnett writes about beliefs when she criticizes the superficiality of one character's claim to her heritage when compared to the "real" respect it is given as lived every day by her mother and sister.

The student essays of Michelle McAuliffe (p. 151) and Julie Fitzmaurice (p. 153) about John Updike's "A & P" at the end of this chapter also illustrate this type of critical response. Both students comment on the protagonist's decision to quit his job, but they disagree about the wisdom of his decision. Michelle criticizes his decision and believes that he will regret it because of the consequences it will have for him and his family. Julie, however, sees his action as an inspiring statement that he will refuse to sell out and live his life like the store manager in the story.

Writing About Stories in Context

To write about literature in context is to consider the work within a framework of cultural, historical, biographical, or other influences. For a more comprehensive explanation of these approaches (including historical, gender, political-economic, psychoanalytic, archetypal, and biographical criticism), see Appendix A: Critical Approaches to Literature, on page 467.

Kevin Chamberlain's essay about James Joyce's "Eveline" on page 345 examines the cultural imperatives of late-nineteenth-century Ireland as they seem to determine the fate of the story's protagonist.

✔ **C H E C K L I S T** • *Choosing a Topic for a Critical Essay*

❑ What work or aspect of a work interests you?

❑ Is there a work or elements of a work (language, form, conflict, plot, characterization, theme) that you would like to analyze or explicate?

❑ Would it be illuminating to compare this work or some aspect of it to another work or works?

❑ Are there beliefs or actions of the narrator or characters that you want to interpret or evaluate?

❑ Do you want to interpret or evaluate the work or aspects of it within a larger historical, cultural, biographical, or other context?

RESPONSE ESSAY OR CRITICAL ESSAY?

TWO READERS ∼ TWO CHOICES

Following Alice Walker's "Everyday Use" on page 112, the complete versions of the two student essays excerpted earlier in this chapter illustrate the difference between a *response essay* (p. 119) and a *critical essay* (p.121).

■ *EXPLORING "Everyday Use"*

Making Connections   One of the more compelling aspects of Alice Walker's short story "Everyday Use" is its reminder that heritage is much more than a coat of arms or a display of historical artifacts. The legacy most of us inherit from our ancestors has been shaped not by glorious and noteworthy achievement but by quiet courage and everyday struggle.

The story reminds us, too, that in the shift from one generation to the next there is often a clash of values and a breaking away. Mama, the story's narrator, has learned and taught her lessons in the school of practical experience, a school where dirt floors and tin roofs dictate the values of physical strength, simple dignity, and humility. For one daughter, Maggie, this environment and its old-time values are a comforting refuge. But for her other daughter, Dee, these conditions are something to escape from, a reference point for how far she has come as she makes her way up through a world of formal education and the values of modern living .

Your Experiences and Beliefs   Before you read "Everyday Use," you may want to consider your own experiences and beliefs as they apply to some of the issues that emerge from this story. How do you feel about your own heritage? Is it a major factor in your identity? Have you ever felt embarrassed by your family? Would you be satisfied to live the life your parents or other close family members have lived? If you have brothers or sisters, do you think of yourself as more or less ambitious than they are? What do you consider to be the measure of success? Do you think there is more to be learned through formal education or practical experience? Do you feel in control of forging your own identity?

ALICE WALKER (b. 1944)

Alice Walker was one of eight children born in rural Georgia to sharecropper parents and was particularly close to her mother. Walker first attended Spelman College, and then transferred to Sarah Lawrence, where she earned a bachelor's degree in 1965. In 1967, she married a white civil rights lawyer (they have since divorced), and the couple settled in Jackson, Mississippi, where they were the first legally married interracial couple in the city. The following year, while she was teaching at Jackson State University, she published the first of her seven volumes of concise and unsentimental verse, Once. *Though she first attracted national attention with her edition of* I Love Myself When I Am Laughing *(1979), an anthology of essays about Zora Neale Hurston, it was her novel,* The Color Purple, *the story of a black woman's struggle in the early twentieth century, that made her the literary equivalent of a superstar. Her other novels include* The Temple of My Familiar *(1989) and* Possessing the Secret of Joy *(1992). Her most recent novel is* By the Light of My Father's Smile *(1999). Walker currently resides in southern California.*

EVERYDAY USE   [1973]

For Your Grandmama

I will wait for her in the yard that Maggie and I made so clean and wavy yesterday afternoon. A yard like this is more comfortable than most people know. It is not just a yard. It is like an extended living room. When the hard clay is swept clean as a floor and the fine sand around the edges lined with tiny, irregular grooves anyone can come and sit and look up into the elm tree and wait for the breezes that never come inside the house.

Maggie will be nervous until after her sister goes: she will stand hopelessly in corners homely and ashamed of the burn scars down her arms and legs, eyeing her sister with a mixture of envy and awe. She thinks her sister has held life always in the palm of one hand, that "no" is a word the world never learned to say to her.

You've no doubt seen those TV shows where the child who has "made it" is confronted, as a surprise, by her own mother and father, tottering in weakly from backstage. (A pleasant surprise, of course: What would they do if parent and child came on the show only to curse out and insult each other?) On TV mother and child embrace and smile into each other's faces. Sometimes the mother and father weep, the child wraps them in her arms and leans across the table to tell how she would not have made it without their help. I have seen these programs.

Sometimes I dream a dream in which Dee and I are suddenly brought together on a TV program of this sort. Out of a dark and soft-seated limousine I am ushered into a bright room filled with many people. There I meet a smiling, gray, sporty man like Johnny Carson who shakes my hand and tells me what a fine girl I have. Then we are on the stage and Dee is embracing me with tears in her eyes. She pins on my dress a large orchid, even though she has told me once that she thinks orchids are tacky flowers.

5   In real life I am a large, big-boned woman with rough, man-working hands. In the winter I wear flannel nightgowns to bed and overalls during the day. I can kill and clean a hog as mercilessly as a man. My fat keeps me hot in zero weather. I can work outside all day, breaking ice to get water for washing; I can eat pork liver cooked over the open fire minutes after it comes steaming from the hog. One winter I knocked a bull calf straight in the brain between the eyes with a sledge hammer and had the meat hung up to chill before nightfall. But of course all this does not show on television. I am the way my daughter would want me to be: a hundred pounds lighter, my skin like an uncooked barley pancake. My hair glistens in the hot bright lights. Johnny Carson has much to do to keep up with my quick and witty tongue.

But that is a mistake. I know even before I wake up. Who ever knew a Johnson with a quick tongue? Who can even imagine me looking a strange white man in the eye? It seems to me I have talked to them always with one foot raised in flight, with my head turned in whichever way is farthest from them. Dee, though. She would always look anyone in the eye. Hesitation was no part of her nature.

"How do I look, Mama?" Maggie says, showing just enough of her thin body enveloped in pink skirt and red blouse for me to know she's there, almost hidden by the door.

"Come out into the yard," I say.

Have you ever seen a lame animal, perhaps a dog run over by some careless person rich enough to own a car, sidle up to someone who is ignorant enough to be kind to him? That is the way my Maggie walks. She has been like this, chin on chest, eyes on ground, feet in shuffle, ever since the fire that burned the other house to the ground.

10 Dee is lighter than Maggie, with nicer hair and a fuller figure. She's a woman now, though sometimes I forget. How long ago was it that the other house burned? Ten, twelve years? Sometimes I can still hear the flames and feel Maggie's arms sticking to me, her hair smoking and her dress falling off her in little black papery flakes. Her eyes seemed stretched open, blazed open by the flames reflected in them. And Dee. I see her standing off under the sweet gum tree she used to dig gum out of, a look of concentration on her face as she watched the last dingy gray board of the house fall in toward the red-hot brick chimney. Why don't you do a dance around the ashes? I'd wanted to ask her. She had hated the house that much.

I used to think she hated Maggie, too. But that was before we raised the money, the church and me, to send her to Augusta to school. She used to read to us without pity; forcing words, lies, other folks' habits, whole lives upon us two, sitting trapped and ignorant underneath her voice. She washed us in a river of make-believe, burned us with a lot of knowledge we didn't necessarily need to know. Pressed us to her with the serious way she read, to shove us away at just the moment, like dimwits, we seemed about to understand.

Dee wanted nice things. A yellow organdy dress to wear to her graduation from high school; black pumps to match a green suit she'd made from an old suit somebody gave me. She was determined to stare down any disaster in her efforts. Her eyelids would not flicker for minutes at a time. Often I fought off the temptation to shake her. At sixteen she had a style of her own: and knew what style was.

I never had an education myself. After second grade the school was closed down. Don't ask me why: in 1927 colored asked fewer questions than they do now. Sometimes Maggie reads to me. She stumbles along good-naturedly but can't see well. She knows she is not bright. Like good looks and money, quickness passed her by. She will marry John Thomas (who has mossy teeth in an earnest face) and then I'll be free to sit here and I guess just sing church songs to myself. Although I never was a good singer. Never could carry a tune. I was always better at a man's job. I used to love to milk till I was hooked in the side in '49. Cows are soothing and slow and don't bother you, unless you try to milk them the wrong way.

I have deliberately turned my back on the house. It is three rooms, just like the one that burned, except the roof is tin; they don't make shingle roofs any more. There are no real windows, just some holes cut in the sides, like the portholes in a ship, but not round and not square, with rawhide holding the shutters up on the outside. This house is in a pasture, too, like the other one. No doubt when Dee sees it she will want to tear it down. She wrote me once that no matter where we "choose" to live, she will manage to come see us. But she will never bring her friends. Maggie and I thought about this and Maggie asked me, "Mama, when did Dee ever *have* any friends?"

15 She had a few. Furtive boys in pink shirts hanging about on washday after school. Nervous girls who never laughed. Impressed with her they worshiped the well-turned phrase, the cute shape, the scalding humor that erupted like bubbles in lye. She read to them.

When she was courting Jimmy T she didn't have much time to pay to us, but turned all her faultfinding power on him. He *flew* to marry a cheap gal from a family of ignorant flashy people. She hardly had time to recompose herself.

When she comes I will meet—but there they are!

Maggie attempts to make a dash for the house, in her shuffling way, but I stay her with my hand. "Come back here," I say. And she stops and tries to dig a well in the sand with her toe.

It is hard to see them clearly through the strong sun. But even the first glimpse of leg out of the car tells me it is Dee. Her feet were always neat-looking, as if God himself had shaped them with a certain style. From the other side of the car comes a short, stocky man. Hair is all over his head a foot long and hanging from his chin like a kinky mule tail. I hear Maggie suck in her breath. "Uhnnnh," is what it sounds like. Like when you see the wriggling end of a snake just in front of your foot on the road. "Uhnnnh."

20   Dee next. A dress down to the ground, in this hot weather. A dress so loud it hurts my eyes. There are yellows and oranges enough to throw back the light of the sun. I feel my whole face warming from the heat waves it throws out. Earrings, too, gold and hanging down to her shoulders. Bracelets dangling and making noises when she moves her arm up to shake the folds of the dress out of her armpits. The dress is loose and flows, and as she walks closer, I like it. I hear Maggie go "Uhnnnh" again. It is her sister's hair. It stands straight up like the wool on a sheep. It is black as night and around the edges are two long pigtails that rope about like small lizards disappearing behind her ears.

"Wa-su-zo-Tean-o!" she says, coming on in that gliding way the dress makes her move. The short stocky fellow with the hair to his navel is all grinning and he follows up with "Asalamalakim, my mother and sister!" He moves to hug Maggie but she falls back, right up against the back of my chair. I feel her trembling there and when I look up I see the perspiration falling off her chin.

"Don't get up," says Dee. Since I am stout it takes something of a push. You can see me trying to move a second or two before I make it. She turns, showing white heels through her sandals, and goes back to the car. Out she peeks next with a Polaroid. She stoops down quickly and lines up picture after picture of me sitting there in front of the house with Maggie cowering behind me. She never takes a shot without making sure the house is included. When a cow comes nibbling around the edge of the yard she snaps it and me and Maggie *and* the house. Then she puts the Polaroid in the back seat of the car, and comes up and kisses me on the forehead.

Meanwhile Asalamalakim is going through the motions with Maggie's hand. Maggie's hand is as limp as a fish, and probably as cold, despite the sweat, and she keeps trying to pull it back. It looks like Asalamalakim wants to shake hands but wants to do it fancy. Or maybe he don't know how people shake hands. Anyhow, he soon gives up on Maggie.

"Well," I say. "Dee."

25   "No, Mama," she says. "Not 'Dee', Wangero Leewanika Kemanjo!"

"What happened to 'Dee'?" I wanted to know.

"She's dead," Wangero said. "I couldn't bear it any longer being named after the people who oppress me."

"You know as well as me you was named after your aunt Dicie," I said. Dicie is my sister. She named Dee. We called her "Big Dee" after Dee was born.

"But who was *she* named after?" asked Wangero.

30   "I guess after Grandma Dee," I said.

"And who was she named after?" asked Wangero.

"Her mother," I said, and saw Wangero was getting tired. "That's about as far back as I can trace it," I said. Though, in fact, I probably could have carried it back beyond the Civil War through the branches.

"Well," said Asalamalakim, "there you are."

"Uhnnnh," I heard Maggie say.

35   "There I was not," I said, "before 'Dicie' cropped up in our family, so why should I try to trace it that far back?"

He just stood there grinning, looking down on me like somebody inspecting Model A car. Every once in a while he and Wangero sent eye signals over my head.

"How do you pronounce this name?" I asked.

"You don't have to call me by it if you don't want to," said Wangero.

"Why shouldn't I?" I asked. "If that's what you want us to call you, we'll call you."

40   "I know it might sound awkward at first," said Wangero.

"I'll get used to it," I said. "Ream it out again."

Well, soon we got the name out of the way. Asalamalakim had a name twice as long and three times as hard. After I tripped over it two or three times he told me to just call him Hakim-a-barber. I wanted to ask him was he a barber, but I didn't really think he was, so I didn't ask.

"You must belong to those beef-cattle peoples down the road," I said. They said "Asalamalakim" when they met you, too, but they didn't shake hands. Always too busy: feeding the cattle, fixing the fences, putting up salt-lick shelters, throwing down hay. When the white folks poisoned some of the herd the men stayed up all night with rifles in their hands. I walked a mile and a half just to see the sight.

Hakim-a-barber said, "I accept some of their doctrines, but farming and rais-ing cattle is not my style." (They didn't tell me, and I didn't ask, whether Wangero [Dee] had really gone and married him.)

45   We sat down to eat and right away he said he didn't eat collards and pork was unclean. Wangero, though, went on through the chitlins and corn bread, the greens and everything else. She talked a blue streak over the sweet potatoes. Everything delighted her. Even the fact that we still used the benches her daddy made for the table when we couldn't afford to buy chairs.

"Oh, Mama!" she cried. Then turned to Hakim-a-barber. "I never knew how lovely these benches are. You can feel the rump prints," she said, running her hands underneath her and along the bench. Then she gave a sigh and her hand closed over Grandma Dee's butter dish. "That's it!" she said. "I knew there was something I wanted to ask you if I could have." She jumped up from the table and went over in the corner where the churn stood, the milk in it clabber by now. She looked at the churn and looked at it.

"This churn top is what I need," she said. "Didn't Uncle Buddy whittle it out of a tree you all used to have?"

"Yes," I said.

"Uh huh," she said happily. "And I want the dasher, too."

50   "Uncle Buddy whittle that, too?" asked the barber.

Dee (Wangero) looked up at me.

"Aunt Dee's first husband whittled the dash," said Maggie so low you almost couldn't hear her. "His name was Henry, but they called him Stash."

"Maggie's brain is like an elephant's," Wangero said, laughing. "I can use the churn top as a centerpiece for the alcove table," she said, sliding a plate over the churn, "and I'll think of something artistic to do with the dasher."

When she finished wrapping the dasher the handle stuck out. I took it for a moment in my hands. You didn't even have to look close to see where hands pushing the dasher up and down to make butter had left a kind of sink in the wood. In fact, there were a lot of small sinks; you could see where thumbs and fingers had sunk into the wood. It was beautiful light yellow wood, from a tree that grew in the yard where Big Dee and Stash had lived.

55   After dinner Dee (Wangero) went to the trunk at the foot of my bed and started rifling through it. Maggie hung back in the kitchen over the dishpan. Out came Wangero with two quilts. They had been pieced by Grandma Dee and then Big Dee and me had hung them on the quilt frames on the front porch and quilted them. One was in the Lone Star pattern. The other was Walk Around the Mountain. In both of them were scraps of dresses Grandma Dee had worn fifty and more years ago. Bits and pieces of Grandpa Jarrell's Paisley shirts. And one teeny faded blue piece, about the size of a penny matchbox, that was from Great Grandpa Ezra's uniform that he wore in the Civil War.

"Mama," Wangero said sweet as a bird. "Can I have these old quilts?"

I heard something fall in the kitchen, and a minute later the kitchen door slammed.

"Why don't you take one or two of the others?" I asked. "These old things was just done by me and Big Dee from some tops your grandma pieced before she died."

"No," said Wangero. "I don't want those. They are stitched around the border by machine."

60   "That'll make them last better," I said.

"That's not the point," said Wangero. "These are all pieces of dresses Grandma used to wear. She did all this stitching by hand. Imagine!" She held the quilts securely in her arms, stroking them.

"Some of the pieces, like those lavender ones, come from old clothes her mother handed down to her," I said, moving up to touch the quilts. Dee (Wangero) moved back just enough so that I couldn't reach the quilts. They already belonged to her.

"Imagine!" she breathed again, clutching them closely to her bosom.

"The truth is," I said, "I promised to give them quilts to Maggie, for when she marries John Thomas."

65   She gasped like a bee had stung her.

"Maggie can't appreciate these quilts!" she said. "She'd probably be backward enough to put them to everyday use."

"I reckon she would," I said. "God knows I been saving 'em for long enough with nobody using 'em. I hope she will!" I didn't want to bring up how I had offered Dee (Wangero) a quilt when she went away to college. Then she had told me they were old-fashioned, out of style.

"But they're *priceless!*" she was saying now, furiously; for she has a temper. "Maggie would put them on the bed and in five years they'd be in rags. Less than that!"

"She can always make some more," I said. "Maggie knows how to quilt."

70   Dee (Wangero) looked at me with hatred. "You just will not understand. The point is these quilts, *these* quilts!"

"Well," I said, stumped. "What would *you* do with them?"

"Hang them," she said. As if that was the only thing you *could* do with quilts.

Maggie by now was standing in the door. I could almost hear the sound her feet made as they scraped over each other.

"She can have them, Mama," she said, like somebody used to never winning anything, or having anything reserved for her. "I can 'member Grandma Dee without the quilts."

75   I looked at her hard. She had filled her bottom lip with checkerbeny snuff and it gave her face a kind of dopey, hangdog look. It was Grandma Dee and Big Dee who taught her how to quilt herself. She stood there with her scarred hands hidden in the folds of her skirt. She looked at her sister with something like fear but she wasn't mad at her. This was Maggie's portion. This was the way she knew God to work.

When I looked at her like that something hit me in the top of my head and ran down to the soles of my feet. Just like when I'm in church and the spirit of God touches me and I get happy and shout. I did something I never had done before: hugged Maggie to me, then dragged her on into the room, snatched the quilts out of Miss Wangero's hands and dumped them into Maggie's lap. Maggie just sat there on my bed with her mouth open.

"Take one or two of the others," I said to Dee.

But she turned without a word and went out to Hakim-a-barber.

"You just don't understand," she said, as Maggie and I came out to the car.

80   "What don't I understand?" I wanted to know.

"Your heritage," she said. And then she turned to Maggie, kissed her, and said, "You ought to try to make something of yourself, too, Maggie. It's really a new day for us. But from the way you and Mama still live you'd never know it."

She put on some sunglasses that hid everything above the tip of her nose and her chin.

Maggie smiled; maybe at the sunglasses. But a real smile, not scared. After we watched the car dust settle I asked Maggie to bring me a dip of snuff. And then the two of us sat there just enjoying, until it was time to go in the house and go to bed.

➤ QUESTIONS FOR READING AND WRITING

1. To what extent does your own background or experience influence your response to "Everyday Use"?
2. This story is told from Mama's point of view. In what way does that affect how and what you are told? If the story were told from Dee's point of view, how would it differ? Cite some examples from the text.

3. The setting of "Everyday Use" seems to mean something different to each of the characters. What does it mean to Mama? To Dee? To Maggie?
4. If you were in Dee's situation, would you have acted differently? Would you see the quilt as a valuable artifact or something to be used every day? Explain.
5. Is the title of the story appropriate? How so? How would you define *everyday use*?

∼ TWO STUDENT ESSAYS ∼

Depending on your experience of it, "Everyday Use" is a story about many different things. You may experience it as a story about heritage and identity, tradition versus change, lack of communication between generations, ingratitude, formal education versus experience, or any number of other issues.

A Response Essay

In his *response essay*, Alejandro Ramos identifies with Dee's search to find her heritage and compares it to his own struggle to find his ethnic identity in his Hispanic and African-American roots.

Alejandro Ramos Jr.

Dr. Madden

English 102

October 15, 200X

The Conflict of Change

History has shown us that as time wears on traditions give way to change. Along with change, conflicts have always emerged between two great forces: the forces of the old and tradition and the forces of the new and change. This conflict is often seen between parents and their children. An excellent example of this conflict of old and new between parent and child is seen in Alice Walker's story "Everyday Use." At the core of this conflict is a search for heritage and identity.

Mama and Maggie represent the old way of living. They live off the land, do things for themselves, and accept life the way it has always been. However, Mama's other daughter Dee (Wangero Leewanika Kemanjo) represents a new way of living and thinking. She is educated and believes in fighting for her rights. She has gone through an identity crisis and says she has found herself. When she is asked by her mother what happened to "Dee," the name she was given at birth (and a name that had been in her family since before the Civil War) she says, "She's dead. I couldn't bear it any longer, being named after the people who oppress me" (115). She not only changed her name, but she changed her hairstyle and way of dressing. She has new ideas, too, and a different attitude toward the world. Mama says, "Who can even imagine me looking a strange white man in the eye? It seems to me I have talked to them always with one foot raised in flight, with my head turned in whichever way is farthest from them. Dee, though. She would always look anyone in the eye. Hesitation was no part of her nature" (113). Dee is not willing to accept things as they have been, especially the old relationship between whites and blacks.

Unlike Dee, Mama and Maggie are not educated. Mama says, "I never had an education myself. After second grade the school was closed down. Don't ask me why: in 1927 colored asked fewer questions than they do now. Sometimes Maggie reads to me. She stumbles along good-naturedly but can't see well. She knows she is not bright" (114). But Dee is bright and educated and won't settle for the life that Mama and Maggie have accepted.

This story reminds me of my own identity crisis. Like Dee's mother, my father believed that life is a certain way and one just accepted it. He was easygoing and believed in working hard and making sure that everything was in order. He was amused by my "identity crisis" and wondered what the fuss was all about.

To me, however, my ethnic identity was very important. My crisis, whether I was African-American or Spanish, came about primarily because of my friends. My Spanish friends said that I was African-American, and my African-American friends claimed that I was Spanish. Since each group defined me as being from the other, I felt very isolated and alone. I didn't feel like I really belonged to either group. Unlike Dee, I didn't resolve my conflict by changing my name, hairstyle, or style of dress. I finally accepted the fact that I was both Spanish and African-American and learned to enjoy being bicultural.

I am sure that Dee's identification problem was not brought about entirely by herself, either. She was influenced by people, like Hakim-a-barber, who were her friends. She was also influenced by her education.

Mama identifies the source of her conflict with Dee best when she says that Dee " . . . used to read to us without pity; forcing words, lies, other folks' habits, whole lives upon us two, sitting trapped and ignorant underneath her voice. She washed us in a river of make-believe, burned us with a lot of knowledge we didn't necessarily need to know" (114). To Mama, this book knowledge is "lies" and "knowledge we didn't . . . need to know." To Dee this knowledge is the source of her heritage and very important to her.

Mama and Maggie don't have sophisticated, knowledgeable friends or a formal education. Their identity is connected to everyday living and the way things have always been--even if some of these things are not as they should be. They represent the forces of the old and tradition. Dee's identity and her sense of heritage come from books and an appreciation of her African culture, not as she has lived them, but as she has read about them. She represents the forces of the new and change. As is usually the case in conflicts between the forces of old and new, both sides would benefit a great deal by listening to and learning from each other.

Work Cited

Walker, Alice. "Everyday Use." <u>Exploring Fiction</u>. Ed. Frank Madden. New
York: Longman, 2002, 112–118.

A Critical Essay

In her *critical* essay, Debora VanCoughnett, disagrees with the beliefs expressed by Dee, and argues that Dee has learned much less about her heritage through her formal education than Mama and Maggie know and understand through their experience. She criticizes the superficiality of Dee's claim to her heritage when compared with the "real" respect it is given as lived every day by her mother and sister.

Debora VanCoughnett

Dr. Madden

English 102

October 16, 200X

Using Heritage Every Day

In the short story "Everyday Use," by Alice Walker, Dee accuses her mother of not understanding her heritage, yet Dee herself denies her own true roots. Not only does she change her name, trying to become someone she isn't, but she criticizes her mother and sister for living the way they do. Maggie and her mother, however, are the only ones in this family who can truly grasp their heritage.

When Dee comes back home after being educated and modernized, she tells her mother that the old "Dee" is dead and that her new name is "Wangero Leewanika Kemanjo." She says "I couldn't bear it any longer being named after the people who oppress me" (115). Despite her educated comment, Dee didn't even know the origin of her own name. Her mother tells her she was named for her aunt and generations of ancestors going back before the Civil War, not a white slaveholder. The name Dee has chosen may be connected to her African ancestry, but it is not connected to her personal heritage. It is she who doesn't understand her heritage, not her mother.

As Mama describes her, Dee seems only concerned with appearances: "At sixteen she had a style of her own: and knew what style was" (114). She is much more physically attractive than Maggie who moves like a " . . . lame animal, perhaps a dog run over by some careless person . . . . [she] walks . . . chin on chest, eyes on the ground, feet in shuffle" (113–114). This is obviously not a style Dee would find acceptable. Mama's style and appearance are no doubt an embarrassment to her as well. Mama describes herself as " . . . a large, big-boned woman with rough, man-working hands. In the winter I wear flannel nightgowns to bed and overalls during the day. I can kill and clean a hog as mercilessly as a man. My fat keeps me hot in zero weather" (113). It's no wonder that Dee wrote to her once that " . . . no matter where we 'choose' to live, she will manage to come see us. But she will never bring her friends" (114). It's obvious that she is ashamed of Mama and Maggie and doesn't want anyone else to know about them except under her terms.

Dee concerns herself too much with appearances. She dresses so others have to take notice. She wears a " . . . dress so loud it hurt [Mama's] eyes" (115). She takes Polaroids of her family, making sure that the house or even a cow was in each shot. She is not taking these pictures because she is proud of where she is from; she only wants to show off--to let her friends know how pitiful her family home is and how far she has come to get where she is.

When Dee asks her mother for the quilts, she comments that Maggie would " . . . probably be backward enough to put them to everyday use" (117). She also wants the churn and the dasher that her mother still uses on a daily basis, but Dee wants to use them " . . . as a centerpiece for the alcove table" (117). That was not what Uncle Buddy whittled them for, or why Grandma stitched the quilts. They are meant for everyday use, not merely for display. It is Dee's total misconception of the real meaning behind the quilts that points to her ignorance, not her family's. In this respect, Mama and Maggie are the educated ones. Her grandmother made them to be used, not to be hung on the wall and admired.

It is very ironic for Dee (Wangero) to have the audacity to tell her mother that she (Mama) does not understand her heritage. It is true that her mother and Maggie do not have a formal education and are not attractive nor stylish, but they experience their heritage every day. No matter what Dee has learned from books and schooling, or how stylish she is with her African name or dress, it was she, not her family, who didn't have a clue to what her heritage was really like.

Work Cited

Walker, Alice. "Everyday Use." <u>Exploring Fiction</u>. Ed. Frank Madden. New
    York: Longman, 2002, 112–118.

CRITICAL THINKING: INDUCTION AND SUBSTANTIATION

Have you ever watched a toddler discover the world? The child crawls through the grass, stops to examine it blade by blade, picks it up, feels it, shakes it, tastes it. The child explores the surroundings and tests them piece by piece, and after several tries, probably comes to a conclusion: Grass is good for crawling but not so great for eating. When someone offers you a type of food you've never eaten before, how do you respond? How do you discover if you like it or not? Well, you probably ask for a taste. If you like the taste, you might ask for more. If you don't like the taste, you may or may not try more. This kind of examining, testing, making tentative observations, retesting, and concluding is a fairly common process in our lives. It is called **inductive reasoning**.

When you think or write inductively, you move from specific observations to conclusions. If you try a new food and like it, the next time it's offered you can respond with more certainty. You've tested it and can come to a tentative conclusion. Each subsequent tasting gives you more information and solidifies your conclusion: I like sushi; it tastes good.

Once you arrive at your conclusion, you are ready to make a generalization: Sushi tastes good. The process of supporting this generalization is called **substantiation**. When we substantiate, we support our conclusion with specific observations. This brings the process full circle. We discover how much we like sushi through specific tastings; we explain why sushi is good with support from those tastings: This sushi sits lightly on my tongue; it's soft and moist with a full seafood flavor and pleasant smell. We arrive at our conclusion inductively; we support, defend, and explain it through substantiation.

Developing Standards

As we examine our reasons for liking something, we also identify and develop standards. We know how good this food can be; we now have certain expectations. (Standards for sushi: 1. Soft. 2. Moist. 3. Full seafood flavor. 4. Pleasant smell.) When something meets our expectations, we can identify why. When it doesn't, we can say where and perhaps why it falls short.

THINKING CRITICALLY ABOUT FICTION

In many ways, thinking and writing about fiction follows a similar induction and substantiation pattern as that described above. As we initially read, respond, discuss, and write about our experience with literature, we build on our specific observations of the text and arrive at our conclusions inductively. With those conclusions in hand, we substantiate them with reference to our specific observations of the text. Writing an effective, convincing essay requires that we have enough evidence to support our conclusions and that we have clearly explained the connection between the two. Finding the evidence and making the connections require a close rereading of the text.

Facts and Opinions

All of us have probably been criticized at some time for not being objective or allowing our personal feelings to influence our judgment. It's not possible, of course, to be entirely objective—to separate the facts from who we are and how we see them. Most of our feelings and prejudgments come from our personalities, backgrounds, and experiences, and they form values we have developed unconsciously over time. In the course of our daily lives, we're not usually required to justify our feelings or our opinions. But writing an effective critical essay requires a rationale for our judgments—reasons derived not only from our feelings and values but from ingredients in the work of literature that prompt those judgments. Although there is no guarantee that everyone will agree with our conclusions, we can make sure that our evidence is recognized and respected as valid.

➤ *GETTING STARTED—YOUR FIRST RESPONSE*
1. Read one of your responses to a story.
2. Which parts are fact, which opinion? How can you tell the difference?
3. To what extent can you support your opinions with facts?
4. To what extent can you explain how the facts support your opinions?

➤ *SUPPORTING CONNECTIONS—"THE STORY OF AN HOUR"*

Remember, "telling" your views alone will not convince readers. Telling what the story means or declaring its effectiveness is not convincing unless you support those views by *showing* what led to your conclusion. Identifying details, giving examples, making comparisons, and quoting from the text of the work are means to this end.

KATE CHOPIN (1851–1906)

Kate Chopin was born in St. Louis, Missouri. Her father, an Irish immigrant, became a successful businessman. Her mother was a prominent member of the French-Creole community and traveled in exclusive social circles. Chopin attended Catholic school and, before her marriage at nineteen to Creole cotton broker Oscar Chopin, was much admired for her beauty and wit. The couple settled first in New Orleans and, following the collapse of Oscar's business, moved to his family's plantations in Natchitoches Parish. Following his unexpected death in 1883, at a doctor's suggestion, Chopin began writing. Her stories, which are set among the Creole people of the Louisiana bayou, were collected and published in two anthologies, Bayou Folk *(1894) and* A Night in Arcadie *(1899). Her greatest work, the novel* The Awakening *(1899), which tells the story of an extramarital affair, was denounced as obscene and was largely ignored until it was reevaluated by critics, beginning in the 1930s, who praised it for its emotional honesty and beautiful prose.*

THE STORY OF AN HOUR   [1891]

Knowing that Mrs. Mallard was afflicted with a heart trouble, great care was taken to break to her as gently as possible the news of her husband's death.

It was her sister Josephine who told her, in broken sentences, veiled hints that revealed in half concealing. Her husband's friend Richards was there, too, near her. It was he who had been in the newspaper office when intelligence of the railroad disaster was received, with Brently Mallard's name leading the list of "killed." He had only taken the time to assure himself of its truth by a second telegram, and had hastened to forestall any less careful, less tender friend in bearing the sad message.

She did not hear the story as many women have heard the same, with a paralyzed inability to accept its significance. She wept at once, with sudden, wild abandonment, in her sister's arms. When the storm of grief had spent itself she went away to her room alone. She would have no one follow her.

There stood, facing the open window, a comfortable, roomy armchair. Into this she sank, pressed down by a physical exhaustion that haunted her body and seemed to reach into her soul.

5   She could see in the open square before her house the tops of trees that were all aquiver with the new spring life. The delicious breath of rain was in the air. In the street below a peddler was crying his wares. The notes of a distant song which some one was singing reached her faintly, and countless sparrows were twittering in the eaves.

There were patches of blue sky showing here and there through the clouds that had met and piled above the other in the west facing her window.

She sat with her head thrown back upon the cushion of the chair quite motionless, except when a sob came up into her throat and shook her, as a child who has cried itself to sleep continues to sob in its dreams.

She was young, with a fair, calm face, whose lines bespoke repression and even a certain strength. But now there was a dull stare in her eyes, whose gaze was fixed away off yonder on one of those patches of blue sky. It was not a glance of reflection, but rather indicated a suspension of intelligent thought.

There was something coming to her and she was waiting for it, fearfully. What was it? She did not know; it was too subtle and elusive to name. But she felt it, creeping out of the sky, reaching toward her through the sounds, the scents, the color that filled the air.

10   Now her bosom rose and fell tumultuously. She was beginning to recognize this thing that was approaching to possess her, and she was striving to beat it back with her will—as powerless as her two white slender hands would have been.

When she abandoned herself a little whispered word escaped her slightly parted lips. She said it over and over under her breath: "Free, free, free!" The vacant stare and the look of terror that had followed it went from her eyes. They stayed keen and bright. Her pulses beat fast, and the coursing blood warmed and relaxed every inch of her body.

She did not stop to ask if it were not a monstrous joy that held her. A clear and exalted perception enabled her to dismiss the suggestion as trivial.

She knew that she would weep again when she saw the kind, tender hands folded in death; the face that had never looked save with love upon her, fixed and gray and dead. But she saw beyond that bitter moment a long procession of years to come that would belong to her absolutely. And she opened and spread her arms out to them in welcome.

There would be no one to live for her during those coming years; she would live for herself. There would be no powerful will bending her in that blind persistence with which men and women believe they have a right to impose a private will upon a fellow creature. A kind intention or a cruel intention made the act seem no less a crime as she looked upon it in that brief moment of illumination.

15   And yet she had loved him—sometimes. Often she had not. What did it matter! What could love, the unsolved mystery, count for in face of this possession of self-assertion which she suddenly recognized as the strongest impulse of her being.

"Free! Body and soul free!" she kept whispering.

Josephine was kneeling before the closed door with her lips to the keyhole, imploring for admission. "Louise, open the door! I beg; open the door—you will make yourself ill. What are you doing, Louise? For heaven's sake open the door."

"Go away. I am not making myself ill." No; she was drinking in a very elixir of life through that open window.

Her fancy was running riot along those days ahead of her. Spring days, and summer days, and all sorts of days that would be her own. She breathed a quick prayer that life might be long. It was only yesterday she had thought with a shudder that life might be long.

20   She arose at length and opened the door to her sister's importunities. There was a feverish triumph in her eyes, and she carried herself unwittingly like a goddess of Victory. She clasped her sister's waist, and together they descended the stairs. Richards stood waiting for them at the bottom.

Some one was opening the front door with a latchkey. It was Brently Mallard who entered, a little travel-stained, composedly carrying his gripsack and umbrella. He had been far from the scene of the accident, and did not even know there had been one. He stood amazed at Josephine's piercing cry; at Richards' quick motion to screen him from the view of his wife.

But Richards was too late.

When the doctors came they said she had died of heart disease—of joy that kills.

➤ QUESTIONS FOR READING AND WRITING

Induction
1. Go back and read "The Story of an Hour" again.
2. As you read, write down as many details about Mrs. Mallard as you can.
3. Review what you wrote down as you finished the story, any questions you jotted down, and your list of details.
4. What conclusion does this information lead you to draw about Mrs. Mallard?

Substantiation
1. Write down your conclusion.
2. Support your conclusion through reference to your details.
3. Are all of these details facts? Would everyone agree that they are facts?
4. Explain how these details support your conclusion.
5. Reread what you've written and answer the following questions:
   a. Do you have enough details to support your conclusion?
   b. Do *all* the details about Mrs. Mallard in the story support your conclusion?
   c. If not, how can you account for those details that do not?
   d. When you consider *all* the details—all the evidence—does your conclusion still hold up? If not, revise your conclusion to match the evidence.

Conclusion
1. Sometimes what seems self-evident to us is not so evident to our readers. Write a statement that explains *how* the details in the story support your conclusion about Mrs. Mallard.

INTERPRETATION: WHAT DOES IT MEAN?

The idea of coming up with an interpretation may seem a bit overwhelming, but in our everyday lives we hear and respond to this request regularly. "What do you make of that?" "What was that all about?" and "What's your read on that?" are among the many ways we might be asked for an interpretation. At the core of all these questions is a basic request for an explanation of "meaning." When we construct and articulate that meaning we are giving our interpretation.

What goes into our explanation of meaning, of course, has a lot to do with who we are. Our interpretations are influenced by many personal factors, but what makes an interpretation convincing or credible is our ability to explain *why*—a why not based on unsupported personal opinion but on support with evidence.

An interpretation of literature may involve almost any aspect of work, from the meaning of a single word, image, character, or place to a statement of its overall meaning. It may even involve more than one work, so don't feel that you must limit yourself to choosing from the possibilities discussed here.

A Defensible Interpretation, Not *the* Right Answer

Stories are not problems to be solved. They don't have one correct answer or interpretation. Remember, what makes an interpretation convincing or defensible is the quality of its support. Your belief about what a story means may change as you move back and forth through the stages of your reading experience. The first time you read a work you may feel one way, but writing down your reflections, rereading the text, and discussing it with others may lead to a different, better-informed understanding and interpretation.

DEVELOPING AN INTERPRETATION

As you consider the statements and questions that follow, think about the stories you've read and how the language, point of view, setting, conflict, or characterization in those pieces influenced your response. Our brief discussion of these elements below is a carryover from a more comprehensive explanation of these terms in Chapter 3. *If you have unanswered questions about these elements, you may find it helpful to refer to that discussion beginning on page 84.*

Language and Form

The diction of the narrator or characters, concrete images, similes, metaphors, and symbols may all contribute in crucial ways to the meaning of literature.

Consider Sammy's slang and concrete descriptions in John Updike's "A & P" (p. 146) and the effect they have on your reading. Try to imagine less powerful images, vague descriptions, unnatural diction, and how your response to these might differ.

Narration: Point of View and Voice

Point of view, the perspective from which the narrator speaks to us, can strongly influence our interpretation. This narrative "lens" controls what we see and know about the setting, the characters, or the conflict in a work. The narrator's *voice* gives us a personality behind the words.

Consider Mama's up close first-person narration and its influence on your interpretation of Alice Walker's "Everyday Use" (p. 112). How is your response to Ernest Hemingway's "Hills Like White Elephants" (p. 334) affected by its distanced third person objective narration? How would a first person point of view from either the man or the woman's perspective change Hemingway's story? Can you imagine "Everyday Use" narrated from the distance of third person objective, or from Dee's perspective, and how it might be different?

Recall other works you've read and how point of view or voice influence your response to the setting, conflict, characters, or the story's meaning. Imagine how a shift in narration might change your interpretation.

Setting

Setting is the environment in which the work takes place. It includes location, time, atmosphere, and mood and has a direct and indirect impact on character and conflict. It supports and emphasizes the story's meaning.

Consider the dreary, dark atmosphere in James Joyce's "Araby," and how it contrasts with the warmth of the boy's feelings for Mangan's sister. Picture the overpowering ocean waves and high cold stars in the black sky of Stephen Crane's "The Open Boat" and their effect on the characters and your reading.

Think about the settings of other works you've read and their impact on conflict, characters, or theme. Try to imagine those stories in a different setting and the difference that would make to the conflicts, the characters, and your response.

Conflict and Plot

Conflict is the struggle of opposing external or internal forces. External conflict may be physical or social. Internal conflict is a struggle of opposing forces within a character. Most good fiction contains both types of conflict, but places greater emphasis on the internal component.

Think about the extraordinary external and internal conflicts in the brutal, racist humiliation experienced by the young man in Ralph Ellison's "Battle Royal" (p. 286). Or consider the ordinary but painful internal conflict that results from the young girl's humiliation in Sandra Cisneros's "Eleven" (p. 40). The first person point of view has a major impact on our understanding of the characters and conflicts in these stories. While the narrators/protagonists in both pieces are young, they are preteen and late-teen and articulate their sense of conflict in very different terms. An oppressive setting in each story increases the pressure and makes them (and us) feel their conflicts more intensely.

Recall other works you've read and look at the ways that conflict is developed or intensified through point of view, voice, setting, or characterization. If any of these elements were changed, imagine how the conflict and your response to it might be affected.

Plot is the structure of the story. Think about the plots of stories you've read. How does the structure of each work convey the setting, the conflict, the characters, and ultimately the story's meaning?

Characterization

Characterization is the creation and development of characters in a work. Well-developed characters come to life. In our own lives, we react to people on the basis of how they look and what they say and do. In most good literature, we're able to observe characters thinking, speaking, and doing—and judge who they are for ourselves.

Think about the description, actions, and reactions of Elisa as her character gradually emerges in John Steinbeck's "The Chrysanthemums" (p. 440). The narration, conversations, settings, and conflicts all provide an opportunity for us to witness these characters thinking, saying, and doing.

Recall other characters in works you've read. How did you get to know them? How did the narrators' point of view, the characters' diction, the setting, or their conflicts influence your understanding of who they are?

The Whole: Theme

Theme is the central idea expressed by a story. Identifying and articulating this idea is not always an easy task. It's true that the whole work's theme or meaning is greater than the sum of its parts, but the support required for your justification of it still calls for an analysis of the work's elements—the language, narration, setting, conflicts, characters, and outcome—and their relationship to the whole.

What conclusion about the work can you draw from its elements? Try to expand your conclusion about the work into a generalization or idea that addresses the human condition. What is the work saying about being human? What is its theme?

Beliefs or Actions Expressed by the Narrator or Characters

It is natural for us to respond to the beliefs and actions of characters through the lenses of our own values, so it's not surprising that, as a subset of characterization, this is one of the more popular topics for interpretation. What's your interpretation of the beliefs or actions (or potential actions) expressed by the man or the woman in Ernest Hemingway's "Hills Like White Elephants" (p. 334)? What is your understanding of the beliefs expressed by the narrator/protagonist in John Updike's "A & P"?

Think about the beliefs or actions of other characters in your reading. What are they? How do you feel about them? How are these beliefs exemplified by what the narrator or characters say or do? How would you interpret them?

For a more comprehensive explanation of this option with references to student samples in this text, see page 110 earlier in this chapter.

The Story in Context

To interpret a story in its context successfully, you must be able to identify the contextual framework that surrounds it and articulate the influence that context has on the work or an element of the work. If you're not very knowledgeable about this background, it may be necessary to do additional reading and research before you begin to write your essay.

What are the cultural imperatives that influence the young woman in James Joyce's "Eveline," or Mrs. Mallard in "The Story of an Hour"? Think of other works you've read, and the historical, cultural, biographical, or other contextual factors that influenced them. How do these factors affect or enrich your reading and interpretation of those works?

For a more comprehensive explanation of this option with references to student samples in this text, see page 111 earlier in this chapter or Appendix A, Critical Approaches to Literature, on page 467.

✔ CHECKLIST • *Developing an Interpretation*

Language and Form

❑ In what ways are diction, imagery, figurative language, or symbolism important to the story and your understanding of it?

Narration: Point of View and Voice

❑ In what ways do point of view and voice affect what you know about the setting, conflict, or characters?

❑ How does the narration influence your understanding of the story's meaning?

❑ How would you interpret the impact of narration on the story?

Setting

❑ In what ways does the story's setting affect conflict and characterization?

❑ How would you interpret the influence of setting on the story's meaning?

Conflict and Plot

❑ In what ways is conflict related to setting and characterization?

❑ How does the plot structure convey the conflict and the story's meaning?

❑ How would you interpret the conflict or the importance of plot in the story?

continued

Characterization

❑ How is characterization related to point of view, setting, and conflict?

❑ How do the characters affect your understanding of the story's meaning?

❑ How would you interpret the characters in the story?

Theme

❑ Describe the elements (language, narration, setting, conflict/plot, characters) of the story.

❑ What conclusion can you draw from these elements?

❑ What comment about the human condition—what generalization about life—does this conclusion lead to?

❑ What is the central idea expressed by the story? What do you think the story means?

Interpreting the Beliefs or Actions of the Narrator or Characters

❑ What beliefs are expressed by the narrator or characters in the story and how does what they say or do exemplify these beliefs or actions?

❑ How would you interpret the effect of these beliefs on the story?

Interpreting a Story in Context

❑ How is the story influenced by historical, cultural, biographical, or other contextual factors?

❑ How would you interpret the story in the light of these contextual factors?

Interpretation or Evaluation?

Like many other classifications in literature, *interpretation* and *evaluation* are not separate and distinct. In our reading, both often occur at the same time. When we write about our reading, however, we can make choices about which to emphasize. Do we want to interpret what the story or an aspect of it means or its worth? While each is a different emphasis, it may be difficult to separate them, and many critical essays are a combination of both.

EVALUATION: HOW WELL DOES IT WORK?

Throughout this book you have been encouraged to identify and write about what you value. Those values or standards directly influence your response to literature. Writing an effective evaluative essay requires that you make these standards explicit and account for the ways in which they have led to your evaluation of a work. You become a credible critic by evaluating in the light of these clearly defined standards.

Developing Standards

Each of us has clearly defined standards about some things and not about others. Every day we are bombarded with advertisements that make great claims without support. They assume our lack of standards. They tell us with glitz rather than showing us with facts. Do we always buy products because we know a lot about them? Do we buy cars, stereos, or computers because we know they are quality products or because we like the ads and the attractive people in them? What are our standards for judging?

You've been evaluating literature since you first started reading. You like it or don't like it, believe it's good or bad. How specific you are about "why" may depend on your experience as a reader. Those of us who read often have probably given some thought to why we like to read some things more than others. Experienced readers are likely to respond to "why" by pointing to particular qualities that are present or absent. Those of us who don't read very much might simply say, "I couldn't get into it" or "It was boring" and leave it at that. Our standards, the principles by which we evaluate literature, tend to be developed through experience and over time.

➤ *QUESTIONS FOR THINKING AND WRITING*

Write down your responses to the following questions. You may even find it interesting to share them with other members of the class in pairs or small groups.

1. Choose a topic you know a lot about (music, dance, sports, cars, computers, etc.). How did you learn about it? By yourself? Did someone show you or teach you? Why do you think you know a lot about it?
2. What are your standards or criteria for evaluating the topic you chose in Question 1? See if you can make a list and explain the importance of each standard.
3. Think back to a large purchase you made recently (clothes, computer, stereo, etc.). What were your standards or criteria for evaluation? Make a list and explain the importance of each of these standards.
4. Do you feel as if you know a lot about fiction? How would you feel if someone asked you to evaluate a story? Explain.
5. What are your standards for evaluating fiction? See if you can make a list of standards and explain the importance of each one. If you can't, what difficulties did you encounter?

Developing Standards for Evaluating Fiction

Our task in this chapter is not only to help you develop new standards but to identify and build on those you already have. You've been developing and applying standards for evaluating fiction throughout your life. They're as familiar to you as your everyday experiences, so familiar you don't usually stop to analyze or spell them out.

We live in the world that fiction reveals. We make judgments about the nature of that world—people's biases, our surroundings, difficult circumstances, and the authenticity of people we meet. In this way we have already experienced and developed standards about point of view, setting, conflict, and character. What may not be so familiar, however, is a systematic way of applying these standards to stories.

Your Own Standards: Expectations and Intentions

When we choose entertainment, we usually know what to expect. When we see a fantasy movie like *Alien* or *Star Wars,* we have very different expectations than when we see a realistic film. Listening to a rock song brings different expectations than listening to an opera. We have different expectations for a Stephen King thriller than for a story like James Joyce's "Araby."

The standards we have for evaluating fiction are directly affected by our expectations. Is the primary purpose of this story to thrill or entertain? To make a social comment? To reveal something essential about the human condition? All of these? Some of these? It would be unfair to apply the same standards to a mystery thriller that we would apply to "Araby." On the other hand, applying our "thrill and entertain" standards to a story that intends to give insight into the human condition seems equally unfair.

Standards for Evaluating Fiction

Of course, we may not always be aware of the type and intentions of the stories we read until after we begin reading. Many of the pieces in this book may put you in that position. Almost all of these stories, however, have been chosen because they seek to reveal something important about the human experience. The expectations and standards discussed below are measured against this intention.

The standards for language, point of view, setting, conflict, character, and theme discussed here are derived from our description of these elements in Chapter 3. The questions and brief explanations that follow are a guide to the kinds of qualities we might look for when evaluating these elements.

Language and Form   When language is used effectively it prompts our imaginations and provides us with clear images, rhythm, and insight. Form complements content and effectively conveys meaning to us.

Point of View   When point of view is used effectively, we see the characters, setting, and events from a perspective that helps us experience the overall meaning of a work.

Setting   An effective setting will help us see and experience the concrete details of a work's environment. We "sense" the sights, sounds, and emotions of the atmosphere as if we were really there. The writer of an effective setting does not settle for vague descriptions. An effective setting complements and clarifies conflict, character, and theme. It seems a natural vehicle to convey the story's meaning.

Conflict and Plot   Unless we feel its reality, we are not drawn into the conflict. For this to happen, we must be able to imagine ourselves or others faced with this situation. In many cases, it is our ability to identify with the *internal nature* (the anxiety, frustration, and disappointment) of the conflict, which gives us a feel for it. We may never have faced this kind of external dilemma, but other experiences we have had may give us an idea of what the dilemma feels like inside.

We won't care about the conflict if it's not important to the characters and to us. As we know from our own lives, a conflict doesn't need to be a life-and-death struggle to have an impact on us. We might want to ask ourselves, "If I were in this circumstance, would this be an important conflict for me?" Well-developed conflict and plot, like a game between two evenly matched teams or players, keeps us involved until the outcome is decided.

Characterization   Effective characters seem lifelike. Like real people, they are not simple, but have depth and complexity. They are believable. When characters are developed most effectively, we don't have to be told who they are. We "see" and experience them through their words, actions, and what others have to say about them.

As in life, well-developed characters have reasons, or motivations, for behaving as they do. They will act in a relatively consistent pattern. They won't behave one way on one occasion and differently on another without adequate motivation.

Theme   An effective theme gives us an insight into human nature. When fiction preaches or teaches a lesson, it doesn't usually account for the complexities of the real world. An effective theme transcends the time and place of its setting. It has universal qualities that make it applicable to human nature in any time or place.

Beliefs or Actions of the Narrator or Characters   Before you evaluate the beliefs or actions of the narrator or characters, be clear about what they are and be clear about your own standards for judging them. Only when you have clarified both will you be able to evaluate the beliefs in the work measured against your own criteria, take a position, and build an argument for or against those beliefs.

The Work in Context   Before you can evaluate the influence of historical, cultural, biographical, or other contextual factors on the story, you must have knowledge of these areas. If you don't have knowledge of these contexts, you must do research and additional reading to give yourself standards and criteria by which to evaluate.

✔ CHECKLIST • *Developing an Evaluation*

Language and Form

❏ How well does the language prompt your imagination and engage your emotions?

❏ How effective are the language and form in conveying the story's meaning?

Narration

❏ How effective is the narrative perspective, or point of view, in helping you understand the story's meaning?

Setting

❏ How effective is the setting in presenting the concrete details and enabling you to feel like you're present?

❏ How well does the setting complement conflict and character and support and emphasize the story's meaning?

Conflict and Plot

❏ How believable is the internal and external conflict?

❏ How important is the conflict?

❏ How challenging is the struggle?

❏ How unified is the conflict? How well do the minor conflicts complement each other and support the major conflicts?

❏ How well does the plot's structure convey the conflict and the story's meaning?

Characterization

❏ How believable are the characters? How complex?

❏ How effectively are the characters developed? Are you shown, not told, who they are? How so?

❏ How motivated and consistent are the characters? Does their behavior make sense?

Theme

❏ Does the theme *reveal* or *preach*? Is it an insight about life or a lesson?

❏ How universal is the theme? Is it limited by time, place, and circumstances?

Beliefs and Actions of the Narrator or Characters

❏ What are the beliefs and actions of the narrator or characters in the story?

❏ What are your standards for evaluating these beliefs or actions?

❏ Why do you agree or disagree with these beliefs or actions?

continued

The Work in Context

❏ How much do you know about the contextual background of the story? What do you need to know? How will you find out more?

❏ What are your standards for evaluating this context?

❏ How well does the story fulfill these standards?

GENERATING IDEAS FOR A CRITICAL ESSAY

The same processes that are so useful in generating ideas for a response essay are just as valuable for giving you ideas and narrowing your topic for a critical essay. Reading literature encourages a variety of responses—and perhaps raises more questions than answers. It is a good idea to generate and explore as many of your questions and ideas as possible before you decide on a topic. Below is a quick review of strategies to get started. For a detailed explanation of these techniques, with examples, see Chapter 2, pages 65–69.

- *Using directed freewriting* can generate ideas. The best time to do this exercise is immediately after you finish reading, while your thoughts and impressions are still fresh. The intention of this exercise is to release what you know without blocking it with pauses for reflection, punctuation, or editing.
- *Asking questions about a general topic* is likely to provide you with new information. Responding with detailed answers to these questions may provide you with ideas for a narrowed thesis and specific support for that thesis.
- *By choosing a few key words or phrases* that apply to your topic and then *listing* as many related details under each as you can, you should be able to generate many concrete details and much specific support for your ideas.
- *Clustering your ideas* or drawing a semantic map may help you discover and understand relationships, and generate and extend ideas better by seeing them spatially rather than linearly.

ARGUMENTATION: WRITING A CRITICAL ESSAY

There are many different ways to plan and structure a critical essay. The suggestions that follow represent one approach. The purpose of this discussion is not to move you step-by-step through a rigid sequence. Constructing an argument is a continuous process of moving forward and returning and moving forward again. The strongest thesis, the most convincing evidence, the most effective structure may occur to you early or late. Let your ideas flow freely throughout the process. Some of your best ideas may come to you when you think you're almost finished.

The Shape of an Argument

The subject

The proposition about the subject (the thesis)

The evidence that supports the proposition about the subject

The explanation that connects the evidence to the proposition about the subject

Planning Your Argument

Determine the Argument's Feasibility   Can you write a critical essay about this? No matter how compelling your proposition, you cannot write an essay about it unless you have enough to say and can find enough evidence to support your argument. If the point you want to make is obvious, abstract, or very general, it may be impossible to come up with a solid argument and develop it into a convincing essay in a reasonable amount of time.

Consider Your Own Motivation   How much do you care about the subject? Will it sustain your enthusiasm long enough for you to complete the essay? Can you identify strongly with the situation in the work? Do you approve or disapprove of a character's action? Do you believe the work has helped you to understand yourself or inspired you to act in a particular way? Have you learned something about your own life through your experience of the story? Finally, do you feel strongly about your ability to convince an audience of your argument?

You will work with more enthusiasm and write with a stronger voice when you care about the subject.

Clarify Your Proposition: Write a Thesis Statement   Do you have a clear understanding of the proposition you are trying to prove? If you don't, you won't be able to express it in a form your readers will understand. Try to put your proposition into the form of a complete sentence that connects it to the subject. This thesis statement will sit at the core of your argument. Everything in your argument must relate back to and support this thesis statement. If you've put it in a form that you and your readers clearly understand, you will know if the evidence you've gathered adequately supports it.

If your thesis is an interpretation, define what you mean by the terms of the proposition or thesis. In the excerpt from her essay at the beginning of this chapter, Debora has identified the subject of "Everyday Use" as "finding heritage." Her proposition about this subject, her thesis statement (what she believes the story is saying about heritage), will not be clear unless she spells out what she means by those terms. What "heritage" means to her may be different from what it means to other readers.

Be careful to distinguish between the *subject* of your essay and your *proposition* about the subject—your thesis statement. Debora's subject is "seeking heritage." What she believes the story is saying about this subject—her thesis statement—(as reflected in the final draft of her essay) is "Maggie and her mother . . . are the only ones in this family who can truly grasp their heritage."

As you consider the evidence you have and gather new evidence, you may discover that your thesis statement must be adjusted to accommodate this new information. Be flexible. Match the statement to the evidence, and the evidence to the statement. Until you submit your final draft, it's never too late to make adjustments to strengthen your thesis.

Know Your Readers   What can you assume about your readers? If you're writing this essay to be read by those in your class, you may already have some idea what your classmates and instructor think about your opinion. If so, does your thesis statement agree with the majority of responses you've heard? If not, it's important to "speak to" these contrary views when you present your own view.

No matter how convincing your evidence may be, if you don't address their contrary position, your readers will always wonder, "Yes, but what about. . . ." This doesn't mean you must change their minds, but it does mean that you must account for all the evidence, especially the evidence that may seem (to some) to go against your thesis statement. If you cannot account for it, it may be time to reexamine your original proposition.

Remember, many interpretations of a story may be acceptable. The strength of your thesis is in its support, not the thesis itself. So don't offend your readers by being inflexible and suggesting that anyone holding a different view is ignorant. Feeling strongly about what you want to prove gives you a stronger voice, but insulting or overpowering your readers is not likely to be persuasive.

Supporting Your Argument

Arrange Your Support Effectively   Substantiation and induction (see "Critical Thinking," pp. 123–124) are the two most common approaches to argumentation. In each case, the order in which the proposition, or thesis statement, and the supporting evidence are presented is different.

You substantiate your argument when you place the thesis statement or proposition at the beginning of the essay and lay out evidence in the rest of the essay to support it. You begin with a generalization and support it with specific examples as evidence. You immediately make it clear to your readers what you intend to prove. Your thesis remains in their minds as they encounter each piece of subsequent evidence. In fact, if what you propose at the outset is interesting enough, your thesis statement may act as a "hook" for your readers and pull them into the essay.

Substantiation

$(a = b + b + b + b + b + b)$

(Your thesis equals the sum of the evidence.)

This approach may not work well if you are trying to convince skeptical readers, that is, readers who have already made up their minds and hold a contrary

view. Encountering a proposition they disagree with at the beginning may interfere with their response through the rest of the essay. Once they know what you
want to prove, they may not give you an open-minded reading. They may be
predisposed to disagree with you no matter how compelling your evidence.

Inductive argumentation moves from specific examples to a generalization
or conclusion. It mimics the process you probably went through when you came
up with your proposition to begin with. As the specifics of the work built up in
your mind, they moved you toward a conclusion and a proposition. A more
effective strategy to convince a skeptical reader may be to withhold your proposition until the end. If you first provide support, before readers know what your
position is, they may withhold judgment and be more likely to accept your thesis
when it comes as the natural conclusion of strong evidence.

Induction

(b + b + b + b + b + b = a)

(The sum of the evidence equals your thesis.)

And, of course, there are variations of these strategies. For example, if
you're stating your thesis up front, you may want to provide background information to "educate" the reader before you present your thesis, and then follow
with supporting evidence. If you are using an inductive approach, you may
want to build your support to a natural conclusion, and then discuss why this
conclusion makes sense. In any case, you should consider your audience and
your intentions before you decide which strategy will work best.

Support Your Thesis with Facts from the Text   Earlier, we discussed the difference between facts and opinions (pp. 123–124). Facts are verifiable. You can
cite them in the text. They should be the core of the evidence that supports your
argument.

A good critical essay requires reasons for your judgments, factual support
derived not only from your feelings and values but from ingredients in the text
that logically combine to prompt them. There is no guarantee, of course, that
everyone will agree with your conclusions, but you should make sure that your
evidence is recognized and respected as valid.

Account for All the Evidence   A strong thesis is constructed from all the evidence, not just the parts that agree with your conclusion. A discerning reader
sees contrary evidence whether you point it out or not.

In Alice Walker's "Everyday Use" (p. 112), if you ignore the fact that the
story is told by Dee's mother, you fail to account for the subjectivity of her
descriptions. By addressing her subjectivity, however, and demonstrating that
she is a reliable narrator by matching her descriptions to Dee's actions in the
story, you may establish credibility for her narration and what she tells you.

None of this is to say that the personal meaning you derive from the work is
not the most important meaning for you—a meaning that is often based on many
factors beyond the text. But for the purposes of a critical essay, you must rely heavily on the text and its factual support to make a convincing case for your reader.

Explain the Connections   Sometimes what seems self-evident to us is not so evident to our readers.

In addition to highlighting the facts to support your argument, explain the connections. Explicitly show your readers *how* the chosen evidence supports your conclusion. For example, if your proposition is that "Maggie and her mother . . . are the only ones in this family who can truly grasp their heritage," it is still necessary to explain the connection between the evidence (what Dee says and does compared with what Maggie and Mama say and do).

Consider the explanation: "While Dee embraces her heritage by renaming herself and other 'purely surface' actions, Maggie and Dee 'live' their heritage every day by actually using what has been passed down to them." This explanation shows the connection between the proposition and the evidence and makes your logic clear to the reader.

Opening, Closing, and Revising Your Argument

Write Your Introduction After You Know Your Argument   It may seem strange to wait until you're almost finished with the first draft of an essay before writing its introduction. However, introducing an essay is a bit like introducing a person. In both cases, you can make a more effective introduction when you know who or what you are introducing. This does not mean you have to mention everything you know. It means that you know your subject well enough to say the essential things.

Make your introduction interesting. You want the reader to continue reading beyond the first paragraph. Remember what seemed so interesting to you about the work, and try to pass that interest on to the reader. Make sure that what you say flows smoothly and maintains the same voice used in the rest of the essay. If you're developing your argument through substantiation, this is the place to state your thesis as clearly as possible.

Close Your Argument Reasonably   Although there is no need to summarize your essay in the conclusion, it may be helpful to remind the reader of the logic of your argument and explain the basic connections between your support and your thesis. Avoid being too ambitious. Only make claims or take credit for connections you've actually established.

If you've developed your argument inductively, this is the place where you want to state your thesis. Remember not to overstate your case. If you've proved your point, the evidence will carry it.

Revise with a Fresh View   If you really want to "re-vision" your essay, to see it again from a fresh perspective, it's best to let some time pass. Try to place yourself in the position of the reader who is reading your essay for the first time.

As with any other essay, it can be very useful to do an after-draft outline. Go back and identify the point of each paragraph. List those points. This should give you a pretty good overview of your essay. How well is your draft organized?

Does the sequence make sense? Are there gaps that need to be filled? Is there enough support?

Within the body of the essay have you explained the connections between your support and your thesis? Have you expressed those connections as clearly as possible? Have you maintained a consistent voice throughout the essay?

Check Against Your Intentions and Organization

- State your thesis clearly. Support and clarify your thesis with enough details and examples from the work of literature. *Show* what you have stated.
- Give the essay a title based on your thesis. If you're having trouble thinking of a title, it may be an indication that the thesis itself is not clear.
- Make sure that your essay is fully developed. Account for all aspects of your thesis statement. All your paragraphs must relate to that central thesis, and the organization of those paragraphs within the essay should be clear.
- Each paragraph should be fully developed too; each of the sentences within your paragraphs should relate to the central idea of that paragraph.
- All your statements should add something to the essay. Are there redundancies, digressions, or meaningless phrases that could be cut?

Proofread Carefully

- Proofreading is a crucial final step in the process of producing an essay. In addition to making any changes that did not occur to you earlier and fine-tuning your writing, check your essay for correct grammar, spelling, punctuation, and typos.
- Make sure all your sentences are complete and punctuated appropriately.
- Check to see that all of your words are spelled correctly. Check for easily confused words (then/than, your/you're, its/it's, etc.), which computerized spell checkers do not pick up.
- Check on the meaning of any words you are not sure of. Make sure the titles of works are underlined or in quotation marks, as appropriate.
- If there are types of errors you personally have a tendency to make, look carefully for them.
- Finally, make sure you've followed the *MLA Handbook for Writers of Research Papers* or another documentation format recommended by your instructor. Have you cited and documented your sources correctly? Do you have a "Work(s) Cited" list at the end of your essay?

✔ CHECKLIST • *Writing a Critical Essay*

Planning Your Argument

Determine Its Feasibility

❏ Can you write a critical essay about this?

❏ Do you have enough to say, and can you find enough evidence to support your case?

continued

Consider Your Motivation

❏ Will this topic sustain your interest long enough for you to do a good job?

Clarify Your Thesis

❏ Do you have a clear understanding of the thesis you want to argue? Can you articulate it in a thesis statement?

Know Your Readers

❏ What assumptions can you make about your readers? Are they likely to agree or disagree with your thesis?

Supporting Your Argument

Arrange Your Support Effectively

❏ Is the support for your thesis arranged in the most effective way?

❏ Is it more effective to develop your argument by stating your thesis first and then supporting it with evidence, or by allowing the evidence to build into your thesis?

Support Your Thesis with Facts from the Text

❏ Is your support based on facts or opinions?

❏ Have you supported your opinions with facts and quotations from the text?

Account for All the Evidence

❏ Have you accounted for *all* the evidence in the text?

❏ Have you accounted for evidence that may not support your thesis?

Explain the Connections

❏ Have you explained *how* the evidence you've chosen supports your thesis?

Opening, Closing, and Revising

Write or Rewrite Your Introduction After Your First Draft

❏ Is your introduction clear, informative, and interesting?

❏ If appropriate, does it map out the journey for the reader?

Close Your Argument Reasonably

❏ Have you explained the connections between the thesis and your support?

❏ Have you claimed anything for which you haven't delivered evidence?

Revise with a Fresh View

❏ Have you reread and reviewed your essay?

❏ How well is your draft organized? Does the sequence make sense?

❏ Are there gaps that need to be filled? Is there enough support? *continued*

❏ Have you explained the connections between your support and your thesis?

❏ Have you expressed those connections as clearly as possible?

❏ Have you maintained a consistent "voice" throughout the essay?

Review Your Intentions and Organization

❏ Is the central thesis of the essay clearly stated? Does the title account for your thesis?

❏ Is the essay fully developed? Have you accounted for all aspects of your thesis statement?

❏ Are there enough details to support or clarify your thesis? Have you *shown* what you've told?

❏ Are there enough quotations from the work to support your thesis?

❏ Do all the paragraphs relate to your thesis? Is the essay fully developed?

❏ Is the organization of the paragraphs within the essay clear?

❏ Are the paragraphs fully developed?

❏ Do each of the sentences within the paragraphs relate to the paragraph's central ideas?

❏ Is the language clear?

❏ Are there redundancies, digressions, or meaningless phrases that could be cut?

Proofread Carefully

❏ Are all your sentences complete sentences?

❏ Are all your sentences punctuated appropriately?

❏ Have you checked for easily confused words (then/than, your/you're, its/it's, etc.)?

❏ Are you sure of the meaning of all the words you've used?

❏ Are the titles of works underlined or in quotation marks as appropriate?

❏ Are there particular errors that you have a tendency to make? Have you looked for those in this essay?

❏ Is the essay written in the format required by your instructor? Have you documented your references to the text and included a list of works cited?

TWO READERS ⌣ TWO INTERPRETATIONS

Following John Updike's "A & P" below are two student samples of critical essays. These essays do not agree about what the story means, yet both present supportable interpretations. Remember, the strength of your interpretation is not based on your thesis but on the evidence you bring to support your thesis. What makes an interpretation convincing or defensible is the quality of its support. In this respect, many different interpretations are valid.

■ *EXPLORING "A & P"*

Making Connections   There is nothing extraordinary about the setting, the characters, or the conflict of John Updike's short story "A & P." The setting, an A & P supermarket in suburban Massachusetts in the 1960s, is as commonplace as it gets. And we experience this setting and the story's conflict through the eyes and mind of the protagonist, Sammy, an ordinary young man enduring the monotony of working a checkout slot. But Sammy checks out more than groceries. Through his narration we view the customers and employees of the supermarket, and witness his conflict, an ordinary conflict, but one that leaves him feeling "how hard the world was going to be to me hereafter."

What is extraordinary about this story is the quality of John Updike's description and his characterization of Sammy and his dilemma. Sammy, the supermarket, the customers, his boss, and his parents come to life for us. Whether we agree or disagree with Sammy's decision, we are reminded of our own choices and their consequences. In the tradition of some of the best fiction, Updike finds the "extraordinary in the ordinary" and reveals a great deal about the hard choices of growing up.

Your Experiences and Beliefs   Before you read "A & P," it may be helpful to think about your own experiences and beliefs in relation to issues that emerge from this story: pleasing or disappointing parents, teachers, employers, or other people you respect; or staying in a job, in school, or in a relationship to avoid disappointing others; or taking responsibility for your actions. If you have ever worked in a supermarket, department store, fast-food restaurant, or similar business, try to remember what that experience was like for you. If you have ever been in charge of other employees, try to recall how that responsibility made you feel.

JOHN UPDIKE (b. 1932)

John Updike was born in Shillington, Pennsylvania. His father was a teacher, and his mother a writer. After graduating from Harvard University in 1954, Updike spent two years in England, where he studied at the Ruskin School of Drawing and Fine Art. After returning to the United States in 1955, he worked as a reporter for the New Yorker, *leaving the magazine two years later to become a full-time writer. Though he is an accomplished critic, essayist, and poet, Updike is best known for his novels, which include* The Centaur

(1963), Couples (1968), S. (1988), and Rabbit Is Rich, *which was awarded the Pulitzer Prize in 1982. His novel* The Witches of Eastwick *(1984) was turned into a film starring Susan Sarandon and Jack Nicholson in 1987. His latest novel,* Gertrude and Cladius, *was published in 2000. Michiko Kakutani, a long time critic for the* New York Times, *has said of Updike's fiction: "His heroes over the years have all suffered from 'the tension and guilt of being human.' Torn between vestigial spiritual yearnings and the new imperatives of self-fulfillment, they hunger for salvation even as they submit to importunate demands of the flesh."*

A & P   [1962]

In walks these three girls in nothing but bathing suits. I'm in the third checkout slot, with my back to the door, so I don't see them until they're over by the bread. The one that caught my eye first was the one in the plaid green two-piece. She was a chunky kid, with a good tan and a sweet broad soft-looking can with those two crescents of white just under it, where the sun never seems to hit, at the top of the backs of her legs. I stood there with my hand on a box of HiHo crackers trying to remember if I rang it up or not. I ring it up again and the customer starts giving me hell. She's one of these cash-register-watchers, a witch about fifty with rouge on her cheekbones and no eyebrows, and I know it made her day to trip me up. She'd been watching cash registers for fifty years and probably never seen a mistake before.

By the time I got her feathers smoothed and her goodies into a bag—she gives me a little snort in passing, if she'd been born at the right time they would have burned her over in Salem—by the time I get her on her way the girls had circled around the bread and were coming back, without a pushcart, back my way along the counters, in the aisle between the checkouts and the Special bins. They didn't even have shoes on. There was this chunky one, with the two-piece—it was bright green and the seams on the bra were still sharp and her belly was still pretty pale so I guessed she just got it (the suit)—there was this one, with one of those chubby berry-faces, the lips all bunched together under her nose, this one, and a tall one, with black hair that hadn't quite frizzed right, and one of these sunburns right across under the eyes, and a chin that was too long—you know, the kind of girl other girls think is very "striking" and "attractive" but never quite makes it, as they very well know, which is why they like her so much—and then the third one, that wasn't quite so tall. She was the queen. She kind of led them, the other two peeking around and making their shoulders round. She didn't look around, not this queen, she just walked straight on slowly, on these long white prima-donna legs. She came down a little hard on her heels, as if she didn't walk in her bare feet that much, putting down her heels and then letting the weight move along to her toes as if she was testing the floor with every step, putting a little deliberate extra action into it. You never know for sure how girls' minds work (do you really think it's a mind in there or just a little buzz like a bee in a glass jar?) but you got the idea she had talked the other two into coming in here with her, and now she was showing them how to do it, walk slow and hold yourself straight.

She had on a kind of dirty-pink—beige maybe, I don't know—bathing suit with a little nubble all over it and, what got me, the straps were down. They were off her shoulders looped loose around the cool tops of her arms, and I guess as a result the suit had slipped a little on her, so all around the top of the cloth there was this shining rim. If it hadn't been there you wouldn't have known there could have been anything whiter than those shoulders. With the straps pushed off, there was nothing between the top of the suit and the top of her head except just *her,* this clean bare plane of the top of her chest down from the shoulder bones like a dented sheet of metal tilted in the light. I mean, it was more than pretty.

She had sort of oaky hair that the sun and salt had bleached, done up in a bun that was unraveling, and a kind of prim face. Walking into the A & P with your straps down, I suppose it's the only kind of face you *can* have. She held her head so high her neck, coming up out of those white shoulders, looked kind of stretched, but I didn't mind. The longer her neck was, the more of her there was.

5   She must have felt in the corner of her eye me and over my shoulder Stokesie in the second slot watching, but she didn't tip. Not this queen. She kept her eyes moving across the racks, and stopped, and turned so slow it made my stomach rub the inside of my apron, and buzzed to the other two, who kind of huddled against her for relief, and then they all three of them went up the cat-and-dog-food-break-fast-cereal-macaroni-rice-raisins-seasonings-spreads-spaghetti-soft-drinks-crack-ers-and-cookies aisle. From the third slot I look straight up this aisle to the meat counter, and I watched them all the way. The fat one with the tan sort of fumbled with the cookies, but on second thought she put the package back. The sheep pushing their carts down the aisle—the girls were walking against the usual traffic (not that we have one-way signs or anything)—were pretty hilarious. You could see them, when Queenie's white shoulders dawned on them, kind of jerk, or hop, or hiccup, but their eyes snapped back to their own baskets and on they pushed. I bet you could set off dynamite in an A & P and the people would by and large keep reaching and checking oatmeal off their lists and muttering "Let me see, there was a third thing, began with A, asparagus, no, ah, yes, applesauce!" or whatever it is they do mutter. But there was no doubt, this jiggled them. A few houseslaves in pin curlers even looked around after pushing their carts past to make sure what they had seen was correct.

You know, it's one thing to have a girl in a bathing suit down on the beach, where what with the glare nobody can look at each other much anyway, and another thing in the cool of the A & P, under the fluorescent lights, against all those stacked packages, with her feet paddling along naked over our checkerboard green-and-cream rubber-tile floor.

"Oh Daddy," Stokesie said beside me. "I feel so faint."

"Darling," I said. "Hold me tight." Stokesie's married, with two babies chalked up on his fuselage already, but as far as I can tell that's the only difference. He's twenty-two, and I was nineteen this April.

"Is it done?" he asks, the responsible married man finding his voice. I forgot to say he thinks he's going to be manager some sunny day, maybe in 1990 when it's called the Great Alexandrov and Petrooshki Tea Company or something.

10   What he meant was, our town is five miles from a beach, with a big summer colony out on the Point, but we're right in the middle of town, and the women generally put on a shirt or shorts or something before they get out of the car into the street. And anyway these are usually women with six children and varicose veins mapping their legs and nobody, including them, could care less. As I say, we're right in the middle of town, and if you stand at our front doors you can see two banks and the Congregational church and the newspaper store and three real-estate offices and about twenty-seven old freeloaders tearing up Central Street because the sewer broke again. It's not as if we're on the Cape; we're north of Boston and there's people in this town haven't seen the ocean for twenty years.

   The girls had reached the meat counter and were asking McMahon something. He pointed, they pointed, and they shuffled out of sight behind a pyramid of Diet Delight peaches. All that was left for us to see was old McMahon patting his mouth and looking after them sizing up their joints. Poor kids, I began to feel sorry for them, they couldn't help it.

   Now here comes the sad part of the story, at least my family says it's sad, but I don't think it's so sad myself. The store's pretty empty, it being Thursday afternoon, so there was nothing much to do except lean on the register and wait for the girls to show up again. The whole store was like a pinball machine and I didn't know which tunnel they'd come out of. After a while they come around out of the far aisle, around the light bulbs, records at discount of the Caribbean Six or Tony Martin Sings or some such gunk you wonder they waste the wax on, sixpacks of candy bars, and plastic toys done up in cellophane that fall apart when a kid looks at them anyway. Around they come, Queenie still leading the way, and holding a little gray jar in her hand. Slots Three through Seven are unmanned, and I could see her wondering between Stokes and me, but Stokesie with his usual luck, draws an old party in baggy gray pants who stumbles up with four giant cans of pineapple juice (what do these bums *do* with all that pineapple juice? I've often asked myself) so the girls come to me. Queenie puts down the jar and I take it into my fingers icy cold. Kingfish Fancy Herring Snacks in Pure Sour Cream: 49¢. Now her hands are empty, not a ring or a bracelet, bare as God made them, and I wonder where the money's coming from. Still with that prim look she lifts a folded dollar bill out of the hollow at the center of her nubbled pink top. The jar went heavy in my hand. Really, I thought that was so cute.

   Then everybody's luck begins to run out. Lengel comes in from haggling with a truck full of cabbages on the lot and is about to scuttle into that door marked MANAGER behind which he hides all day when the girls touch his eye. Lengel's pretty dreary, teaches Sunday school and the rest, but he doesn't miss that much. He comes over and says, "Girls, this isn't the beach."

   Queenie blushes, though maybe it's just a brush of sunburn I was noticing for the first time, now that she was so close. "My mother asked me to pick up a jar of herring snacks." Her voice kind of startled me, the way voices do when you see the people first, coming out so flat and dumb yet kind of tony, too, the way it ticked over "pick up" and "snacks." All of a sudden I slid right down her voice into her living room. Her father and the other men were standing around in ice-cream coats and bow ties and the women were in sandals picking up herring snacks on toothpicks off a big plate and they were all holding drinks the color of water with olives and sprigs of mint in them. When my parents have somebody over they get lemonade and if it's a real racy affair Schlitz in tall glasses with "They'll Do It Every Time" cartoons stenciled on.

15   "That's all right," Lengel said. "But this isn't the beach." His repeating this struck me as funny, as if it had just occurred to him, and he had been thinking all these years the A & P was a great big dune and he was the head lifeguard. He didn't like my smiling—as I say he doesn't miss much—but he concentrates on giving the girls that sad Sunday-school-superintendent stare.

Queenie's blush is no sunburn now, and the plump one in plaid, that I liked better from the back—a really sweet can—pipes up, "We weren't doing any shopping. We just came in for the one thing."

"That makes no difference," Lengel tells her, and I could see from the way his eyes went that he hadn't noticed she was wearing a two-piece before. "We want you decently dressed when you come in here."

"We *are* decent," Queenie says suddenly, her lower lip pushing, getting sore now that she remembers her place, a place from which the crowd that runs the A & P must look pretty crummy. Fancy Herring Snacks flashed in her very blue eyes.

"Girls, I don't want to argue with you. After this come in here with your shoulders covered. It's our policy." He turns his back. That's policy for you. Policy is what the kingpins want. What the others want is juvenile delinquency.

20   All this while, the customers had been showing up with their carts but, you know, sheep, seeing a scene, they had all bunched up on Stokesie, who shook open a paper bag as gently as peeling a peach, not wanting to miss a word. I could feel in the silence everybody getting nervous, most of all Lengel, who asks me, "Sammy, have you rung up their purchase?"

I thought and said, "No" but it wasn't about that I was thinking. I go through the punches, 4, 9, GROC, TOT—it's more complicated than you think, and after you do it often enough, it begins to make a little song, that you hear words to, in my case "Hello (*bing*) there, you (*gung*) hap-py *pee*-pul (*splat*)!"—the *splat* being the drawer flying out. I uncrease the bill, tenderly as you may imagine, it just having come from between the two smoothest scoops of vanilla I had ever known were there, and pass a half and a penny into her narrow pink palm, and nestle the herrings in a bag and twist its neck and hand it over, all the time thinking.

The girls, and who'd blame them, are in a hurry to get out, so I say "I quit" to Lengel quick enough for them to hear, hoping they'll stop and watch me, their unsuspected hero. They keep right on going, into the electric eye; the door flies open and they flicker across the lot to their car, Queenie and Plaid and Big Tall Goony-Goony (not that as raw material she was so bad), leaving me with Lengel and a kink in his eyebrow.

"Did you say something, Sammy?"

"I said I quit."

25   "I thought you did."

"You didn't have to embarrass them."

"It was they who were embarrassing us."

I started to say something that came out "Fiddle-de-doo." It's a saying of my grandmother's, and I know she would have been pleased.

"I don't think you know what you're saying," Lengel said.

30 "I know you don't," I said. "But I do." I pull the bow at the back of my apron and start shrugging it off my shoulders. A couple customers that had been heading for my slot begin to knock against each other, like scared pigs in a chute.

Lengel sighs and begins to look very patient and old and gray. He's been a friend of my parents for years. "Sammy, you don't want to do this to your Mom and Dad," he tells me. It's true, I don't. But it seems to me that once you begin a gesture it's fatal not to go through with it. I fold the apron, "Sammy" stitched in red on the pocket, and put it on the counter, and drop the bow tie on top of it. The bow tie is theirs, if you've ever wondered. "You'll feel this for the rest of your life," Lengel says, and I know that's true, too, but remembering how he made that pretty girl blush makes me so scrunchy inside I punch the No Sale tab and the machine whirs "pee-pul" and the drawer splats out. One advantage to this scene taking place in summer, I can follow this up with a clean exit, there's no fumbling around getting your coat and galoshes, I just saunter into the electric eye in my white shirt that my mother ironed the night before, and the door heaves itself open, and outside the sunshine is skating around on the asphalt.

I look around for my girls, but they're gone, of course. There wasn't anybody but some young married screaming with her children about some candy they didn't get by the door of a powder-blue Falcon station wagon. Looking back in the big windows, over the bags of peat moss and aluminum lawn furniture stacked on the pavement, I could see Lengel in my place in the slot, checking the sheep through. His face was dark gray and his back stiff, as if he'd just had an injection of iron, and my stomach kind of fell as I felt how hard the world was going to be to me hereafter.

► QUESTIONS FOR READING AND WRITING

1. To what extent can you connect "A & P" with your own background and experience? How did this influence your response?
2. How would you describe the narrator, Sammy? What is your reaction to his description of the girls and what he says about the customers?
3. How are you affected by the concrete description of the setting?
4. What do you think Sammy means when he says, "Now here comes the sad part of the story, at least my family says it's sad, but I don't think it's so sad myself"?
5. If you were in his position, would you have made the same decision?
6. What does Sammy mean at the end of the story when he says, ". . . my stomach kind of fell as I felt how hard the world was going to be to me hereafter"?

∽ TWO CRITICAL ESSAYS: TWO DIFFERENT VIEWS ∽

Depending on your experience of it, "A & P" is a story about many different things. You may experience it as a story about family pressure, rebellion, loss of innocence, immaturity, or any number of other issues.

In the student essays that follow, Michelle and Julie both emphasize the importance of Sammy's decision to quit, but come to different conclusions about what it means. Michelle sees it as a loss of innocence—a realization by Sammy that his actions will have negative consequences for him and his family. Julie also sees Sammy's action as significant, but as a defining moment for the rest of his life, a clear statement that Sammy will refuse to live his life like Lengel.

Michelle's Essay

Michelle McAuliffe

Dr. Madden

English 102

April 10, 200X

Ironed Shirts and Bathing Suits

We all have moments in our lives when we find ourselves alone and forced to see the world and ourselves in a new and painful light. In the short story "A & P," John Updike illustrates how a seemingly unimportant experience becomes this kind of moment in the life of his main character, Sammy.

Sammy is a lively, cynical, young guy who seems more than familiar with the grocery sciences, anatomy of the store, and psychology of the customer mind: "The girls had circled around the bread and were coming back, without a pushcart, back my way along the counters, in the aisle between the checkouts and the Special bins" (146). Sammy spends a lot of time analyzing the store and the people in it: "I bet you could set off dynamite in an A & P and the people would by and large keep reaching and checking oatmeal off their lists and muttering, 'Let me see, there was a third thing, began with an A, asparagus, no, ah, yes, applesauce!' or whatever it is they do mutter." (147). He doesn't hesitate to pass judgment on them either: "What do these bums <u>do</u> with all that pineapple juice?" (148). This seems to be the primary mental activity of his day.

On this particular day, Sammy's focus is on three young girls who enter the store wearing bathing suits. Besides ogling their every move, he gets a kick out of how they are dressed and people's reactions to it: "You could see them, when Queenie's white shoulders dawned on them, kind of jerk, or hop, or hiccup, but their eyes snapped back to their own baskets and on they pushed" (147). But Lengel, the store manager, is not so amused. He exclaims, "Girls, this isn't the beach" (148). And the fun begins.

When the confrontation with the girls and the manager occurs, Sammy sees it as time to act instead of watching passively. We can't really say what motivates his action. It may be something noble, or simply an excuse to be rid of a stifling job. Even Sammy might not be able to tell us. He has the initial urge to quit in the presence of the girls, but when they're gone, he still feels strongly about something. Once he says he quits, it's too late to turn back. Even though Lengel, the store manager, is giving him the chance to stay, "You don't want to do this to your Mom and Dad" (150), his decision is final. Sammy admits to us that he doesn't want to do this to his parents, but adds, "It seems to me that once you begin a gesture it's fatal not to go through with it" (150). He has his personal dignity to consider. Lengel speaks prophetically when he says, "You'll feel this for the rest of your life" (150). Sammy knows this too, but feels his decision is one of liberation. He even likes the idea of this taking place in the summertime, so he can make a quick exit.

Sammy, however, is also aware of Lengel's reaction. He notices that "Lengel sighs and begins to look very patient and old and gray" (150). His need for a quick exit is a result of feeling some shame and guilt in the face of a family friend and an understanding man. When Sammy gets outside, the desolation of the parking lot takes away the glory of his act in the war between youth and responsibility. His righteous decision is not so simple any-more. Without something to rebel against he feels alone. Sammy may be expressing his sympathy for Lengel when he says, "I could see Lengel in my place in the slot, checking the sheep through. His face was dark gray and his back stiff, as if he'd just had an injection of iron, and my stomach kind of fell as I felt how hard the world was going to be to me hereafter" (150). He feels that Lengel and his parents, and perhaps the entire adult world, must be dis-appointed in him. He has let them down.

Although we can't say what immediate consequence Sammy will face, we know that he recognizes the effects of his action beyond himself. This realization of how we affect others through our actions is not a lesson to be learned in books; we must experience it. We are often surprised when we see how what we do, say, or think affects others. At moments like this we know we have learned something valuable. Although we don't always understand it, we know that it's something that will influence our outlook on life. At the end of this story, Sammy is all alone to contemplate a decision and thoughts that only a half hour before were very far from his mind. Such is the introduction of insight and wisdom into our lives--when we least expect it, and in the most unlikely situations.

Work Cited

Updike, John. "A & P." <u>Exploring Fiction</u>. Ed. Frank Madden. New York:

> Longman, 2002. 146–150.

Julie's Essay

Julie Fitzmaurice

Dr. Madden

English 102

April 6, 200X

What Makes Sammy Quit?

In John Updike's short story "A & P," we see the world through the eyes of a nineteen-year-old. Sammy, the main character, is also the narrator, and his narration creates the tone and atmosphere of the story. When Sammy quits his job for no obvious reason we are left with a question: Why? Was it his impatience with older people, rebellion against authority, or just boredom? It was not one of these alone that made him quit, but the synergy of them all which, once in motion, could not be stopped.

First, let us consider Sammy and what we learn about his character in the story. Updike doesn't actually give us many details about him. From the text we learn that Sammy is nineteen years old and lives in a small town north of Boston, five miles from the beach. The most important key to Sammy's character, however, is how he sees everyone else.

Virtually everything we learn in this story, we learn through Sammy's thoughts. Sammy comes from a working-class background: "When my parents have somebody over they get lemonade and if it's a real racy affair Schlitz in tall glasses with 'They'll Do It Every Time' cartoons stenciled on" (149). Another indication of a working-class background is in his comment, "Now here comes the sad part of the story, at least my family says it's sad, but I don't think it's so sad myself" (148). This statement tells us that Sammy's parents placed importance on his job at the A & P.

His comments about Lengel tell us more about Sammy than they do about his boss at the A & P. Lengel is older and the manager of the A & P. He teaches Sunday school and has been a friend of Sammy's parents for years. Sammy thinks Lengel is "pretty dreary," and "doesn't miss that much" (148), and describes him as giving the girls that "sad Sunday-school-superintendent stare" (149). His descriptions of the customers also tell us a lot about him: "one of these cash-register-watchers, a witch about fifty" (146), "The sheep pushing their carts down the aisle" (147), and "A few houseslaves in pin curlers" (147). These comments reveal Sammy's impatience with adults and his rebellious streak.

Sammy's description of the A & P itself turns the store into a quasi character. The A & P has its own pulse and comes alive for us. He tells us what the store looks and sounds like. The cash register even sings a song as Sammy tediously pushes its keys: "Hello (bing) there, you (gung) hap-py pee-pul (splat)!" (149). Almost everyone has experienced the setting of a food store. There is a certain universality about them. But Sammy's description of the "cat-and-dog-food-breakfast-cereal-macaroni-rice-raisins-seasonings-spreads-spaghetti-soft-drinks-crackers-and-cookies aisle" (147) brings this familiar place to dull but fresh life.

Sammy goes into great detail about the girls, too. Had he been busy he would not have noticed so much about them. The store was slow, and Sammy leans on the register looking at the girls. He is so bored that he sees the store as a pinball machine. The girls are the balls, and the aisles are the chutes that the balls travel through.

His detailed description has a strong impact on our reading of the story. It makes it easy for us to imagine being nineteen and working in a store on a hot summer day. Sammy describes what the atmosphere is like: "The store's pretty empty, it being Thursday afternoon, so there was nothing much to do except lean on the register and wait for the girls to show up again" (148).

At the climax of the story, when Lengel confronts the girls about their bathing suits, Sammy is already bored and frustrated to exhaustion. He thinks that Lengel is a pompous bag of wind, so he says, "I quit" (149). He says this to Lengel to save himself, not the girls. The girls are simply the final impetus for Sammy's quitting, he needs them as his excuse. He would like to have the girls think that he is quitting his job in indignation over the way Lengel treated them.

At this moment, Lengel is everything that Sammy detests. He represents all the things that Sammy wants to rebel against: age, authority, his working-class background, Sunday school teachers, and the voice of righteousness. He realizes that if he stays at the A & P he will become a Lengel. In one brief moment all his emotions synergize. The two words "I quit" leave his lips, and Sammy changes the course of his life forever.

Work Cited

Updike, John. "A & P." <u>Exploring Fiction</u>. Ed. Frank Madden. New York: Longman, 2002, 146–150.

PART III

An Anthology
of Short Fiction

❧

CHINUA ACHEBE (b. 1930)

The son of a mission schoolteacher, Chinua Achebe was born and raised in eastern Nigeria, a British colony that later became the Republic of Nigeria after gaining independence in 1963. Educated both in Africa and England, he first burst into prominence with his 1958 novel Things Fall Apart, *a moving portrayal of the conflicts between traditional tribal customs and European culture in colonial Africa. He has since become one of the most influential African voices of his generation. Much of his later work, including the novels* Man of the People *(1964) and* Anthills of the Savannah *(1988), explores the corruption and conflicts of contemporary Nigeria. He currently resides both in Nigeria and the United States, holding teaching positions at Stanford University, the University of Massachusetts at Amherst, and Bard College.*

MARRIAGE IS A PRIVATE AFFAIR [1972]

"Have you written to your dad yet?" asked Nene one afternoon as she sat with Nnaemeka in her room at 16 Kasanga Street, Lagos.

"No. I've been thinking about it. I think it's better to tell him when I get home on leave!"

"But why? Your leave is such a long way off yet—six whole weeks. He should be let into our happiness now."

Nnaemeka was silent for a while, and then began very slowly as if he groped for his words: "I wish I were sure it would be happiness to him."

5 "Of course it must," replied Nene, a little surprised. "Why shouldn't it?"

"You have lived in Lagos all your life, and you know very little about people in remote parts of the country."

"That's what you always say. But I don't believe anybody will be so unlike other people that they will be unhappy when their sons are engaged to marry."

"Yes. They are most unhappy if the engagement is not arranged by them. In our case it's worse—you are not even an Ibo."

This was said so seriously and so bluntly that Nene could not find speech immediately. In the cosmopolitan atmosphere of the city it had always seemed to her something of a joke that a person's tribe could determine whom he married.

10 At last she said, "You don't really mean that he will object to your marrying me simply on that account? I had always thought you Ibos were kindly disposed to other people."

"So we are. But when it comes to marriage, well, it's not quite so simple. And this," he added, "is not peculiar to the Ibos. If your father were alive and lived in the heart of lbibio-land he would be exactly like my father."

"I don't know. But anyway, as your father is so fond of you, I'm sure he will forgive you soon enough. Come on then, be a good boy and send him a nice lovely letter. . ."

"It would not be wise to break the news to him by writing. A letter will bring it upon him with a shock. I'm quite sure about that."

"All right, honey, suit yourself. You know your father."

15   As Nnaemeka walked home that evening he turned over in his mind the different ways of overcoming his father's opposition, especially now that he had gone and found a girl for him. He had thought of showing his letter to Nene but decided on second thought not to, at least for the moment. He read it again when he got home and couldn't help smiling to himself. He remembered Ugoye quite well, an Amazon of a girl who used to beat up all the boys, himself included, on the way to the stream, a complete dunce at school.

> I have found a girl who will suit you admirably—Ugoye Nweke, the eldest daughter of our neighbor, Jacob Nweke. She has a proper Christian upbringing. When she stopped schooling some years ago her father (a man of sound judgment) sent her to live in the house of a pastor where she has received all the training a wife could need. Her Sunday School teacher has told me that she reads her Bible very fluently. I hope we shall begin negotiations when you come home in December.

On the second evening of his return from Lagos Nnaemeka sat with his father under a cassia tree. This was the old man's retreat where he went to read his Bible when the parching December sun had set and a fresh, reviving wind blew on the leaves.

"Father," began Nnaemeka suddenly, "I have come to ask forgiveness."

"Forgiveness? For what, my son?" he asked in amazement.

20   "It's about this marriage question!"

"Which marriage question."

"I can't—we must—I mean it is impossible for me to marry Nweke's daughter."

"Impossible? Why?" asked his father.

"I don't love her."

25   "Nobody said you did. Why should you?" he asked.

"Marriage today is different. . ."

"Look here, my son," interrupted his father, "nothing is different. What one looks for in a wife are a good character and a Christian background."

Nnaemeka saw there was no hope along the present line of argument.

"Moreover," he said, "I am engaged to marry another girl who has all of Ugoye's good qualities, and who. . ."

30   His father did not believe his ears. "What did you say?" he asked slowly and disconcertingly.

"She is a good Christian," his son went on, "and a teacher in a girls' school in Lagos."

"Teacher, did you say? If you consider that a qualification for a good wife I should like to point out to you, Emeka, that no Christian woman should teach. St. Paul in his letter to the Corinthians says that women should keep silence." He rose

slowly from his seat and paced forwards and backwards. This was his pet subject,
and he condemned vehemently those church leaders who encouraged women to
teach in their schools. After he had spent his emotion on a long homily, he at last
came back to his son's engagement, in a seemingly milder tone.

"Whose daughter is she, anyway?"

"She is Nene Atang."

35   "What!" All the mildness was gone again. "Did you say Neneatang? What does
that mean?"

"Nene Atang from Calabar. She is the only girl I can marry." This was a very
rash reply and Nnaemeka expected the storm to burst. But it did not. His father
merely walked away into his room. This was most unexpected and perplexed
Nnaemeka. His father's silence was infinitely more menacing than a flood of threatening speech. That night the old man did not eat.

When he sent for Nnaemeka a day later he applied all possible ways of dissua-
sion. But the young man's heart was hardened, and his father eventually gave him
up as lost.

"I owe it to you, my son, as a duty to show you what is right and what is wrong.
Whoever put this idea into your head might as well have cut your throat. It is
Satan's work." He waved his son away.

"You will change your mind, Father, when you know Nene."

40   "I shall never see her" was the reply. From that night the father scarcely spoke
to his son. He did not, however, cease hoping that he would realize how serious was
the danger he was heading for. Day and night he put him in his prayers.

Nnaemeka, for his own part, was very deeply affected by his father's grief. But
he kept hoping that it would pass away. If it had occurred to him that never in the
history of his people had a man married a woman who spoke a different tongue, he
might have been less optimistic. "It has never been heard," was the verdict of an old
man speaking a few weeks later. In that short sentence he spoke for all of his people.
This man had come with others to commiserate with Okeke when news went round
about his son's behavior. By that time the son had gone back to Lagos.

"It has never been heard," said the old man again with a sad shake of his head.

"What did Our Lord say?" asked another gentleman. "Sons shall rise against
their Fathers; it is there in the Holy Book."

"It is the beginning of the end," said another.

45   The discussion thus tending to become theological, Madubogwu, a highly
practical man, brought it down once more to the ordinary level.

"Have you thought of consulting a native doctor about your son?" he asked
Nnaemeka's father.

"He isn't sick," was the reply.

"What is he then? The boy's mind is diseased and only a good herbalist can
bring him back to his right senses. The medicine he requires is *Amalile,* the same
that women apply with success to recapture their husbands' straying affection."

"Madubogwu is right," said another gentleman. "This thing calls for medicine."

50   "I shall not call in a native doctor." Nnaemeka's father was known to be obsti-
nately ahead of his more superstitious neighbors in these matters. "I will not be
another Mrs. Ochuba. If my son wants to kill himself let him do it with his own
hands. It is not for me to help him."

"But it was her fault," said Madubogwu. "She ought to have gone to an honest herbalist. She was a clever woman, nevertheless."

"She was a wicked murderess," said Jonathan who rarely argued with his neighbors because, he often said, they were incapable of reasoning. "The medicine was prepared for her husband, it was his name they called in its preparation and I am sure it would have been perfectly beneficial to him. It was wicked to put it into the herbalist's food, and say you were only trying it out."

Six months later, Nnaemeka was showing his young wife a short letter from his father:

> It amazes me that you could be so unfeeling as to send me your wedding picture. I would have sent it back. But on further thought I decided just to cut off your wife and sent it back to you because I have nothing to do with her. How I wish that I had nothing to do with you either.

55   When Nene read through this letter and looked at the mutilated picture her eyes filled with tears, and she began to sob.

"Don't cry, my darling," said her husband. "He is essentially good natured and will one day look more kindly on our marriage." But years passed and that one day did not come.

For eight years, Okeke would have nothing to do with his son, Nnaemeka. Only three times (when Nnaemeka asked to come home and spend his leave) did he write to him.

"I can't have you in my house," he replied on one occasion. "It can be of no interest to me where or how you spend your leave—or your life, for that matter."

The prejudice against Nnaemeka's marriage was not confined to his little village. In Lagos, especially among his people who worked there, it showed itself in a different way. Their women, when they met at their village meeting were not hostile to Nene. Rather, they paid her such excessive deference as to make her feel she was not one of them. But as time went on, Nene gradually broke through some of this prejudice and even began to make friends among them. Slowly and grudgingly they began to admit that she kept her home much better than most of them.

60   The story eventually got to the little village in the heart of the Ibo country that Nnaemeka and his young wife were a most happy couple. But his father was one of the few people who knew nothing about this. He always displayed so much temper whenever his son's name was mentioned that everyone avoided it in his presence. By a tremendous effort of will he had succeeded in pushing his son to the back of his mind. The strain had nearly killed him but he had persevered, and won.

Then one day he received a letter from Nene, and in spite of himself he began to glance through it perfunctorily until all of a sudden the expression on his face changed and he began to read more carefully.

> ... Our two sons, from the day they learnt that they have a grandfather, have insisted on being taken to him. I find it impossible to tell them that you will not see them. I implore you to allow Nnaemeka to bring them home for a short time during his leave next month. I shall remain here in Lagos ...

The old man at once felt the resolution he had built up over so many years falling in. He was telling himself that he must not give in. He tried to steel his heart against all emotional appeals. It was a reenactment of that other struggle. He leaned against a window and looked out. The sky was overcast with heavy black clouds and a high wind began to blow filling the air with dust and dry leaves. It was one of those rare occasions when even Nature takes a hand in a human fight. Very soon it began to rain, the first rain in the year. It came down in large sharp drops and was accompanied by the lightning and thunder which mark a change of season. Okeke was trying hard not to think of his two grandsons. But he knew he was now fighting a losing battle. He tried to hum a favorite hymn but the pattering of large rain drops on the roof broke up the tune. His mind immediately returned to the children. How could he shut his door against them? By a curious mental process he imagined them standing, sad and forsaken, under the harsh angry weather—shut out from his house.

That night he hardly slept, from remorse—and a vague fear that he might die without making it up to them.

▶ QUESTIONS FOR READING AND WRITING

1. At the start of the story Nnaemeka has a letter from his father that he doesn't share with Nene. Why does he conceal its contents? Is he justified in not sharing such information with his fiancée?

2. Nnaemeka's father objects to his marriage to Nene because she is not an Ibo. Are there any groups whose members it would be difficult for you to marry?

3. What do you think of the way that Okeke treats his son and daughter-in-law? Is it ever appropriate to disown a child? How does your culture affect how you answer that question?

4. Throughout the story, Nnaemeka seems optimistic that his father will come to accept his marriage. Do Okeke's reactions to Nene's letter at the end of the story validate his son's optimism? Why?

5. What do you think the rain near the end of the story symbolizes?

6. It is commonly assumed that marriages are based upon love, but even in our society people marry for reasons other than love. Is marriage for a motive other than love justifiable? Might it even be preferable? Explain.

SHERMAN ALEXIE (b. 1966)

Sherman Alexie achieved a goal by having ten books of poetry and fiction published before he turned 30. In 2000, he added another two.

His very first book, The Business of Fancydancing *(1992), was chosen as a New York Times Notable Book of the Year, and reviewer James R. Kincaid wrote, "Mr. Alexie's is one of the major lyric voices of our time." Alexie's latest poetry collection is* One Stick Song *(2000) and his latest fiction collection is* The Toughest Indian in the World *(2000). A film,* Smoke Signals, *for which he wrote a script adapted from the short story* The Lone Ranger and Tonto Fistfight in Heaven, *has won rave reviews and large audiences. He is presently involved with new film projects and a new novel. He has also written criticism and articles.*

Alexie's poems and stories have appeared very widely, and he has read from his work in virtually every state as well as in several European countries. Among many awards, he has won a Lila Wallace-Reader's Digest Writer's Award, an American Book Award, and a Creative Writing Fellowship from the National Endowment for the Arts.

An enrolled Spokane/Coeur d'Alene Indian, Alexie was born on the Spokane reservation in Wellpinit, Washington, in 1966. He is very active in the American Indian community and frequently gives workshops. He now lives in Seattle with his wife and infant son.

THE LONE RANGER AND TONTO FISTFIGHT IN HEAVEN [1993]

Too hot to sleep so I walked down to the Third Avenue 7-11 for a Creamsicle and the company of a graveyard-shift cashier. I know the game. I worked graveyard for a Seattle 7-11 and got robbed once too often. The last time the bastard locked me in the cooler. He even took my money and basketball shoes.

The graveyard-shift worker in the Third Avenue 7-11 looked like they all do. Acne scars and a bad haircut, work pants that showed off his white socks, and those cheap black shoes that have no support. My arches still ache from my year at the Seattle 7-11.

"Hello," he asked when I walked into his store. "How you doing?"

I gave him a half-wave as I headed back to the freezer. He looked me over so he could describe me to the police later. I knew the look. One of my old girlfriends said I started to look at her that way, too. She left me not long after that. No, I left her and don't blame her for anything. That's how it happened. When one person starts to look at another like a criminal, then the love is over. It's logical.

5   "I don't trust you," she said to me. "You get too angry."

She was white and I lived with her in Seattle. Some nights we fought so bad that I would just get in my car and drive all night, only stop to fill up on gas. In fact, I worked the graveyard shift to spend as much time away from her as possible. But I learned all about Seattle that way, driving its back ways and dirty alleys.

Sometimes, though, I would forget where I was and get lost. I'd drive for hours, searching for something familiar. Seems like I'd spent my whole life that way, looking for anything I recognized. Once, I ended up in a nice residential neighborhood and somebody must have been worried because the police showed up and pulled me over.

"What are you doing out here?" the police officer asked me as he looked over my license and registration.

"I'm lost."

10 "Well, where are you supposed to be?" he asked me, and I knew there were plenty of places I wanted to be, but none where I was supposed to be.

"I got in a fight with my girlfriend," I said. "I was just driving around, blowing off steam, you know?"

"Well, you should be more careful where you drive," the officer said. "You're making people nervous. You don't fit the profile of the neighborhood."

I wanted to tell him that I didn't really fit the profile of the country but I knew it would just get me into trouble.

"Can I help you?" the 7-11 clerk asked me loudly, searching for some response that would reassure him that I wasn't an armed robber. He knew this dark skin and long, black hair of mine was dangerous. I had potential.

15 "Just getting a Creamsicle," I said after a long interval. It was a sick twist to pull on the guy, but it was late and I was bored. I grabbed my Creamsicle and walked back to the counter slowly, scanned the aisles for effect. I wanted to whistle low and menacingly but I never learned to whistle.

"Pretty hot out tonight?" he asked, that old rhetorical weather bullshit question designed to put us both as ease.

"Hot enough to make you go crazy," I said and smiled. He swallowed hard like a white man does in those situations. I looked him over. Same old green, red, and white 7-11 jacket and thick glasses. But he wasn't ugly, just misplaced and marked by loneliness. If he wasn't working there that night, he'd be home alone, flipping through channels and wishing he could afford HBO or Showtime.

"Will this be all?" he asked me, in that company effort to make me do some impulse shopping. Like adding a clause onto a treaty. *We'll take Washington and Oregon, and you get six pine trees and a brand-new Chrysler Cordoba.* I knew how to make and break promises.

"No," I said and paused. "Give me a Cherry Slushie, too."

20 "What size?" he asked, relieved.

"Large," I said, and he turned his back to me to make the drink. He realized his mistake but it was too late. He stiffened, ready for the gunshot or the blow behind the ear. When it didn't come, he turned back to me.

"I'm sorry," he said. "What size did you say?"

"Small," I said and changed the story.

"But I thought you said large."

25 "If you knew I wanted a large, then why did you ask me again?" I asked him and laughed. He looked at me, couldn't decide if I was giving him serious shit or just goofing. There was something about him I liked, even if it was three in the morning and he was white.

"Hey," I said. "Forget the Slushie. What I want to know is if you know all the words to the theme from 'The Brady Bunch'?"

He looked at me, confused at first, then laughed.

"Shit," he said. "I was hoping you weren't crazy. You were scaring me."

"Well, I'm going to get crazy if you don't know the words."

30   He laughed loudly then, told me to take the Creamsicle for free. He was the graveyard-shift manager and those little demonstrations of power tickled him. All seventy-five cents of it. I knew how much everything cost.

"Thanks," I said to him and walked out the door. I took my time walking home, let the heat of the night melt the Creamsicle all over my hand. At three in the morning I could act just as young as I wanted to act. There was no one around to ask me to grow up.

In Seattle, I broke lamps. She and I would argue and I'd break a lamp, just pick it up and throw it down. At first she'd buy replacement lamps, expensive and beautiful. But after a while she'd buy lamps from Goodwill or garage sales. Then she just gave up the idea entirely and we'd argue in the dark.

"You're just like your brother," she'd yell. "Drunk all the time and stupid."

"My brother don't drink that much."

35   She and I never tried to hurt each other physically. I did love her, after all, and she loved me. But those arguments were just as damaging as the fist. Words can be like that, you know? Whenever I get into arguments now, I remember her and I also remember Muhammad Ali. He knew the power of his fists but, more importantly, he knew the power of his words, too. Even though he only had an IQ of 80 or so, Ali was a genius. And she was a genius, too. She knew exactly what to say to cause me the most pain.

But don't get me wrong. I walked through that relationship with an executioner's hood. Or more appropriately, with war paint and sharp arrows. She was a kindergarten teacher and I continually insulted her for that.

"Hey, schoolmarm," I asked. "Did your kids teach you anything new today?"

And I always had crazy dreams. I always have had them, but it seemed they became nightmares more often in Seattle.

In one dream, she was a missionary's wife and I was a minor war chief. We fell in love and tried to keep it secret. But the missionary caught us fucking in the barn and shot me. As I lay dying, my tribe learned of the shooting and attacked the whites all across the reservation. I died and my soul drifted above the reservation.

40   Disembodied, I could see everything that was happening. Whites killing Indians and Indians killing whites. At fist it was small, just my tribe and the few whites who lived there. But my dream grew, intensified. Other tribes arrived on horseback to continue the slaughter of whites, and the United States Cavalry rode into battle.

The most vivid image of that dream stays with me. Three mounted soldiers played polo with a dead Indian woman's head. When I first dreamed it, I thought it was just a product of my anger and imagination. But since then, I've read similar accounts of that kind of evil in the old West. Even more terrifying, though, is the fact that those kinds of brutal things are happening today in places like El Salvador.

All I know for sure, though, is that I woke from that dream in terror, packed up all my possessions, and left Seattle in the middle of the night.

"I love you," she said as I left her. "And don't ever come back."

I drove through the night, over the Cascades, down into the plains of central Washington, and back home to the Spokane Indian Reservation.

. . .

45   When I finished the Creamsicle that the 7-11 clerk gave me, I held the wooden stick up into the air and shouted out very loudly. A couple of lights flashed on in windows and a police car cruised by me a few minutes later. I waved to the men in blue and they wave back accidentally. When I got home it was still too hot to sleep so I picked up a week-old newspaper from the floor and read.

There was another civil war, another terrorist bomb exploded, and one more plane crashed and all aboard were presumed dead. The crime rate was rising in every city with populations larger than 100,000, and a farmer in Iowa shot his banker after foreclosure on his 1,000 acres.

A kid from Spokane won the local spelling bee by spelling the word *rhinoceros*.

When I got back to the reservation, my family wasn't surprised to see me. They'd been expecting me back since the day I left for Seattle. There's an old Indian poet who said that Indians can reside in the city, but they can never live there. That's as close to the truth as any of us can get.

Mostly I watched television. For weeks I flipped through channels, searched for answers in the game shows and soap operas. My mother would circle the want ads in red and hand the paper to me.

50   "What are you going to do with the rest of your life?" she asked.

"Don't know," I said, and normally, for almost any other Indian in the country, that would have been a perfectly fine answer. But I was special, a former college student, a smart kid. I was one of those Indians who was supposed to make it, to rise above the rest of the reservation like a fucking eagle or something. I was the new kind of warrior.

For a few months I didn't even look at the want ads my mother circled, just left the newspaper where she had set it down. After a while, though, I got tired of television and started to play basketball again. I'd been a good player in high school, nearly great, and almost played at the college I attended for a couple of years. But I'd been too out of shape from drinking and sadness to ever be good again. Still, I liked the way the ball felt in my hands and the away my feet felt inside my shoes.

At first I just shot baskets by myself. It was selfish, and I also wanted to learn the game again before I played against anybody else. Since I had been good before and embarrassed fellow tribal members, I knew they would want to take revenge on me. Forget about the cowboys versus Indians business. The most intense competition on any reservation is Indians versus Indians.

But on the night I was ready to play for real, there was this white guy at the gym, playing with all the Indians.

55   "Who is that?" I asked Jimmy Seyler.

"He's the new BIA[1] chief's kid."

"Can he play?"

"Oh, yeah."

And he could play. He played Indian ball, fast and loose, better than all the Indians there.

60   "How long's he been playing here?" I asked.

[1] Bureau of Indian Affairs

"Long enough."

I stretched my muscles, and everybody watched me. All these Indians watched one of their old and dusty heroes. Even though I had played most of my ball at the white high school I went to, I was still all Indian, you know? I was Indian when it counted, and this BIA kid needed to be beaten by an Indian, any Indian.

I jumped into the game and played well for a little while. It felt good. I hit a few shots, grabbed a rebound or two, played enough defense to keep the other team honest. Then that white kid took over the game. He was too good. Later, he'd play college ball back East and would nearly make the Knicks team a couple years on. But we didn't know any of that would happen. We just knew he was better that day and every other day.

The next morning I woke up tired and hungry, so I grabbed the want ads, found a job I wanted, and drove to Spokane to get it. I've been working at the high school exchange program ever since, typing and answering phones. Sometimes I wonder if the people on the other end of the line know that I'm Indian and if their voices would change if they did know.

65   One day I picked up the phone and it was her, calling from Seattle.

"I got your number from you mom," she said. "I'm glad you're working."

"Yeah, nothing like a regular paycheck."

"Are you drinking?"

"No, I've been on the wagon for almost a year."

70   "Good."

The connection was good. I could hear her breathing in the spaces between our words. How do you talk to the real person whose ghost has haunted you? How do you tell the differences between the two?

"Listen," I said. "I'm sorry for everything."

"Me, too."

"What's going to happen to us?" I asked her and wished I had the answer for myself.

75   "I don't know," she said. "I want to change the world."

These days, living alone in Spokane, I wish I lived closer to the river, to the falls where ghosts of salmon jump. I wish I could sleep. I put down my paper or book and turn off all the lights, lie quietly in the dark. It may take hours, even years, for me to sleep again. There's nothing surprising or disappointing in that.

I know how all my dreams end anyway.

► QUESTIONS FOR READING AND WRITING

1. To what extent is your response to this story influenced by your own experience?
2. What do you think the protagonist means when he says, "When one person starts to look at another like a criminal, then the love is over"?
3. Why do you think he is so angry?
4. At the end of the story he says, "I know how all my dreams end anyway." What do you think he means?

5. Do you think "The Lone Ranger and Tonto Fistfight in Heaven" is an appropriate title for this story? Explain.

MARGARET ATWOOD (b. 1939)

Margaret Atwood was born in Ottawa, Canada, and took extensive trips during her childhood through the wilds of Canada with her father, an entomologist. In 1962, the same year she graduated from the University of Toronto, she published her first book of poetry, Double Persephone. *She has since published numerous works of fiction, poetry, and criticism, including the novels* Surfacing *(1972),* Cat's Eye *(1988),* The Handmaid's Tale *(1985), which was made into a film, and* Alias Grace *(1996). Her most recent novel is* The Blind Assassin *(2000). A fierce proponent of Canadian literature as well as an ardent feminist, Atwood has been instrumental in forging a Canadian cultural identity separate from that of England and the United States. She told an interviewer in* Ms. *magazine, "I began as a profoundly apolitical writer, but then I began to do what all novelists and some poets do: I began to describe the world around me."*

HAPPY ENDINGS   [1983]

John and Mary meet.
What happens next?
If you want a happy ending, try A.

A

John and Mary fall in love and get married. They both have worthwhile and remunerative jobs which they find stimulating and challenging. They buy a charming house. Real estate values go up. Eventually, when they can afford live-in help, they have two children, to whom they are devoted. The children turn out well. John and Mary have a stimulating and challenging sex life and worthwhile friends. They go on fun vacations together. They retire. They both have hobbies which they find stimulating and challenging. Eventually they die. This is the end of the story.

B

Mary falls in love with John but John doesn't fall in love with Mary. He merely uses her body for selfish pleasure and ego gratification of a tepid kind. He comes to her apartment twice a week and she cooks him dinner, you'll notice that he doesn't ever consider her worth the price of a dinner out, and after he's eaten the dinner he fucks her and after that he falls asleep, while she does the dishes so he won't think she's untidy, having all those dirty dishes lying around, and puts on fresh lipstick so she'll look good when he wakes up, but when he wakes up he doesn't even notice, he puts on his socks and his shorts and his pants and his shirt and his tie and his shoes, the reverse order from the one in which he took them off. He doesn't take off Mary's clothes, she takes them off herself, she acts as if she's dying for it every time, not because she likes sex exactly, she doesn't, but she wants John to think she does because if they do often enough surely he'll get used to her, he'll come to depend on her and they will get married, but John goes out the door with hardly so much as a good-night and three days later he turns up at six o'clock and they do the whole thing over again.

Mary gets run-down. Crying is bad for your face, everyone knows that and so does Mary but she can't stop. People at work notice. Her friends tell her John is a rat, a pig, a dog, he isn't' good enough for her, but she can't believe it. Inside John, she thinks, is another John, who is much nicer. This other John will emerge like a butterfly from a cocoon, a Jack from the box, a pit from a prune, if the first John is only squeezed enough.

One evening John complains about the food. He has never complained about the food before. Mary is hurt.

5   Her friends tell her they've seen him in a restaurant with another woman, whose name is Madge. It's not even Madge that finally gets to Mary; it's the restaurant. John has never taken Mary to a restaurant. Mary collects all the sleeping pills and aspirins she can find, and takes them and a half of bottle of sherry. You can see what kind of a woman she is by the fact that it's not even whiskey. She leaves a note for John. She hopes he'll discover her and get her to the hospital in time and repent and then they can get married, but this fails to happen and she dies.

John marries Madge and everything continues as in A.

C

John, who is an older man, falls in love with Mary, and Mary, who is only twenty-two, feels sorry for him because he's worried about his hair falling out. She sleeps with him even though she's not in love with him. She met him at work. She's in love with someone called James, who is twenty-two also and not yet ready to settle down.

John on the contrary settled down long ago: this is what is bothering him. John has a steady, respectable job and is getting ahead in his field, but Mary isn't impressed by him, she's impressed by James, who has a motorcycle and a fabulous record collection. But James is often away on his motorcycle, being free. Freedom isn't the same for girls, so in the meantime Mary spends Thursday evenings with John. Thursdays are the only days John can get away.

John is married to a woman called Madge and they have two children, a charming house which they bought just before the real estate values went up, and hobbies which they find stimulating and challenging, when they have the time. John tells Mary how important she is to him, but of course he can't leave his wife because a commitment is a commitment. He goes on about this more than is necessary and Mary finds if boring, but older men can keep it up longer so on the whole she has a fairly good time.

10   One day James breezes in on his motorcycle with some top-grade California hybrid and James and Mary get higher than you'd believe possible and they climb into bed. Everything becomes very underwater, but along comes John, who has a key to Mary's apartment. He finds them stoned and entwined. He's hardly in any position to be jealous, considering Madge, but nevertheless he's overcome with despair. Finally, he's middle-aged, in two years he'll be bald as an egg and he can't stand it. He purchases a handgun, saying he needs it for target practice—this is the thin part of the plot, but it can be dealt with later—and shoots the two of them and himself.

Madge, after a suitable period of mourning, marries an understanding man called Fred and everything continues as in A, but under different names.

D

Fred and Madge have no problems. They get along exceptionally well and are good at working out any little difficulties that may arise. But their charming house is by the seashore and one day a giant tidal wave approaches. Real estate values go down. The rest of the story is about what caused the tidal wave and how they escape from it. They do, though thousands drown, but Fred and Madge are virtuous and luck. Finally on high ground they clasp each other, wet and dripping and grateful, and continue as in A.

E

Yes, but Fred has a bad heart. The rest of the story is about how kind and understanding they both are until Fred dies. Then Madge devotes herself to charity work until the end of A. If you like, it can be "Madge," "cancer," "guilty and confused," and "bird watching."

F

If you think this is all too bourgeois, make John a revolutionary and Mary a counterespionage agent and see how far that gets you. Remember, this is Canada. You'll still end up with A, though in between you may get a lustful brawling saga of passionate involvement, a chronicle of our times, sort of.

15   You'll have to face it, the endings are the same however you slice it. Don't be deluded by any other endings, they're all fake, either deliberately fake, with malicious intent to deceive, or just motivated by excessive optimism if not by downright sentimentality.

The only authentic ending is the one provided her:
John and Mary die. John and Mary die. John and Mary die.

So much for endings. Beginnings are always more fun. True connoisseurs, however, are known to favor the stretch in between, since it's the hardest to do anything with.

That's about all that can be said for plots, which anyway are just one thing after another, a what and a what and a what.

20   Now they How and Why.

➤ *QUESTIONS FOR READING AND WRITING*

1. To what extent is your response to these different scenarios affected by your own experience?
2. The narrator says, "Beginnings are always more fun" and the endings are always the same. But the "stretch in between" is "the hardest to do anything with." Do you agree? Explain.
3. In what way is "How and Why" most difficult?

JAMES BALDWIN (1924–1987)

James Baldwin grew up in poverty in Harlem with his mother, eight half-brothers and -sisters, and a stepfather whom he hated. He became a preacher at the age of 14, but after graduating from high school he left the ministry disillusioned. Turning to writing, he struggled for over ten years to complete his first novel, the autobiographical Go Tell It on the Mountain *(1953), a publication which instantly made Baldwin one of the most important American writers of his time. In his subsequent work, which included numerous novels, plays, and essays, Baldwin continually explored issues of racial and sexual identity, and the problems of the civil rights movement, often writing of his own experiences of his family and Harlem. Unhappy with racial conditions in the United States, Baldwin spent most of his adult life in Paris, returning to the United States only occasionally.*

SONNY'S BLUES   [1957]

I read about it in the paper, in the subway, on my way to work. I read it, and I couldn't believe it, and I read it again. Then perhaps I just stared at it, at the newsprint spelling out his name, spelling out the story. I stared at it in the swinging lights of the subway car, and in the faces and bodies of the people, and in my own face, trapped in the darkness which roared outside.

It was not to be believed and I kept telling myself that, as I walked from the subway station to the high school. And at the same time I couldn't doubt it. I was scared, scared for Sonny. He became real to me again. A great block of ice got settled in my belly and kept melting there slowly all day long, while I taught my classes algebra. It was a special kind of ice. It kept melting, sending trickles of ice water all up and down my veins, but it never got less. Sometimes it hardened and seemed to expand until I felt my guts were going to come spilling out or that I was going to choke or scream. This would always be at a moment when I was remembering some specific thing Sonny had once said or done.

When he was about as old as the boys in my classes his face had been bright and open, there was a lot of copper in it; and he'd had wonderfully direct brown eyes, and great gentleness and privacy. I wondered what he looked like now. He had been picked up, the evening before, in a raid on an apartment downtown, for peddling and using heroin.

I couldn't believe it: but what I mean by that is that I couldn't find any room for it anywhere inside me. I had kept it outside me for a long time. I hadn't wanted to know. I had had suspicions, but I didn't name them, I kept putting them away. I told myself that Sonny was wild, but he wasn't crazy. And he'd always been a good boy, he hadn't ever turned hard or evil or disrespectful, the way kids can, so quick, so quick, especially in Harlem. I didn't want to believe that I'd ever see my brother going down, coming to nothing, all that light in his face gone out, in the condition I'd already seen so many others. Yet it had happened and here I was, talking about algebra to a lot of boys who might, every one of them for all I knew, be popping off needles every time they went to the head. Maybe it did more for them than algebra could.

5   I was sure that the first time Sonny had ever had horse, he couldn't have been much older than these boys were now. These boys, now, were living as we'd been living then, they were growing up with a rush and their heads bumped abruptly against the low ceiling of their actual possibilities. They were filled with rage. All they really knew were two darknesses, the darkness of their lives, which was now closing in on them, and the darkness of the movies, which had blinded them to that other darkness, and in which they now, vindictively, dreamed, at once more together than they were at any other time, and more alone.

When the last bell rang, the last class ended, I let out my breath. It seemed I'd been holding it for all that time. My clothes were wet—I may have looked as though I'd been sitting in a steam bath, all dressed up, all afternoon. I sat alone in the classroom a long time. I listened to the boys outside, downstairs, shouting and cursing and laughing. Their laughter struck me for perhaps the first time. It was not the joyous laughter which—God knows why—one associates with children. It was mocking and insular, its intent was to denigrate. It was disenchanted, and in this, also, lay the authority of their curses. Perhaps I was listening to them because I was thinking about my brother and in them I heard my brother. And myself.

One boy was whistling a tune, at once very complicated and very simple, it seemed to be pouring out of him as though he were a bird, and it sounded very cool and moving through all that harsh, bright air, only just holding its own through all those other sounds.

I stood up and walked over to the window and looked down into the courtyard. It was the beginning of the spring and the sap was rising in the boys. A teacher passed through them every now and again, quickly, as though he or she couldn't wait to get out of that courtyard, to get those boys out of their sight and off their minds. I started collecting my stuff. I thought I'd better get home and talk to Isabel.

The courtyard was almost deserted by the time I got downstairs. I saw this boy standing in the shadow of a doorway, looking just like Sonny. I almost called his name. Then I saw that it wasn't Sonny, but somebody we used to know, a boy from around our block. He'd been Sonny's friend. He'd never been mine, having been too young for me, and, anyway, I'd never liked him. And now, even though he was a grown-up man, he still hung around that block, still spent hours on the street corners, was always high and raggy. I used to run into him from time to time and he'd often work around to asking me for a quarter or fifty cents. He always had some real good excuse, too, and I always gave it to him, I don't know why.

10   But now, abruptly, I hated him. I couldn't stand the way he looked at me, partly like a dog, partly like a cunning child. I wanted to ask him what the hell he was doing in the school courtyard.

He sort of shuffled over to me, and he said, "I see you got the papers. So you already know about it."

"You mean about Sonny? Yes, I already know about it. How come they didn't get you?"

He grinned. It made him repulsive and it also brought to mind what he'd looked like as a kid. "I wasn't there. I stay away from them people."

"Good for you." I offered him a cigarette and I watched him through the smoke. "You come all the way down here just to tell me about Sonny?"

15   "That's right." He was sort of shaking his head and his eyes looked strange, as though they were about to cross. The bright sun deadened his damp dark brown skin and it made his eyes look yellow and showed up the dirt in his kinked hair. He smelled funky. I moved a little away from him and I said, "Well, thanks. But I already know about it and I got to get home."

"I'll walk you a little ways," he said. We started walking. There were a couple of kids still loitering in the courtyard and one of them said goodnight to me and looked strangely at the boy beside me.

"What're you going to do?" he asked me. "I mean, about Sonny?"

"Look. I haven't seen Sonny for over a year, I'm not sure I'm going to do anything. Anyway, what the hell *can* I do?"

"That's right," he said quickly, "ain't nothing you can do. Can't much help old Sonny no more, I guess."

20   It was what I was thinking and so it seemed to me he had no right to say it.

"I'm surprised at Sonny, though," he went on—he had a funny way of talking, he looked straight ahead as though he were talking to himself—"I thought Sonny was a smart boy, I thought he was too smart to get hung."

"I guess he thought so too," I said sharply, "and that's how he got hung. And how about you? You're pretty goddamn smart, I bet."

Then he looked directly at me, just for a minute. "I ain't smart," he said. "If I was smart, I'd have reached for a pistol a long time ago."

"Look. Don't tell *me* your sad story, if it was up to me, I'd give you one." Then I felt guilty—guilty, probably, for never having supposed that the poor bastard *had* a story of his own, much less a sad one, and I asked, quickly, "What's going to happen to him now?"

25   He didn't answer this. He was off by himself some place. "Funny thing," he said, and from his tone we might have been discussing the quickest way to get to Brooklyn, "when I saw the papers this morning, the first thing I asked myself was if I had anything to do with it. I felt sort of responsible."

I began to listen more carefully. The subway station was on the corner, just before us, and I stopped. He stopped, too. We were in front of a bar and he ducked slightly, peering in, but whoever he was looking for didn't seem to be there. The juke box was blasting away with something black and bouncy and I half watched the barmaid as she danced her way from the juke box to her place behind the bar. And I watched her face as she laughingly responded to something someone said to her, still keeping time to the music. When she smiled one saw the little girl, one sensed the doomed, still-struggling woman beneath the battered face of the semi-whore.

"I never *give* Sonny nothing," the boy said finally, "but a long time ago I come to school high and Sonny asked me how it felt." He paused, I couldn't bear to watch him, I watched the barmaid, and I listened to the music which seemed to be causing the pavement to shake. "I told him it felt great." The music stopped, the barmaid paused and watched the juke box until the music began again. "It did."

All this was carrying me some place I didn't want to go. I certainly didn't want to know how it felt. It filled everything, the people, the houses, the music, the dark, quicksilver barmaid, with menace; and this menace was their reality.

"What's going to happen to him now?" I asked again.

30   "They'll send him away some place and they'll try to cure him." He shook his head. "Maybe he'll even think he's kicked the habit. Then they'll let him loose"—he gestured, throwing his cigarette into the gutter. "That's all."

"What do you mean, that's *all?*"

But I knew what he meant.

"I *mean,* that's *all.*" He turned his head and looked at me, pulling down the corners of his mouth. "Don't you know what I mean?" he asked, softly.

"How the hell *would* I know what you mean?" I almost whispered it, I don't know why.

35   "That's right," he said to the air, "how would *he* know what I mean?" He turned toward me again, patient and calm, and yet I somehow felt him shaking, shaking as though he were going to fall apart. I felt that ice in my guts again, the dread I'd felt all afternoon; and again I watched the barmaid, moving about the bar, washing glasses, and singing. "Listen. They'll let him out and then it'll just start all over again. That's what I mean."

"You mean—they'll let him out. And then he'll just start working his way back in again. You mean he'll never kick the habit. Is that what you mean?"

"That's right," he said, cheerfully. "*You* see what I mean."

"Tell me," I said at last, "why does he want to die? He must want to die, he's killing himself, why does he want to die?"

He looked at me in surprise. He licked his lips. "He don't want to die. He wants to live. Don't nobody want to die, ever."

40   Then I wanted to ask him—too many things. He could not have answered, or if he had, I could not have borne the answers. I started walking. "Well, I guess it's none of my business."

"It's going to be rough on old Sonny," he said. We reached the subway station. "This is your station?" he asked. I nodded. I took one step down. "Damn!" he said, suddenly. I looked up at him. He grinned again. "Damn it if I didn't leave all my money home. You ain't got a dollar on you, have you? Just for a couple of days, is all."

All at once something inside gave and threatened to come pouring out of me. I didn't hate him any more. I felt that in another moment I'd start crying like a child.

"Sure," I said. "Don't sweat." I looked in my wallet and didn't have a dollar, I only had a five. "Here," I said. "That hold you?"

He didn't look at it—he didn't want to look at it. A terrible closed look came over his face, as though he were keeping the number on the bill a secret from him and me. "Thanks," he said, and now he was dying to see me go. "Don't worry about Sonny. Maybe I'll write him or something."

45   "Sure," I said. "You do that. So long."

"Be seeing you," he said. I went on down the steps.

And I didn't write Sonny or send him anything for a long time. When I finally did, it was just after my little girl died, he wrote me back a letter which made me feel like a bastard.

Here's what he said:

Dear brother,

50   You don't know how much I needed to hear from you. I wanted to write you many a time but I dug how much I must have hurt you and so I didn't write. But now I feel like a man who's been trying to climb up out of some deep, real deep and funky hole and just saw the sun up there, outside. I got to get outside.

I can't tell you much about how I got here. I mean I don't know how to tell you. I guess I was afraid of something or I was trying to escape from something and you know I have never been very strong in the head (smile). I'm glad Mama and Daddy are dead and can't see what's happened to their son and I swear if I'd known what I was doing I would never have hurt you so, you and a lot of other fine people who were nice to me and who believed in me.

I don't want you to think it had anything to do with me being a musician. It's more than that. Or maybe less than that. I can't get anything straight in my head down here and I try not to think about what's going to happen to me when I get outside again. Sometime I think I'm going to flip and *never* get outside and sometime I think I'll come straight back. I tell you one thing, though, I'd rather blow my brains out than go through this again. But that's what they all say, so they tell me. If I tell you when I'm coming to New York and if you could meet me, I sure would appreciate it. Give my love to Isabel and the kids and I was sure sorry to hear about little Gracie. I wish I could be like Mama and say the Lord's will be done, but I don't know it seems to me that trouble is the one thing that never does get stopped and I don't know what good it does to blame it on the Lord. But maybe it does some good if you believe it.

Your brother,
Sonny

55   Then I kept in constant touch with him and I sent him whatever I could and I went to meet him when he came back to New York. When I saw him many things I

thought I had forgotten came flooding back to me. This was because I had begun, finally, to wonder about Sonny, about the life that Sonny lived inside. This life, whatever it was, had made him older and thinner and it had deepened the distant stillness in which he had always moved. He looked very unlike my baby brother. Yet, when he smiled, when we shook hands, the baby brother I'd never known looked out from the depths of his private life, like an animal waiting to be coaxed into the light.

"How you been keeping?" he asked me.

"All right. And you?"

"Just fine." He was smiling all over his face. "It's good to see you again."

"It's good to see you."

60   The seven years' difference in our ages lay between us like a chasm: I wondered if these years would ever operate between us as a bridge. I was remembering, and it made it hard to catch my breath, that I had been there when he was born; and I had heard the first words he had ever spoken. When he started to walk, he walked from our mother straight to me. I caught him just before he fell when he took the first steps he ever took in this world.

"How's Isabel?"

"Just fine. She's dying to see you."

"And the boys?"

"They're fine, too. They're anxious to see their uncle."

65   "Oh, come on. You know they don't remember me."

"Are you kidding? Of course they remember you."

He grinned again. We got into a taxi. We had a lot to say to each other, far too much to know how to begin.

As the taxi began to move, I asked, "You still want to go to India?"

He laughed. "You still remember that. Hell, no. This place is Indian enough for me."

70   "It used to belong to them," I said.

And he laughed again. "They damn sure knew what they were doing when they got rid of it."

Years ago, when he was around fourteen, he'd been all hipped on the idea of going to India. He read books about people sitting on rocks, naked, in all kinds of weather, but mostly bad, naturally, and walking barefoot through hot coals and arriving at wisdom. I used to say that it sounded to me as though they were getting away from wisdom as fast as they could. I think he sort of looked down on me for that.

"Do you mind," he asked, "if we have the driver drive alongside the park? On the west side—I haven't seen the city in so long."

"Of course not," I said. I was afraid that I might sound as though I were humoring him, but I hoped he wouldn't take it that way.

75   So we drove along, between the green of the park and the stony, lifeless elegance of hotels and apartment buildings, toward the vivid, killing streets of our childhood. These streets hadn't changed, though housing projects jutted up out of them now like rocks in the middle of a boiling sea. Most of the houses in which we had grown up had vanished, as had the stores from which we had stolen, the basements in which we had first tried sex, the rooftops from which we had hurled tin cans and bricks. But houses exactly like the houses of our past yet dominated the landscape,

boys exactly like the boys we once had been found themselves smothering in these houses, came down into the streets for light and air and found themselves encircled by disaster. Some escaped the trap, most didn't. Those who got out always left something of themselves behind, as some animals amputate a leg and leave it in the trap. It might be said, perhaps, that I had escaped, after all, I was a school teacher; or that Sonny had, he hadn't lived in Harlem for years. Yet, as the cab moved uptown through streets which seemed, with a rush, to darken with dark people, and as I covertly studied Sonny's face, it came to me that what we both were seeking through our separate cab windows was that part of ourselves which had been left behind. It's always at the hour of trouble and confrontation that the missing member aches.

We hit 110th Street and started rolling up Lenox Avenue. And I'd known this avenue all my life, but it seemed to me again, as it had seemed on the day I'd first heard about Sonny's trouble, filled with a hidden menace which was its very breath of life.

"We almost there," said Sonny.

"Almost." We were both too nervous to say anything more.

We live in a housing project. It hasn't been up long. A few days after it was up it seemed uninhabitably new, now, of course, it's already rundown. It looks like a parody of the good, clean, faceless life—God knows the people who live in it do their best to make it a parody. The beat-looking grass lying around isn't enough to make their lives green, the hedges will never hold out the streets, and they know it. The big windows fool no one, they aren't big enough to make space out of no space. They don't bother with the windows, they watch the TV screen instead. The playground is most popular with the children who don't play at jacks, or skip rope, or roller skate, or swing, and they can be found in it after dark. We moved in partly because it's not too far from where I teach, and partly for the kids; but it's really just like the houses in which Sonny and I grew up. The same things happen, they'll have the same things to remember. The moment Sonny and I started into the house I had the feeling that I was simply bringing him back into the danger he had almost died trying to escape.

80   Sonny has never been talkative. So I don't know why I was sure he'd be dying to talk to me when supper was over the first night. Everything went fine, the oldest boy remembered him, and the youngest boy liked him, and Sonny had remembered to bring something for each of them; and Isabel, who is really much nicer than I am, more open and giving, had gone to a lot of trouble about dinner and was genuinely glad to see him. And she's always been able to tease Sonny in a way that I haven't. It was nice to see her face so vivid again and to hear her laugh and watch her make Sonny laugh. She wasn't, or, anyway, she didn't seem to be, at all uneasy or embarrassed. She chatted as though there were no subject which had to be avoided and she got Sonny past his first, faint stiffness. And thank God she was there, for I was filled with that icy dread again. Everything I did seemed awkward to me, and everything I said sounded freighted with hidden meaning. I was trying to remember everything I'd heard about dope addiction and I couldn't help watching Sonny for signs. I wasn't doing it out of malice. I was trying to find out something about my brother. I was dying to hear him tell me he was safe.

"Safe!" my father grunted, whenever Mama suggested trying to move to a neighborhood which might be safer for children. "Safe, hell! Ain't no place safe for kids, nor nobody."

He always went on like this, but he wasn't, ever, really as bad as he sounded, not even on weekends, when he got drunk. As a matter of fact, he was always on the lookout for "something a little better," but he died before he found it. He died suddenly, during a drunken weekend in the middle of the war, when Sonny was fifteen. He and Sonny hadn't ever got on too well. And this was partly because Sonny was the apple of his father's eye. It was because he loved Sonny so much and was frightened for him, that he was always fighting with him. It doesn't do any good to fight with Sonny. Sonny just moves back, inside himself, where he can't be reached. But the principal reason that they never hit it off is that they were so much alike. Daddy was big and rough and loud-talking, just the opposite of Sonny, but they both had —that same privacy.

Mama tried to tell me something about this, just after Daddy died. I was home on leave from the army.

This was the last time I ever saw my mother alive. Just the same, this picture gets all mixed up in my mind with pictures I had of her when she was younger. The way I always see her is the way she used to be on a Sunday afternoon, say, when the old folks were talking after the big Sunday dinner. I always see her wearing pale blue. She'd be sitting on the sofa. And my father would be sitting in the easy chair, not far from her. And the living room would be full of church folks and relatives. There they sit, in chairs all around the living room, and the night is creeping up outside, but nobody knows it yet. You can see the darkness growing against the window-panes and you hear the street noises every now and again, or maybe the jangling beat of a tambourine from one of the churches close by, but it's real quiet in the room. For a moment nobody's talking, but every face looks darkening, like the sky outside. And my mother rocks a little from the waist, and my father's eyes are closed. Everyone is looking at something a child can't see. For a minute they've forgotten the children. Maybe a kid is lying on the rug, half asleep. Maybe somebody's got a kid in his lap and is absent-mindedly stroking the kid's head. Maybe there's a kid, quiet and big-eyed, curled up in a big chair in the corner. The silence, the darkness coming, and the darkness in the faces frighten the child obscurely. He hopes that the hand which strokes his forehead will never stop—will never die. He hopes that there will never come a time when the old folks won't be sitting around the living room, talking about where they've come from, and what they've seen, and what's happened to them and their kinfolk.

85   But something deep and watchful in the child knows that this is bound to end, is already ending. In a moment someone will get up and turn on the light. Then the old folks will remember the children and they won't talk any more that day. And when light fills the room, the child is filled with darkness. He knows that every time this happens he's moved just a little closer to that darkness outside. The darkness outside is what the old folks have been talking about. It's what they've come from. It's what they endure. The child knows that they won't talk any more because if he knows too much about what's happened to *them,* he'll know too much too soon, about what's going to happen to *him.*

The last time I talked to my mother, I remember I was restless. I wanted to get out and see Isabel. We weren't married then and we had a lot to straighten out between us.

There Mama sat, in black, by the window. She was humming an old church song, *Lord, you brought me from a long ways off.* Sonny was out somewhere. Mama kept watching the streets.

"I don't know," she said, "if I'll ever see you again, after you go off from here. But I hope you'll remember the things I tried to teach you."

"Don't talk like that," I said, and smiled. "You'll be here a long time yet."

90   She smiled, too, but she said nothing. She was quiet for a long time. And I said, "Mama, don't you worry about nothing. I'll be writing all the time, and you be getting the checks. . . ."

"I want to talk to you about your brother," she said, suddenly. "If anything happens to me he ain't going to have nobody to look out for him."

"Mama," I said, "ain't nothing going to happen to you *or* Sonny. Sonny's all right. He's a good boy and he's got good sense."

"It ain't a question of his being a good boy," Mama said, "nor of his having good sense. It ain't only the bad ones, nor yet the dumb ones that gets sucked under." She stopped, looking at me. "Your Daddy once had a brother," she said, and she smiled in a way that made me feel she was in pain. "You didn't never know that, did you?"

"No," I said, "I never knew that," and I watched her face.

95   "Oh, yes," she said, "your Daddy had a brother." She looked out of the window again. "I know you never saw your Daddy cry. But *I* did—many a time, through all these years."

I asked her, "What happened to his brother? How come nobody's ever talked about him?"

This was the first time I ever saw my mother look old.

"His brother got killed," she said, "when he was just a little younger than you are now. I knew him. He was a fine boy. He was maybe a little full of the devil, but he didn't mean nobody no harm."

Then she stopped and the room was silent, exactly as it had sometimes been on those Sunday afternoons. Mama kept looking out into the streets.

100   "He used to have a job in the mill," she said, "and, like all young folks, he just liked to perform on Saturday nights. Saturday nights, him and your father would drift around to different places, go to dances and things like that, or just sit around with people they knew, and your father's brother would sing, he had a fine voice, and play along with himself on his guitar. Well, this particular Saturday night, him and your father was coming home from some place, and they were both a little drunk and there was a moon that night, it was bright like day. Your father's brother was feeling kind of good, and he was whistling to himself, and he had his guitar slung over his shoulder. They was coming down a hill and beneath them was a road that turned off from the highway. Well, your father's brother, being always kind of frisky, decided to run down this hill, and he did, with that guitar banging and clanging behind him, and he ran across the road, and he was making water behind a tree. And your father was sort of amused at him and he was still coming down the hill, kind of slow. Then he heard a car motor and that same minute his brother stepped

from behind the tree, into the road, in the moonlight. And he started to cross the road. And your father started to run down the hill, he says he don't know why. This car was full of white men. They was all drunk, and when they seen your father's brother they let out a great whoop and holler and they aimed the car straight at him. They was having fun, they just wanted to scare him, the way they do sometimes, you know. But they was drunk. And I guess the boy, being drunk, too, and scared, kind of lost his head. By the time he jumped it was too late. Your father says he heard his brother scream when the car rolled over him, and he heard the wood of that guitar when it give, and he heard them strings go flying, and he heard them white men shouting, and the car kept on a-going and it ain't stopped till this day. And, time your father got down the hill, his brother weren't nothing but blood and pulp."

Tears were gleaming on my mother's face. There wasn't anything I could say.

"He never mentioned it," she said, "because I never let him mention it before you children. Your Daddy was like a crazy man that night and for many a night thereafter. He says he never in his life seen anything as dark as that road after the lights of that car had gone away. Weren't nothing, weren't nobody on that road, just your Daddy and his brother and that busted guitar. Oh, yes. Your Daddy never did really get right again. Till the day he died he weren't sure but that every white man he saw was the man that killed his brother."

She stopped and took out her handkerchief and dried her eyes and looked at me.

"I ain't telling you all this," she said, "to make you scared or bitter or to make you hate nobody. I'm telling you this because you got a brother. And the world ain't changed."

105   I guess I didn't want to believe this. I guess she saw this in my face. She turned away from me, toward the window again, searching those streets.

"But I praise my Redeemer," she said at last, "that He called your Daddy home before me. I ain't saying it to throw no flowers at myself, but, I declare, it keeps me from feeling too cast down to know I helped your father get safely through this world. Your father always acted like he was the roughest, strongest man on earth. And everybody took him to be like that. But if he hadn't had me there—to see his tears!"

She was crying again. Still, I couldn't move. I said, "Lord, Lord, Mama, I didn't know it was like that."

"Oh, honey," she said, "there's a lot that you don't know. But you are going to find out." She stood up from the window and came over to me. "You got to hold on to your brother," she said, "and don't let him fall, no matter what it looks like is happening to him and no matter how evil you gets with him. You going to be evil with him many a time. But don't you forget what I told you, you hear?"

"I won't forget," I said. "Don't you worry, I won't forget. I won't let nothing happen to Sonny."

110   My mother smiled as though she were amused at something she saw in my face. Then, "You may not be able to stop nothing from happening. But you got to let him know you's *there*."

Two days later I was married, and then I was gone. And I had a lot of things on my mind and I pretty well forgot my promise to Mama until I got shipped home on a special furlough for her funeral.

And, after the funeral, with just Sonny and me alone in the empty kitchen, I tried to find out something about him.

"What do you want to do?" I asked him.

"I'm going to be a musician," he said.

115 For he had graduated, in the time I had been away, from dancing to the juke box to finding out who was playing what, and what they were doing with it, and he had bought himself a set of drums.

"You mean, you want to be a drummer?" I somehow had the feeling that being a drummer might be all right for other people but not for my brother Sonny.

"I don't think," he said, looking at me very gravely, "that I'll ever be a good drummer. But I think I can play a piano."

I frowned. I'd never played the role of the older brother quite so seriously before, had scarcely ever, in fact, *asked* Sonny a damn thing. I sensed myself in the presence of something I didn't really know how to handle, didn't understand. So I made my frown a little deeper as I asked: "What kind of musician do you want to be?"

He grinned. "How many kinds do you think there are?"

120 "Be *serious*," I said.

He laughed, throwing his head back, and then looked at me. "I *am* serious."

"Well, then, for Christ's sake, stop kidding around and answer a serious question. I mean, do you want to be a concert pianist, you want to play classical music and all that, or—or what?" Long before I finished he was laughing again. "For Christ's *sake*, Sonny!"

He sobered, but with difficulty. "I'm sorry. But you sound so—*scared!*" and he was off again.

"Well, you may think it's funny now, baby, but it's not going to be so funny when you have to make your living at it, let me tell you *that*." I was furious because I knew he was laughing at me and I didn't know why.

125 "No," he said, very sober now, and afraid, perhaps, that he'd hurt me, "I don't want to be a classical pianist. That isn't what interests me. I mean"—he paused, looking hard at me, as though his eyes would help me to understand, and then gestured helplessly, as though perhaps his hand would help—"I mean, I'll have a lot of studying to do, and I'll have to study *everything*, but, I mean, I want to play *with*— jazz musicians." He stopped. "I want to play jazz," he said.

Well, the word had never before sounded as heavy, as real, as it sounded that afternoon in Sonny's mouth. I just looked at him and I was probably frowning a real frown by this time. I simply couldn't see why on earth he'd want to spend his time hanging around nightclubs, clowning around on bandstands, while people pushed each other around a dance floor. It seemed—beneath him, somehow. I had never thought about it before, had never been forced to, but I suppose I had always put jazz musicians in a class with what Daddy called "good-time people."

"Are you *serious*?"

"Hell, *yes*, I'm serious."

He looked more helpless than ever, and annoyed, and deeply hurt.

130 I suggested, helpfully: "You mean—like Louis Armstrong?"

His face closed as though I'd struck him. "No. I'm not talking about none of that old-time, down home crap."

"Well, look, Sonny, I'm sorry, don't get mad. I just don't altogether get it, that's all. Name somebody—you know, a jazz musician you admire."

"Bird."

"Who?"

135 "Bird! Charlie Parker! Don't they teach you nothing in the goddamn army?"

I lit a cigarette. I was surprised and then a little amused to discover that I was trembling. "I've been out of touch," I said. "You'll have to be patient with me. Now. Who's this Parker character?"

"He's just one of the greatest jazz musicians alive," said Sonny, sullenly, his hands in his pockets, his back to me. "Maybe *the* greatest," he added, bitterly, "that's probably why *you* never heard of him."

"All right," I said, "I'm ignorant. I'm sorry. I'll go out and buy all the cat's records right away, all right?"

"It don't," said Sonny, with dignity, "make any difference to me. I don't care what you listen to. Don't do me no favors."

140 I was beginning to realize that I'd never seen him so upset before. With another part of my mind I was thinking that this would probably turn out to be one of those things kids go through and that I shouldn't make it seem important by pushing it too hard. Still, I didn't think it would do any harm to ask: "Doesn't all this take a lot of time? Can you make a living at it?"

He turned back to me and half leaned, half sat, on the kitchen table. "Everything takes time," he said, "and—well, yes, sure, I can make a living at it. But what I don't seem to be able to make you understand is that it's the only thing I want to do."

"Well, Sonny," I said, gently, "you know people can't always do exactly what they *want* to do—"

"*No*, I don't know that," said Sonny, surprising me. "I think people *ought* to do what they want to do, what else are they alive for?"

"You getting to be a big boy," I said desperately, "it's time you started thinking about your future."

145 "I'm thinking about my future," said Sonny, grimly. "I think about it all the time."

I gave up. I decided, if he didn't change his mind, that we could always talk about it later. "In the meantime," I said, "you got to finish school." We had already decided that he'd have to move in with Isabel and her folks. I knew this wasn't the ideal arrangement because Isabel's folks are inclined to be dicty and they hadn't especially wanted Isabel to marry me. But I didn't know what else to do. "And we have to get you fixed up at Isabel's."

There was a long silence. He moved from the kitchen table to the window. "That's a terrible idea. You know it yourself."

"Do you have a *better* idea?"

He just walked up and down the kitchen for a minute. He was as tall as I was. He had started to shave. I suddenly had the feeling that I didn't know him at all.

150 He stopped at the kitchen table and picked up my cigarettes. Looking at me with a kind of mocking, amused defiance, he put one between his lips. "You mind?"

"You smoking already?"

He lit the cigarette and nodded, watching me through the smoke. "I just wanted to see if I'd have the courage to smoke in front of you." He grinned and blew a great cloud of smoke to the ceiling. "It was easy." He looked at my face. "Come on, now. I bet you was smoking at my age, tell the truth."

I didn't say anything but the truth was on my face, and he laughed. But now there was something very strained in his laugh. "Sure. And I bet that ain't all you was doing."

He was frightening me a little. "Cut the crap," I said. "We already decided that you was going to go and live at Isabel's. Now what's got into you all of a sudden?"

155 "*You* decided it," he pointed out. "*I* didn't decide nothing." He stopped in front of me, leaning against the stove, arms loosely folded. "Look, brother. I don't want to stay in Harlem no more, I really don't." He was very earnest. He looked at me, then over toward the kitchen window. There was something in his eyes I'd never seen before, some thoughtfulness, some worry all his own. He rubbed the muscle of one arm. "It's time I was getting out of here."

"Where do you want to *go*, Sonny?"

"I want to join the army. Or the navy, I don't care. If I say I'm old enough, they'll believe me."

Then I got mad. It was because I was so scared. "You must be crazy. You goddamn fool, what the hell do you want to go and join the *army* for?"

"I just told you. To get out of Harlem."

160 "Sonny, you haven't even finished *school*. And if you really want to be a musician, how do you expect to study if you're in the *army?*"

He looked at me, trapped, and in anguish. "There's ways. I might be able to work out some kind of deal. Anyway, I'll have the G.I. Bill when I come out."

"*If* you come out." We stared at each other. "Sonny, please. Be reasonable. I know the setup is far from perfect. But we got to do the best we can."

"I ain't learning nothing in school," he said. "Even when I go." He turned away from me and opened the window and threw his cigarette out into the narrow alley. I watched his back. "At least, I ain't learning nothing you'd want me to learn." He slammed the window so hard I thought the glass would fly out, and turned back to me. "And I'm sick of the stink of these garbage cans!"

"Sonny," I said, "I know how you feel. But if you don't finish school now, you're going to be sorry later that you didn't." I grabbed him by the shoulders. "And you only got another year. It ain't so bad. And I'll come back and I swear I'll help you do *whatever* you want to do. Just try to put up with it till I come back. Will you please do that? For me?"

165 He didn't answer and he wouldn't look at me.

"Sonny. You hear me?"

He pulled away. "I hear you. But you never hear anything I say."

I didn't know what to say to that. He looked out of the window and then back at me. "OK," he said, and sighed. "I'll try."

Then I said, trying to cheer him up a little, "They got a piano at Isabel's. You can practice on it."

170   And as a matter of fact, it did cheer him up for a minute. "That's right," he said to himself. "I forgot that." His face relaxed a little. But the worry, the thoughtfulness, played on it still, the way shadows play on a face which is staring into the fire.

But I thought I'd never hear the end of that piano. At first, Isabel would write me, saying how nice it was that Sonny was so serious about his music and how, as soon as he came in from school, or wherever he had been when he was supposed to be at school, he went straight to that piano and stayed there until suppertime. And, after supper, he went back to that piano and stayed there until everybody went to bed. He was at the piano all day Saturday and all day Sunday. Then he bought a record player and started playing records. He'd play one record over and over again, all day long sometimes, and he'd improvise along with it on the piano. Or he'd play one section of the record, one chord, one change, one progression, then he'd do it on the piano. Then back to the record. Then back to the piano.

Well, I really don't know how they stood it. Isabel finally confessed that it wasn't like living with a person at all, it was like living with sound. And the sound didn't make any sense to her, didn't make any sense to any of them—naturally. They began, in a way, to be afflicted by this presence that was living in their home. It was as though Sonny were some sort of god, or monster. He moved in an atmosphere which wasn't like theirs at all. They fed him and he ate, he washed himself, he walked in and out of their door; he certainly wasn't nasty or unpleasant or rude, Sonny isn't any of those things; but it was as though he were all wrapped up in some cloud, some fire, some vision all his own; and there wasn't any way to reach him.

At the same time, he wasn't really a man yet, he was still a child, and they had to watch out for him in all kinds of ways. They certainly couldn't throw him out. Neither did they dare to make a great scene about that piano because even they dimly sensed, as I sensed, from so many thousands of miles away, that Sonny was at that piano playing for his life.

But he hadn't been going to school. One day a letter came from the school board and Isabel's mother got it—there had, apparently, been other letters but Sonny had torn them up. This day, when Sonny came in, Isabel's mother showed him the letter and asked where he'd been spending his time. And she finally got it out of him that he'd been down in Greenwich Village, with musicians and other characters, in a white girl's apartment. And this scared her and she started to scream at him and what came up, once she began—though she denies it to this day—was what sacrifices they were making to give Sonny a decent home and how little he appreciated it.

175   Sonny didn't play the piano that day. By evening, Isabel's mother had calmed down but then there was the old man to deal with, and Isabel herself. Isabel says she did her best to be calm but she broke down and started crying. She says she just watched Sonny's face. She could tell, by watching him, what was happening with him. And what was happening was that they penetrated his cloud, they had reached him. Even if their fingers had been a thousand times more gentle than human fingers ever are, he could hardly help feeling that they had stripped him naked and were spitting on that nakedness. For he also had to see that his presence, that music, which was life or death to him, had been torture for them and that they had

endured it, not at all for his sake, but only for mine. And Sonny couldn't take that. He can take it a little better today than he could then but he's still not very good at it and, frankly, I don't know anybody who is.

The silence of the next few days must have been louder than the sound of all the music ever played since time began. One morning, before she went to work, Isabel was in his room for something and she suddenly realized that all of his records were gone. And she knew for certain that he was gone. And he was. He went as far as the navy would carry him. He finally sent me a postcard from some place in Greece and that was the first I knew that Sonny was still alive. I didn't see him any more until we were both back in New York and the war had long been over.

He was a man by then, of course, but I wasn't willing to see it. He came by the house from time to time, but we fought almost every time we met. I didn't like the way he carried himself, loose and dreamlike all the time, and I didn't like his friends, and his music seemed to be merely an excuse for the life he led. It sounded just that weird and disordered.

Then we had a fight, a pretty awful fight, and I didn't see him for months. By and by I looked him up, where he was living, in a furnished room in the Village, and I tried to make it up. But there were lots of people in the room and Sonny just lay on his bed, and he wouldn't come downstairs with me, and he treated these other people as though they were his family and I weren't. So I got mad and then he got mad, and then I told him that he might just as well be dead as live the way he was living. Then he stood up and he told me not to worry about him any more in life, that he *was* dead as far as I was concerned. Then he pushed me to the door and the other people looked on as though nothing were happening, and he slammed the door behind me. I stood in the hallway, staring at the door. I heard somebody laugh in the room and then the tears came to my eyes. I started down the steps, whistling to keep from crying, I kept whistling to myself, *You going to need me, baby, one of these cold, rainy days.*

I read about Sonny's trouble in the spring. Little Grace died in the fall. She was a beautiful little girl. But she only lived a little over two years. She died of polio and she suffered. She had a slight fever for a couple of days, but it didn't seem like anything and we just kept her in bed. And we would certainly have called the doctor, but the fever dropped, she seemed to be all right. So we thought it had just been a cold. Then, one day, she was up, playing, Isabel was in the kitchen fixing lunch for the two boys when they'd come in from school, and she heard Grace fall down in the living room. When you have a lot of children you don't always start running when one of them falls, unless they start screaming or something. And, this time, Grace was quiet. Yet, Isabel says that when she heard that *thump* and then that silence, something happened in her to make her afraid. And she ran to the living room and there was little Grace on the floor, all twisted up, and the reason she hadn't screamed was that she couldn't get her breath. And when she did scream, it was the worst sound, Isabel says, that she'd ever heard in all her life, and she still hears it sometimes in her dreams. Isabel will sometimes wake me up with a low, moaning, strangled sound and I have to be quick to awaken her and hold her to me and where Isabel is weeping against me seems a mortal wound.

I think I may have written Sonny the very day that little Grace was buried. I was sitting in the living room in the dark, by myself, and I suddenly thought of Sonny. My trouble made his real.

One Saturday afternoon, when Sonny had been living with us, or, anyway, been in our house, for nearly two weeks, I found myself wandering aimlessly about the living room, drinking from a can of beer, and trying to work up the courage to search Sonny's room. He was out, he was usually out whenever I was home, and Isabel had taken the children to see their grandparents. Suddenly I was standing still in front of the living room window, watching Seventh Avenue. The idea of searching Sonny's room made me still. I scarcely dared to admit to myself what I'd be searching for. I didn't know what I'd do if I found it. Or if I didn't.

On the sidewalk across from me, near the entrance to a barbecue joint, some people were holding an old-fashioned revival meeting. The barbecue cook, wearing a dirty white apron, his conked hair reddish and metallic in the pale sun, and a cigarette between his lips, stood in the doorway, watching them. Kids and older people paused in their errands and stood there, along with some older men and a couple of very tough-looking women who watched everything that happened on the avenue, as though they owned it, or were maybe owned by it. Well, they were watching this, too. The revival was being carried on by three sisters in black, and a brother. All they had were their voices and their Bibles and a tambourine. The brother was testifying and while he testified two of the sisters stood together, seeming to say, amen, and the third sister walked around with the tambourine outstretched and a couple of people dropped coins into it. Then the brother's testimony ended and the sister who had been taking up the collection dumped the coins into her palm and transferred them to the pocket of her long black robe. Then she raised both hands, striking the tambourine against the air, and then against one hand, and she started to sing. And the two other sisters and the brother joined in.

It was strange, suddenly, to watch, though I had been seeing these street meetings all my life. So, of course, had everybody else down there. Yet, they paused and watched and listened and I stood still at the window. "*'Tis the old ship of Zion,*" they sang, and the sister with the tambourine kept a steady, jangling beat, "*it has rescued many a thousand!*" Not a soul under the sound of their voices was hearing this song for the first time, not one of them had been rescued. Nor had they seen much in the way of rescue work being done around them. Neither did they especially believe in the holiness of the three sisters and the brother, they knew too much about them, knew where they lived, and how. The woman with the tambourine, whose voice dominated the air, whose face was bright with joy, was divided by very little from the woman who stood watching her, a cigarette between her heavy, chapped lips, her hair a cuckoo's nest, her face scarred and swollen from many beatings, and her black eyes glittering like coal. Perhaps they both knew this, which was why, when, as rarely, they addressed each other, they addressed each other as Sister. As the singing filled the air the watching, listening faces underwent a change, the eyes focusing on something within; the music seemed to soothe a poison out of them; and time seemed, nearly, to fall away from the sullen, belligerent, battered faces, as though they were fleeing back to their first condition, while dreaming of their last. The barbecue cook half shook his head and smiled, and dropped his cigarette and disappeared into his joint. A man fumbled in his pockets for change and stood holding it in his hand impatiently, as though he had just remembered a pressing appointment further up the avenue. He looked furious. Then I saw Sonny, standing on the edge of the crowd. He was carrying a wide, flat notebook with a green cover, and it made him look, from where I was standing, almost like a schoolboy. The coppery sun brought out the copper in his skin, he was very faintly smiling, standing very still. Then the singing stopped, the tambourine turned into a collection plate again. The furious man dropped in his coins and vanished, so did a couple of the women, and Sonny dropped some change in the plate, looking directly at the woman with a little smile. He started across the avenue, toward the house. He has a slow, loping walk, something like the way Harlem hipsters walk, only he's imposed on this his own half-beat. I had never really noticed it before.

I stayed at the window, both relieved and apprehensive. As Sonny disappeared from my sight, they began singing again. And they were still singing when his key turned in the lock.

185 "Hey," he said.

"Hey, yourself. You want some beer?"

"No. Well, maybe." But he came up to the window and stood beside me, looking out. "What a warm voice," he said.

They were singing *If I could only hear my mother pray again!*

"Yes," I said, "and she can sure beat that tambourine."

190 "But what a terrible song," he said, and laughed. He dropped his notebook on the sofa and disappeared into the kitchen. "Where's Isabel and the kids?"

"I think they went to see their grandparents. You hungry?"

"No." He came back into the living room with his can of beer. "You want to come some place with me tonight?"

I sensed, I don't know how, that I couldn't possibly say no. "Sure. Where?"

He sat down on the sofa and picked up his notebook and started leafing through it. "I'm going to sit in with some fellows in a joint in the Village."

195 "You mean, you're going to play, tonight?"

"That's right." He took a swallow of his beer and moved back to the window. He gave me a sidelong look. "If you can stand it."

"I'll try," I said.

He smiled to himself and we both watched as the meeting across the way broke up. The three sisters and the brother, heads bowed, were singing *God be with you till we meet again.* The faces around them were very quiet. Then the song ended. The small crowd dispersed. We watched the three women and the lone man walk slowly up the avenue.

"When she was singing before," said Sonny, abruptly, "her voice reminded me for a minute of what heroin feels like sometimes—when it's in your veins. It makes you feel sort of warm and cool at the same time. And distant. And—and sure." He sipped his beer, very deliberately not looking at me. I watched his face. "It makes you feel—in control. Sometimes you've got to have that feeling."

200 "Do you?" I sat down slowly in the easy chair.

"Sometimes." He went to the sofa and picked up his notebook again. "Some people do."

"In order," I asked, "to play?" And my voice was very ugly, full of contempt and anger.

"Well"—he looked at me with great, troubled eyes, as though, in fact, he hoped his eyes would tell me things he could never otherwise say—"they *think* so. And *if* they think so—!"

"And what do *you* think?" I asked.

He sat on the sofa and put his can of beer on the floor. "I don't know," he said, and I couldn't be sure if he were answering my question or pursuing his thoughts. His face didn't tell me. "It's not so much to *play*. It's to *stand* it, to be able to make it at all. On any level." He frowned and smiled: "In order to keep from shaking to pieces."

"But these friends of yours," I said, "they seem to shake themselves to pieces pretty goddamn fast."

"Maybe." He played with the notebook. And something told me that I should curb my tongue, that Sonny was doing his best to talk, that I should listen. "But of course you only know the ones that've gone to pieces. Some don't—or at least they haven't *yet* and that's just about all *any* of us can say." He paused. "And then there are some who just live, really, in hell, and they know it and they see what's happening and they go right on. I don't know." He sighed, dropped the notebook, folded his arms. "Some guys, you can tell from the way they play, they on something *all* the time. And you can see that, well, it makes something real for them. But of course," he picked up his beer from the floor and sipped it and put the can down again, "they *want* to, too, you've got to see that. Even some of them that say they don't—*some*, not all."

"And what about you?" I asked—I couldn't help it. "What about you? Do *you* want to?"

He stood up and walked to the window and remained silent for a long time. Then he sighed. "Me," he said. Then: "While I was downstairs before, on my way here, listening to that woman sing, it struck me all of a sudden how much suffering she must have had to go through—to sing like that. It's *repulsive* to think you have to suffer that much."

I said: "But there's no way not to suffer—is there, Sonny?"

"I believe not," he said and smiled, "but that's never stopped anyone from trying." He looked at me. "Has it?" I realized, with this mocking look, that there stood between us, forever, beyond the power of time or forgiveness, the fact that I had held silence—so long!—when he had needed human speech to help him. He turned back to the window. "No, there's no way not to suffer. But you try all kinds of ways to keep from drowning in it, to keep on top of it, and to make it seem—well, like *you*. Like you did something, all right, and now you're suffering for it. You know?" I said nothing. "Well you know," he said, impatiently, "why *do* people suffer? Maybe it's better to do something to give it a reason, *any* reason."

"But we just agreed," I said, "that there's no way not to suffer. Isn't it better, then, just to—take it?"

"But nobody just takes it," Sonny cried, "that's what I'm telling you! *Everybody* tries not to. You're just hung up on the *way* some people try—it's not *your* way!"

The hair on my face began to itch, my face felt wet. "That's not true," I said, "that's not true. I don't give a damn what other people do, I don't even care how they suffer. I just care how *you* suffer." And he looked at me. "Please believe me," I said, "I don't want to see you—die—trying not to suffer."

215 "I won't," he said, flatly, "die trying not to suffer. At least, not any faster than anybody else."

"But there's no need," I said, trying to laugh, "is there? in killing yourself."

I wanted to say more, but I couldn't. I wanted to talk about will power and how life could be—well, beautiful. I wanted to say that it was all within; but was it? or, rather, wasn't that exactly the trouble? And I wanted to promise that I would never fail him again. But it would all have sounded—empty words and lies.

So I made the promise to myself and prayed that I would keep it.

"It's terrible sometimes, inside," he said, "that's what's the trouble. You walk these streets, black and funky and cold, and there's not really a living ass to talk to, and there's nothing shaking, and there's no way of getting it out—that storm inside. You can't talk it and you can't make love with it, and when you finally try to get with it and play it, you realize *nobody's* listening. So *you've* got to listen. You got to find a way to listen."

220 And then he walked away from the window and sat on the sofa again, as though all the wind had suddenly been knocked out of him. "Sometimes you'll do *anything* to play, even cut your mother's throat." He laughed and looked at me. "Or your brother's." Then he sobered. "Or your own." Then: "Don't worry. I'm all right now and I think I'll *be* all right. But I can't forget—where I've been. I don't mean just the physical place I've been, I mean where I've *been*. And *what* I've been."

"What have you been, Sonny?" I asked.

He smiled—but sat sideways on the sofa, his elbow resting on the back, his fingers playing with his mouth and chin, not looking at me. "I've been something I didn't recognize, didn't know I could be. Didn't know anybody could be." He stopped, looking inward, looking helplessly young, looking old. "I'm not talking about it now because I feel *guilty* or anything like that—maybe it would be better if I did, I don't know. Anyway, I can't really talk about it. Not to you, not to anybody," and now he turned and faced me. "Sometimes, you know, and it was actually when I was most *out* of the world, I felt that I was in it, that I was *with* it, really, and I could play or I didn't really have to *play*, it just came out of me, it was there. And I don't know how I played, thinking about it now, but I know I did awful things, those times, sometimes, to people. Or it wasn't that I *did* anything to them—it was that they weren't real." He picked up the beer can; it was empty; he rolled it between his palms: "And other times—well, I needed a fix, I needed to find a place to lean, I needed to clear a space to *listen*—and I couldn't find it, and I—went crazy, I did terrible things to *me*, I was terrible *for* me." He began pressing the beer can between his hands, I watched the metal begin to give. It glittered, as he played with it, like a knife, and I was afraid he would cut himself, but I said nothing. "Oh well. I can never tell you. I was all by myself at the bottom of something, stinking and sweating and crying and shaking, and I smelled it, you know? *my* stink, and I thought I'd die if I couldn't get away from it and yet, all the same, I knew that everything I was doing was just locking me in with it. And I didn't know," he paused, still flattening the beer can, "I didn't know, I still *don't* know, something kept telling me that maybe it was good to smell your own stink, but I didn't think that *that* was what I'd been trying to do—and—who can stand it?" and he abruptly dropped the ruined beer can, looking at me with a small, still smile, and then rose, walking to the window as though it were the lodestone rock. I watched his face, he watched the avenue. "I couldn't tell you when Mama died—but the reason I wanted to leave Harlem so bad was to get away from drugs. And then, when I ran away, that's what I was running from—really. When I came back, nothing had changed, *I* hadn't changed, I was just—older." And he stopped, drumming with his fingers on the windowpane. The sun had vanished, soon darkness would fall. I watched his face. "It can come again," he said, almost as though speaking to himself. Then he turned to me. "It can come again," he repeated. "I just want you to know that."

"All right," I said, at last. "So it can come again. All right."

He smiled, but the smile was sorrowful. "I had to try to tell you," he said.

225   "Yes," I said. "I understand that."

"You're my brother," he said, looking straight at me, and not smiling at all.

"Yes," I repeated, "yes. I understand that."

He turned back to the window, looking out. "All that hatred down there," he said, "all that hatred and misery and love. It's a wonder it doesn't blow the avenue apart."

We went to the only nightclub on a short, dark street, downtown. We squeezed through the narrow, chattering, jam-packed bar to the entrance of the big room, where the bandstand was. And we stood there for a moment, for the lights were very dim in this room and we couldn't see. Then, "Hello, boy," said a voice and an enormous black man, much older than Sonny or myself, erupted out of all that atmospheric lighting and put an arm around Sonny's shoulder. "I been sitting right here," he said, "waiting for you."

230   He had a big voice, too, and heads in the darkness turned toward us.

Sonny grinned and pulled a little away, and said, "Creole, this is my brother. I told you about him."

Creole shook my hand. "I'm glad to meet you, son," he said, and it was clear that he was glad to meet me *there*, for Sonny's sake. And he smiled, "You got a real musician in *your* family," and he took his arm from Sonny's shoulder and slapped him, lightly, affectionately, with the back of his hand.

"Well. Now I've heard it all," said a voice behind us. This was another musician, and a friend of Sonny's, a coal-black, cheerful-looking man, built close to the ground. He immediately began confiding to me, at the top of his lungs, the most terrible things about Sonny, his teeth gleaming like a lighthouse and his laugh coming up out of him like the beginning of an earthquake. And it turned out that everyone at the bar knew Sonny, or almost everyone; some were musicians, working there, or nearby, or not working, some were simply hangers-on, and some were there to hear Sonny play. I was introduced to all of them and they were all very polite to me. Yet, it was clear that, for them, I was only Sonny's brother. Here, I was in Sonny's world. Or, rather: his kingdom. Here, it was not even a question that his veins bore royal blood.

They were going to play soon and Creole installed me, by myself, at a table in a dark corner. Then I watched them, Creole, and the little black man, and Sonny, and the others, while they horsed around, standing just below the bandstand. The light from the bandstand spilled just a little short of them and, watching them laughing and gesturing and moving about, I had the feeling that they, nevertheless, were being most careful not to step into that circle of light too suddenly: that if they moved into the light too suddenly, without thinking, they would perish in flame. Then, while I watched, one of them, the small black man, moved into the light and crossed the bandstand and started fooling around with his drums. Then—being funny and being, also, extremely ceremonious—Creole took Sonny by the arm and led him to the piano. A woman's voice called Sonny's name and a few hands started clapping. And Sonny, also being funny and being ceremonious, and so touched, I think, that he could have cried, but neither hiding it nor showing it, riding it like a man, grinned, and put both hands to his heart and bowed from the waist.

235   Creole then went to the bass fiddle and a lean, very bright-skinned brown man jumped up on the bandstand and picked up his horn. So there they were, and the atmosphere on the bandstand and in the room began to change and tighten. Someone stepped up to the microphone and announced them. Then there were all kinds of murmurs. Some people at the bar shushed others. The waitress ran around, frantically getting in the last orders, guys and chicks got closer to each other, and the lights on the bandstand, on the quartet, turned to a kind of indigo. Then they all looked different there. Creole looked about him for the last time, as though he were making certain that all his chickens were in the coop, and then he—jumped and struck the fiddle. And there they were.

All I know about music is that not many people ever really hear it. And even then, on the rare occasions when something opens within, and the music enters, what we mainly hear, or hear corroborated, are personal, private, vanishing evocations. But the man who creates the music is hearing something else, is dealing with the roar rising from the void and imposing order on it as it hits the air. What is evoked in him, then, is of another order, more terrible because it has no words, and triumphant, too, for that same reason. And his triumph, when he triumphs, is ours. I just watched Sonny's face. His face was troubled, he was working hard, but he wasn't with it. And I had the feeling that, in a way, everyone on the bandstand was waiting for him, both waiting for him and pushing him along. But as I began to watch Creole, I realized that it was Creole who held them all back. He had them on a short rein. Up there, keeping the beat with his whole body, wailing on the fiddle, with his eyes half closed, he was listening to everything, but he was listening to Sonny. He was having a dialogue with Sonny. He wanted Sonny to leave the shoreline and strike out for the deep water. He was Sonny's witness that deep water and drowning were not the same thing—he had been there, and he knew. And he wanted Sonny to know. He was waiting for Sonny to do the things on the keys which would let Creole know that Sonny was in the water.

And, while Creole listened, Sonny moved, deep within, exactly like someone in torment. I had never before thought of how awful the relationship must be between the musician and his instrument. He has to fill it, this instrument, with the breath of life, his own. He has to make it do what he wants it to do. And a piano is just a piano. It's made out of so much wood and wires and little hammers and big ones, and ivory. While there's only so much you can do with it, the only way to find this out is to try; to try and make it do everything.

And Sonny hadn't been near a piano for over a year. And he wasn't on much better terms with his life, not the life that stretched before him now. He and the piano stammered, started one way, got scared, stopped; started another way, panicked, marked time, started again; then seemed to have found a direction, panicked again, got stuck. And the face I saw on Sonny I'd never seen before. Everything had been burned out of it, and, at the same time, things usually hidden were being burned in, by the fire and fury of the battle which was occurring in him up there.

Yet, watching Creole's face as they neared the end of the first set, I had the feeling that something had happened, something I hadn't heard. Then they finished, there was scattered applause, and then, without an instant's warning, Creole started into something else, it was almost sardonic, it was *Am I Blue.* And, as though he commanded, Sonny began to play. Something began to happen. And Creole let out the reins. The dry, low, black man said something awful on the drums, Creole answered, and the drums talked back. Then the horn insisted, sweet and high, slightly detached perhaps, and Creole listened, commenting now and then, dry, and driving, beautiful and calm and old. Then they all came together again, and Sonny was part of the family again. I could tell this from his face. He seemed to have found, right there beneath his fingers, a damn brand-new piano. It seemed that he couldn't get over it. Then, for a while, just being happy with Sonny, they seemed to be agreeing with him that brand-new pianos certainly were a gas.

240   Then Creole stepped forward to remind them that what they were playing was the blues. He hit something in all of them, he hit something in me, myself, and the music tightened and deepened, apprehension began to beat the air. Creole began to tell us what the blues were all about. They were not about anything very new. He and his boys up there were keeping it new, at the risk of ruin, destruction, madness, and death, in order to find new ways to make us listen. For, while the tale of how we suffer, and how we are delighted, and how we may triumph is never new, it always must be heard. There isn't any other tale to tell, it's the only light we've got in all this darkness.

And this tale, according to that face, that body, those strong hands on those strings, has another aspect in every country, and a new depth in every generation. Listen, Creole seemed to be saying, listen. Now these are Sonny's blues. He made the little black man on the drums know it, and the bright, brown man on the horn. Creole wasn't trying any longer to get Sonny in the water. He was wishing him Godspeed. Then he stepped back, very slowly, filling the air with the immense suggestion that Sonny speak for himself.

Then they all gathered around Sonny and Sonny played. Every now and again one of them seemed to say, amen. Sonny's fingers filled the air with life, his life. But that life contained so many others. And Sonny went all the way back, he really began with the spare, flat statement of the opening phrase of the song. Then he began to make it his. It was very beautiful because it wasn't hurried and it was no longer a lament. I seemed to hear with what burning he had made it his, with what burning we had yet to make it ours, how we could cease lamenting. Freedom lurked around us and I understood, at last, that he could help us to be free if we would listen, that he would never be free until we did. Yet, there was no battle in his face now. I heard what he had gone through, and would continue to go through until he came to rest in earth. He had made it his: that long line, of which we knew only

Mama and Daddy. And he was giving it back, as everything must be given back, so that, passing through death, it can live forever. I saw my mother's face again, and felt, for the first time, how the stones of the road she had walked on must have bruised her feet. I saw the moonlit road where my father's brother died. And it brought something else back to me, and carried me past it. I saw my little girl again and felt Isabel's tears again, and I felt my own tears begin to rise. And I was yet aware that this was only a moment, that the world waited outside, as hungry as a tiger, and that trouble stretched above us, longer than the sky.

Then it was over. Creole and Sonny let out their breath, both soaking wet, and grinning. There was a lot of applause and some of it was real. In the dark, the girl came by and I asked her to take drinks to the bandstand. There was a long pause, while they talked up there in the indigo light and after awhile I saw the girl put a Scotch and milk on top of the piano for Sonny. He didn't seem to notice it, but just before they started playing again, he sipped from it and looked toward me, and nodded. Then he put it back on top of the piano. For me, then, as they began to play again, it glowed and shook above my brother's head like the very cup of trembling.

▶ QUESTIONS FOR READING AND WRITING

1. Who is the narrator? What kind of relationship does he have with Sonny?
2. How does the tale of the narrator's father and his father's brother shed light on this story?
3. How would you interpret the statement "All they knew were two darknesses, the darkness of their lives, which was now closing in on them, and the darkness of the movies, which had blinded them to that other darkness"?
4. Why do you think the narrator writes to Sonny after his daughter, Grace, dies? What does he mean by "My trouble made his real"?
5. Describe the relationship between Sonny and his music. Why does it mean so much to him?
6. The relationship between Sonny and his brother changes. What helps the narrator to understand Sonny better?
7. In what way do you think "Sonny's Blues" is an appropriate title for this story?

TONI CADE BAMBARA (1939–1995)

Toni Cade Bambara was born in New York City and raised in the impoverished neighborhoods of Harlem and Bedford-Stuyvesant, New York, and Jersey City, New Jersey. Born Toni Cade, she added the name Bambara after discovering it as part of a signature in her great-grandmother's sketchbook. She attended Queen's College, where she majored in theater arts and English, graduating in 1959. Before turning to writing, she worked for the New York Department of Welfare, served as a director of recreation in a psychiatric ward, studied theater at the famous Commedia dell'Arte in Italy, ran a local community center, and earned a master's degree from the City University of New York. She began her writing career editing anthologies of black women writers and

African-American stories, but first attracted
attention with her collections of short stories
Gorilla, My Love *(1972) and* The Sea Birds
are Still Alive *(1977). She died of cancer in
1995. Her most recent publication,* Deep
Sightings and Rescue Missions: Fiction,
Essays, and Conversations *(1996), was published posthumously. In an interview in* Black
Women Writers at Work, *she said, "It's a
tremendous responsibility—responsibility and
honor—to be a writer, an artist, a cultural
worker . . . One's got to see what the factory
worker sees, what the prisoner sees, what the
welfare children see, what the scholar sees, got
to see what the ruling-class mythmakers see as
well, in order to tell the truth and not get trapped."*

THE LESSON   [1972]

Back in the days when everyone was old and stupid or young and foolish and me
and Sugar were the only ones just right, this lady moved on our block with nappy
hair and proper speech and no makeup. And quite naturally we laughed at her,
laughed the way we did at the junk man who went about his business like he was
some big-time president and his sorry-ass horse his secretary. And we kinda hated
her too, hated the way we did the winos who cluttered up our parks and pissed on
our handball walls and stank up our hallways and stairs so you couldn't halfway play
hide-and-seek without a goddamn gas mask. Miss Moore was her name. The only
woman on the block with no first name. And she was black as hell, cept for her feet,
which were fish-white and spooky. And she was always planning these boring-ass
things for us to do, us being my cousin, mostly, who lived on the block cause we all
moved North the same time and to the same apartment then spread out gradual to
breathe. And our parents would yank our heads into some kinda shape and crisp up
our clothes so we'd be presentable for travel with Miss Moore, who always looked
like she was going to church, though she never did. Which is just one of the things
the grownups talked about when they talked behind her back like a dog. But when
she came calling with some sachet she'd sewed up or some gingerbread she'd made
or some book, why then they'd all be too embarrassed to turn her down and we'd
get handed over all spruced up. She'd been to college and said it was only right that
she should take responsibility for the young ones' education, and she not even
related by marriage or blood. So they'd go for it. Specially Aunt Gretchen. She was
the main gofer in the family. You got some ole dumb shit foolishness you want
somebody to go for, you send for Aunt Gretchen. She been screwed into the go-
along for so long, it's a blood-deep natural thing with her. Which is how she got sad-
dled with me and Sugar and Junior in the first place while our mothers were in a
la-de-da apartment up the block having a good ole time.

So this one day, Miss Moore rounds us all up at the mailbox and it's puredee hot and she's knockin herself out about arithmetic. And school suppose to let up in summer I heard, but she don't never let up. And the starch in my pinafore scratching the shit outta me and I'm really hating this nappy-head bitch and her goddamn college degree. I'd much rather go to the pool or to the show where it's cool. So me and Sugar leaning on the mailbox being surly, which is a Miss Moore word. And Flyboy checking out what everybody brought for lunch. And Fat Butt already wasting his peanut-butter-and-jelly sandwich like the pig he is. And Junebug punchin on Q. T.'s arm for potato chips. And Rosie Giraffe shifting from one hip to the other waiting for somebody to step on her foot or ask her if she from Georgia so she can kick ass, preferably Mercedes'. And Miss Moore asking us do we know what money is, like we a bunch of retards. I mean real money, she say, like it's only poker chips or monopoly papers we lay on the grocer. So right away I'm tired of this and say so. And would much rather snatch Sugar and go to the Sunset and terrorize the West Indian kids and take their hair ribbons and their money too. And Miss Moore files that remark away for next week's lesson on brotherhood, I can tell. And finally I say we oughta get to the subway cause it's cooler and besides we might meet some cute boys. Sugar done swiped her mama's lipstick, so we ready.

So we heading down the street and she's boring us silly about what things cost and what our parents make and how much goes for rent and how money ain't divided up right in this country. And then she gets to the part about we all poor and live in the slums, which I don't feature. And I'm ready to speak on that, but she steps out in the street and hails two cabs just like that. Then she hustles half the crew in with her and hands me a five-dollar bill and tells me to calculate 10 percent tip for the driver. And we're off. Me and Sugar and Junebug and Flyboy hangin out the window and hollering to everybody, putting lipstick on each other cause Flyboy a faggot anyway, and making farts with our sweaty armpits. But I'm mostly trying to figure how to spend this money. But they all fascinated with the meter ticking and Junebug starts laying bets as to how much it'll read when Flyboy can't hold his breath no more. Then Sugar lays bets as to how much it'll be when we get there. So I'm stuck. Don't nobody want to go for my plan, which is to jump out at the next light and run off to the first bar-b-que we can find. Then the driver tells us to get the hell out cause we there already. And the meter reads eighty-five cents. And I'm stalling to figure out the tip and Sugar say give him a dime. And I decide he don't need it bad as I do, so later for him. But then he tries to take off with Junebug foot still in the door so we talk about his mamma something ferocious. Then we check out that we on Fifth Avenue and everybody dressed up in stockings. One lady in a fur coat, hot as it is. White folks crazy.

"This is the place," Miss Moore say, presenting it to us in the voice she uses at the museum. "Let's look in the windows before we go in."

5   "Can we steal?" Sugar asks very serious like she's getting the ground rules squared away before she plays. "I beg your pardon," say Miss Moore, and we fall out. So she leads us around the windows of the toy store and me and Sugar screamin, "This is mine, that's mine, I gotta have that, that was made for me, I was born for that," till Big Butt drowns us out.

"Hey, I'm goin to buy that there."

"That there? You don't even know what it is, stupid."

"I do so," he say punchin on Rosie Giraffe. "It's a microscope."

"Whatcha gonna do with a microscope, fool?"

10   "Look at things."

"Like what, Ronald?" ask Miss Moore. And Big Butt ain't got the first notion. So here go Miss Moore gabbing about the thousands of bacteria in a drop of water and the somethinorother in a speck of blood and the million and one living things in the air around us is invisible to the naked eye. And what she say that for? Junebug go to town on that "naked" and we rolling. Then Miss Moore ask what it cost. So we all jam into the window smudgin it up and the price tag say $300. So then she ask how long'd take for Big Butt and Junebug to save up their allowances. "Too long," I say. "Yeh," adds Sugar, "outgrown it by that time." And, Miss Moore say no, you never outgrow learning instruments. "Why, even medical students and interns and," blah, blah, blah. And we ready to choke Big Butt for bringing it up in the first damn place.

"This here costs four hundred eighty dollars," say Rosie Giraffe. So we pile up all over her to see what she pointin out. My eyes tell me it's a chunk of glass cracked with something heavy, and different-color inks dripped into the splits, then the whole thing put into a oven or something. But for $480 it don't make sense.

"That's a paperweight made of semi-precious stones fused together under tremendous pressure," she explains slowly, with her hands doing the mining and all the factory work.

"So what's a paperweight?" ask Rosie Giraffe.

15   "To weigh paper with, dumbbell," say Flyboy, the wise man from the East.

"Not exactly," say Miss Moore, which is what she say when you warm or way off too. "It's to weigh paper down so it won't scatter and make your desk untidy." So right away me and Sugar curtsy to each other and then to Mercedes who is more the tidy type.

"We don't keep paper on top of the desk in my class," say Junebug, figuring Miss Moore crazy or lyin one.

"At home, then," she say. "Don't you have a calendar and a pencil case and a blotter and a letter-opener on your desk at home where you do your homework?" And she know damn well what our homes look like cause she nosys around in them every chance she gets.

"I don't even have a desk," say Junebug. "Do we?"

20   "No. And I don't get no homework neither," says Big Butt.

"And I don't even have a home," says Flyboy like he do at school to keep the white folks off his back and sorry for him. Send this poor kid to camp posters, is his specialty.

"I do," says Mercedes. "I have a box of stationery on my desk and a picture of my cat. My godmother bought the stationery and the desk. There's a big rose on each sheet and the envelopes smell like roses."

"Who wants to know about your smelly-ass stationery," say Rosie Giraffe fore I can get my two cents in.

"It's important to have a work area all your own so that . . ."

25   "Will you look at this sailboat, please," say Flyboy, cuttin her off and pointin to the thing like it was his. So once again we tumble all over each other to gaze at this magnificent thing in the toy store which is just big enough to maybe sail two kittens across the pond if you strap them to the posts tight. We all start reciting the price tag like we in assembly. "Handcrafted sailboat of fiberglass at one thousand one hundred ninety-five dollars."

"Unbelievable," I hear myself say and am really stunned. I read it again for myself just in case the group recitation put me in a trance. Same thing. For some reason this pisses me off. We look at Miss Moore and she lookin at us, waiting for I dunno what.

"Who'd pay all that when you can buy a sailboat set for a quarter at Pop's, a tube of glue for a dime, and a ball of string for eight cents? It must have a motor and a whole lot else besides," I say. "My sailboat cost me about fifty cents."

"But will it take water?" say Mercedes with her smart ass.

"Took mine to Alley Pond Park once," say Flyboy. "String broke. Lost it. Pity."

30   "Sailed mine in Central Park and it keeled over and sank. Had to ask my father for another dollar."

"And you got the strap," laugh Big Butt. "The jerk didn't even have a string on it. My old man wailed on his behind."

Little Q. T. was staring hard at the sailboat and you could see he wanted it bad. But he too little and somebody'd just take it from him. So what the hell. "This boat for kids, Miss Moore?"

"Parents silly to buy something like that just to get all broke up," say Rosie Giraffe.

"That much money it should last forever," I figure.

35   "My father'd buy it for me if I wanted it."

"Your father, my ass," say Rosie Giraffe getting a chance to finally push Mercedes.

"Must be rich people shop here," say Q. T.

"You are a very bright boy," say Flyboy. "What was your first clue?" And he rap him on the head with the back of his knuckles, since Q. T. the only one he could get away with. Though Q. T. liable to come up behind you years later and get his licks in when you half expect it.

"What I want to know is," I says to Miss Moore though I never talk to her, I wouldn't give the bitch that satisfaction, "is how much a real boat costs? I figure a thousand'd get you a yacht any day."

40   "Why don't you check that out," she says, "and report back to the group?" Which really pains my ass. If you gonna mess up a perfectly good swim day least you could do is have some answers. "Let's go in," she say like she got something up her sleeve. Only she don't lead the way. So me and Sugar turn the corner to where the entrance is, but when we get there I kinda hang back. Not that I'm scared, what's there to be afraid of, just a toy store. But I feel funny, shame. But what I got to be shamed about? Got as much right to go in as anybody. But somehow I can't seem to get hold of the door, so I step away from Sugar to lead. But she hangs back too. And I look at her and she looks at me and this is ridiculous. I mean, damn, I

have never ever been shy about doing nothing or going nowhere. But then Mercedes steps up and then Rosie Giraffe and Big Butt crowd in behind and shove, and next thing we all stuffed into the doorway with only Mercedes squeezing past us, smoothing out her jumper and walking right down the aisle. Then the rest of us tumble in like a glued-together jigsaw done all wrong. And people lookin at us. And it's like the time me and Sugar crashed into the Catholic church on a dare. But once we got in there and everything so hushed and holy and the candles and the bowin and the handkerchiefs on all the drooping heads, I just couldn't go through with the plan. Which was for me to run up to the altar and do a tap dance while Sugar played the nose flute and messed around in the holy water. And Sugar kept given me the elbow. Then later teased me so bad I tied her up in the shower and turned it on and locked her in. And she'd be there till this day if Aunt Gretchen hadn't finally figured I was lyin about the boarder takin a shower.

Same thing in the store. We all walkin on tiptoe and hardly touchin the games and puzzles and things. And I watched Miss Moore who is steady watchin us like she waitin for a sign. Like Mama Drewery watches the sky and sniffs the air and takes note of just how much slant is in the bird formation. Then me and Sugar bump smack into each other, so busy gazing at the toys, 'specially the sailboat. But we don't laugh and go into our fat-lady bump-stomach routine. We just stare at that price tag. Then Sugar run a finger over the whole boat. And I'm jealous and want to hit her. Maybe not her, but I sure want to punch somebody in the mouth.

"Watcha bring us here for, Miss Moore?"

"You sound angry, Sylvia. Are you mad about something?" Givin me one of them grins like she tellin a grown-up joke that never turns out to be funny. And she's lookin very closely at me like maybe she plannin to do my portrait from memory. I'm mad, but I won't give her that satisfaction. So I slouch around the store bein very bored and say, "Let's go."

Me and Sugar at the back of the train watchin the tracks whizzin by large then small then gettin gobbled up in the dark. I'm thinkin about this tricky toy I saw in the store. A clown that somersaults on a bar then does chin-ups just cause you yank lightly at his leg. Cost $35. I could see me askin my mother for a $35 birthday clown. "You wanna who that costs what?" she'd say, cocking her head to the side to get a better view of the hole in my head. Thirty-five dollars could buy new bunk beds for Junior and Gretchen's boy. Thirty-five dollars and the whole household could go visit Granddaddy Nelson in the country. Thirty-five dollars would pay for the rent and the piano bill too. Who are these people that spend that much for performing clowns and $1000 for toy sailboats? What kinda work they do and how they live and how come we ain't in on it? Where we are is who we are, Miss Moore always pointin out. But it don't necessarily have to be that way, she always adds then waits for somebody to say that poor people have to wake up and demand their share of the pie and don't none of us know what kind of pie she talking about in the first damn place. But she ain't so smart cause I still got her four dollars from the taxi and she sure ain't gettin it. Messin up my day with this shit. Sugar nudges me in my pocket and winks.

45   Miss Moore lines us up in front of the mailbox where we started from, seem like years ago, and I got a headache for thinkin so hard. And we lean all over each

other so we can hold up under the draggy-ass lecture she always finishes us off with at the end before we thank her for borin us to tears. But she just looks at us like she readin tea leaves. Finally she say, "Well, what did you think of F. A. O. Schwartz?"

Rosie Giraffe mumbles, "White folks crazy."

"I'd like to go there again when I get my birthday money," says Mercedes, and we shove her out the pack so she has to lean on the mailbox by herself.

"I'd like a shower. Tiring day," say Flyboy.

Then Sugar surprises me by sayin, "You know, Miss Moore, I don't think all of us here put together eat in a year what that sailboat costs." And Miss Moore lights up like somebody goosed her. "And?" she say, urging Sugar on. Only I'm standin on her foot so she don't continue.

50   "Imagine for a minute what kind of society it is in which some people can spend on a toy what it would cost to feed a family of six or seven. What do you think?"

"I think," say Sugar pushing me off her feet like she never done before, cause I whip her ass in a minute, "that this is not much of a democracy if you ask me. Equal chance to pursue happiness means an equal crack at the dough, don't it?" Miss Moore is besides herself and I am disgusted with Sugar's treachery. So I stand on her foot one more time to see if she'll shove me. She shuts up, and Miss Moore looks at me, sorrowfully I'm thinkin. And somethin weird is goin on, I can feel it in my chest.

"Anybody else learn anything today?" lookin dead at me. I walk away and Sugar has to run to catch up and don't even seem to notice when I shrug her arm off my shoulder.

"Well, we got four dollars anyway," she says.

"Uh hunh."

55   "We could go to Hascombs and get half a chocolate layer and then go to the Sunset and still have plenty money for potato chips and ice cream sodas."

"Uh hunh."

"Race you to Hascombs," she say.

We start down the block and she gets ahead which is O.K. by me cause I'm going to the West End and then over to the Drive to think this day through. She can run if she want to and even run faster. But ain't nobody gonna beat me at nuthin.

➤ QUESTIONS FOR READING AND WRITING

1. Think about the final paragraph of the story. Has the narrator changed? If so, why? What does she tell us about herself and her future?

2. You might say that this story is told from the point of view of a "hostile witness." How did you respond to the speaker? To the events she describes? How would the story change if told from Miss Moore's point of view?

3. Describe the narrator's relationship to Sugar. In what ways is this relationship important to the narrator? How is the relationship developed throughout the story?

4. What is Miss Moore's central message? Why does she bring poor inner-city adolescents to a store where they can't afford anything? Do you think this is an effective lesson?

DONALD BARTHELME (1931–1989)

Donald Barthelme was born in Philadelphia and raised in Texas. In her Twayne series biography Donald Barthelme, *Lois Gordon claims that Barthelme "rejects traditional chronology, plot, character, time, space, grammar, syntax, metaphor, and simile, as well as the traditional distinctions between fact and fiction." Larry McCaffery writes, "If there is a sense of optimism in [Barthelme's] work, it does not derive from the familiar modernist belief that art offers the possibility of escape from the disorders of the modern world or that art can change existing conditions; Barthelme overtly mocks these beliefs along with most other modern representation of that world." The short story collection* Sixty Stories *(1981), which won the PEN/Faulkner Award for fiction, contains much of the short fiction for which Barthelme is remembered. In addition to his short fiction, he published two novels during his lifetime,* Snow White *(1967) and* The Dead Father *(1975), and one posthumously,* The King *(1992). Among other awards, he received a Guggenheim Fellowship, the National Book Award, and the National Institute of Arts and Letters Zabel Award.*

AT THE TOLSTOY MUSEUM [1987]

At the Tolstoy Museum we sat and wept. Paper streamers came out of our eyes. Our gaze drifted toward the pictures. They were placed too high on the wall. We suggested to the director that they be lowered six inches at least. He looked unhappy but said he would see to it. The holdings of the Tolstoy Museum consist principally of some thirty thousand pictures of Count Leo Tolstoy.

After they had lowered the pictures we went back to the Tolstoy Museum. I don't think you can peer into one man's face too long—for too long a period. A great many human passions could be discerned, behind the skin.

Tolstoy means "fat" in Russian. His grandfather sent his linen to Holland to be washed. His mother *did not know* any bad words. As a youth he shaved off his eyebrows, hoping they would grow back bushier. He first contracted gonorrhea in 1847. He was once bitten on the face by a bear. He became a vegetarian in 1885. To make himself interesting, he occasionally bowed backward.

I was eating a sandwich at the Tolstoy Museum. The Tolstoy Museum is made of stone—many stones, cunningly wrought. Viewed from the street, it has the aspect of three stacked boxes: the first, second, and third levels. These are of increasing size. The first level is, say, the size of a shoebox, the second level the size of a case

of whiskey, and the third level the size of a box that contained a new overcoat. The amazing cantilever of the third level has been much talked about. The glass floor there allows one to look straight down and provides a "floating" feeling. The entire building, viewed from the street, suggests that it is about to fall on you. This the architects relate to Tolstoy's moral authority.

5   In the basement of the Tolstoy Museum carpenters uncrated new pictures of Count Leo Tolstoy. The huge crates stenciled FRAGILE in red ink . . .

The guards at the Tolstoy Museum carry buckets in which there are stacks of clean white pocket handkerchiefs. More than any other museum, the Tolstoy Museum induces weeping. Even the bare title of a Tolstoy work, with its burden of love, can induce weeping—for example, the article titled "Who Should Teach Whom to Write, We the Peasant Children or the Peasant Children Us?" Many people stand before this article, weeping. Too, those who are caught by Tolstoy's eyes, in the various portraits, room after room after room, are not unaffected by the experience. It is like, people, say, committing a small crime and being discovered at it by your father, who stands in four doorways, looking at you.

Tolstoy's Coat

Tolstoy as a Youth

I was reading a story of Tolstoy's at the Tolstoy Museum. In this story a bishop is sailing on a ship. One of his fellow-passengers tells the Bishop about an island on which three hermits live. The hermits are said to be extremely devout. The Bishop is seized with a desire to see and talk with the hermits. He persuades the captain of the ship to anchor near the island. He goes ashore in a small boat. He speaks to the hermits. The hermits tell the Bishop how they worship God. They have a prayer that goes: "Three of You, three of us, have mercy on us." The Bishop feels that this is a prayer prayed in the wrong way. He undertakes to teach the hermits the Lord's Prayer. The hermits learn the Lord's Prayer but with the greatest difficulty. Night has fallen by the time they have got it correctly.

The Bishop returns to his ship, happy that he has been able to assist the hermits in their worship. The ship sails on. The Bishop sits alone on the deck, thinking about the experiences of the day. He sees a light in the sky, behind the ship. The light is cast by the three hermits floating over the water, hand in hand, without moving their feet. They catch up with the ship, saying: "We have forgotten, servant of God, we have forgotten your teaching!" They ask him to teach them again. The Bishop

At Starogladkovskaya about 1852

Tiger Hunt, Siberia

The Anna-Vronsky Pavilion

crosses himself. Then he tells the hermits that their prayer, too, reaches God. "It is not for me to teach you. Pray for us sinners!" The Bishop bows to the deck. The hermits fly back over the sea, hand in hand, to their island.

The story is written in a very simple style. It is said to originate in a folk tale. There is a version of it in St. Augustine. I was incredibly depressed by reading this story. Its beauty. Distance.

10   At the Tolstoy Museum, sadness grasped the 741 Sunday visitors. The Museum was offering a series of lectures on the text "Why Do Men Stupefy Themselves?" The visitors were made sad by these eloquent speakers, who were probably right.

People stared at tiny pictures of Turgenev, Nekrasov, and Fet. These and other small pictures hung alongside extremely large pictures of Count Leo Tolstoy.

In the plaza, a sinister musician played a wood trumpet while two children watched.

We considered the 640,086 pages (Jubilee Edition) of the author's published work. Some people wanted him to go away, but other people were glad we had him. "He has been a lifelong source of inspiration to me," one said.

I haven't made up my mind. Standing here in the "Summer in the Country" Room, several hazes passed over my eyes. Still, I think I will march on to "A Landlord's Morning." Perhaps something vivifying will happen to me there.

At the Disaster (Arrow indicates Tolstoy)

Museum Plaza with Monumental Head (Closed Monday)

▶ QUESTIONS FOR READING AND WRITING

1. Describe your experience reading this story. Did you find it serious, humorous, or sad? Explain.
2. Were you surprised to find the pictures? How did you "read" them? What did you think their purpose was?
3. Barthelme has compared his short story writing with creating artistic collages. Do you think "At the Tolstoy Museum" fits this description? Explain.

T. CORAGHESSAN BOYLE (b. 1948)

T. Coraghessan Boyle is the author of 14 books of fiction, including A Friend of the Earth *(2000) and his most recent collection,* After the Plague *(2001). He received a Ph.D. degree in nineteenth-century British literature from the University of Iowa in 1977, his master of fine arts degree from the University of Iowa Writers' Workshop in 1974, and his bachelor's degree in English and history from SUNY Potsdam in 1968. He has been a member of the English department at the University of Southern California since 1978. His stories have appeared in most of the major American magazines, including* The New Yorker, Harper's, Esquire, The Atlantic Monthly, Playboy, The Paris Review, GQ, Antaeus, *and* Granta, *and he has been the recipient of a number of literary awards. He currently lives near Santa Barbara, California, with his wife and three children.*

GREASY LAKE

[1985]

It's about a mile down on the dark side of Route 8.
                    —Bruce Springsteen

There was a time when courtesy and winning ways went out of style, when it was good to be bad, when you cultivated decadence like a taste. We were all dangerous characters then. We wore torn-up leather jackets, slouched around with toothpicks in our mouths, sniffed glue and ether and what somebody claimed was cocaine. When we wheeled our parents' whining station wagons out onto the street we left a patch of rubber half a block long. We drank gin and grape juice, Tango, Thunderbird, and Bali Hai. We were nineteen. We were bad. We read André Gide[1] and struck elaborate poses to show that we didn't give a shit about anything. At night, we went up to Greasy Lake.

---

[1] **André Gide** controversial French writer (1869–1951) whose novels, including *The Counterfeiters* and *Lafcadio's Adventures*, often show individuals in conflict with accepted morality.

Through the center of town, up the strip, past the housing developments and shopping malls, street lights giving way to the thin streaming illumination of the headlights, trees crowding the asphalt in a black unbroken wall: that was the way out to Greasy Lake. The Indians had called it Wakan, a reference to the clarity of its waters. Now it was fetid and murky, the mud banks glittering with broken glass and strewn with beer cans and the charred remains of bonfires. There was a single ravaged island a hundred yards from shore, so stripped of vegetation it looked as if the air force had strafed it. We went up to the lake because everyone went there, because we wanted to snuff the rich scent of possibility on the breeze, watch a girl take off her clothes and plunge into the festering murk, drink beer, smoke pot, howl at the stars, savor the incongruous full-throated roar of rock and roll against the primeval susurrus of frogs and crickets. This was nature.

I was there one night, late, in the company of two dangerous characters. Digby wore a gold star in his right ear and allowed his father to pay his tuition at Cornell; Jeff was thinking of quitting school to become a painter/musician/head-shop proprietor. There were both expert in the social graces, quick with a sneer, able to manage a Ford with lousy shocks over a rutted and gutted blacktop road at eighty-five while rolling a joint as compact as a Tootsie Roll Pop stick. They could lounge against a bank of booming speakers and trade "man's" with the best of them or roll out across the dance floor as if their joints worked on bearing. They were slick and quick and they wore their mirror shades at breakfast and dinner, in the shower, in closets and caves. In short, they were bad.

I drove. Digby pounded the dashboard and shouted along with Toots & the Maytals with Jeff hung his head out the window and streaked the side of my mothers Bel Air with vomit. It was early June, the air soft as a hand on your cheek, the third night of summer vacation. The first two nights we'd been out till dawn, looking for something we never found. On this, the third night, we'd cruised the strip sixty-seven times, been in and out of every bar and club we could think of in a twenty-mile radius, stopped twice for bucket chicken and forty-cent hamburgers, debated going to a party at the house of a girl Jeff's sister knew, and chucked two dozen raw eggs at mailboxes and hitchhikers. It was 2:00 A.M.; the bars were closing. There was nothing to do but take a bottle of lemon-flavored gin up to Greasy Lake.

5   The taillights of a single car winked at us as we swung into the dirt lot with its tufts of weed and washboard corrugations; '57 Chevy, mint, metallic blue. On the far side of the lot, like the exoskeleton of some gaunt chrome insect, a chopper leaned against its kickstand. And that was it for excitement; some junkie halfwit biker and a car freak pumping his girlfriend. Whatever it was we were looking for, we weren't about to find it at Greasy Lake. Not that night.

But then all of a sudden Digby was fighting for the wheel. "Hey, that's Tony Lovett's car! Hey!" he shouted, while I stabbed at the brake pedal and the Bel Air nosed up to the gleaming bumper of the parked Chevy. Digby leaned on the horn, laughing, and instructed me to put my bright lights on. I flicked on the brights. This was hilarious. A joke. Tony would experience premature withdrawal and expect to be confronted by grim-looking state troopers with flashlights. We hit the horn, strobed the lights, and then jumped out of the car to press our witty faces to Tony's windows; for all we knew we might even catch a glimpse of some little fox's tit, and then we could slap backs with red-faced Tony, roughhouse a little, and go on to new heights of adventure and daring.

The first mistake, the one that opened the whole floodgate, was losing my grip on the keys. In the excitement, leaping from the car with the gin in one hand and a roach clip in the other, I spilled them in the grass—in the dark, rank, mysterious nighttime grass of Greasy Lake. This was a tactical error, as damaging and irreversible in its way as Westmoreland's decision to dig in at Khe Sanh.[2] I felt it like a jab of intuition, and I stopped there by the open door, peering vaguely into the night that puddled up round my feet.

The second mistake—and this was inextricably bound up with the first—was identifying the car as Tony Lovett's. Even before the very bad character in greasy jeans and engineer boots ripped out of the driver's door, I began to realize that this chrome blue was much lighter than the robin's-egg of Tony's car, and that Tony's car didn't have rear-mounted speakers. Judging from their expressions, Digby and Jeff were privately groping toward the same inevitable and unsettling conclusion as I was.

In any case, there was no reasoning with this bad greasy character—clearly he was a man of action. The first lusty Rockette[3] kick of his steel-toed boot caught me under the chin, chipped my favorite tooth, and left me sprawled in the dirt. Like a fool, I'd gone down on one knee to comb the stiff cracked grass for my keys, my mind making connections in the most dragged-out, testudineous way, knowing that things had gone wrong, that I was in a lot of trouble, and that the lost ignition key was my grail and my salvation. The three or four succeeding blows were mainly absorbed by my right buttock and the tough piece of bone at the base of my spine.

10   Meanwhile, Digby vaulted the kissing bumpers and delivered a savage kung-fu blow to the greasy character's collarbone. Digby had just finished a course in martial arts for phys-ed credit and had spent the better part of the past two nights telling us apocryphal tales of Bruce Lee types and of the raw power invested in lightning blows shot from coiled wrists, ankles, and elbows. The greasy character was unimpressed. He merely backed off a step, his face like a Toltec mask, and laid Digby out with a single whistling roundhouse blow . . . but by now Jeff had got into the act, and I was beginning to extricate myself from the dirt, a tinny compound of shock, rage, and impotence wadded in my throat.

Jeff was on the guy's back, biting his ear. Digby was on the ground, cursing. I went for the tire iron I kept under the driver's seat. I kept it there because bad characters always keep tire irons under the driver's seat, for just such an occasion as this. Never ming that I hadn't been involved in a fight since sixth grade, when a kid with a sleepy eye and two streams of mucus descending from his nostrils hit me in the knee with a Louisville slugger,[4] never mind that I'd touched the tire iron exactly twice before, to change tires: it was there. And I went for it.

I was terrified. Blood was beating in my ears, my hands were shaking, my heart turning over like a dirtbike in the wrong gear. My antagonist was shirtless, and a single cord of muscle flashed across his chest as he bent forward to peel Jeff from his

[2] **Westmoreland's decision . . . Khe Sanh** General William C. Westmoreland commanded United States troops in Vietnam (1964–1968). In late 1967 the North Vietnamese and Viet Cong forces attacked Khe Sanh (or Khesanh) with a show of strength, causing Westmoreland to expend great effort to defend a plateau of relatively little tactical importance.   [3] **Rockette** member of a dancing troupe in the stage show at Radio City Music Hall, New York, famous for its ability to kick fast and high with wonderful coordination.   [4] **Louisville slugger** a brand of baseball bat

back like a wet overcoat. "Motherfucker," he spat, over and over, and I was aware in that instant that all four of us—Digby, Jeff, and myself included—were chanting, "motherfucker, motherfucker," as if it were a battle cry. (What happened next? the detective asks the murderer from beneath the turned-down brim of his porkpie hat. I don't know, the murderer says, something came over me. Exactly.)

Digby poked the flat of his hand in the bad character's face and I came at him like a kamikaze, mindless, raging, stung with humiliation—the whole thing, from the initial boot in the chin to this murderous primal instant involving no more than sixty hyperventilating, gland-flooding seconds—I came at him and brought the tire iron down across his ear. The effect was instantaneous, astonishing. He was a stunt man and this was Hollywood, he was a big grimacing toothy balloon and I was a man with a straight pin. He collapsed. Wet his pants. Went loose in his boots.

A single second, big as a zeppelin, floated by. We were standing over him in a circle, gritting our teeth, jerking our necks, our limbs and hands and feet twitching with glandular discharges. No one said anything. We just stared down at the guy, the car freak, the lover, the bad greasy character laid low. Digby looked at me; so did Jeff. I was still holding the tire iron, a tuft of hair clinging to the crook like dandelion fluff, like down. Rattled, I dropped it in the dirt, already envisioning the headlines, the pitted faces of the police inquisitors, the gleam of handcuffs, clank of bars, the big black shadows rising from the back of the cell . . . when suddenly a raw torn shriek cut through me like all the juice in all the electric chairs in the country.

15   It was the fox. She was short, barefoot, dressed in panties and a man's shirt. "Animals!" she screamed, running at us with her fists clenched and wisps of blow-dried hair in her face. There was a silver chain round her ankle, and her toenails flashed in the glare of the headlights. I think it was the toenails that did it. Sure, the gin and the cannabis and even the Kentucky Fried may have had a hand in it, but it was the sight of those flaming toes that set us off—the toad emerging from the loaf in *Virgin Spring*,[5] lipstick smeared on a child; she was already tainted. We were on her like Bergman's deranged brothers—see no evil, hear none, speak none—panting, wheezing, tearing at her clothes, grabbing for flesh. We were bad characters, and we were scared and hot and three steps over the line—anything could have happened.

It didn't.

Before we could pin her to the hood of the car, our eyes masked with lust and greed and the purest primal badness, a pair of headlights swung into the lot. There we were, dirty, bloody, guilty, dissociated from humanity and civilization, the first of the Ur-crimes behind us, the second in progress, shreds of nylon panty and spandex brassiere dangling from our fingers, our flies open, lips licked—there we were, caught in the spotlight. Nailed.

We bolted. First for the car, and then, realizing we had no way of starting it, for the woods. I thought nothing. I thought escape. The headlights came at me like accusing fingers. I was gone.

Ram-bam-bam, across the parking lot, past the chopper and into the feculent undergrowth of the lake's edge, insects flying up in my face, weeds whipping, frogs and snakes and red-eyed turtles splashing off into the night: I was already

---

[5] **Virgin Spring** film by Swedish director Ingmar Bergman.

ankle-deep in muck and tepid water and still going strong. Behind me, the girl's screams rose in intensity, disconsolate, incriminating, the screams of the Sabine women[6], the Christian martyrs, Anne Frank[7] dragged from the garret. I kept going, pursued by the cries, imagining cops and bloodhounds. The water was up to my knees when I realized what I was doing: I was going to swim for it. Swim the breadth of Greasy Lake and hide myself in the thick clot of woods on the far side. They'd never find me there.

20   I was breathing in sobs, in gasps. The water lapped at my waist as I looked out over the moon-burnished ripples, the mats of algae that clung to the surface like scabs. Digby and Jeff had vanished. I paused. Listened. The girl was quieter now, screams tapering to sobs, but there were male voices, angry, excited, and the high-pitched ticking of the second car's engine. I waded deeper, stealthy, hunted, the ooze sucking at my sneakers. As I was about to take the plunge—at the very instant I dropped my shoulder for the first slashing stroke—I blundered into something. Something unspeakable, obscene, something soft, wet, moss-grown. A patch of weed? A log? When I reached out to touch it, it gave like a rubber duck, it gave like flesh.

In one of those nasty little epiphanies, for which we are prepared by films and TV and childhood visits to the funeral home to ponder the shrunken painted forms of dead grandparents, I understood what it was that bobbed there so inadmissibly in the dark. Understood, and stumbled back in horror and revulsion, my mind yanked in six different directions (I was nineteen, a mere child, an infant, and here in the space of five minutes I'd struck down on greasy character and blundered into the waterlogged carcass of a second), thinking, The keys, the keys, why did I have to go and lose the keys? I stumbled back, but the muck took hold of my feet—a sneaker snagged, balance lost—and suddenly I was pitching face forward into the buoyant black mass, throwing out my hands in desperation while simultaneously conjuring the image of reeking frogs and muskrats revolving in slicks of their own deliquescing juices. AAAAArrrgh! I shot from the water like a torpedo, the dead man rotating to expose a mossy beard and eyes as cold as the moon. I must have shouted out, thrashing around in the weeds, because the voices behind me suddenly became animated.

"What was that?"

"It's them, it's them: they tried to , tried to . . . *rape* me!" Sobs.

A man's voice, flat Midwestern accent. "You sons of bitches, we'll kill you!" Frogs, crickets.

25   Then another voice, harsh, *r*-less, Lower East Side: "Motherfucker!" I recognized the verbal virtuosity of the bad greasy character in the engineer boots. Tooth chipped, sneakers gone, coated in mud and slime and worse, crouching breathless in the weeds waiting to have my ass thoroughly and definitively kicked and fresh from the hideous stinking embrace of a three-days-dead-corpse, I suddenly felt a

[6] **Sabine Women** members of an ancient tribe in Italy, according to legend, forcibly carried off by the early Romans under Romulus to be their wives. The incident is depicted in a famous painting, "The Rape of the Sabine Women," by seventeenth-century French artist Nicolas Poussin.   [7] **Anne Frank** German Jewish girl (1929–1945) whose diary written during the Nazi occupation of the Netherlands later became world famous. She hid with her family in a secret attic in Amsterdam, but was caught by storm troopers and sent to the concentration camp at Belsen, where she died.

rush of joy and vindication: the son of a bitch was alive! Just as quickly, my bowels turned to ice. "Come on out of there, you pansy mothers!" the bad greasy character was screaming. He shouted curses till he was out of breath.

The crickets started up again, then the frogs. I held my breath. All at once was a sound in the reeds, a swishing, a splash: thunk-a-thunk. They were throwing rocks. The frogs fell silent. I cradled my head. Swish, swish, thunk-a-thunk. A wedge of feldspar the size of a cue ball glanced off my knee. I bit my finger.

It was then that they turned to the car. I heard a door slam, a curse, and then the sound of the headlights shattering—almost a good-natured sound, celebratory, like corks popping from the necks of bottles. This was succeeded by the dull booming of the fenders, metal on metal, and then the icy crash of the windshield. I inched forward, elbows and knees, my belly pressed to the muck, thinking of guerrillas and commandos and *The Naked and the Dead*.[8] I parted the weeds and squinted the length of the parking lot.

The second car—it was a Trans-Am—was still running, its high beams washing the scene in a lurid stagy light. Tire iron flailing, the greasy bad character was laying into the side of my mother's Bel Air like an avenging demon, his shadow riding up the trunks of the trees. Whomp. Whomp. Whomp-whomp. The other two guys—blond types, in fraternity jackets—were helping out with tree branches and skull-sized boulders. One of them was gathering up bottles, rocks, muck, candy wrappers, used condoms, poptops, and other refuse and pitching it through the window of the driver's side. I could see the fox, a white bulb behind the windshield of the '57 Chevy. "Bobby," she whined over the thumping, "come *on*." The greasy character paused a moment, took one good swipe at the left taillight, and then heaved the tire iron halfway across the lake. Then he fired up the '57 and was gone.

Blond head nodded at blond head. One said something to the other, too low for me to catch. They were no doubt thinking that in helping to annihilate my mother's car they'd committed a fairly rash act, and thinking too that there were three bad characters connected with that very car watching them from the woods. Perhaps other possibilities occurred to them as well—police, jail cells, justices of the peace, reparations, lawyers, irate parents, fraternal censure. Whatever they were thinking, they suddenly dropped branches, bottles, and rocks and sprang for their car in unison, as if they'd choreographed it. Five seconds. That's all it took. The engine shrieked, the tires squealed, a cloud of dust rose from the rutted lot and then settled back on darkness.

30 I don't know how long I lay there, the bad breath of decay all around me, my jacket heavy as a bear, the primordial ooze subtly reconstituting itself to accommodate my upper thighs and testicles. My jaws ached, my knee throbbed, my coccyx was on fire. I contemplated suicide, wondered if I'd need bridgework, scraped the recesses of my brain for some sort of excuse to give my parents—a tree had fallen on the car, I was blinded by a bread truck, hit and run, vandals had got to it while we were playing chess at Digby's. Then I thought of the dead man. He was probably the only person on the planet worse off than I was. I thought about him, fog on the lake, insects chirring eerily, and felt the tug of fear, felt the darkness opening up inside me like a set of jaws. Who was he, I wondered, this victim of time and

---

[8] **The Naked and the Dead** novel (1948) by Norman Mailer, of U.S. Army life in World War II.

circumstance bobbing sorrowfully in the lake at my back. The owner of the chopper, no doubt, a bad older character come to this. Shot during a murky drug deal, drowned while drunkenly frolicking in the lake. Another headline. My car was wrecked; he was dead.

When the eastern half of the sky went from black to cobalt and the trees began to separate themselves from the shadows, I pushed myself up from the mud and stepped out into the open. By now the birds had begun to take over for the crickets, and dew lay slick on the leaves. There was a smell in the air, raw and sweet at the same time, the smell of the sun firing buds and opening blossoms. I contemplated the car. It lay there like a wreck along the highway, like a steel sculpture left over from a vanished civilization. Everything was still. This was nature.

I was circling the car, as dazed and bedraggled as the sole survivor of an air blitz, when Digby and Jeff emerged from the trees behind me. Digby's face was crosshatched with smears of dirt; Jeff's jacket was gone and his shirt was torn across the shoulder. They slouched across the lot, looking sheepish, and silently came up beside me to gape at the ravaged automobile. No one said a word. After a while Jeff swung open the driver's door and began to scoop the broken glass and garbage off the seat. I looked at Digby. He shrugged. "At least they didn't slash the tires," he said.

It was true: the tires were intact. There was no windshield, the headlights were staved in, and the body looked as if it had been sledge-hammered for a quarter a shot at the county fair, but the tires were inflated to regulation pressure. The car was drivable. In silence, all three of us bent to scrape the mud and shattered glass from the interior. I said nothing about the biker. When we were finished, I reached in my pocket for the keys, experienced a nasty stab of recollection, cursed myself, and turned to search the grass. I spotted them almost immediately, no more than five feet from the open door, glinting like jewels in the first tapering shaft of sunlight. There was no reason to get philosophical about it: I eased into the seat and turned the engine over.

It was at that precise moment that the silver Mustang with the flame decals rumbled into the lot. All three of us froze; then Digby and Jeff slid into the car and slammed the door. We watched as the Mustang rocked and bobbed across the ruts and finally jerked to a halt beside the forlorn chopper at the far end of the lot. "Let's go," Digby said. I hesitated, the Bel Air wheezing beneath me.

35   Two girls emerged from the Mustang. Tight jeans, stiletto heels, hair like frozen fur. They bent over the motorcycle, paced back and forth aimlessly, glanced once or twice at us, and then ambled over to where the reeds sprang up in a green fence round the perimeter of the lake. One of them cupped her hands to her mouth. "Al," she called. "Hey, Al!"

"Come on," Digby hissed. "Let's get out of here."

But it was too late. The second girl was picking her way across the lot, unsteady on her heels, looking up at us and then away. She was older—twenty-five or -six— and as she came closer we could see there was something wrong with her: she was stoned or drunk, lurching now and waving her arms for balance. I gripped the steering wheel as if it were the ejection lever of a flaming jet, and Digby spat out my name, twice, terse and impatient.

"Hi," the girl said.

We looked at her like zombies, like war veterans, like deaf-and-dumb pencil peddlers.

40   She smiled, her lips cracked and dry. "Listen," she said, bending from the waist to look in the window, "you guys seen Al?" Her pupils were pinpoints, her eyes glass. She jerked her neck. "That's his bike over there—Al's. You seen him?"

Al. I didn't know what to say. I wanted to get out of the car and retch, I wanted to go home to my parents' house and crawl into bed. Digby poked me in the ribs. "We haven't seen anybody," I said.

The girl seemed to consider this, reaching out a slim veiny arm to brace herself against the car. "No matter," she said, slurring the *t*'s, "he'll turn up." And then, as if she'd just taken stock of the whole scene—the ravaged car and our battered faces, the desolation of the place— she said: "Hey, you guys look like some pretty bad characters—been fightin', huh?" We stared straight ahead, rigid as catatonics. She was fumbling in her pocket and muttering something. Finally she held out a handful of tablets in glassine wrappers: "Hey, you want to party, you want to do some of these with me and Sarah?"

I just looked at her. I thought I was going to cry. Digby broke the silence. "No, thanks," he said, leaning over me. "Some other time."

I put the car in gear and it inched forward with a groan, shaking off pellets of glass like an old dog shedding water after a bath, heaving over the ruts on its worn springs, creeping toward the highway. There was a sheen of sun on the lake. I looked back. The girl was still standing there, watching us, her shoulders slumped, hand outstretched.

➤ QUESTIONS FOR READING AND WRITING

1. To what extent does your own experience influence your response to this story?
2. How would you describe the setting of the story? How important is it?
3. Are the narrator, Digby, and Jeff dynamic characters? To what extent do you think they change as a result of this incident?

ROBERT OLEN BUTLER (b. 1945)

Robert Olen Butler was born in Granite City, Illinois. He learned the Vietnamese language and culture when he served in the Vietnam War from 1969 to 1972. He has received grants from the National Endowment for the Arts and a Guggenheim Fellowship. "Snow" is taken from a collection of stories, A Good Scent from a Strange Mountain, *which earned Butler Pulitzer Prize for Fiction in 1993. His most recent collection of stories,* Tabloid Dreams, *was published in 1996. He lives in Louisiana and teaches at McNeese State University.*

SNOW

[1992]

I wonder how long he watched me sleeping. I still wonder that. He sat and he did not wake me to ask about his carry-out order. Did he watch my eyes move as I dreamed? When I finally knew he was there and I turned to look at him, I could not make out his whole face at once. His head was turned a little to the side. His beard was neatly trimmed, but the jaw it covered was long and its curve was like a sampan sail and it held my eyes the way a sail always did when I saw one on the sea. Then I raised my eyes and looked at his nose. I am Vietnamese, you know, and we have a different sense of these proportions. Our noses are small and his was long and it also curved, gently, a reminder of his jaw, which I looked at again. His beard was dark gray, like he'd crawled out of a charcoal kiln. I make these comparisons to things from my country and village, but it is only to clearly say what this face was like. It is not that he reminded me of home. That was the farthest thing from my mind when I first saw Mr. Cohen. And I must have stared at him in those first moments with a strange look because when his face turned full to me and I could finally lift my gaze to his eyes, his eyebrows made a little jump like he was asking me, What is it? What's wrong?

I was at this same table before the big window at the front of the restaurant. The Plantation Hunan does not look like a restaurant, though. No one would give it a name like that unless it really was an old plantation house. It's very large and full of antiques. It's quiet right now. Not even five, and I can hear the big clock—I had never seen one till I came here. No one in Vietnam has a clock as tall as a man. Time isn't as important as that in Vietnam. But the clock here is very tall and they call it Grandfather, which I like, and Grandfather is ticking very slowly right now, and he wants me to fall asleep again. But I won't.

This plantation house must feel like a refugee. It is full of foreign smells, ginger and Chinese pepper and fried shells for wonton, and there's a motel on one side and a gas station on the other, not like the life the house once knew, though there are very large oak trees surrounding it, trees that must have been here when this was still a plantation. The house sits on a busy street and the Chinese family who owns it changed it from Plantation Seafood into a place that could hire a Vietnamese woman like me to be a waitress. They are very kind, this family, though we know we are different from each other. They are Chinese and I am Vietnamese and they are very kind, but we are both here in Louisiana and they go somewhere with the other Chinese in town—there are four restaurants and two laundries and some people, I think, who work as engineers at the oil refinery. They go off to themselves and they don't seem to even notice where they are.

I was sleeping that day he came in here. It was late afternoon of the day before Christmas. Almost Christmas Eve. I am not a Christian. My mother and I are Buddhist. I live with my mother and she is very sad for me because I am thirty-four years old and I am not married. There are other Vietnamese here in Lake Charles, Louisiana, but we are not a community. We are all too sad, perhaps, or too tired. But maybe not. Maybe that's just me saying that. Maybe the others are real Americans already. My mother has two Vietnamese friends, old women like her, and her two friends look at me with the same sadness in their faces because of what they see as my life. They know that once I might have been married, but the fiancé I had in my town in Vietnam went away in the Army and though he is still alive in Vietnam, the last I heard, he is driving a cab in Hô Chí Minh City and he is married to someone else. I never really knew him, and I don't feel any loss. It's just that he's the only boy my mother ever speaks of when she gets frightened for me.

5   I get frightened for me, too, sometimes, but it's not because I have no husband. That Christmas Eve afternoon I woke slowly. The front tables are for cocktails and for waiting for carry-out, so the chairs are large and stuffed so that they are soft. My head was very comfortable against one of the high wings of the chair and I opened my eyes without moving. The rest of me was still sleeping, but my eyes opened and the sky was still blue, though the shreds of cloud were turning pink. It looked like a warm sky. And it was. I felt sweat on my throat and I let my eyes move just a little and the live oak in front of the restaurant was quivering—all its leaves were shaking and you might think that it would look cold doing that, but it was a warm wind, I knew. The air was thick and wet, and cutting through the ginger and pepper smell was the fuzzy smell of mildew.

       Perhaps it was from my dream but I remembered my first Christmas Eve in America. I slept and woke just like this, in a Chinese restaurant. I was working there. But it was in a distant place, in St. Louis. And I woke to snow. The first snow I had ever seen. It scared me. Many Vietnamese love to see their first snow, but it frightened me in some very deep way that I could not explain, and even remembering that moment—especially as I woke from sleep at the front of another restaurant—frightened me. So I turned my face sharply from the window in the Plantation Hunan and that's when I saw Mr. Cohen.

       I stared at those parts of his face, like I said, and maybe this was a way for me to hide from the snow, maybe the strangeness that he saw in my face had to do with the snow. But when his eyebrows jumped and I did not say anything to explain what was going on inside me, I could see him wondering what to do. I could feel him thinking: Should I ask her what is wrong or should I just ask her for my carry-out? I am not an especially shy person, but I hoped he would choose to ask for the carry-out. I came to myself with a little jolt and I stood up and faced him—he was sitting in one of the stuffed chairs at the next table. "I'm sorry," I said, trying to turn us both from my dreaming. "Do you have an order?"

       He hesitated, his eyes holding fast on my face. These were very dark eyes, as dark as the eyes of any Vietnamese, but turned up to me like this, his face seemed so large that I had trouble taking it in. Then he said, "Yes. For Cohen." His voice was deep, like a movie actor who is playing a grandfather, the kind of voice that if he asked what it was that I had been dreaming, I would tell him at once.

       But he did not ask anything more. I went off to the kitchen and the order was not ready. I wanted to complain to them. There was no one else in the restaurant, and everyone in the kitchen seemed like they were just hanging around. But I don't make any trouble for anybody. So I just went back out to Mr. Cohen. He rose when he saw me, even though he surely also saw that I had no carry-out with me.

10   "It's not ready yet," I said. "I'm sorry."

       "That's okay," he said, and he smiled at me, his gray beard opening and showing teeth that were very white.

"I wanted to scold them," I said. "You should not have to wait for a long time on Christmas Eve."

"It's okay," he said. "This is not my holiday."

I tilted my head, not understanding. He tilted his own head just like mine, like he wanted to keep looking straight into my eyes. Then he said, "I am Jewish."

15   I straightened my head again, and I felt a little pleasure at knowing that his straightening his own head was caused by me. I still didn't understand, exactly, and he clearly read that in my face. He said, "A Jew doesn't celebrate Christmas."

"I thought all Americans celebrated Christmas," I said.

"Not all. Not exactly." He did a little shrug with his shoulders, and his eyebrows rose like the shrug, as he tilted his head to the side once more, for just a second. It all seemed to say, What is there to do, it's the way the world is and I know it and it all makes me just a little bit weary. He said, "We all stay home, but we don't all celebrate."

He said no more, but he looked at me and I was surprised to find that I had no words either on my tongue or in my head. It felt a little strange to see this very American man who was not celebrating the holiday. In Vietnam we never miss a holiday and it did not make a difference if we were Buddhist or Cao Đái or Catholic. I thought of this Mr. Cohen sitting in his room tonight alone while all the other Americans celebrated Christmas Eve. But I had nothing to say and he didn't either and he kept looking at me and I glanced down at my hands twisting at my order book and I didn't even remember taking the book out. So I said, "I'll check on your order again," and I turned and went off to the kitchen and I waited there till the order was done, though I stood over next to the door away from the chatter of the cook and the head waiter and the mother of the owner.

Carrying the white paper bag out to the front, I could not help but look inside to see how much food there was. There was enough for two people. So I did not look into Mr. Cohen's eyes as I gave him the food and rang up the order and took his money. I was counting his change into his palm—his hand, too, was very large—and he said, "You're not Chinese, are you?"

20   I said, "No. I am Vietnamese," but I did not raise my face to him, and he went away.

Two days later, it was even earlier in the day when Mr. Cohen came in. About four-thirty. The Grandfather had just chimed the half hour like a man who is really crazy about one subject and talks of it at any chance he gets. I was sitting in my chair at the front once again and my first thought when I saw Mr. Cohen coming through the door was that he would think I am a lazy girl. I started to jump up, but he saw me and he motioned with his hand for me to stay where I was, a single heavy pat in the air, like he'd just laid this large hand of his on the shoulder of an invisible child before him. He said, "I'm early again."

"I am not a lazy girl," I said.

"I know you're not," he said and he sat down in the chair across from me.

"How do you know I'm not?" This question just jumped out of me. I can be a cheeky girl sometimes. My mother says that this was one reason I am not married, that this is why she always talks about the boy I was once going to marry in Vietnam, because he was a shy boy, a weak boy, who would take whatever his wife said and not complain. I myself think this is why he is driving a taxi in Hô Chí Minh City. But as soon as this cheeky thing came out of my mouth to Mr. Cohen, I found that I was afraid. I did not want Mr. Cohen to hate me.

25   But he was smiling. I could even see his white teeth in this smile. He said, "You're right. I have no proof."

"I am always sitting here when you come in," I said, even as I asked myself, Why are you rubbing on this subject?

I saw still more teeth in his smile, then he said, "And the last time you were even sleeping."

I think at this I must have looked upset, because his smile went away fast. He did not have to help me seem a fool before him. "It's all right," he said. "This is a slow time of day. I have trouble staying awake myself. Even in court."

I looked at him more closely, leaving his face. He seemed very prosperous. He was wearing a suit as gray as his beard and it had thin blue stripes, almost invisible, running through it. "You are a judge?"

30   "A lawyer," he said.

"You will defend me when the owner fires me for sleeping."

This made Mr. Cohen laugh, but when he stopped, his face was very solemn. He seemed to lean nearer to me, though I was sure he did not move. "You had a bad dream the last time," he said.

How did I know he would finally come to ask about my dream? I had known it from the first time I'd heard his voice. "Yes," I said. "I think I was dreaming about the first Christmas Eve I spent in America. I fell asleep before a window in a restaurant in St. Louis, Missouri. When I woke, there was snow on the ground. It was the first snow I'd ever seen. I went to sleep and there was still only a gray afternoon, a thin little rain, like a mist. I had no idea things could change like that. I woke and everything was covered and I was terrified."

I suddenly sounded to myself like a crazy person. Mr. Cohen would think I was lazy and crazy both. I stopped speaking and I looked out the window. A jogger went by in the street, a man in shorts and a T-shirt, and his body glistened with sweat. I felt beads of sweat on my own forehead like little insects crouching there and I kept my eyes outside, wishing now that Mr. Cohen would go away.

35   "Why did it terrify you?" he said.

"I don't know," I said, though this wasn't really true. I'd thought about it now and then, and though I'd never spoken them, I could imagine reasons.

Mr. Cohen said, "Snow frightened me, too, when I was a child. I'd seen it all my life, but it still frightened me."

I turned to him and now he was looking out the window.

"Why did it frighten you?" I asked, expecting no answer.

40   But he turned from the window and looked at me and smiled just a little bit, like he was saying that since he had asked this question of me, I could ask him, too. He answered, "It's rather a long story. Are you sure you want to hear it?"

"Yes," I said. Of course I did.

"It was far away from here," he said. "My first home and my second one. Poland and then England. My father was a professor in Warsaw. It was early in 1939. I was eight years old and my father knew something was going wrong. All the talk about the corridor to the sea was just the beginning. He had ears. He knew. So he sent me and my mother to England. He had good friends there. I left that February and there was snow everywhere and I had my own instincts, even at eight. I cried in the courtyard of our apartment building. I threw myself into the snow there and I would not move. I cried like he was sending us away from him forever. He and my mother said it was only for some months, but I didn't believe it. And I was right. They had to lift me bodily and carry me to the taxi. But the snow was in my clothes and as we pulled away and I scrambled up to look out the back window at my father, the snow was melting against my skin and I began to shake. It was as much from my fear as from the cold. The snow was telling me he would die. And he did. He waved at me in the street and he grew smaller and we turned a corner and that was the last I saw of him."

Maybe it was foolish of me, but I thought not so much of Mr. Cohen losing his father. I had lost a father, too, and I knew that it was something that a child lives through. In Vietnam we believe that our ancestors are always close to us, and I could tell that about Mr. Cohen, that his father was still close to him. But what I thought about was Mr. Cohen going to another place, another country, and living with his mother. I live with my mother, just like that. Even still.

He said, "So the snow was something I was afraid of. Every time it snowed in England I knew that my father was dead. It took a few years for us to learn this from others, but I knew it whenever it snowed."

45 "You lived with your mother?" I said.

"Yes. In England until after the war and then we came to America. The others from Poland and Hungary and Russia that we traveled with all came in through New York City and stayed there. My mother loved trains and she'd read a book once about New Orleans, and so we stayed on the train and we came to the South. I was glad to be in a place where it almost never snowed."

I was thinking how he was a foreigner, too. Not an American, really. But all the talk about the snow made this little chill behind my thoughts. Maybe I was ready to talk about that. Mr. Cohen had spoken many words to me about his childhood and I didn't want him to think I was a girl who takes things without giving something back. He was looking out the window again, and his lips pinched together so that his mouth disappeared in his beard. He seemed sad to me. So I said, "You know why the snow scared me in St. Louis?"

He turned at once with a little humph sound and a crease on his forehead between his eyes and then a very strong voice saying, "Tell me," and it felt like he was scolding himself inside for not paying attention to me. I am not a vain girl, always thinking that men pay such serious attention to me that they get mad at themselves for ignoring me even for a few moments. This is what it really felt like and it surprised me. If I was a vain girl, it wouldn't have surprised me. He said it again: "Tell me why it scared you."

I said, "I think it's because the snow came so quietly and everything was underneath it, like this white surface was the real earth and everything had died—all the trees and the grass and the streets and the houses—everything had died and was buried. It was all lost. I knew there was snow above me, on the roof, and I was dead, too."

50 "Your own country was very different," Mr. Cohen said.

It pleased me that he thought just the way I once did. You could tell that he wished there was an easy way to make me feel better, make the dream go away. But I said to him, "This is what I also thought. If I could just go to a warm climate, more like home. So I came down to New Orleans, with my mother, just like you, and then we came over to Lake Charles. And it is something like Vietnam here. The rice fields and the heat and the way the storms come in. But it makes no difference. There's no snow to scare me here, but I still sit alone in this chair in the middle of the afternoon and I sleep and I listen to the Grandfather over there ticking."

I stopped talking and I felt like I was making no sense at all, so I said, "I should check on your order."

Mr. Cohen's hand came out over the table. "May I ask your name?"

"I'm Miss Giàu," I said.

55 "Miss Giàu?" he asked, and when he did that, he made a different word, since Vietnamese words change with the way your voice sings them.

I laughed. "My name is Giàu, with the voice falling. It means 'wealthy' in Vietnamese. When you say the word like a question, you say something very different. You say I am Miss Pout."

Mr. Cohen laughed and there was something in the laugh that made me shiver just a little, like a nice little thing, like maybe stepping into the shower when you are covered with dust and feeling the water expose you. But in the back of my mind was his carry-out and there was a bad little feeling there, something I wasn't thinking about, but it made me go off now with heavy feet to the kitchen. I got the bag and it was feeling different as I carried it back to the front of the restaurant. I went behind the counter and I put it down and I wished I'd done this a few moments before, but even with his eyes on me, I looked into the bag. There was one main dish and one portion of soup.

Then Mr. Cohen said, "Is this a giau I see on your face?" And he pronounced the word exactly right, with the curling tone that made it "pout."

I looked up at him and I wanted to smile at how good he said the word, but even wanting to do that made the pout worse. I said, "I was just thinking that your wife must be sick. She is not eating tonight."

60 He could have laughed at this. But he did not. He laid his hand for a moment on his beard, he smoothed it down. He said, "The second dinner on Christmas Eve was for my son passing through town. My wife died some years ago and I am not remarried."

I am not a hard-hearted girl because I knew that a child gets over the loss of a father and because I also knew that a man gets over the loss of a wife. I am a good girl, but I did not feel sad for Mr. Cohen. I felt very happy. Because he laid his hand on mine and he asked if he could call me. I said yes, and as it turns out, New Year's Eve seems to be a Jewish holiday. The Vietnamese New Year comes at a different time, but people in Vietnam know to celebrate whatever holiday comes along. So tonight Mr. Cohen and I will go to some restaurant that is not Chinese, and all I have to do now is sit here and listen very carefully to Grandfather as he talks to me about time.

➤ *QUESTIONS FOR READING AND WRITING*

1. Who is the narrator of this story? Why is her background important?
2. Describe Mr. Cohen.
3. In what way does the setting of this story matter?
4. Why is the narrator's mother frightened for her? Why is she frightened for herself?
5. Why do you think the first snowfall she saw frightened her "in some very deep way"? Why does snow frighten Mr. Cohen?
6. It's clear at the end of the story that a spark has been lit between the narrator and Mr. Cohen. Do you think they make a good couple? Explain.

ITALO CALVINO (1923–1985)

Italo Calvino was born in Cuba but grew up in Italy. His experimental writing made him one of the most important Italian fiction writers of the twentieth century. Calvino's career as a writer spanned nearly four decades. In The Uses of Literature *(1980), Calvino noted that there should be a time "in adult life devoted to revisiting the most important books of our youth. Even if the books have remained the same (though they do change, in the light of an altered historical perspective), we have most certainly changed, and our encounter will be an entirely new thing." Of Calvino's* If on a winter's night a traveler *(1979), Salman Rushdie declared, "He is writing down what you have always known except that you've never thought of it before."*

IF ON A WINTER'S NIGHT A TRAVELER [1981]

Translated by William Weaver

The novel begins in a railway station, a locomotive huffs, steam from a piston covers the opening of the chapter, a cloud of smoke hides part of the first paragraph. In the odor of the station there is a passing whiff of station café odor. There is someone looking through the befogged glass, he opens the glass door of the bar, everything is misty, inside, too, as if seen by nearsighted eyes, or eyes irritated by coal dust. The pages of the book are clouded like the windows of an old train, the cloud of smoke rests on the sentences. It is a rainy evening; the man enters the bar; he unbuttons his damp overcoat; a cloud of steam enfolds him; a whistle dies away along tracks that are glistening with rain, as far as the eye could see.

   A whistling sound, like a locomotive's, and a cloud of steam rise from the coffee machine that the old counterman puts under pressure, as if he were sending up a signal, or at least so it seems from the series of sentences in the second paragraph, in which the players at the table close the fans of cards against their chests and turn toward the newcomer with a triple twist of their necks, shoulders, and chairs, while the customers at the counter raise their little cups and blow on the surface of the coffee, lips and eyes half shut, or suck the head of their mugs of beer, taking exaggerated care not to spill. The cat arches its back, the cashier closes her cash register and it goes pling. All these signs converge to inform us that this is a little provincial station, where anyone is immediately noticed.

Stations are all alike; it doesn't matter if the lights cannot illuminate beyond their blurred halo, all of this is a setting you know by heart, with the odor of train that lingers even after all the trains have left, the special odor of stations after the last train has left. The lights of the station and the sentences you are reading seem to have the job of dissolving more than of indicating the things that surface from a veil of darkness and fog. I have landed in this station tonight for the first time in my life, entering and leaving this bar, moving from the odor of the platform to the odor of wet sawdust in the toilets, all mixed in a single odor which is that of waiting, the odor of telephone booths when all you can do is reclaim your tokens because the number called has shown no signs of life.

I am the man who comes and goes between the bar and the telephone booth. Or, rather: that man is called "I" and you know nothing else about him, just as this station is called only "station" and beyond it there exists nothing except the unanswered signal of a telephone ringing in a dark room of a distant city. I hang up the receiver, I await the rattling flush, down through the metallic throat, I push the glass door again, head toward the cups piled up to dry in a cloud of steam.

5   The espresso machines in station cafés boast their kinship with the locomotives, the espresso machines of yesterday and today with the locomotives and steam engines of today and yesterday. It's all very well for me to come and go, shift and turn: I am caught in a trap, in that nontemporal trap which all stations unfailingly set. A cloud of coal dust still hovers in the air of stations all these years after the lines have been totally electrified, and a novel that talks about trains and stations cannot help conveying this odor of smoke. For a couple of pages now you have been reading on, and this would be the time to tell you clearly whether this station where I have got off is a station of the past or a station of today; instead the sentences continue to move in vagueness, grayness, in a kind of no man's land of experience reduced to the lowest common denominator. Watch out: it is surely a method of involving you gradually, capturing you in the story before you realize it—a trap. Or perhaps the author still has not made up his mind, just as you, reader, for that matter, are not sure what you would most like to read: whether it is the arrival at an old station, which would give you a sense of going back, a renewed concern with lost times and places, or else a flashing of lights and sounds, which would give you the sense of being alive today, in the world where people today believe it is a pleasure to be alive. This bar (or "station buffet," as it is also called) could seem dim and misty only to my eyes, nearsighted or irritated, whereas it could also be steeped in light diffused by tubes the color of lightning and reflected by mirrors in such a way as to fill completely every passage and interstice, and the shadowless space might be overflowing with music exploding at top volume from a vibrant silent-killing machine, and the pinballs and the other electric games simulating horse races and manhunts are all in

action, and colored shadows swim in the transparency of a TV and in that of an aquarium of tropical fish enlivened by a vertical stream of air bubbles. And my arm might not hold a briefcase, swollen and a bit worn, but might be pushing a square suitcase of plastic material supplied with little wheels, guided by a chrome stick that can be folded up.

You, reader, believe that there, on the platform, my gaze was glued to the hands of the round clock of an old station, hands pierced like halberds, in the vain attempt to turn them back, to move backward over the cemetery of spent hours, lying life-less in their circular pantheon. But who can say that the clock's numbers aren't peeping from rectangular windows, where I see every minute fall on me with a click like the blade of a guillotine? However, the result would not change much: even advancing in a polished, sliding world, my hand contracted on the light rudder of the wheeled suitcase would still express an inner refusal, as if that carefree luggage represented for me an unwelcome and exhausting burden.

Something must have gone wrong for me: some misinformation, a delay, a missed connection; perhaps on arriving I should have found a contact, probably linked with this suitcase that seems to worry me so much, though whether because I am afraid of losing it or because I can't wait to be rid of it is not clear. What seems certain is that it isn't just ordinary baggage, something I can check or pretend to forget in the waiting room. There's no use my looking at my watch; if anyone had come and waited for me he would have gone away again long ago, there's no point in my furiously racking my brain to turn back clocks and calendars in the hope of reaching again the moment before something that should not have happened did happen. If I was to meet someone in this station, someone who perhaps had noth-ing to do with this station but was simply to get off one train and leave on another train, as I was to have done, and one of the two was to pass something to the other—for example, if I was supposed to give the other this wheeled suitcase which instead has been left on my hands and is scorching them—then the only thing to do is to try to reestablish the lost contact.

I have already crossed the café a couple of times and have looked out of the front door onto the invisible square, and each time the wall of darkness has driven back inside this sort of illuminated limbo suspended between the two darknesses, the bundle of tracks and the foggy city. Where would I go out to? The city outside there has no name yet, we don't know if it will remain outside the novel or whether the whole story will be contained within its inky blackness. I know only that this first chapter is taking a while to break free of the station and the bar: it is not wise for me to move away from here where they might still come looking for me, or for me to be seen by other people with this burdensome suitcase. And so I continue to cram tokens into the public telephone, which spits them back at me every time. Many tokens, as if for a long-distance call: God knows where they are now, the people from whom I am to receive instructions or, rather—let's come right out and say it—take orders. If is obvious that I am a subordinate, I do not seem the sort of man who is traveling for personal reasons or who is in business for himself; you would say, on the contrary, that I am doing a job, a pawn in a very complicated game, a little cog in a huge gear, so little that it should not even be seen: if fact, it was established that I would go through here without leaving any traces; and instead, every minute I spend here I am leaving more traces. I leave traces if I do not speak with anyone, since I stick out as a man who won't open his mouth; I leave traces if I speak with someone because every word spoken is a word that remains and can crop up again later, with quotation marks or without. Perhaps this is why the author piles supposition on supposition in long paragraphs without dialogue, a thick, opaque layer of lead where I may pass unnoticed, disappear.

I am not at all the sort of person who attracts attention, I am an anonymous presence against an even more anonymous background. If you, reader, couldn't help picking me out among the people getting off the train and continued following me in my to-and-fro-ing between bar and telephone, this is simply because I am called "I" and this is the only thing you know about me, but this alone is reason enough for you to invest a part of yourself in the stranger "I." Just as the author, since he has no intention of telling about himself, decided to call the character "I" as if to conceal him, not having to name him or describe him, because any other name or attribute would define him more than this stark pronoun; still, by the very fact of writing "I" the author feels driven to put into this "I" a bit of himself, of what he feels or imagines he feels. Nothing could be easier for him than to identify himself with me; for the moment my external behavior is that of a traveler who has missed a connection, a situation that is part of everyone's experience. But a situation that takes place at the opening of a novel always refers you to something else that has happened or is about to happen, and it is this something else that makes it risky to identify with me, risky for you the reader and for him the author; and the more gray and ordinary and undistinguished and commonplace the beginning of this novel is, the more you and the author feel a hint of danger looming over that fraction of "I" that you have heedlessly invested in the "I" of a character whose inner history you know nothing about, as you know nothing about the contents of that suitcase he is so anxious to be rid of.

10   Getting rid of the suitcase was to be the first condition for re-establishing the previous situation: previous to everything that happened afterward. This is what I mean when I say I would like to swim against the stream of time: I would like to erase the consequences of certain events and restore an initial condition. But every moment of my life brings with it an accumulation of new facts, and each of these new facts brings with it its consequences; so the more I seek to return to the zero moment from which I set out, the further I move away from it: though all my actions are bent on erasing the consequences of previous actions and though I manage to achieve appreciable results in this erasure, enough to open my heart to hopes of immediate relief, I must, however, bear in mind that my every move to erase previous events provokes a rain of new events, which complicate the situation worse that before and which I will then, in their turn, have to try to erase. Therefore I must calculate carefully every move so as to achieve the maximum of erasure with the minimum of recomplication.

A man whom I do not know was to meet me as soon as I got off the train, if everything hadn't gone wrong. A man with a suitcase on wheels, exactly like mine, empty. The two suitcases would bump into each other as if accidentally in the bustle of travelers on the platform, between one train and another. An event that can happen by chance, but there would have been a password that that man would have said to me, a comment on the headline of the newspaper sticking out of my pocket, on the results of the horse races. "Ah, Zeno of Elea[1] came in first!" And at the same time we would disentangle our suitcases, shifting the metal poles, perhaps also exchanging some remarks about horses, forecasts, odds; and we would then go off toward different trains, each pushing his suitcase in his own direction. No one would have noticed, but I would have been left with the other man's suitcase and he would have taken away mine.

A perfect plan, so perfect that a trivial complication sufficed to spoil it. Now I am here not knowing what to do next, the last traveler waiting in this station where no more trains arrive or leave before tomorrow morning. It is the hour when the little provincial city crawls into its shell again. At the station bar the only people left are locals who all know one another, people who have no connection with the station but come this far through the dark square perhaps because there is no other place open in the neighborhood, or perhaps because of the attraction that stations still exercise in provincial cities, that bit of novelty that can be expected from stations, or perhaps only in recollection of the time when a station was the single point of contact with the rest of the world.

It's all very well for me to tell myself there are no provincial cities any more and perhaps there never were any: all places communicate instantly with all other places, a sense of isolation is felt only during the trip between one place and the other, that is, when you are in no place. I, in fact, find myself here without a here or an elsewhere, recognized as an outsider by the nonoutsiders at least as clearly as I recognize the nonoutsiders and envy them. Yes, envy. I am looking from the outside at the life of an ordinary evening in an ordinary little city, and I realize I am cut off from ordinary evenings for God knows how long, and I think of thousands of cities like this, of hundreds of thousands of lighted places where at this hour people allow the evening's darkness to descend and have none of the thoughts in their head that I have in mine; maybe they have other thoughts that aren't at all enviable, but at this moment I would be willing to trade with any one of them. For example, with one of these young men who are making the rounds of local shopkeepers collecting signatures on a petition to City Hall, concerning the tax on neon signs, and who are now reading it to the barman.

The novel here repeats fragments of conversation that seem to have no function beyond that of depicting the daily life of a provincial city. "What about you, Armida? Have you signed yet?" they ask a woman I can see only from behind, a belt hanging from a long overcoat trimmed with fur, the collar turned up, a thread of smoke rising from the fingers gripping the stem of a glass. "Who says I want to put a neon sign over my shop?" she answers. "If the City is planning to save money on street lights, they certainly aren't going to light the streets with my money! Anyway, everybody knows where Armida's Leather Goods is. And when I've pulled down the metal blind, the street will just stay dark, and that's that."

15   "That's a good reason for you to sign," they say to her. They address her familiarly, as *tu*; they all call one another *tu*; their speech is half in dialect; these are people used to seeing one another daily year after year; everything they say is the

[1] **Zeno of Elea** Also the name of a Greek philosopher (495–430 B.C.) who described paradoxes of time and space

continuation of things already said. They tease one another, even crudely: "Admit it, you like the street dark so nobody can see who comes to your place! Who visits you in the back of the shop after you've locked up?"

These remarks form a murmuring of indistinct voices from which a word or phrase might emerge, decisive for what comes afterward. To read properly you must take in both the murmuring effect and the effect of the hidden intention, which you (and I, too) are as yet in no position to perceive. In reading, therefore, you must remain both oblivious and highly alert, as I am abstracted but prick up my ears, with my elbow on the counter of the bar and my cheek on my fist. And if now the novel begins to abandon its misty vagueness and give some details about the appearance of the people, the sensation it wants to transmit to you is that of faces seen for the first time but also faces that seem to have been seen thousands of times. We are in a city in whose streets the same people often run into one another; the faces bear a weight of habit which is communicated even to someone like me, who, though I have never been here before, realizes these are habitual faces, whose features the bar mirror has watched thicken or sag, whose expressions evening after evening have become wrinkled or puffy. This woman was perhaps the beauty of the city; even now I feel, seeing her for the first time, she could be called an attractive woman; but if I imagine looking at her with the eyes of the other customers at the bar, then a kind of weariness settles on her, perhaps only the shadow of their weariness (or my weariness, or yours). They have known her since she was a girl, they know everything there is to know about her, some of them may have been involved with her, now water under the bridge, over and done with; in other words, there is a veil of other images that settles on her image and blurs it, a weight of memories that keep me from seeing her as a person seen for the first time, other people's memories suspended like the smoke under the lamps.

The great pastime of these customers at the bar seems to be betting: betting on trivial events of daily life. For example, one says, "Let's bet on who comes first to the bar here tonight, Dr. Marne or Chief Gorin." And another says, "And when Dr. Marne does get here, what will he do to avoid meeting his ex-wife? Will he play billiards or fill in the football-pool form?"

In an existence like mine forecasts could not be made: I never know what could happen to me in the next half hour, I can't imagine a life all made up of minimal alternatives, carefully circumscribed, on which bets can be made: either this or that.

"I don't know," I say in a low voice.

20   "Don't know what?" she asks.

It's a thought I feel I can also say now and not keep for myself as I do with all my thoughts, say it to the woman who is here beside me at the bar, the owner of the leather-goods shop, with whom I have a slight hankering to strike up a conversation. "Is that how it is, here in your town?"

"No, it's not true," she answers me, and I knew this was how she would answer me. She insists that nothing can be foreseen, here or anywhere else: of course, every evening at this hour Dr. Marne closes his office and Chief Gorin comes off duty at the police station; and they always drop by here, first one or first the other; but what does that signify?

"In any case, nobody seems to doubt the fact that the doctor will try to avoid the former Madame Marne," I say to her.

"I am the former Madame Marne," she answers. "Don't listen to them."

25   Your attention, as reader, is now completely concentrated on the woman, already for several pages you have been circling around her, I have—no, the author has—been circling around the feminine presence, for several pages you have been expecting this female shadow to take shape the way female shadows take shape on the written page, and it is your expectation, reader, that drives the author toward her; and I, too, though I have other things to think about, there I let myself go, I speak to her, I strike up a conversation that I should break off as quickly as I can, in order to go away, disappear. You surely would want to know more about what she's like, but instead only a few elements surface on the written page, her face remains hidden by the smoke and her hair, you would need to understand beyond the bitter twist of her mouth what there is that isn't bitter and twisted.

"What stories do they tell?" I ask. "I don't know a thing. I know that you have a shop, without a neon sign. But I don't even know where it is."

She explains to me. It is a leather-goods shop, selling suitcases and travel articles. It isn't in the station square but on a side street, near the grade crossing of the freight station.

"But why are you interested?"

"I wish I had arrived earlier. I would walk along the dark street, I would see your shop all lighted up, I would go inside, I would say to you: If you like, I'll help you pull down the shutter."

30   She tells me she has already pulled down the shutter, but she has to go back to the shop to take inventory, and she will be staying there till late.

The men in the bar are exchanging wisecracks and slaps on the back. One bet has already been decided: the doctor is coming into the place.

"The chief's late tonight. I wonder why."

The doctor comes in and waves a general greeting; his gaze does not stop on his wife, but he has certainly noticed that a man is talking with her. He goes on to the end of the room, turning his back on the bar; he thrusts a coin into the pinball machine. Now I, who should have remained unnoticed, have been scrutinized, photographed by eyes that I cannot deceive myself I have eluded, eyes that forget nothing and no one connected with the object of jealousy and pain. Those slightly heavy, slightly watery eyes are enough to make me realize that the drama between the two has not yet ended: he continues coming to this café every evening to see her, to open the old wound again, perhaps also to know who is walking her home this evening; and she comes to this café every evening perhaps deliberately to make him suffer, or perhaps hoping that the habit of suffering will become for him a habit like any other, that it will take on the flavor of the nothingness that has coated her mouth and her life for years.

"The thing I'd like most in the world," I say to her, since at this point I might as well go on talking with her, "is to make clocks run backwards."

35   The woman gives some ordinary answer, such as, "You only have to move the hands." "No, with thought, by concentrating until I force time to move back," I say; or, rather, it isn't clear whether I really say it or would like to say it or whether the author interprets in this way the half sentence I am muttering. "When I got here my first thought was: Maybe I achieved such an effort with my thoughts that time has made a complete revolution; here I am at the station from which I left on my first

journey, it has remained as it was then, without any change. All the lives that I could have led begin here; there is the girl who could have been my girl and wasn't, with the same eyes, the same hair . . . ."

She looks around, as if making fun of me; I point my chin at her; she raises the corners of her mouth as if to smile, then stops: because she has changed her mind, or because this is the only way she smiles. "I don't know if that's a compliment, but I'll take it as one. And then what?"

"Then I am here, I am the I of the present, with this suitcase."

This is the first time I mention the suitcase, even though I never stop thinking about it.

And she says, "This is the evening of square suitcases on wheels."

40   I remain calm, impassive. I ask, "What do you mean?"

"I sold one today, a suitcase like that."

"Who bought it?"

"A stranger. Like you. He was on his way to the station, he was leaving. With an empty suitcase, just bought. Exactly like yours."

"What's odd about that? Don't you sell suitcases?"

45   "I have a lot of this model in stock at the shop, but nobody here buys them. People don't like them, or they're no use. Or people don't know them. But they must be convenient."

"Not for me. For example, just when I'm thinking that this evening could be a beautiful evening for me, I remember I have to drag this suitcase after me, and I can't think about anything else."

"Then why don't you leave it somewhere?"

"Like a suitcase shop," I say.

"Why not? Another suitcase, more or less."

50   She stands up from the stool, adjusts the collar of her overcoat in the mirror, the belt.

"If I come by later on and rap on the shutter, will you hear me?"

"Try."

She doesn't say good-bye to anyone. She is already outside in the square.

Dr. Marne leaves the pinball machine and approaches the bar. He wants to look at me in the face, perhaps overhear some remarks from the others, or only a snicker. But they are talking of bets, the bets on him, not caring if he listens. There is a stirring of gaiety and intimacy, of slaps on the back, which surrounds Dr. Marne, a business of old jokes and teasing; but at the center of this merriment there is a zone of respect that is never breached, not only because Marne is a physician, public health officer or something of the sort, but also because he is a friend, or perhaps he's a poor bastard who bears his misfortunes while remaining a friend.

55   "Chief Gorin is arriving later that all predictions tonight," someone says, because at that moment the chief enters the bar.

He enters. "Good evening, one and all!" He comes over to me, lowers his eyes to the suitcase, the newspaper, mutters through clenched teeth, "Zeno of Elea," then goes to the cigarette machine.

Have they thrown me to the police? Is he a policeman who is working for our organization? I go over to the machine as if I were also buying cigarettes.

He says, "They've killed Jan. Clear out."

"The suitcase?" I ask.

60   "Take it away again. We want nothing to do with it now. Catch the eleven o'clock express."

"But it doesn't stop here . . ."

"It will. Go to track six. Opposite the freight station. You have three minutes."

"But . . ."

"Move, or I'll have to arrest you."

65   The organization is powerful. It can command the police, the railroad. I trail my suitcase along the passages between the tracks until I reach track six. I walk along the platform. The freight section is at the end, with the grade crossing that opens into the fog and the darkness. The chief is at the door of the station bar, keeping an eye on me. The express arrives at top speed. It slows down, stops, erases me from the chief's sight, pulls out again.

▶ *QUESTIONS FOR READING AND WRITING*

1. The narrator/protagonist refers to us as his "reader." How are you (his reader) affected by his acknowledgement of your presence?
2. Several times he refers to his adventure as a novel. How does this announcement that he is part of a work of fiction influence your response? How does this acknowledgement differ from what narrators usually tell you?
3. This story has been classified as "metafiction" (see p. 487 for a definition). How does the author's "self-conciousness" affect your experience of the story? Would you prefer a more conventional approach? Explain.

RAYMOND CARVER (1938–1988)

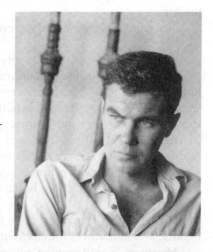

Raymond Carver was born in Clatskanie, Oregon, and raised in Yakima, Washington. After working at a series of low-paying jobs, he entered Humboldt State University in 1963, where he first began to write poetry and short stories, and then went on to earn an master of fine arts degree from the University of Iowa in 1966. Usually set among working-class people, his stories, like "Cathedral," often hinge on moments of sudden insight. His collections include Put Yourself in My Shoes *(1974),* Will You Please Be Quiet, Please? *(1977),* What We Talk About When We Talk About Love *(1981),* Cathedral *(1984), and* Where I'm Calling from: New and Collected Stories *(1988). His stories inspired* Short Takes, *the critically acclaimed 1993 film directed by Robert Altman. Carver died of lung cancer in 1988. Unlike many writers who came of age in the 1970s, Carver did not see the writing of fiction as a political act: "It just has*

to be there for the pleasure we take in doing it, and the different kind of pleasure that's taken in reading something that's durable and made to last, as well as beautiful in and of itself. Something that throws off these sparks—a persistent and steady glow, however dim."

WHAT WE TALK ABOUT WHEN WE TALK ABOUT LOVE   [1981]

My friend Mel McGinnis was talking. Mel McGinnis is a cardiologist, and sometimes that gives him the right.

The four of us were sitting around his kitchen table drinking gin. Sunlight filled the kitchen from the big window behind the sink. There were Mel and me and his second wife, Teresa—Terri, we called her—and my wife, Laura. We lived in Albuquerque then. But we were all from somewhere else.

There was an ice bucket on the table. The gin and the tonic water kept going around, and we somehow got on the subject of love. Mel thought real love was nothing less than spiritual love. He said he'd spent five years in a seminary before quitting to go to medical school. He said he still looked back on those years in the seminary as the most important years in his life.

Terri said the man she lived with before she lived with Mel loved her so much he tried to kill her. Then Terri said, "He beat me up one night. He dragged me around the living room by my ankles. He kept saying, 'I love you, I love you, you bitch.' He went on dragging me around the living room. My head kept knocking on things." Terri looked around the table. "What do you do with love like that?"

5   She was a bone-thin woman with a pretty face, dark eyes, and brown hair that hung down her back. She liked necklaces made of turquoise, and long pendant earrings.

"My God, don't be silly. That's not love, and you know it," Mel said. "I don't know what you'd call it, but I sure know you wouldn't call it love."

"Say what you want to, but I know it was," Terri said. "It may sound crazy to you, but it's true just the same. People are different, Mel. Sure, sometimes he may have acted crazy. Okay. But he loved me. In his own way maybe, but he loved me. There was love there, Mel. Don't say there wasn't."

Mel let out his breath. He held his glass and turned to Laura and me. "The man threatened to kill me," Mel said. He finished his drink and reached for the gin bottle. "Terri's a romantic. Terri's of the kick-me-so-I'll-know-you-love-me school. Terri, hon, don't look that way." Mel reached across the table and touched Terri's cheek with his fingers. He grinned at her.

"Now he wants to make up," Terri said.

10   "Make up what?" Mel said. "What is there to make up? I know what I know. That's all."

"How'd we get started on this subject, anyway?" Terri said. She raised her glass and drank from it. "Mel always has love on his mind," she said. "Don't you, honey?" She smiled, and I thought that was the last of it.

"I just wouldn't call Ed's behavior love. That's all I'm saying, honey," Mel said. "What about you guys?" Mel said to Laura and me. "Does that sound like love to you?"

"I'm the wrong person to ask," I said. "I didn't even know the man. I've only heard his name mentioned in passing. I wouldn't know. You'd have to know the particulars. But I think what you're saying is that love is an absolute."

Mel said, "This kind of love I'm talking about is. The kind of love I'm talking about, you don't try to kill people."

15   Laura said, "I don't know anything about Ed, or anything about the situation. But who can judge anyone else's situation?"

I touched the back of Laura's hand. She gave me a quick smile. I picked up Laura's hand. It was warm, the nails polished, perfectly manicured. I encircled the broad wrist with my fingers, and I held her.

"When I left, he drank rat poison." Terri said. She clasped her arms with her hands. "They took him to the hospital in Santa Fe. That's where we lived then, about ten miles out. They saved his life. But his gums went crazy from it. I mean they pulled away from his teeth. After that, his teeth stood out like fangs. My God," Terry said. She waited a minute, then let go of her arms and picked up her glass.

"What people won't do!" Laura said.

"He's out of the action now," Mel said. "He's dead."

20   Mel handed me the saucer of limes. I took a section, squeezed it over my drink, and stirred the ice cubes with my finger.

"It gets worse," Terri said. "He shot himself in the mouth. But he bungled that too. Poor Ed," she said. Terri shook her head.

"Poor Ed nothing," Mel said. "He was dangerous."

Mel was forty-five years old. He was tall and rangy with curly soft hair. His face and arms were brown from the tennis he played. When he was sober, his gestures, all his movements, were precise, very careful.

"He did love me though, Mel. Grant me that," Terri said. "That's all I'm asking. He didn't love me the way you love me. I'm not saying that. But he loved me. You can grant me that, can't you?"

25   "What do you mean, he bungled it?" I said.

Laura leaned forward with her glass. She put her elbows on the table and held her glass in both hands. She glanced from Mel to Terri and waited with a look of bewilderment on her open face, as if amazed that such things happened to people you were friendly with.

"How'd he bungle it when he killed himself?" I said.

"I'll tell you what happened," Mel said. "He took this twenty-two pistol he'd bought to threaten Terri and me with. Oh, I'm serious, the man was always threatening. You should have seen the way we lived in those days. Like fugitives. I even bought a gun myself. Can you believe it? A guy like me? But I did. I bought one for self-defense and carried it in the glove compartment. Sometimes I'd have to leave the apartment in the middle of the night. To go to the hospital, you know? Terri and I weren't married then, and my first wife had the house and kids, the dog, everything, and Terri and I were living in this apartment here. Sometimes, as I say, I'd get a call in the middle of the night and have to go in to the hospital at two or three in the morning. It'd be dark out there in the parking lot, and I'd break into a sweat before I could even get to my car. I never knew if he was going to come up out of the shrubbery or from behind a car and start shooting. I mean, the man was crazy. He was capable of wiring a bomb, anything. He used to call my service at all hours and say he needed to talk to the doctor, and when I'd return the call, he'd say, 'Son of a bitch, your days are numbered.' Little things like that. It was scary, I'm telling you."

"I still feel sorry for him," Terri said.

30   "It sounds like a nightmare," Laura said. "But what exactly happened after he shot himself?"

Laura is a legal secretary. We'd met in a professional capacity. Before we knew it, it was a courtship. She's thirty-five, three years younger than I am. In addition to being in love, we like each other and enjoy one another's company. She's easy to be with.

"What happened?" Laura said.

Mel said, "He shot himself in the mouth in his room. Someone heard the shot and told the manager. They came in with a passkey, saw what had happened, and called an ambulance. I happened to be there when they brought him in, alive but past recall. The man lived for three day. His head swelled up to twice the size of a normal head. I'd never seen anything like it, and I hope I never do again. Terri wanted to go in and sit with him when she found out about it. We had a fight over it. I didn't think she should see him like that. I didn't think she should see him, and I still don't."

"Who won the fight?" Laura said.

35   "I was in the room with him when he died," Terri said. "He never came up out of it. But I sat with him. He didn't have anyone else."

"He was dangerous," Mel said. "If you call that love, you can have it."

"It was love," Terri said. "Sure, it's abnormal in most people's eyes. But he was willing to die for it. He did die for it."

"I sure as hell wouldn't call it love," Mel said. "I mean, no one knows what he did it for. I've seen a lot of suicides, and I couldn't say anyone ever knew what they did it for."

Mel put his hands behind his neck and tilted his chair back. "I'm not interested in that kind of love," he said. "If that's love, you can have it."

40   Terri said, "We were afraid. Mel even made a will out and wrote to his brother in California who used to be a Green Beret. Mel told him who to look for if something happened to him."

Terri drank from her glass. She said, "But Mel's right—we lived like fugitives. We were afraid. Mel was, weren't you, honey? I even called the police at one point, but they were no help. They said they couldn't do anything until Ed actually did something. Isn't that a laugh?" Terri said.

She poured the last of the gin into her glass and waggled the bottle. Mel got up from the table and went to the cupboard. He took down another bottle.

"Well, Nick and I know what love is," Laura said. "For us, I mean," Laura said. She bumped my knee with her knee. "You're supposed to say something now," Laura said, and turned her smile on me.

For an answer, I took Laura's hand and raised it to my lips. I made a big production out of kissing her hand. Everyone was amused.

45   "We're lucky," I said.

"You guys," Terri said. "Stop that now. You're making me sick. You're still on the honeymoon, for God's sake. You're still gaga, for crying out loud. Just wait. How long have you been together now? How long has it been? A year? Longer than a year?"

"Going on a year and a half," Laura said, flushed and smiling.

"Oh, now," Terri said. "Wait awhile."

She held her drink and gazed at Laura.

50   "I'm only kidding," Terri said.

Mel opened the gin and went around the table with the bottle.

"Here, you guys," he said. "Let's have a toast. I want to propose a toast. A toast to love. To true love," Mel said.

We touched glasses.

"To love," we said.

55   Outside in the backyard, one of the dogs began to bark. The leaves of the aspen that leaned past the window ticked against the glass. The afternoon sun was like a presence in this room, the spacious light of ease and generosity. We could have been anywhere, somewhere enchanted. We raised our glasses again and grinned at each other like children who had agreed on something forbidden.

"I'll tell you what real love is," Mel said. "I mean, I'll give you a good example. And then you can draw your own conclusions." He poured some more gin into his glass. He added an ice cube and a sliver of lime. We waited and sipped our drinks. Laura and I touched knees again. I put a hand on her warm thigh and left it there.

"What do any of us really know about love?" Mel said. "It seems to me we're just beginners at love. We say we love each other and we do, I don't doubt it. I love Terri and Terri loves me, and you guys love each other too. You know the kind of love I'm talking about now. Physical love, that impulse that drives you to someone special, as well as love of the other person's being, his or her essence, as it were. Carnal love and, well, call it sentimental love, the day-to-day caring about the other person. But sometimes I have a hard time accounting for the fact that I must have loved my first wife too. But I did, I know I did. So I suppose I am like Terri in that regard. Terri and Ed." He thought about it and then he went on. "There was a time when I thought I loved my first wife more than life itself. But now I hate her guts. I do. How do you explain that? What happened to that love? What happened to it, is what I'd like to know. I wish someone could tell me. Then there's Ed. Okay, we're back to Ed. He loves Terri so much he tries to kill her and he winds up killing himself." Mel stopped talking and swallowed from his glass. "You guys have been together eighteen months and you love each other. It shows all over you. You glow with it. But you both loved other people before you met each other. You've both been married before, just like us. And you probably loved other people before that too, even. Terri and I have been together five years, been married for four. And the terrible thing, the terrible thing is, but the good thing too, the saving grace, you might say, is that if something happened to one of us—excuse me for saying this—but if something happened to one of us tomorrow, I think the other one, the other person would grieve for a while, you know, but then the surviving party would go out and love again, have someone else soon enough. All this, all of this love we're talking about, it would just be a memory. Maybe not even a memory. Am I wrong? Am I way off base? Because I want you to set me straight if you think I'm wrong. I want to know. I mean, I don't know anything, and I'm the first one to admit it."

"Mel, for God's sake," Terri said. She reached out and took hold of his wrist. "Are you getting drunk? Honey? Are you drunk?"

"Honey, I'm just talking," Mel said. "All right? I don't have to be drunk to say what I think. I mean, we're all just talking, right?" Mel said. He fixed his eyes on her.

60 "Sweetie, I'm not criticizing," Terri said.

She picked up her glass.

"I'm not on call today," Mel said. "Let me remind you of that. I am not on call," he said.

"Mel, we love you," Laura said.

Mel looked at Laura. He looked at her as if he could not place her, as if she was not the woman she was.

65 "Love you too, Laura," Mel said. "And you, Nick, love you too. You know something?" Mel said. "You guys are our pals," Mel said.

He picked up his glass.

Mel said, "I was going to tell you about something. I mean, I was going to prove a point. You see, this happened a few months ago, but it's still going on right now, and it ought to make us feel ashamed when we talk like we know what we're talking about when we talk about love."

"Come on now," Terri said. "Don't talk like you're drunk if you're not drunk."

"Just shut up for once in your life," Mel said very quietly. "Will you do me a favor and do that for a minute? So as I was saying, there's this old couple who had this car wreck out on the interstate. A kid hit them and they were all torn to shit and nobody was giving them much chance to pull through."

70 Terri looked at us and then back at Mel. She seemed anxious, or maybe that's too strong a word.

Mel was handing the bottle around the table.

"I was on call that night," Mel said. "It was May or maybe it was June. Terri and I had just sat down to dinner when the hospital called. There'd been this thing out on the interstate. Drunk kid, teenager, plowed his dad's pickup into this camper with this old couple in it. They were up in their mid-seventies, that couple. The kid—eighteen, nineteen, something—he was DOA. Taken the steering wheel through his sternum. The old couple, they were alive, you understand. I mean, just barely. But they had everything. Multiple fractures, internal injuries, hemorrhaging, contusions, lacerations, the works, and they each of them had concussions. They were in a bad way, believe me. And, of course, their age was two strikes against them. I'd say she was worse off than he was. Ruptured spleen along with everything else. Both kneecaps broken. But they'd been wearing their seatbelts and, God knows, that's what saved them for the time being."

"Folks, this is an advertisement for the National Safety Council," Terri said. "This is your spokesman, Dr. Melvin R. McGinnis, talking." Terri laughed. "Mel," she said, "sometimes you're just too much. But I love you, hon," she said.

"Honey, I love you," Mel said.

75   He leaned across the table. Terri met him halfway. They kissed.

"Terri's right," Mel said as he settled himself again. "Get those seatbelts on. But seriously, they were in some shape, those oldsters. By the time I got down there, the kid was dead, as I said. He was off in a corner, laid out on a gurney. I took one look at the old couple and told the ER nurse to get me a neurologist and an orthopedic man and a couple of surgeons down there right away."

He drank from his glass. "I'll try to keep this short," he said. "So we took the two of them up to the OR and worked like fuck on them most of the night. They had these incredible reserves, those two. You see that once in a while. So we did everything that could be done, and toward morning we're giving them a fifty-fifty chance, maybe less than that for her. So here they are, still alive the next morning. So, okay, we move them into the ICU, which is where they both kept plugging away at it for two weeks, hitting it better and better on all the scopes. So we transfer them out to their own room."

Mel stopped talking. "Here," he said, "let's drink this cheapo gin the hell up. Then we're going to dinner, right? Terri and I know a new place. That's where we'll go, to this new place we know about. But were not going until we finish up this cut-rate, lousy gin."

Terri said, "We haven't actually eaten there yet. But it looks good. From the outside, you know."

80   "I like food," Mel said. "If I had it to do all over again, I'd be a chef, you know? Right, Terri?" Mel said.

He laughed. He fingered the ice in his glass.

"Terri knows," he said. "Terri can tell you. But let me say this. If I could come back again in a different life, a different time and all, you know what? I'd like to come back as a knight. You were pretty safe wearing all that armor. It was all right being a knight until gunpowder and muskets and pistols came along."

"Mel would like to ride a horse and carry a lance," Terri said.

"Carry a woman's scarf with you everywhere," Laura said.

85   "Or just a woman," Mel said.

"Shame on you," Laura said.

Terri said, "Suppose you came back as a serf. The serfs didn't have it so good in those days," Terri said.

"The serfs never had it good," Mel said. "But I guess even the knights were vessels to someone. Isn't that the way it worked? But then everyone is always a vessel to someone. Isn't that right? Terri? But what I liked about knights, beside their ladies, was that they had that suit of armor, you know, and they couldn't get hurt very easy. No cars in those days, you know? No drunk teenagers to tear into your ass."

"Vassals," Terri said.

90   "What?" Mel said.

"Vassals," Terri said. "They were called vassals, not vessels."

"Vassals, vessels," Mel said, "what the fuck's the difference? You knew what I meant anyway. All right," Mel said. "So I'm not educated. I learned my stuff. I'm a heart surgeon, sure, but I'm just a mechanic. I go in and fuck around and I fix things. Shit," Mel said.

"Modesty doesn't become you," Terri said.

"He's just a humble sawbones," I said. "But sometimes they suffocated in all that armor, Mel. They'd even have heart attacks if it got too hot and they were too tired and worn out. I read somewhere that they'd fall off their horses and not be able to get up because they were too tired to stand with all that armor on them. They got trampled by their own horses sometimes."

95 "That's terrible," Mel said. "That's a terrible thing, Nicky. I guess they'd just lay there and wait until somebody came along and made a shish kebab out of them."

"Some other vessel," Terri said.

"That's right," Mel said. "Some vassal would come along and spear the bastard in the name of love. Or whatever the fuck it was they fought over in those days."

"Same things we fight over these days," Terri said.

Laura said, "Nothing's changed."

100 The color was still high in Laura's cheeks. Her eyes were bright. She brought her glass to her lips.

Mel poured himself another drink. He looked at the label closely as if studying a long row of numbers. Then he slowly put the bottle down on the table and slowly reached for the tonic water.

"What about the old couple?" Laura said. "You didn't finish that story you started."

Laura was having a hard time lighting her cigarette. Her matches kept going out.

The sunshine inside the room was different now, changing, getting thinner. But the leaves outside the window were still shimmering, and I stared at the pattern they made on the panes and on the Formica counter. They weren't the same patterns, of course.

105 "What about the old couple?" I said.

"Older but wiser," Terri said.

Mel stared at her.

Terri said, "Go on with your story, hon. I was only kidding. Then what happened?"

"Terri, sometimes," Mel said.

110 "Please, Mel," Terri said. "Don't always be so serious, sweetie. Can't you take a joke?"

"Where's the joke?" Mel said.

He held his glass and gazed steadily at his wife.

"What happened?" Laura said.

Mel fastened his eyes on Laura. He said, "Laura, if I didn't have Terri and if I didn't love her so much, and if Nick wasn't my best friend, I'd fall in love with you. I'd carry you off, honey," he said.

115 "Tell your story," Terri said. "Then we'll go to that new place, okay?"

"Okay," Mel said. "Where was I?" he said. He stared at the table and then he began again.

"I dropped in to see each of them every day, sometimes twice a day if I was up doing other calls anyway. Casts and bandages, head to foot, the both of them. You know, you've seen it in the movies. That's just the way they looked, just like in the movies. Little eye-holes and nose-holes and mouth-holes. And she had to have her legs slung up on top of it. Well, the husband was very depressed for the longest while. Even after he found out that his wife was going to pull through, he was still very depressed. Not about the accident, though. I mean, the accident was one thing, but it wasn't everything. I'd get up to his mouth-hole, you know, and he'd so no, it wasn't the accident exactly but it was because he couldn't see her through his eye-holes. He said that was what was making him feel so bad. Can you imagine? I'm telling you, the man's heart was breaking because he couldn't turn his goddamn head and *see* his goddamn wife."

Mel looked around the table and shook his head at what he was going to say.

"I mean, it was killing the old fart just because he couldn't *look* at the fucking woman."

120   We all looked at Mel.

"Do you see what I'm saying?" he said.

Maybe we were a little drunk by then. I know it was hard keeping things in focus. The light was draining out of the room, going back through the window where it had come from. Yet nobody made a move to get up from the table to turn on the overhead light.

"Listen," Mel said. "Let's finish this fucking gin. There's about enough here for one shooter all around. Then let's go eat. Let's go to the new place."

"He's depressed," Terri said. "Mel, why don't you take a pill?"

125   Mel shook his head. "I've taken everything there is."

"We all need a pill now and then," I said.

"Some people are born needing them," Terri said.

She was using her finger to rub at something on the table. Then she stopped rubbing.

"I think I want to call my kids," Mel said. "Is that all right with everybody? I'll call my kids," he said.

130   Terri said, "What if Marjorie answers the phone? You guys, you've heard us on the subject of Marjorie? Honey, you know you don't want to talk to Marjorie. It'll make you feel even worse."

"I don't want to talk to Marjorie," Mel said. "But I want to talk to my kids."

"There isn't a day goes by that Mel doesn't say he wishes she'd get married again. Or else die," Terri said. "For one thing," Terri said, "she's bankrupting us. Mel says it's just to spite him that she won't get married again. She has a boyfriend who lives with her and the kids, so Mel is supporting the boyfriend too."

"She's allergic to bees," Mel said. "If I'm not praying she'll get married again, I'm praying she'll get herself stung to death by a swarm of fucking bees."

"Shame on you," Laura said.

135   "Bzzzzz," Mel said, turning his fingers into bees and buzzing them at Terri's throat. Then he let his hands drop all the way to his sides.

"She's vicious," Mel said. "Sometimes I think I'll go up there dressed like a beekeeper. You know, that hat that's like a helmet with the plate that comes down over your face, the big gloves, and the padded coat? I'll knock on the door and let loose a hive of bees in the house. But first I'd make sure the kids were out, of course."

He crossed one leg over the other. It seemed to take him a lot of time to do it. Then he put bother feet on the floor and leaned forward, elbows on the table, his chin cupped in his hands.

"Maybe I won't call the kids, after all. Maybe it isn't such a hot idea. Maybe we'll just go eat. How does that sound?

"Sounds fine to me," I said. "Eat or not eat. Or keep drinking. I could head right on out into the sunset."

140   "What does that mean, honey?" Laura said.

"It just means what I said," I said. "It means I could just keep going. That's all it means."

"I could eat something myself," Laura said. "I don't think I've ever been so hungry in my life. Is there something to nibble on?"

"I'll put out some cheese and crackers," Terri said.

But Terri just sat there. She did not get up to get anything.

145   Mel turned his glass over. He spilled it out on the table.

"Gin's gone," Mel said.

Terri said, "Now what?"

I could hear my heart beating. I could hear everyone's heart. I could hear the human noise we sat there making, not one of us moving, not even when the room went dark.

➤ QUESTIONS FOR READING AND WRITING

1. How would you define "love"?
2. If you were a participant in this discussion, would you have agreed with Mel or with Terri about Ed's love for Terri?
3. Why is everyone so still at the end of the story? What do you think they are wondering? What are you wondering?

WILLA CATHER (1873–1947)

Willa Cather was born in the Shenandoah Valley of Virginia, but moved with her family to Red Cloud, Nebraska, a young community made up primarily of European immigrants, when she was 9 years old. She attended the University of Nebraska, and after graduation in 1895 moved back East, first to Pittsburgh and then to New York City, where she worked as a reporter, high school teacher, and editor, writing and publishing occasional poems and short stories. In 1912, following the publication of her first novel, Alexander's Bridge, *Cather left her job as managing editor of* McClure's *magazine, deciding to devote herself exclusively to writing fiction. Much of her great-est work, including the novels* O Pioneers! *(1913),* The Song of the Lark *(1915), and* My Antonia *(1918), is set in the rural frontier of her childhood. "Paul's Case," which explores the artistic temperament and power of the human imagination in an inhos-pitable world, is taken from* The Troll Garden *(1905), Cather's first collection of short stories.*

PAUL'S CASE   [1905]

A Study in Temperament

It was Paul's afternoon to appear before the faculty of the Pittsburgh High School to account for his various misdemeanors. He had been suspended a week ago, and his father had called at the Principal's office and confessed his perplexity about his son. Paul entered the faculty room suave and smiling. His clothes were a trifle out-grown and the tan velvet on the collar of his open overcoat was frayed and worn; but for all that there was something of the dandy about him, and he wore an opal pin in his neatly knotted black four-in-hand, and a red carnation in his buttonhole. This latter adornment the faculty somehow felt was not properly significant of the contrite spirit befitting a boy under the ban of suspension.

Paul was tall for his age and very thin, with high, cramped shoulders and a narrow chest. His eyes were remarkable for a certain hysterical brilliancy, and he continually used them in a conscious, theatrical sort of way, peculiarly offensive in a boy. The pupils were abnormally large, as though he were addicted to belladonna, but there was a glassy glitter about them which that drug does not produce.

When questioned by the Principal as to why he was there, Paul stated, politely enough, that he wanted to come back to school. This was a lie, but Paul was quite accustomed to lying; found it, indeed, indispensable for overcoming friction. His teachers were asked to state their respective charges against him, which they did with such a rancor and aggrievedness as evinced that this was not a usual case. Disorder and impertinence were among the offenses named, yet each of his instructors felt that it was scarcely possible to put into words the real cause of the trouble, which lay in a sort of hysterically defiant manner of the boy's; in the con-tempt which they all knew he felt for them, and which he seemingly made not the least effort to conceal. Once, when he had been making a synopsis of a paragraph at the blackboard, his English teacher had stepped to his side and attempted to guide his hand. Paul had started back with a shudder and thrust his hands violently behind him. The astonished woman could scarcely have been more hurt and embarrassed had he struck at her. The insult was so involuntary and definitely per-sonal as to be unforgettable. In one way and another, he had made all his teachers, men and women alike, conscious of the same feeling of physical aversion. In one class he habitually sat with his hand shading his eyes; in another he always looked out of the window during the recitation; in another he made a running commen-tary on the lecture, with humorous intention.

His teachers felt this afternoon that his whole attitude was symbolized by his shrug and his flippantly red carnation flower, and they fell upon him without mercy, his English teacher leading the pack. He stood through it smiling, his pale lips parted over his white teeth. (His lips were continually twitching, and he had a habit of raising his eyebrows that was contemptuous and irritating to the last degree.) Older boys than Paul had broken down and shed tears under that baptism of fire, but his set smile did not once desert him, and his only sign of discomfort was the nervous trembling of the fingers that toyed with the buttons of his overcoat, and an occasional jerking of the other hand that held his hat. Paul was always smiling, always glancing about him, seeming to feel that people might be watching him and trying to detect something. This conscious expression, since it was as far as possible from boyish mirthfulness, was usually attributed to insolence or "smartness."

5   As the inquisition proceeded, one of his instructors repeated an impertinent remark of the boy's, and the Principal asked him whether he thought that a courteous speech to make to a woman. Paul shrugged his shoulders slightly and his eyebrows twitched.

"I don't know," he replied. "I didn't mean to be polite or impolite, either. I guess it's a sort of way I have of saying things regardless."

The Principal, who was a sympathetic man, asked him whether he didn't think that a way it would be well to get rid of. Paul grinned and said he guessed so. When he was told that he could go, he bowed gracefully and went out. His bow was but a repetition of the scandalous red carnation.

His teachers were in despair, and his drawing master voiced the feeling of them all when he declared there was something about the boy which none of them understood. He added: "I don't really believe that smile of his comes altogether from insolence; there's something sort of haunted about it. The boy is not strong, for one thing. I happen to know that he was born in Colorado, only a few months' before his mother died out there of a long illness. There is something wrong about the fellow."

The drawing master had come to realize that, in looking at Paul, one saw only his white teeth and the forced animation of his eyes. One warm afternoon the boy had gone to sleep at his drawing board, and his master had noted with amazement what a white, blue-veined face it was; drawn and wrinkled like an old man's about the eyes, the lips twitching even in his sleep, and stiff with a nervous tension that drew them back from his teeth.

10   His teachers left the building dissatisfied and unhappy; humiliated to have felt so vindictive toward a mere boy, to have uttered this feeling in cutting terms, and to have set each other on, as it were, in the gruesome game of intemperate reproach. Some of them remembered having seen a miserable street cat set at bay by a ring of tormentors.

As for Paul, he ran down the hill whistling the Soldiers' Chorus from *Faust*,[1] looking wildly behind him now and then to see whether some of his teachers were not there to writhe under his light-heartedness. As it was now late in the afternoon and Paul was on duty that evening as usher at Carnegie Hall[2], he decided that he would not go home to supper. When he reached the concert hall the doors were not yet open and, as it was chilly outside, he decided to go up into the picture gallery— always deserted at this hour—where there were some of Raffaëlli's[3] gay studies of

---

[1] **Faust** a popular opera   [2] **Carnegie Hall** in Pittsburgh, not New York   [3] **Raffaëlli** an impressionist painter, sculptor, and engraver

Paris streets and an airy blue Venetian scene or two that always exhilarated him. He was delighted to find no one in the gallery but the old guard, who sat in one corner, a newspaper on his knee, a black patch over one eye and the other closed. Paul possessed himself of the place and walked confidently up and down, whistling under his breath. After a while he sat down before a blue Rico[4] and lost himself. When he bethought him to look at his watch, it was after seven o'clock, and he rose with a start and ran downstairs, making a face at Augustus[5], peering out from the cast-room, and an evil gesture at the Venus of Milo as he passed her on the stairway.

When Paul reached the ushers' dressing-room half a dozen boys were there already, and he began excitedly to tumble into his uniform. It was one of the few that at all approached fitting, and Paul thought it very becoming—though he knew that the tight, straight coat accentuated his narrow chest, about which he was exceedingly sensitive. He was always considerably excited while he dressed, twanging all over to the tuning of the strings and the preliminary flourishes of the horns in the music-room; but tonight he seemed quite beside himself, and he teased and plagued the boys until, telling him that he was crazy, they put him down on the floor and sat on him.

Somewhat calmed by his suppression, Paul dashed out to the front of the house to seat the early comers. He was a model usher; gracious and smiling he ran up and down the aisles; nothing was too much trouble for him; he carried messages and brought programs as though it were his greatest pleasure in life, and all the people in his section thought him a charming boy, feeling that he remembered and admired them. As the house filled, he grew more and more vivacious and animated, and the color came to his cheeks and lips. It was very much as though this were a great reception and Paul were the host. Just as the musicians came out to take their places, his English teacher arrived with checks for the seats which a prominent manufacturer had taken for the season. She betrayed some embarrassment when she handed Paul the tickets, and a *hauteur* which subsequently made her feel very foolish. Paul was startled for a moment, and had the feeling of wanting to put her out; what business had she here among all these fine people and gay colors? He looked her over and decided that she was not appropriately dressed and must be a fool to sit downstairs in such togs. The tickets had probably been sent her out of kindness, he reflected as he put down a seat for her, and she had about as much right to sit there as he had.

When the symphony began Paul sank into one of the rear seats with a long sigh of relief, and lost himself as he had done before the Rico. It was not that symphonies, as such, meant anything in particular to Paul, but the first sigh of the instruments seemed to free some hilarious and potent spirit within him; something that struggled there like the genie in the bottle found by the Arab fisherman.[6] He felt a sudden zest of life; the lights danced before his eyes and the concert hall blazed into unimaginable splendor. When the soprano soloist came on, Paul forgot even the nastiness of his teacher's being there and gave himself up to the peculiar

---

[4] **Rico** a Spanish landscape painter   [5] **Augustus . . . Milo** copies of the famous statues of Augustus and the Venus de Milo   [6] **Arab fisherman** reference to a tale from *The Arabian Nights*

stimulus such personages always had for him. The soloist chanced to be a German woman, by no means in her first youth, and the mother of many children; but she wore an elaborate gown and a tiara, and above all she had that indefinable air of achievement, that world-shine upon her, which, in Paul's eyes, made her a veritable queen of romance.

15   After a concert was over Paul was always irritable and wretched until he got to sleep, and tonight he was even more than usually restless. He had the feeling of not being able to let down, of its being impossible to give up this delicious excitement which was the only thing that could be called living at all. During the last number he withdrew and, after hastily changing his clothes in the dressing-room, slipped out to the side door where the soprano's carriage stood. Here he began pacing rapidly up and down the walk, waiting to see her come out.

Over yonder the Schenley, in its vacant stretch, loomed big and square through the fine rain, the windows of its twelve stories glowing like those of a lighted cardboard house under a Christmas tree. All the actors and singers of the better class stayed there when they were in the city, and a number of the big manufacturers of the place lived there in the winter. Paul had often hung about the hotel, watching the people go in and out, longing to enter and leave schoolmasters and dull care behind him forever.

At last the singer came out, accompanied by the conductor, who helped her into her carriage and closed the door with a cordial *auf Wiedersehen*[7] which set Paul to wondering whether she were not an old sweetheart of his. Paul followed the carriage over to the hotel, walking so rapidly as not to be far from the entrance when the singer alighted and disappeared behind the swinging glass doors that were opened by a Negro in a tall hat and a long coat. In the moment that the door was ajar it seemed to Paul that he, too, entered. He seemed to feel himself go after her up the steps, into the warm, lighted building, into an exotic, a tropical world of shiny, glistening surfaces and basking ease. He reflected upon the mysterious dishes that were brought into the dining-room, the green bottles in buckets of ice, as he had seen them in the supper party pictures of the *Sunday World* supplement. A quick gust of wind brought the rain down with sudden vehemence, and Paul was startled to find that he was still outside in the slush of the gravel driveway; that his boots were letting in the water and his scanty overcoat was clinging wet about him; that the lights in front of the concert hall were out and that the rain was driving in sheets between him and the orange glow of the windows above him. There it was, what he wanted—tangibly before him, like the fairy world of a Christmas pantomime—but mocking spirits stood guard at the doors, and, as the rain beat in his face, Paul wondered whether he were destined always to shiver in the black night outside, looking up at it.

He turned and walked reluctantly toward the car[8] tracks. The end had to come sometime; his father in his night-clothes at the top of the stairs, explanations that did not explain, hastily improvised fictions that were forever tripping him up, his upstairs room and its horrible yellow wallpaper, the creaking bureau with the greasy

---

[7] **auf Wiedersehen** German for "good-bye"   [8] **car** streetcar

plush collar-box, and over his painted wooden bed the pictures of George Washington and John Calvin,[9] and the framed motto, "Feed my Lambs,"[10] which had been worked in red worsted by his mother.

Half an hour later, Paul alighted from his car and went slowly down one of the side streets off the main thoroughfare. It was a highly respectable street, where all the houses were exactly alike, and where businessmen of moderate means begot and reared large families of children, all of whom went to Sabbath school and learned the shorter catechism, and were interested in arithmetic; all of whom were as exactly alike as their homes, and of a piece with the monotony in which they lived. Paul never went up Cordelia Street without a shudder of loathing. His home was next to the house of the Cumberland[11] minister. He approached it tonight with the nerveless sense of defeat, the hopeless feeling of sinking back forever into ugliness and commonness that he had always had when he came home. The moment he turned into Cordelia Street he felt the waters close above his head. After each of these orgies of living, he experienced all the physical depression which follows a debauch; the loathing of respectable beds, of common food, of a house permeated by kitchen odors; a shuddering repulsion for the flavorless, colorless mass of everyday existence; a morbid desire for cool things and soft lights and fresh flowers.

20   The nearer he approached the house, the more absolutely unequal Paul felt to the sight of it all: his ugly sleeping chamber; the cold bathroom with the grimy zinc tub, the cracked mirror, the dripping spigots; his father, at the top of the stairs, his hairy legs sticking out from his nightshirt, his feet thrust into carpet slippers. He was so much later than usual that there would certainly be inquiries and reproaches. Paul stopped short before the door. He felt that he could not be accosted by his father tonight; that he could not toss again on that miserable bed. He would not go in. He would tell his father that he had no car fare, and it was raining so hard he had gone home with one of the boys and stayed all night.

Meanwhile, he was wet and cold. He went around to the back of the house and tried one of the basement windows, found it open, raised it cautiously, and scrambled down the cellar wall to the floor. There he stood, holding his breath, terrified by the noise he had made, but the floor above him was silent, and there was no creak on the stairs. He found a soap-box, and carried it over to the soft ring of light that streamed from the furnace door, and sat down. He was horribly afraid of rats, so he did not try to sleep, but sat looking distrustfully at the dark, still terrified lest he might have awakened his father. In such reactions, after one of the experiences which made days and nights out of the dreary blanks of the calendar, when his senses were deadened, Paul's head was always singularly clear. Suppose his father had heard him getting in at the window and had come down and shot him for a burglar? Then, again, suppose his father had come down, pistol in hand, and he had cried out in time to save himself, and his father had been horrified to think how nearly he had killed him? Then, again, suppose a day should come when his father would remember that night, and wish there had been no warning cry to stay his hand? With this last supposition Paul entertained himself until daybreak.

[9] **John Calvin** an early leader of the Protestant Reformation   [10] **"Feed my Lambs"** from John 21:15–17
[11] **Cumberland** an Evangelical branch of the Presbyterian church

The following Sunday was fine; the sodden November chill was broken by the last flash of autumnal summer. In the morning Paul had to go to church and Sabbath school, as always. On seasonable Sunday afternoons the burghers of Cordelia Street always sat out on their front "stoops," and talked to their neighbors on the next stoop, or called to those across the street in neighborly fashion. The men usually sat on gay cushions placed upon the steps that led down to the sidewalk, while the women, in their Sunday "waists,"[12] sat in rockers on the cramped porches, pretending to be greatly at their ease. The children played in the streets; there were so many of them that the place resembled the recreation grounds of a kindergarten. The men on the steps—all in their shirt sleeves, their vests unbuttoned—sat with their legs well apart, their stomachs comfortably protruding, and talked of the prices of things, or told anecdotes of the sagacity of their various chiefs and overlords. They occasionally looked over the multitude of squabbling children, listened affectionately to their high-pitched, nasal voices, smiling to see their own proclivities reproduced in their offspring, and interspersed their legends of the iron kings with remarks about their sons' progress at school, their grades in arithmetic, and the amounts they had saved in their toy banks.

On this last Sunday of November, Paul sat all the afternoon on the lowest step of his "stoop," staring into the street, while his sisters, in their rockers, were talking to the minister's daughters next door about how many shirtwaists they had made in the last week, and how many waffles someone had eaten at the last church supper. When the weather was warm, and his father was in a particularly jovial frame of mind, the girls made lemonade, which was always brought out in a red-glass pitcher, ornamented with forget-me-nots in blue enamel. This the girls thought very fine, and the neighbors always joked about the suspicious color of the pitcher.

Today Paul's father sat on the top step, talking to a young man who shifted a restless baby from knee to knee. He happened to be the young man who was daily held up to Paul as a model, and after whom it was his father's dearest hope that he would pattern. This young man was of a ruddy complexion, with a compressed, red mouth, and faded, nearsighted eyes, over which he wore thick spectacles, with gold bows that curved about his ears. He was clerk to one of the magnates of a great steel corporation, and was looked upon in Cordelia Street as a young man with a future. There was a story that, some five years ago—he was now barely twenty-six—he had been a trifle dissipated, but in order to curb his appetites and save the loss of time and strength that a sowing of wild oats might have entailed, he had taken his chief's advice, oft reiterated to his employees, and at twenty-one had married the first woman whom he could persuade to share his fortunes. She happened to be an angular schoolmistress, much older than he, who also wore thick glasses, and who had now borne him four children, all nearsighted, like herself.

25   The young man was relating how his chief, now cruising in the Mediterranean, kept in touch with all the details of the business, arranging his office hours on his yacht just as though he were at home, and "knocking off work enough to keep two stenographers busy." His father told, in turn, the plan his corporation was considering, of putting in an electric railway plant at Cairo. Paul snapped his teeth; he had

[12] **waists** laced, close-fitting vests or jackets

an awful apprehension that they might spoil it all before he got there. Yet he rather liked to hear these legends of the iron kings, that were told and retold on Sundays and holidays; these stories of palaces in Venice, yachts on the Mediterranean, and high play at Monte Carlo appealed to his fancy, and he was interested in the triumphs of these cash boys[13] who had become famous, though he had no mind for the cash-boy stage.

After supper was over, and he had helped to dry the dishes, Paul nervously asked his father whether he could go to George's to get some help in his geometry, and still more nervously asked for car fare. This latter request he had to repeat, as his father, on principle, did not like to hear requests for money, whether much or little. He asked Paul whether he could not go to some boy who lived nearer, and told him that he ought not to leave his school work until Sunday; but he gave him the dime. He was not a poor man, but he had a worthy ambition to come up in the world. His only reason for allowing Paul to usher was that he thought a boy ought to be earning a little.

Paul bounded upstairs, scrubbed the greasy odor of the dishwater from his hands with the ill-smelling soap he hated, and then shook over his fingers a few drops of violet water from the bottle he kept hidden in his drawer. He left the house with his geometry conspicuously under his arm, and the moment he got out of Cordelia Street and boarded a downtown car, he shook off the lethargy of two deadening days, and began to live again.

The leading juvenile of the permanent stock company which played at one of the downtown theaters was an acquaintance of Paul's, and the boy had been invited to drop in at the Sunday-night rehearsals whenever he could. For more than a year Paul had spent every available moment loitering about Charley Edwards's dressing-room. He had won a place among Edwards's following not only because the young actor, who could not afford to employ a dresser, often found him useful, but because he recognized in Paul something akin to what churchmen term "vocation."

It was at the theater and at Carnegie Hall that Paul really lived; the rest was but a sleep and a forgetting. This was Paul's fairy tale, and it had for him all the allurement of a secret love. The moment he inhaled the gassy, painty, dusty odor behind the scenes, he breathed like a prisoner set free, and felt within him the possibility of doing or saying splendid, brilliant, poetic things. The moment the cracked orchestra beat out the overture from *Martha*,[14] or jerked at the serenade from *Rigoletto*, [15] all stupid and ugly things slid from him, and his senses were deliciously, yet delicately fired.

30   Perhaps it was because, in Paul's world, the natural nearly always wore the guise of ugliness, that a certain element of artificiality seemed to him necessary in beauty. Perhaps it was because his experience of life elsewhere was so full of Sabbath school picnics, petty economies, wholesome advice as to how to succeed in life, and the unescapable odors of cooking, that he found this existence so alluring, these smartly clad men and women so attractive, that he was so moved by these starry apple orchards that bloomed perennially under the limelight.

---

[13] **cash boys** *The Cash Boy*, a "rags to riches" novel by Horatio Alger   [14] **Martha** opera by Friedrick von Flotow and the source of "The Last Rose of Summer"   [15] **Rigoletto** a well-known opera by Giuseppe Verdi

It would be difficult to put it strongly enough how convincingly the stage entrance of that theater was for Paul the actual portal of Romance. Certainly none of the company ever suspected it, least of all Charley Edwards. It was very like the old stories that used to float about London of fabulously rich Jews, who had subterranean halls, with palms, and fountains, and soft lamps and richly appareled women who never saw the disenchanting light of London day. So, in the midst of that smoke-palled city, enamored of figures and grimy toil, Paul had his secret temple, his wishing carpet, his bit of blue-and-white Mediterranean shore bathed in perpetual sunshine.

Several of Paul's teachers had a theory that his imagination had been perverted by garish fiction, but the truth was, that he scarcely ever read at all. The books at home were not such as would either tempt or corrupt a youthful mind, and as for reading the novels that some of his friends urged upon him—well, he got what he wanted much more quickly from music; any sort of music, from an orchestra to a barrel organ. He needed only the spark, the indescribable thrill that made his imagination master of his senses, and he could make plots and pictures enough of his own. It was equally true that he was not stagestruck—not, at any rate, in the usual acceptation of that expression. He had no desire to become an actor, any more than he had to become a musician. He felt no necessity to do any of these things; what he wanted was to see, to be in the atmosphere, float on the wave of it, to be carried out, blue league after blue league, away from everything.

After a night behind the scenes, Paul found the school-room more than ever repulsive; the bare floors and naked walls; the prosy men who never wore frock coats, or violets in their buttonholes; the women with their dull gowns, shrill voices, and pitiful seriousness about prepositions that govern the dative. He could not bear to have the other pupils think, for a moment, that he took these people seriously; he must convey to them that he considered it all trivial, and was there only by way of a jest, anyway. He had autographed pictures of all the members of the stock company which he showed his classmates, telling them the most incredible stories of his familiarity with these people, of his acquaintance with the soloists who came to Carnegie Hall, his suppers with them and the flowers he sent them. When these stories lost their effect, and his audience grew listless, he became desperate and would bid all the boys good-bye, announcing that he was going to travel for a while; going to Naples, to Venice, to Egypt. Then, next Monday, he would slip back, conscious and nervously smiling; his sister was ill, and he should have to defer his voyage until spring.

Matters went steadily worse with Paul at school. In the itch to let his instructors know how heartily he despised them and their homilies, and how thoroughly he was appreciated elsewhere, he mentioned once or twice that he had no time to fool with theorems; adding—with a twitch of the eyebrows and a touch of that nervous bravado which so perplexed them—that he was helping the people down at the stock company; they were old friends of his.

35   The upshot of the matter was that the Principal went to Paul's father, and Paul was taken out of school and put to work. The manager at Carnegie Hall was told to get another usher in his stead; the door-keeper at the theater was warned not to admit him to the house; and Charley Edwards remorsefully promised the boy's father not to see him again.

The members of the stock company were vastly amused when some of Paul's stories reached them—especially the women. They were hard-working women, most of them supporting indigent husbands or brothers, and they laughed rather bitterly at having stirred the boy to such fervid and florid inventions. They agreed with the faculty and with his father that Paul's was a bad case.

The east-bound train was plowing through a January snowstorm; the dull dawn was beginning to show gray when the engine whistled a mile out of Newark.[16] Paul started up from the seat where he had lain curled in uneasy slumber, rubbed the breath-misted window glass with his hand, and peered out. The snow was whirling in curling eddies above the white bottom lands, and the drifts lay already deep in the fields and along the fences, while here and there the long dead grass and dried weed stalks protruded black above it. Lights shone from the scattered houses, and a gang of laborers who stood beside the track waved their lanterns.

Paul had slept very little, and he felt grimy and uncomfortable. He had made the all-night journey in a day coach, partly because he was ashamed, dressed as he was, to go into a Pullman, and partly because he was afraid of being seen there by some Pittsburgh businessman who might have noticed him in Denny & Carson's office. When the whistle awoke him, he clutched quickly at his breast pocket, glancing about him with an uncertain smile. But the little, clay-bespattered Italians were still sleeping, the slatternly women across the aisle were in open-mouthed oblivion, and even the crumby, crying babies were for the nonce stilled. Paul settled back to struggle with his impatience as best as he could.

When he arrived at the Jersey City station, he hurried through his breakfast, manifestly ill at ease and keeping a sharp eye about him. After he reached the Twenty-third Street station,[17] he consulted a cabman, and had himself driven to a men's furnishing establishment that was just opening for the day. He spent upward of two hours there, buying with endless reconsidering and great care. His new street suit he put on in the fitting-room; the frock coat and dress clothes he had bundled into the cab with his linen. Then he drove to a hatter's and a shoe house. His next errand was at Tiffany's, where he selected his silver-mounted brushes[18] and a new scarf-pin. He would not wait to have his silver marked, he said. Lastly, he stopped at a trunk shop on Broadway, and had his purchases packed into various traveling bags.

40   It was a little after one o'clock when he drove up to the Waldorf, and after settling with the cabman, went into the office. He registered from Washington; said his mother and father had been abroad, and that he had come down to await the arrival of their steamer. He told his story plausibly and had no trouble, since he volunteered to pay for them in advance, in engaging his rooms; a sleeping-room, sitting room, and bath.

Not once, but a hundred times, Paul had planned this entry into New York. He had gone over every detail of it with Charley Edwards, and in his scrap book at home there were pages of description about New York hotels, cut from the Sunday papers. When he was shown to his sitting-room on the eighth floor, he saw at a

---

[16] **Newark** New Jersey city about 20 miles from New York   [17] **Twenty-third Street station** Paul's destination in Manhattan   [18] **brushes** hairbrushes

glance that everything was as it should be; there was but one detail in his mental picture that the place did not realize, so he rang for the bell boy and sent him down for flowers. He moved about nervously until the boy returned, putting away his new linen and fingering it delightedly as he did so. When the flowers came, he put them hastily into water, and then tumbled into a hot bath. Presently he came out of his white bathroom, resplendent in his new silk underwear, and playing with the tassels of his red robe. The snow was whirling so fiercely outside his windows that he could scarcely see across the street, but within the air was deliciously soft and fragrant. He put the violets and jonquils on the taboret beside the couch, and threw himself down, with a long sigh, covering himself with a Roman blanket. He was thoroughly tired; he had been in such haste, he had stood up to such a strain, covered so much ground in the last twenty-four hours, that he wanted to think how it had all come about. Lulled by the sound of the wind, the warm air, and the cool fragrance of the flowers, he sank into deep, drowsy retrospection.

It had been wonderfully simple; when they had shut him out of the theater and concert hall, when they had taken away his bone, the whole thing was virtually determined. The rest was a mere matter of opportunity. The only thing that at all surprised him was his own courage—for he realized well enough that he had always been tormented by fear, a sort of apprehensive dread that, of late years, as the meshes of the lies he had told closed about him, had been pulling the muscles of his body tighter and tighter. Until now, he could not remember the time when he had not been dreading something. Even when he was a little boy, it was always there— behind him, or before, or on either side. There had always been the shadowed corner, the dark place into which he dared not look, but from which something seemed always to be watching him—and Paul had done things that were not pretty to watch, he knew.

But now he had a curious sense of relief, as though he had at last thrown down the gauntlet to the thing in the corner.

Yet it was but a day since he had been sulking in the traces; but yesterday afternoon that he had been sent to the bank with Denny & Carson's deposit, as usual— but this time he was instructed to leave the book to be balanced. There was above two thousand dollars in checks, and nearly a thousand in the bank notes which he had taken from the book and quietly transferred to his pocket. At the bank he had made out a new deposit slip. His nerves had been steady enough to permit of his returning to the office, where he had finished his work and asked for a full day's holiday tomorrow, Saturday, giving a perfectly reasonable pretext. The bank book, he knew, would not be returned before Monday or Tuesday, and his father would be out of town for the next week. From the time he slipped the bank notes into his pocket until he boarded the night train for New York, he had not known a moment's hesitation. It was not the first time Paul had steered through treacherous waters.

45   How astonishingly easy it had all been; here he was, the thing done; and this time there would be no awakening, no figure at the top of the stairs. He watched the snow flakes whirling by his window until he fell asleep.

When he awoke, it was three o'clock in the afternoon. He bounded up with a start; half of one of his precious days gone already! He spent more than an hour in dressing, watching every stage of his toilet carefully in the mirror. Everything was quite perfect; he was exactly the kind of boy he had always wanted to be.

When he went downstairs, Paul took a carriage and drove up Fifth Avenue toward the Park.[19] The snow had somewhat abated; carriages and tradesmen's wagons were hurrying soundlessly to and fro in the winter twilight; boys in woolen mufflers were shoveling off the doorsteps; the avenue stages[20] made fine spots of color against the white street. Here and there on the corners were stands, with whole flower gardens blooming under glass cases against the sides of which the snow flakes stuck and melted; violets, roses, carnations, lilies of the valley—somehow vastly more lovely and alluring that they blossomed thus unnaturally in the snow. The Park itself was a wonderful stage winterpiece.

When he returned, the pause of the twilight had ceased, and the tune of the streets had changed. The snow was falling faster, lights streamed from the hotels that reared their dozen stories fearlessly up into the storm, defying the raging Atlantic winds. A long, black stream of carriages poured down the avenue, intersected here and there by other streams, tending horizontally. There were a score of cabs about the entrance of this hotel, and his driver had to wait. Boys in livery were running in and out of the awning stretched across the sidewalk, up and down the red velvet carpet laid from the door to the street. Above, about, within it all was the rumble and roar, the hurry and toss of thousands of human beings as hot for pleasure as himself, and on every side of him towered the glaring affirmation of the omnipotence of wealth.

The boy set his teeth and drew his shoulders together in a spasm of realization; the plot of all dramas, the text of all romances, the nerve-stuff of all sensations was whirling about him like the snow flakes. He burnt like a faggot in a tempest.

50   When Paul went down to dinner, the music of the orchestra came floating up the elevator shaft to greet him. His head whirled as he stepped into the thronged corridor, and he sank back into one of the chairs against the wall to get his breath. The lights, the chatter, the perfumes, the bewildering medley of color—he had, for a moment, the feeling of not being able to stand it. But only for a moment; these were his own people, he told himself. He went slowly about the corridors, through the writing-rooms, smoking-rooms, reception-rooms, as though he were exploring the chambers of an enchanted palace, built and peopled for him alone.

When he reached the dining room he sat down at a table near a window. The flowers, the white linen, the many-colored wine glasses, the gay toilettes of the women, the low popping of corks, the undulating repetitions of the *Blue Danube*[21] from the orchestra, all flooded Paul's dream with bewildering radiance. When the roseate tinge of his champagne was added—that cold, precious, bubbling stuff that creamed and foamed in his glass—Paul wondered that there were honest men in the world at all. This was what all the world was fighting for, he reflected; this was what all the struggle was about. He doubted the reality of his past. Had he ever known a place called Cordelia Street, a place where fagged-looking businessmen got on the early car; mere rivets in a machine they seemed to Paul—sickening men, with combings of children's hair always hanging to their coats, and the smell of

---

[19] **the Park** Central Park   [20] **avenue stages** shop display windows   [21] ***Blue Danube*** "The Blue Danube" is the best-known waltz of composer Johann Strauss

cooking in their clothes. Cordelia Street—Ah! that belonged to another time and country; had he not always been thus, had he not sat here night after night, from as far back as he could remember, looking pensively over just such shimmering textures, and slowly twirling the stem of a glass like this one between his thumb and middle finger? He rather thought he had.

He was not in the least abashed or lonely. He had no especial desire to meet or to know any of these people; all he demanded was the right to look on and conjecture, to watch the pageant. The mere stage properties were all he contended for. Nor was he lonely later in the evening, in his loge at the Metropolitan. He was now entirely rid of his nervous misgivings, of his forced aggressiveness, of the imperative desire to show himself different from his surroundings. He felt now that his surroundings explained him. Nobody questioned the purple;[22] he had only to wear it passively. He had only to glance down at his attire to reassure himself that here it would be impossible for anyone to humiliate him.

He found it hard to leave his beautiful sitting room to go to bed that night, and sat long watching the raging storm from his turret window. When he went to sleep it was with the lights turned on in his bedroom; partly because of his old timidity, and partly so that, if he should wake in the night, there would be no wretched moment of doubt, no horrible suspicion of yellow wallpaper, or of Washington and Calvin above his bed.

Sunday morning the city was practically snow-bound. Paul breakfasted late, and in the afternoon he fell in with a wild San Francisco boy, a freshman at Yale, who said he had run down for a "little flyer" over Sunday. The young man offered to show Paul the night side of the town, and the two boys went out together after dinner, not returning to the hotel until seven o'clock the next morning. They had started out in the confiding warmth of a champagne friendship, but their parting in the elevator was singularly cool. The freshman pulled himself together to make his train, and Paul went to bed. He awoke at two o'clock in the afternoon, very thirsty and dizzy, and rang for ice-water, coffee, and the Pittsburgh papers.

55   On the part of the hotel management, Paul excited no suspicion. There was this to be said for him, that he wore his spoils with dignity and in no way made himself conspicuous. Even under the glow of his wine he was never boisterous, though he found the stuff like a magician's wand for wonder-buildings. His chief greediness lay in his ears and eyes, and his excesses were not offensive ones. His dearest pleasures were the gray winter twilights in his sitting room; his quiet enjoyment of his flowers, his clothes, his wide divan, his cigarette, and his sense of power. He could not remember a time when he had felt so at peace with himself. The mere release from the necessity of petty lying, lying every day and every day, restored his self-respect. He had never lied for pleasure, even at school; but to be noticed and admired, to assert his difference from other Cordelia Street boys; and he felt a good deal more manly, more honest, even, now that he had no need for boastful pretensions, now that he could, as his actor friends used to say, "dress the part." It was characteristic that remorse did not occur to him. His golden days went by without a shadow, and he made each as perfect as he could.

---

[22] **purple** a color fit for royalty

On the eighth day after his arrival in New York, he found the whole affair exploited in the Pittsburgh papers, exploited with a wealth of detail which indicated that local news of a sensational nature was at a low ebb. The firm of Denny & Carson announced that the boy's father had refunded the full amount of the theft, and that they had no intention of prosecuting. The Cumberland minister had been interviewed, and expressed his hope of yet reclaiming the motherless lad, and his Sabbath-school teacher declared that she would spare no effort to that end. The rumor had reached Pittsburgh that the boy had been seen in a New York hotel, and his father had gone East to find him and bring him home.

Paul had just come in to dress for dinner; he sank into a chair, weak to the knees, and clasped his head in his hands. It was to be worse than jail, even; the tepid waters of Cordelia Street were to close over him finally and forever. The gray monotony stretched before him in hopeless, unrelieved years; Sabbath school, Young People's Meeting, the yellow-papered room, the damp dish-towels; it all rushed back upon him with a sickening vividness. He had the old feeling that the orchestra had suddenly stopped, the sinking sensation that the play was over. The sweat broke out on his face, and he sprang to his feet, looked about him with his white, conscious smile, and winked at himself in the mirror. With something of the old childish belief in miracles with which he had so often gone to class, all his lessons unlearned, Paul dressed and dashed whistling down the corridor to the elevator.

He had no sooner entered the dining room and caught the measure of the music, than his remembrance was lightened by his old elastic power of claiming the moment, mounting with it, and finding it all sufficient. The glare and glitter about him, the mere scenic accessories had again, and for the last time, their old potency. He would show himself that he was game, he would finish the thing splendidly. He doubted, more than ever, the existence of Cordelia Street, and for the first time he drank his wine recklessly. Was he not, after all, one of those fortunate beings born to the purple, was he not still himself and in his own place? He drummed a nervous accompaniment to the Pagliacci music and looked about him, telling himself over and over that it had paid.

He reflected drowsily, to the swell of the music and the chill sweetness of his wine, that he might have done it more wisely. He might have caught an outbound steamer and been well out of their clutches before now. But the other side of the world had seemed too far away and too uncertain then; he could not have waited for it; his need had been too sharp. If he had to choose over again, he would do the same thing tomorrow. He looked affectionately about the dining room, now gilded with a soft mist. Ah, it had paid indeed!

60 Paul was awakened next morning by a painful throbbing in his head and feet. He had thrown himself across the bed without undressing, and had slept with his shoes on. His limbs and hands were lead heavy, and his tongue and throat were parched and burnt. There came upon him one of those fateful attacks of clear-headedness that never occurred except when he was physically exhausted and his nerves hung loose. He lay still and closed his eyes and let the tide of things wash over him.

His father was in New York; "stopping at some joint or other," he told himself. The memory of successive summers on the front stoop fell upon him like a weight of black water. He had not a hundred dollars left, and he knew now, more than ever, that money was everything, the wall that stood between all he loathed and all he wanted. The thing was winding itself up; he had thought of that on his first glorious day in New York, and had even provided a way to snap the thread. It lay on his dressing-table now; he had got it out last night when he came blindly up from dinner, but the shiny metal hurt his eyes, and he disliked the looks of it.

He rose and moved about with a painful effort, succumbing now and again to attacks of nausea. It was the old depression exaggerated; all the world had become Cordelia Street. Yet somehow he was not afraid of anything, was absolutely calm; perhaps because he had looked into the dark corner at last and knew. It was bad enough, what he saw there, but somehow not so bad as his long fear of it had been. He saw everything clearly now. He had a feeling that he had made the best of it, that he had lived the sort of life he was meant to live, and for half an hour he sat staring at the revolver. But he told himself that was not the way, so he went downstairs and took a cab to the ferry.

When Paul arrived at Newark, he got off the train and took another cab, directing the driver to follow the Pennsylvania tracks out of the town. The snow lay heavy on the roadways and had drifted deep in the open fields. Only here and there the dead grass or dried weed stalks projected, singularly black, above it. Once well into the country, Paul dismissed the carriage and walked, floundering along the tracks, his mind a medley of irrelevant things. He seemed to hold in his brain an actual picture of everything he had seen that morning. He remembered every feature of both his drivers, of the toothless old woman from whom he had bought the red flowers in his coat, the agent from whom he had got his ticket, and all of his fellow-passengers on the ferry. His mind, unable to cope with vital matters near at hand, worked feverishly and deftly at sorting and grouping these images. They made for him a part of the ugliness of the world, of the ache in his head, and the bitter burning on his tongue. He stooped and put a handful of snow into his mouth as he walked, but that, too, seemed hot. When he reached a little hillside, where the tracks ran through a cut some twenty feet below him, he stopped and sat down.

The carnations in his coat were drooping with the cold, he noticed; their red glory all over. It occurred to him that all the flowers he had seen in the glass cases that first night must have gone the same way, long before this. It was only one splendid breath they had, in spite of their brave mockery at the winter outside the glass; and it was a losing game in the end, it seemed, this revolt against the homilies by which the world is run. Paul took one of the blossoms carefully from his coat and scooped a little hole in the snow, where he covered it up. Then he dozed a while, from his weak condition, seemingly insensible to the cold.

65   The sound of an approaching train awoke him, and he started to his feet, remembering only his resolution, and afraid lest he should be too late. He stood watching the approaching locomotive, his teeth chattering, his lips drawn away from them in a frightened smile; once or twice he glanced nervously sidewise, as though he were being watched. When the right moment came, he jumped. As he fell, the folly of his haste occurred to him with merciless clearness, the vastness of what he had left undone. There flashed through his brain, clearer than ever before, the blue of Adriatic water, the yellow of Algerian sands.

He felt something strike his chest, and that his body was being thrown swiftly through the air, on and on, immeasurably far and fast, while his limbs were gently relaxed. Then, because the picture-making mechanism was crushed, the disturbing visions flashed into black, and Paul dropped back into the immense design of things.

► QUESTIONS FOR READING AND WRITING

1. Early in the story the teachers gather to reprimand Paul. What are their motives? Although they don't have the effect on Paul that they intend, they still feel strange about what they have done. Why?
2. What do the theater and concert hall offer Paul that school and home don't? How does Paul's enthusiasm for these arts differ from the enthusiasm of typical supporters?
3. Is Paul antisocial, or is there a sense in which he needs other people? What sort of relationships does he form? Cite evidence from the story.
4. Many people think they know what is in Paul's best interest—including Paul. Who really knows what's best? Should Paul be trusted to pursue his interests, or are his father and teachers right to seek ways to make him conform?
5. Is Paul's an avoidable tragedy? Who is to blame for Paul's fate? Are there some people who just can't be helped?
6. If you were a character in this story or if Paul were a real person in your life, you'd probably respond much less sympathetically to the act of his stealing money from his father's firm. What is different for you as a reader of this story? How does fiction allow you to see events from a different point of view? As you read the story, where do your sympathies lie?
7. Near the end of the story, Paul has a number of options open to him. For one, he could turn himself in; he could also resolve to identify and pursue a career that would allow him to lead the life he desires. What prevents him from exploring these options? What do you think he realizes in his last moment?

ANTON CHEKHOV (1860–1904)

Considered the father of the modern short story and the modern play, Anton Pavlovich Chekhov was born in the town of Taganrog, near the Black Sea, in Russia. His grandfather was a serf who bought his family's freedom. Chekhov attended the University of Moscow on a scholarship, eventually earning a degree in medicine. In an effort to support himself and his impoverished family during this period, Chekhov began writing short pieces, first sketches and jokes, and later short stories for newspapers and journals. By 1886, Chekhov

had gained enough recognition to make writing his chief interest and occupation. His long association with the famed Moscow Arts Theater began with its acclaimed production of The Seagull *in 1898 (which had a disastrous premiere two years earlier in St. Petersburg), and continued with productions of his greatest plays,* The Three Sisters, Uncle Vanya, *and* The Cherry Orchard. *In his later years, which were plagued by ill health, Chekhov married Olga Knipper, a star of the theater company. He died in 1904 of tuberculosis. His short stories, which he continued to write even after he became a successful playwright, are characterized not only by their economical prose style, but also by a love of humanity that is often set against a pervading mood of sadness.*

THE LADY WITH THE PET DOG [1899]

Translated by Avrahm Yarmolinsky

I

A new person, it was said, had appeared on the esplanade: a lady with a pet dog. Dmitry Dmitrich Gurov, who had spent a fortnight at Yalta and had got used to the place, had also begun to take an interest in new arrivals. As he sat in Vernet's confectionery shop, he saw, walking on the esplanade, a fair-haired young woman of medium height, wearing a beret; a white Pomeranian was trotting behind her.

And afterwards he met her in the public garden and in the square several times a day. She walked alone, always wearing the same beret and always with the white dog; no one knew who she was and everyone called her simply "the lady with the pet dog."

"If she is here alone without husband or friends," Gurov reflected, "it wouldn't be a bad thing to make her acquaintance."

He was under forty, but he already had a daughter twelve years old, and two sons at school. They had found a wife for him when he was very young, a student in his second year, and by now she seemed half as old again as he. She was a tall, erect woman with dark eyebrows, stately and dignified and, as she said of herself, intellectual. She read a great deal, used simplified spelling in her letters, called her husband, not Dmitry, but Dimitry, while he privately considered her of limited intelligence, narrow-minded, dowdy, was afraid of her, and did not like to be at home. He had begun being unfaithful to her long ago—had been unfaithful to her often and, probably for that reason, almost always spoke ill of women, and when they were talked of in his presence used to call them "the inferior race."

5   It seemed to him that he had been sufficiently tutored by bitter experience to call them what he pleased, and yet he could not have lived without "the inferior race" for two days together. In the company of men he was bored and ill at ease, he was chilly and uncommunicative with them; but when he was among women he felt free, and knew what to speak to them about and how to comport himself; and even to be silent with them was no strain on him. In his appearance, in his character, in his whole make-up there was something attractive and elusive that disposed women in his favor and allured them. He knew that, and some force seemed to draw him to them, too.

Oft-repeated and really bitter experience had taught him long ago that with decent people—particularly Moscow people—who are irresolute and slow to move, every affair which at first seems a light and charming adventure inevitably grows into a whole problem of extreme complexity, and in the end a painful situation is created. But at every new meeting with an interesting woman this lesson of experience seemed to slip from his memory, and he was eager for life, and everything seemed so simple and diverting.

One evening while he was dining in the public garden the lady in the beret walked up without haste to take the next table. Her expression, her gait, her dress, and the way she did her hair told him that she belonged to the upper class, that she was married, that she was in Yalta for the first time and alone, and that she was bored there. The stories told of the immorality in Yalta are to a great extent untrue; he despised them, and knew that such stories were made up for the most part by persons who would have been glad to sin themselves if they had had the chance; but when the lady sat down at the next table three paces from him, he recalled these stories of easy conquests, of trips to the mountains, and the tempting thought of a swift, fleeting liaison, a romance with an unknown woman of whose very name he was ignorant suddenly took hold of him.

He beckoned invitingly to the Pomeranian, and when the dog approached him, shook his finger at it. The Pomeranian growled; Gurov threatened it again.

The lady glanced at him and at once dropped her eyes.

10 "He doesn't bite," she said and blushed.

"May I give him a bone?" he asked; and when she nodded he inquired affably, "Have you been in Yalta long?"

"About five days."

"And I am dragging out the second week here."

There was a short silence.

15 "Time passes quickly, and yet it is so dull here!" she said, not looking at him.

"It's only the fashion to say it's dull here. A provincial will live in Belyov or Zhizdra and not be bored, but when he comes here it's 'Oh, the dullness! Oh, the dust!' One would think he came from Granada."

She laughed. Then both continued eating in silence, like strangers, but after dinner they walked together and there sprang up between them the light banter of people who are free and contented, to whom it does not matter where they go or what they talk about. They walked and talked of the strange light on the sea: the water was a soft, warm, lilac color, and there was a golden band of moonlight upon it. They talked of how sultry it was after a hot day. Gurov told her that he was a native of Moscow, that he had studied languages and literature at the university, but had a post in a bank; that at one time he had trained to become an opera singer but had given it up, that he owned two houses in Moscow. And he learned from her that she had grown up in Petersburg, but had lived in S_____ since her marriage two years previously, that she was going to stay in Yalta for about another month, and that her husband, who needed a rest, too, might perhaps come to fetch her. She was not certain whether her husband was a member of a Government Board or served on a Zemstvo Council, and this amused her. And Gurov learned that her name was Anna Sergeyevna.

Afterwards in his room at the hotel he thought about her—and was certain that he would meet her the next day. It was bound to happen. Getting into bed he recalled that she had been a schoolgirl only recently, doing lessons like his own daughter; he thought how much timidity and angularity there was still in her laugh and her manner of talking with a stranger. It must have been the first time in her life that she was alone in a setting in which she was followed, looked at, and spoken to for one secret purpose alone, which she could hardly fail to guess. He thought of her slim, delicate throat, her lovely gray eyes.

"There's something pathetic about her, though," he thought, and dropped off.

II

20 A week had passed since they had struck up an acquaintance. It was a holiday. It was close indoors, while in the street the wind whirled the dust about and blew people's hats off. One was thirsty all day, and Gurov often went into the restaurant and offered Anna Sergeyevna a soft drink or ice cream. One did not know what to do with oneself.

In the evening when the wind had abated they went out on the pier to watch the steamer come in. There were a great many people walking about the dock; they had come to welcome someone and they were carrying bunches of flowers. And two peculiarities of a festive Yalta crowd stood out: the elderly ladies were dressed like young ones and there were many generals.

Owing to the choppy sea, the steamer arrived late, after sunset, and it was a long time tacking about before it put in at the pier. Anna Sergeyevna peered at the steamer and the passengers through her lorgnette as though looking for acquaintances, and whenever she turned to Gurov her eyes were shining. She talked a great deal and asked questions jerkily, forgetting the next moment what she had asked; then she lost her lorgnette in the crush.

The festive crowd began to disperse; it was now too dark to see people's faces; there was no wind any more, but Gurov and Anna Sergeyevna still stood as though waiting to see someone else come off the steamer. Anna Sergeyevna was silent now, and sniffed her flowers without looking at Gurov.

"The weather has improved this evening," he said. "Where shall we go now? Shall we drive somewhere?"

25   She did not reply.

Then he looked at her intently, and suddenly embraced her and kissed her on the lips, and the moist fragrance of her flowers enveloped him; and at once he looked round him anxiously, wondering if anyone had seen them.

"Let us go to your place," he said softly. And they walked off together rapidly.

The air in her room was close and there was the smell of the perfume she had bought at the Japanese shop. Looking at her, Gurov thought: "What encounters life offers!" From the past he preserved the memory of carefree, good-natured women whom love made gay and who were grateful to him for the happiness he gave them, however brief it might be; and of women like his wife who loved without sincerity, with too many words, affectedly, hysterically, with an expression that it was not love or passion that engaged them but something more significant; and of two or three others, very beautiful, frigid women, across whose faces would suddenly flit a rapacious expression—an obstinate desire to take from life more than it could give, and these were women no longer young, capricious, unreflecting, domineering, unintelligent, and when Gurov grew cold to them their beauty aroused his hatred, and the lace on their lingerie seemed to him to resemble scales.

But here there was the timidity, the angularity of inexperienced youth, a feeling of awkwardness; and there was a sense of embarrassment, as though someone had suddenly knocked at the door. Anna Sergeyevna, "the lady with the pet dog," treated what had happened in a peculiar way, very seriously, as though it were her fall—so it seemed, and this was odd and inappropriate. Her features drooped and faded, and her long hair hung down sadly on either side of her face; she grew pensive and her dejected pose was that of a Magdalene in a picture by an old master.

30   "It's not right," she said. "You don't respect me now, you first of all."

There was a watermelon on the table. Gurov cut himself a slice and began eating it without haste. They were silent for at least half an hour.

There was something touching about Anna Sergeyevna; she had the purity of a well-bred, naive woman who has seen little of life. The single candle burning on the table barely illumined her face, yet it was clear that she was unhappy.

"Why should I stop respecting you, darling?" asked Gurov. "You don't know what you're saying."

"God forgive me," she said, and her eyes filled with tears. "It's terrible."

35   "It's as though you were trying to exonerate yourself."

"How can I exonerate myself? No. I am a bad, low woman; I despise myself and I have no thought of exonerating myself. It's not my husband but myself I have deceived. And not only just now; I have been deceiving myself for a long time. My husband may be a good, honest man, but he is a flunkey! I don't know what he does, what his work is, but I know he is a flunkey! I was twenty when I married him. I was tormented by curiosity; I wanted something better. 'There must be a different sort of life,' I said to myself. I wanted to live! To live, to live! Curiosity kept eating at me— you don't understand, but I swear to God I could no longer control myself; some- thing was going on in me; I could not be held back. I told my husband I was ill, and came here. And here I have been walking about as though in a daze, as though I were mad; and now I have become a vulgar, vile woman whom anyone may despise."

Gurov was already bored with her; he was irritated by her naive tone, by her repentance, so unexpected and so out of place, but for the tears in her eyes he might have thought she was joking or play-acting.

"I don't understand, my dear," he said softly. "What do you want?"

She hid her face on his breast and pressed close to him.

40   "Believe me, believe me, I beg you," she said, "I love honesty and purity, and sin is loathsome to me; I don't know what I'm doing. Simple people say, 'The Evil One has led me astray.' And I may say of myself now that the Evil One has led me astray."

"Quiet, quiet," he murmured.

He looked into her fixed, frightened eyes, kissed her, spoke to her softly and affectionately, and by degrees she calmed down, and her gaiety returned; both began laughing.

Afterwards when they went out there was not a soul on the esplanade. The town with its cypresses looked quite dead, but the sea was still sounding as it broke upon the beach; a single launch was rocking on the waves and on it a lantern was blinking sleepily.

They found a cab and drove to Oreanda.

45   "I found out your surname in the hall just now; it was written on the board—von Dideritz," said Gurov. "Is your husband German?"

"No; I believe his grandfather was German, but he is Greek Orthodox himself."

At Oreanda they sat on a bench not far from the church, looked down at the sea, and were silent. Yalta was barely visible through the morning mist; white clouds rested motionlessly on the mountaintops. The leaves did not stir on the trees, cicadas twanged, and the monotonous muffled sound of the sea that rose from below spoke of the peace, the eternal sleep awaiting us. So it rumbled below when there was no Yalta, no Oreanda here; so it rumbles now, and it will rumble as indifferently and as hollowly when we are no more. And in this constancy, in this complete indifference to the life and death of each of us, there lies, perhaps, a pledge of our eternal salvation, of the unceasing advance of life upon earth, of unceasing movement towards perfection. Sitting beside a young woman who in the dawn seemed so lovely, Gurov, soothed and spellbound by these magical surroundings—the sea, the mountains, the clouds, the wide sky—thought how everything is really beautiful in this world when one reflects: everything except what we think or do ourselves when we forget the higher aims of life and our own human dignity.

A man strolled up to them—probably a guard—looked at them and walked away. And this detail, too, seemed so mysterious and beautiful. They saw a steamer arrive from Feodosia, its lights extinguished in the glow of dawn.

"There is dew on the grass," said Anna Sergeyevna, after a silence.

50   "Yes, it's time to go home."

They returned to the city.

Then they met every day at twelve o'clock on the esplanade, lunched and dined together, took walks, admired the sea. She complained that she slept badly, that she had palpitations, asked the same questions, troubled now by jealousy and now by the fear that he did not respect her sufficiently. And often in the square or the public garden, when there was no one near them, he suddenly drew her to him and kissed her passionately. Complete idleness, these kisses in broad daylight exchanged furtively in dread of someone's seeing them, the heat, the smell of the sea, and the continual flitting before his eyes of idle, well-dressed, well-fed people, worked a complete change in him; he kept telling Anna Sergeyevna how beautiful she was, how seductive, was urgently passionate; he would not move a step away from her, while she was often pensive and continually pressed him to confess that he did not respect her, did not love her in the least, and saw in her nothing but a common woman. Almost every evening rather late they drove somewhere out of town, to Oreanda or to the waterfall; and the excursion was always a success, the scenery invariably impressed them as beautiful and magnificent.

They were expecting her husband, but a letter came from him saying that he had eye-trouble, and begging his wife to return home as soon as possible. Anna Sergeyevna made haste to go.

"It's a good thing I am leaving," she said to Gurov. "It's the hand of Fate!"

55   She took a carriage to the railway station, and he went with her. They were driving the whole day. When she had taken her place in the express, and when the second bell had rung, she said, "Let me look at you once more—let me look at you again. Like this."

She was not crying but was so sad that she seemed ill and her face was quivering.

"I shall be thinking of you—remembering you," she said. "God bless you; be happy. Don't remember evil against me. We are parting forever—it has to be, for we ought never to have met. Well, God bless you."

The train moved off rapidly, its lights soon vanished, and a minute later there was no sound of it, as though everything had conspired to end as quickly as possible that sweet trance, that madness. Left alone on the platform, and gazing into the dark distance, Gurov listened to the twang of the grasshoppers and the hum of the telegraph wires, feeling as though he had just waked up. And he reflected, musing, that there had now been another episode or adventure in his life, and it, too, was at an end, and nothing was left of it but a memory. He was moved, sad, and slightly remorseful: this young woman whom he would never meet again had not been happy with him; he had been warm and affectionate with her, but yet in his manner, his tone, and his caresses there had been a shade of light irony, the slightly coarse arrogance of a happy male who was, besides, almost twice her age. She had constantly called him kind, exceptional, high-minded; obviously he had seemed to her different from what he really was, so he had involuntarily deceived her.

Here at the station there was already a scent of autumn in the air; it was a chilly evening.

60   "It is time for me to go north, too," thought Gurov as he left the platform. "High time!"

III

At home in Moscow the winter routine was already established; the stoves were heated, and in the morning it was still dark when the children were having breakfast and getting ready for school, and the nurse would light the lamp for a short time. There were frosts already. When the first snow falls, on the first day the sleighs are out, it is pleasant to see the white earth, the white roofs; one draws easy, delicious breaths, and the season brings back the days of one's youth. The old limes and birches, white with hoar-frost, have a good-natured look; they are closer to one's heart than cypresses and palms, and near them one no longer wants to think of mountains and the sea.

Gurov, a native of Moscow, arrived there on a fine frosty day, and when he put on his fur coat and warm gloves and took a walk along Petrovka, and when on Saturday night he heard the bells ringing, his recent trip and the places he had visited lost all charm for him. Little by little he became immersed in Moscow life, greedily read three newspapers a day, and declared that he did not read the Moscow papers on principle. He already felt a longing for restaurants, clubs, formal dinners, anniversary celebrations, and it flattered him to entertain distinguished lawyers and actors, and to play cards with a professor at the physicians' club. He could eat a whole portion of meat stewed with pickled cabbage and served in a pan, Moscow style.

A month or so would pass and the image of Anna Sergeyevna, it seemed to him, would become misty in his memory, and only from time to time he would dream of her with her touching smile as he dreamed of others. But more than a month went by, winter came into its own, and everything was still clear in his memory as though he had parted from Anna Sergeyevna only yesterday. And his memories glowed more and more vividly. When in the evening stillness the voices of his children preparing their lessons reached his study, or when he listened to a song or to an organ playing in a restaurant, or when the storm howled in the chimney, suddenly everything would rise up in his memory; what had happened on the pier and the early morning with the mist on the mountains, and the steamer coming from Feodosia, and the kisses. He would pace about his room a long time, remembering and smiling; then his memories passed into reveries, and in his imagination the past would mingle with what was to come. He did not dream of Anna Sergeyevna, but she followed him about everywhere and watched him. When he shut his eyes he saw her before him as though she were there in the flesh, and she seemed to him lovelier, younger, tenderer than she had been, and he imagined himself a finer man than he had been in Yalta. Of evenings she peered out at him from the bookcase, from the fireplace, from the corner—he heard her breathing, the caressing rustle of her clothes. In the street he followed the women with his eyes, looking for someone who resembled her.

Already he was tormented by a strong desire to share his memories with someone. But in his home it was impossible to talk of his love, and he had no one to talk to outside; certainly he could not confide in his tenants or in anyone at the bank. And what was there to talk about? He hadn't loved her then, had he? Had there been anything beautiful, poetical, edifying, or simply interesting in his relations with Anna Sergeyevna? And he was forced to talk vaguely of love, of women, and no one guessed what he meant; only his wife would twitch her black eyebrows and say, "The part of a philanderer does not suit you at all, Dimitry."

65 One evening, coming out of the physicians' club with an official with whom he had been playing cards, he could not resist saying:

"If you only knew what a fascinating woman I became acquainted with at Yalta!"

The official got into his sledge and was driving away, but turned suddenly and shouted:

"Dmitry Dmitrich!"

"What is it?"

70 "You were right this evening: the sturgeon was a bit high."

These words, so commonplace, for some reason moved Gurov to indignation, and struck him as degrading and unclean. What savage manners, what mugs! What stupid nights, what dull, humdrum days! Frenzied gambling, gluttony, drunkenness, continual talk always about the same thing! Futile pursuits and conversations always about the same topics take up the better part of one's time, the better part of one's strength, and in the end there is left a life clipped and wingless, an absurd mess, and there is no escaping or getting away from it—just as though one were in a madhouse or a prison.

Gurov, boiling with indignation, did not sleep all night. And he had a headache all the next day. And the following nights too he slept badly; he sat up in bed, thinking, or paced up and down his room. He was fed up with his children, fed up with the bank; he had no desire to go anywhere or to talk of anything.

In December during the holidays he prepared to take a trip and told his wife he was going to Petersburg to do what he could for a young friend—and he set off for S_____. What for? He did not know, himself. He wanted to see Anna Sergeyevna and talk with her, to arrange a rendezvous if possible.

He arrived at S_____ in the morning, and at the hotel took the best room, in which the floor was covered with gray army cloth, and on the table there was an ink-stand, gray with dust and topped by a figure on horseback, its hat in its raised hand and its head broken off. The porter gave him the necessary information: von Dideritz lived in a house of his own on Staro-Goncharnaya Street, not far from the hotel: he was rich and lived well and kept his own horses; everyone in the town knew him. The porter pronounced the name: "Dridiritz."

75   Without haste Gurov made his way to Staro-Goncharnaya Street and found the house. Directly opposite the house stretched a long gray fence studded with nails.

"A fence like that would make one run away," thought Gurov, looking now at the fence, now at the windows of the house.

He reflected: this was a holiday, and the husband was apt to be at home. And in any case, it would be tactless to go into the house and disturb her. If he were to send her a note, it might fall into her husband's hands, and that might spoil everything. The best thing was to rely on chance. And he kept walking up and down the street and along the fence, waiting for the chance. He saw a beggar go in at the gate and heard the dogs attack him; then an hour later he heard a piano, and the sound came to him faintly and indistinctly. Probably it was Anna Sergeyevna playing. The front door opened suddenly, and an old woman came out, followed by the familiar white Pomeranian. Gurov was on the point of calling to the dog, but his heart began beating violently, and in his excitement he could not remember the Pomeranian's name.

He kept walking up and down, and hated the gray fence more and more, and by now he thought irritably that Anna Sergeyevna had forgotten him, and was perhaps already diverting herself with another man, and that that was very natural in a young woman who from morning till night had to look at that damn fence. He went back to his hotel room and sat on the couch for a long while, not knowing what to do, then he had dinner and a long nap.

"How stupid and annoying all this is!" he thought when he woke and looked at the dark windows: it was already evening. "Here I've had a good sleep for some reason. What am I going to do at night?"

80   He sat on the bed, which was covered with a cheap gray blanket of the kind seen in hospitals, and he twitted himself in his vexation:

"So there's your lady with the pet dog. There's your adventure. A nice place to cool your heels in."

That morning at the station a playbill in large letters had caught his eye. *The Geisha* was to be given for the first time. He thought of this and drove to the theater.

"It's quite possible that she goes to first nights," he thought.

The theater was full. As in all provincial theaters, there was a haze above the chandelier, the gallery was noisy and restless; in the front row, before the beginning of the performance the local dandies were standing with their hands clasped behind their backs; in the Governor's box the Governor's daughter, wearing a boa, occupied the front seat, while the Governor himself hid modestly behind the portiere and only his hands were visible; the curtain swayed; the orchestra was a long time tuning up. While the audience was coming in and taking their seats, Gurov scanned the faces eagerly.

85   Anna Sergeyevna, too, came in. She sat down in the third row, and when Gurov looked at her his heart contracted, and he understood clearly that in the whole world there was no human being so near, so precious, and so important to him; she, this little, undistinguished woman, lost in a provincial crowd, with a vulgar lorgnette in her hand, filled his whole life now, was his sorrow and his joy, the only happiness that he now desired for himself, and to the sounds of the bad orchestra, of the miserable local violins, he thought how lovely she was. He thought and dreamed.

A young man with small side-whiskers, very tall and stooped, came in with Anna Sergeyevna and sat down beside her; he nodded his head at every step and seemed to be bowing continually. Probably this was the husband whom at Yalta, in an access of bitter feeling, she had called a flunkey. And there really was in his lanky figure, his side-whiskers, his small bald patch, something of a flunkey's retiring manner; his smile was mawkish, and in his buttonhole there was an academic badge like a waiter's number.

During the first intermission the husband went out to have a smoke; she remained in her seat. Gurov, who was also sitting in the orchestra, went up to her and said in a shaky voice, with a forced smile:

"Good evening!"

She glanced at him and turned pale, then looked at him again in horror, unable to believe her eyes, and gripped the fan and the lorgnette tightly together in her hands, evidently trying to keep herself from fainting. Both were silent. She was sitting, he was standing, frightened by her distress and not daring to take a seat beside her. The violins and the flute that were being tuned up sang out. He suddenly felt frightened: it seemed as if all the people in the boxes were looking at them. She got up and went hurriedly to the exit; he followed her, and both of them walked blindly along the corridors and up and down stairs, and figures in the uniforms prescribed for magistrates, teachers, and officials of the Department of Crown Lands, all wearing badges, flitted before their eyes, as did also ladies, and fur coats on hangers; they were conscious of drafts and the smell of stale tobacco. And Gurov, whose heart was beating violently, thought:

90   "Oh, Lord! Why are these people here and this orchestra!"

And at that instant he suddenly recalled how when he had seen Anna Sergeyevna off at the station he had said to himself that all was over between them and that they would never meet again. But how distant the end still was!

On the narrow, gloomy staircase over which it said "To the Amphitheatre," she stopped.

"How you frightened me!" she said, breathing hard, still pale and stunned. "Oh, how you frightened me! I am barely alive. Why did you come? Why?"

"But do understand, Anna, do understand—" he said hurriedly, under his breath. "I implore you, do understand—"

95   She looked at him with fear, with entreaty, with love; she looked at him intently, to keep his features more distinctly in her memory.

"I suffer so," she went on, not listening to him. "All this time I have been thinking of nothing but you; I live only by the thought of you. And I wanted to forget, to forget; but why, oh, why have you come?"

On the landing above them two high school boys were looking down and smoking, but it was all the same to Gurov; he drew Anna Sergeyevna to him and began kissing her face and hands.

"What are you doing, what are you doing!" she was saying in horror, pushing him away. "We have lost our senses. Go away today; go away at once—I conjure you by all that is sacred, I implore you—People are coming this way!"

Someone was walking up the stairs.

100   "You must leave," Anna Sergeyevna went on in a whisper. "Do you hear, Dmitry Dmitrich? I will come and see you in Moscow. I have never been happy; I am unhappy now, and I never, never shall be happy, never! So don't make me suffer still more! I swear I'll come to Moscow. But now let us part. My dear, good, precious one, let us part!"

She pressed his hand and walked rapidly downstairs, turning to look round at him, and from her eyes he could see that she really was unhappy. Gurov stood for a while, listening, then when all grew quiet, he found his coat and left the theater.

IV

And Anna Sergeyevna began coming to see him in Moscow. Once every two or three months she left S_____ telling her husband that she was going to consult a doctor about a woman's ailment from which she was suffering—and her husband did and did not believe her. When she arrived in Moscow she would stop at the Slavyansky Bazar Hotel, and at once send a man in a red cap to Gurov. Gurov came to see her, and no one in Moscow knew of it.

Once he was going to see her in this way on a winter morning (the messenger had come the evening before and not found him in). With him walked his daughter, whom he wanted to take to school; it was on the way. Snow was coming down in big wet flakes.

"It's three degrees above zero,[1] and yet it's snowing," Gurov was saying to his daughter. "But this temperature prevails only on the surface of the earth; in the upper layers of the atmosphere there is quite a different temperature."

105   "And why doesn't it thunder in winter, papa?"

He explained that, too. He talked, thinking all the while that he was on his way to a rendezvous, and no living soul knew of it, and probably no one would ever know. He had two lives, an open one, seen and known by all who needed to know it, full of conventional truth and conventional falsehood, exactly like the lives of his friends and acquaintances; and another life that went on in secret. And through some strange, perhaps accidental, combination of circumstances, everything that was of interest and importance to him, everything that was essential to him, everything about which he felt sincerely and did not deceive himself, everything that constituted the core of his life, was going on concealed from others; while all that was false, the shell in which he hid to cover the truth—his work at the bank, for instance, his discussions at the club, his references to the "inferior race," his appearances at anniversary celebrations with his wife—all that went on in the open.

---

[1] **three degrees above zero** about 37 degrees Fahrenheit

Judging others by himself, he did not believe what he saw, and always fancied that every man led his real, most interesting life under cover of secrecy as under cover of night. The personal life of every individual is based on secrecy, and perhaps it is partly for that reason that civilized man is so nervously anxious that personal privacy should be respected.

Having taken his daughter to school, Gurov went on to the Slavyansky Bazar Hotel. He took off his fur coat in the lobby, went upstairs, and knocked gently at the door. Anna Sergeyevna, wearing his favorite gray dress, exhausted by the journey and by waiting, had been expecting him since the previous evening. She was pale, and looked at him without a smile, and he had hardly entered when she flung herself on his breast. That kiss was a long, lingering one, as though they had not seen one another for two years.

"Well, darling, how are you getting on there?" he asked. "What news?"

"Wait; I'll tell you in a moment—I can't speak."

110   She could not speak; she was crying. She turned away from him, and pressed her handkerchief to her eyes.

"Let her have her cry; meanwhile I'll sit down," he thought, and he seated himself in an armchair.

Then he rang and ordered tea, and while he was having his tea she remained standing at the window with her back to him. She was crying out of sheer agitation, in the sorrowful consciousness that their life was so sad; that they could only see each other in secret and had to hide from people like thieves! Was it not a broken life?

"Come, stop now, dear!" he said.

It was plain to him that this love of theirs would not be over soon, that the end of it was not in sight. Anna Sergeyevna was growing more and more attached to him. She adored him, and it was unthinkable to tell her that their love was bound to come to an end some day; besides, she would not have believed it!

115   He went up to her and took her by the shoulders, to fondle her and say something diverting, and at that moment he caught sight of himself in the mirror.

His hair was already beginning to turn gray. And it seemed odd to him that he had grown so much older in the last few years, and lost his looks. The shoulders on which his hands rested were warm and heaving. He felt compassion for this life, still so warm and lovely, but probably already about to begin to fade and wither like his own. Why did she love him so much? He always seemed to women different from what he was, and they loved in him not himself, but the man whom their imagination created and whom they had been eagerly seeking all their lives; and afterwards, when they saw their mistake, they loved him nevertheless. And not one of them had happy with him. In the past he had met women, come together with them, parted from them, but he had never once loved; it was anything you please, but not love. And only now when his head was gray he had fallen in love, really, truly—for the first time in his life.

Anna Sergeyevna and he loved each other as people do who are very close and intimate, like man and wife, like tender friends; it seemed to them that Fate itself had meant them for one another, and they could not understand why he had a wife and she a husband; and it was as though they were a pair of migratory birds, male and female, caught and forced to live in different cages. They forgave each other what they were ashamed of in their past, they forgave everything in the present, and felt that this love of theirs had altered them both.

Formerly in moments of sadness he had soothed himself with whatever logical arguments came into his head, but now he no longer cared for logic; he felt profound compassion, he wanted to be sincere and tender.

"Give it up now, my darling," he said. "You've had your cry; that's enough. Let us have a talk now, we'll think up something."

120   Then they spent a long time taking counsel together, they talked of how to avoid the necessity for secrecy, for deception, for living in different cities, and not seeing one another for long stretches of time. How could they free themselves from these intolerable fetters?

"How? How?" he asked, clutching his head. "How?"

And it seemed as though in a little while the solution would be found, and then a new and glorious life would begin; and it was clear to both of them that the end was still far off, and that what was to be most complicated and difficult for them was only just beginning.

▶ QUESTIONS FOR READING AND WRITING

1. Why do you think that most of the action takes place away from Moscow?
2. What attracts Gurov to Anna Sergeyevna in the first place? During their time in Yalta, she is concerned with whether or not he respects her. Does he?
3. There are no scenes between Gurov and his wife. Why? Would it change how you feel about Gurov and Anna Sergeyevna if you knew more about his wife?
4. Is there a sense in which the central characters behave nobly? Do you think that infidelity is ever justified? Is love for a mistress the same as love for a wife?
5. What does the last paragraph mean? What has happened to make the time ahead "to be most complicated and difficult"? Explain.

STEPHEN CRANE (1871–1900)

Stephen Crane was the youngest of 14 children born to a Methodist minister in Newark, New Jersey. After briefly attending LaFayette College and Syracuse University, Crane moved to New York City to work as a freelance journalist. He lived a bohemian (and often impoverished) existence and came to know life in the slums firsthand. These experiences inspired his first novel, Maggie, a Girl on the Streets, *which he published at his own expense under a pseudonym. While not widely read due to its realistic language, which was considered shocking at the time, the novel impressed members of New*

York's literary elite, setting the stage for the publication of his second novel, The Red Badge of Courage *(1895). The story of a young man's initiation into the horrors of war, the book was hailed for its realism—all the more remarkable because Crane had never been in a battle—and catapulted Crane into literary prominence. Also in 1895, Crane published a book of short poems,* The Black Riders, *and* Other Line, *which would later prove influential but went largely unnoticed until after his death. For the rest of his short life, Crane continued working as a journalist while producing a series of masterful short stories, including "The Open Boat" (1898) and "The Blue Hotel" (1899), as well as four less regarded novels and another collection of poetry,* War Is Kind *(1899). Plagued by ill health and growing financial difficulties, Crane died of tuberculosis when he was only 28. "The Open Boat" is based on Crane's real-life experiences: in 1897, he was on assignment on a ship bound for Cuba that sank off the coast of Florida. Crane and four other men spent 30 hours in a dinghy before finally reaching the shore.*

THE OPEN BOAT   [1898]

A Tale Intended to be after the Fact, Being the Experience of Four Men from the Sunk Steamer COMMODORE

I

None of them knew the color of the sky. Their eyes glanced level, and were fastened upon the waves that swept toward them. These waves were of the hue of slate, save for the tops, which were of foaming white, and all of the men knew the colors of the sea. The horizon narrowed and widened, and dipped and rose, and at all times its edge was jagged with waves that seemed thrust up in points like rocks.

Many a man ought to have a bathtub larger than the boat which here rode upon the sea. These waves were most wrongfully and barbarously abrupt and tall, and each froth-top was a problem in small-boat navigation.

The cook squatted in the bottom, and looked with both eyes at the six inches of gunwale which separated him from the ocean. His sleeves were rolled over his fat forearms, and the two flaps of his unbuttoned vest dangled as he bent to bail out the boat. Often he said, "Gawd! that was a narrow clip." As he remarked it he invariably gazed eastward over the broken sea.

The oiler, steering with one of the two oars in the boat, sometimes raised himself suddenly to keep clear of water that swirled in over the stern. It was a thin little oar, and it seemed often ready to snap.

5   The correspondent, pulling at the other oar, watched the waves and wondered why he was there.

The injured captain, lying in the bow, was at this time buried in that profound dejection and indifference which comes, temporarily at least, to even the bravest and most enduring when, willy-nilly, the firm fails, the army loses, the ship goes down. The mind of the master of a vessel is rooted deep in the timbers of her, though he command for a day or a decade; and this captain had on him the stern impression of a scene in the grays of dawn of seven turned faces, and later a stump of a topmast with a white ball on it, that slashed to and fro at the waves, went low and lower, and down. Thereafter there was something strange in his voice. Although steady, it was deep with mourning, and of a quality beyond oration or tears.

"Keep 'er a little more south, Billie," said he.

"A little more south, sir," said the oiler in the stern.

A seat in this boat was not unlike a seat upon a bucking broncho, and by the same token a broncho is not much smaller. The craft pranced and reared and plunged like an animal. As each wave came, and she rose for it, she seemed like a horse making at a fence outrageously high. The manner of her scramble over these walls of water is a mystic thing, and, moreover, at the top of them were ordinarily these problems in white water, the foam racing down from the summit of each wave requiring a new leap, and a leap from the air. Then, after scornfully bumping a crest, she would slide and race and splash down a long incline, and arrive bobbing and nodding in front of the next menace.

10   A singular disadvantage of the sea lies in the fact that after successfully surmounting one wave you discover that there is another behind it just as important and just as nervously anxious to do something effective in the way of swamping boats. In a ten-foot dinghy one can get an idea of the resources of the sea in the line of waves that is not probable to the average experience, which is never at sea in a dinghy. As each slaty wall of water approached, it shut all else from the view of the men in the boat, and it was not difficult to imagine that this particular wave was the final outburst of the ocean, the last effort of the grim water. There was a terrible grace in the move of the waves, and they came in silence, save for the snarling of the crests.

In the wan light the faces of the men must have been gray. Their eyes must have glinted in strange ways as they gazed steadily astern. Viewed from a balcony, the whole thing would doubtless have been weirdly picturesque. But the men in the boat had no time to see it, and if they had had leisure, there were other things to occupy their minds. The sun swung steadily up the sky, and they knew it was broad day because the color of the sea changed from slate to emerald-green, streaked with amber lights, and the foam was like tumbling snow. The process of the breaking day was unknown to them. They were aware only of this effect upon the color of the waves that rolled toward them.

In disjointed sentences the cook and the correspondent argued as to the difference between a life-saving station and a house of refuge. The cook had said: "There's a house of refuge just north of the Mosquito Inlet Light, and as soon as they see us they'll come off in their boat and pick us up."

"As soon as who see us?" said the correspondent.

"The crew," said the cook.

15   "Houses of refuge don't have crews," said the correspondent. "As I understand them, they are only places where clothes and grub are stored for the benefit of shipwrecked people. They don't carry crews."

"Oh, yes, they do," said the cook.

"No, they don't," said the correspondent.

"Well, we're not there yet, anyhow," said the oiler, in the stern.

"Well," said the cook, "perhaps it's not a house of refuge that I'm thinking of as being near Mosquito Inlet Light; perhaps it's a life-saving station."

20   "We're not there yet," said the oiler in the stern.

II

As the boat bounced from the top of each wave the wind tore through the hair of the hatless men, and as the craft plopped her stern down again the spray slashed past them. The crest of each of these waves was a hill, from the top of which the men surveyed for a moment a broad tumultuous expanse, shining and wind-riven. It was probably splendid, it was probably glorious, this play of the free sea, wild with lights of emerald and white and amber.

"Bully good thing it's an on-shore wind," said the cook. "If not, where would we be? Wouldn't have a show."

"That's right," said the correspondent.

The busy oiler nodded his assent.

25   Then the captain, in the bow, chuckled in a way that expressed humor, contempt, tragedy, all in one. "Do you think we've got much of a show now, boys?" said he.

Whereupon the three were silent, save for a trifle of hemming and hawing. To express any particular optimism at this time they felt to be childish and stupid, but they all doubtless possessed this sense of the situation in their minds. A young man thinks doggedly at such times. On the other hand, the ethics of their condition was decidedly against any open suggestion of hopelessness. So they were silent.

"Oh, well," said the captain, soothing his children, "we'll get ashore all right."

But there was that in his tone which made them think; so the oiler quoth, "Yes! if this wind holds."

The cook was bailing. "Yes! if we don't catch hell in the surf."

30   Canton-flannel gulls flew near and far. Sometimes they sat down on the sea, near patches of brown seaweed that rolled over the waves with a movement like carpets on a line in a gale. The birds sat comfortably in groups, and they were envied by some in the dinghy, for the wrath of the sea was no more to them than it was to a covey of prairie chickens a thousand miles inland. Often they came very close and stared at the men with black bead-like eyes. At these times they were uncanny and sinister in their unblinking scrutiny, and the men hooted angrily at them, telling them to be gone. One came, and evidently decided to alight on the top of the captain's head. The bird flew parallel to the boat and did not circle, but made short sidelong jumps in the air in chicken-fashion. His black eyes were wistfully fixed upon the captain's head. "Ugly brute," said the oiler to the bird. "You look as if you were made with a jackknife." The cook and the correspondent swore darkly at the creature. The captain naturally wished to knock it away with the end of the heavy painter, but he did not dare do it, because anything resembling an emphatic gesture would have capsized this freighted boat; and so, with his open hand, the captain gently and carefully waved the gull away. After it had been discouraged from the pursuit the captain breathed easier on account of his hair, and others breathed easier because the bird struck their minds at this time as being somehow gruesome and ominous.

In the meantime the oiler and the correspondent rowed. And also they rowed. They sat together in the same seat, and each rowed an oar. Then the oiler took both oars; then the correspondent took both oars; then the oiler; then the correspondent.

They rowed and they rowed. The very ticklish part of the business was when the time came for the reclining one in the stern to take his turn at the oars. By the very last star of truth, it is easier to steal eggs from under a hen than it was to change seats in the dinghy. First the man in the stern slid his hand along the thwart and moved with care, as if he were of Sèvres. Then the man in the rowing-seat slid his hand along the other thwart. It was all done with the most extraordinary care. As the two sidled past each other, the whole party kept watchful eyes on the coming wave, and the captain cried: "Look out, now! Steady, there!"

The brown mats of seaweed that appeared from time to time were like islands, bits of earth. They were travelling, apparently, neither one way nor the other. They were, to all intents, stationary. They informed the men in the boat that it was making progress slowly toward the land.

The captain, rearing cautiously in the bow after the dinghy soared on a great swell, said that he had seen the lighthouse at Mosquito Inlet. Presently the cook remarked that he had seen it. The correspondent was at the oars then, and for some reason he too wished to look at the lighthouse; but his back was toward the far shore, and the waves were important, and for some time he could not seize an opportunity to turn his head. But at last there came a wave more gentle than the others, and when at the crest of it he swiftly scoured the western horizon.

"See it?" said the captain.

35 "No," said the correspondent, slowly; "I didn't see anything."

"Look again," said the captain. He pointed. "It's exactly in that direction."

At the top of another wave the correspondent did as he was bid, and this time his eyes chanced on a small, still thing on the edge of the swaying horizon. It was precisely like the point of a pin. It took an anxious eye to find a lighthouse so tiny.

"Think we'll make it, Captain?"

"If this wind holds and the boat don't swamp, we can't do much else," said the captain.

40 The little boat, lifted by each towering sea and splashed viciously by the crests, made progress that in the absence of seaweed was not apparent to those in her. She seemed just a wee thing wallowing, miraculously top up, at the mercy of five oceans. Occasionally a great spread of water, like white flames, swarmed into her.

"Bail her, cook," said the captain, serenely.

"All right, Captain," said the cheerful cook.

III

It would be difficult to describe the subtle brotherhood of men that was here established on the seas. No one said that it was so. No one mentioned it. But it dwelt in the boat, and each man felt it warm him. They were a captain, an oiler, a cook, and a correspondent, and they were friends—friends in a more curiously iron-bound degree than may be common. The hurt captain, lying against the water-jar in the bow, spoke always in a low voice and calmly; but he could never command a more ready and swiftly obedient crew than the motley three of the dinghy. It was more than a mere recognition of what was best for the common safety. There was surely in it a quality that was personal and heart-felt. And after this devotion to the commander of the boat, there was this comradeship, that the correspondent, for instance, who had been taught to be cynical of men, knew even at the time was the best experience of his life. But no one said that it was so. No one mentioned it.

"I wish we had a sail," remarked the captain. "We might try my overcoat on the end of an oar, and give you two boys a chance to rest." So the cook and the correspondent held the mast and spread wide the overcoat, the oiler steered; and the little boat made good way with her new rig. Sometimes the oiler had to scull sharply to keep a sea from breaking into the boat, but otherwise sailing was a success.

45   Meanwhile the lighthouse had been growing slowly larger. It had now almost assumed color, and appeared like a little gray shadow on the sky. The man at the oars could not be prevented from turning his head rather often to try for a glimpse of this little gray shadow.

At last, from the top of each wave, the men in the tossing boat could see land. Even as the lighthouse was an upright shadow on the sky, this land seemed but a long black shadow on the sea. It certainly was thinner than paper. "We must be about opposite New Smyrna," said the cook, who had coasted this shore often in schooners. "Captain, by the way, I believe they abandoned that life-saving station there about a year ago."

"Did they?" said the captain.

The wind slowly died away. The cook and the correspondent were not now obliged to slave in order to hold high the oar. But the waves continued their old impetuous swooping at the dinghy, and the little craft, no longer under way, struggled woundily over them. The oiler or the correspondent took the oars again.

Shipwrecks are *apropos* of nothing. If men could only train for them and have them occur when the men had reached pink condition, there would be less drowning at sea. Of the four in the dinghy none had slept any time worth mentioning for two days and two nights previous to embarking in the dinghy, and in the excitement of clambering about the deck of a foundering ship they had also forgotten to eat heartily.

50   For these reasons, and for others, neither the oiler nor the correspondent was fond of rowing at this time. The correspondent wondered ingenuously how in the name of all that was sane could there be people who thought it amusing to row a boat. It was not an amusement; it was a diabolical punishment, and even a genius of mental aberrations could never conclude that it was anything but a horror to the muscles and a crime against the back. He mentioned to the boat in general how the amusement of rowing struck him, and the weary-faced oiler smiled in full sympathy. Previously to the foundering, by the way, the oiler had worked a double-watch in the engine-room of the ship.

"Take her easy now, boys," said the captain. "Don't spend yourselves. If we have to run a surf you'll need all your strength, because we'll sure have to swim for it. Take your time."

Slowly the land arose from the sea. From a black line it became a line of black and a line of white—trees and sand. Finally the captain said that he could make out a house on the shore. "That's the house of refuge, sure," said the cook. "They'll see us before long, and come out after us."

The distant lighthouse reared high. "The keeper ought to be able to make us out now, if he's looking through a glass," said the captain. "He'll notify the life-saving people."

"None of those other boats could have got ashore to give word of this wreck," said the oiler, in a low voice, "else the life-boat would be out hunting us."

55   Slowly and beautifully the land loomed out of the sea. The wind came again. It had veered from the northeast to the southeast. Finally a new sound struck the ears of the men in the boat. It was the low thunder of the surf on the shore. "We'll never be able to make the lighthouse now," said the captain. "Swing her head a little more north, Billie."

"A little more north, sir," said the oiler.

Whereupon the little boat turned her nose once more down the wind, and all but the oarsman watched the shore grow. Under the influence of this expansion doubt and direful apprehension were leaving the minds of the men. The management of the boat was still most absorbing, but it could not prevent a quiet cheerfulness. In an hour, perhaps, they would be ashore.

Their backbones had become thoroughly used to balancing in the boat, and they now rode this wild colt of a dinghy like circus men. The correspondent thought that he had been drenched to the skin, but happening to feel in the top pocket of his coat, he found therein eight cigars. Four of them were soaked with sea-water; four were perfectly scatheless. After a search, somebody produced three dry matches; and thereupon the four waifs rode impudently in their little boat and, with an assurance of an impending rescue shining in their eyes, puffed at the big cigars, and judged well and ill of all men. Everybody took a drink of water.

IV

"Cook," remarked the captain, "there don't seem to be any signs of life about your house of refuge."

60   "No," replied the cook. "Funny they don't see us!"

A broad stretch of lowly coast lay before the eyes of the men. It was of low dunes topped with dark vegetation. The roar of the surf was plain, and sometimes they could see the white lip of a wave as it spun up the beach. A tiny house was blocked out black upon the sky. Southward, the slim lighthouse lifted its little gray length.

Tide, wind, and waves were swinging the dinghy northward. "Funny they don't see us," said the men.

The surf's roar was here dulled, but its tone was nevertheless thunderous and mighty. As the boat swam over the great rollers the men sat listening to this roar. "We'll swamp sure," said everybody.

It is fair to say here that there was not a life-saving station within twenty miles in either direction; but the men did not know this fact, and in consequence they made dark and opprobrious remarks concerning the eyesight of the nation's lifesavers. Four scowling men sat in the dinghy and surpassed records in the invention of epithets.

65   "Funny they don't see us."

The light-heartedness of a former time had completely faded. To their sharpened minds it was easy to conjure pictures of all kinds of incompetency and blindness and, indeed, cowardice. There was the shore of the populous land, and it was bitter and bitter to them that from it came no sign.

"Well," said the captain, ultimately, "I suppose we'll have to make a try for ourselves. If we stay out here too long, we'll none of us have strength left to swim after the boat swamps."

And so the oiler, who was at the oars, turned the boat straight for the shore. There was a sudden tightening of muscles. There was some thinking.

"If we don't all get ashore," said the captain—"if we don't all get ashore, I suppose you fellows know where to send news of my finish?"

70   They then briefly exchanged some addresses and admonitions. As for the reflections of the men, there was a great deal of rage in them. Perchance they might be formulated thus: "If I am going to be drowned—if I am going to be drowned—if I am going to be drowned, why, in the name of the seven mad gods who rule the sea, was I allowed to come thus far and contemplate sand and trees? Was I brought here merely to have my nose dragged away as I was about to nibble the sacred cheese of life? It is preposterous. If this old ninny-woman, Fate, cannot do better than this, she should be deprived of the management of men's fortunes. She is an old hen who knows not her intention. If she has decided to drown me, why did she not do it in the beginning and save me all this trouble? The whole affair is absurd. . . . But no; she cannot mean to drown me. She dare not drown me. She cannot drown me. Not after all this work." Afterward the man might have had an impulse to shake his fist at the clouds. "Just you drown me, now, and then hear what I call you!"

The billows that came at this time were more formidable. They seemed always just about to break and roll over the little boat in a turmoil of foam. There was a preparatory and long growl in the speech of them. No mind unused to the sea would have concluded that the dinghy could ascend these sheer heights in time. The shore was still afar. The oiler was a wily surfman. "Boys," he said swiftly, "she won't live three minutes more, and we're too far out to swim. Shall I take her to sea again, Captain?"

"Yes; go ahead!" said the captain.

This oiler, by a series of quick miracles and fast and steady oarsmanship, turned the boat in the middle of the surf and took her safely to sea again.

There was a considerable silence as the boat bumped over the furrowed sea to deeper water. Then somebody in gloom spoke. "Well, anyhow, they must have seen us from the shore by now."

75   The gulls went in slanting flight up the wind toward the gray, desolate east. A squall, marked by dingy clouds and clouds brick-red, like smoke from a burning building, appeared from the southeast.

"What do you think of those life-saving people? Ain't they peaches?"

"Funny they haven't seen us."

"Maybe they think we're out here for sport! Maybe they think we're fishin'. Maybe they think we're damned fools."

It was a long afternoon. A changed tide tried to force them southward, but wind and wave said northward. Far ahead, where coast-line, sea, and sky formed their mighty angle, there were little dots which seemed to indicate a city on the shore.

80   "St. Augustine?"

The captain shook his head. "Too near Mosquito Inlet."

And the oiler rowed, and then the correspondent rowed; then the oiler rowed. It was a weary business. The human back can become the seat of more aches and pains than are registered in books for the composite anatomy of a regiment. It is a limited area, but it can become the theatre of innumerable muscular conflicts, tangles, wrenches, knots, and other comforts.

"Did you ever like to row, Billie?" asked the correspondent.

"No," said the oiler; "hang it!"

85   When one exchanged the rowing-seat for a place in the bottom of the boat, he suffered a bodily depression that caused him to be careless of everything save an obligation to wiggle one finger. There was cold sea-water swashing to and fro in the boat, and he lay in it. His head, pillowed on a thwart, was within an inch of the swirl of a wave-crest, and sometimes a particularly obstreperous sea came inboard and drenched him once more. But these matters did not annoy him. It is almost certain that if the boat had capsized he would have tumbled comfortably out upon the ocean as if he felt sure that it was a great soft mattress.

"Look! There's a man on the shore!"

"Where?"

"There! See 'im? See 'im?"

"Yes, sure! He's walking along."

90   "Now he's stopped. Look! He's facing us!"

"He's waving at us!"

"So he is! By thunder!"

"Ah, now we're all right! Now we're all right! There'll be a boat out here for us in half an hour."

"He's going on. He's running. He's going up to that house there."

95   The remote beach seemed lower than the sea, and it required a searching glance to discern the little black figure. The captain saw a floating stick, and they rowed to it. A bath towel was by some weird chance in the boat, and, tying this on the stick, the captain waved it. The oarsman did not dare turn his head, so he was obliged to ask questions.

"What's he doing now?"

"He's standing still again. He's looking, I think. . . . There he goes again— toward the house. . . . Now he's stopped again."

"Is he waving at us?"

"No, not now; he was, though."

100   "Look! There comes another man!"

"He's running."

"Look at him go, would you!"

"Why, he's on a bicycle. Now he's met the other man. They're both waving at us. Look!"

"There comes something up the beach."

105   "What the devil is that thing?"

"Why, it looks like a boat."

"Why, certainly, it's a boat."

"No; it's on wheels."

"Yes, so it is. Well, that must be the life-boat. They drag them along shore on a wagon."

110   "That's the life-boat, sure."

"No, by God, it's—it's an omnibus."

"I tell you it's a life-boat."

"It is not! It's an omnibus. I can see it plain. See? One of the these big hotel omnibuses."

"By thunder, you're right. It's an omnibus, sure as fate. What do you suppose they are doing with an omnibus? Maybe they are going around collecting the life-crew, hey?"

115   "That's it, likely. Look! There's a fellow waving a little black flag. He's standing on the steps of the omnibus. There come those other two fellows. Now they're all talking together. Look at the fellow with the flag. Maybe he ain't waving it!"

"That ain't a flag, is it? That's his coat. Why, certainly, that's his coat."

"So it is; it's his coat. He's taken it off and is waving it around his head. But would you look at him swing it!"

"Oh, say, there isn't any life-saving station there. That's just a winter resort hotel omnibus that has brought over some of the boarders to see us drown."

"What's that idiot with the coat mean? What's he signaling, anyhow?"

120   "It looks as if he were trying to tell us to go north. There must be a life-saving station up there."

"No; he thinks we're fishing. Just giving us a merry hand. See? Ah, there, Willie!"

"Well, I wish I could make something out of those signals. What do you suppose he means?"

"He don't mean anything; he's just playing."

"Well, if he'd just signal us to try the surf again, or to go to sea and wait, or go north, or go south, or go to hell, there would be some reason in it. But look at him! He just stands there and keeps his coat revolving like a wheel. The ass!"

125   "There come more people."

"Now there's quite a mob. Look! Isn't that a boat?"

"Where? Oh, I see where you mean. No, that's no boat."

"That fellow is still waving his coat."

"He must think we like to see him do that. Why don't he quit it? It don't mean anything."

130   "I don't know. I think he is trying to make us go north. It must be that there's a life-saving station there somewhere."

"Say, he ain't tired yet. Look at 'im wave!"

"Wonder how long he can keep that up. He's been revolving his coat ever since he caught sight of us. He's an idiot. Why aren't they getting men to bring a boat out? A fishing boat—one of those big yawls—could come out here all right. Why don't he do something?"

"Oh, it's all right now."

"They'll have a boat out here for us in less than no time, now that they've seen us."

135   A faint yellow tone came into the sky over the low land. The shadows on the sea slowly deepened. The wind bore coldness with it, and the men began to shiver.

"Holy smoke!" said one, allowing his voice to express his impious mood, "if we keep on monkeying out here! If we've got to flounder out here all night!"

"Oh, we'll never have to stay here all night! Don't you worry. They've seen us now, and it won't be long before they'll come chasing out after us."

The shore grew dusky. The man waving a coat blended gradually into this gloom, and it swallowed in the same manner the omnibus and the group of people. The spray, when it dashed uproariously over the side, made the voyagers shrink and swear like men who were being branded.

"I'd like to catch the chump who waved the coat. I feel like socking him one, just for luck."

140   "Why? What did he do?"

"Oh, nothing, but then he seemed so damned cheerful."

In the meantime the oiler rowed, and then the correspondent rowed, and then the oiler rowed. Gray-faced and bowed forward, they mechanically, turn by turn, plied the leaden oars. The form of the lighthouse had vanished from the southern horizon, but finally a pale star appeared, just lifting from the sea. The streaked saffron in the west passed before the all-merging darkness, and the sea to the east was black. The land had vanished, and was expressed only by the low and drear thunder of the surf.

"If I am going to be drowned—if I am going to be drowned—if I am going to be drowned, why, in the name of the seven mad gods who rule the sea, was I allowed to come thus far and contemplate sand and trees? Was I brought here merely to have my nose dragged away as I was about to nibble the sacred cheese of life?"

The patient captain, drooped over the water-jar, was sometimes obliged to speak to the oarsman.

145   "Keep her head up! Keep her head up!"

"Keep her head up, sir." The voices were weary and low.

This was surely a quiet evening. All save the oarsman lay heavily and listlessly in the boat's bottom. As for him, his eyes were just capable of noting the tall black waves that swept forward in a most sinister silence, save for an occasional subdued growl of a crest.

The cook's head was on a thwart, and he looked without interest at the water under this nose. He was deep in other scenes. Finally he spoke. "Billie," he murmured, dreamfully, "what kind of pie do you like best?"

V

"Pie!" said the oiler and the correspondent, agitatedly. "Don't talk about those things, blast you!"

150   "Well," said the cook, "I was just thinking about ham sandwiches, and—"

A night on the sea in an open boat is a long night. As darkness settled finally, the shine of the light, lifting from the sea in the south, changed to full gold. On the northern horizon a new light appeared, a small bluish gleam on the edge of the waters. These two lights were the furniture of the world. Otherwise there was nothing but waves.

Two men huddled in the stern, and distances were so magnificent in the dinghy that the rower was enabled to keep his feet partly warm by thrusting them under his companions. Their legs indeed extended far under the rowing-seat until they touched the feet of the captain forward. Sometimes, despite the efforts of the tired oarsman, a wave came piling into the boat, an icy wave of the night, and the chilling water soaked them anew. They would twist their bodies for a moment and groan, and sleep the dead sleep once more, while the water in the boat gurgled about them as the craft rocked.

The plan of the oiler and the correspondent was for one to row until he lost the ability, and then arouse the other from his sea-water couch in the bottom of the boat.

The oiler plied the oars until his head drooped forward and the overpowering sleep blinded him; and he rowed yet afterward. Then he touched a man in the bottom of the boat, and called his name. "Will you spell me for a little while?" he said meekly.

155   "Sure, Billie," said the correspondent, awaking and dragging himself to a sitting position. They exchanged places carefully, and the oiler, cuddling down in the sea-water at the cook's side, seemed to go to sleep instantly.

The particular violence of the sea had ceased. The waves came without snarling. The obligation of the man at the oars was to keep the boat headed so that the tilt of the rollers would not capsize her, and to preserve her from filling when the crests rushed past. The black waves were silent and hard to be seen in the darkness. Often one was almost upon the boat before the oarsman was aware.

In a low voice the correspondent addressed the captain. He was not sure that the captain was awake, although this iron man seemed to be always awake. "Captain, shall I keep her making for that light north, sir?"

The same steady voice answered him. "Yes. Keep it about two points off the port bow."

The cook had tied a life-belt around himself in order to get even the warmth which this clumsy cork contrivance could donate, and he seemed almost stove-like when a rower, whose teeth invariably chattered wildly as soon as he ceased his labor, dropped down to sleep.

160   The correspondent, as he rowed, looked down at the two men sleeping underfoot. The cook's arm was around the oiler's shoulders, and, with their fragmentary clothing and haggard faces, they were the babes of the sea—a grotesque rendering of the old babes in the wood.

Later he must have grown stupid at his work, for suddenly there was a growling of water, and a crest came with a roar and a swash into the boat, and it was a wonder that it did not set the cook afloat in his life-belt. The cook continued to sleep, but the oiler sat up, blinking his eyes and shaking with the new cold.

"Oh, I'm awful sorry, Billie," said the correspondent, contritely.

"That's all right, old boy," said the oiler, and lay down again and was asleep.

Presently it seemed that even the captain dozed, and the correspondent thought that he was the one man afloat on all the ocean. The wind had a voice as it came over the waves, and it was sadder than the end.

165   There was a long, loud swishing astern of the boat, and a gleaming trail of phosphorescence, like blue flame, was furrowed on the black waters. It might have been made by a monstrous knife.

Then there came a stillness, while the correspondent breathed with open mouth and looked at the sea.

Suddenly there was another swish and another long flash of bluish light, and this time it was alongside the boat, and might almost have been reached with an oar. The correspondent saw an enormous fin speed like a shadow through the water, hurling the crystalline spray and leaving the long glowing trail.

The correspondent looked over his shoulder at the captain. His face was hidden, and he seemed to be asleep. He looked at the babes of the sea. They certainly were asleep. So, being bereft of sympathy, he leaned a little way to one side and swore softly into the sea.

But the thing did not then leave the vicinity of the boat. Ahead or astern, on one side or the other, at intervals long or short, fled the long sparkling streak, and there was to be heard the *whirroo* of the dark fin. The speed and power of the thing was greatly to be admired. It cut the water like a gigantic and keen projectile.

170   The presence of this biding thing did not affect the man with the same horror that it would if he had been a picnicker. He simply looked at the sea dully and swore in an undertone.

Nevertheless, it is true that he did not wish to be alone with the thing. He wished one of his companions to awake by chance and keep him company with it. But the captain hung motionless over the water-jar, and the oiler and the cook in the bottom of the boat were plunged in slumber.

VI

"If I am going to be drowned—if I am going to be drowned—if I am going to be drowned, why, in the name of the seven mad gods who rule the sea, was I allowed to come thus far and contemplate sand and trees?"

During this dismal night, it may be remarked that a man would conclude that it was really the intention of the seven mad gods to drown him, despite the abominable injustice of it. For it was certainly an abominable injustice to drown a man who had worked so hard, so hard. The man felt it would be a crime most unnatural. Other people had drowned at sea since galleys swarmed with painted sails, but still—

When it occurs to a man that nature does not regard him as important, and that she feels she would not maim the universe by disposing of him, he at first wishes to throw bricks at the temple, and he hates deeply the fact that there are no bricks and no temples. Any visible expression of nature would surely be pelleted with his jeers.

175   Then, if there be no tangible thing to hoot, he feels, perhaps, the desire to confront a personification and indulge in pleas, bowed to one knee, and with hands supplicant, saying, "Yes, but I love myself."

A high cold star on a winter's night is the word he feels that she says to him. Thereafter he knows the pathos of his situation.

The men in the dinghy had not discussed these matters, but each had, no doubt, reflected upon them in silence and according to his mind. There was seldom any expression upon their faces save the general one of complete weariness. Speech was devoted to the business of the boat.

To chime the notes of his emotion, a verse mysteriously entered the correspondent's head. He had even forgotten that he had forgotten this verse, but it suddenly was in his mind.

A soldier of the Legion lay dying in Algiers;
There was lack of woman's nursing, there was dearth of woman's tears;
But a comrade stood beside him, and he took that comrade's hand,
And he said, "I never more shall see my own, my native land."

180   In his childhood the correspondent had been made acquainted with the fact that a soldier of the Legion lay dying in Algiers, but he had never regarded it as important. Myriads of his school-fellows had informed him of the soldier's plight, but the dinning had naturally ended by making him perfectly indifferent. He had never considered it his affair that a soldier of the Legion lay dying in Algiers, nor had it appeared to him as a matter for sorrow. It was less to him than the breaking of a pencil's point.

Now, however, it quaintly came to him as a human, living thing. It was no longer merely a picture of a few throes in the breast of a poet, meanwhile drinking tea and warming his feet at the grate; it was an actuality—stern, mournful, and fine.

The correspondent plainly saw the soldier. He lay on the sand with his feet out straight and still. While his pale left hand was upon his chest in an attempt to thwart the going of his life, the blood came between his fingers. In the far Algerian distance, a city of low square forms was set against a sky that was faint with the last sunset hues. The correspondent, plying the oars and dreaming of the slow and slower movements of the lips of the soldier, was moved by a profound and perfectly impersonal comprehension. He was sorry for the soldier of the Legion who lay dying in Algiers.

The thing which had followed the boat and waited had evidently grown bored at the delay. There was no longer to be heard the slash of the cutwater, and there was no longer the flame of the long trail. The light in the north still glimmered, but it was apparently no nearer to the boat. Sometimes the boom of the surf rang in the correspondent's ears, and he turned the craft seaward then and rowed harder. Southward, some one had evidently built a watch-fire on the beach. It was too low and too far to be seen, but it made a shimmering, roseate reflection upon the bluff in back of it, and this could be discerned from the boat. The wind came stronger, and sometimes a wave suddenly raged out like a mountain-cat, and there was to be seen the sheen and sparkle of a broken crest.

The captain, in the bow, moved on his water-jar and sat erect. "Pretty long night," he observed to the correspondent. He looked at the shore. "Those life-saving people take their time."

185   "Did you see that shark playing around?"

"Yes, I saw him. He was a big fellow, all right."

"Wish I had known you were awake."

Later the correspondent spoke into the bottom of the boat. "Billie!" There was a slow and gradual disentanglement. "Billie, will you spell me?"

"Sure," said the oiler.

190   As soon as the correspondent touched the cold, comfortable sea-water in the bottom of the boat and had huddled close to the cook's life-belt he was deep in sleep, despite the fact that his teeth played all the popular airs. This sleep was so good to him that it was but a moment before he heard a voice call his name in a tone that demonstrated the last stages of exhaustion. "Will you spell me?"

"Sure, Billie."

The light in the north had mysteriously vanished, but the correspondent took his course from the wide-awake captain.

Later in the night they took the boat farther out to sea, and the captain directed the cook to take one oar at the stern and keep the boat facing the seas. He was to call out if he should hear the thunder of the surf. This plan enabled the oiler and the correspondent to get respite together. "We'll give those boys a chance to get into shape again," said the captain. They curled down and, after a few preliminary chatterings and trembles, slept once more the dead sleep. Neither knew they had bequeathed to the cook the company of another shark, or perhaps the same shark.

As the boat caroused on the waves, spray occasionally bumped over the side and gave them a fresh soaking, but this had no power to break their repose. The ominous slash of the wind and the water affected them as it would have affected mummies.

195   "Boys," said the cook, with the notes of every reluctance in his voice, "she's drifted in pretty close. I guess one of you had better take her to sea again." The correspondent, aroused, heard the crash of the toppled crests.

As he was rowing, the captain gave him some whisky-and-water, and this steadied the chills out of him. "If I ever get ashore and anybody shows me even a photograph of an oar—"

At last there was a short conversation.

"Billie! . . . Billie, will you spell me?"

"Sure," said the oiler.

VII

200 When the correspondent again opened his eyes, the sea and sky were each of the gray hue of the dawning. Later, carmine and gold was painted upon the waters. The morning appeared finally, in its splendor, with a sky of pure blue, and the sunlight flamed on the tips of the waves.

On the distant dunes were set many little black cottages, and a tall white windmill reared above them. No man, nor dog, nor bicycle appeared on the beach. The cottages might have formed a deserted village.

The voyagers scanned the shore. A conference was held in the boat. "Well," said the captain, "if no help is coming, we might better try a run through the surf right away. If we stay out here much longer we will be too weak to do anything for ourselves at all." The others silently acquiesced in this reasoning. The boat was headed for the beach. The correspondent wondered if none ever ascended the tall windtower, and if then they never looked seaward. This tower was a giant, standing with its back to the plight of the ants. It represented in a degree, to the correspondent, the serenity of nature amid the struggles of the individual—nature in the wind, and nature in the vision of men. She did not seem cruel to him then, nor beneficent, nor treacherous, nor wise. But she was indifferent, flatly indifferent. It is, perhaps, plausible that a man in this situation, impressed with the unconcern of the universe, should see the innumerable flaws of life, and have them taste wickedly in his mind, and wish for another chance. A distinction between right and wrong seems absurdly clear to him, then, in this new ignorance of the grave-edge, and he understands that if he were given another opportunity he would mend his conduct and his words, and be better and brighter during an introduction or at a tea.

"Now, boys," said the captain, "she is going to swamp sure. All we can do is to work her in as far as possible, and then when she swamps, pile out and scramble for the beach. Keep cool now, and don't jump until she swamps sure."

The oiler took the oars. Over his shoulders he scanned the surf. "Captain," he said, "I think I'd better bring her about, and keep her head-on to the seas and back her in."

205   "All right, Billie," said the captain. "Back her in." The oiler swung the boat then, and, seated in the stern, the cook and the correspondent were obliged to look over their shoulders to contemplate the lonely and indifferent shore.

The monstrous inshore rollers heaved the boat high until the men were again enabled to see the white sheets of water scudding up the slanted beach. "We won't get in very close," said the captain. Each time a man could wrest his attention from the rollers, he turned his glance toward the shore, and in the expression of the eyes during this contemplation there was a singular quality. The correspondent, observing the others, knew that they were not afraid, but the full meaning of their glances was shrouded.

As for himself, he was too tired to grapple fundamentally with the fact. He tried to coerce his mind into thinking of it, but the mind was dominated at this time by the muscles, and the muscles said they did not care. It merely occurred to him that if he should drown it would be a shame.

There were no hurried words, no pallor, no plain agitation. The men simply looked at the shore. "Now, remember to get well clear of the boat when you jump," said the captain.

Seaward the crest of a roller suddenly fell with a thunderous crash, and the long white comber came roaring down upon the boat.

210   "Steady now," said the captain. The men were silent. They turned their eyes from the shore to the comber and waited. The boat slid up the incline, leaped at the furious top, bounced over it, and swung down the long back of the wave. Some water had been shipped and the cook bailed it out.

But the next crest crashed also. The tumbling, boiling flood of white water caught the boat and whirled it almost perpendicular. Water swarmed in from all sides. The correspondent had his hands on the gunwale at this time, and when the water entered at that place he swiftly withdrew his fingers, as if he objected to wetting them.

The little boat, drunken with this weight of water, reeled and snuggled deeper into the sea.

"Bail her out, cook! Bail her out!" said the captain.

"All right, Captain," said the cook.

215   "Now, boys, the next one will do for us sure," said the oiler. "Mind to jump clear of the boat."

The third wave moved forward, huge, furious, implacable. It fairly swallowed the dinghy, and almost simultaneously the men tumbled into the sea. A piece of life-belt had lain in the bottom of the boat, and as the correspondent went overboard he held this to his chest with his left hand.

The January water was icy, and he reflected immediately that it was colder than he had expected to find it off the coast of Florida. This appeared to his dazed mind as a fact important enough to be noted at the time. The coldness of the water was sad; it was tragic. This fact was somehow mixed and confused with his opinion of his own situation, so that it seemed almost a proper reason for tears. The water was cold.

When he came to the surface he was conscious of little but the noisy water. Afterward he saw his companions in the sea. The oiler was ahead in the race. He was swimming strongly and rapidly. Off to the correspondent's left, the cook's great white and corked back bulged out of the water, and in the rear the captain was hanging with his one good hand to the keel of the overturned dinghy.

There is a certain immovable quality to a shore, and the correspondent wondered at it amid the confusion of the sea.

220   It seemed also very attractive; but the correspondent knew that it was a long journey, and he paddled leisurely. The piece of life-preserver lay under him, and sometimes he whirled down the incline of a wave as if he were on a hand-sled.

But finally he arrived at a place in the sea where travel was beset with difficulty. He did not pause swimming to inquire what manner of current had caught him, but there his progress ceased. The shore was set before him like a bit of scenery on a stage, and he looked at it and understood with his eyes each detail of it.

As the cook passed, much farther to the left, the captain was calling to him, "Turn over on your back, cook! Turn over on your back and use the oar."

"All right, sir." The cook turned on his back, and, paddling with an oar, went ahead as if he were a canoe.

Presently the boat also passed to the left of the correspondent, with the captain clinging with one hand to the keel. He would have appeared like a man raising himself to look over a board fence if it were not for the extraordinary gymnastics of the boat. The correspondent marveled that the captain could still hold to it.

225   They passed on nearer to shore—the oiler, the cook, the captain—and following them went the water-jar, bouncing gaily over the seas.

The correspondent remained in the grip of this strange new enemy—a current. The shore, with its white slope of sand and its green bluff topped with little silent cottages, was spread like a picture before him. It was very near to him then, but he was impressed as one who, in a gallery, looks at a scene from Brittany or Algiers.

He thought: "I am going to drown? Can it be possible? Can it be possible? Can it be possible?" Perhaps an individual must consider his own death to be the final phenomenon of nature.

But later a wave perhaps whirled him out of this small deadly current, for he found suddenly that he could again make progress toward the shore. Later still he was aware that the captain, clinging with one hand to the keel of the dinghy, had his face turned away from the shore and toward him, and was calling his name. "Come to the boat! Come to the boat!"

In his struggle to reach the captain and the boat, he reflected that when one gets properly wearied drowning must really be a comfortable arrangement—a cessation of hostilities accompanied by a large degree of relief; and he was glad of it, for the main thing in his mind for some moments had been horror of the temporary agony. He did not wish to be hurt.

230   Presently he saw a man running along the shore. He was undressing with most remarkable speed. Coat, trousers, shirt, everything flew magically off him.

"Come to the boat!" called the captain.

"All right, Captain." As the correspondent paddled, he saw the captain let himself down to bottom and leave the boat. Then the correspondent performed his one little marvel of the voyage. A large wave caught him and flung him with ease and supreme speed completely over the boat and far beyond it. It struck him even then as an event in gymnastics and a true miracle of the sea. An overturned boat in the surf is not a plaything to a swimming man.

The correspondent arrived in water that reached only to his waist, but his condition did not enable him to stand for more than a moment. Each wave knocked him into a heap, and the undertow pulled at him.

Then he saw the man who had been running and undressing, and undressing and running, come bounding into the water. He dragged ashore the cook, and then waded toward the captain; but the captain waved him away and sent him to the correspondent. He was naked—naked as a tree in winter; but a halo was about his head, and he shone like a saint. He gave a strong pull, and a long drag, and a bully heave at the correspondent's hand. The correspondent, schooled in the minor formulae, said, "Thanks, old man." But suddenly the man cried, "What's that?" He pointed a swift finger. The correspondent said, "Go."

235   In the shallows, face downward, lay the oiler. His forehead touched sand that was periodically, between each wave, clear of the sea.

The correspondent did not know all that transpired afterward. When he achieved safe ground he fell, striking the sand with each particular part of his body. It was as if he had dropped from a roof, but the thud was grateful to him.

It seems that instantly the beach was populated with men with blankets, clothes, and flasks, and women with coffee-pots and all the remedies sacred to their minds. The welcome of the land to the men from the sea was warm and generous; but a still and dripping shape was carried slowly up the beach, and the land's welcome for it could only be the different and sinister hospitality of the grave.

When it came night, the white waves paced to and fro in the moonlight, and the wind brought the sound of the great sea's voice to the men on the shore, and they felt that they could then be interpreters.

➤ *QUESTIONS FOR READING AND WRITING*

1. How are you affected by the tone and description in the first paragraph? Have you ever experienced something like this? Explain.

2. This story is based on an actual event that Crane experienced and subsequently described as a reporter for a newspaper, *The New York World.*
How do you suppose that news story differed from this work of fiction?
3. What is the relationship between the men and nature in this story?
4. Given the difficulty of their situation, why does the correspondent believe
(in Section 3, Parargraph 1) that this "was the best experience of his life"?
5. Why does the correspondent wonder, "Was I brought here merely to have
my nose dragged away as I was about to nibble the sacred cheese of life?"
6. The correspondent remembers a poem he learned as a schoolboy. Why
does the poem about the soldier dying in Algiers have so much more
meaning now? Have you ever had something you read long ago brought to
life in a subsequent experience? Explain.
7. What do you think the last paragraph means? In what way are the survivors
now able to be interpreters?

DON DELILLO (b.1936)

*Don DeLillo was born and grew up in New
York City. He published his first novel,*
Americana, *in 1971 and has won the
American Book Award for* White Noise *(1985)
and the PEN/Faulkner Award for* Mao II
*(1991). While writing his novels he published a
number of stories in* Esquire, Harper's, *and*
Sports Illustrated. *In 1999, he became the first
American recipient of the Jerusalem Prize,
awarded to writers "whose work expresses the
theme of the freedom of the individual in society." Reviewer John Aldridge has said of DeLillo
that he has "the rarest of creative gifts, the abil-
ity to identify and describe, as if from the perspective of another galaxy, the exact look
and feel of contemporary reality." In keeping with his short story "Videotape," DeLillo
has said that "fiction is all about reliving things. It is our second chance."*

VIDEOTAPE   [1996]

It shows a man driving a car. It is the simplest sort of family video. You see a man
at the wheel of a medium Dodge.

It is just a kid aiming her camera through the rear window of the family car at
the windshield of the car behind her.

You know about families and their video cameras. You know how kids get
involved, how the camera shows them that every subject is potentially charged, a
million things they never see with the unaided eye. They investigate the meaning of

inert objects and dumb pets and they poke at family privacy. They learn to see things twice.

It is the kid's own privacy that is being protected here. She is twelve years old and her name is being withheld even though she is neither the victim nor the perpetrator of the crime but only the means of recording it.

5 It shows a man in a sport shirt at the wheel of his car. There is nothing else to see. The car approaches briefly, then falls back.

You know how children with cameras learn to work the exposed moments that define the family cluster. They break every trust, spy out the undefended space, catching Mom coming out of the bathroom in her cumbrous robe and turbaned towel, looking bloodless and plucked. It is not a joke. They will shoot you sitting on the pot if they can manage a suitable vantage.

The tape has the jostled sort of noneventness that marks the family product. Of course the man in this case is not a member of the family but a stranger in a car, a random figure, someone who has happened along in the slow lane.

It shows a man in his forties wearing a pale shirt open at the throat, the image washed by reflections and sunglint, with many jostled moments.

It is not just another video homicide. It is a homicide recorded by a child who thought she was doing something simple and maybe halfway clever, shooting some tape of a man in a car.

10 He sees the girl and waves briefly, wagging a hand without taking it off the wheel—an underplayed reaction that makes you like him.

It is unrelenting footage that rolls on and on. It has an aimless determination, a persistence that lives outside the subject matter. You are looking into the mind of home video. It is innocent, it is aimless, it is determined, it is real.

He is bald up the middle of his head, a nice guy in his forties whose whole like seems to open to the hand-held camera.

But there is also an element of suspense. You keep on looking not because you know something is going to happen—of course you do know something is going to happen and you do look for that reason but you might also keep on looking if you came across this footage for the first time without knowing the outcome. There is a crude power operating here. You keep on looking because things combine to hold you fast—a sense of the random, the amateurish, the accidental, the impending. You don't think of the tape as boring or interesting. It is crude, it is blunt, it is relentless. It is the jostled part of your mind, the film that runs through your hotel brain under all the thoughts you know you're thinking.

The world is lurking in the camera, already framed, waiting for the boy or girl who will come along and take up the device, learn the instrument, shooting old Granddad at breakfast, all stroked out so his nostrils gape, the cereal spoon baby-gripped in his pale fist.

15 It shows a man alone in a medium Dodge. It seems to go on forever.

There's something about the nature of the tape, the grain of the image, the sputtering black-and-white tones, the starkness—you think this is more real, truer-to-life, than anything around you. The things around you have a rehearsed and layered and cosmetic look. The tape is superreal, or maybe underreal is the way you want to put it. It is what lies at the scraped bottom of all the layers you have added. And this is another reason why you keep on looking. The tape has a searing realness.

It shows him giving an abbreviated wave, stiff-palmed, like a signal flag at a siding.

You know how families make up games. This is just another game in which the child invents the rules as she goes along. She likes the idea of videotaping a man in his car. She has probably never done it before and she sees no reason to vary the format or terminate early or pan to another car. This is her game and she is learning it and playing it at the same time. She feels halfway clever and inventive and maybe slightly intrusive as well, a little bit brazenness that spices any game.

And you keep on looking. You look because this is the nature of the footage, to make a channeled path through time, to give things a shape and a destiny.

20   Of course if she had panned to another car, the right car at the precise time, she would have caught the gunman as he fired.

The chance quality of the encounter. The victim, the killer, and the child with a camera. Random energies that approach a common point. There's something here that speaks to you directly, saying terrible things about forces beyond your control, lines of intersection that cut thorough history and logic and every reasonable layer of human expectation.

She wandered into it. The girl got lost and wandered clear-eyed into horror. This is a children's story about straying too far from home. But it isn't the family car that serves as the instrument of the child's curiosity, her inclination to explore. It is the camera that puts her in the tale.

You know about holidays and family celebrations and how somebody shows up with a camcorder and the relatives stand around and barely react because they're numbingly accustomed to the process of being taped and decked and shown on the VCR with the coffee and cake.

He is hit soon after. If you've seen the tape many times you know from the handwave exactly when he will be hit. It is something, naturally, that you wait for. You say to your wife, if you're at home and she is there, Now here is where he gets it. You say, Janet, hurry up, this is where it happens.

25   Now here is where he gets it. You see him jolted, sort of wire-shocked—then he seizes up and falls toward the door or maybe leans or slides into the door is the proper way to put it. It is awful and unremarkable at the same time. The car stays in the slow lane. It approaches briefly, then falls back.

You don't usually call your wife over to the TV set. She has her programs and you have yours. But there's a certain urgency here. You want her to see how it looks. The tape has been running forever and now the thing is finally going to happen and you want her to be here when he's shot.

Here it comes, all right. He is shot, head-shot, and the camera reacts, the child reacts—there is a jolting movement but she keeps on taping, there is a sympathetic response, a nerve response, her heart is beating faster but she keeps the camera trained on the subject as he slides into the door and even as you see him die you're thinking of the girl. At some level the girl has to be present here, watching what you're watching, unprepared—the girl is seeing this cold and you have to marvel at the fact that she keeps the tape rolling.

It shows something awful and unaccompanied. You want your wife to see it because it is real this time, not fancy movie violence—the realness beneath the layers of cosmetic perception. Hurry up, Janet, here it comes. He dies so fast. There is no accompaniment of any kind. It is very stripped. You want to tell her it is realer than real but then she will ask what that means.

The way the camera reacts to the gunshot—a startled reaction that brings pity and terror into the frame, the girl's own shock, the girl's identification with the victim.

30   You don't see the blood, which is probably trickling behind his ear and down the back of his neck. The way his head is twisted away from the door, the twist of the head gives you only a partial profile and it's the wrong side, it's not the side where he was hit.

And maybe you're being a little aggressive here, practically forcing your wife to watch. Why? What are you telling her? Are you making a little statement? Like I'm going to ruin your day out of ordinary spite. Or a big statement? Like this is the risk of existing. Either way you're rubbing her face in this tape and you don't know why.

It shows the car drifting toward the guardrail and then there's a jostling sense of two other lanes and part of another car, a split-second blur, and then tape ends here, either because the girl stopped shooting or because some central authority, the police or the district attorney or the TV station, decided there was nothing else you had to see.

This is either the tenth or eleventh homicide committed by the Texas Highway Killer. The number is uncertain because the police believe that one of the shootings may have been a copycat crime.

And there is something about videotape, isn't there, and this particular kind of serial crime? This is a crime designed for random taping and immediate playing. You sit there and wonder if this kind of crime became more possible when the means of taping and playing an event—playing it immediately after the taping— became part of the culture. The principal doesn't necessarily commit the sequence of crimes in order to see them taped and played. He commits the crimes as if they were a form of taped-and-played event. The crimes are inseparable from the idea of taping and playing. You sit there thinking that this is a crime that has found its medium, or vice versa—cheap mass production, the sequence of repeated images and victims, stark and glary and more or less unremarkable.

35   It shows very little in the end. It is a famous murder because it is on tape and because the murderer has done it many times and because the crime was recorded by a child. So the child is involved, the Video Kid as she is sometimes called because the have to call her something. The tape is famous and so is she. She is famous in the modern manner of people whose names are strategically withheld. They are famous without names or faces, spirits living apart from their bodies, the victims and witnesses, the underage criminals, out there somewhere at the edges of perception.

Seeing someone at the moment he dies, dying unexpectedly. This is reason alone to stay fixed to the screen. It is instructional, watching a man shot dead as he drives along on a sunny day. It demonstrates an elemental truth, that every breath you take has two possible endings. And that's another thing. There's a joke locked away here, a note of cruel slapstick that you are completely willing to appreciate.

Maybe the victim's a chump, a dope, classically unlucky. He had it coming, in a way, like an innocent fool in a silent movie.

You don't want Janet to give you any crap about it's on all the time, they show it a thousand times a day. They show it because it exists, because they have to show it, because this is why they're out there. The horror freezes your soul but this doesn't mean that you want them to stop.

▶ QUESTIONS FOR READING AND WRITING

1. The dominant pronoun in the story is "it." What is "it"? How does this continual reference to "it" affect your response to this story?
2. At the end of the story, the narrator says, "The horror freezes your soul but this doesn't mean that you want them to stop." What does he mean? Do you agree? Explain.

RALPH ELLISON (1914–1994)

Ralph Ellison was born in Oklahoma. "Battle Royal" is an excerpt from his novel Invisible Man, *which won the National Book Award in 1953 and was widely praised for its depiction of the plight of African-Americans. In addition to his fiction writing, Ellison frequently wrote essays and gave interviews about race relations, and was Albert Schweitzer Professor of the Humanities at New York University. The* Collected Essays of Ralph Ellison *was published in 1995, and an unfinished novel,* Juneteenth *(completed by John Callahan), was published in 1999.*

BATTLE ROYAL

[1953]

It goes a long way back, some twenty years. All my life I had been looking for something, and everywhere I turned someone tried to tell me what it was. I accepted their answers too, though they were often in contradiction and even self-contradictory. I was naïve. I was looking for myself and asking everyone except myself questions which I, and only I, could answer. It took me a long time and much painful boomeranging of my expectations to achieve a realization everyone else appears to have been born with: That I am nobody but myself. But first I had to discover that I am an invisible man!

And yet I am no freak of nature, nor of history. I was in the cards, other things having been equal (or unequal) eighty-five years ago. I am not ashamed of my grandparents for having been slaves. I am only ashamed of myself for having at one time been ashamed. About eighty-five years ago they were told they were free, united with others of our country in everything pertaining to the common good, and, in everything social, separate like the fingers of the hand. And they believed it. They exulted in it. They stayed in their place, worked hard, and brought up my father to do the same. But my grandfather is the one. He was an odd old guy, my grandfather, and I am told I take after him. It was he who caused the trouble. On his deathbed he called my father to him and said, "Son, after I'm gone I want you to keep up the good fight. I never told you, but our life is a war and I have been a traitor all my born days, a spy in the enemy's country ever since I give up my gun back in the Reconstruction. Live with your head in the lion's mouth. I want you to overcome 'em with yeses, undermine 'em with grins, agree 'em to death and destruction, let 'em swoller you till they vomit or bust wide open." They thought the old man had gone out of his mind. He had been the meekest of men. The younger children were rushed from the room, the shades drawn and the flame of the lamp turned so low that it sputtered on the wick like the old man's breathing. "Learn it to the younguns," he whispered fiercely; then he died.

But my folks were more alarmed over his last words than over his dying. It was as though he had not died at all, his words caused so much anxiety. I was warned emphatically to forget what he had said and, indeed, this is the first time it has been mentioned outside the family circle. It had a tremendous effect upon me, however. I could never be sure of what he meant. Grandfather had been a quiet old man who never made any trouble, yet on his deathbed he had called himself a traitor and a spy, and he had spoken of his meekness as a dangerous activity. It became a constant puzzle which lay unanswered in the back of my mind. And whenever things went well for me I remembered my grandfather and felt guilty and uncomfortable. It was as though I was carrying out his advice in spite of myself. And to make it worse, everyone loved me for it. I was praised by the most lily-white men in town. I was considered an example of desirable conduct—just as my grandfather had been. And what puzzled me was that the old man had defined it as *treachery*. When I was praised for my conduct I felt a guilt that in some way I was doing something that was really against the wishes of the white folks, that if they had understood they would have desired me to act just the opposite, that I should have been sulky and mean, and that that really would have been what they wanted, even though they were fooled and thought they wanted me to act as I did. It made me afraid that some day they would look upon me as a traitor and I would be lost. Still I was more afraid to act any other way because they didn't like that at all. The old man's words were like a curse. On my graduation day I delivered an oration in which I showed that humility was the secret, indeed, the very essence of progress. (Not that I believed this—how could I, remembering my grandfather?—I only believed that it worked.) It was a great success. Everyone praised me and I was invited to give the speech at a gathering of the town's leading white citizens. It was a triumph for the whole community.

It was in the main ballroom of the leading hotel. When I got there I discovered that it was on the occasion of a smoker, and I was told that since I was to be there anyway I might as well take part in the battle royal to be fought by some of my schoolmates as part of the entertainment. The battle royal came first.

5   All of the town's big shots were there in their tuxedoes, wolfing down the buffet foods, drinking beer and whiskey and smoking black cigars. It was a large room with a high ceiling. Chairs were arranged in neat rows around three sides of a portable boxing ring. The fourth side was clear, revealing a gleaming space of polished floor. I had some misgivings over the battle royal, by the way. Not from a distaste for fighting, but because I didn't care too much for the other fellows who were to take part. They were tough guys who seemed to have no grandfather's curse worrying their minds. No one could mistake their toughness. And besides, I suspected that fighting a battle royal might distract from the dignity of my speech. In those pre-invisible days I visualized myself as a potential Booker T. Washington. But the other fellows didn't care too much for me either, and there were nine of them. I felt superior to them in my way, and I didn't like the manner in which we were all crowded together in the servants' elevator. Nor did they like my being there. In fact, as the warmly lighted floors flashed past the elevator we had words over the fact that I, by taking part in the fight, had knocked one of their friends out of a night's work.

We were led out of the elevator through a rococo hall into an anteroom and told to get into our fighting togs. Each of us was issued a pair of boxing gloves and ushered out into the big mirrored hall, which we entered looking cautiously about us and whispering, lest we might accidentally be heard above the noise of the room. It was foggy with cigar smoke. And already the whiskey was taking effect. I was shocked to see some of the most important men of the town quite tipsy. They were all there—bankers, lawyers, judges, doctors, fire chiefs, teachers, merchants. Even one of the more fashionable pastors. Something we could not see was going on up front. A clarinet was vibrating sensuously and the men were standing up and moving eagerly forward. We were a small tight group, clustered together, our bare upper bodies touching and shining with anticipatory sweat; while up front the big shots were becoming increasingly excited over something we still could not see. Suddenly I heard the school superintendent, who had told me to come, yell, "Bring up the shines, gentlemen! Bring up the little shines!"

We were rushed up to the front of the ballroom, where it smelled even more strongly of tobacco and whiskey. Then we were pushed into place. I almost wet my pants. A sea of faces, some hostile, some amused, ringed around us, and in the center, facing us, stood a magnificent blonde—stark naked. There was dead silence. I felt a blast of cold air chill me. I tried to back away, but they were behind me and around me. Some of the boys stood with lowered heads, trembling. I felt a wave of irrational guilt and fear. My teeth chattered, my skin turned to goose flesh, my knees knocked. Yet I was strongly attracted and looked in spite of myself. Had the price of looking been blindness, I would have looked. The hair was yellow like that of a circus kewpie doll, the face heavily powdered and rouged, as though to form an abstract mask, the eyes hollow and smeared a cool blue, the color of a baboon's butt. I felt a desire to spit upon her as my eyes brushed slowly over her body. Her breasts were firm and round as the domes of East Indian temples, and I stood so close as to see the fine skin texture and beads of pearly perspiration glistening like dew around the pink and erected buds of her nipples. I wanted at one and the same time to run from the room, to sink through the floor, or go to her and cover her from my eyes and the eyes of the others with my body; to feel the soft thighs, to caress her and destroy her, to love her and murder her, to hide from her, and yet to stroke where below the small American flag tattooed upon her belly her thighs formed a capital V. I had a notion that of all in the room she saw only me with her impersonal eyes.

And then she began to dance, a slow sensuous movement; the smoke of a hundred cigars clinging to her like the thinnest of veils. She seemed like a fair bird-girl girdled in veils calling to me from the angry surface of some gray and threatening sea. I was transported. Then I became aware of the clarinet playing and the big shots yelling at us. Some threatened us if we looked and others if we did not. On my right I saw one boy faint. And now a man grabbed a silver pitcher from a table and stepped close as he dashed ice water upon him and stood him up and forced two of us to support him as his head hung and moans issued from his thick bluish lips. Another boy began to plead to go home. He was the largest of the group, wearing dark red fighting trunks much too small to conceal the erection which projected from him as though in answer to the insinuating low-registered moans of the clarinet. He tried to hide himself with his boxing gloves.

And all the while the blonde continued dancing, smiling faintly at the big shots who watched her with fascination, and faintly smiling at our fear. I noticed a certain merchant who followed her hungrily, his lips loose and drooling. He was a large man who wore diamond studs in a shirtfront which swelled with the ample paunch underneath, and each time the blonde swayed her undulating hips he ran his hand through the thin hair of his bald head and, with his arms upheld, his posture clumsy like that of an intoxicated panda, wound his belly in a slow and obscene grind. This creature was completely hypnotized. The music had quickened. As the dancer flung herself about with a detached expression on her face, the men began reaching out to touch her. I could see their beefy fingers sink into her soft flesh. Some of the others tried to stop them and she began to move around the floor in graceful circles, as they gave chase, slipping and sliding over the polished floor. It was mad. Chairs went crashing, drinks were spilt, as they ran laughing and howling after her. They caught her just as she reached a door, raised her from the floor, and tossed her as college boys are tossed at a hazing, and above her red, fixed-smiling lips I saw the terror and disgust in her eyes, almost like my own terror and that which I saw in some of the other boys. As I watched, they tossed her twice and her soft breasts seemed to flatten against the air and her legs flung wildly as she spun. Some of the more sober ones helped her to escape. And I started off the floor, heading for the anteroom with the rest of the boys.

10   Some were still crying and in hysteria. But as we tried to leave we were stopped and ordered to get into the ring. There was nothing to do but what we were told. All ten of us climbed under the ropes and allowed ourselves to be blindfolded with broad bands of white cloth. One of the men seemed to feel a bit sympathetic and tried to cheer us up as we stood with our backs against the ropes. Some of us tried to grin. "See that boy over there?" one of the men said. "I want you to run across at the bell and give it to him right in the belly. If you don't get him, I'm going to get you. I don't like his looks." Each of us was told the same. The blindfolds were put on. Yet even then I had been going over my speech. In my mind each word was as bright as a flame. I felt the cloth pressed into place, and frowned so that it would be loosened when I relaxed.

But now I felt a sudden fit of blind terror. I was unused to darkness. It was as though I had suddenly found myself in a dark room filled with poisonous cottonmouths. I could hear the bleary voices yelling insistently for the battle royal to begin.

"Get going in there!"

"Let me at that big nigger!"

I strained to pick up the school superintendent's voice, as though to squeeze some security out of that slightly more familiar sound.

15   "Let me at those black sonsabitches!" someone yelled.

"No, Jackson, no!" another voice yelled. "Here, somebody, help me hold Jack."

"I want to get at that ginger-colored nigger. Tear him limb from limb," the first voice yelled.

I stood against the ropes trembling. For in those days I was what they called ginger-colored, and he sounded as though he might crunch me between his teeth like a crisp ginger cookie.

Quite a struggle was going on. Chairs were being kicked about and I could hear voices grunting as with a terrific effort. I wanted to see, to see more desperately than ever before. But the blindfold was as tight as a thick skin-puckering scab and when I raised my gloved hands to push the layers of white aside a voice yelled, "Oh, no you don't, black bastard! Leave that alone!"

20   "Ring the bell before Jackson kills him a coon!" someone boomed in the sudden silence. And I heard the bell clang and the sound of the feet scuffling forward.

A glove smacked against my head. I pivoted, striking out stiffly as someone went past, and felt the jar ripple along the length of my arm to my shoulder. Then it seemed as though all nine of the boys had turned upon me at once. Blows pounded me from all sides while I struck out as best I could. So many blows landed upon me that I wondered if I were not the only blindfolded fighter in the ring, or if the man called Jackson hadn't succeeded in getting me after all.

Blindfolded, I could no longer control my motions. I had no dignity. I stumbled about like a baby or a drunken man. The smoke had become thicker and with each new blow it seemed to sear and further restrict my lungs. My saliva became like hot bitter glue. A glove connected with my head, filling my mouth with warm blood. It was everywhere. I could not tell if the moisture I felt upon my body was sweat or blood. A blow landed hard against the nape of my neck. I felt myself going over, my head hitting the floor. Streaks of blue light filled the black world behind the blindfold. I lay prone, pretending that I was knocked out, but felt myself seized by hands and yanked to my feet. "Get going, black boy! Mix it up!" My arms were like lead, my head smarting from blows. I managed to feel my way to the ropes and held on, trying to catch my breath. A glove landed in my midsection and I went over again, feeling as though the smoke had become a knife jabbed into my guts. Pushed this way and that by the legs milling around me, I finally pulled erect and discovered that I could see the black, sweat-washed forms weaving in the smoky-blue atmosphere like drunken dancers weaving to the rapid drum-like thuds of blows.

Everyone fought hysterically. It was complete anarchy. Everybody fought everybody else. No group fought together for long. Two, three, four, fought one, then turned to fight each other, were themselves attacked. Blows landed below the belt and in the kidney, with the gloves open as well as closed, and with my eye partly opened now there was not so much terror. I moved carefully, avoiding blows, although not too many to attract attention, fighting group to group. The boys groped about like blind, cautious crabs crouching to protect their midsections, their heads pulled in short against their shoulders, their arms stretched nervously before them, with their fists testing the smoke-filled air like the knobbed feelers of hypersensitive snails. In one corner I glimpsed a boy violently punching the air and heard him scream in pain as he smashed his hand against a ring post. For a second I saw him bent over holding his hand, then going down as a blow caught his unprotected head. I played one group against the other, slipping in and throwing a punch then stepping out of range while pushing the others into the melee to take the blows blindly aimed at me. The smoke was agonizing and there were no rounds, no bells at three minute intervals to relieve our exhaustion. The room spun round me, a swirl of lights, smoke, sweating bodies surrounded by tense white faces. I bled from both nose and mouth, the blood spattering upon my chest.

The men kept yelling, "Slug him, black boy! Knock his guts out!"

25   "Uppercut him! Kill him! Kill that big boy!"

Taking a fake fall, I saw a boy going down heavily beside me as though we were felled by a single blow, saw a sneaker-clad foot shoot into his groin as the two who had knocked him down stumbled upon him. I rolled out of range, feeling a twinge of nausea.

The harder we fought the more threatening the men became. And yet, I had begun to worry about my speech again. How would it go? Would they recognize my ability? What would they give me?

I was fighting automatically when suddenly I noticed that one after another of the boys were leaving the ring. I was surprised, filled with panic, as though I had been left alone with an unknown danger. Then I understood. The boys had arranged it among themselves. It was the custom for the two men left in the ring to slug it out for the winner's prize. I discovered this too late. When the bell sounded two men in tuxedoes leaped into the ring and removed the blindfold. I found myself facing Tatlock, the biggest of the gang. I felt sick at my stomach. Hardly had the bell stopped ringing in my ears than it clanged again and I saw him moving swiftly toward me. Thinking of nothing else to do I hit him smash on the nose. He kept coming, bringing the rank sharp violence of stale sweat. His face was a black bank of a face, only his eyes alive—with hate of me and aglow with a feverish terror from what had happened to us all. I became anxious. I wanted to deliver my speech and he came at me as though he meant to beat it out of me. I smashed him again and again, taking his blows as they came. Then on a sudden impulse I struck him lightly as we clinched, I whispered, "Fake like I knocked you out, you can have the prize."

"I'll break your behind," he whispered hoarsely.

30   "For *them?*"

"For *me,* sonafabitch!"

They were yelling for us to break it up and Tatlock spun me half around with a blow, and as a joggled camera sweeps in a reeling scene, I saw the howling red faces crouching tense beneath the cloud of blue-gray smoke. For a moment the world wavered, unraveled, flowed, then my head cleared and Tatlock bounced before me. That fluttering shadow before my eyes was his jabbing left hand. Then falling forward, my head against his damp shoulder, I whispered,

"I'll make it five dollars more."

"Go to hell!"

35   But his muscles relaxed a trifle beneath my pressure and I breathed, "Seven!"

"Give it to your ma," he said, ripping me beneath the heart.

And while I still held him I butted him and moved away. I felt myself bombarded with punches. I fought back with hopeless desperation. I wanted to deliver my speech more than anything else in the world, because I felt that only these men could judge truly my ability, and now this stupid clown was ruining my chances. I began fighting carefully now, moving in to punch him and out again with my greater speed. A lucky blow to his chin and I had him going too—until I heard a loud voice yell, "I got my money on the big boy."

Hearing this, I almost dropped my guard. I was confused: Should I try to win against the voice out there? Would not this go against my speech, and was not this a moment for humility, for nonresistance? A blow to my head as I danced about sent my right eye popping like a jack-in-the-box and settled my dilemma. The room went red as I fell. It was a dream fall, my body languid and fastidious as to where to land, until the floor became impatient and smashed up to meet me. A moment later I came to. An hypnotic voice said FIVE emphatically. And I lay there, hazily watching a dark red spot of my own blood shaping itself into a butterfly, glistening and soaking into the soiled gray world of the canvas.

When the voice drawled TEN I was lifted up and dragged to a chair. I sat dazed. My eye pained and swelled with each throb of my pounding heart and I wondered if now I would be allowed to speak. I was wringing wet, my mouth still bleeding. We were grouped along the wall now. The other boys ignored me as they congratulated Tatlock and speculated as to how much they would be paid. One boy whimpered over his smashed hand. Looking up front, I saw attendants in white jackets rolling the portable ring away and placing a small square rug in the vacant space surrounded by chairs. Perhaps, I thought, I will stand on the rug to deliver my speech.

40   Then the M.C. called to us, "Come on up here boys and get your money."

We ran forward to where the men laughed and talked in their chairs, waiting. Everyone seemed friendly now.

"There it is on the rug," the man said. I saw the rug covered with coins of all dimensions and a few crumpled bills. But what excited me, scattered here and there, were the gold pieces.

"Boys, it's all yours," the man said. "You get all you grab."

"That's right, Sambo," a blond man said, winking at me confidentially.

45   I trembled with excitement, forgetting my pain. I would get the gold and the bills, I thought. I would use both hands. I would throw my body against the boys nearest me to block them from the gold.

"Get down around the rug now," the man commanded, "and don't anyone touch it until I give the signal."

"This ought to be good," I heard.

As told, we got around the square rug on our knees. Slowly the man raised his freckled hand as we followed it upward with our eyes.

I heard, "These niggers look like they're about to pray!"

50   Then, "Ready," the man said. "Go!"

I lunged for a yellow coin lying on the blue design of the carpet, touching it and sending a surprised shriek to join those around me. I tried frantically to remove my hand but could not let go. A hot, violent force tore through my body, shaking me like a wet rat. The rug was electrified. The hair bristled up on my head as I shook myself free. My muscles jumped, my nerves jangled, writhed. But I saw that this was not stopping the other boys. Laughing in fear and embarrassment, some were holding back and scooping up the coins knocked off by the painful contortions of the others. The men roared above us as we struggled.

"Pick it up, goddamnit, pick it up!" someone called like a bass-voiced parrot. "Go on, get it!"

I crawled rapidly around the floor, picking up the coins, trying to avoid the coppers and to get greenbacks and the gold. Ignoring the shock by laughing, as I brushed the coins off quickly, I discovered that I could contain the electricity—a contradiction but it works. Then the men began to push us onto the rug. Laughing embarrassedly, we struggled out of their hands and kept after the coins. We were all wet and slippery and hard to hold. Suddenly I saw a boy lifted into the air, glistening with sweat like a circus seal, and dropped, his wet back landing flush upon the charged rug, heard him yell and saw him literally dance upon his back, his elbows beating a frenzied tattoo upon the floor, his muscles twitching like the flesh of a horse stung by many flies. When he finally rolled off, his face was gray and no one stopped him when he ran from the floor amid booming laughter.

"Get the money," the M.C. called. "That's good hard American cash!"

55   And we snatched and grabbed, snatched and grabbed. I was careful not to come too close to the rug now, and when I felt the hot whiskey breath descend upon me like a cloud of foul air I reached out and grabbed the leg of a chair. It was occupied and I held on desperately.

"Leggo, nigger! Leggo!"

The huge face wavered down to mine as he tried to push me free. But my body was slippery and he was too drunk. It was Mr. Colcord, who owned a chain of movie houses and "entertainment palaces." Each time he grabbed me I slipped out of his hands. It became a real struggle. I feared the rug more than I did the drunk, so I held on, surprising myself for a moment by trying to topple *him* upon the rug. It was such an enormous idea that I found myself actually carrying it out. I tried not to be obvious, yet when I grabbed his leg, trying to tumble him out of the chair, he raised up roaring with laughter, and, looking at me with soberness dead in the eye, kicked me viciously in the chest. The chair leg flew out of my hand. I felt myself going and rolled. It was as though I had rolled through a bed of hot coals. It seemed a whole century would pass before I would roll free, a century in which I was seared through the deepest levels of my body to the fearful breath within me and the breath seared and heated to the point of explosion. It'll all be over in a flash, I thought as I rolled clear. It'll all be over in a flash.

But not yet, the men on the other side were waiting, red faces swollen as though from apoplexy as they bent forward in their chairs. Seeing their fingers coming toward me I rolled away as a fumbled football rolls off the receiver's fingertips, back into the coals. That time I luckily sent the rug sliding out of place and heard the coins ringing against the floor and the boys scuffling to pick them up and the M.C. calling, "All right, boys, that's all. Go get dressed and get your money."

I was limp as a dish rag. My back felt as though it had been beaten with wires.

60   When we had dressed the M.C. came in and gave us each five dollars, except Tatlock, who got ten for being the last in the ring. Then he told us to leave. I was not to get a chance to deliver my speech, I thought. I was going out into the dim alley in despair when I was stopped and told to go back. I returned to the ballroom, where the men were pushing back their chairs and gathering in groups to talk.

The M.C. knocked on a table for quiet. "Gentlemen," he said, "we almost forgot an important part of the program. A most serious part, gentlemen. This boy was brought here to deliver a speech which he made at his graduation yesterday. . . ."

"Bravo!"

"I'm told that he is the smartest boy we've got out there in Greenwood. I'm told that he knows more big words than a pocket-sized dictionary."

Much applause and laughter.

65   "So now, gentlemen, I want you to give him your attention."

There was still laughter as I faced them, my mouth dry, my eyes throbbing. I began slowly, but evidently my throat was tense, because they began shouting, "Louder! Louder!"

"We of the younger generation extol the wisdom of that great leader and educator," I shouted, "who first spoke these flaming words of wisdom: 'A ship lost at sea for many days suddenly sighted a friendly vessel. From the mast of the unfortunate vessel was seen a signal: "Water, water; we die of thirst!" The answer from the friendly vessel came back: "Cast down your bucket where you are." The captain of the distressed vessel, at last heeding the injunction, cast down his bucket, and it came up full of fresh sparkling water from the mouth of the Amazon River.' And like him I say, and in his words, 'To those of my race who depend upon bettering their condition in a foreign land, or who underestimate the importance of cultivating friendly relations with the Southern white man, who is his next-door neighbor, I would say: "Cast down your bucket where you are"—cast it down in making friends in every manly way of the people of all races by whom we are surrounded. . . .'"

I spoke automatically and with such fervor that I did not realize that the men were still talking and laughing until my dry mouth, filling up with blood from the cut, almost strangled me. I coughed, wanting to stop and go to one of the tall brass, sand-filled spittoons to relieve myself, but a few of the men, especially the superintendent, were listening and I was afraid. So I gulped it down, blood, saliva and all, and continued. (What power of endurance I had during those days! What enthusiasm! What a belief in the rightness of things!) I spoke even louder in spite of the pain. But still they talked and still they laughed, as though deaf with cotton in dirty ears. So I spoke with greater emotional emphasis. I closed my ears and swallowed blood until I was nauseated. The speech seemed a hundred times as long as before, but I could not leave out a single word. All had to be said, each memorized nuance considered, rendered. Nor was that all. Whenever I uttered a word of three or more syllables a group of voices would yell for me to repeat it. I used the phrase "social responsibility" and they yelled:

"What's the word you say, boy?"

70 "Social responsibility," I said.

"What?"

"Social . . . "

"Louder."

" . . . responsibility."

75 "More!"

"Respon—"

"Repeat!"

"—sibility."

The room filled with the uproar of laughter until, no doubt, distracted by having to gulp down my blood, I made a mistake and yelled a phrase I had often seen denounced in newspaper editorials, heard debated in private.

80 "Social . . . "

"What?" they yelled.

" . . . equality—"

The laughter hung smokelike in the sudden stillness. I opened my eyes, puzzled. Sounds of displeasure filled the room. The M.C. rushed forward. They shouted hostile phrases at me. But I did not understand.

A small dry mustached man in the front row blared out, "Say that slowly, son!"

85 "What sir?"

"What you just said!"

"Social responsibility, sir." I said.

"You weren't being smart, were you, boy?" he said, not unkindly.

"No, sir!"

90 "You sure that about 'equality' was a mistake?"

"Oh, yes, sir," I said. "I was swallowing blood."

"Well, you had better speak more slowly so we can understand. We mean to do right by you, but you've got to know your place at all times. All right, now, go on with your speech."

I was afraid. I wanted to leave but I wanted also to speak and I was afraid they'd snatch me down.

"Thank you, sir," I said, beginning where I had left off, and having them ignore me as before.

95 Yet when I finished there was a thunderous applause. I was surprised to see the superintendent come forth with a package wrapped in white tissue paper, and, gesturing for quiet, address the men.

"Gentlemen, you see that I did not overpraise the boy. He makes a good speech and some day he'll lead his people in the proper paths. And I don't have to tell you that that is important in these days and times. This is a good, smart boy, and so to encourage him in the right direction, in the name of the Board of Education I wish to present him a prize in the form of this . . . "

He paused, removing the tissue paper and revealing a gleaming calfskin briefcase.

" . . . in the form of this first-class article from Shad Whitmore's shop."

"Boy," he said, addressing me, "take this prize and keep it well. Consider it a badge of office. Prize it. Keep developing as you are and some day it will be filled with important papers that will help shape the destiny of your people."

100   I was so moved that I could hardly express my thanks. A rope of bloody saliva forming a shape like an undiscovered continent drooled upon the leather and I wiped it quickly away. I felt an importance that I had never dreamed.

"Open it and see what's inside," I was told.

My fingers a-tremble, I complied, smelling the fresh leather and finding an official-looking document inside. It was a scholarship to the state college for Negroes. My eyes filled with tears and I ran awkwardly off the floor.

I was overjoyed; I did not even mind when I discovered the gold pieces I had scrambled for were brass pocket tokens advertising a certain make of automobile.

When I reached home everyone was excited. Next day the neighbors came to congratulate me. I even felt safe from grandfather, whose deathbed curse usually spoiled my triumphs. I stood beneath his photograph with my briefcase in hand and smiled triumphantly into his stolid black peasant's face. It was a face that fascinated me. The eyes seemed to follow everywhere I went.

105   That night I dreamed I was at a circus with him and that he refused to laugh at the clowns no matter what they did. Then later he told me to open my briefcase and read what was inside and I did, finding an official envelope stamped with the state seal; and inside the envelope I found another and another, endlessly, and I thought I would fall of weariness. "Them's years," he said. "Now open that one." And I did and in it I found an engraved stamp containing a short message in letters of gold. "Read it," my grandfather said. "Out loud."

"To Whom It May Concern," I intoned. "Keep This Nigger-Boy Running."

I awoke with the old man's laughter ringing in my ears.

(It was a dream I was to remember and dream again for many years after. But at the time I had no insight into its meaning. First I had to attend college.)

➤ QUESTIONS FOR READING AND WRITING

1. Have you ever found yourself in a humiliating circumstance and were afraid to protest? If so, how did that experience affect your response to this story?
2. The narrator is the protagonist. In what way does this point of view influence how you experience the story?
3. If you were placed in the same situation as the narrator, would you have acted the same way? Explain.
4. Describe the setting of the story. What aspects of the description were most effective in conveying the atmosphere?
5. Why does the audience react so strongly to the narrator's use of the terms "social responsibility" and "social equality"?

6. What is the primary conflict in the story? Is it external, internal, both? Explain.
7. What is the theme of "Battle Royal"?

LOUISE ERDRICH (b. 1954)

The daughter of a Chippewa Indian mother and a German-American father, Louise Erdrich was raised in Wahpeton, North Dakota, near the Turtle Mountain Reservation. Her parents both worked in the Bureau of Indian Affairs boarding school. From an early age, she was encouraged to write stories (she says, "My father used to give me a nickel for every story I wrote"). She graduated from Dartmouth College in 1976 and earned a master's degree from Johns Hopkins University in 1979. Her works include Love Medicine *(1984, and an expanded edition, 1993),* The Beet Queen *(1986),* Tracks *(1988),* The Crown of Columbus *(1991), which she coauthored with her late husband, Michael Dorris,* The Bingo Palace *(1995), and* The Antelope Wife *(1998). Her most recent novel,* The Last Report on the Miracles of Little No Horse, *was published in 2001.*

THE RED CONVERTIBLE   [1984]

Lyman Lamartine

I was the first one to drive a convertible on my reservation. And of course it was red, a red Olds. I owned that car along with my brother Henry Junior. We owned it together until his boots filled with water on a windy night and he bought out my share. Now Henry owns the whole car, and his youngest brother Lyman (that's myself), Lyman walks everywhere he goes.

How did I earn enough money to buy my share in the first place? My own talent was I could always make money. I had a touch for it, unusual in a Chippewa. From the first I was different that way, and everyone recognized it. I was the only kid they let in the American Legion Hall to shine shoes, for example, and one Christmas I sold spiritual bouquets for the mission door to door. The nuns let me keep a percentage. Once I started, it seemed the more money I made the easier the money came. Everyone encouraged it. When I was fifteen I got a job washing dishes at the Joliet Café, and that was where my first big break happened.

It wasn't long before I was promoted to bussing tables, and then the short-order cook quit and I was hired to take her place. No sooner than you know it I was managing the Joliet. The rest is history. I went on managing. I soon became part owner, and of course there was no stopping me then. It wasn't long before the whole thing was mine.

After I'd owned the Joliet for one year, it blew over in the worst tornado ever seen around here. The whole operation was smashed to bits. A total loss. The fryalator was up in a tree, the grill torn in half like it was paper. I was only sixteen. I had it all in my mother's name, and I lost it quick, but before I lost it I had every one of my relatives, and their relatives, to dinner, and I also bought that red Olds I mentioned, along with Henry.

5   The first time we saw it! I'll tell you when we first saw it. We had gotten a ride up to Winnipeg, and both of us had money. Don't ask me why, because we never mentioned a car or anything, we just had all our money. Mine was cash, a big bankroll from the Joliet's insurance. Henry had two checks—a week's extra pay for being laid off, and his regular check from the Jewel Bearing Plant.

We were walking down Portage anyway, seeing the sights, when we saw it. There it was, parked, large as life. Really as *if* it was alive. I thought of the word *repose,* because the car wasn't simply stopped, parked, or whatever. That car reposed, calm and gleaming, a FOR SALE sign in its left front window. Then, before we had thought it over at all, the car belonged to us and our pockets were empty. We had just enough money for gas back home.

We went places in that car, me and Henry. We took off driving all one whole summer. We started off toward the Little Knife River and Mandaree in Fort Berthold and then we found ourselves down in Wakpala somehow, and then suddenly we were over in Montana on the Rocky Boys, and yet the summer was not even half over. Some people hang on to details when they travel, but we didn't let them bother us and just lived our everyday lives here to there.

I do remember this one place with willows. I remember I laid under those trees and it was comfortable. So comfortable. The branches bent down all around me like a tent or a stable. And quiet, it was quiet, even though there was a powwow close enough so I could see it going on. The air was not too still, not too windy either. When the dust rises up and hangs in the air around the dancers like that, I feel good. Henry was asleep with his arms thrown wide. Later on, he woke up and we started driving again. We were somewhere in Montana, or maybe on the Blood Reserve—it could have been anywhere. Anyway it was where we met the girl.

All her hair was in buns around her ears, that's the first thing I noticed about her. She was posed alongside the road with her arm out, so we stopped. That girl was short, so short her lumber shirt looked comical on her, like a nightgown. She had jeans on and fancy moccasins and she carried a little suitcase.

10   "Hop on in," says Henry. So she climbs in between us.

"We'll take you home," I says. "Where do you live?"

"Chicken," she says.

"Where the hell's that?" I ask her.

"Alaska."

15   "Okay," says Henry, and we drive.

We got up there and never wanted to leave. The sun doesn't truly set there in summer, and the night is more a soft dusk. You might doze off, sometimes, but before you know it you're up again, like an animal in nature. You never feel like you have to sleep hard or put away the world. And things would grow up there. One day just dirt or moss, the next day flowers and long grass. The girl's name was Susy. Her family really took to us. They fed us and put us up. We had our own tent to live in by their house, and the kids would be in and out of there all day and night. They couldn't get over me and Henry being brothers, we looked so different. We told them we knew we had the same mother, anyway.

One night Susy came in to visit us. We sat around in the tent talking of this thing and that. The season was changing. It was getting darker by that time, and the cold was even getting just a little mean. I told her it was time for us to go. She stood up on a chair.

"You never seen my hair," Susy said.

That was true. She was standing on a chair, but still, when she unclipped her buns the hair reached all the way to the ground. Our eyes opened. You couldn't tell how much hair she had when it was rolled up so neatly. Then my brother Henry did something funny. He went up to the chair and said, "Jump on my shoulders." So she did that, and her hair reached down past his waist, and he started twirling, this way and that, so her hair was flung out from side to side.

20 "I always wondered what it was like to have long pretty hair," Henry says. Well we laughed. It was a funny sight, the way he did it. The next morning we got up and took leave of those people.

On to greener pastures, as they say. It was down through Spokane and across Idaho then Montana and very soon we were racing the weather right along under the Canadian border through Columbus, Des Lacs, and then we were in Bottineau County and soon home. We'd made most of the trip, that summer, without putting up the car hood at all. We got home just in time, it turned out, for the army to remember Henry had signed up to join it.

I don't wonder that the army was so glad to get my brother that they turned him into a Marine. He was built like a brick outhouse anyway. We liked to tease him that they really wanted him for his Indian nose. He had a nose big and sharp as a hatchet, like the nose on Red Tomahawk, the Indian who killed Sitting Bull, whose profile is on signs all along the North Dakota highways. Henry went off to training camp, came home once during Christmas, then the next thing you know we got an overseas letter from him. It was 1970, and he said he was stationed up in the northern hill country. Whereabouts I did not know. He wasn't such a hot letter writer, and only got off two before the enemy caught him. I could never keep it straight, which direction those good Vietnam soldiers were from.

I wrote him back several times, even though I didn't know if those letters would get through. I kept him informed all about the car. Most of the time I had it up on blocks in the yard or half taken apart, because that long trip did a hard job on it under the hood.

I always had good luck with numbers, and never worried about the draft myself. I never even had to think about what my number was. But Henry was never lucky in the same way as me. It was at least three years before Henry came home. By then I guess the whole war was solved in the government's mind, but for him it would keep on going. In those years I'd put his car into almost perfect shape. I always thought of it as his car while he was gone, even though when he left he said, "Now it's yours," and threw me his key.

25   "Thanks for the extra key," I'd say. "I'll put it up in your drawer just in case I need it." He laughed.

When he came home, though, Henry was very different, and I'll say this: the change was no good. You could hardly expect him to change for the better, I know. But he was quiet, so quiet, and never comfortable sitting still anywhere but always up and moving around. I thought back to times we'd sat still for whole afternoons, never moving a muscle, just shifting our weight along the ground, talking to whoever sat with us, watching things. He'd always had a joke, then, too, and now you couldn't get him to laugh, or when he did it was more the sound of a man choking, a sound that stopped up the throats of other people around him. They got to leaving him alone most of the time, and I didn't blame them. It was a fact: Henry was jumpy and mean.

I'd bought a color TV set for my mom and the rest of us while Henry was away. Money still came very easy. I was sorry I'd ever bought it though, because of Henry. I was also sorry I'd bought color, because with black-and-white the pictures seem older and farther away. But what are you going to do? He sat in front of it, watching it, and that was the only time he was completely still. But it was the kind of stillness that you see in a rabbit when it freezes and before it will bolt. He was not easy. He sat in his chair gripping the armrests with all his might, as if the chair itself was moving at a high speed and if he let go at all he would rocket forward and maybe crash right through the set.

Once I was in the room watching TV with Henry and I heard his teeth click at something. I looked over, and he'd bitten through his lip. Blood was going down his chin. I tell you right then I wanted to smash that tube to pieces. I went over to it but Henry must have known what I was up to. He rushed from his chair and shoved me out of the way, against the wall. I told myself he didn't know what he was doing.

My mom came in, turned the set off real quiet, and told us she had made something for supper. So we went and sat down. There was still blood going down Henry's chin, but he didn't notice it and no one said anything, even though every time he took a bite of his bread his blood fell onto it until he was eating his own blood mixed in with the food.

30   While Henry was not around we talked about what was going to happen to him. There were no Indian doctors on the reservation, and my mom was afraid of trusting Old Man Pillager because he courted her long ago and was jealous of her husbands. He might take revenge through her son. We were afraid that if we brought Henry to a regular hospital they would keep him.

"They don't fix them in those places," Mom said; "they just give them drugs."

"We wouldn't get him there in the first place," I agreed, "so let's just forget about it."

Then I thought about the car.

Henry had not even looked at the car since he'd gotten home, though like I said, it was in tip-top condition and ready to drive. I thought the car might bring the old Henry back somehow. So I bided my time and waited for my chance to interest him in the vehicle.

35   One night Henry was off somewhere. I took myself a hammer. I went out to that car and I did a number on its underside. Whacked it up. Bent the tail pipe double. Ripped the muffler loose. By the time I was done with the car it looked worse than any typical Indian car that has been driven all its life on reservation roads, which they always say are like government promises—full of holes. It just about hurt me, I'll tell you that! I threw dirt in the carburetor and I ripped all the electric tape off the seats. I made it look just as beat up as I could. Then I sat back and waited for Henry to find it.

Still, it took him over a month. That was all right, because it was just getting warm enough, not melting, but warm enough to work outside.

"Lyman," he says, walking in one day, "that red car looks like shit."

"Well it's old," I says. "You got to expect that."

"No way!" says Henry. "That car's a classic! But you went and ran the piss right out of it, Lyman, and you know it don't deserve that. I kept that car in A-one shape. You don't remember. You're too young. But when I left, that car was running like a watch. Now I don't even know if I can get it to start again, let alone get it anywhere near its old condition."

40   "Well you try," I said, like I was getting mad, "but I say it's a piece of junk."

Then I walked out before he could realize I knew he'd strung together more than six words at once.

After that I thought he'd freeze himself to death working on that car. He was out there all day, and at night he rigged up a little lamp, ran a cord out the window, and had himself some light to see by while he worked. He was better than he had been before, but that's still not saying much. It was easier for him to do the things the rest of us did. He ate more slowly and didn't jump up and down during the meal to get this or that or look out the window. I put my hand in the back of the TV set, I admit, and fiddled around with it good, so that it was almost impossible now to get a clear picture. He didn't look at it very often anyway. He was always out with that car or going off to get parts for it. By the time it was really melting outside, he had it fixed.

I had been feeling down in the dumps about Henry around this time. We had always been together before. Henry and Lyman. But he was such a loner now that I didn't know how to take it. So I jumped at the chance one day when Henry seemed friendly. It's not that he smiled or anything. He just said, "Let's take that old shitbox for a spin." Just the way he said it made me think he could be coming around.

We went out to the car. It was spring. The sun was shining very bright. My only sister, Bonita, who was just eleven years old, came out and made us stand together for a picture. Henry leaned his elbow on the red car's windshield, and he took his other arm and put it over my shoulder, very carefully, as though it was heavy for him to lift and he didn't want to bring the weight down all at once.

45   "Smile," Bonita said, and he did.

That picture, I never look at it anymore. A few months ago, I don't know why, I got his picture out and tacked it on the wall. I felt good about Henry at the time, close to him. I felt good having his picture on the wall, until one night when I was looking at television(I was a little drunk and stoned.)I looked up at the wall and Henry was staring at me. I don't know what it was, but his smile had changed, or maybe it was gone. All I know is I couldn't stay in the same room with that picture. I was shaking. I got up, closed the door, and went into the kitchen. A little later my friend Ray came over and we both went back into that room. We put the picture in a brown bag, folded the bag over and over tightly, then put it way back in a closet.

I still see that picture now, as if it tugs at me, whenever I pass that closet door. The picture is very clear in my mind. It was so sunny that day Henry had to squint against the glare. Or maybe the camera Bonita held flashed like a mirror, blinding him, before she snapped the picture. My face is right out in the sun, big and round. But he might have drawn back, because the shadows on his face are deep as holes. There are two shadows curved like little hooks around the ends of his smile, as if to frame it and try to keep it there—that one, first smile that looked like it might have hurt his face. He has his field jacket on and the worn-in clothes he'd come back in and kept wearing ever since. After Bonita took the picture, she went into the house and we got into the car. There was a full cooler in the trunk. We started off, east, toward Pembina and the Red River because Henry said he wanted to see the high water.

The trip over there was beautiful. When everything starts changing, drying up, clearing off, you feel like your whole life is starting. Henry felt it, too. The top was down and the car hummed like a top. He'd really put it back in shape, even the tape on the seats was very carefully put down and glued back in layers. It's not that he smiled again or even joked, but his face looked to me as if it was clear, more peaceful. It looked as though he wasn't thinking of anything in particular except the bare fields and windbreaks and houses we were passing.

The river was high and full of winter trash when we got there. The sun was still out, but it was colder by the river. There were still little clumps of dirty snow here and there on the banks. The water hadn't gone over the banks yet, but it would, you could tell. It was just at its limit, hard swollen, glossy like an old gray scar. We made ourselves a fire, and we sat down and watched the current go. As I watched it I felt something squeezing inside me and tightening and trying to let go all at the same time. I knew I was not just feeling it myself; I knew I was feeling what Henry was going through at that moment. Except that I couldn't stand it, the closing and opening. I jumped to my feet. I took Henry by the shoulders and I started shaking him. "Wake up," I says, "wake up, wake up, wake up!" I didn't know what had come over me. I sat down beside him again.

50   His face was totally white and hard. Then it broke, like stones break all of a sudden when water boils up inside them.

"I know it," he says. "I know it. I can't help it. It's no use."

We start talking. He said he knew what I'd done with the car. It was obvious it had been whacked out of shape and not just neglected. He said he wanted to give the car to me for good now, it was no use. He said he'd fixed it just to give it back and I should take it.

"No way," I says. "I don't want it."

"That's okay," he says, "you take it."

55   "I don't want it, though," I says back to him, and then to emphasize, just to emphasize, you understand, I touch his shoulder. He slaps my hand off.

"Take that car," he says.

"No," I say, "make me," I say, and then he grabs my jacket and rips the arm loose. That jacket is a class act, suede with tags and zippers. I push Henry backwards, off the log. He jumps up and bowls me over. We go down in a clinch and come up swinging hard, for all we're worth, with our fists. He socks my jaw so hard I feel like it swings loose. Then I'm at his rib cage and land a good one under his chin so his head snaps back. He's dazzled. He looks at me and I look at him and then his eyes are full of tears and blood and at first I think he's crying. But no, he's laughing. "Ha! Ha!" he says. "Ha! Ha! Take good care of it."

"Okay," I says, "okay, no problem. Ha! Ha!"

I can't help it, and I start laughing, too. My face feels fat and strange, and after a while I get a beer from the cooler in the trunk, and when I hand it to Henry he takes his shirt and wipes my germs off. "Hoof-and-mouth disease," he says. For some reason this cracks me up, and so we're really laughing for a while, and then we drink all the rest of the beers one by one and throw them in the river and see how far, how fast, the current takes them before they fill up and sink.

60   "You want to go on back?" I ask after a while. "Maybe we could snag a couple nice Kashpaw girls."

He says nothing. But I can tell his mood is turning again.

"They're all crazy, the girls up here, every damn one of them."

"You're crazy too," I say, to jolly him up. "Crazy <u>Lamartine</u> boys!"

He looks as though he will take this wrong at first. His face twists, then clears, and he jumps up on his feet. "That's right!" he says. "Crazier 'n hell. Crazy Indians!"

65   I think it's the old Henry again. He throws off his jacket and starts swinging his legs out from the knees like a fancy dancer. He's down doing something between a grouse dance and a bunny hop, no kind of dance I ever saw before, but neither has anyone else on all this green growing earth. He's wild. He wants to pitch whoopee! He's up and at me and all over. All this time I'm laughing so hard, so hard my belly is getting tied up in a knot.

"Got to cool me off!" he shouts all of a sudden. Then he runs over to the river and jumps in.

There's boards and other things in the current. It's so high. No sound comes from the river after the splash he makes, so I run right over. I look around. It's getting dark. I see he's halfway across the water already, and I know he didn't swim there but the current took him. It's far. I hear his voice, though, very clearly across it.

"My boots are filling," he says.

He says this in a normal voice, like he just noticed and he doesn't know what to think of it. Then he's gone. A branch comes by. Another branch. And I go in.

70   By the time I get out of the river, off the snag I pulled myself onto, the sun is down. I walk back to the car, turn on the high beams, and drive it up the bank. I put

it in first gear and then I take my foot off the clutch. I get out, close the door, and watch it plow softly into the water. The headlights reach in as they go down, searching, still lighted even after the water swirls over the back end. I wait. The wires short out. It is all finally dark. And then there is only the water, the sound of it going and running and going and running and running.

> **QUESTIONS FOR READING AND WRITING**

1. In the first paragraph the narrator, Lyman, says of the red convertible, "We owned it together until his boots filled with water." Were you puzzled by this comment? In what way does it make sense at the end of the story?
2. Why do you suppose Lyman refers to himself in the third person at the end of the first paragraph?
3. What do you think happened to Henry in Vietnam that changed him?
4. Why is the red convertible so important to Lyman? To Henry? To their relationship?
5. Why does Lyman push the car into the water after Henry?

WILLIAM FAULKNER (1897–1962)

William Faulkner was born into a genteel Southern family and was raised in Oxford, Mississippi, where he attended the University of Mississippi. Following World War I, during which he served in the Canadian Air Force, he settled in Oxford, Mississippi, and worked for a time in the post office until he was forced to resign—he was lax in his duties and often became absorbed in writing or reading. By 1930 he had published a book of verse and a number of novels, including two of his greatest, The Sound and The Fury *(1929) and* As I Lay Dying *(1930), but he did not reach a wide readership until the publication of the novel* Sanctuary, *in 1931. Fifteen of his novels, as well as many of his short stories, are set in fictional Yoknapatawpha County, Mississippi, and concern themselves with the interconnected fortunes of a group of families of different social classes from the Civil War to modern times. Other major works include* Light in August *(1931),* Absalom! Absalom! *(1939),* The Hamlet *(1940), and* Collected Stories *(1950). Faulkner was awarded the Nobel Prize in 1950. When asked about his inspiration for "A Rose for Emily," which originally appeared in* These Thirteen *(1931), a collection of short stories, Faulkner said, "That came from a picture of the strand of hair on the pillow. It was a ghost story. Simply a picture of a strand of hair on the pillow in the abandoned house."*

A ROSE FOR EMILY

[1931]

I

When Miss Emily Grierson died, our whole town went to her funeral: the men through a sort of respectful affection for a fallen monument, the women mostly out of curiosity to see the inside of her house, which no one save an old manservant— a combined gardener and cook—had seen in at least ten years.

It was a big, squarish frame house that had once been white, decorated with cupolas and spires and scrolled balconies in the heavily lightsome style of the seventies, set on what had once been our most select street. But garages and cotton gins had encroached and obliterated even the august names of that neighborhood; only Miss Emily's house was left, lifting its stubborn and coquettish decay above the cotton wagons and the gasoline pumps—an eyesore among eyesores. And now Miss Emily had gone to join the representatives of those august names where they lay in the cedar-bemused cemetery among the ranked and anonymous graves of Union and Confederate soldiers who fell at the battle of Jefferson.

Alive, Miss Emily had been a tradition, a duty, and a care; a sort of hereditary obligation upon the town, dating from that day in 1894 when Colonel Sartoris, the mayor—he who fathered the edict that no Negro woman should appear on the streets without an apron—remitted her taxes, the dispensation dating from the death of her father on into perpetuity. Not that Miss Emily would have accepted charity. Colonel Sartoris invented an involved tale to the effect that Miss Emily's father had loaned money to the town, which the town, as a matter of business, preferred this way of repaying. Only a man of Colonel Sartoris' generation and thought could have invented it, and only a woman could have believed it.

When the next generation, with its more modern ideas, became mayors and aldermen, this arrangement created some little dissatisfaction. On the first of the year they mailed her a tax notice. February came, and there was no reply. They wrote her a formal letter, asking her to call at the sheriff's office at her convenience. A week later the mayor wrote her himself, offering to call or to send his car for her, and received in reply a note on paper of an archaic shape, in a thin, flowing calligraphy in faded ink, to the effect that she no longer went out at all. The tax notice was also enclosed, without comment.

5   They called a special meeting of the Board of Aldermen. A deputation waited upon her, knocked at the door through which no visitor had passed since she ceased giving china-painting lessons eight or ten years earlier. They were admitted by the old Negro into a dim hall from which a staircase mounted into still more shadow. It smelled of dust and disuse—a close, dank smell. The Negro led them into the parlor. It was furnished in heavy, leather-covered furniture. When the Negro opened the blinds of one window, they could see that the leather was cracked; and when they sat down, a faint dust rose sluggishly about their thighs, spinning with slow motes in the single sunray. On a tarnished gilt easel before the fireplace stood a crayon portrait of Miss Emily's father.

They rose when she entered—a small, fat woman in black, with a thin gold chain descending to her waist and vanishing into her belt, leaning on an ebony cane with a tarnished gold head. Her skeleton was small and spare; perhaps that was why what would have been merely plumpness in another was obesity in her. She looked bloated, like a body long submerged in motionless water, and of that pallid hue. Her eyes, lost in the fatty ridges of her face, looked like two small pieces of coal pressed into a lump of dough as they moved from one face to another while the visitors stated their errand.

She did not ask them to sit. She just stood in the door and listened quietly until the spokesman came to a stumbling halt. Then they could hear the invisible watch ticking at the end of the gold chain.

Her voice was dry and cold. "I have no taxes in Jefferson. Colonel Sartoris explained it to me. Perhaps one of you can gain access to the city records and satisfy yourselves."

"But we have. We are the city authorities, Miss Emily. Didn't you get a notice from the sheriff, signed by him?"

10   "I received a paper, yes," Miss Emily said. "Perhaps he considers himself the sheriff . . . . I have no taxes in Jefferson."

"But there is nothing on the books to show that, you see. We must go by the—"

"See Colonel Sartoris. I have no taxes in Jefferson."

"But, Miss Emily—"

"See Colonel Sartoris." (Colonel Sartoris had been dead almost ten years.) "I have no taxes in Jefferson. Tobe!" The Negro appeared. "Show these gentlemen out."

II

15 So she vanquished them, horse and foot, just as she had vanquished their fathers thirty years before about the smell. That was two years after her father's death and a short time after her sweetheart—the one we believed would marry her—had deserted her. After her father's death she went out very little; after her sweetheart went away, people hardly saw her at all. A few of the ladies had the temerity to call, but were not received, and the only sign of life about the place was the Negro man—a young man then—going in and out with a market basket.

"Just as if a man—any man—could keep a kitchen properly," the ladies said; so they were not surprised when the smell developed. It was another link between the gross, teeming world and the high and mighty Griersons.

A neighbor, a woman, complained to the mayor, Judge Stevens, eighty years old.

"But what will you have me do about it, madam?" he said.

"Why, send her word to stop it," the woman said. "Isn't there a law?"

20   "I'm sure that won't be necessary," Judge Stevens said. "It's probably just a snake or a rat that nigger of hers killed in the yard. I'll speak to him about it."

The next day he received two more complaints, one from a man who came in diffident deprecation. "We really must do something about it, Judge, I'd be the last one in the world to bother Miss Emily, but we've got to do something." That night the Board of Aldermen met—three gray-beards and one younger man, a member of the rising generation.

"It's simple enough," he said. "Send her word to have her place cleaned up. Give her a certain time to do it in, and if she don't . . . "

"Dammit, sir," Judge Stevens said, "will you accuse a lady to her face of smelling bad?"

So the next night, after midnight, four men crossed Miss Emily's lawn and slunk about the house like burglars, sniffing along the base of the brickwork and at the cellar openings while one of them performed a regular sowing motion with his hand out of a sack slung from his shoulder. They broke open the cellar door and sprinkled lime there, and in all the outbuildings. As they recrossed the lawn, a window that had been dark was lighted and Miss Emily sat in it, the light behind her, and her upright torso motionless as that of an idol. They crept quietly across the lawn and into the shadow of the locusts that lined the street. After a week or two the smell went away.

25   That was when people had begun to feel really sorry for her. People in our town, remembering how old lady Wyatt, her great-aunt, had gone completely crazy at last, believed that the Griersons held themselves a little too high for what they really were. None of the young men were quite good enough for Miss Emily and such. We had long thought of them as a tableau; Miss Emily a slender figure in white in the background, her father a spraddled silhouette in the foreground, his back to her and clutching a horsewhip, the two of them framed by the back-flung front door. So when she got to be thirty and was still single, we were not pleased exactly, but vindicated; even with insanity in the family she wouldn't have turned down all of her chances if they had really materialized.

When her father died, it got about that the house was all that was left to her; and in a way, people were glad. At last they could pity Miss Emily. Being left alone, and a pauper, she had become humanized. Now she too would know the old thrill and the old despair of a penny more or less.

The day after his death all the ladies prepared to call at the house and offer condolence and aid, as is our custom. Miss Emily met them at the door, dressed as usual and with no trace of grief on her face. She told them that her father was not dead. She did that for three days, with the ministers calling on her, and the doctors, trying to persuade her to let them dispose of the body. Just as they were about to resort to law and force, she broke down, and they buried her father quickly.

We did not say she was crazy then. We believed she had to do that. We remembered all the young men her father had driven away, and we knew that with nothing left, she would have to cling to that which had robbed her, as people will.

III

She was sick for a long time. When we saw her again, her hair was cut short, making her look like a girl, with a vague resemblance to those angels in colored church windows—sort of tragic and serene.

30   The town had just let the contracts for paving the sidewalks, and in the summer after her father's death they began to work. The construction company came with niggers and mules and machinery, and a foreman named Homer Barron, a Yankee—a big, dark, ready man, with a big voice and eyes lighter than his face. The little boys would follow in groups to hear him cuss the niggers, and the niggers singing in time to the rise and fall of picks. Pretty soon he knew everybody in town. Whenever you heard a lot of laughing anywhere about the square, Homer

Barron would be in the center of the group. Presently we began to see him and Miss Emily on Sunday afternoons driving in the yellow-wheeled buggy and the matched team of bays from the livery stable.

At first we were glad that Miss Emily would have an interest, because the ladies all said, "Of course a Grierson would not think seriously of a Northerner, a day laborer." But there were still others, older people, who said that even grief could not cause a real lady to forget *noblesse oblige*—without calling it *noblesse oblige*. They just said, "Poor Emily. Her kinsfolk should come to her." She had some kin in Alabama; but years ago her father had fallen out with them over the estate of old lady Wyatt, the crazy woman, and there was no communication between the two families. They had not even been represented at the funeral.

And as soon as the old people said, "Poor Emily," the whispering began. "Do you suppose it's really so?" they said to one another. "Of course it is. What else could . . . ." This behind their hands; rustling of craned silk and satin behind jalousies closed upon the sun of Sunday afternoon as the thin, swift clop-clop-clop of the matched team passed: "Poor Emily."

She carried her head high enough—even when we believed that she was fallen. It was as if she demanded more than ever the recognition of her dignity as the last Grierson; as if it had wanted that touch of earthiness to reaffirm her imperviousness. Like when she bought the rat poison, the arsenic. That was over a year after they had begun to say "Poor Emily," and while the two female cousins were visiting her.

"I want some poison," she said to the druggist. She was over thirty then, still a slight woman, though thinner than usual, with cold, haughty black eyes in a face the flesh of which was strained across the temples and about the eyesockets as you imagine a lighthouse-keeper's face ought to look. "I want some poison," she said.

35 "Yes, Miss Emily. What kind? For rats and such? I'd recom—"

"I want the best you have. I don't care what kind."

The druggist named several. "They'll kill anything up to an elephant. But what you want is—"

"Arsenic," Miss Emily said. "Is that a good one?"

"Is . . . arsenic? Yes ma'am. But what you want—"

40 "I want arsenic."

The druggist looked down at her. She looked back at him, erect, her face like a strained flag. "Why, of course," the druggist said. "If that's what you want. But the law requires you to tell what you are going to use it for."

Miss Emily just stared at him, her head tilted back in order to look him eye for eye, until he looked away and went and got the arsenic and wrapped it up. The Negro delivery boy brought her the package; the druggist didn't come back. When she opened the package at home there was written on the box, under the skull and bones: "For rats."

IV

So the next day we all said, "She will kill herself"; and we said it would be the best thing. When she had first begun to be seen with Homer Barron, we had said, "She will marry him." Then we said, "She will persuade him yet," because Homer himself had remarked—he liked men, and it was known that he drank with the younger men in the Elk's Club—that he was not a marrying man. Later we said, "Poor Emily," behind the jalousies as they passed on Sunday afternoon in the glittering buggy, Miss Emily with her head high and Homer Barron with his hat cocked and a cigar in his teeth, reins and whip in a yellow glove.

Then some of the ladies began to say that it was a disgrace to the town and a bad example to the young people. The men did not want to interfere, but at last the ladies forced the Baptist minister—Miss Emily's people were Episcopal—to call upon her. He would never divulge what happened during that interview, but he refused to go back again. The next Sunday they again drove about the streets, and the following day the minister's wife wrote to Miss Emily's relations in Alabama.

45   So she had blood-kin under her roof again and we sat back to watch developments. At first nothing happened. Then we were sure that they were to be married. We learned that Miss Emily had been to the jeweler's and ordered a man's toilet set in silver, with the letters H. B. on each piece. Two days later we learned that she had bought a complete outfit of men's clothing, including a nightshirt, and we said, "They are married." We were really glad. We were glad because the two female cousins were even more Grierson than Miss Emily had ever been.

So we were not surprised when Homer Barron—the streets had been finished some time since—was gone. We were a little disappointed that there was not a public blowing-off, but we believed that he had gone on to prepare for Miss Emily's coming, or to give her a chance to get rid of the cousins. (By that time it was a cabal, and we were all Miss Emily's allies to help circumvent the cousins.) Sure enough, after another week they departed. And, as we had expected all along, within three days Homer Barron was back in town. A neighbor saw the Negro man admit him at the kitchen door at dusk one evening.

And that was the last we saw of Homer Barron. And of Miss Emily for some time. The Negro man went in and out with the market basket, but the front door remained closed. Now and then we would see her at a window for a moment, as the men did that night when they sprinkled the lime, but for almost six months she did not appear on the streets. Then we knew that this was to be expected too; as if that quality of her father which had thwarted her woman's life so many times had been too virulent and too furious to die.

When we next saw Miss Emily, she had grown fat and her hair was turning gray. During the next few years it grew grayer and grayer until it attained an even pepper-and-salt iron-gray, when it ceased turning. Up to the day of her death at seventy-four it was still that vigorous iron-gray, like the hair of an active man.

From that time on her front door remained closed, save for a period of six or seven years, when she was about forty, during which she gave lessons in china-painting. She fitted up a studio in one of the downstairs rooms, where the daughters and granddaughters of Colonel Sartoris' contemporaries were sent to her with the same regularity and in the same spirit that they were sent on Sundays with a twenty-five cent piece for the collection plate. Meanwhile her taxes had been remitted.

50   Then the newer generation became the backbone and the spirit of the town, and the painting pupils grew up and fell away and did not send their children to her

with boxes of color and tedious brushes and pictures cut from the ladies' magazines. The front door closed upon the last one and remained closed for good. When the town got free postal delivery, Miss Emily alone refused to let them fasten the metal numbers above her door and attach a mailbox to it. She would not listen to them.

Daily, monthly, yearly we watched the Negro grow grayer and more stooped, going in and out with the market basket. Each December we sent her a tax notice, which would be returned by the post office a week later, unclaimed. Now and then we would see her in one of the downstairs windows—she had evidently shut up the top floor of the house—like the carven torso of an idol in a niche, looking or not looking at us, we could never tell which. Thus she passed from generation to generation—dear, inescapable, impervious, tranquil, and perverse.

And so she died. Fell ill in the house filled with dust and shadows, with only a doddering Negro man to wait on her. We did not even know she was sick; we had long since given up trying to get any information from the Negro. He talked to no one, probably not even to her, for his voice had grown harsh and rusty, as if from disuse.

She died in one of the downstairs rooms, in a heavy walnut bed with a curtain, her gray head propped on a pillow yellow and moldy with age and lack of sunlight.

V

The Negro met the first of the ladies at the front door and let them in, with their hushed, sibilant voices and their quick, curious glances, and then he disappeared. He walked right through the house and out the back and was not seen again.

55   The two female cousins came at once. They held the funeral on the second day, with the town coming to look at Miss Emily beneath a mass of bought flowers, with the crayon face of her father musing profoundly above the bier and the ladies sibilant and macabre; and the very old men—some in their brushed Confederate uniforms—on the porch and the lawn, talking of Miss Emily as if she had been a contemporary of theirs, believing that they had danced with her and courted her perhaps, confusing time with its mathematical progression, as the old do, to whom all the past is not a diminishing road, but, instead, a huge meadow which no winter ever quite touches, divided from them now by the narrow bottleneck of the most recent decade of years.

Already we knew that there was one room in that region above stairs which no one had seen in forty years, and which would have to be forced. They waited until Miss Emily was decently in the ground before they opened it.

The violence of breaking down the door seemed to fill this room with pervading dust. A thin, acrid pall as of the tomb seemed to lie everywhere upon this room decked and furnished as for a bridal: upon the valance curtains of faded rose color, upon the rose-shaded lights, upon the dressing table, upon the delicate array of crystal and the man's toilet things backed with tarnished silver, silver so tarnished that the monogram was obscured. Among them lay a collar and tie, as if they had just been removed, which, lifted, left upon the surface a pale crescent in the dust. Upon a chair hung the suit, carefully folded; beneath it the two mute shoes and the discarded socks.

The man himself lay in the bed.

For a long while we just stood there, looking down at the profound and flesh-less grin. The body had apparently once lain in the attitude of an embrace, but now the long sleep that outlasts love, that conquers even the grimace of love, had cuck-olded him. What was left of him, rotted beneath what was left of the nightshirt, had become inextricable from the bed in which he lay; and upon him and upon the pillow beside him lay that even coating of the patient and biding dust.

60   Then we noticed that in the second pillow was the indentation of a head. One of us lifted something from it, and leaning forward, that faint and invisible dust dry and acrid in the nostrils, we saw a long strand of iron-gray hair.

➤ *QUESTIONS FOR READING AND WRITING*

1. Who is the narrator? How does the narrator's point of view influence what you know in the story? What difference does it make that the story is told in flashbacks instead of from beginning to end? What is the narrator's atti-tude toward Emily?
2. How do you feel about Emily Grierson? What is her conflict?
3. Who is Homer Barron? How does his characterization differ from Emily's?
4. At the end of the story, what is the significance of the iron-gray strand of hair on the second pillow? Are there indications earlier in the story that foreshadow this outcome?
5. Why is Emily such a formidable force in the town? Why does she seem to get away with so much?
6. In what way is the setting (the house, the town, Mississippi) of this story important? What is the relationship between the setting and the characters?
7. To what extent is this a story about change—or the inability to change?

CHARLOTTE PERKINS GILMAN

(1860–1935)

Charlotte Perkins Gilman was born in Hartford, Connecticut. Because her father, the writer Frederick Beecher Perkins, abandoned the family when she was only an infant, she was often left in the company of relatives, who included Harriet Beecher Stowe, the author of Uncle Tom's Cabin, *and the feminist activists Isabella Beecher Hooker and Catherine Beecher. These women instilled in Gilman the ideas of equality and independence, which formed the basis for the political activism that made her famous later in life. Though she wrote numerous works about the conditions of women, her reputation as a writer of literature rests almost solely on her short story "The Yellow Wallpaper," which adds a feminist twist to the psychological horror story pioneered by Edgar Allan Poe. The*

story, written in 1899, was based on her own experiences. During her unhappy first marriage, Gilman suffered a severe depression following the birth of her daughter. A noted doctor of the time prescribed a regimen of bed rest and minimal intellectual stimulation. Her condition only worsened. Eventually she rebelled, and taking responsibility for her own cure, separated from her husband and moved to California. In 1900, she married again, this time happily to her cousin George Houghton Gilman. She remained active politically until she took her own life in 1935, after fighting a losing battle with breast cancer.

THE YELLOW WALLPAPER [1899]

It is very seldom that mere ordinary people like John and myself secure ancestral halls for the summer.

A colonial mansion, a hereditary estate, I would say a haunted house and reach the height of romantic felicity—but that would be asking too much of fate!

Still I will proudly declare that there is something queer about it.

Else, why should it be let so cheaply? And why have stood so long untenanted?

5 John laughs at me, of course, but one expects that.

John is practical in the extreme. He has no patience with faith, an intense horror of superstition, and he scoffs openly at any talk of things not to be felt and seen and put down in figures.

John is a physician, and *perhaps*—(I would not say it to a living soul, of course, but this is dead paper and a great relief to my mind)—*perhaps* that is one reason I do not get well faster.

You see, he does not believe I am sick! And what can one do?

If a physician of high standing, and one's own husband, assures friends and relatives that there is really nothing the matter with one but temporary nervous depression—a slight hysterical tendency—what is one to do?

10 My brother is also a physician, and also of high standing, and he says the same thing.

So I take phosphates or phosphites—whichever it is—and tonics, and air and exercise, and journeys, and am absolutely forbidden to "work" until I am well again.

Personally, I disagree with their ideas.

Personally, I believe that congenial work, with excitement and change, would do me good.

But what is one to do?

15 I did write for a while in spite of them; but it *does* exhaust me a good deal— having to be so sly about it, or else meet with heavy opposition.

I sometimes fancy that in my condition, if I had less opposition and more society and stimulus—but John says the very worst thing I can do is to think about my condition, and I confess it always makes me feel bad.

So I will let it alone and talk about the house.

The most beautiful place! It is quite alone, standing well back from the road, quite three miles from the village. It makes me think of English places that you read about, for there are hedges and walls and gates that lock, and lots of separate little houses for the gardeners and people.

There is a *delicious* garden! I never saw such a garden—large and shady, full of box-bordered paths, and lined with long grape-covered arbors with seats under them.

20   There were greenhouses, but they are all broken now.

There was some legal trouble, I believe, something about the heirs and co-heirs; anyhow, the place has been empty for years.

That spoils my ghostliness, I am afraid, but I don't care—there is something strange about the house—I can feel it.

I even said so to John one moonlight evening, but he said what I felt was a draught, and shut the window.

I get unreasonably angry with John sometimes. I'm sure I never used to be so sensitive. I think it is due to this nervous condition.

25   But John says if I feel so I shall neglect proper self-control; so I take pains to control myself—before him, at least, and that makes me very tired.

I don't like our room a bit. I wanted one downstairs that opened onto the piazza and had roses all over the window, and such pretty old-fashioned chintz hangings! But John would not hear of it.

He said there was only one window and not room for two beds, and no near room for him if he took another.

He is very careful and loving, and hardly lets me stir without special direction.

I have a schedule prescription for each hour in the day; he takes all care from me, and so I feel basely ungrateful not to value it more.

30   He said he came here solely on my account, that I was to have perfect rest and all the air I could get. "Your exercise depends on your strength, my dear," said he, "and your food somewhat on your appetite; but air you can absorb all the time." So we took the nursery at the top of the house.

It is a big, airy room, the whole floor nearly, with windows that look all ways, and air and sunshine galore. It was nursery first, and then playroom and gymnasium, I should judge, for the windows are barred for little children, and there are rings and things in the walls.

The paint and paper look as if a boys' school had used it. It is stripped off—the paper—in great patches all around the head of my bed, about as far as I can reach, and in a great place on the other side of the room low down. I never saw a worse paper in my life. One of those sprawling, flamboyant patterns committing every artistic sin.

It is dull enough to confuse the eye in following, pronounced enough to constantly irritate and provoke study, and when you follow the lame uncertain curves for a little distance they suddenly commit suicide—plunge off at outrageous angles, destroy themselves in unheard-of contradictions.

The color is repellent, almost revolting: a smouldering unclean yellow, strangely faded by the slow-turning sunlight. It is a dull yet lurid orange in some places, a sickly sulphur tint in others.

35   No wonder the children hated it! I should hate it myself if I had to live in this room long.

There comes John, and I must put this away—he hates to have me write a word.

We have been here two weeks, and I haven't felt like writing before, since that first day.

I am sitting by the window now, up in this atrocious nursery, and there is nothing to hinder my writing as much as I please, save lack of strength.

John is away all day, and even some nights when his cases are serious.

40   I am glad my case is not serious!

But these nervous troubles are dreadfully depressing.

John does not know how much I really suffer. He knows there is no reason to suffer, and that satisfies him.

Of course it is only nervousness. It does weigh on me so not to do my duty in any way!

I meant to be such a help to John, such a real rest and comfort, and here I am a comparative burden already!

45   Nobody would believe what an effort it is to do what little I am able—to dress and entertain, and order things.

It is fortunate Mary is so good with the baby. Such a dear baby!

And yet I *cannot* be with him, it makes me so nervous.

I suppose John never was nervous in his life. He laughs at me so about this wallpaper!

At first he meant to repaper the room, but afterward he said that I was letting it get the better of me, and that nothing was worse for a nervous patient than to give way to such fancies.

50   He said that after the wallpaper was changed it would be the heavy bedstead, and then the barred windows, and then that gate at the head of the stairs, and so on.

"You know the place is doing you good," he said, "and really, dear, I don't care to renovate the house just for a three months' rental."

"Then do let us go downstairs," I said, "there are such pretty rooms there."

Then he took me in his arms and called me a blessed little goose, and said he would go down to the cellar, if I wished, and have it whitewashed into the bargain.

But he is right enough about the beds and windows and things.

55   It is as airy and comfortable a room as anyone need wish, and, of course, I would not be so silly as to make him uncomfortable just for a whim.

I'm really getting quite fond of the big room, all but that horrid paper.

Out of one window I can see the garden—those mysterious deep-shaded arbors, the riotous old-fashioned flowers, and bushes and gnarly trees.

Out of another I get a lovely view of the bay and a little private wharf belonging to the estate. There is a beautiful shaded lane that runs down there from the house. I always fancy I see people walking in these numerous paths and arbors, but John has cautioned me not to give way to fancy in the least. He says that with my imaginative power and habit of story-making, a nervous weakness like mine is sure to lead to all manner of excited fancies, and that I ought to use my will and good sense to check the tendency. So I try.

I think sometimes that if I were only well enough to write a little it would relieve the press of ideas and rest me.

60   But I find I get pretty tired when I try.

It is so discouraging not to have any advice and companionship about my work. When I get really well, John says we will ask Cousin Henry and Julia down for a long visit; but he says he would as soon put fireworks in my pillow-case as to let me have those stimulating people about now.

I wish I could get well faster.

But I must not think about that. This paper looks to me as if it *knew* what a vicious influence it had!

There is a recurrent spot where the pattern lolls like a broken neck and two bulbous eyes stare at you upside down.

65   I get positively angry with the impertinence of it and the everlastingness. Up and down and sideways they crawl, and those absurd, unblinking eyes are everywhere. There is one place where two breadths didn't match, and the eyes go all up and down the line, one a little higher than the other.

I never saw so much expression in an inanimate thing before, and we all know how much expression they have! I used to lie awake as a child and get more entertainment and terror out of blank walls and plain furniture than most children could find in a toy-store.

I remember what a kindly wink the knobs of our big, old bureau used to have, and there was one chair that always seemed like a strong friend.

I used to feel that if any of the other things looked too fierce I could always hop into that chair and be safe.

The furniture in this room is no worse than inharmonious, however, for we had to bring it all from downstairs. I suppose when this was used as a playroom they had to take the nursery things out, and no wonder! I never saw such ravages as the children have made here.

70   The wallpaper, as I said before, is torn off in spots, and it sticketh closer than a brother—they must have had perseverance as well as hatred.

Then the floor is scratched and gouged and splintered, the plaster itself is dug out here and there, and this great heavy bed, which is all we found in the room, looks as if it had been through the wars.

But I don't mind it a bit—only the paper.

There comes John's sister. Such a dear girl as she is, and so careful of me! I must not let her find me writing.

She is a perfect and enthusiastic housekeeper, and hopes for no better profession. I verily believe she thinks it is the writing which made me sick!

75   But I can write when she is out, and see her a long way off from these windows.

There is one that commands the road, a lovely shaded winding road, and one that just looks off over the country. A lovely country, too, full of great elms and velvet meadows.

This wallpaper has a kind of sub-pattern in a different shade, a particularly irritating one, for you can only see it in certain lights, and not clearly then.

But in the places where it isn't faded and where the sun is just so—I can see a strange, provoking, formless sort of figure that seems to skulk about behind that silly and conspicuous front design.

There's sister on the stairs!

80 Well, the Fourth of July is over! The people are all gone and I am tired out. John thought it might do me good to see a little company, so we just had Mother and Nellie and the children down for a week.

Of course I didn't do a thing. Jennie sees to everything now.

But it tired me all the same.

John says if I don't pick up faster he shall send me to Weir Mitchell[1] in the fall.

But I don't want to go there at all. I had a friend who was in his hands once, and she says he is just like John and my brother, only more so!

85 Besides, it is such an undertaking to go so far.

I don't feel as if it was worth while to turn my hand over for anything, and I'm getting dreadfully fretful and querulous.

I cry at nothing, and cry most of the time.

Of course I don't when John is here, or anybody else, but when I am alone.

And I am alone a good deal just now. John is kept in town very often by serious cases, and Jennie is good and lets me alone when I want her to.

90 So I walk a little in the garden or down that lovely lane, sit on the porch under the roses, and lie down up here a good deal.

I'm getting really fond of the room in spite of the wallpaper. Perhaps *because* of the wallpaper.

It dwells in my mind so!

I lie here on this great immovable bed—it is nailed down. I believe—and follow that pattern about by the hour. It is as good as gymnastics, I assure you. I start, we'll say, at the bottom, down in the corner over there where it has not been touched, and I determine for the thousandth time that I *will* follow that pointless pattern to some sort of a conclusion.

I know a little of the principle of design, and I know this thing was not arranged on any laws of radiation, or alternation, or repetition, or symmetry, or anything else that I ever heard of.

95 It is repeated, of course, by the breadths, but not otherwise.

Looked at in one way each breadth stands alone; the bloated curves and flourishes—a kind of "debased Romanesque" with delirium tremens go waddling up and down in isolated columns of fatuity.

But, on the other hand, they connect diagonally, and the sprawling outlines run off in great slanting waves of optic horror, like a lot of wallowing sea-weeds in full chase.

The whole thing goes horizontally, too, at least it seems so, and I exhaust myself in trying to distinguish the order of its going in that direction.

They have used a horizontal breadth for a frieze, and that adds wonderfully to the confusion.

100 There is one end of the room where it is almost intact, and there, when the crosslights fade and the low sun shines directly upon it, I can almost fancy radiation after all—the interminable grotesque seems to form around a common center and rush off in headlong plunges of equal distraction.

---

[1]**Weir Mitchell** a physician known for his "rest cure" for psychoneurosies

It makes me tired to follow it. I will take a nap, I guess.

I don't know why I should write this.
I don't want to.
I don't feel able.

105   And I know John would think it absurd. But I *must* say what I feel and think in some way—it is such a relief.

But the effort is getting to be greater than the relief!

Half the time now I am awfully lazy, and lie down ever so much. John says I mustn't lose my strength, and has me take cod liver oil and lots of tonics and things, to say nothing of ale and wine and rare meat.

Dear John! He loves me very dearly, and hates to have me sick. I tried to have a real earnest reasonable talk with him the other day, and tell him how I wish he would let me go and make a visit to Cousin Henry and Julia.

But he said I wasn't able to go, nor able to stand it after I got there; and I did not make out a very good case for myself, for I was crying before I had finished.

110   It is getting to be a great effort for me to think straight. Just this nervous weakness, I suppose.

And dear John gathered me up in his arms, and just carried me upstairs and laid me on the bed, and sat by me and read to me till it tired my head.

He said I was his darling and his comfort and all he had, and that I must take care of myself for his sake, and keep well.

He says no one but myself can help me out of it, that I must use my will and self-control and not let any silly fancies run away with me.

There's one comfort—the baby is well and happy, and does not have to occupy this nursery with the horrid wallpaper.

115   If we had not used it, that blessed child would have! What a fortunate escape! Why, I wouldn't have a child of mine, an impressionable little thing, live in such a room for worlds.

I never thought of it before, but it is lucky that John kept me here after all; I can stand it so much easier than a baby, you see.

Of course I never mention it to them any more—I am too wise—but I keep watch for it all the same.

There are things in that wallpaper that nobody knows but me, or ever will.

Behind that outside pattern the dim shapes get clearer every day.

120   It is always the same shape, only very numerous.

And it is like a woman stooping down and creeping about behind that pattern. I don't like it a bit. I wonder—I begin to think—I wish John would take me away from here!

It is so hard to talk with John about my case, because he is so wise, and because he loves me so.

But I tried last night.

It was moonlight. The moon shines in all around just as the sun does.

125   I hate to see it sometimes, it creeps so slowly, and always comes in by one window or another.

John was asleep and I hated to waken him, so I kept still and watched the moonlight on that undulating wallpaper till I felt creepy.

The faint figure behind seemed to shake the pattern, just as if she wanted to get out.

I got up softly and went to feel and see if the paper *did* move, and when I came back John was awake.

"What is it, little girl?" he said. "Don't go walking about like that—you'll get cold."

130   I thought it was a good time to talk, so I told him that I really was not gaining here, and that I wished he would take me away.

"Why, darling!" said he, "our lease will be up in three weeks, and I can't see how to leave before."

"The repairs are not done at home, and I cannot possibly leave town just now. Of course if you were in any danger, I could and would, but you really are better, dear, whether you can see it or not. I am a doctor, dear, and I know. You are gaining flesh and color, your appetite is better, I feel really much easier about you."

"I don't weigh a bit more," said I, "nor as much; and my appetite may be better in the evening when you are here but it is worse in the morning when you are away!"

"Bless her little heart!" said he with a big hug. "She shall be as sick as she pleases! But now let's improve the shining hours by going to sleep, and talk about it in the morning!"

135   "And you won't go away?" I asked gloomily.

"Why, how can I, dear? It is only three weeks more and then we will take a nice little trip of a few days while Jennie is getting the house ready. Really, dear, you are better!"

"Better in body perhaps—" I began, and stopped short, for he sat up straight and looked at me with such a stern, reproachful look that I could not say another word.

"My darling," said he, "I beg of you, for my sake and for our child's sake, as well as for your own, that you will never for one instant let that idea enter your mind! There is nothing so dangerous, so fascinating, to a temperament like yours. It is a false and foolish fancy. Can you not trust me as a physician when I tell you so?"

So of course I said no more on that score, and we went to sleep before long. He thought I was asleep first, but I wasn't, and lay there for hours trying to decide whether that front pattern and the back pattern really did move together or separately.

140   On a pattern like this, by daylight, there is a lack of sequence, a defiance of law, that is a constant irritant to a normal mind.

The color is hideous enough, and unreliable enough, and infuriating enough, but the pattern is torturing.

You think you have mastered it, but just as you get well under way in following, it turns a back-somersault and there you are. It slaps you in the face, knocks you down, and tramples upon you. It is like a bad dream.

The outside pattern is a florid arabesque, reminding one of a fungus. If you can imagine a toadstool in joints, an interminable string of toadstools, budding and sprouting in endless convolutions—why, that is something like it.

That is, sometimes!

145 There is one marked peculiarity about this paper, a thing nobody seems to notice but myself, and that is that it changes as the light changes.

When the sun shoots in through the east window—I always watch for that first long, straight ray—it changes so quickly that I never can quite believe it.

That is why I watch it always.

By moonlight—the moon shines in all night when there is a moon—I wouldn't know it was the same paper.

At night in any kind of light, in twilight, candlelight, lamplight, and worst of all by moonlight, it becomes bars! The outside pattern, I mean, and the woman behind it is as plain as can be.

150 I didn't realize for a long time what the thing was that showed behind, that dim sub-pattern, but now I am quite sure it is a woman.

By daylight she is subdued, quiet. I fancy it is the pattern that keeps her so still. It is so puzzling. It keeps me quiet by the hour.

I lie down ever so much now. John says it is good for me, and to sleep all I can.

Indeed he started the habit by making me lie down for an hour after each meal.

It is a very bad habit, I am convinced, for you see, I don't sleep.

155 And that cultivates deceit, for I don't tell them I'm awake—oh, no!

The fact is I am getting a little afraid of John.

He seems very queer sometimes, and even Jennie has an inexplicable look.

It strikes me occasionally, just as a scientific hypothesis, that perhaps it is the paper!

I have watched John when he did not know I was looking, and come into the room suddenly on the most innocent excuses, and I've caught him several times *looking at the paper!* And Jennie too. I caught Jennie with her hand on it once.

160 She didn't know I was in the room, and when I asked her in a quiet, a very quiet voice, with the most restrained manner possible, what she was doing with the paper, she turned around as if she had been caught stealing, and looked quite angry—asked me why I should frighten her so!

Then she said that the paper stained everything it touched, that she had found yellow smooches on all my clothes and John's, and she wished we would be more careful!

Did not that sound innocent? But I know she was studying that pattern, and I am determined that nobody shall find it out but myself!

Life is very much more exciting now than it used to be. You see, I have something more to expect, to look forward to, to watch. I really do eat better, and am more quiet than I was.

John is so pleased to see me improve! He laughed a little the other day, and said I seemed to be flourishing in spite of my wallpaper.

165 I turned it off with a laugh. I had no intention of telling him it was *because* of the wallpaper—he would make fun of me. He might even want to take me away.

I don't want to leave now until I have found it out. There is a week more, and I think that will be enough.

I'm feeling so much better!

I don't sleep much at night, for it is so interesting to watch developments; but I sleep a good deal during the daytime.

In the daytime it is tiresome and perplexing.

170   There are always new shoots on the fungus, and new shades of yellow all over it. I cannot keep count of them, though I have tried conscientiously.

It is the strangest yellow, that wallpaper! It makes me think of all the yellow things I ever saw—not beautiful ones like buttercups, but old, foul, bad yellow things.

But there is something else about that paper—the smell! I noticed it the moment we came into the room, but with so much air and sun it was not bad. Now we have had a week of fog and rain, and whether the windows are open or not, the smell is here.

It creeps all over the house.

I find it hovering in the dining-room, skulking in the parlor, hiding in the hall, lying in wait for me on the stairs.

175   It gets into my hair.

Even when I go to ride, if I turn my head suddenly and surprise it—there is that smell!

Such a peculiar odor, too! I have spent hours in trying to analyze it, to find what it smelled like.

It is not bad—at first—and very gentle, but quite the subtlest, most enduring odor I ever met.

In this damp weather it is awful. I wake up in the night and find it hanging over me.

180   It used to disturb me at first. I thought seriously of burning the house—to reach the smell.

But now I am used to it. The only thing I can think of that it is like is the *color* of the paper! A yellow smell.

There is a very funny mark on this wall, low down, near the mopboard. A streak that runs round the room. It goes behind every piece of furniture, except the bed, a long, straight, even *smooch,* as if it had been rubbed over and over.

I wonder how it was done and who did it, and what they did it for. Round and round and round—round and round and round—it makes me dizzy!

I really have discovered something at last.

185   Through watching so much at night, when it changes so, I have finally found out.

The front pattern *does* move—and no wonder! The woman behind shakes it!

Sometimes I think there are a great many women behind, and sometimes only one, and she crawls around fast, and her crawling shakes it all over.

Then in the very bright spots she keeps still, and in the very shady spots she just takes hold of the bars and shakes them hard.

And she is all the time trying to climb through. But nobody could climb through that pattern—it strangles so; I think that is why it has so many heads.

190   They get through, and then the pattern strangles them off and turns them upside down, and makes their eyes white!

If those heads were covered or taken off it would not be half so bad.

I think that woman gets out in the daytime!

And I'll tell you why—privately—I've seen her!

I can see her out of every one of my windows!

195   It is the same woman, I know, for she is always creeping, and most women do not creep by daylight.

I see her in that long shaded lane, creeping up and down. I see her in those dark grape arbors, creeping all around the garden.

I see her on that long road under the trees, creeping along, and when a carriage comes she hides under the blackberry vines.

I don't blame her a bit. It must be very humiliating to be caught creeping by daylight!

I always lock the door when I creep by daylight. I can't do it at night, for I know John would suspect something at once.

200   And John is so queer now that I don't want to irritate him. I wish he would take another room! Besides, I don't want anybody to get that woman out at night but myself.

I often wonder if I could see her out of all the windows at once.

But, turn as fast as I can, I can only see out of one at one time.

And though I always see her, she *may* be able to creep faster than I can turn! I have watched her sometimes away off in the open country, creeping as fast as a cloud shadow in a wind.

If only that top pattern could be gotten off from the under one! I mean to try it, little by little.

205   I have found out another funny thing, but I shan't tell it this time! It does not do to trust people too much.

There are only two more days to get this paper off, and I believe John is beginning to notice. I don't like the look in his eyes.

And I heard him ask Jennie a lot of professional questions about me. She had a very good report to give.

She said I slept a good deal in the daytime.

John knows I don't sleep very well at night, for all I'm so quiet!

210   He asked me all sorts of questions, too, and pretended to be very loving and kind.

As if I couldn't see through him!

Still, I don't wonder he acts so, sleeping under this paper for three months.

It only interests me, but I feel sure John and Jennie are affected by it.

Hurrah! This is the last day, but it is enough. John is to stay in town over night, and won't be out until this evening.

215   Jennie wanted to sleep with me—the sly thing; but I told her I should undoubtedly rest better for a night all alone.

That was clever, for really I wasn't alone a bit! As soon as it was moonlight and that poor thing began to crawl and shake the pattern, I got up and ran to help her.

I pulled and she shook. I shook and she pulled, and before morning we had peeled off yards of that paper.

A strip about as high as my head and half around the room.

And then when the sun came and that awful pattern began to laugh at me, I declared I would finish it today!

220   We go away tomorrow, and they are moving all my furniture down again to leave things as they were before.

Jennie looked at the wall in amazement, but I told her merrily that I did it out of pure spite at the vicious thing.

She laughed and said she wouldn't mind doing it herself, but I must not get tired.

How she betrayed herself that time!

But I am here, and no person touches this paper but Me—not *alive!*

225   She tried to get me out of the room—it was too patent! But I said it was so quiet and empty and clean now that I believed I would lie down again and sleep all I could, and not to wake me even for dinner—I would call when I woke.

So now she is gone, and the servants are gone, and the things are gone, and there is nothing left but that great bedstead nailed down, with the canvas mattress we found on it.

We shall sleep downstairs tonight, and take the boat home tomorrow.

I quite enjoy the room, now it is bare again.

How those children did tear about here!

230   This bedstead is fairly gnawed!

But I must get to work.

I have locked the door and thrown the key down into the front path.

I don't want to go out, and I don't want to have anybody come in, till John comes.

I want to astonish him.

235   I've got a rope up here that even Jennie did not find. If that woman does get out, and tries to get away, I can tie her!

But I forgot I could not reach far without anything to stand on!

This bed will *not* move!

I tried to lift and push it until I was lame, and then I got so angry I bit off a little piece at one corner—but it hurt my teeth.

Then I peeled off all the paper I could reach standing on the floor. It sticks horribly and the pattern just enjoys it! All those strangled heads and bulbous eyes and waddling fungus growths just shriek with derision!

240   I am getting angry enough to do something desperate. To jump out of the window would be admirable exercise, but the bars are too strong even to try.

Besides I wouldn't do it. Of course not. I know well enough that a step like that is improper and might be misconstrued.

I don't like to *look* out of the windows even—there are so many of those creeping women, and they creep so fast.

I wonder if they all come out of that wallpaper as I did?

But I am securely fastened now by my well-hidden rope—you don't get *me* out in the road there!

245   I suppose I shall have to get back behind the pattern when it comes night, and that is hard!

It is so pleasant to be out in this great room and creep around as I please!

I don't want to go outside. I won't, even if Jennie asks me to.

For outside you have to creep on the ground, and everything is green instead of yellow.

But here I can creep smoothly on the floor, and my shoulder just fits in that long smooch around the wall, so I cannot lose my way.

250   Why, there's John at the door!

It is no use, young man, you can't open it!

How he does call and pound!

Now he's crying to Jennie for an axe.

It would be a shame to break down that beautiful door!

255   "John, dear!" said I in the gentlest voice, "The key is down by the front steps, under a plantain leaf!"

That silenced him for a few moments.

Then he said, very quietly indeed, "Open the door, my darling!"

"I can't," said I. "The key is down by the front door under a plantain leaf!" And then I said it again, several times, very gently and slowly, and said it so often that he had to go and see, and he got it of course, and came in. He stopped short by the door.

"What is the matter?" he cried. "For God's sake, what are you doing?"

260   I kept on creeping just the same, but I looked at him over my shoulder.

"I've got out at last," said I, "in spite of you and Jennie. And I've pulled off most of the paper, so you can't put me back!"

Now why should that man have fainted? But he did, and right across my path by the wall, so that I had to creep over him every time!

➤ *QUESTIONS FOR READING AND WRITING*

1. The narrator is the main character in the story. To what extent does this influence what you are told in this story? Can you describe the narrator? Do you think she is reliable? Explain

2. Describe her relationship with her husband, John. What is he like? How does he treat her?

3. What kind of illness does the narrator say she has? What does her physician-husband prescribe as a cure? Do you think it's an appropriate cure? Why or why not?

4. In what way is the yellow wallpaper symbolic in this story? To what extent does the narrator's description of it change as the story progresses? Do you see any other symbols in the story?

5. To what extent does the narrator change as the story progresses? What are the indications of that in the story?

6. Near the end of the story, the narrator says, "I've got out at last." Has she? Explain.

NATHANIEL HAWTHORNE

(1804–1864)

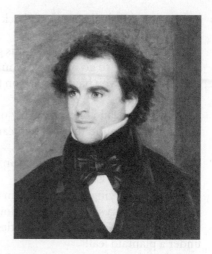

Nathaniel Hawthorne was born in Salem, Massachusetts, to a once-influential Puritan family. Two of his ancestors had served as judges: one in the persecution of Quakers, the other in the Salem witch trials. His father, a ship's captain, died when he was 4, and his mother, after moving the family back to her parents' house, became a recluse, emerging from her room only for meals. Following an injury that left him lame, Hawthorne was mostly educated at home. After attending Bowdoin College in Maine, he returned home to live with his sisters and mother, where he began writing and publishing stories. In 1828, he published a little-read novel about his college experiences, Fanshawe. *His next publication,* Twice-Told Tales *(1837), a collection of stories, fared better. After his marriage in 1842 and the birth of a daughter, Hawthorne wrote less, working as a customs inspector at various times to support his young family. In 1849, following the death of his mother, Hawthorne moved back to Salem, where he wrote his masterpiece* The Scarlet Letter. *The book was an enormous critical and financial success, as was his next novel,* The House of the Seven Gables *(1851). Hawthorne was then financially able to devote himself fully to his writing. Later in his life, following the election of his college friend Franklin Pierce to the presidency, Hawthorne served as American consul at Liverpool from 1853 to 1857, and then remained in Europe until 1860, where he wrote his final novel,* The Marble Faun *(1860). He died in Concord, Massachusetts, in 1864.*

YOUNG GOODMAN BROWN [1828]

Young Goodman Brown came forth at sunset into the street at Salem village; but put his head back, after crossing the threshold, to exchange a parting kiss with his young wife. And Faith, as the wife was aptly named, thrust her own pretty head into the street, letting the wind play with the pink ribbons of her cap while she called to Goodman Brown.

"Dearest heart," whispered she, softly and rather sadly, when her lips were close to his ear, "prithee put off your journey until sunrise and sleep in your own bed to-night. A lone woman is troubled with such dreams and such thoughts that she's afeard of herself sometimes. Pray tarry with me this night, dear husband, of all nights in the year."

"My love and my Faith," replied young Goodman Brown, "of all nights in the year, this one night must I tarry away from thee. My journey, as thou callest it, forth and back again, must needs be done 'twixt now and sunrise. What, my sweet, pretty wife, dost thou doubt me already, and we but three months married?"

"Then God bless you!" said Faith, with the pink ribbons; "and may you find all well when you come back."

5   "Amen!" cried Goodman Brown. "Say thy prayers, dear Faith, and go to bed at dusk, and no harm will come to thee."

So they parted; and the young man pursued his way until, being about to turn the corner by the meeting-house, he looked back and saw the head of Faith still peeping after him with a melancholy air, in spite of her pink ribbons.

"Poor little Faith!" thought he, for his heart smote him. "What a wretch am I to leave her on such an errand! She talks of dreams, too. Methought as she spoke there was trouble in her face, as if a dream had warned her what work is to be done to-night. But no, no; 'twould kill her to think it. Well, she's a blessed angel on earth; and after this one night I'll cling to her skirts and follow her to heaven."

With this excellent resolve for the future, Goodman Brown felt himself justified in making more haste on his present evil purpose. He had taken a dreary road, darkened by all the gloomiest trees of the forest, which barely stood aside to let the narrow path creep through, and closed immediately behind. It was all as lonely as could be; and there is this peculiarity in such a solitude, that the traveller knows not who may be concealed by the innumerable trunks and the thick boughs overhead; so that with lonely footsteps he may yet be passing through an unseen multitude.

"There may be a devilish Indian behind every tree," said Goodman Brown to himself; and he glanced fearfully behind him as he added, "What if the devil himself should be at my very elbow!"

10   His head being turned back, he passed a crook of the road, and, looking forward again, beheld the figure of a man, in grave and decent attire, seated at the foot of an old tree. He arose at Goodman Brown's approach and walked onward side by side with him.

"You are late, Goodman Brown," said he. "The clock of the Old South was striking as I came through Boston, and that is full fifteen minutes agone."

"Faith kept me back a while," replied the young man, with a tremor in his voice, caused by the sudden appearance of his companion, though not wholly unexpected.

It was now deep dusk in the forest, and deepest in that part of it where these two were journeying. As nearly as could be discerned, the second traveller was about fifty years old, apparently in the same rank of life as Goodman Brown, and bearing a considerable resemblance to him, though perhaps more in expression than features. Still they might have been taken for father and son. And yet, though the elder person was as simply clad as the younger, and as simple in manner too, he had an indescribable air of one who knew the world, and who would not have felt abashed at the governor's dinner table or in King William's court, were it possible that his affairs should call him thither. But the only thing about him that could be fixed upon as remarkable was his staff, which bore the likeness of a great black snake, so curiously wrought that it might almost be seen to twist and wriggle itself like a living serpent. This, of course, must have been an ocular deception, assisted by the uncertain light.

"Come, Goodman Brown," cried his fellow-traveller, "this is a dull pace for the beginning of a journey. Take my staff, if you are so soon weary."

15   "Friend," said the other, exchanging his slow pace for a full stop, "having kept covenant by meeting thee here, it is my purpose now to return whence I came. I have scruples touching the matter thou wot'st of."

"Sayest thou so?" replied he of the serpent, smiling apart. "Let us walk on, nevertheless, reasoning as we go; and if I convince thee not thou shalt turn back. We are but a little way in the forest yet."

"Too far! too far!" exclaimed the goodman, unconsciously resuming his walk. "My father never went into the woods on such an errand, nor his father before him. We have been a race of honest men and good Christians since the days of the martyrs; and shall I be the first of the name of Brown that ever took this path and kept"—

"Such company, thou wouldst say," observed the elder person, interpreting his pause. "Well said, Goodman Brown! I have been as well acquainted with your family as with ever a one among the Puritans; and that's no trifle to say. I helped your grandfather, the constable, when he lashed the Quaker woman so smartly through the streets of Salem; and it was I that brought your father a pitch-pine knot, kindled at my own hearth, to set fire to an Indian village, in King Philip's war. They were my good friends, both; and many a pleasant walk have we had along this path, and returned merrily after midnight. I would fain be friends with you for their sake."

"If it be as thou sayest," replied Goodman Brown, "I marvel they never spoke of these matters: or, verily, I marvel not, seeing that the least rumor of the sort would have driven them from New England. We are a people of prayer, and good works to boot, and abide no such wickedness."

20   "Wickedness or not," said the traveller with the twisted staff, "I have a very general acquaintance here in New England. The deacons of many a church have drunk the communion wine with me; the selectmen of divers towns make me their chairman; and a majority of the Great and General Court are firm supporters of my interest. The governor and I, too—But these are state secrets."

"Can this be so?" cried Goodman Brown, with a stare of amazement at his undisturbed companion. "Howbeit, I have nothing to do with the governor and council; they have their own ways, and are no rule for a simple husbandman like me. But, were I to go on with thee, how should I meet the eye of that good old man, our minister, at Salem village? Oh, his voice would make me tremble both Sabbath day and lecture day."

Thus far the elder traveller had listened with due gravity; but now burst into a fit of irrepressible mirth, shaking himself so violently that his snake-like staff actually seemed to wriggle in sympathy.

"Ha! ha! ha!" shouted he again and again; then composing himself, "Well, go on, Goodman Brown, go on; but, prithee, don't kill me with laughing."

"Well, then, to end the matter at once," said Goodman Brown, considerably nettled, "there is my wife, Faith. It would break her dear little heart; and I'd rather break my own."

25   "Nay, if that be the case," answered the other, "e'en go thy ways, Goodman Brown. I would not for twenty old women like the one hobbling before us that Faith should come to any harm."

As he spoke he pointed his staff at a female figure on the path, in whom Goodman Brown recognized a very pious and exemplary dame, who had taught him his catechism in youth, and was still his moral and spiritual adviser, jointly with the minister and Deacon Gookin.

"A marvel, truly, that Goody Cloyse should be so far in the wilderness at nightfall," said he. "But with your leave, friend, I shall take a cut through the woods until we have left this Christian woman behind. Being a stranger to you, she might ask whom I was consorting with and whither I was going."

"Be it so," said his fellow-traveller. "Betake you the woods, and let me keep the path."

Accordingly the young man turned aside, but took care to watch his companion, who advanced softly along the road until he had come within a staff's length of the old dame. She, meanwhile, was making the best of her way, with singular speed for so aged a woman, and mumbling some indistinct words—a prayer, doubtless— as she went. The traveller put forth his staff and touched her withered neck with what seemed the serpent's tail.

30   "The devil!" screamed the pious old lady.

"Then Goody Cloyse knows her old friend?" observed the traveller, confronting her and leaning on his writhing stick.

"Ah, forsooth, and is it your worship indeed?" cried the good dame. "Yea, truly is it, and in the very image of my old gossip, Goodman Brown, the grandfather of the silly fellow that now is. But—would your worship believe it?—my broomstick hath strangely disappeared, stolen, as I suspect, by that unhanged witch, Goody Cory, and that, too, when I was all anointed with the juice of smallage, and cinquefoil, and wolf's bane"—

"Mingled with fine wheat and the fat of a new-born babe," said the shape of old Goodman Brown.

"Ah, your worship knows the recipe," cried the old lady, cackling aloud. "So, as I was saying, being all ready for the meeting, and no horse to ride on, I made up my mind to foot it; for they tell me there is a nice young man to be taken into communion to-night. But now your good worship will lend me your arm, and we shall be there in a twinkling."

35   "That can hardly be," answered her friend. "I may not spare you my arm, Goody Cloyse; but here is my staff, if you will."

So saying, he threw it down at her feet, where, perhaps, it assumed life, being one of the rods which its owner had formerly lent to the Egyptian magi. Of this fact, however, Goodman Brown could not take cognizance. He had cast up his eyes in astonishment, and, looking down again, beheld neither Goody Cloyse nor the serpentine staff, but his fellow-traveller alone, who waited for him as calmly as if nothing had happened.

"That old woman taught me my catechism," said the young man; and there was a world of meaning in this simple comment.

They continued to walk onward, while the elder traveller exhorted his companion to make good speed and persevere in the path, discoursing so aptly that his arguments seemed rather to spring up in the bosom of his auditor than to be suggested by himself. As they went, he plucked a branch of maple to serve for a walking stick, and began to strip it of the twigs and little boughs, which were wet with evening dew. The moment his fingers touched them they became strangely withered and dried up as with a week's sunshine. Thus the pair proceeded, at a good free pace, until suddenly, in a gloomy hollow of the road, Goodman Brown sat himself down on the stump of a tree and refused to go any farther.

"Friend," said he, stubbornly, "my mind is made up. Not another step will I budge on this errand. What if a wretched old woman do choose to go to the devil when I thought she was going to heaven: is that any reason why I should quit my dear Faith and go after her?"

40   "You will think better of this by and by," said his acquaintance, composedly. "Sit here and rest yourself a while; and when you feel like moving again, there is my staff to help you along."

Without more words, he threw his companion the maple stick, and was as speedily out of sight as if he had vanished into the deepening gloom. The young man sat a few moments by the roadside, applauding himself greatly, and thinking with how clear a conscience he should meet the minister in his morning walk, nor shrink from the eye of good old Deacon Gookin. And what calm sleep would be his that very night, which was to have been spent so wickedly, but so purely and sweetly now, in the arms of Faith! Amidst these pleasant and praiseworthy meditations, Goodman Brown heard the tramp of horses along the road, and deemed it advisable to conceal himself within the verge of the forest, conscious of the guilty purpose that had brought him thither, though now so happily turned from it.

On came the hoof tramps and the voices of the riders, two grave old voices, conversing soberly as they drew near. These mingled sounds appeared to pass along the road, within a few yards of the young man's hiding-place; but, owing doubtless to the depth of the gloom at that particular spot, neither the travellers nor their steeds were visible. Though their figures brushed the small boughs by the wayside, it could not be seen that they intercepted, even for a moment, the faint gleam from the strip of bright sky athwart which they must have passed. Goodman Brown alternately crouched and stood on tiptoe, pulling aside the branches and thrusting forth his head as far as he durst without discerning so much as a shadow. It vexed him the more, because he could have sworn, were such a thing possible, that he recognized the voices of the minister and Deacon Gookin, jogging along quietly, as they were wont to do, when bound to some ordination or ecclesiastical council. While yet within hearing, one of the riders stopped to pluck a switch.

"Of the two, reverend sir," said the voice like the deacon's, "I had rather miss an ordination dinner than to-night's meeting. They tell me that some of our community are to be here from Falmouth and beyond, and others from Connecticut and Rhode Island, besides several of the Indian powwows, who, after their fashion, know almost as much deviltry as the best of us. Moreover, there is a goodly young woman to be taken into communion."

"Mighty well, Deacon Gookin!" replied the solemn old tones of the minister. "Spur up, or we shall be late. Nothing can be done, you know, until I get on the ground."

45   The hoofs clattered again; and the voices, talking so strangely in the empty air, passed on through the forest, where no church had ever been gathered or solitary

Christian prayed. Whither, then, could these holy men be journeying so deep into the heathen wilderness? Young Goodman Brown caught hold of a tree for support, being ready to sink down on the ground, faint and overburdened with the heavy sickness of his heart. He looked up to the sky, doubting whether there really was a heaven above him. Yet there was the blue arch, and the stars brightening in it.

"With heaven above and Faith below, I will yet stand firm against the devil!" cried Goodman Brown.

While he still gazed upward into the deep arch of the firmament and had lifted his hands to pray, a cloud, though no wind was stirring, hurried across the zenith and hid the brightening stars. The blue sky was still visible, except directly overhead, where this black mass of cloud was sweeping swiftly northward. Aloft in the air, as if from the depths of the cloud, came a confused and doubtful sound of voices. Once the listener fancied that he could distinguish the accents of townspeople of his own, men and women, both pious and ungodly, many of whom he had met at the communion table, and had seen others rioting at the tavern. The next moment, so indistinct were the sounds, he doubted whether he had heard aught but the murmur of the old forest, whispering without a wind. Then came a stronger swell of those familiar tones, heard daily in the sunshine at Salem village, but never until now from a cloud of night. There was one voice, of a young woman, uttering lamentations, yet with an uncertain sorrow, and entreating for some favor, which, perhaps, it would grieve her to obtain; and all the unseen multitude, both saints and sinners, seemed to encourage her onward.

"Faith!" shouted Goodman Brown, in a voice of agony and desperation; and the echoes of the forest mocked him, crying, "Faith! Faith!" as if bewildered wretches were seeking her all through the wilderness.

The cry of grief, rage, and terror was yet piercing the night, when the unhappy husband held his breath for a response. There was a scream, drowned immediately in a louder murmur of voices, fading into far-off laughter, as the dark cloud swept away, leaving the clear and silent sky above Goodman Brown. But something fluttered lightly down through the air and caught on the branch of a tree. The young man seized it, and beheld a pink ribbon.

50   "My Faith is gone!" cried he, after one stupefied moment. "There is no good on earth; and sin is but a name. Come, devil; for to thee is this world given."

And, maddened with despair, so that he laughed loud and long, did Goodman Brown grasp his staff and set forth again, at such a rate that he seemed to fly along the forest path rather than to walk or run. The road grew wilder and drearier and more faintly traced, and vanished at length, leaving him in the heart of the dark wilderness, still rushing onward with the instinct that guides mortal man to evil. The whole forest was peopled with frightful sounds—the creaking of the trees, the howling of wild beasts, and the yell of Indians; while sometimes the wind tolled like a distant church bell, and sometimes gave a broad roar around the traveller, as if all Nature were laughing him to scorn. But he was himself the chief horror of the scene, and shrank not from its other horrors.

"Ha! ha! ha!" roared Goodman Brown when the wind laughed at him. "Let us hear which will laugh loudest. Think not to frighten me with your deviltry. Come witch, come wizard, come Indian powwow, come devil himself, and here comes Goodman Brown. You may as well fear him as he fear you."

In truth, all through the haunted forest there could be nothing more frightful than the figure of Goodman Brown. On he flew among the black pines, brandishing his staff with frenzied gestures, now giving vent to an inspiration of horrid blasphemy, and now shouting forth such laughter as set all the echoes of the forest laughing like demons around him. The fiend in his own shape is less hideous than when he rages in the breast of man. Thus sped the demoniac on his course, until, quivering among the trees, he saw a red light before him, as when the felled trunks and branches of a clearing have been set on fire, and throw up their lurid blaze against the sky, at the hour of midnight. He paused, in a lull of the tempest that had driven him onward, and heard the swell of what seemed a hymn, rolling solemnly from a distance with the weight of many voices. He knew the tune; it was a familiar one in the choir of the village meeting-house. The verse died heavily away, and was lengthened by a chorus, not of human voices, but of all the sounds of the benighted wilderness pealing in awful harmony together. Goodman Brown cried out, and his cry was lost to his own ear by its unison with the cry of the desert.

In the interval of silence he stole forward until the light glared full upon his eyes. At one extremity of an open space, hemmed in by the dark wall of the forest, arose a rock, bearing some rude, natural resemblance either to an altar or a pulpit, and surrounded by four blazing pines, their tops aflame, their stems untouched, like candles at an evening meeting. The mass of foliage that had overgrown the summit of the rock was all on fire, blazing high into the night and fitfully illuminating the whole field. Each pendent twig and leafy festoon was in a blaze. As the red light arose and fell, a numerous congregation alternately shone forth, then disappeared in shadow, and again grew, as it were, out of the darkness, peopling the heart of the solitary woods at once.

55   "A grave and dark-clad company," quoth Goodman Brown.

In truth they were such. Among them, quivering to and fro between gloom and splendor, appeared faces that would be seen next day at the council board of the province, and others which, Sabbath after Sabbath, looked devoutly heavenward, and benignantly over the crowded pews, from the holiest pulpits in the land. Some affirm that the lady of the governor was there. At least there were high dames well known to her, and wives of honored husbands, and widows, a great multitude, and ancient maidens, all of excellent repute, and fair young girls, who trembled lest their mothers should espy them. Either the sudden gleams of light flashing over the obscure field bedazzled Goodman Brown, or he recognized a score of the church members of Salem village famous for their especial sanctity. Good old Deacon Gookin had arrived, and waited at the skirts of that venerable saint, his revered pastor. But, irreverently consorting with these grave, reputable, and pious people, these elders of the church, these chaste dames and dewy virgins, there were men of dissolute lives and women of spotted fame, wretches given over to all mean and filthy vice, and suspected even of horrid crimes. It was strange to see that the good shrank not from the wicked, nor were the sinners abashed by the saints. Scattered also among their pale-faced enemies were the Indian priests, or powwows, who had often scared their native forest with more hideous incantations than any known to English witchcraft.

"But where is Faith?" thought Goodman Brown; and, as hope came into his heart, he trembled.

Another verse of the hymn arose, a slow and mournful strain, such as the pious love, but joined to words which expressed all that our nature can conceive of sin, and darkly hinted at far more. Unfathomable to mere mortals is the lore of fiends. Verse after verse was sung; and still the chorus of the desert swelled between like the deepest tone of a mighty organ; and with the final peal of that dreadful anthem there came a sound, as if the roaring wind, the rushing streams, the howling beasts, and every other voice of the unconcerted wilderness were mingling and according with the voice of guilty man in homage to the prince of all. The four blazing pines threw up a loftier flame, and obscurely discovered shapes and visages of horror on the smoke wreaths above the impious assembly. At the same moment the fire on the rock shot redly forth and formed a glowing arch above its base, where now appeared a figure. With reverence be it spoken, the figure bore no slight similitude, both in garb and manner, to some grave divine of the New England churches.

"Bring forth the converts!" cried a voice that echoed through the field and rolled into the forest.

60   At the word, Goodman Brown stepped forth from the shadow of the trees and approached the congregation, with whom he felt a loathful brotherhood by the sympathy of all that was wicked in his heart. He could have well-nigh sworn that the shape of his own dead father beckoned him to advance, looking downward from a smoke wreath, while a woman, with dim features of despair, threw out her hand to warn him back. Was it his mother? But he had no power to retreat one step, nor to resist, even in thought, when the minister and good old Deacon Gookin seized his arms and led him to the blazing rock. Thither came also the slender form of a veiled female, led between Goody Cloyse, that pious teacher of the catechism, and Martha Carrier, who had received the devil's promise to be queen of hell. A rampant hag was she. And there stood the proselytes beneath the canopy of fire.

"Welcome, my children," said the dark figure, "to the communion of your race. Ye have found thus young your nature and your destiny. My children, look behind you!"

They turned; and flashing forth, as it were, in a sheet of flame, the fiend worshippers were seen; the smile of welcome gleamed darkly on every visage.

"There," resumed the sable form, "are all whom ye have reverenced from youth. Ye deemed them holier than yourselves, and shrank from your own sin, contrasting it with their lives of righteousness and prayerful aspirations heavenward. Yet here are they all in my worshipping assembly. This night it shall be granted you to know their secret deeds: how hoary-bearded elders of the church have whispered wanton words to the young maids of their households; how many a woman, eager for widows' weeds, has given her husband a drink at bedtime and let him sleep his last sleep in her bosom; how beardless youths have made haste to inherit their fathers' wealth; and how fair damsels—blush not, sweet ones—have dug little graves in the garden, and bidden me, the sole guest, to an infant's funeral. By the sympathy of your human hearts for sin ye shall scent out all the places—whether in church, bed-chamber, street, field, or forest—where crime has been committed, and shall exult to behold the whole earth one stain of guilt, one mighty blood spot. Far more than this. It shall be yours to penetrate, in every bosom, the deep mystery of sin, the fountain of all wicked arts, and which inexhaustibly supplies more evil impulses than human power—than my power at its utmost—can make manifest in deeds. And now, my children, look upon each other."

They did so; and, by the blaze of the hell-kindled torches, the wretched man beheld his Faith, and the wife her husband, trembling before that unhallowed altar.

65 "Lo, there ye stand, my children," said the figure, in a deep and solemn tone, almost sad with its despairing awfulness, as if his once angelic nature could yet mourn for our miserable race. "Depending upon one another's hearts, ye had still hoped that virtue were not all a dream. Now are ye undeceived. Evil is the nature of mankind. Evil must be your only happiness. Welcome again, my children, to the communion of your race."

"Welcome," repeated the fiend worshippers, in one cry of despair and triumph.

And there they stood, the only pair, as it seemed, who were yet hesitating on the verge of wickedness in this dark world. A basin was hollowed, naturally, in the rock. Did it contain water, reddened by the lurid light? or was it blood? or, per-chance, a liquid flame? Herein did the shape of evil dip his hand and prepare to lay the mark of baptism upon their foreheads, that they might be partakers of the mystery of sin, more conscious of the secret guilt of others, both in deed and thought, than they could now be of their own. The husband cast one look at his pale wife, and Faith at him. What polluted wretches would the next glance show them to each other, shuddering alike at what they disclosed and what they saw!

"Faith! Faith!" cried the husband, "look up to heaven, and resist the wicked one."

Whether Faith obeyed he knew not. Hardly had he spoken when he found himself amid calm night and solitude, listening to a roar of the wind which died heavily away through the forest. He staggered against the rock, and felt it chill and damp; while a hanging twig, that had been all on fire, besprinkled his cheek with the coldest dew.

70 The next morning young Goodman Brown came slowly into the street of Salem village, staring around him like a bewildered man. The good old minister was taking a walk along the graveyard to get an appetite for breakfast and meditate his sermon, and bestowed a blessing, as he passed, on Goodman Brown. He shrank from the ven-erable saint as if to avoid an anathema. Old Deacon Gookin was at domestic wor-ship, and the holy words of his prayer were heard through the open window. "What God doth the wizard pray to?" quoth Goodman Brown. Goody Cloyse, that excellent old Christian, stood in the early sunshine at her own lattice, catechizing a little girl who had brought her a pint of morning's milk. Goodman Brown snatched away the child as from the grasp of the fiend himself. Turning the corner by the meeting-house, he spied the head of Faith, with the pink ribbons, gazing anxiously forth, and bursting into such joy at sight of him that she skipped along the street and almost kissed her husband before the whole village. But Goodman Brown looked sternly and sadly into her face, and passed on without a greeting.

Had Goodman Brown fallen asleep in the forest and only dreamed a wild dream of a witch-meeting?

Be it so if you will; but alas! it was a dream of evil omen for young Goodman Brown. A stern, a sad, a darkly meditative, a distrustful, if not a desperate man did he become from the night of that fearful dream. On the Sabbath day, when the congregation were singing a holy psalm, he could not listen because an anthem of sin rushed loudly upon his ear and drowned all the blessed strain. When the minister spoke from the pulpit with power and fervid eloquence, and, with his hand on the open Bible, of the sacred truths of our religion, and of saint-like lives and triumphant deaths, and of future bliss or misery unutterable, then did Goodman Brown turn pale, dreading lest the roof should thunder down upon the gray blasphemer and his hearers. Often, awaking suddenly at midnight, he shrank from the bosom of Faith; and at morning or eventide, when the family knelt down at prayer, he scowled and muttered to himself, and gazed sternly at his wife, and turned away. And when he had lived long, and was borne to his grave a hoary corpse, followed by Faith, an aged woman, and children and grandchildren, a goodly procession, besides neighbors not a few, they carved no hopeful verse upon his tombstone, for his dying hour was gloom.

▶ QUESTIONS FOR READING AND WRITING

1. What is the significance of the names in this story? For example, is Faith aptly named? Explain.
2. In what way does the setting of this story, Puritan New England, influence your response?
3. Why do you suppose the stranger in the woods looks like Goodman Brown himself?
4. Do you think Brown's experience was real or a dream? Explain.
5. This is a story about good and evil. How are they defined here? In what way is this story about human nature? How would you interpret the story's theme?

ERNEST HEMINGWAY (1899–1961)

Ernest Hemingway was born in Oak Park, Illinois, and began his writing career as a newspaper reporter. He was an active participant in World War I, the Spanish Civil War, and World War II, and often used his personal experiences as the source of his work. His direct, spare writing style was a major influence on many writers in the twentieth century. His writing includes A Farewell to Arms *(1929),* For Whom the Bell Tolls *(1940), and* The Old Man and the Sea *(1954). He received the Nobel Prize for literature in 1954.*

HILLS LIKE WHITE ELEPHANTS

[1927]

The hills across the valley of the Ebro were long and white. On this side there was no shade and no trees and the station was between two lines of rails in the sun. Close against the side of the station there was the warm shadow of the building and a curtain, made of strings of bamboo beads, hung across the open door into the bar, to keep out flies. The American and the girl with him sat at a table in the shade, outside the building. It was very hot and the express from Barcelona would come in forty minutes. It stopped at this junction for two minutes and went on to Madrid.

"What should we drink?" the girl asked. She had taken off her hat and put it on the table.

"It's pretty hot," the man said.

"Let's drink beer."

5 "Dos cervezas," the man said into the curtain.

"Big ones?" a woman asked from the doorway.

"Yes. Two big ones."

The woman brought two glasses of beer and two felt pads. She put the felt pads and the beer glasses on the table and looked at the man and the girl. The girl was looking off at the line of hills. They were white in the sun and the country was brown and dry.

"They look like white elephants," she said.

10 "I've never seen one," the man drank his beer.

"No, you wouldn't have."

"I might have," the man said. "Just because you say I wouldn't have doesn't prove anything."

The girl looked at the bead curtain. "They've painted something on it," she said. "What does it say?"

"Anis del Toro. It's a drink."

15 "Could we try it?"

The man called "Listen" through the curtain. The woman came out from the bar.

"Four reales."

"We want two Anis del Toro."

"With water?"

20 "Do you want it with water?"

"I don't know," the girl said. "Is it good with water?"

"It's all right."

"You want them with water?" asked the woman.

"Yes, with water."

25 "It tastes like licorice," the girl said and put the glass down.

"That's the way with everything."

"Yes," said the girl. "Everything tastes of licorice. Especially all the things you've waited so long for, like absinthe."

"Oh, cut it out."

"You started it," the girl said. "I was being amused. I was having a fine time."

30 "Well, let's try and have a fine time."

"All right. I was trying. I said the mountains looked like white elephants. Wasn't that bright?"

"That was bright."

"I wanted to try this new drink. That's all we do, isn't it—look at things and try new drinks?"

"I guess so."

35 The girl looked across at the hills.

"They're lovely hills," she said. "They don't really look like white elephants. I just meant the coloring of their skin through the trees."

"Should we have another drink?"

"All right."

The warm wind blew the bead curtain against the table.

40 "The beer's nice and cool," the man said.

"It's lovely," the girl said.

"It's really an awfully simple operation, Jig," the man said. "It's not really an operation at all."

The girl looked at the ground the table legs rested on.

"I know you wouldn't mind it, Jig. It's really not anything. It's just to let the air in."

45 The girl did not say anything.

"I'll go with you and I'll stay with you all the time. They just let the air in and then it's all perfectly natural."

"Then what will we do afterward?"

"We'll be fine afterward. Just like we were before."

"What makes you think so?"

50 "That's the only thing that bothers us. It's the only thing that's made us unhappy."

The girl looked at the bead curtain, put her hand out and took hold of two of the strings of beads.

"And you think then we'll be all right and be happy."

"I know we will. You don't have to be afraid. I've known lots of people that have done it."

"So have I," said the girl. "And afterward they were all so happy."

55 "Well," the man said, "if you don't want to you don't have to. I wouldn't have you do it if you didn't want to. But I know it's perfectly simple."

"And you really want to?"

"I think it's the best thing to do. But I don't want you to do it if you don't really want to."

"And if I do it you'll be happy and things will be like they were and you'll love me?"

"I love you now. You know I love you."

60 "I know. But if I do it, then it will be nice again if I say things are like white elephants, and you'll like it?"

"I'll love it. I love it now but I just can't think about it. You know how I get when I worry."

"If I do it you won't ever worry?"

"I won't worry about that because it's perfectly simple."

"Then I'll do it. Because I don't care about me."

65   "What do you mean?"

"I don't care about me."

"Well, I care about you."

"Oh, yes. But I don't care about me. And I'll do it and then everything will be fine."

"I don't want you to do it if you feel that way."

70   The girl stood up and walked to the end of the station. Across, on the other side, were fields of grain and trees along the banks of the Ebro. Far away, beyond the river, were mountains. The shadow of a cloud moved across the field of grain and she saw the river through the trees.

"And we could have all this," she said. "And we could have everything and every day we make it more impossible."

"What did you say?"

"I said we could have everything."

"We can have everything."

75   "No, we can't."

"We can have the whole world."

"No, we can't."

"We can go everywhere."

"No, we can't. It isn't ours any more."

80   "It's ours."

"No, it isn't. And once they take it away, you never get it back."

"But they haven't taken it away."

"We'll wait and see."

"Come on back in the shade," he said. "You mustn't feel that way."

85   "I don't feel any way," the girl said. "I just know things."

"I don't want you to do anything that you don't want to do—"

"Nor that isn't good for me," she said. "I know. Could we have another beer?"

"All right. But you've got to realize—"

"I realize," the girl said. "Can't we maybe stop talking?"

90   They sat down at the table and the girl looked across at the hills on the dry side of the valley and the man looked at her and at the table.

"You've got to realize," he said, "that I don't want you to do it if you don't want to. I'm perfectly willing to go through with it if it means anything to you."

"Doesn't it mean anything to you? We could get along."

"Of course it does. But I don't want anybody but you. I don't want any one else. And I know it's perfectly simple."

"Yes, you know it's perfectly simple."

95   "It's all right for you to say that, but I do know it."

"Would you do something for me now?"

"I'd do anything for you."

"Would you please please please please please please please stop talking?"

He did not say anything but looked at the bags against the wall of the station. There were labels on them from all the hotels where they had spent nights.

100 "But I don't want you to," he said, "I don't care anything about it."

"I'll scream," the girl said.

The woman came out through the curtains with two glasses of beer and put them down on the damp felt pads. "The train comes in five minutes," she said.

"What did she say?" asked the girl.

"That the train is coming in five minutes."

105 The girl smiled brightly at the woman, to thank her.

"I'd better take the bags over to the other side of the station," the man said. She smiled at him.

"All right. Then come back and we'll finish the beer."

He picked up the two heavy bags and carried them around the station to the other tracks. He looked up the tracks but could not see the train. Coming back, he walked through the barroom, where people waiting for the train were drinking. He drank an Anis at the bar and looked at the people. They were all waiting reasonably for the train. He went out through the bead curtain. She was sitting at the table and smiled at him.

"Do you feel better?" he asked.

110 "I feel fine," she said. "There's nothing wrong with me. I feel fine."

➤ QUESTIONS FOR READING AND WRITING

1. What are the man and woman discussing? Do you have strong feelings about this topic? If so, how does that influence your response? If you were placed in this situation, what would you say or do?
2. From what point of view is the story told? How does that affect your response?
3. What is the conflict in the story? Is it external, internal, both?
4. Some researchers have suggested that men and women talk to each other with different intentions. Do you see any indication of this in the story? How are you affected by the language of the conversation?
5. What does their conversation tell you about these characters and their relationship? Do you think this relationship has a positive future? Why?

CASE STUDY IN RESEARCH

Thinking About Interpretation, Culture, and Research

James Joyce and *Eveline*

JAMES JOYCE (1882–1941)

James Joyce was one of ten children born into a middle-class family of declining fortunes in a suburb of Dublin, Ireland. In spite of an unhappy childhood dominated by a drunken father, Joyce managed to receive a thorough classical education, first in Jesuit schools and then at University College, Dublin. Though he spent most of his adult life living outside of Ireland, Dublin is the backdrop for nearly all of his work. His three innovative novels, Portrait of the Artist as a Young Man *(1916),* Ulysses *(1922), and* Finnegans Wake *(1939), established him as one of the greatest writers of modern times. "Araby" (p. 51) and "Eveline" are taken from his collection of short stories,* Dubliners, *which appeared in 1914 after an eight-year battle with publishers who feared it would offend important residents of the city.*

EVELINE

[1914]

She sat at the window watching the evening invade the avenue. Her head was leaned against the window curtains and in her nostrils was the odour of dusty cretonne[1]. She was tired.

Few people passed. The man out of the last house passed on his way home; she heard his footsteps clacking along the concrete pavement and afterwards crunching on the cinder path before the new red houses. One time there used to be a field there in which they used to play every evening with other people's children. Then a man from Belfast bought the field and built houses in it—not like their little

---

[1] **cretonne** cotton or linen cloth used for curtains

brown houses but bright brick houses with shining roofs. The children of the avenue used to play together in that field—the Devines, the Waters, the Dunns, little Keogh the cripple, she and her brothers and sisters. Ernest, however, never played: he was too grown up. Her father used often to hunt them in out of the field with his blackthorn stick; but usually little Keogh used to keep nix and call out when he saw her father coming. Still they seemed to have been rather happy then. Her father was not so bad then; and besides, her mother was alive. That was a long time ago; she and her brothers and sisters were all grown up; her mother was dead. Tizzie Dunn was dead, too, and the Waters had gone back to England. Everything changes. Now she was going to go away like the others, to leave her home.

Home! She looked around the room, reviewing all its familiar objects which she had dusted once a week for so many years, wondering where on earth all the dust came from. Perhaps she would never see again those familiar objects from which she had never dreamed of being divided. And yet during all those years she had never found out the name of the priest whose yellowing photograph hung on the wall above the broken harmonium beside the coloured print of the promises made to Blessed Margaret Mary Alacoque. He had been a school friend of her father. Whenever he showed the photograph to a visitor her father used to pass it with a casual word:

—He is in Melbourne now.

5   She had consented to go away, to leave her home. Was that wise? She tried to weigh each side of the question. In her home anyway she had shelter and food; she had those whom she had known all her life about her. Of course she had to work hard both in the house and at business. What would they say of her in the Stores when they found out that she had run away with a fellow? Say she was a fool, perhaps; and her place would be filled up by advertisement. Miss Gavan would be glad. She had always had an edge on her, especially whenever there were people listening.

—Miss Hill, don't you see these ladies are waiting?

—Look lively, Miss Hill, please.

She would not cry many tears at leaving the Stores.

But in her new home, in a distant unknown country, it would not be like that. Then she would be married—she, Eveline. People would treat her with respect then. She would not be treated as her mother had been. Even now, though she was over nineteen, she sometimes felt herself in danger of her father's violence. She knew it was that that had given her the palpitations. When they were growing up he had never gone for her, like he used to go for Harry and Ernest, because she was a girl; but latterly he had begun to threaten her and say what he would do to her only for her dead mother's sake. And now she had nobody to protect her. Ernest was dead and Harry, who was in the church decorating business, was nearly always down somewhere in the country. Besides, the invariable squabble for money on Saturday nights had begun to weary her unspeakably. She always gave her entire wages—seven shillings—and Harry always sent up what he could but the trouble was to get any money from her father. He said she used to squander the money, that she had no head, that he wasn't going to give her his hard-earned money to throw about the streets, and much more, for he was usually fairly bad of a Saturday night. In the end he would give her the money and ask her had she any intention of buying Sunday's dinner. Then she had to rush out as quickly as she could and do her marketing, holding her black leather purse tightly in her hand as she elbowed her way through the crowds and returning home late under her load of provisions. She had hard work to keep the house together and to see that the two young children who had been left to her charge went to school regularly and got their meals regularly. It was hard work—a hard life—but now that she was about to leave it she did not find it a wholly undesirable life.

10   She was about to explore another life with Frank. Frank was very kind, manly, open-hearted. She was to go away with him by the night-boat to be his wife and to live with him in Buenos Ayres where he had a home waiting for her. How well she remembered the first time she had seen him; he was lodging in a house on the main road where she used to visit. It seemed a few weeks ago. He was standing at the gate, his peaked cap pushed back on his head and his hair tumbled forward over a face of bronze. Then they had come to know each other. He used to meet her outside the Stores every evening and see her home. He took her to see *The Bohemian Girl* and she felt elated as she sat in an unaccustomed part of the theatre with him. He was awfully fond of music and sang a little. People knew that they were courting and, when he sang about the lass that loves a sailor, she always felt pleasantly confused. He used to call her Poppens out of fun. First of all it had been an excitement for her to have a fellow and then she had begun to like him. He had tales of distant countries. He had started as a deck boy at a pound a month on a ship of the Allan Line going out to Canada. He told her the names of the ships he had been on and the names of the different services. He had sailed through the Straits of Magellan and he told her stories of the terrible Patagonians. He had fallen on his feet in Buenos Ayres, he said, and had come over to the old country just for a holiday. Of course, her father had found out the affair and had forbidden her to have anything to say to him.

—I know these sailor chaps, he said.

One day he had quarreled with Frank and after that she had to meet her lover secretly.

The evening deepened in the avenue. The white of two letters in her lap grew indistinct. One was to Harry; the other was to her father. Ernest had been her favourite but she liked Harry too. Her father was becoming old lately, she noticed; he would miss her. Sometimes he could be very nice. Not long before, when she had been laid up for a day, he had read her out a ghost story and made toast for her at the fire. Another day, when their mother was alive, they had all gone for a picnic to the Hill of Howth. She remembered her father putting on her mother's bonnet to make the children laugh.

Her time was running out but she continued to sit by the window, leaning her head against the window curtain, inhaling the odour of dusty cretonne. Down far in the avenue she could hear a street organ playing. She knew the air. Strange that it should come that very night to remind her of the promise to her mother, her promise to keep the home together as long as she could. She remembered the last night of her mother's illness; she was again in the close dark room at the other side of the hall and outside she heard a melancholy air of Italy. The organ-player had been ordered to go away and given sixpence. She remembered her father strutting back into the sickroom saying:

15   ✍ —Damned Italians! coming over here!

As she mused the pitiful vision of her mother's life laid its spell on the very quick of her being—that life of commonplace sacrifices closing in final craziness. She trembled as she heard again her mother's voice saying constantly with foolish insistence:

—Derevaun Seraun! Derevaun Seraun!

She stood up in a sudden impulse of terror. Escape! She must escape! Frank would save her. He would give her life, perhaps love, too. But she wanted to live. Why should she be unhappy? She had a right to happiness. Frank would take her in his arms, fold her in his arms. He would save her.

She stood among the swaying crowd in the station at the North Wall. He held her hand and she knew that he was speaking to her, saying something about the passage over and over again. The station was full of soldiers with brown baggages. Through the wide doors of the sheds she caught a glimpse of the black mass of the boat, lying in beside the quay wall, with illumined portholes. She answered nothing. She felt her cheek pale and cold and, out of a maze of distress, she prayed to God to direct her, to show her what was her duty. The boat blew a long mournful whistle into the mist. If she went, to-morrow she would be on the sea with Frank, steaming towards Buenos Ayres. Their passage had been booked. Could she still draw back after all he had done for her? Her distress awoke a nausea in her body and she kept moving her lips in silent fervent prayer.

20   A bell clanged upon her heart. She felt him seize her hand:

—Come!

All the seas of the world tumbled about her heart. He was drawing her into them: he would drown her. She gripped with both hands at the iron railing.

—Come!

No! No! No! It was impossible. Her hands clutched the iron in frenzy. Amid the seas she sent a cry of anguish!

25   —Eveline! Evvy!

He rushed beyond the barrier and called to her to follow. He was shouted at to go on but he still called to her. She set her white face to him, passive, like a helpless animal. Her eyes gave him no sign of love or farewell or recognition.

➤ QUESTIONS FOR READING AND WRITING

1. To what extent is your response to this story influenced by your own background or experience?
2. Were you hoping that Eveline would leave or stay? Why?
3. Describe Frank. What does he represent to Eveline?
4. To what extent is Eveline a prisoner of her setting? Of her own culture?
5. Do you think Eveline really has a choice at the end of the story? Explain.

Interpretation, Culture, and Research

As we have emphasized throughout this book, writing an effective essay is not always a straightforward process. Many factors may influence the choices we make along the way. This is particularly true when using secondary source research in our writing. One possible topic, and a rich source for research, may be the connection we find between our own backgrounds or culture and that presented in the work. The best research springs from our need to know more—to fill in the gaps in our knowledge. This research is not imposed on our writing but evolves naturally from it.

Below is the commentary of Prof. Alan Devenish, followed by the research essay of his student, Kevin Chamberlain. Dr. Devenish recalls their conferences and the process Kevin experienced while writing his research essay. He explains that Kevin did not set out to do research. While reading James Joyce's short story "Eveline," Kevin found similarities between himself and the protagonist. He started to write a personal essay, but his interest in her as a character inspired him to want to know more. He sought information about the conditions of her background. This, in turn, led him to do research about the author and to read more of Joyce's work. What began as a personal response developed naturally into an informative and personally meaningful research essay.

All readers may not have such a strong personal identification with the work or, like Kevin, follow up their reading of one work by reading other works by the same author. But the process Kevin followed is a strong model for anyone doing secondary source research. He did not begin by gathering all the information he could and refashioning it into an essay. He began by writing a draft of his own response. In the process, he identified the issues he wanted to explore and generated the questions he needed to answer to make this exploration successful. The objective of his search was not to gather the most information, but to gather answers to his questions. His search was motivated by his "need to know," and it was only through his early writing and reflection that *what* he needed to know became clear to him.

Professor Devenish's Commentary

Before beginning my commentary on his essay "Leaving Home," I met with Kevin Chamberlain to discuss his paper. In preparation for our informal interview I asked him to write a short "process reflection" describing the researching, writing and revising of his essay. I am tempted to delete this last phrase—"researching, writing, and revising"—because Kevin's actual process did not follow this neat, if unnatural, progression of discrete steps or stages. His process was rich in recursions and excursions, in rethinkings that led to new inquiries, which in turn led to further thinking and writing. The finished essay is not the one Kevin thought he was going to write when he started out.

So, how *did* he start out? Why did he choose to write on James Joyce's "Eveline," a story about a young woman's unsuccessful struggle to leave home, when he had any number of literary works and authors from which to select? "I was drawn to this story because I, too, am attached to my home and family," Kevin writes in his essay. "I have lived in the same house all my life, and I often dread the thought of leaving." In his process reflection Kevin writes similarly: "I was able to empathize with Eveline because I am at a similar point in my life— too long in the nest." Kevin's impetus for this paper was at heart a personal one. He responded emotionally to the title character's fears and desires, to the terrible conflict between home and self. Kevin also notes that he had read other works by Joyce and enjoyed his "writing style." Clearly, however, "Eveline" struck a special chord.

In our conversation, Kevin spoke of his initial impatience with the character Eveline, how he felt "anxious to push this person out of her home—to do what I would do." On further reading and research, however, he tempered this impulse, as he looked more closely at the conditions and culture that gave rise to Eveline's quandry. Reading Joyce's *Portrait of the Artist as a Young Man* and *Dubliners*, along with relevant critical research on the author and Ireland itself, brought Kevin to a more complex and empathetic understanding of the character. No doubt, too, rereading the story reminded Kevin of his own unresolved tensions between loyalties to home and family on one hand, and change and "beginning my own life" on the other.

Along with Kevin's intimate connection with the story's protagonist must be added another: culture. Eveline is not only a person struggling with fierce inner conflicts, she is a person living in a particular place and time, Ireland of the early twentieth century. Again, in his process, Kevin writes of "being part Irish" and how this cultural heritage leads him to share similar values with Eveline in regard to family, religion, and change. At the same time, he realized that he needed to know more of the particular Ireland of Joyce's "Eveline" and how the author "intertwines political, social, religious, and economic themes into his writing . . . That is where the research began."

Cultural relevance, then, became a starting point for inquiry into the important complexities that form the backdrop of Joyce's story. Interestingly, Kevin did not presume that his own Irish heritage gave him a satisfactory understanding of the character or story. Being part Irish did, however, stir his interest in the Ireland that gave rise to Eveline, and indeed to Joyce himself. In our interview, Kevin made the surprising assertion that in Joyce the characters are "the least important things in the story. The characters show one whole side of life, are representative of a whole class of people." What Kevin meant by this, I believe, is that "Eveline," far from being the idiosyncratic story of a particularly troubled young woman, is the story of many an Irish woman of Joyce's day, these Evelines holding fast to the dock railing as their figurative or real ships left for distant ports. In his essay, Kevin makes amply clear the enormous historical, economic, religious, and familial forces that converged into a sort of paralysis in Eveline and so many like her, and how these selfsame forces acted more centrifugally on Joyce and others like him who broke from home, and "the old sow" of Ireland "that eats her farrow," as Kevin quotes Joyce's biting indictment. Most notable in this analysis is that Kevin undertook his research from a need to now more of the very culture whose personal relevance first connected him to the story.

Here I would like to quote Kevin's description of how his initial intent to write an interpretive essay relying solely on his reading of "Eveline" evolved rather organically into a more complete inquiry:

> My first step was to respond to the story, writing an essay that examined the primary source [the story "Eveline"] without any outside influences such as literary criticism. Once the draft was completed I made a list of things in the story that I did not understand but felt were important to understanding the work as a whole . . . . . . By making a list of things I did not understand, I had something to look for in the outside sources . . . . . . Once I felt I had enough information to revise my first draft, I added in the research to my already existing essay . . . without letting my research write the paper for me. I simply used the research to support my already existing thesis.

Clearly, Kevin did not start out with either the requirement or the intention of writing a research paper. His method was not to get books out of the library and then figure out a way to incorporate all the research into a readable—or writable—essay. Rather, as his process reflection here and his finished essay demonstrate, he *grew* into the research, beginning with that important personal connection, that moment of recognition between himself and the text. He saw something of himself in Eveline, as he did in the Ireland that lived in her. From this recognition he wrote his first draft, a draft that led him to other questions. These questions, in turn, led him to further reading and writing, thereby strengthening the original connection between himself and the story. He repeated this process through several revisions, each time returning to the library when he felt "there were things that were still not strong enough," until he had satisfied the questions raised by his reading and writing. What started, then, as a response to a short story related to his own life grew to a larger inquiry into cultural contexts, literary criticism, and the author's work. That initial personal response, however, was not simply a starting point for the "real" work of research and writing. From Kevin's process reflections, as from his completed essay, I am convinced that his ongoing—indeed deepened—connection with the character and culture of this story sustained his research, writing, and revision throughout.

By citing Kevin's approach to writing about a literary work I am not claiming that students need to share a cultural identity with an author or text, or find exact parallels with the circumstances of their own lives. What I do believe Kevin's example illustrates is the importance of a personal connection with the work. Clearly, Kevin did not need a male protagonist in a familiar, contemporary setting in order to "relate." He did, however, feel a need to find in the work something that touched him. As it happened, he found this through cultural and psychological perspectives. More important, he then broadened these perspectives, questioning what he read and wrote, adding to it, seeing what was previously unseen. In the process, he learned about women in Joyce's Ireland; he read other works by the author; he saw historical and political patterns in Eveline's painful stasis; he deciphered religious references as significant symbols; he studied the human heart through the particulars of one fictive but very human creation. As important, I think, is that Kevin came to experience this story and his response to it as integral to his own life.

A Student Essay—Research and Culture

Kevin Chamberlain

Dr. Devenish

English 102

March 20, 200X

✗ Leaving Home

James Joyce's short story "Eveline" is the story of a girl who turns down a marriage proposal because of her attachment to her home and family. I was drawn to this story because I, too, am attached to my home and family. I have lived in the same house all of my life, and I often dread the thought of leaving. I live along with my mother and we depend on each other in many ways. I take care of the house, inside and out, in return for room and board. The problem is that if I were to move out, my mother would not be able to maintain the house. Such a change would alter both our lives in different ✗ ways. It would be the beginning of my own life but the end of hers. I know that this must happen sooner or later, but I sometimes feel it is my duty to stay and help out even if it only prolongs the inevitable. Eveline, the main character in Joyce's story, is faced with a similar dilemma. Should she abandon her father and begin her own life? Or should she stay home and take care of her father, but give up her own future in the process?

Eveline's devotion to her father stems from a promise to her deceased mother to keep her home together. Even after the home falls apart, Eveline feels that she must stay. On the surface, it is Eveline's tale of how and why she can not leave. Beneath the surface, the story is a metaphor for womens' conditions in turn-of-the-century Ireland. There are many factors that influence

Eveline's decision, but the most compelling are religion, family, and fear of change.

There is not much to the story on the surface. It appears to be nothing more than the story of a girl who makes a bad decision, but Joyce has neatly interwoven a metaphor for what keeps Irish people in an idle state. He is using his story to point out how Irish people, especially women, let themselves be trapped. He does not entirely blame the individual, because conditions gave people a poor foundation to build on. Finally, when there is some certainty, they cling to it, and are reluctant to change. This is the plight of Eveline.

In the 1890s, when this story was set, Ireland was still suffering the effects of the potato famine of the 1840s. Around this time, the country had lost millions of its people to starvation and emigration. The people left behind suffered many effects. "For a full century after 1845, poverty was widespread, jobs were few and precarious, salaries meager, and opportunities for advancement rare" (Walzl 33). This was especially true for women, who were relegated to more traditional roles.

Lack of financial resources led people to put off marriage. Postponing marriages kept women with their families longer, causing them to become dependent on that lifestyle. As one becomes more devoted to family, the option of marriage becomes less likely. Eveline's chance to marry Frank, her fiancé, is important because it may be her only chance to marry and leave the country. By deciding not to marry Frank, she identifies herself as one woman who will not leave her homeland. In this sense, Eveline is representative of many of her fellow citizens. "Even when emigration had become established as an almost automatic part of rural life, it conflicted sharply with the high value that Irish country people put upon communalism, kinship and a sense of place. To leave here meant a psychic disruption" (Foster 351).

The story opens with Eveline sitting motionless, contemplating leaving the home she has known. After her mother's death, Eveline takes over her duties in the home and tends to her abusive father. "Growing up he had never gone for her . . . but latterly he had begun to threaten her" (Dubliners 38). Usually, his rage is about money and the idea that she squanders it. The truth is that after working at her job all week, she gives her wages to him, ultimately to support his drinking habits. A family that has a minimal income

[ís]

should treat alcohol as a luxury, yet "he was usually fairly bad of a Saturday night" (38).

This kind of life should create a fear of remaining at home, yet Eveline feels that the unknown is much more frightening. It is clear that her social paralysis is self-inflicted and reinforced by her beliefs. Perhaps it is the thought that her father cannot survive without her that keeps her from leaving. She expends herself and her earnings just to support him. In a way she is acting more like a wife or mother than like a daughter: "She had to work hard both in the house and at business" (37), but her marriage to Frank
[will]
would change all that. He offers to take her to Buenos Aires, where she could live a comfortable life, but she finally chooses not to go with him because of her attachment to the life she has known. She is paralyzed by her fear of change and her devotion to her family.

During the scene that depicts her mother's final moments, when the promise to keep the home together is made, Eveline muses that her mother's life is a "life of commonplace sacrifices closing in final craziness" (40). This describes Eveline's life as well. Her own commonplace sacrifice is staying in her home and tending to her father. To her, it is a necessary sacrifice for her family's sake not to take interest in her own future. Her final craziness happens when she tries to escape. In the final scene at the station, she "clutched [clutches] the iron [railing] in frenzy" trying to hold on to the life she has known (41). Her decision could mark the end of her social existence. She will probably *delete last sentence* never have this kind of opportunity again. Even if the opportunity again were to arise she would most likely act the same way.

It is obvious that religion plays a role in Eveline's decision as well. In his description of her home, Joyce includes a "coloured print of the promises made to Blessed Margaret Alacoque" (37). This is a symbol of devotion to home and family in the Catholic church. The promises that are made by Jesus himself include, "I will establish peace in their homes. / I will comfort them in all their afflictions. / I will be their secure refuge during life, and above all in death" (Gifford 49). Joyce refers to this in his narration because Eveline's promise to her mother parallels these promises. He does this to show how religion only increases the guilt felt by someone who leaves home to make a life for herself. Since Eveline's promise was to keep her family together, it becomes impossible for her to leave. In the final scene, she stands at the station, unable to board the boat: "she prayed to God to direct her, to show here what was her duty" (40). It is clear that she feels it is her duty to stay at home and give up her only chance at starting a life of her own.

There is great emphasis on the promise that Eveline made to her mother, "to keep the home together as long as she could" (40). This might be seen, metaphorically, as the people of Ireland promising to stay together as long as possible because their own country has been taken from them. Weakened by the famine and exploited by the British, the country was in shambles. Although Ireland did not have control of its own government, the people maintained collective unity.

During this time, one of the country's worst periods, people depended on each other to survive. Afterward, the people had trouble getting back on their feet and relied mostly on religion to guide them. Joyce reacted against this. He felt that people should get out of Ireland and writes that "Ireland is the old sow that eats her farrow" (Portrait 220). He makes his feelings very clear in this story by drawing on Eveline's promise to her mother.

Throughout the story, Eveline is tormented by the thought of leaving her home and it ultimately consumes her. Her home life is not at all desirable, yet she stays. It is a condition often depicted by Joyce in his stories: "[Joyce] expresses the fragmentation experienced by individuals unable to rely on old certainties, whether religious, economic, or political" (Werner 27). It is these certainties that Eveline and many others were unable to part with. Her faith and bond to her family helped instill a fear of change that, for her, is too great to overcome.

I know from my own experience that this is true. One of the main reasons that I still live at home is that I am dependent on the security and simplicity of being where I have always been. By living with what little family I have, I know that I will never go hungry or worry about where I will sleep. I know what is around every corner because I most likely put it there. I am also concerned about what will happen to my home and family when I am gone. There is always the proud fear that people cannot survive without me, and the belittling fear that I can't survive without them. Perhaps it is one or both of these fears that influence Eveline's actions and ultimately control them.

Works Cited

Foster, Roy F. <u>Modern Ireland 1600–1972</u>. London: Penguin, 1988.

Gifford, Don. <u>Joyce Annotated</u>. Calif.: University of California Press, 1982,
   48–52.

Joyce, James. <u>Dubliners: Text, Criticism, and Notes</u>. ed. Robert Scholes and
   A. Walton Litz. New York: Penguin, 1969.

—. <u>Portrait of the Artist as a Young Man</u>. New York: Penguin, 1987.

Walzl, Florence L. "Dubliners: Women in Irish Society." <u>Women in Joyce</u>.
   Suzette Hanke and Elaine Unkless. Champaign-Urbana, Illinois:
   University of Illinois Press, 1982, 31–54.

Werner, Craig Hanson. <u>Dubliners. A Student's Companion to the Stories</u>.
   Robert Lecker. Boston: Twayne Publishers, 1988.

FRANZ KAFKA (1883–1924)

*A German-Jew born and raised in Bohemia
(today the Czech Republic), Franz Kafka lived
most of his unhappy life in a tiny apartment
with his parents in the city of Prague. Trained
in the law, Kafka worked for the state insurance
company, and wrote at night, in part to combat
his lifelong insomnia. He was often reluctant to
submit his work for publication, and during
his lifetime, he published only a few short stories and two novellas—*The Metamorphosis
(1915) and In the Penal Colony *(1919). When
Kafka died of tuberculosis in 1924, he left
instructions in his will asking his longtime
friend and editor, Max Brod, to destroy his unpublished manuscripts. Ignoring his
wishes, Brod edited and published his paper, which included three novels:* The Trial
(1925), The Castle *(1926), and* Amerika *(1927). Kafka's work is invariably dark, and,
like the protagonist in "The Hunger Artist," full of characters who search for purity or
goodness in an irrational world.*

A HUNGER ARTIST [1924]

During these last decades the interest in professional fasting has markedly dimin-
ished. It used to pay very well to stage such great performances under one's own
management, but today that is quite impossible. We live in a different world now.
At one time the whole town took a lively interest in the hunger artist; from day to

day of his fast the excitement mounted; everybody wanted to see him at least once a day; there were people who bought season tickets for the last few days and sat from morning till night in front of his small barred cage; even in the nighttime there were visiting hours, when the whole effect was heightened by torch flares; on fine days the cage was set out in the open air, and then it was the children's special treat to see the hunger artist; for their elders he was often just a joke that happened to be in fashion, but the children stood open-mouthed, holding each other's hands for greater security, marveling at him as he sat there pallid in black tights, with his ribs sticking out so prominently, not even on a seat but down among straw on the ground, sometimes giving a courteous nod, answering questions with a constrained smile, or perhaps stretching an arm through the bars so that one might feel how thin it was, and then again withdrawing deep into himself, paying no attention to anyone or anything, not even to the all-important striking of the clock that was the only piece of furniture in his cage, but merely staring into vacancy with half-shut eyes, now and then taking a sip from a tiny glass of water to moisten his lips.

Besides casual onlookers there were also relays of permanent watchers selected by the public, usually butchers, strangely enough, and it was their task to watch the hunger artist day and night, three of them at a time, in case he should have some secret recourse to nourishment. This was nothing but a formality, instituted to reassure the masses, for the initiates knew well enough that during his fast the artist would never in any circumstances, not even under forcible compulsion, swallow the smallest morsel of food: the honor of his profession forbade it. Not every watcher, of course, was capable of understanding this, there were often groups of night watchers who were very lax in carrying out their duties and deliberately huddled together in a retired corner to play cards with great absorption, obviously intending to give the hunger artist the chance of a little refreshment, which they supposed he could draw from some private hoard. Nothing annoyed the artist more than such watchers; they made him miserable; they made his fast seem unendurable; sometimes he mastered his feebleness sufficiently to sing during their watch for as long as he could keep going, to show them how unjust their suspicions were. But that was of little use; they only wondered at his cleverness in being able to fill his mouth even while singing. Much more to his taste were the watchers who sat close up to the bars, who were not content with the dim night lighting of the hall but focused him in the full glare of the electric pocket torch given them by the impresario. The harsh light did not trouble him at all, in any case he could never sleep properly, and he could always drowse a little, whatever the light, at any hour, even when the hall was thronged with noisy onlookers. He was quite happy at the prospect of spending a sleepless night with such watchers; he was ready to exchange jokes with them, to tell them stories out of his nomadic life, anything at all to keep them awake and demonstrate to them again that he had no eatables in his cage and that he was fasting as not one of them could fast. But his happiest moment was when the morning came and an enormous breakfast was brought them, at his expense, on which they flung themselves with the keen appetite of healthy men after a weary night of wakefulness. Of course there were people who argued that this breakfast was an unfair attempt to bribe the watchers, but that was going rather too far, and when they were invited to take on a night's vigil without a breakfast, merely for the sake of the cause, they made themselves scarce, although they stuck stubbornly to their suspicions.

Such suspicions, anyhow, were a necessary accompaniment to the profession of fasting. No one could possibly watch the hunger artist continuously, day and night, and so no one could produce first-hand evidence that the fast had really been rigorous and continuous; only the artist himself could know that, he was therefore bound to be the sole completely satisfied spectator of his own fast. Yet for other reasons he was never satisfied; it was not perhaps mere fasting that had brought him to such skeleton thinness that many people had regretfully to keep away from his exhibitions, because the sight of him was too much for them, perhaps it was dissatisfaction with himself that had worn him down. For he alone knew, what no other initiate knew, how easy it was to fast. It was the easiest thing in the world. He made no secret of this, yet people did not believe him, at the best they set him down as modest, most of them however, thought he was out for publicity or else was some kind of cheat who found it easy to fast because he had discovered a way of making it easy, and then had the impudence to admit the fact, more or less. He had to put up with all that, and in the course of time had got used to it, but his inner dissatisfaction always rankled, and never yet, after any term of fasting—this must be granted to his credit—had he left the cage of his own free will. The longest period of fasting was fixed by his impresario at forty days, beyond that term he was not allowed to go, not even in great cities, and there was good reason for it, too. Experience had proved that for forty days the interest of the public could be stimulated by a steadily increasing pressure of advertisement, but after that the town began to lose interest, sympathetic support began notably to fall off; there were of course local variations as between one town and another or one country and another, but as a general rule forty days marked the limit. So on the fortieth day the flower-bedecked cage was opened, enthusiastic spectators filled the hall, a military band played, two doctors entered the cage to measure the results of the fast, which were announced through a megaphone, and finally two young ladies appeared blissful at having been selected for the honor, to help the hunger artist down the few steps leading to a small table on which was spread a carefully chosen invalid repast. And at this very moment the artist always turned stubborn. True, he would entrust his bony arms to the outstretched helping hands of the ladies bending over him, but stand up he would not. Why stop fasting at this particular moment, after forty days of it? He had held out for a long time, an illimitably long time; why stop now, when he was in his best fasting form, or rather, not yet quite in his best fasting form? Why should he be cheated of the fame he would get for fasting longer, for being not only the record hunger artist of all time, which presumably he was already, but for beating his own record by a performance beyond human imagination, since he felt that there were no limits to his capacity for fasting? His public pretended to admire him so much, why should it have so little patience with him; if he could endure fasting longer, why shouldn't the public endure it? Besides, he was tired, he was comfortable sitting in the straw, and now he was supposed to lift himself to his full height and go down to a meal the very thought of which gave him a nausea that only the presence of the ladies kept him from betraying, and even that with an effort. And he looked up into the eyes of the ladies who were apparently so friendly and in reality so cruel, and shook his head, which felt too heavy on its strengthless neck. But then there happened yet again what always happened. The impresario came forward, without a word—for the band made speech impossible—lifted his arms in the air above the artist, as if inviting Heaven to look down upon its creature here in the straw, this suffering martyr, which indeed he was, although in quite another sense; grasped him round the emaciated waist, with exaggerated caution, so that the frail condition he was in might be appreciated; and committed him to the care of the blenching ladies, not without secretly giving him a shaking so that his legs and body tottered and swayed. The artist now submitted completely; his head lolled on his breast as if it had landed there by chance; his body was hollowed out; his legs in a spasm of self-preservation clung close to each other at the knees, yet scraped on the ground as if it were not really solid ground, as if they were only trying to find solid ground; and the whole weight of his body, a feather-weight after all, relapsed onto one of the ladies, who, looking around for help and panting a little—this post of honor was not at all what she had expected it to be—first stretched her neck as far as she could to keep her face at least free from contact with the artist, then finding this impossible, and her more fortunate companion not coming to her aid but merely holding extended in her own trembling hand the little bunch of knucklebones that was the artist's, to the great delight of the spectators burst into tears and had to be replaced by an attendant who had long been stationed in readiness. Then came the food, a little of which the impresario managed to get between the artist's lips, while he sat in a kind of half-fainting trance, to the accompaniment of cheerful patter designed to distract the public's attention from the artist's condition; after that, a toast was drunk to the public, supposedly prompted by a whisper from the artist in the impresario's ear; the band confirmed it with a mighty flourish, the spectators melted away, and no one had any cause to be dissatisfied with the proceedings, no one except the hunger artist himself, he only, as always.

So he lived for many years, with small regular intervals of recuperation, in visible glory, honored by the world, yet in spite of that troubled in spirit, and all the more troubled because no one would take his trouble seriously. What comfort could he possibly need? What more could he possibly wish for? And if some good-natured person, feeling sorry for him, tried to console him by pointing out that his melancholy was probably caused by fasting, it could happen, especially when he had been fasting for some time, that he reacted with an outburst of fury and to the general alarm began to shake the bars of his cage like a wild animal. Yet the impresario had a way of punishing these outbreaks which he rather enjoyed putting into operation. He would apologize publicly for the artist's behavior, which was only to be excused, he admitted, because of the irritability caused by fasting; a condition hardly to be understood by well-fed people; then by natural transition he went on to mention the artist's equally incomprehensible boast that he could fast for much longer than he was doing; he praised the high ambition, the good will, the great self-denial undoubtedly implicit in such a statement; and then quite simply countered it by bringing out photographs, which were also on sale to the public, showing the artist on the fortieth day of a fast lying in bed almost dead from exhaustion. This perversion of the truth, familiar to the artist though it was, always unnerved him afresh and proved too much for him. What was a consequence of the premature ending of his fast was here presented as the cause of it! To fight against this lack of understanding, against a whole world of nonunderstanding, was impossible. Time and again in good faith he stood by the bars listening to the impresario, but as soon as the photographs appeared he always let go and sank with a groan back on to his straw, and the reassured public could once more come close and gaze at him.

5   A few years later when the witnesses of such scenes called them to mind, they often failed to understand themselves at all. For meanwhile the aforementioned change in public interest had set in; it seemed to happen almost overnight; there may have been profound causes for it, but who was going to bother about that; at any rate the pampered hunger artist suddenly found himself deserted one fine day by the amusement-seekers, who went streaming past him to more favored attractions. For the last time the impresario hurried him over half Europe to discover whether the old interest might still survive here and there; all in vain; everywhere, as if by secret agreement, a positive revulsion from professional fasting was in evidence. Of course it could not really have sprung up so suddenly as all that, and many premonitory symptoms which had not been sufficiently remarked or suppressed during the rush and glitter of success now came retrospectively to mind, but it was now too late to take any countermeasures. Fasting would surely come into fashion again at some future date, yet that was no comfort for those living in the present. What, then, was the hunger artist to do? He had been applauded by thousands in his time and could hardly come down to showing himself in a street booth at village fairs, and as for adopting another profession, he was not only too old for that but too fanatically devoted to fasting. So he took leave of the impresario, his partner in an unparalleled career, and hired himself to a large circus; in order to spare his own feelings he avoided reading the conditions of his contract.

A large circus with its enormous traffic in replacing and recruiting men, animals, and apparatus can always find a use for people at any time, even for a hunger artist, provided of course that he does not ask too much, and in this particular case anyhow it was not only the artist who was taken on but his famous and long-known name as well, indeed considering the peculiar nature of his performance, which was not impaired by advancing age, it could not be objected that here was an artist past his prime, no longer at the height of his professional skill, seeking a refuge in some quiet corner of a circus; on the contrary, the hunger artist averred that he could fast as well as ever, which was entirely credible, he even alleged that if he were allowed to fast as he liked and this was at once promised him without more ado, he could astound the world by establishing a record never yet achieved, a statement that certainly provoked a smile among the other professionals, since it left out of account the change in public opinion, which the hunger artist in his zeal conveniently forgot.

He had not, however, actually lost his sense of the real situation and took it as a matter of course that he and his cage should be stationed, not in the middle of the ring as a main attraction, but outside, near the animal cages, on a site that was after all easily accessible. Large and gaily painted placards made a frame for the cage and announced what was to be seen inside it. When the public came thronging out in the intervals to see the animals, they could hardly avoid passing the hunger artist's cage and stopping there for a moment, perhaps they might even have stayed longer had not those pressing behind them in the narrow gangway, who did not understand why they should be held up on their way toward the excitements of the menagerie, made it impossible for anyone to stand gazing quietly for any length of time. And that was the reason why the hunger artist, who had of course been looking forward to these visiting hours as the main achievement of his life, began instead to shrink from them. At first he could hardly wait for the intervals; it was exhilarating to watch the crowds come streaming his way, until only too soon—not even the most obstinate self-deception, clung to almost consciously, could hold out against the fact—the conviction was borne in upon him that these people, most of them, to judge from their actions, again and again, without exception, were all on their way to the menagerie. And the first sight of them from the distance remained the best. For when they reached his cage he was at once deafened by the storm of shouting and abuse that arose from the two contending factions, which renewed themselves continuously, of those who wanted to stop and stare at him—he soon began to dislike them more than the others—not out of real interest but only out of obstinate self-assertiveness, and those who wanted to go straight on to the animals. When the first great rush was past, the stragglers came along, and these, whom nothing could have prevented from stopping to look at him as long as they had breath, raced past with long strides, hardly even glancing at him, in their haste to get to the menagerie in time. And all too rarely did it happen that he had a stroke of luck, when some father of a family fetched up before him with his children, pointed a finger at the hunger artist and explained at length what the phenomenon meant, telling stories of earlier years when he himself had watched similar but much more thrilling performances, and the children, still rather uncomprehending, since neither inside nor outside school had they been sufficiently prepared for this lesson—what did they care about fasting?—yet showed by the brightness of their intent eyes that new and better times might be coming. Perhaps, said the hunger artist to himself many a time, things would be a little better if his cage were set not quite so near the menagerie. That made it too easy for people to make their choice, to say nothing of what he suffered from the stench of the menagerie, the animals' restlessness by night, the carrying past of raw lumps of flesh for the beasts of prey, the roaring at feeding times, which depressed him continually. But he did not dare to lodge a complaint with the management; after all, he had the animals to thank for the troops of people who passed his cage, among whom there might always be one here and there to take an interest in him, and who could tell where they might seclude him if he called attention to his existence and thereby to the fact that, strictly speaking, he was only an impediment on the way to the menagerie.

A small impediment, to be sure, one that grew steadily less. People grew familiar with the strange idea that they could be expected, in times like these, to take an interest in a hunger artist, and with this familiarity the verdict went out against him. He might fast as much as he could, and he did so; but nothing could save him now, people passed him by. Just try to explain to anyone the art of fasting! Anyone who has no feeling for it cannot be made to understand it. The fine placards grew dirty and illegible, they were torn down; the little notice board telling the number of fast days achieved, which at first was changed carefully every day, had long stayed at the same figure, for after the first few weeks even this small task seemed pointless to the staff; and so the artist simply fasted on and on, as he had once dreamed of doing, and it was no trouble to him, just as he had always foretold, but no one counted the days, no one, not even the artist himself knew what records he was already breaking, and his heart grew heavy. And when once in a while some leisurely passer-by stopped, made merry over the old figure on the board, and spoke of swindling, that was in its way the stupidest lie ever invented by indifference and inborn malice, since it was not the hunger artist who was cheating, he was working honestly, but the world was cheating him of his reward.

Many more days went by, however, and that too came to an end. An overseer's eye fell on the cage one day and he asked the attendants why this perfectly good cage should be left standing there unused with dirty straw inside it; nobody knew, until one man, helped out by the notice board, remembered about the hunger artist. They poked the straw with sticks and found him in it. "Are you still fasting?" asked the overseer. "When on earth do you mean to stop?" "Forgive me, everybody," whispered the hunger artist; only the overseer, who had his ears to the bars, understood him. "Of course," said the overseer, and tapped his forehead with a finger to let the attendants know what state the man was in, "we forgive you." "I always wanted you to admire my fasting," said the hunger artist. "We do admire it," said the overseer, affably. "But you shouldn't admire it," said the hunger artist. "Well, then we don't admire it," said the overseer, "but why shouldn't we admire it?" "Because I have to fast, I can't help it," said the hunger artist. "What a fellow you are," said the overseer, "and why can't you help it?" "Because," said the hunger artist, lifting his head a little and speaking, with his lips pursed, as if for a kiss, right into the overseer's ear, so that no syllable might be lost, "because I couldn't find the food I liked. If I had found it, believe me, I should have made no fuss and stuffed myself like you or anyone else." These were his last words, but in his dimming eyes remained the firm though no longer proud persuasion that he was still continuing to fast.

10   "Well, clear this out now!" said the overseer, and they buried the hunger artist, straw and all. Into the cage they put a young panther. Even the most insensitive felt it refreshing to see this wild creature leaping around the cage that had so long been dreary. The panther was all right. The food he liked was brought him without hesitation by the attendants; he seemed not even to miss his freedom; his noble body, furnished almost to the bursting point with all that it needed, seemed to carry freedom around with it too; somewhere in his jaws it seemed to lurk; and the joy of life streamed with such ardent passion from his throat that for the onlookers it was not easy to stand the shock of it. But they braced themselves, crowded around the cage, and did not want ever to move away.

➤ QUESTIONS FOR READING AND WRITING

1. What do you think the protagonist means when he says that fasting is "the easiest thing in the world" for him?
2. Do you agree that the protagonist is an "artist"? Explain.
3. How were you affected by the demise of the hunger artist and his replacement by a panther? Do you, like the crowd, think it's an improvement? Explain.

D. H. LAWRENCE (1885–1930)

D[avid] H[erbert] Lawrence was born in Nottinghamshire, England. In the largely auto-biographical novel Sons and Lovers *(1913), Lawrence wrote about his difficult childhood as the son of a coarse (and often drunken) coal miner and an overprotective and demanding mother. After earning a teaching degree while on a scholarship at Nottingham University College in 1908, Lawrence taught school while he worked on his first novel,* The White Peacock *(1910), and published his first poems and short stories in the* English Review*. In 1912, he quit teaching after meeting and falling in love with Frieda von Richthofen, the sister of the German flying ace the Red Baron. They were married in 1914, following her divorce. In 1915, Lawrence published his novel,* The Rainbow, *the story of three generations of a family in Nottinghamshire. Like much of his following work, the novel was extremely controversial for its frank depiction of sexual relationships and was banned by the English courts. Lawrence spent the rest of his life in self-imposed exile with his wife, traveling around the world. Though he wrote numerous novels, poems, and essays, many critics consider Lawrence's best work to be his short stories.*

THE HORSE DEALER'S DAUGHTER   [1922]

"Well, Mabel, and what are you going to do with yourself?" asked Joe, with foolish flippancy. He felt quite safe himself. Without listening for an answer, he turned aside, worked a grain of tobacco to the tip of his tongue, and spat it out. He did not care about anything, since he felt safe himself.

The three brothers and the sister sat round the desolate breakfast-table, attempting some sort of desultory consultation. The morning's post had given the final tap to the family fortune and all was over. The dreary dining-room itself, with its heavy mahogany furniture, looked as if it were waiting to be done away with.

But the consultation amounted to nothing. There was a strange air of ineffec-tuality about the three men, as they sprawled at table, smoking and reflecting vaguely on their own condition. The girl was alone, a rather short, sullen-looking young woman of twenty-seven. She did not share the same life as her brothers. She would have been good-looking, save for the impressive fixity of her face, "bull-dog," as her brothers called it.

There was a confused tramping of horses' feet outside. The three men all sprawled round in their chairs to watch. Beyond the dark holly bushes that separated the strip of lawn from the highroad, they could see a cavalcade of shire horses swinging out of their own yard, being taken for exercise. This was the last time. These were the last horses that would go through their hands. The young men watched with critical, callous looks. They were all frightened at the collapse of their lives, and the sense of disaster in which they were involved left them no inner freedom.

5   Yet they were three fine, well-set fellows enough. Joe, the eldest, was a man of thirty-three, broad and handsome in a hot, flushed way. His face was red, he twisted his black moustache over a thick finger, his eyes were shallow and restless. He had a sensual way of uncovering his teeth when he laughed, and his bearing was stupid. Now he watched the horses with a glazed look of helplessness in his eyes, a certain stupor of downfall.

The great draught-horses swung past. They were tied head to tail, four of them, and they heaved along to where a lane branched off from the highroad, planting their great hoofs floutingly in the fine black mud, swinging their great rounded haunches sumptuously, and trotting a few sudden steps as they were led into the lane, round the corner. Every movement showed a massive, slumbrous strength, and a stupidity which held them in subjection. The groom at the head looked back, jerking the leading rope. And the cavalcade moved out of sight up the lane, the tail of the last horse, bobbed up tight and stiff, held out taut from the swinging great haunches as they rocked behind the hedges in a motion-like sleep.

Joe watched with glazed hopeless eyes. The horses were almost like his own body to him. He felt he was done for now. Luckily he was engaged to a woman as old as himself, and therefore her father, who was steward of a neighboring estate, would provide him with a job. He would marry and go into harness. His life was over, he would be a subject animal now.

He turned uneasily aside, the retreating steps of the horses echoing in his ears. Then, with foolish restlessness, he reached for the scraps of bacon-rind from the plates, and making a faint whistling sound, flung them to the terrier that lay against the fender. He watched the dog swallow them, and waited till the creature looked into his eyes. Then a faint grin came on his face, and in a high, foolish voice he said:

"You won't get much more bacon, shall you, you little bitch?"

10   The dog faintly and dismally wagged its tail, then lowered its haunches, circled round, and lay down again.

There was another helpless silence at the table. Joe sprawled uneasily in his seat, not willing to go till the family conclave was dissolved. Fred Henry, the second brother, was erect, clean-limbed, alert. He had watched the passing of the horses with more *sangfroid*. If he was an animal, like Joe, he was an animal which controls, not one which is controlled. He was master of any horse, and he carried himself with a well-tempered air of mastery. But he was not master of the situations of life. He pushed his coarse brown moustache upwards, off his lip, and glanced irritably at his sister, who sat impassive and inscrutable.

"You'll go and stop with Lucy for a bit, shan't you?" he asked. The girl did not answer.

"I don't see what else you can do," persisted Fred Henry.

"Go as a skivvy," Joe interpolated laconically.

15   The girl did not move a muscle.

"If I was her, I should go in for training for a nurse," said Malcolm, the youngest of them all. He was the baby of the family, a young man of twenty-two, with a fresh, jaunty *museau*.[1]

But Mabel did not take any notice of him. They had talked at her and round her for so many years, that she hardly heard them at all.

The marble clock on the mantelpiece softly chimed the half-hour, the dog rose uneasily from the hearth-rug and looked at the party at the breakfast-table. But still they sat on in ineffectual conclave.

"Oh, all right," said Joe suddenly, apropos of nothing. "I'll get a move on."

20   He pushed back his chair, straddled his knees with a downward jerk, to get them free, in horsey fashion, and went to the fire. Still he did not go out of the room; he was curious to know what the others would do or say. He began to charge his pipe, looking down at the dog and saying, in a high, affected voice:

"Going wi' me? Going wi' me are ter? Tha'rt goin' further than tha counts on just now, dost hear?"

The dog faintly wagged its tail, the man stuck out his jaw and covered his pipe with his hands, and puffed intently, losing himself in the tobacco, looking down all the while at the dog with an absent brown eye. The dog looked up at him in mournful distrust. Joe stood with his knees stuck out, in real horsey fashion.

"Have you had a letter from Lucy?" Fred Henry asked of his sister.

"Last week," came the neutral reply.

25   "And what does she say?"

There was no answer.

"Does she *ask* you to go and stop there?" persisted Fred Henry.

"She says I can if I like."

"Well, then, you'd better. Tell her you'll come on Monday."

30   This was received in silence.

"That's what you'll do then, is it?" said Fred Henry, in some exasperation.

But she made no answer. There was a silence of futility and irritation in the room. Malcolm grinned fatuously.

"You'll have to make up your mind between now and next Wednesday," said Joe loudly, "or else find yourself lodgings on the kerbstone."

The face of the young woman darkened, but she sat on immutable.

35   "Here's Jack Fergusson!" exclaimed Malcolm, who was looking aimlessly out of the window.

"Where?" exclaimed Joe loudly.

"Just gone past."

"Coming in?"

Malcolm craned his neck to see the gate.

---

[1] **museau** muzzle or snout; slang for "face"

40   "Yes," he said.

There was a silence. Mabel sat on like one condemned, at the head of the table. Then a whistle was heard from the kitchen. The dog got up and barked sharply. Joe opened the door and shouted:

"Come on."

After a moment a young man entered. He was muffled up in overcoat and a purple woolen scarf, and his tweed cap, which he did not remove, was pulled down on his head. He was of medium height, his face was rather long and pale, his eyes looked tired.

"Hello, Jack! Well, Jack!" exclaimed Malcolm and Joe. Fred Henry merely said: "Jack."

45   "What's doing?" asked the newcomer, evidently addressing Fred Henry.

"Same. We've got to be out by Wednesday. Got a cold?"

"I have—got it bad, too."

"Why don't you stop in?"

"*Me* stop in? When I can't stand on my legs, perhaps I shall have a chance." The young man spoke huskily. He had a slight Scotch accent.

50   "It's a knock-out, isn't it," said Joe, boisterously, "if a doctor goes round croaking with a cold. Looks bad for the patients, doesn't it?"

The young doctor looked at him slowly.

"Anything the matter with *you*, then?" he asked sarcastically.

"Not as I know of. Damn your eyes, I hope not. Why?"

"I thought you were very concerned about the patients, wondered if you might be one yourself."

55   "Damn it, no, I've never been patient to no flaming doctor, and hope I never shall be," returned Joe.

At this point Mabel rose from the table, and they all seemed to become aware of her existence. She began putting the dishes together. The young doctor looked at her, but did not address her. He had not greeted her. She went out of the room with the tray, her face impassive and unchanged.

"When are you off then, all of you?" asked the doctor.

"I'm catching the eleven-forty," replied Malcolm. "Are you goin' down wi' th' trap, Joe?"

"Yes, I've told you I'm going down wi' th' trap, haven't I?"

60   "We'd better be getting her in then. So long, Jack, if I don't see you before I go," said Malcolm, shaking hands.

He went out, followed by Joe, who seemed to have his tail between his legs.

"Well, this is the devil's own," exclaimed the doctor, when he was left alone with Fred Henry. "Going before Wednesday, are you?"

"That's the orders," replied the other.

"Where, to Northampton?"

65   "That's it."

"The devil!" exclaimed Fergusson, with quiet chagrin.

And there was silence between the two.

"All settled up, are you?" asked Fergusson.

"About."

70   There was another pause.

"Well, I shall miss yer, Freddy, boy," said the young doctor.

"And I shall miss thee, Jack," returned the other.

"Miss you like hell," mused the doctor.

Fred Henry turned aside. There was nothing to say. Mabel came in again, to finish clearing the table.

75   "What are *you* going to do, then, Miss Pervin?" asked Fergusson. "Going to your sister's, are you?"

Mabel looked at him with her steady, dangerous eyes, that always made him uncomfortable, unsettling his superficial ease.

"No," she said.

"Well, what in the name of fortune *are* you going to do? Say what you mean to do," cried Fred Henry, with futile intensity.

But she only averted her head, and continued her work. She folded the white table-cloth, and put on the chenille cloth.

80   "The sulkiest bitch that ever trod!" muttered her brother.

But she finished her task with perfectly impassive face, the young doctor watching her interestedly all the while. Then she went out.

Fred Henry stared after her, clenching his lips, his blue eyes fixing in sharp antagonism, as he made a grimace of sour exasperation.

"You could bray her into bits, and that's all you'd get out of her," he said, in a small, narrowed tone.

The doctor smiled faintly.

85   "What's she *going* to do, then?" he asked.

"Strike me if *I* know!" returned the other.

There was a pause. Then the doctor stirred.

"I'll be seeing you to-night, shall I?" he said to his friend.

"Ay—where's it to be? Are we going over to Jessdale?"

90   "I don't know. I've got such a cold on me. I'll come round to the 'Moon and Stars,' anyway."

"Let Lizzie and May miss their night for once, eh?"

"That's it—if I feel as I do now."

"All's one—"

The two young men went through the passage and down to the back door together. The house was large, but it was servantless now, and desolate. At the back was a small bricked house-yard, and beyond that a big square, gravelled fine and red, and having stables on two sides. Sloping, dank, winter-dark fields stretched away on the open sides.

95   But the stables were empty. Joseph Pervin, the father of the family, had been a man of no education, who had become a fairly large horse dealer. The stables had been full of horses, there was a great turmoil and come-and-go of horses and of dealers and grooms. Then the kitchen was full of servants. But of late things had declined. The old man had married a second time, to retrieve his fortunes. Now he was dead and everything was gone to the dogs, there was nothing but debt and threatening.

For months, Mabel had been servantless in the big house, keeping the home together in penury for her ineffectual brothers. She had kept house for ten years. But previously it was with unstinted means. Then, however brutal and coarse everything was, the sense of money had kept her proud, confident. The men might be foul-mouthed, the women in the kitchen might have bad reputations, her brothers might have illegitimate children. But so long as there was money, the girl felt herself established, and brutally proud, reserved.

No company came to the house, save dealers and coarse men. Mabel had no associates of her own sex, after her sister went away. But she did not mind. She went regularly to church, she attended to her father. And she lived in the memory of her mother, who had died when she was fourteen, and whom she had loved. She had loved her father, too, in a different way, depending upon him, and feeling secure in him, until at the age of fifty-four he married again. And then she had set hard against him. Now he had died and left them all hopelessly in debt.

She had suffered badly during the period of poverty. Nothing, however, could shake the curious, sullen, animal pride that dominated each member of the family. Now, for Mabel, the end had come. Still she would not cast about her. She would follow her own way just the same. She would always hold the keys of her own situation. Mindless and persistent, she endured from day to day. Why should she think? Why should she answer anybody? It was enough that this was the end, and there was no way out. She need not pass any more darkly along the main street of the small town, avoiding every eye. She need not demean herself any more, going into the shops and buying the cheapest food. This was at an end. She thought of nobody, not even of herself. Mindless and persistent, she seemed in a sort of ecstasy to be coming nearer to her fulfillment, her own glorification, approaching her dead mother, who was glorified.

In the afternoon she took a little bag, with shears and sponge and a small scrubbing brush, and went out. It was a grey, wintry day, with saddened, dark green fields and an atmosphere blackened by the smoke of foundries not far off. She went quickly, darkly along the causeway, heeding nobody, through the town to the churchyard.

100   There she always felt secure, as if no one could see her, although as a matter of fact she was exposed to the stare of everyone who passed along under the churchyard wall. Nevertheless, once under the shadow of the great looming church, among the graves, she felt immune from the world, reserved within the thick churchyard wall as in another country.

Carefully she clipped the grass from the grave, and arranged the pinky white, small chrysanthemums in the tin cross. When this was done, she took an empty jar from a neighbouring grave, brought water, and carefully, most scrupulously sponged the marble head-stone and the coping-stone.

It gave her sincere satisfaction to do this. She felt in immediate contact with the world of her mother. She took minute pains, went through the park in a state bordering on pure happiness, as if in performing this task she came into a subtle, intimate connection with her mother. For the life she followed here in the world was far less real than the world of death she inherited from her mother.

The doctor's house was just by the church. Fergusson, being a mere hired assistant, was slave to the country-side. As he hurried now to attend to the out-patients in the surgery, glancing across the graveyard with his quick eye, he saw the girl at her task at the grave. She seemed so intent and remote, it was like looking into another world. Some mystical element was touched in him. He slowed down as he walked, watching her as if spellbound.

She lifted her eyes, feeling him looking. Their eyes met. And each looked away again at once, each feeling, in some way, found out by the other. He lifted his cap and passed on down the road. There remained distinct in his consciousness, like a vision, the memory of her face, lifted from the tombstone in the churchyard, and looking at him with slow, large, portentous eyes. It *was* portentous, her face. It seemed to mesmerize him. There was a heavy power in her eyes which laid hold of his whole being, as if he had drunk some powerful drug. He had been feeling weak and done before. Now the life came back into him, he felt delivered from his own fretted, daily self.

105   He finished his duties at the surgery as quickly as might be, hastily filling up the bottles of the waiting people with cheap drugs. Then, in perpetual haste, he set off again to visit several cases in another part of his round, before tea-time. At all times he preferred to walk if he could, but particularly when he was not well. He fancied the motion restored him.

The afternoon was falling. It was grey, deadened, and wintry, with a slow, moist, heavy coldness sinking in and deadening all the faculties. But why should he think or notice? He hastily climbed the hill and turned across the dark green fields, following the black cinder-track. In the distance, across a shallow dip in the country, the small town was clustered like smouldering ash, a tower, a spire, a heap of low, raw, extinct houses. And on the nearest fringe of the town, sloping into the dip, was Oldmeadow, the Pervins' house. He could see the stables and the outbuildings distinctly, as they lay towards him on the slope. Well, he would not go there many more times! Another resource would be lost to him, another place gone: the only company he cared for in the alien, ugly little town he was losing. Nothing but work, drudgery, constant hastening from dwelling to dwelling among the colliers and the iron-workers. It wore him out, but at the same time he had a craving for it. It was a stimulant to him to be in the homes of the working people, moving, as it were, through the innermost body of their life. His nerves were excited and grati-fied. He could come so near, into the very lives of the rough, inarticulate, powerfully emotional men and women. He grumbled, he said he hated the hellish hole. But as a matter of fact it excited him, the contact with the rough, strongly-feeling people was a stimulant applied direct to his nerves.

Below Oldmeadow, in the green, shallow, soddened hollow of fields, lay a square, deep pond. Roving across the landscape, the doctor's quick eye detected a figure in black passing through the gate of the field, down towards the pond. He looked again. It would be Mabel Pervin. His mind suddenly became alive and attentive.

Why was she going down there? He pulled up on the path on the slope above, and stood staring. He could just make sure of the small black figure moving in the hollow of the failing day. He seemed to see her in the midst of such obscurity, that he was like a clairvoyant, seeing rather with the mind's eye than with ordinary sight. Yet he could see her positively enough, whilst he kept his eye attentive. He felt, if he looked away from her, in the thick, ugly falling dusk, he would lose her altogether.

He followed her minutely as she moved, direct and intent, like something transmitted rather than stirring in voluntary activity, straight down the field towards the pond. There she stood on the bank for a moment. She never raised her head. Then she waded slowly into the water.

110 He stood motionless as the small black figure walked slowly and deliberately towards the centre of the pond, very slowly, gradually moving deeper into the motionless water, and still moving forward as the water got up to her breast. Then he could see her no more in the dusk of the dead afternoon.

"There!" he exclaimed. "Would you believe it?"

And he hastened straight down, running over the wet, soddened fields, pushing through the hedges, down into the depression of callous wintry obscurity. It took him several minutes to come to the pond. He stood on the bank, breathing heavily. He could see nothing. His eyes seemed to penetrate the dead water. Yes, perhaps that was the dark shadow of her black clothing beneath the surface of the water.

He slowly ventured into the pond. The bottom was deep, soft clay, he sank in, and the water clasped dead cold round his legs. As he stirred he could smell the cold, rotten clay that fouled up into the water. It was objectionable in his lungs. Still, repelled and yet not heeding, he moved deeper into the pond. The cold water rose over his thighs, over his loins, upon his abdomen. The lower part of his body was all sunk in the hideous cold element. And the bottom was so deeply soft and uncertain, he was afraid of pitching with his mouth underneath. He could not swim, and was afraid.

He crouched a little, spreading his hands under the water and moving them round, trying to feel for her. The dead cold pond swayed upon his chest. He moved again, a little deeper, and again, with his hands underneath, he felt all around under the water. And he touched her clothing. But it evaded his fingers. He made a desperate effort to grasp it.

115 And so doing he lost his balance and went under, horribly, suffocating in the foul earthy water, struggling madly for a few moments. At last, after what seemed an eternity, he got his footing, rose again into the air and looked around. He gasped, and knew he was in the world. Then he looked at the water. She had risen near him. He grasped her clothing, and drawing her nearer, turned to take his way to land again.

He went very slowly, carefully, absorbed in the slow progress. He rose higher, climbing out of the pond. The water was now only about his legs; he was thankful, full of relief to be out of the clutches of the pond. He lifted her and staggered onto the bank, out of the horror of wet, grey clay.

He laid her down on the bank. She was quite unconscious and running with water. He made the water come from her mouth, he worked to restore her. He did not have to work very long before he could feel the breathing begin again in her; she was breathing naturally. He worked a little longer. He could feel her live beneath his hands; she was coming back. He wiped her face, wrapped her in his overcoat, looked round into the dim, dark grey world, then lifted her and staggered down the bank and across the fields.

It seemed an unthinkably long way, and his burden so heavy he felt he would never get to the house. But at last he was in the stable-yard, and then in the house-yard. He opened the door and went into the house. In the kitchen he laid her down on the hearth-rug, and called. The house was empty. But the fire was burning in the grate.

Then again he kneeled to attend to her. She was breathing regularly, her eyes were wide open and as if conscious, but there seemed something missing in her look. She was conscious in herself, but unconscious of her surroundings.

120 He ran upstairs, took blankets from a bed, and put them before the fire to warm. Then he removed her saturated, earthy-smelling clothing, rubbed her dry with a towel, and wrapped her naked in the blankets. Then he went into the dining-room, to look for spirits. There was a little whisky. He drank a gulp himself, and put some into her mouth.

The effect was instantaneous. She looked full into his face, as if she had been seeing him for some time, and yet had only just become conscious of him.

"Dr. Fergusson?" she said.

"What?" he answered.

He was divesting himself of his coat, intending to find some dry clothing upstairs. He could not bear the smell of the dead, clayey water, and he was mortally afraid for his own health.

125 "What did I do?" she asked.

"Walked into the pond," he replied. He had begun to shudder like one sick, and could hardly attend to her. Her eyes remained full on him, he seemed to be going dark in his mind, looking back at her helplessly. The shuddering became quieter in him, his life came back to him, dark and unknowing, but strong again.

"Was I out of my mind?" she asked, while her eyes were fixed on him all the time.

"Maybe, for the moment," he replied. He felt quiet, because his strength had come back. The strange fretful strain had left him.

"Am I out of my mind now?" she asked.

130 "Are you?" he reflected a moment. "No," he answered truthfully. "I don't see that you are." He turned his face aside. He was afraid now, because he felt dazed, and felt dimly that her power was stronger than his, in this issue. And she continued to look at him fixedly all the time. "Can you tell me where I shall find some dry things to put on?" he asked.

"Did you dive into the pond for me?" she asked.

"No," he answered. "I walked in. But I went in overhead as well."

There was silence for a moment. He hesitated. He very much wanted to go upstairs to get into dry clothing. But there was another desire in him. And she seemed to hold him. His will seemed to have gone to sleep, and left him, standing there slack before her. But he felt warm inside himself. He did not shudder at all, though his clothes were sodden on him.

"Why did you?" she asked.

135 "Because I didn't want you to do such a foolish thing," he said.

"It wasn't foolish," she said, still gazing at him as she lay on the floor, with a sofa cushion under her head. "It was the right thing to do. *I* knew best, then."

"I'll go and shift these wet things," he said. But still he had not the power to move out of her presence, until she sent him. It was as if she had the life of his body in her hands, and he could not extricate himself. Or perhaps he did not want to.

Suddenly she sat up. Then she became aware of her own immediate condition. She felt the blankets about her, she knew her own limbs. For a moment it seemed as if her reason were going. She looked round, with wild eye, as if seeking something. He stood still with fear. She saw her clothing lying scattered.

"Who undressed me?" she asked, her eyes resting full and inevitable on his face.

140 "I did," he replied, "to bring you round."

For some moments she sat and gazed at him awfully, her lips parted.

"Do you love me, then?" she asked.

He only stood and stared at her, fascinated. His soul seemed to melt.

She shuffled forward on her knees, and put her arms round him, round his legs, as he stood there, pressing her breasts against his knees and thighs, clutching him with strange, convulsive certainty, pressing his thighs against her, drawing him to her face, her throat, as she looked up at him with flaring, humble eyes of transfiguration, triumphant in first possession.

145 "You love me," she murmured, in strange transport, yearning and triumphant and confident. "You love me. I know you love me, I know."

And she was passionately kissing his knees, through the wet clothing, passionately and indiscriminately kissing his knees, his legs, as if unaware of everything.

He looked down at the tangled wet hair, the wild, bare, animal shoulders. He was amazed, bewildered, and afraid. He had never thought of loving her. He had never wanted to love her. When he rescued her and restored her, he was a doctor, and she was a patient. He had had no single personal thought of her. Nay, this introduction of the personal element was very distasteful to him, a violation of his professional honour. It was horrible to have her there embracing his knees. It was horrible. He revolted from it, violently. And yet—and yet—he had not the power to break away.

She looked at him again, with the same supplication of powerful love, and that same transcendent, frightening light of triumph. In view of the delicate flame which seemed to come from her face like a light, he was powerless. And yet he had never intended to love her. He had never intended. And something stubborn in him could not give way.

"You love me," she repeated, in a murmur of deep, rhapsodic assurance. "You love me."

150 Her hands were drawing him, drawing him down to her. He was afraid, even a little horrified. For he had, really, no intention of loving her. Yet her hands were drawing him towards her. He put out his hand quickly to steady himself, and grasped her bare shoulder. A flame seemed to burn the hand that grasped her soft shoulder. He had no intention of loving her: his whole will was against his yielding. It was horrible. And yet wonderful was the touch of her shoulders, beautiful the shining of her face. Was she perhaps mad? He had a horror of yielding to her. Yet something in him ached also.

He had been staring away at the door, away from her. But his hand remained on her shoulder. She had gone suddenly very still. He looked down at her. Her eyes were now wide with fear, with doubt, the light was dying from her face, a shadow of terrible greyness was returning. He could not bear the touch of her eyes' question upon him, and the look of death behind the question.

With an inward groan he gave way, and let his heart yield towards her. A sudden gentle smile came on his face. And her eyes, which never left his face, slowly, slowly filled with tears. He watched the strange water rise in her eyes, like some slow fountain coming up. And his heart seemed to burn and melt away in his breast.

He could not bear to look at her any more. He dropped on his knees and caught her head with his arms and pressed her face against his throat. She was very still. His heart, which seemed to have broken, was burning with a kind of agony in his breast. And he felt her slow, hot tears wetting his throat. But he could not move.

He felt the hot tears wet his neck and the hollows of his neck, and he remained motionless, suspended through one of man's eternities. Only now it had become indispensable to him to have her face pressed close to him; he could never let her go again. He could never let her head go away from the close clutch of his arm. He wanted to remain like that for ever, with his heart hurting him in a pain that was also life to him. Without knowing, he was looking down on her damp, soft brown hair.

155   Then, as it were suddenly, he smelt the horrid stagnant smell of that water. And at the same moment she drew away from him and looked at him. Her eyes were wistful and unfathomable. He was afraid of them, and he fell to kissing her, not knowing what he was doing. He wanted her eyes not to have that terrible, wistful, unfathomable look.

When she turned her face to him again, a faint delicate flush was glowing, and there was again dawning that terrible shining of joy in her eyes, which really terrified him, and yet which he now wanted to see, because he feared the look of doubt still more.

"You love me?" she said, rather faltering.

"Yes." The word cost him a painful effort. Not because it wasn't true. But because it was too newly true, the *saying* seemed to tear open again his newly torn heart. And he hardly wanted it to be true, even now.

She lifted her face to him, and he bent forward and kissed her on the mouth, gently, with the one kiss that is an eternal pledge. And as he kissed her his heart strained again in his breast. He never intended to love her. But now it was over. He had crossed over the gulf to her, and all that he had left behind had shrivelled and become void.

160   After the kiss, her eyes again slowly filled with tears. She sat still, away from him, with her face drooped aside, and her hands folded in her lap. The tears fell very slowly. There was complete silence. He too sat there motionless and silent on the hearth-rug. The strange pain of his heart that was broken seemed to consume him. That he should love her? That this was love! That he should be ripped open in this way! Him, a doctor! How they would all jeer if they knew! It was agony to him to think they might know.

In the curious naked pain of the thought he looked again to her. She was sitting there drooped into a muse. He saw a tear fall, and his heart flared hot. He saw for the first time that one of her shoulders was quite uncovered, one arm bare, he could see one of her small breasts; dimly, because it had become almost dark in the room.

"Why are you crying?" he asked, in an altered voice.

She looked up at him, and behind her tears the consciousness of her situation for the first time brought a dark look of shame to her eyes.

"I'm not crying, really," she said, watching him, half frightened.

165 He reached his hand, and softly closed it on her bare arm.

"I love you! I love you!" he said in a soft, low vibrating voice, unlike himself.

She shrank, and dropped her head. The soft, penetrating grip of his hand on her arm distressed her. She looked up at him.

"I want to go," she said. "I want to go and get you some dry things."

"Why?" he said. "I'm all right."

170 "But I want to go," she said. "And I want you to change your things."

He released her arm, and she wrapped herself in the blanket, looking at him rather frightened. And still she did not rise.

"Kiss me," she said wistfully.

He kissed her, but briefly, half in anger.

Then, after a second, she rose nervously, all mixed up in the blanket. He watched her in her confusion, as she tried to extricate herself and wrap herself up so that she could walk. He watched her relentlessly, as she knew. And as she went, the blanket trailing, and as he saw a glimpse of her feet and her white leg, he tried to remember her as she was when he had wrapped her in the blanket. But then he didn't want to remember, because she had been nothing to him then, and his nature revolted from remembering her as she was when she was nothing to him.

175 A tumbling, muffled noise from within the dark house startled him. Then he heard her voice: "There are clothes." He rose and went to the foot of the stairs, and gathered up the garments she had thrown down. Then he came back to the fire, to rub himself down and dress. He grinned at his own appearance when he had finished.

The fire was sinking, so he put on coal. The house was now quite dark, save for the light of a street-lamp that shone in faintly from beyond the holly trees. He lit the gas with matches he found on the mantelpiece. Then he emptied the pockets of his own clothes, and threw all his wet things in a heap into the scullery. After which he gathered up her sodden clothes, gently, and put them in a separate heap on the copper-top in the scullery.

It was six o'clock on the clock. His own watch had stopped. He ought to go back to the surgery. He waited, and still she did not come down. So he went to the foot of the stairs and called:

"I shall have to go."

Almost immediately he heard her coming down. She had on her best dress of black voile, and her hair was tidy, but still damp. She looked at him—and in spite of herself, smiled.

180 "I don't like you in those clothes," she said.

"Do I look a sight?" he answered.

They were shy of one another.

"I'll make you some tea," she said.

"No, I must go."

185 "Must you?" And she looked at him again with the wide, strained, doubtful eyes. And again, from the pain of his breast, he knew how he loved her. He went and bent to kiss her, gently, passionately, with his heart's painful kiss.

"And my hair smells so horrible," she murmured in distraction. "And I'm so awful, I'm so awful! Oh no, I'm too awful." And she broke into bitter, heart-broken sobbing. "You can't want to love me, I'm horrible."

"Don't be silly, don't be silly," he said, trying to comfort her, kissing her, holding her in his arms. "I want you, I want to marry you, we're going to be married, quickly, quickly—tomorrow if I can."

But she only sobbed terribly, and cried:

"I feel awful. I feel awful. I feel I'm horrible to you."

190 "No, I want you, I want you," was all he answered, blindly, with that terrible intonation which frightened her almost more than her horror lest he should *not* want her.

► QUESTIONS FOR READING AND WRITING

1. In what way is the setting of the story a factor? How would you describe the surroundings and their effect on Mabel and Fergusson?
2. Describe Mabel. What is her everyday existence like? How is she treated by her father and brothers? In what ways does she differ from them?
3. Describe Fergusson. What is his everyday existence like?
4. What is the conflict in this story? To what extent is it related to setting and characterization?
5. At the end of the story Fergusson cries out, "I want you, I want you." Why does he seem to want Mabel so much? Do you think they are really in love? Explain.

GABRIEL GARCIA MARQUEZ

(b. 1928)

Gabriel Garcia Marquez was born in Aracataca, Colombia. Marquez published "A Very Old Man with Enormous Wings" as part of his first book, Leaf Storm and Other Stories, *in 1955. Typical of his fiction, including "A Very Old Man with Enormous Wings," is the mingling of realistic fiction and magical or fantastic elements. The author of several novels and collections of stories, including the International best-selling* One Hundred Years of Solitude *and* Love in the Time of Cholera, *he was awarded the Nobel Prize for Literature in 1982.*

A VERY OLD MAN WITH ENORMOUS WINGS [1955]

Translated by Gregory Rabassa

On the third day of rain they had killed so many crabs inside the house that Pelayo had to cross his drenched courtyard and throw them into the sea, because the newborn child had a temperature all night and they thought it was due to the stench. The world had been sad since Tuesday. Sea and sky were a single ash-gray thing and the sands of the beach, which on March nights glimmered like powdered light, had become a stew of mud and rotten shellfish. The light was so weak at noon that when Pelayo was coming back to the house after throwing away the crabs, it was hard for him to see what it was that was moving and groaning in the rear of the courtyard. He had to go very close to see that it was an old man, a very old man, lying face down in the mud, who, in spite of his tremendous efforts, couldn't get up, impeded by his enormous wings.

Frightened by that nightmare, Pelayo ran to get Elisenda, his wife, who was putting compresses on the sick child, and he took her to the rear of the court-yard. They both looked at the fallen body with mute stupor. He was dressed like a ragpicker. There were only a few faded hairs left on his bald skull and very few teeth in his mouth, and his pitiful condition of a drenched great-grandfather had taken away any sense of grandeur he might have had. His huge buzzard wings, dirty and half-plucked, were forever entangled in the mud. They looked at him so long and so closely that Pelayo and Elisenda very soon overcame their surprise and in the end found him familiar. Then they dared speak to him, and he answered in an incomprehensible dialect with a strong sailor's voice. That was how they skipped over the inconvenience of the wings and quite intelli-gently concluded that he was a lonely castaway from some foreign ship wrecked by the storm. And yet, they called in a neighbor woman who knew everything about life and death to see him, and all she needed was one look to show them their mistake.

"He's an angel," she told them. "He must have been coming for the child, but the poor fellow is so old that the rain knocked him down."

On the following day everyone knew that a flesh-and-blood angel was held captive in Pelayo's house. Against the judgment of the wise neighbor woman, for whom angels in those times were the fugitive survivors to a celestial conspiracy, they did not have the heart to club him to death. Pelayo watched over him all afternoon from the kitchen, armed with his bailiff's club, and before going to bed he dragged him out of the mud and locked him up with the hens in the wire chicken coop. In the middle of the night, when the rain stopped, Pelayo and Elisenda were still killing crabs. A short time afterward the child woke up without a fever and with a desire to eat. Then they felt magnanimous and decided to put the angel on a raft with fresh water and provisions for three days and leave him to his fate on the high seas. But when they went out into the courtyard with the first light of dawn, they found the whole neighborhood in front of the chicken coop having fun with the angel, without the slightest reverence, tossing him things to eat through the openings in the wire as if he weren't a supernatural creature but a circus animal.

5   Father Gonzaga arrived before seven o'clock, alarmed at the strange news. By that time onlookers less frivolous than those at dawn had already arrived and they were making all kinds of conjectures concerning the captive's future. The simplest among them thought that he should be named mayor of the world. Others of sterner mind felt that he should be promoted to the rank of five-star general in order to win all wars. Some visionaries hoped that he could be put to stud in order to implant on earth a race of winged wise men who could take charge of the universe. But Father Gonzaga, before becoming a priest, had been a robust woodcutter. Standing by the wire, he reviewed his catechism in an instant and asked them to open the door so that he could take a close look at that pitiful man who looked more like a huge decrepit hen among the fascinated chickens. He was lying in a corner drying his open wings in the sunlight among the fruit peels and breakfast leftovers that they early risers have thrown him. Alien to the impertinences of the world, he only lifted his antiquarian eyes and murmured something in his dialect when Father Gonzaga went into the chicken coop and said good morning to him in Latin. The parish priest had his first suspicion of an impostor when he saw that he did not understand the language of God or know how to greet His ministers. Then he noticed that seen close up he was much too human: he had an unbearable smell of the outdoors, the back side of his wings was strewn with parasites and his main feathers had been mistreated by terrestrial winds, and nothing about him measured up to the proud dignity of angels. Then he came out of the chicken coop and in a brief sermon warned the curious against the risks of being ingenuous. He reminded them that the devil had the bad habit of making use of carnival tricks in order to confuse the unwary. He argued that if wings were not the essential element in determining the difference between a hawk and an airplane, they were even less so in the recognition of angels. Nevertheless, he promised to write a letter to his bishop so that the latter would write to his primate so that the latter would write to the Supreme Pontiff in order to get the final verdict from the highest courts.

His prudence fell on sterile hearts. The news of the captive angel spread with such rapidity that after a few hours the courtyard had the bustle of a marketplace and they had to call in troops with fixed bayonets to disperse the mob that was about to knock the house down. Elisenda, her spine all twisted from sweeping up so much marketplace trash, then got the idea of fencing in the yard and charging five cents admission to see the angel.

The curious came from far away. A traveling carnival arrived with a flying acrobat who buzzed over the crowd several times, but no one paid any attention to him because his wings were not those of an angel, but rather, those of a sidereal[1] bat. The most unfortunate invalids on earth came in search of health: a poor woman who since childhood had been counting her heartbeats and had run out of numbers; a Portuguese man who couldn't sleep because the noise of the stars disturbed him; a sleepwalker who got up at night to undo the things he had done while awake; and many others with less serious ailments. In the midst of that shipwreck disorder that made the earth tremble, Pelayo and Elisenda were happy with

---

[1] **sidereal** coming from the stars

fatigue, for in less than a week they had crammed their rooms with money and the line of pilgrims waiting their turn to enter still reached beyond the horizon.

The angel was the only one who took no part in his own act. He spent his time trying to get comfortable in his borrowed nest, befuddled by the hellish heat of the oil lamps and sacramental candles that had been placed along the wire. At first they tried to make him eat some mothballs, which, according to the wisdom of the wise neighbor woman, were the food prescribed for angels. But he turned them down, just as he turned down the papal lunches that the penitents brought him, and they never found out whether it was because he was an angel or because he was an old man that in the end he ate nothing but eggplant mush. His only supernatural virture seemed to be patience. Especially during the first days, when the hens pecked at him, searching for the stellar parasites that proliferated in his wings, and the cripples pulled out feathers to touch their defective parts with, and even the merciful threw stones at him, trying to get him to rise so they could see him standing. The only time they succeeded in arousing him was when they burned his side with an iron for branding steers, for he had been motionless for so many hours that they thought he was dead. He awoke with a start, ranting in his hermetic language and with tears in his eyes, and he flapped his wings a couple of times, which brought on a whirlwind of chicken dung and lunar dust and a gale of panic that did not seem to be of this world. Although many thought that his reaction had been one not of rage but of pain, from then on they were careful not to annoy him, because the majority understood that his passivity was not that of a hero taking his ease but that of a cataclysm in repose.

Father Gonzaga held back the crowd's frivolity with formulas of maidservant inspiration while awaiting the arrival of a final judgment on the nature of the captive. But the mail from Rome showed no sense of urgency. They spent their time finding out if the prisoner had a navel, if his dialect had any connection with Aramaic, how many times he could fit on the head of a pin, or whether he wasn't just a Norwegian with wings. Those meager letters might have come and gone until the end of time if a providential event had not put an end to the priest's tribulations.

10   It so happened that during those days, among so many other carnival attractions, there arrived in town the traveling show of the woman who had been changed into a spider for having disobeyed her parents. The admission to see her was not only less than the admission to see the angel, but people were permitted to ask her all manner of questions about her absurd state and to examine her up and down so that no one would ever doubt the truth of her horror. She was a frightful tarantula the size of a ram and with the head of a sad maiden. What was most heart-rending, however, was not her outlandish shape but the sincere affliction with which she recounted the details of her misfortune. While still practically a child she had sneaked out of her parents' house to go to a dance, and while she was coming back through the woods after having danced all night without permission, a fearful thunderclap rent the sky in two and through the crack came the lightning bolt of brimstone that changed her into a spider. Her only nourishment came from the meatballs that charitable souls chose to toss into her mouth. A spectacle like that, full of so much human truth and which such a fearful lesson, was bound to defeat

without even trying that of a haughty angel who scarcely deigned to look at mortals. Besides, the few miracles attributed to the angel showed a certain metal disorder, like the blind man who didn't recover his sight but grew three new teeth, or the paralytic who didn't get to walk but almost won the lottery, and the leper whose sores sprouted sunflowers. Those consolation miracles, which were more like mocking fun, had already ruined the angel's reputation when the woman who had been changed into a spider finally crushed him completely. That was how Father Gonzaga was cured forever of his insomnia and Pelayo's courtyard went back to being as empty as during the time it had rained for three days and crabs walked through the bedrooms.

The owners of the house had no reason to lament. With the money they saved they built a two-story mansion with balconies and gardens and high netting so that crabs wouldn't get in during the winter, and with iron bars on the windows so that angels wouldn't get in. Pelayo also set up a rabbit warren close to town and gave up his job as bailiff for good, and Elisenda bought some satin pumps with high heels and many dresses of iridescent silk, the kind worn on Sunday by the most desirable women in those times. The chicken coop was the only thing that didn't receive any attention. If they washed it down with creolin and burned tears of myrrh inside it every so often, it was not in homage to the angel but to drive away the dung heap stench that still hung everywhere like a ghost and was turning the new house into an old one. At first, when the child learned to walk, they were careful that he not get too close to the chicken coop. But then they began to lose their fears and got used to the smell, and before the child got his second teeth he'd gone inside the chicken coop to play, where the wires were falling apart. The angel was no less standoffish with him than with other mortals, but he tolerated the most ingenious infamies with the patience of dog who had no illusions. They both came down with chicken pot at the same time. The doctor who took care of the child couldn't resist the temptation to listen to the angel's heart, and he found so much whistling in the heart and so many sounds in his kidneys that it seemed impossible for him to be alive. What surprised him most, however, was the logic of his wings. They seemed so natural on that completely human organism that he couldn't understand why other men didn't have them too.

When the child began school it had been some time since the sun and rain had caused the collapse of the chicken coop. The angel went dragging himself about here and there like a stray dying man. They would drive him out of the bedroom with a broom and a moment later find him in the kitchen. He seemed to be in so many places at the same time that they grew to think that he'd been duplicated, that he was reproducing himself all through the house, and the exasperated and unhinged Elisenda shouted that it was awful living in that hell full of angels. He could scarcely eat and his antiquarian eyes had also become so foggy that he went about bumping into posts. All he had left were the bare cannulae[2] of his last feathers. Pelayo threw a blanket over him and extended him the charity of letting him sleep in the shed, and only then did they notice that he had temperature at night, and was delirious with the tongue twisters of an old Norwegian. That was one of

[2] **cannulae** the tubular pieces by which feathers are attached to a body

the few times they became alarmed, for they thought he was going to die and not even the wise neighbor woman had been able to tell them what to do with dead angels.

And yet he not only survived his worst winter, but seemed improved with the first sunny days. He remained motionless for several days in the farthest corner of the courtyard, where no one would see him, and at the beginning of December some large, stiff feathers began to grow on his wings, the feathers of a scarecrow, which looked more like another misfortune decrepitude. But he must have known the reason for those changes, for he was quite careful that no one should notice them, that no one should hear the sea chanteys that he sometimes sang under the stars. One morning Elisenda was cutting some bunches of onions for lunch when a wind that seemed to come from the high seas blew into the kitchen. Then she went to the window and caught the angel in his first attempts at flight. They were so clumsy that his fingernails opened a furrow in the vegetable patch and he was on the point of knocking the shed down the ungainly flapping that slipped on the light and couldn't get a grip on the air. But he did manage to gain altitude. Elisenda let out a sigh of relief, for herself and for him, when she saw him pass over the last houses, holding himself up in some way with the risky flapping of a senile vulture. She kept watching him even when she was through cutting the onions and she kept on watching until it was no longer possible for her to see him, because then he was no longer an annoyance in her life but an imaginary dot on the horizon of the sea.

➤ QUESTIONS FOR READING AND WRITING

1. To what extent were you affected by Marquez's mingling of fantastic and realistic elements?
2. Does the description of this angel bother you? Does it meet your expectations for what an angel should be? Explain.
3. There are many humorous elements to this story. Do you think it has anything meaningful to say about reality? Explain.

BOBBIE ANN MASON (b. 1940)

Bobbie Ann Mason grew up in rural Kentucky on a dairy farm. An excellent student, Mason was encouraged in her studies by her parents, who never finished high school. She attended college at the University of Kentucky, where she majored in journalism, and later earned a master's degree from the State University of Kentucky, a master's degree from the State University of New York at Binghamton, and a doctorate from the University of Connecticut. Her first collection of short stories, Shiloh and Other Stories *(1982), was enormously well received, winning the Ernest Hemingway*

Foundation Award in 1982 for the year's most distinguished work of fiction. Her 1985 novel, In Country, *was made into a film. Her most recent novel,* Clear Springs, *appeared in 2000. Mason has described her work, which is usually set in the South and filled with popular culture references, as "southern Gothic going to the supermarket."*

SHILOH   [1982]

Leroy Moffitt's wife, Norma Jean, is working on her pectorals. She lifts three-pound dumbbells to warm up, then progresses to a twenty-pound barbell. Standing with her legs apart, she reminds Leroy of Wonder Woman.

"I'd give anything if I could just get these muscles to where they're real hard," says Norma Jean. "Feel this arm. It's not as hard as the other one."

"That's 'cause you're right-handed," says Leroy, dodging as she swings the barbell in an arc.

"Do you think so?"

"Sure."

5   Leroy is a truckdriver. He injured his leg in a highway accident four months ago, and his physical therapy, which involves weights and a pulley, prompted Norma Jean to try building herself up. Now she is attending a body-building class. Leroy has been collecting temporary disability since his tractor-trailer jack-knifed in Missouri, badly twisting his left leg in its socket. He has a steel pin in his hip. He will probably not be able to drive his rig again. It sits in the backyard, like a gigantic bird that has flown home to roost. Leroy has been home in Kentucky for three months, and his leg is almost healed, but the accident frightened him and he does not want to drive any more long hauls. He is not sure what to do next. In the meantime, he makes things from craft kits. He started by building a miniature log cabin from notched Popsicle sticks. He varnished it and placed it on the TV set, where it remains. It reminds him of a rustic Nativity scene. Then he tried string art (sailing ships on black velvet), a macramé owl kit, a snap-together B-17 Flying Fortress, and a lamp made out of a model truck, with a light fixture screwed in the top of the cab. At first the kits were diversions, something to kill time, but now he is thinking about building a full-scale log house from a kit. It would be considerably cheaper than building a regular house, and besides, Leroy has grown to appreciate how things are put together. He has begun to realize that in all the years he was on the road he never took time to examine anything. He was always flying past scenery.

"They won't let you build a log cabin in any of the new subdivisions," Norma Jean tells him.

"They will if I tell them it's for you," he says, teasing her. Ever since they were married, he has promised Norma Jean he would build her a new home one day. They have always rented, and the house they live in is small and nondescript. It does not even feel like a home, Leroy realizes now.

Norma Jean works at the Rexall drugstore, and she has acquired an amazing amount of information about cosmetics. When she explains to Leroy the three stages of complexion care, involving creams, toners, and moisturizers, he thinks happily of other petroleum products—axle grease, diesel fuel. This is a connection between him and Norma Jean. Since he has been home, he has felt unusually tender about his wife and guilty over his long absences. But he can't tell what she feels about him. Norma Jean has never complained about his traveling; she has never made hurt remarks, like calling his truck a "widow-maker." He is reasonably certain she has been faithful to him, but he wishes she would celebrate his perma- nent homecoming more happily. Norma Jean is often startled to find Leroy at home, and he thinks she seems a little disappointed about it. Perhaps he reminds her too much of the early days of their marriage, before he went on the road. They had a child who died as an infant, years ago. They never speak about their memo- ries of Randy, which have almost faded, but now that Leroy is home all the time, they sometimes feel awkward around each other, and Leroy wonders if one of them should mention the child. He has the feeling that they are waking up out of a dream together—that they must create a new marriage, start afresh. They are lucky they are still married. Leroy has read that for most people losing a child destroys the marriage—or else he heard this on *Donahue*. He can't always remem- ber where he learns things anymore.

10   At Christmas, Leroy bought an electric organ for Norma Jean. She used to play the piano when she was in high school. "It don't leave you," she told him once. "It's like riding a bicycle."

The new instrument had so many keys and buttons that she was bewildered by it at first. She touched the keys tentatively, pushed some buttons, then pecked out "Chopsticks." It came out in an amplified fox-trot rhythm, with marimba sounds.

"It's an orchestra!" she cried.

The organ had a pecan-look finish and eighteen preset chords, with optional flute, violin, trumpet, clarinet, and banjo accompaniments. Norma Jean mastered the organ almost immediately. At first she played Christmas songs. Then she bought *The Sixties Songbook* and learned every tune in it, adding variations to each with the rows of brightly colored buttons.

"I didn't like these old songs back then," she said. "But I have this crazy feeling I missed something."

15   "You didn't miss a thing," said Leroy.

Leroy likes to lie on the couch and smoke a joint and listen to Norma Jean play "Can't Take My Eyes Off You" and "I'll Be Back." He is back again. After fifteen years on the road, he is finally settling down with the woman he loves. She is still pretty. Her skin is flawless. Her frosted curls resemble pencil trimmings.

Now that Leroy has come home to stay, he notices how much the town has changed. Subdivisions are spreading across western Kentucky like an oil slick. The sign at the edge of town says "Pop: 11,500"—only seven hundred more than it said twenty years before. Leroy can't figure out who is living in all the new houses. The farmers who used to gather around the courthouse square on Saturday afternoons to play checkers and spit tobacco juice have gone. It has been years since Leroy has thought about the farmers, and they have disappeared without his noticing.

Leroy meets a kid named Stevie Hamilton in the parking lot at the new shop- ping center. While they pretend to be strangers meeting over a stalled car, Stevie tosses an ounce of marijuana under the front seat of Leroy's car. Stevie is wearing orange jogging shoes and a T-shirt that says CHATTAHOOCHEE SUPER-RAT. His father is a prominent doctor who lives in one of the expensive subdivisions in a new white-columned brick house that looks like a funeral parlor. In the phone book under his name there is a separate number, with the listing "Teenagers."

"Where do you get this stuff?" asks Leroy. "From your pappy?"

20   "That's for me to know and you to find out," Stevie says. He is slit-eyed and skinny.

"What else you got?"

"What you interested in?"

"Nothing special. Just wondered."

Leroy used to take speed on the road. Now he has to go slowly. He needs to be mellow. He leans back against the car and says, "I'm aiming to build me a log house, soon as I get time. My wife, though, I don't think she likes the idea."

25   "Well, let me know when you want me again," Stevie says. He has a cigarette in his cupped palm, as though sheltering it from the wind. He takes a long drag, then stomps it on the asphalt and slouches away.

Stevie's father was two years ahead of Leroy in high school. Leroy is thirty-four. He married Norma Jean when they were both eighteen, and their child Randy was born a few months later, but he died at the age of four months and three days. He would be about Stevie's age now. Norma Jean and Leroy were at the drive-in, watching a double feature (*Dr. Strangelove* and *Lover Come Back*), and the baby was sleeping in the back seat. When the first movie ended, the baby was dead. It was the sudden infant death syndrome. Leroy remembers handing Randy to a nurse at the emergency room, as though he were offering her a large doll as a present. A dead baby feels like a sack of flour. "It just happens sometimes," said the doctor, in what Leroy always recalls as a nonchalant tone. Leroy can hardly remember the child anymore, but he still sees vividly a scene from *Dr. Strangelove* in which the President of the United States was talking in a folksy voice on the hot line to the Soviet premier about the bomber accidentally headed toward Russia. He was in the War Room, and the world map was lit up. Leroy remembers Norma Jean standing catatonically beside him in the hospital and himself thinking: Who is this strange girl? He had forgotten who she was. Now scientists are saying that crib death is caused by a virus. Nobody knows anything, Leroy thinks. The answers are always changing.

When Leroy gets home from the shopping center, Norma Jean's mother, Mabel Beasley, is there. Until this year, Leroy has not realized how much time she spends with Norma Jean. When she visits, she inspects the closets and then the plants, informing Norma Jean when a plant is droopy or yellow. Mabel calls the plants "flowers," although there are never any blooms. She also notices if Norma Jean's laundry is piling up. Mabel is a short, overweight woman whose tight, brown-dyed curls look more like a wig than the actual wig she sometimes wears. Today she has brought Norma Jean an off-white dust ruffle she made for the bed; Mabel works in a custom-upholstery shop.

"This is the tenth one I made this year," Mabel says. "I got started and couldn't stop."

"It's real pretty," says Norma Jean.

30   "Now we can hide things under the bed," says Leroy, who gets along with his mother-in-law primarily by joking with her. Mabel has never really forgiven him for disgracing her by getting Norma Jean pregnant. When the baby died, she said that fate was mocking her.

    "What's that thing?" Mabel says to Leroy in a loud voice, pointing to a tangle of yarn on a piece of canvas.

    Leroy holds it up for Mabel to see. "It's my needlepoint," he explains. "This is a *Star Trek* pillow cover."

    "That's what a woman would do," says Mabel. "Great day in the morning!"

    "All the big football players on TV do it," he says.

35   "Why, Leroy, you're always trying to fool me. I don't believe you for one minute. You don't know what to do with yourself—that's the whole trouble. Sewing!"

    "I'm aiming to build us a log house," says Leroy. "Soon as my plans come."

    "Like *heck* you are," says Norma Jean. She takes Leroy's needlepoint and shoves it into a drawer. "You have to find a job first. Nobody can afford to build now anyway."

    Mabel straightens her girdle and says, "I still think before you get tied down y'all ought to take a little run to Shiloh."

    "One of these days, Mama," Norma Jean says impatiently.

40   Mabel is talking about Shiloh, Tennessee. For the past few years, she has been urging Leroy and Norma Jean to visit the Civil War battleground there. Mabel went there on her honeymoon—the only real trip she ever took. Her husband died of a perforated ulcer when Norma Jean was ten, but Mabel, who was accepted into the United Daughters of the Confederacy in 1975, is still preoccupied with going back to Shiloh.

    "I've been to kingdom come and back in that truck out yonder," Leroy says to Mabel, "but we never yet set foot in that battleground. Ain't that something? How did I miss it?"

    "It's not even that far," Mabel says.

    After Mabel leaves, Norma Jean reads to Leroy from a list she has made. "Things you could do," she announces. "You could get a job as a guard at Union Carbide, where they'd let you set on a stool. You could get on at the lumberyard. You could do a little carpenter work, if you want to build so bad. You could—"

    "I can't do something where I'd have to stand up all day."

45   "You ought to try standing up all day behind a cosmetics counter. It's amazing that I have strong feet, coming from two parents that never had strong feet at all." At the moment Norma Jean is holding on to the kitchen counter, raising her knees one at a time as she talks. She is wearing two-pound ankle weights.

    "Don't worry," says Leroy. "I'll do something."

    "You could truck calves to slaughter for somebody. You wouldn't have to drive any big old truck for that."

    "I'm going to build you this house," says Leroy. "I want to make you a real home."

    "I don't want to live in any log cabin."

50   "It's not a cabin. It's a house."

"I don't care. It looks like a cabin."

"You and me together could lift those logs. It's just like lifting weights."

Norma Jean doesn't answer. Under her breath, she is counting. Now she is marching through the kitchen. She is doing goose steps.

Before his accident, when Leroy came home he used to stay in the house with Norma Jean, watching TV in bed and playing cards. She would cook fried chicken, picnic ham, chocolate pie—all his favorites. Now he is home alone much of the time. In the mornings, Norma Jean disappears, leaving a cooling place in the bed. She eats a cereal called Body Buddies, and she leaves the bowl on the table, with the soggy tan balls floating in a milk puddle. He sees things about Norma Jean that he never realized before. When she chops onions, she stares off into a corner, as if she can't bear to look. She puts on her house slippers almost precisely at nine o'clock every evening and nudges her jogging shoes under the couch. She saves bread heels for the birds. Leroy watches the birds at the feeder. He notices the peculiar way goldfinches fly past the window. They close their wings, then fall, then spread their wings to catch and lift themselves. He wonders if they close their eyes when they fall. Norma Jean closes her eyes when they are in bed. She wants the lights turned out. Even then, he is sure she closes her eyes.

55   He goes for long drives around town. He tends to drive a car rather carelessly. Power steering and an automatic shift make a car feel so small and inconsequential that his body is hardly involved in the driving process. His injured leg stretches out comfortably. Once or twice he has almost hit something, but even the prospect of an accident seems minor in a car. He cruises the new subdivisions, feeling like a criminal rehearsing for a robbery. Norma Jean is probably right about a log house being inappropriate here in the new subdivisions. All the houses look grand and complicated. They depress him.

One day when Leroy comes home from a drive he finds Norma Jean in tears. She is in the kitchen making a potato and mushroom-soup casserole, with grated cheese topping. She is crying because her mother caught her smoking.

"I didn't hear her coming. I was standing here puffing away pretty as you please," Norma Jean says, wiping her eyes.

"I knew it would happen sooner or later," says Leroy, putting his arm around her.

"She don't know the meaning of the word 'knock,'" says Norma Jean. "It's a wonder she hadn't caught me years ago."

60   "Think of it this way," Leroy says. "What if she caught me with a joint?"

"You better not let her!" Norma Jean shrieks. "I'm warning you, Leroy Moffitt!"

"I'm just kidding. Here, play me a tune. That'll help you relax."

Norma Jean puts the casserole in the oven and sets the timer. Then she plays a ragtime tune, with horns and banjo, as Leroy lights up a joint and lies on the couch, laughing to himself about Mabel's catching him at it. He thinks of Stevie Hamilton—a doctor's son pushing grass. Everything is funny. The whole town seems crazy and small. He is reminded of Virgil Mathis, a boastful policeman Leroy used to shoot pool with. Virgil recently led a drug bust in a back room at a bowling alley, where he seized ten thousand dollars worth of marijuana. The newspaper had a picture of him holding up the bags of grass and grinning widely. Right now, Leroy can imagine Virgil breaking down the door and arresting him with a lungful of smoke. Virgil would probably have been alerted to the scene because of all the racket Norma Jean is making. Now she sounds like a hard-rock band. Norma Jean is terrific. When she switches to a Latin-rhythm version of "Sunshine Superman," Leroy hums along. Norma Jean's foot goes up and down, up and down.

"Well, what do you think?" Leroy says, when Norma Jean pauses to search through her music.

65   "What do I think about what?"

His mind has gone blank. Then he says, "I'll sell my rig and build us a house." That wasn't what he wanted to say. He wanted to know what she thought—what she *really* thought—about them.

"Don't start in on that again," says Norma Jean. She begins playing "Who'll Be the Next in Line?"

Leroy used to tell hitchhikers his whole life story—about his travels, his hometown, the baby. He would end with a question: "Well, what do you think?" It was just a rhetorical question. In time, he had the feeling that he'd been telling the same story over and over to the same hitchhikers. He quit talking to hitchhikers when he realized how his voice sounded—whining and self-pitying, like some teenage-tragedy song. Now Leroy has the sudden impulse to tell Norma Jean about himself, as if he had just met her. They have known each other so long they have forgotten a lot about each other. They could become reacquainted. But when the oven timer goes off and she runs to the kitchen, he forgets why he wants to do this.

The next day, Mabel drops by. It is Saturday and Norma Jean is cleaning. Leroy is studying the plans of his log house, which have finally come in the mail. He has them spread out on the table—big sheets of stiff blue paper, with diagrams and numbers printed in white. While Norma Jean runs the vacuum, Mabel drinks coffee. She sets her coffee cup on a blueprint.

70   "I'm just waiting for time to pass," she says to Leroy, drumming her fingers on the table.

As soon as Norma Jean switches off the vacuum, Mabel says in a loud voice, "Did you hear about the datsun dog that killed the baby?"

Norma Jean says, "The word is 'dachshund.'"

"They put the dog on trial. It chewed the baby's legs off. The mother was in the next room all the time." She raises her voice. "They thought it was neglect."

Norma Jean is holding her ears. Leroy manages to open the refrigerator and get some Diet Pepsi to offer Mabel. Mabel still has some coffee and she waves away the Pepsi.

75   "Datsuns are like that," Mabel says. "They're jealous dogs. They'll tear a place to pieces if you don't keep an eye on them."

"You better watch out what you're saying, Mabel," says Leroy.

"Well, facts is facts."

Leroy looks out the window at his rig. It is like a huge piece of furniture gathering dust in the backyard. Pretty soon it will be an antique. He hears the vacuum cleaner. Norma Jean seems to be cleaning the living room rug again.

Later, she says to Leroy, "She just said that about the baby because she caught me smoking. She's trying to pay me back."

"What are you talking about?" Leroy says, nervously shuffling blueprints.

"You know good and well," Norma Jean says. She is sitting in a kitchen chair with her feet up and her arms wrapped around her knees. She looks small and helpless. She says, "The very idea, her bringing up a subject like that! Saying it was neglect."

"She didn't mean that," Leroy says.

"She might not have *thought* she meant it. She always says things like that. You don't know how she goes on."

"But she didn't really mean it. She was just talking."

Leroy opens a king-sized bottle of beer and pours it into two glasses, dividing it carefully. He hands a glass to Norma Jean and she takes it from him mechanically. For a long time, they sit by the kitchen window watching the birds at the feeder.

Something is happening. Norma Jean is going to night school. She has graduated from her six-week body-building course, and now she is taking an adult-education course in composition at Paducah Community College. She spends her evenings outlining paragraphs.

"First you have a topic sentence," she explains to Leroy. "Then you divide it up. Your secondary topic has to be connected to your primary topic."

To Leroy, this sounds intimidating. "I never was any good in English," he says.

"It makes a lot of sense."

"What are you doing this for, anyhow?"

She shrugs. "It's something to do." She stands up and lifts her dumbbells a few times.

"Driving a rig, nobody cared about my English."

"I'm not criticizing your English."

Norma Jean used to say, "If I lose ten minutes' sleep, I just drag all day." Now she stays up late, writing compositions. She got a B on her first paper—a how-to theme on soup-based casseroles. Recently Norma Jean has been cooking unusual foods—tacos, lasagna, Bombay chicken. She doesn't play the organ anymore, though her second paper was called "Why Music Is Important to Me." She sits at the kitchen table, concentrating on her outlines, while Leroy plays with his log house plans, practicing with a set of Lincoln Logs. The thought of getting a truckload of notched, numbered logs scares him, and he wants to be prepared. As he and Norma Jean work together at the kitchen table, Leroy has the hopeful thought that they are sharing something, but he knows he is a fool to think this. Norma Jean is miles away. He knows he is going to lose her. Like Mabel, he is just waiting for time to pass.

One day, Mabel is there before Norma Jean gets home from work, and Leroy finds himself confiding in her. Mabel, he realizes, must know Norma Jean better than he does.

"I don't know what's got into that girl," Mabel says. "She used to go to bed with the chickens. Now you say she's up all hours. Plus her a-smoking. I like to died."

"I want to make her this beautiful home," Leroy says, indicating the Lincoln Logs. "I don't think she even wants it. Maybe she was happier with me gone."

"She don't know what to make of you, coming home like this."

"Is that it?"

100   Mabel takes the roof off his Lincoln Log cabin. "You couldn't get *me* in a log cabin," she says. "I was raised in one. It's no picnic, let me tell you."

"They're different now," says Leroy.

"I tell you what," Mabel says, smiling oddly at Leroy.

"What?"

"Take her on down to Shiloh. Y'all need to get out together, stir a little. Her brain's all balled up over them books."

105   Leroy can see traces of Norma Jean's features in her mother's face. Mabel's worn face has the texture of crinkled cotton, but suddenly she looks pretty. It occurs to Leroy that Mabel has been hinting all along that she wants them to take her with them to Shiloh.

"Let's all go to Shiloh," he says. "You and me and her. Come Sunday."

Mabel throws up her hands in protest. "Oh, no, not me. Young folks want to be by theirselves."

When Norma Jean comes in with groceries, Leroy says excitedly. "Your mama here's been dying to go to Shiloh for thirty-five years. It's about time we went, don't you think?"

"I'm not going to butt in on anybody's second honeymoon," Mabel says.

110   "Who's going on a honeymoon, for Christ's sake?" Norma Jean says loudly.

"I never raised no daughter of mine to talk that-a-way," Mabel says.

"You ain't seen nothing yet," says Norma Jean. She starts putting away boxes and cans, slamming cabinet doors.

"There's a log cabin at Shiloh," Mabel says. "It was there during the battle. There's bullet holes in it."

"When are you going to *shut up* about Shiloh, Mama?" asks Norma Jean.

115   "I always thought Shiloh was the prettiest place, so full of history," Mabel goes on. "I just hoped y'all could see it once before I die, so you could tell me about it."

Later, she whispers to Leroy, "You do what I said. A little change is what she needs."

"Your name means 'the king,'" Norma Jean says to Leroy that evening. He is trying to get her to go to Shiloh, and she is reading a book about another century.

"Well, I reckon I ought to be right proud."

"I guess so."

"Am I still king around here?"

120   Norma Jean flexes her biceps and feels them for hardness. "I'm not fooling around with anybody, if that's what you mean," she says.

"Would you tell me if you were?"

"I don't know."

"What does *your* name mean?"

"It was Marilyn Monroe's real name."

125   "No kidding!"

"Norma comes from the Normans. They were invaders," she says. She closes her book and looks hard at Leroy. "I'll go to Shiloh with you if you'll stop staring at me."

On Sunday, Norma Jean packs a picnic and they go to Shiloh. To Leroy's relief Mabel says she does not want to come with them. Norma Jean drives, and Leroy, sitting beside her, feels like some boring hitchhiker she has picked up. He tries some conversation, but she answers him in monosyllables. At Shiloh, she drives aimlessly through the park, past bluffs and trails and steep ravines. Shiloh is an immense place, and Leroy cannot see it as a battleground. It is not what he expected. He thought it would look like a golf course. Monuments are everywhere, showing through the thick clusters of trees. Norma Jean passes the log cabin Mabel mentioned. It is surrounded by tourists looking for bullet holes.

"That's not the kind of log house I've got in mind," says Leroy apologetically.

"I know *that*."

130   "This is a pretty place. Your mama was right."

"It's O.K.," says Norma Jean. "Well, we've seen it. I hope she's satisfied."

They burst out laughing together.

At the park museum, a movie on Shiloh is shown every half hour, but they decide that they don't want to see it. They buy a souvenir Confederate flag for Mabel, and then they find a picnic spot near the cemetery. Norma Jean has brought a picnic cooler, with pimento sandwiches, soft drinks, and Yodels. Leroy eats a sandwich and then smokes a joint, hiding it behind the picnic cooler. Norma Jean has quit smoking altogether. She is picking cake crumbs from the cellophane wrapper, like a fussy bird.

Leroy says, "So the boys in gray ended up in Corinth. The Union soldiers zapped 'em finally. April 7, 1862."

135   They both know that he doesn't know any history. He is just talking about some of the historical plaques they have read. He feels awkward, like a boy on a date with an older girl. They are still just making conversation.

"Corinth is where Mama eloped to," says Norma Jean.

They sit in silence and stare at the cemetery for the Union dead and, beyond, at a tall cluster of trees. Campers are parked nearby, bumper to bumper, and small children in bright clothing are cavorting and squealing. Norma Jean wads up the cake wrapper and squeezes it tightly in her hand. Without looking at Leroy, she says, "I want to leave you."

Leroy takes a bottle of Coke out of the cooler and flips off the cap. He holds the bottle poised near his mouth but cannot remember to take a drink. Finally he says, "No, you don't."

"Yes, I do."

140   "I won't let you."

"You can't stop me."

"Don't do me that way."

Leroy knows Norma Jean will have her own way. "Didn't I promise to be home from now on?" he says.

"In some ways, a woman prefers a man who wanders," says Norma Jean. "That sounds crazy, I know."

145   "You're not crazy."

Leroy remembers to drink from his Coke. Then he says, "Yes, you *are* crazy. You and me could start all over again. Right back at the beginning."

"We *have* started all over again," says Norma Jean. "And this is how it turned out."

"What did I do wrong?"

"Nothing."

150   "Is this one of those women's lib things?" Leroy asks.

"Don't be funny."

The cemetery, a green slope dotted with white markers, looks like a subdivision site. Leroy is trying to comprehend that his marriage is breaking up, but for some reason he is wondering about white slabs in a graveyard.

"Everything was fine till Mama caught me smoking," says Norma Jean, standing up. "That set something off."

"What are you talking about?"

155   "She won't leave me alone—*you* won't leave me alone." Norma Jean seems to be crying, but she is looking away from him. "I feel eighteen again. I can't face that all over again." She starts walking away. "No, it *wasn't* fine. I don't know what I'm saying. Forget it."

Leroy takes a lungful of smoke and closes his eyes as Norma Jean's words sink in. He tries to focus on the fact that thirty-five hundred soldiers died on the grounds around him. He can only think of that war as a board game with plastic soldiers. Leroy almost smiles, as he compares the Confederates' daring attack on the Union camps and Virgil Mathis's raid on the bowling alley. General Grant, drunk and furious, shoved the Southerners back to Corinth, where Mabel and Jet Beasley were married years later, when Mabel was still thin and good-looking. The next day, Mabel and Jet visited the battleground, and then Norma Jean was born, and then she married Leroy and they had a baby, which they lost, and now Leroy and Norma Jean are here at the same battleground. Leroy knows he is leaving out a lot. He is leaving out the insides of history. History was always just names and dates to him. It occurs to him that building a house of logs is similarly empty—too simple. And the real inner workings of a marriage, like most of history, have escaped him. Now he sees that building a log house is the dumbest idea he could have had. It was clumsy of him to think Norma Jean would want a log house. It was a crazy idea. He'll have to think of something else, quickly. He will wad the blueprints into tight balls and fling them into the lake. Then he'll get moving again. He opens his eyes. Norma Jean has moved away and is walking through the cemetery, following a serpentine brick path.

Leroy gets up to follow his wife, but his good leg is asleep and his bad leg still hurts him. Norma Jean is far away, walking rapidly toward the bluff by the river, and he tries to hobble toward her. Some children run past him, screaming noisily. Norma Jean has reached the bluff, and she is looking out over the Tennessee River. Now she turns toward Leroy and waves her arms. Is she beckoning to him? She seems to be doing an exercise for her chest muscles. The sky is unusually pale—the color of the dust ruffle Mabel made for their bed.

➤ QUESTIONS FOR READING AND WRITING

1. To what extent does your own background or experience influence your response to this story? Have you ever had the experience of "growing away" from someone? Explain.
2. The two main characters, Leroy and Norma Jean, seem to change as the story progresses. What do you think is happening to each of them? To their relationship?
3. Norma Jean and Leroy don't seem to have much to say to each other. Why? Are there times when you expect them to say more? What do you think remains unsaid?
4. Shiloh was the site of a major Civil War battle won by Union forces. Do you think this is an appropriate setting for this story? Explain.
5. What do you think is the theme of this story? To what extent does the title of the story account for that theme?

GUY DE MAUPASSANT (1850–1893)

Considered by many to be France's greatest writer of short fiction, Guy de Maupassant has had a major influence on the development of the modern short story and some of its most successful writers. His stories are distinguished by concise, engaging, well-structured plots that often result in ironic consequences for their characters. In the short span of 13 years, he wrote more than 360 short stories, six novels, and three travel books before he died of the complications of (then incurable) syphilis before he reached his forty-third birthday.

THE NECKLACE

[1884]

Translated by Majorie Laurie

She was one of those pretty and charming girls who are sometimes, as if by a mistake of destiny, born in a family of clerks. She had no dowry, no expectations, no means of being known, understood, loved, wedded by any rich and distinguished man; and she let herself be married to a little clerk at the Ministry of Public Instruction.

She dressed plainly because she could not dress well, but she was as unhappy as though she had really fallen from her proper station, since with women there is neither caste nor rank: and beauty, grace, and charm act instead of family and birth.

Natural fineness, instinct for what is elegant, suppleness of wit, are the sole hierarchy, and make from women of the people the equals of the very greatest ladies.

She suffered ceaselessly feeling herself born for all the delicacies and all the luxuries. She suffered from the poverty of her dwelling, from the wretched look of the walls, from the worn-out chairs, from the ugliness of the curtains. All those things, of which another woman of her rank would never even have been conscious, tortured her and made her angry. The sight of the little Breton peasant who did her humble housework aroused in her regrets which were despairing, and distracted dreams. She thought of the silent antechambers hung with Oriental tapestry, lit by tall bronze candelabra, and of the two great footmen in knee breeches who sleep in the big armchairs, made drowsy by the heavy warmth of the hot-air stove. She thought of the long salons[1] fitted up with ancient silk, of the delicate furniture carrying priceless curiosities, and of the coquettish perfumed boudoirs made for talks at five o'clock with intimate friends, with men famous and sought after, whom all women envy and whose attention they all desire.

When she sat down to dinner, before the round table covered with a tablecloth three days old, opposite her husband, who uncovered the soup tureen and declared with an enchanted air, "Ah, the good pot-au-feu![2] I don't know anything better than that," she thought of dainty dinners, of shining silverware, of tapestry which peopled the walls with ancient personages and with strange birds flying in the midst of a fairy forest; and she thought of delicious dishes served on marvelous plates, and of the whispered gallantries which you listen to with a sphinxlike smile, while you are eating the pink flesh of a trout or the wings of a quail.

5   She had no dresses, no jewels, nothing. And she loved nothing but that; she felt made for that. She would so have liked to please, to be envied, to be charming, to be sought after.

She had a friend, a former schoolmate at the convent, who was rich, and whom she did not like to go and see any more, because she suffered so much when she came back.

But one evening, her husband returned home with a triumphant air, and holding a large envelope in his hand.

"There," said he. "Here is something for you."

She tore the paper sharply, and drew out a printed card which bore these words:

10   "The Minister of Public Instruction and Mme. Georges Ramponneau request the honor of M. and Mm. Loisel's company at the palace of the Ministry on Monday evening, January eighteenth."

Instead of being delighted, as her husband hoped, she threw the invitation on the table with disdain, murmuring:

"What do you want me to do with that?"

"But my dear, I thought you would be glad. You never go out, and this is such a fine opportunity. I had awful trouble to get it. Everyone wants to go; it is very select, and they are not giving many invitations to clerks. The whole official world will be there."

[1] **salon** drawing-rooms   [2] **pot-au-feu** stew

15 She looked at him with an irritated glance, and said, impatiently:

"And what do you want me to put on my back?"

He had not thought of that; he stammered:

"Why, the dress you go to the theater in. It looks very well, to me."

He stopped, distracted, seeing his wife was crying. Two great tears descended slowly from the corners of her eyes toward the corners of her mouth. He stuttered:

"What's the matter? What's the matter?"

20 But, by violent effort, she had conquered her grief, and she replied, with a calm voice, while she wiped her wet cheeks:

"Nothing. Only I have no dress and therefore I can't go to this ball. Give your card to some colleague whose wife is better equipped than I."

He was in despair. He resumed:

"Come, let us see, Mathilde. How much would it cost, a suitable dress, which you could use on other occasions, something very simple?"

She reflected several seconds, making her calculations and wondering also what sum she could ask without drawing on herself an immediate refusal and a frightened exclamation from the economical clerk.

25 Finally, she replied, hesitatingly:

"I don't know exactly, but I think I could manage it with four hundred francs."

He had grown a little pale, because he was laying aside just that amount to buy a gun and treat himself to a little shooting next summer on the plain of Nanterre, with several friends who went to shoot larks down there, of a Sunday.

But he said:

"All right. I will give you four hundred francs. And try to have a pretty dress."

30 The day of the ball drew near, and Mme. Loisel seemed sad, uneasy, anxious. Her dress was ready, however. Her husband said to her one evening:

"What is the matter? Come, you've been so queer these last three days."

And she answered:

"It annoys me not to have a single jewel, not a single stone, nothing to put on. I shall look like distress. I should almost rather not go at all."

He resumed:

35 "You might wear natural flowers. It's very stylish at this time of the year. For ten francs you can get two or three magnificent roses."

She was not convinced.

No; there's nothing more humiliating than to look poor among other women who are rich."

But her husband cried:

"How stupid you are! Go look up your friend Mme. Forestier, and ask her to lend you some jewels. You're quite thick enough with her to do that."

40 She uttered a cry of joy:

"It's true. I never thought of it."

The next day she went to her friend and told of her distress.

Mme. Forestier went to a wardrobe with a glass door, took out a large jewel-box, brought it back, opened it, and said to Mme. Loisel:

"Choose, my dear."

45 She saw first of all bracelets, then a pearl necklace, then a Venetian cross, gold and precious stones of admirable workmanship. She tried on the ornaments before

the glass, hesitated, could not make up her mind to part with them, to give them back. She kept asking:

"Haven't you any more?"

"Why, yes. Look. I Don't know what you like."

All of a sudden she discovered, in a black satin box, a superb necklace of diamonds, and her heart began to beat with an immoderate desire. Her hands trembled as she took it. She fastened it around her throat, outside her high-necked dress, and remained lost in ecstasy at the sight of herself.

Then she asked, hesitating, filled with anguish:

50 "Can you lend me that, only that?"

"Why, yes, certainly."

She sprang upon the neck of her friend, kissed her passionately, then fled with her treasure.

The day of the ball arrived. Mme. Loisel made a great success. She was prettier than them all, elegant, gracious, smiling, and crazy with joy. All the men looked at her, asked her name, endeavored to be introduced. All the attachés of the Cabinet wanted to waltz with her. She was remarked by the minister himself.

She danced with intoxication, with passion, made drunk by pleasure, forgetting all, in the triumph of her beauty, in the glory of her success, in a sort of cloud of happiness composed of all this homage, of all this admiration, of all these awakened desires, and of that sense of complete victory which is so sweet to a woman's heart.

55 She went away about four o'clock in the morning. Her husband had been sleeping since midnight, in a little deserted anteroom, with three other gentlemen whose wives were having a very good time. He threw over her shoulders the wraps which he had brought, modest wraps of common life, whose poverty contrasted with the elegance of the ball dress. She felt this, and wanted to escape so as not to be remarked by the other women, who were enveloping themselves in costly furs.

Loisel held her back.

"Wait a bit. You will catch cold outside. I will go and call a cab."

But she did not listen to him, and rapidly descended the stairs. When they were in the street they did not find a carriage; and they began to look for one, shouting after the cabmen whom they saw passing by at a distance.

They went down toward the Seine, in despair, shivering with cold. At last they found on the quay one of those ancient noctambulant coupés which, exactly as if they were ashamed to show their misery during the day, are never seen round Paris until after nightfall.

60 It took them to their door in the Rue des Martyrs, and once more, sadly, they climbed up homeward. All was ended, for her. And as to him, he reflected that he must be at the Ministry at ten o'clock.

She removed the wraps which covered her shoulders, before the glass, so as once more to see herself in all her glory. But suddenly she uttered a cry. She no longer had the necklace around her neck!

Her husband, already half undressed, demanded:

"What is the matter with you?"

She turned madly towards him:

65 "I have—I have—I've lost Mme. Forestier's necklace."

He stood up, distracted.

"What!—how?—impossible!

And they looked in the folds of her dress, in the folds of her cloak, in her pockets, everywhere. They did not find it.

He asked:

70 "You're sure you had it on when you left the ball?"

"Yes, I felt it in the vestibule of the palace."

"But if you had lost it in the street we should have heard it fall. It must be in the cab."

"Yes. Probably. Did you take his number?"

"No. And you, didn't you notice it?"

75 "No,"

They looked, thunderstruck, at one another. At last Loisel put on his clothes.

"I shall go back on foot," said he, "over the whole route which we have taken to see if I can find it."

And he went out. She sat waiting on a chair in her ball dress, without strength to go to bed, overwhelmed, without fire, without a thought.

Her husband came back about seven o'clock. He had found nothing.

80 He went to Police Headquarters, to the newspaper offices, to offer a reward; he went to the cab companies—everywhere, in fact, whither he was urged by the least suspicion of hope.

She waited all day, in the same condition of mad fear before this terrible calamity.

Loisel returned at night with a hollow, pale face; he had discovered nothing.

"You must write to your friend, "said he, "that you have broken the clasp of her necklace and that you are having it mended. That will give us time to turn round."

She wrote at his dictation.

85 At the end of a week they had lost all hope.

And Loisel, who had aged five years, declared:

"We must consider how to replace that ornament."

The next day they took the box which had contained it, and they went to the jeweler whose name was found within. He consulted his books.

"It was not I, madame, who sold that necklace; I must simply have furnished the case."

90 Then they went from jeweler to jeweler, searching for a necklace like the other, consulting their memories, sick both of them with chagrin and anguish.

They found, in a shop at the Palais Royal, a string of diamonds which seemed to them exactly like the one they looked for. It was worth forty thousands francs. They could have it for thirty-six.

So they begged the jeweler not to sell it for three days yet. And they made a bargain that he should buy it back for thirty-four thousand francs, in case they found the other one before the end of February.

Loisel possessed eighteen thousand francs which his father had left him. He would borrow the rest.

He did borrow, asking a thousand francs of one, five hundred of another, five louis here, three louis there. He gave notes, took up ruinous obligations, dealt with usurers and all the race of lenders. He compromised all the rest of his life, risked his signature without even knowing if he could meet it; and, frightened by the pains yet to come, by the black misery which was about to fall upon him, by the prospect of all the physical privation and of all the moral tortures which he was to suffer, he went to get the new necklace, putting down upon the merchant's counter thirty-six thousand francs.

95   When Mme. Loisel took back the necklace, Mme. Forestier said to her, with a chilly manner:

"You should have returned it sooner; I might have needed it."

She did not open the case, as her friend had so much feared. If she had detected the substitution, what would she have thought, what would she have said? Would she not have taken Mme. Loisel for a thief?

Mme. Loisel now knew the horrible existence of the needy. She took her part, moreover, all of a sudden, with heroism. That dreadful debt must be paid. She would pay it. The dismissed their servant; they changed their lodgings; they rented a garret under the roof.

She came to know what heavy housework meant and the odious cares of the kitchen. She washed the dishes, using her rosy nails on the greasy pots and pans. She washed the dirty linen, the shirts, and the dishcloths, which she dried upon a line; she carried the slops down to the street every morning, and carried up the water, stopping for breath at every landing. And, dressed like a woman of the people, she went to the fruiterer, the grocer, the butcher, her basket on her arm, bargaining, insulted, defending her miserable money sou by sou.

100   Each month they had to meet some notes, renew others, obtain more time.

Her husband worked in the evening making a fair copy of some tradesman's accounts, and late at night he often copied manuscript for five sous a page.

And this life lasted for ten years.

At the end of ten years, they had paid everything, everything, with the rates of usury, and the accumulations of the compound interest.

Mme. Loisel looked old now. She had become the woman of impoverished households—strong and hard and rough. With frowsy hair, skirts askew, and red hands, she talked loud while washing the floor with great swishes of water. But sometimes, when her husband was at the office, she sat down near the window, and she thought of that gay evening of long ago, of the ball where she had been so beautiful and so fêted.

105   What would have happened if she had not lost that necklace? Who knows? Who knows? How life is strange and changeful! How little a thing is needed for us to be lost or to be saved!

But, one Sunday, having gone to take a walk in the Champs Elysées to refresh herself from the labor of the week, she suddenly perceived a woman who was leading a child. It was Mme. Forestier, still young, still beautiful, still charming.

Mme. Loisel felt moved. Was she going to speak to her? Yes, certainly. And now that she had paid, she was going to tell her all about it. Why not?

She went up.

"Good day, Jeanne."

110   The other, astonished to be familiarly addressed by this plain goodwife, did not recognize her at all, and stammered:

"But—madam!—I do not know—You must be mistaken."

"No, I am Mathilde Loisel."

Her friend uttered a cry.

"Oh, my poor Mathilde! How you are changed!"

115   "Yes, I have had days hard enough, since I have seen you, days wretched enough—and that because of you!"

"Of me! How so?"

"Do you remember that diamond necklace which you lent me to wear at the ministerial ball?"

"Yes. Well?"

"Well, I lost it."

120   "What do you mean? You brought it back."

"I brought you back another just like it. And for this we have been ten years paying. You can understand that it was not easy for us, us who had nothing. At last it is ended, and I am very glad."

Mme. Forestier had stopped.

"You say that you bought a necklace of diamonds to replace mine?"

"Yes. You never noticed it then! They were very like."

125   And she smiled with a joy which was proud and naïve at once.

Mme. Forestier, strongly moved, took her two hands.

"Oh, my poor Mathilde! Why, my necklace was paste. It was worth at most five hundred francs!"

➤ QUESTIONS FOR READING AND WRITING

1. Describe Mme. Loisel. What motivates her? What does she seem to fear most?
2. Why doesn't she tell her friend right away about the loss of the necklace? Do you think this is consistent with her character? Explain.
3. In what way is the ending ironic? Do you think it's fair?
4. Do you think there is anything else ironic about this story?

ROSARIO MORALES

With her daughter Aurora Levins Morales, Rosario Morales coauthored Getting Home Alive, *a collection of poetry and prose published in 1986 and described by one critic as the most important book to come out of the Puerto Rican diaspora in a generation. "The Day It Happened" was published in* Callaloo.

THE DAY IT HAPPENED   [1992]

The day it happened I was washing my hair. I had long hair then that went halfway down my back and I washed it once a week and rinsed it with lemon juice "to bring out the blond highlights" Mami said. Then I'd set it into pincurls that took an age to do because there was so much to wind around and around my finger. But if Mami was in a good mood, and she looked like she might be that day, she curled the back for me. I usually did all this on Saturday so I would look great for church on Sunday, and for a date Saturday night if I ever had one. ¡ojala!

Naturally the moment when it all began I was rinsing the big soapy mess. Nosy Maria was leaning out the window drying her dark red fingernails in the breeze when Josie stepped out of our apartment house doorway with a suitcase in her hand. Maria sucked in her breath so hard the sound brought my mother who took one look, crossed herself, or so Maria says, and started praying. Someone needed to pray for Josie. It was five o'clock and Ramón was due home any minute.

I wouldn't have known anything about any of this if Olga next door hadn't rung our doorbell and banged on the door just when Mami was too deep in prayer to hear and Maria was leaning out over the sill with her eyes bugging out. I cursed, very quietly of course, because if Mami or Papi heard me curse I'd get a slap across my face. I wrapped my sopping head in a towel and opened the door to Olga's "Oh my goodness, oh my dear. Oh honey, did you see? Look out the window this minute. I wouldn't have believed it if I hadn't seen it with my own two eyes. That poor little kid. I hate to think . . ." and on and on as we crossed the apartment to look out on the street.

Little Mikey from across the way was telling the rest of the kids how he'd found a taxi for Josie the minute he'd hit Southern Boulevard and how he'd hailed it and how the driver had let him ride back to Brook Street in the front seat—even though all of them had seen him arrive and step out with his back stiff with pride. Meantime Josie was back down in the street with Doña Toña from across the hall and Betty Murphy upstairs right behind her, all of them loaded down with two lamps, a typewriter and a big box of books. Doña Toña was muttering something we couldn't hear up here on the second story but it was probably either the prayer I was hearing on my right or the " . . . hurry oh hurry oh God he'll be here any minute are you mad girl, are you mad" that came at me from the left.

5   It was hard not to be scared as well as glad that Josie was packing up and leaving Ramón. They'd been married only six months but already they were in a pattern, like the Garcias down the block who did everything the same way on the same day, all year. Ramón worked late till seven every week day and five on Saturday. When he arrived he expected a good dinner to be on the table at the right temperature exactly five minutes after he walked in the door. He yelled if she didn't get it right and sometimes even if she did.

Saturday evening they went out to a party or the bar down the avenue, both of them dressed up and Ramón looking proud and cheerful for a change. Josie always looked great. She's so cute. Small and plump with long lashes on her dark eyes and, get this, naturally curly hair. She smiled a lot when she was happy but she hadn't been happy much lately and not at all since she got pregnant. I wasn't supposed to know this. God, I was almost thirteen! But Maria, who was fourteen and a half and thought she was twenty, listened in on conversations in the living room by open-ing the door a sliver and she told me all about it.

Saturday nights there was sure to be a fight. Either it was that Josie was "no fun, a man can't be a man with such a wet rag around." Or it was that Josie was "a tramp. Why else was that guy staring at you, eating you up with his eyes?" The first time it happened, soon after they moved in, it woke me up from a deep sleep and I was so scared I crept into Maria's bed. I'd never heard such yelling in my life. When my parents fight it's during the day and in angry whispers. It sounds like a snake con-vention in my parents' bedroom. That's bad enough. Maria and I get real nervous and nothing's right until they make up and talk in normal voices again. But Ramón could be heard right through the floor at two in the morning. And then he took to throwing things and then he started hitting her. The first time that happened Josie didn't go to morning mass at St. Francis and Mami went down to her apartment to see if she was sick or something. Josie came to the door with a big bruise on her face. After that Mami went to fetch her every Sunday and stayed with her if she was too ashamed to go to church.

After she found out she was pregnant Josie had talked it over with Doña Toña and Doña Toña had talked it over with Mami and by and by we all knew she was scared he would hurt the little baby growing inside of her and worried about the child growing up with Ramón for a father. He expected too much of everyone and little kids hurt so when a parent thinks whatever they do is all wrong. Ha! Tell that to Mami and Papi, will you.

I don't think there was anyone in the neighborhood on Ramón's side not even Joe who liked to bully his wife and daughters but didn't realize he did or Tito who talked all the time about "wearing the pants in this family." Ramón was too much, even for them. Josie was so clearly a fine person, a quiet homebody, a sweetypie. Ramón was out of his mind, that's what most of us thought. I mean you had to be to be so regularly mean to a person who adored you. And she did, at least at first. You could see it in the way she looked at him, boasted about his strength, his good job, his brains. The way she excused his temper. "He can't help himself. He doesn't mean it."

10   And now she was packed up and sitting in the taxi. Waiting for him to come home, I guess. That was too much for Mami and she scooted out the door with Olga, Maria, Papi, no less, and me right behind her with that soaked blue towel wrapped sloppily around my head. "Ai Mamita! Jesus, Maria y José. Jesus Maria y José," came faintly up the stairs in the front of the hurrying line. I knew Mami and I knew she meant to stand in front of Josie to protect her from that bully and, sure as shooting, Papi was going to protect Mami who was going so fast in her house slippers she almost fell down except that Olga gripped her hard and kept her upright.

When we streamed out the door into the small crowd that had gathered by now it was to see Ramón coming down the street with a sour look on his face. He looked up once or twice but mostly just stared at his feet as he strode up the block. He swept past us and almost into the house the way he did when he came home weary from the shipyard and the long ride home. He would have missed seeing Josie for sure, as I was praying he would, except that she called to him.

"Ramón," she said in her soft voice, stepping out of the taxi. "Ramón." He looked up and around then, took in the crowd, the taxi with a tall lamp lying on the back seat and Josie in her good suit. He stood looking at all this and especially at Josie for a long time. When he spoke it was only to Josie, as if we weren't there at all. He had to clear his throat to say "Josie?"

I was totally surprised and confused. He sounded so small, you know. So uncertain. It was Josie looked tall now and hard. If I hadn't known what I knew I would've said Josie was the bully in the family. She looked him straight in the eye and said stiffly, as if they were lines someone had given her to memorize, "I warned you. I said I would leave if you ever hit me again. I am not safe with you. Our child is not safe with you. I'm going now. I left arroz con pollo on the stove and the electric bill on the table." He didn't answer so she turned to hug Doña Toña and Mami before sitting herself back down. It was then that Ramón acted. Before I could blink he'd hurled himself at her, thrown himself on his knees and gripped her around her stockinged legs. "No! No te vayas. Tu no comprendes. Eres muy joven para comprender. Tu no puedes dejarme asi. Estamos casados para la vida. Te amo para siempre, para siempre. Josita, mi amor, no te vayas. Si te vas me mato. Te lo juro. No te puedes ir. No te puedes ir . . . " and on and on in a hoarse voice while Josie stood there frozen, fear on her face. There was no sound but Maria whispering occasional translations into Olga's impatient ear: "Don't go." "You're too young to understand." "We're married for life." "I'll love you always." "I'll kill myself, I swear it."

It went on forever, Josie standing there, Ramón kneeling, all of us listening, tears running down my face, Josie's face, Mami's face. It was Olga who ended it, who walked up to Ramón, knelt down beside him, put an arm around him, and started talking, telling him Josie was a mother now and had to think about what was best for her baby, that it was his baby too, that he had to let her go now so she could bear a baby healthy in body and soul, that she knew he loved Josie, that his love would let him do what was best for them all. He was crying now, arguing with her while he slowly let go while he said he never could let her go that she was his whole life, that he would die without her, while Josie kissed Toña quickly on the cheek and climbed in next to the taxi driver who sat there looking the way I probably looked, dazed, like he'd stumbled into a movie screen and couldn't get out. She had to tell him to drive off.

► QUESTIONS FOR READING AND WRITING

1. Who is the narrator? How does her point of view influence your response to the story?
2. Describe Ramón. Why is Josie leaving him? Why is Josie upset that she is pregnant?
3. Why does Ramón sound so small when he realizes Josie is leaving? Do you believe what he says in response? Explain.
4. Do you think Josie will eventually take Ramón back? Do you think she should? Why or why not?

TIM O'BRIEN (b. 1946)

Tim O'Brien was born in Austin, Minnesota. He was drafted immediately after he gradu- ated from Macalester College in 1968, and served in the infantry for two years during the Vietnam War. He has since published four novels and a book of anecdotes, all based on his war experiences. He told an interviewer in Publishers Weekly *that for him, writing "requires a sense of passion, and my passion as a human being and as a writer intersect in Vietnam, not in the physical stuff but in the issue of Vietnam—of courage, rectitude, enlightenment, holiness, trying to do the right thing in the world." The following story is taken from his collection* The Things They Carried *(1990), narrated by a character named "Tim O'Brien." His novel* In the Lake of the Woods *was named by* Time *magazine as the best novel of 1994. His most recent novel is* Tomcat in Love *(1998).*

THE THINGS THEY CARRIED

[1990]

First Lieutenant Jimmy Cross carried letters from a girl named Martha, a junior at Mount Sebastian College in New Jersey. They were not love letters, but Lieutenant Cross was hoping, so he kept them folded in plastic at the bottom of his rucksack. In the late afternoon, after a day's march, he would dig his foxhole, wash his hands under a canteen, unwrap the letters, hold them with the tips of his fingers, and spend the last hour of light pretending. He would imagine romantic camping trips into the White Mountains in New Hampshire. He would sometimes taste the enve- lope flaps, knowing her tongue had been there. More than anything, he wanted Martha to love him as he loved her, but the letters were mostly chatty, elusive on the matter of love. She was a virgin, he was almost sure. She was an English major at Mount Sebastian, and she wrote beautifully about her professors and roommates and midterm exams, about her respect for Chaucer and her great affection for Virginia Woolf. She often quoted lines of poetry; she never mentioned the war, except to say, Jimmy, take care of yourself. The letters weighed ten ounces. They were signed Love, Martha, but Lieutenant Cross understood that Love was only a way of signing and did not mean what he sometimes pretended it meant. At dusk, he would carefully return the letters to his rucksack. Slowly, a bit distracted, he would get up and move among his men, checking the perimeter, then at full dark he would return to his hole and watch the night and wonder if Martha was a virgin.

The things they carried were largely determined by necessity. Among the necessities or near-necessities were P-38 can openers, pocket knives, heat tabs, wristwatches, dog tags, mosquito repellent, chewing gum, candy, cigarettes, salt tablets, packets of Kool-Aid, lighters, matches, sewing kits, Military Payment Certificates, C rations, and two or three canteens of water. Together, these items weighed between fifteen and twenty pounds, depending upon a man's habits or rate of metabolism. Henry Dobbins, who was a big man, carried extra rations; he was especially fond of canned peaches in heavy syrup over pound cake. Dave Jensen, who practiced field hygiene, carried a toothbrush, dental floss, and several hotel-sized bars of soap he'd stolen on R&R[1] in Sydney, Australia. Ted Lavender, who was scared, carried tranquilizers until he was shot in the head outside the village of Than Khe in mid-April. By necessity, and because it was SOP,[2] they all carried steel helmets that weighed five pounds including the liner and camouflage cover. They carried the standard fatigue jackets and trousers. Very few carried underwear. On their feet they carried jungle boots—2.1 pounds—and Dave Jensen carried three pairs of socks and a can of Dr. Scholl's foot powder as a precaution against trench foot. Until he was shot, Ted Lavender carried six or seven ounces of premium dope, which for him was a necessity. Mitchell Sanders, the RTO, carried condoms. Norman Bowker carried a diary. Rat Kiley carried comic books. Kiowa, a devout Baptist, carried an illustrated New Testament that had been presented to him by his father, who taught Sunday school in Oklahoma City, Oklahoma. As a hedge against bad times, however, Kiowa also carried his grandmother's distrust of the white man, his grandfather's old hunting hatchet. Necessity dictated. Because the land was mined and booby-trapped, it was SOP for each man to carry a steel-centered, nylon-covered flak jacket, which weighed 6.7 pounds, but which on hot days seemed much heavier. Because you could die so quickly, each man carried at least one large compress bandage, usually in the helmet band for easy access. Because the nights were cold, and because the monsoons were wet, each carried a green plastic poncho that could be used as a raincoat or groundsheet or makeshift tent. With its quilted liner, the poncho weighed almost two pounds, but it was worth every ounce. In April, for instance, when Ted Lavender was shot, they used his poncho to wrap him up, then to carry him across the paddy, then to lift him into the chopper that took him away.

They were called legs or grunts.

To carry something was to hump it, as when Lieutenant Jimmy Cross humped his love for Martha up the hills and through the swamps. In its intransitive form, to hump meant to walk, or to march, but it implied burdens far beyond the intransitive.

5   Almost everyone humped photographs. In his wallet, Lieutenant Cross carried two photographs of Martha. The first was a Kodachrome snapshot signed Love, though he knew better. She stood against a brick wall. Her eyes were gray and neutral, her lips slightly open as she stared straight-on at the camera. At night, sometimes, Lieutenant Cross wondered who had taken the picture, because he knew she had boyfriends, because he loved her so much, and because he could see the shadow of the picture-taker spreading out against the brick wall. The second photograph had been clipped from the 1968 Mount Sebastian yearbook. It was an

---

[1] **R&R** rest and recreation   [2] **SOP** standard operating procedure

action shot—women's volleyball—and Martha was bent horizontal to the floor, reaching, the palms of her hands in sharp focus, the tongue taut, the expression frank and competitive. There was no visible sweat. She wore white gym shorts. Her legs, he thought, were almost certainly the legs of a virgin, dry and without hair, the left knee cocked and carrying her entire weight, which was just over one hundred pounds. Lieutenant Cross remembered touching that left knee. A dark theater, he remembered, and the movie was *Bonnie and Clyde,* and Martha wore a tweed skirt, and during the final scene, when he touched her knee, she turned and looked at him in a sad, sober way that made him pull his hand back, but he would always remember the feel of the tweed skirt and the knee beneath it and the sound of the gunfire that killed Bonnie and Clyde, how embarrassing it was, how slow and oppressive. He remember kissing her good night at the dorm door. Right then, he thought, he should've done something brave. He should've carried her up the stairs to her room and tied her to the bed and touched that left knee all night long. He should've risked it. Whenever he looked at the photographs, he thought of new things he should've done.

What they carried was partly a function of rank, partly of field specialty.

As a first lieutenant and platoon leader, Jimmy Cross carried a compass, maps, code books, binoculars, and a .45-caliber pistol that weighted 2.9 pounds fully loaded. He carried a strobe light and the responsibility for the lives of his men.

As an RTO, Mitchell Sanders carried the PRC-25 radio, a killer, twenty-six pounds with its battery.

As a medic, Rat Kiley carried a canvas satchel filled with morphone and plasma and malaria tablets and surgical tape and comic books and all the things a medic must carry, including M&M's for especially bad wounds, for a total weight of nearly twenty pounds.

10   As a big man, therefore a machine gunner, Henry Dobbins carried the M-60, which weighed twenty-three pounds unloaded, but which was almost always loaded. In addition, Dobbins carried between ten and fifteen pounds of ammunition draped in belts across his chest and shoulders.

As PFCs or Spec 4s, most of them were common grunts and carried the standard M-16 gas-operated assault rifle. The weapon weighed 7.5 pounds unloaded, 8.2 pounds with its full twenty-round magazine. Depending on numerous factors, such as topography and psychology, the riflemen carried anywhere from twelve to twenty magazines, usually in cloth bandoliers, adding on another 8.4 pounds at mininimum, fourteen pounds at maximum. When it was available, they also carried M-16 maintenance gear—rods and steel brushes and swabs and tubes of LSA oil—all of which weighed about a pound. Among the grunts, some carried the M-79 grenade launcher, 5.9 pounds unloaded, a reasonably light weapon except for the ammunition, which was heavy. A single round weighed ten ounces. The typical load was twenty-five rounds. But Ted Lavender, who was scared, carried thirty-four rounds when he was shot and killed outside Than Khe, and he went down under an exceptional burden, more than twenty pounds of ammunition, plus the flak jacket and helmet and rations and water and toilet paper and tranquilizers and all the rest, plus the unweighed fear. He was dead weight. There was no twitching or flopping.

Kiowa, who saw it happen, said it was like watching a rock fall, or a big sandbag or something—just boom, then down—not like the movies where the dead guy rolls around and does fancy spins and goes ass over teakettle—not like that, Kiowa said, the poor bastard just flat-fuck fell. Boom. Down. Nothing else. It was a bright morning in mid-April. Lieutenant Cross felt the pain. He blamed himself. They stripped off Lavendar's canteens and ammo, all the heavy things, and Rat Kiley said the obvious, the guy's dead, and Mitchell Sanders used his radio to report one U.S. KIA and to request a chopper. Then they wrapped Lavender in his poncho. They carried him out to a dry paddy, established security, and sat smoking the dead man's dope until the chopper came. Lieutenant Cross kept to himself. He pictured Martha's smooth young face, thinking he loved her more than anything, more than his men, and now Ted Lavender was dead because he loved her so much and could not stop thinking about her. When the dustoff arrived, they carried Lavender aboard. Afterward they burned Than Khe. They marched until dusk, then dug their holes, and that night Kiowa kept explaining how you had to be there, how fast it was, how the poor guy just dropped like so much concrete. Boom-down, he said. Like cement.

In addition to the three standard weapons—the M-60, M-16, and M-79—they carried whatever presented itself, or whatever seemed appropriate as a means of killing or staying alive. They carried catch-as-catch-can. At various times, in various situations, they carried M-14s and CAR-15s and Swedish Ks and grease guns and captured AK-47s and Chi-Coms and RPGs and Simonov carbines and black market Uzis and .38-caliber Smith & Wesson handguns and 66 mm LAWs and shotguns and silencers and blackjacks and bayonets and C-4 plastic explosives. Lee Strunk carried a slingshot; a weapon of last resort, he called it. Mitchell Sanders carried brass knuckles. Kiowa carried his grandfather's feathered hatchet. Every third or fourth man carried a Claymore antipersonnel mine—3.5 pounds with its firing device. They all carried fragmentation grenades—fourteen ounces each. They all carried at least one M-18 colored smoke grenade—twenty-four ounces. Some carried CS or tear gas grenades. Some carried white phosphorus grenades. They carried all they could bear, and then some, including a silent awe for the terrible power of the things they carried.

In the first week of April, before Lavendar died, Lieutenant Jimmy Cross received a good-luck charm from Martha. It was a simple pebble, an ounce at most. Smooth to the touch, it was a milky white color with flecks of orange and violet, oval-shaped, like a miniature egg. In the accompanying letter, Martha wrote that she had found the pebble on the Jersey shoreline, precisely where the land touched water at high tide, where things came together but also separated. It was this separate-but-together quality, she wrote, that had inspired her to pick up the pebble and to carry it in her breast pocket for several days, where it seemed weightless, and then to send it through the mail, by air, as a token of her truest feelings for him. Lieutenant Cross found this romantic. But he wondered what her truest feelings were, exactly, and what she meant by separate-but-together. He wondered how the tides and waves had come into play on that afternoon along the Jersey shoreline when Martha saw the pebble and bent down to rescue it from geology. He imagined bare feet. Martha was a poet, with the poet's sensibilities, and her feet would be brown and bare, the toenails unpainted, the eyes chilly and somber like the ocean in March, and though it was painful, he wondered who had been with her that afternoon. He imagined a pair of shadows moving along the strip of sand where things came together but also separated. It was phantom jealousy, he knew,

but he couldn't help himself. He loved her so much. On the march, through the hot days of early April, he carried the pebble in his mouth, turning it with his tongue, tasting sea salt and moisture. His mind wandered. He had difficulty keeping his attention on the war. On occasion he would yell at his men to spread out the column, to keep their eyes open, but then he would slip away into daydreams, just pretending, walking barefoot along the Jersey shore, with Martha, carrying nothing. He would feel himself rising. Sun and waves and gentle winds, all love and lightness.

What they carried varied by mission.

15   When a mission took them to the mountains, they carried mosquito netting, machetes, canvas tarps, and extra bug juice.

If a mission seemed especially hazardous, or if it involved a place they knew to be bad, they carried everything they could. In certain heavily mined AOs, where the land was dense with Toe Poppers and Bouncing Betties, they took turns humping a twenty-eight pound mine detector. With its headphones and big sensing plate, the equipment was a stress on the lower back and shoulders, awkward to handle, often useless because of the shrapnel in the earth, but they carried it anyway, partly for safety, partly for the illusion of safety.

On ambush, or other night missions, they carried peculiar little odds and ends. Kiowa always took along his New Testament and a pair of moccasins for silence. Dave Jensen carried night-sight vitamins high in carotene. Lee Strunk carried his slingshot; ammo, he claimed, would never be a problem. Rat Kiley carried brandy and M&M's candy. Until he was shot, Ted Lavender carried the starlight scope, which weighed 6.3 pounds with its aluminum carrying case. Henry Dobbins carried his girlfriend's pantyhose wrapped around his neck as a comforter. They all carried ghosts. When dark came, they would move out single file across the meadows and paddies to their ambush coordinates, where they would quietly set up the Claymores and lie down and spend the night waiting.

Other missions were more complicated and required special equipment. In mid-April, it was their mission to search out and destroy the elaborate tunnel complexes in the Than Khe area south of Chu Lai. To blow the tunnels, they carried one-pound blocks of pentrite high explosives, four blocks to a man, sixty-eight pounds in all. They carried wiring, detonators, and battery-powered clackers. Dave Jensen carried earplugs. Most often, before blowing the tunnels, they were ordered by higher command to search them, which was considered bad news, but by and large they just shrugged and carried out orders. Because he was a big man, Henry Dobbins was excused from tunnel duty. The others would draw numbers. Before Lavender died there were seventeen men in the platoon, and whoever drew the number seventeen would strip off his gear and crawl in headfirst with a flashlight and Lieutenant Cross's .45-caliber pistol. The rest of them would fan out as security. They would sit down or kneel, not facing the hole, listening to the ground beneath them, imagining cobwebs and ghosts, whatever was down there—the tunnel walls squeezing in—how the flashlight seemed impossibly heavy in the hand and how it was tunnel vision in the very strictest sense, compression in all ways, even time, and how you had to wiggle in—ass and elbows—a swallowed-up feeling—and how you found yourself worrying about odd things: Will your flashlight go dead? Do rats carry rabies? If you screamed, how far would the sound carry? Would your buddies hear it? Would they have the courage to drag you out? In some respects, though not many, the waiting was worse than the tunnel itself. Imagination was a killer.

On April 16, when Lee Strunk drew the number seventeen, he laughed and muttered something and went down quickly. The morning was hot and very still. Not good, Kiowa said. He looked at the tunnel opening, then out across a dry paddy toward the village of Than Khe. Nothing moved. No clouds or birds or people. As they waited, the men smoked and drank Kool-Aid, not talking much, feeling sympathy for Lee Strunk but also feeling the luck of the draw. You win some, you lose some, said Mitchell Sanders, and sometimes you settle for a rain check. It was a tired line and no one laughed.

20   Henry Dobbins ate a tropical chocolate bar. Ted Lavender popped a tranquilizer and went off to pee.

After five minutes, Lieutenant Jimmy Cross moved to the tunnel, leaned down, and examined the darkness. Trouble, he thought—a cave-in maybe. And then suddenly, without willing it, he was thinking about Martha. The stresses and fractures, the quick collapse, the two of them buried alive under all that weight. Dense, crushing love. Kneeling, watching the hole, he tried to concentrate on Lee Strunk and the war, all the dangers, but his love was too much for him, he felt paralyzed, he wanted to sleep inside her lungs and breathe her blood and be smothered. He wanted her to be a virgin and not a virgin, all at once. He wanted to know her. Intimate secrets: Why poetry? Why so sad? Why that grayness in her eyes? Why so alone? Not lonely, just alone—riding her bike across campus or sitting off by herself in the cafeteria— even dancing, she danced alone—and it was the aloneness that filled him with love. He remembered telling her that one evening. How she nodded and looked away. And how, later, when he kissed her, she received the kiss without returning it, her eyes wide open, not afraid, not a virgin's eyes, just flat and uninvolved.

Lieutenant Cross gazed at the tunnel. But he was not there. He was buried with Martha under the white sand at the Jersey shore. They were pressed together, and the pebble in his mouth was her tongue. He was smiling. Vaguely, he was aware of how quiet the day was, the sullen paddies, yet he could not bring himself to worry about matters of security. He was beyond that. He was just a kid at war, in love. He was twenty-four years old. He couldn't help it.

A few moments later Lee Strunk crawled out of the tunnel. He came up grinning, filthy but alive. Lieutenant Cross nodded and closed his eyes while the others clapped Strunk on the back and made jokes about rising from the dead.

Worms, Rat Kiley said. Right out of the grave. Fuckin' zombie.

25   The men laughed. They all felt great relief.

Spook city, said Mitchell Sanders.

Lee Strunk made a funny ghost sound, a kind of moaning, yet very happy, and right then, when Strunk made that high happy moaning sound, when he went *Ahhooooo,* right then Ted Lavender was shot in the head on his way back from peeing. He lay with his mouth open. The teeth were broken. There was a swollen black bruise under his left eye. The cheekbone was gone. Oh shit, Rat Kiley said, the guy's dead. The guy's dead, he kept saying, which seemed profound—the guy's dead. I mean really.

The things they carried were determined to some extent by superstition. Lieutenant Cross carried his good-luck pebble. Dave Jensen carried a rabbit's foot. Norman Bowker, otherwise a very gentle person, carried a thumb that had been presented to him as a gift by Mitchell Sanders. The thumb was dark brown, rubbery to the touch, and weighed four ounces at most. It had been cut from a VC corpse, a boy of fifteen or sixteen. They'd found him at the bottom of an irrigation ditch, badly burned, flies in his mouth and eyes. The boy wore black shorts and sandals. At the time of his death he had been carrying a pouch of rice, a rifle, and three magazines of ammunition.

You want my opinion, Mitchell Sanders said, there's a definite moral here.

30   He put his hand on the dead boy's wrist. He was quiet for a time, as if counting a pulse, then he patted the stomach, almost affectionately, and used Kiowa's hunting hatchet to remove the thumb.

Henry Dobbins asked what the moral was.

Moral?

You know. *Moral.*

Sanders wrapped the thumb in toilet paper and handed it across to Norman Bowker. There was no blood. Smiling, he kicked the boy's head, watched the flies scatter, and said, It's like with that old TV show—Paladin. Have gun, will travel.

35   Henry Dobbins thought about it.

Yeah, well, he finally said. I don't see no moral.

There it *is,* man.

Fuck off.

They carried USO stationery and pencils and pens. They carried Sterno, safety pins, trip flares, signal flares, spools of wire, razor blades, chewing tobacco, liberated joss sticks and statuettes of the smiling Buddha, candles, grease pencils, *The Stars and Stripes,* fingernail clippers, Psy Ops leaflets, bush hats, bolos, and much more. Twice a week, when the resupply choppers came in, they carried hot chow in green mermite cans and large canvas bags filled with iced beer and soda pop. They carried plastic water containers, each with a two-gallon capacity. Mitchell Sanders carried a set of starched tiger fatigues for special occasions. Henry Dobbins carried Black Flag insecticide. Dave Jensen carried empty sandbags that could be filled at night for added protection. Lee Strunk carried tanning lotion. Some things they carried in common. Taking turns, they carried the big PRC-77 scrambler radio, which weighed thirty pounds with its battery. They shared the weight of memory.

They took up what others could no longer bear. Often, they carried each other, the wounded or weak. They carried infections. They carried chess sets, basketballs, Vietnamese-English dictionaries, insignia of rank, Bronze Stars and Purple Hearts, plastic cards imprinted with the Code of Conduct. They carried diseases, among them malaria and dysentery. They carried lice and ringworm and leeches and paddy algae and various rots and molds. They carried the land itself—Vietnam, the place, the soil—a powdery orange-red dust that covered their boots and fatigues and faces. They carried the sky. The whole atmosphere, they carried it, the humidity, the monsoons, the stink of fungus and decay, all of it, they carried gravity. They moved like mules. By daylight they took sniper fire, at night they were mortared, but it was not battle, it was just the endless march, village to village, without purpose, nothing won or lost. They marched for the sake of the march. They plodded along slowly, dumbly, leaning forward against the heat, unthinking, all blood and bone, simple grunts, soldiering with their legs, toiling up the hills and down into the paddies and across the rivers and up again and down, just humping, one step and then the next and then another, but no volition, no will, because it was automatic, it was anatomy, and the war was entirely a matter of posture and carriage, the hump was everything, a kind of inertia, a kind of emptiness, a dullness of desire and intellect and conscience and hope and human sensibility. Their principles were in their feet. Their calculations were biological. They had no sense of strategy or mission. They searched the villages without knowing what to look for, not caring, kicking over jars of rice, frisking children and old men, blowing tunnels, sometimes setting fires and sometimes not, then forming up and moving on to the next village, then other villages, where it would always be the same. They carried their own lives. The pressures were enormous. In the heat of early afternoon, they would remove their helmets and flak jackets, walking bare, which was dangerous but which helped ease the strain. They would often discard things along the route of march. Purely for comfort, they would throw away rations, blow their Claymores and grenades, no matter, because by nightfall the resupply choppers would arrive with more of the same, then a day or two later still more, fresh watermelons and crates of ammunition and sunglasses and woolen sweaters—the resources were stunning—sparklers for the Fourth of July, colored eggs for Easter—it was the great American war chest—the fruits of science, the smokestacks, the canneries, the arsenals at Hartford, the Minnesota forests, the machine shops, the vast fields of corn and wheat—they carried like freight trains; they carried it on their backs and shoulders—and for all the ambiguities of Vietnam, all the mysteries and unknowns, there was at least the single abiding certainty that they would never be at a loss for things to carry.

40   After the chopper took Lavender away, Lieutenant Jimmy Cross led his men into the village of Than Khe. They burned everything. They shot chickens and dogs, they trashed the village well, they called in artillery and watched the wreckage, then they marched for several hours through the hot afternoon, and then at dusk, while Kiowa explained how Lavender died, Lieutenant Cross found himself trembling.

He tried not to cry. With his entrenching tool, which weighed five pounds, he began digging a hole in the earth.

He felt shame. He hated himself. He had loved Martha more than his men, and as a consequence Lavender was now dead, and this was something he would have to carry like a stone in his stomach for the rest of the war.

All he could do was dig. He used his entrenching tool like an ax, slashing, feeling both love and hate, and then later, when it was full dark, he sat at the bottom of his foxhole and wept. It went on for a long while. In part, he was grieving for Ted Lavender, but mostly it was for Martha, and for himself, because she belonged to another world, which was not quite real, and because she was a junior at Mount Sebastian College in New Jersey, a poet and a virgin and uninvolved, and because he realized she did not love him and never would.

Like cement, Kiowa whispered in the dark. I swear to God—boom, down. Not a word.

45   I've heard this, said Norman Bowker.

A pisser, you know? Still zipping himself up. Zapped while zipping.

All right, fine. That's enough.

Yeah, but you had to see it, the guy just—

I *heard,* man. Cement. So why not shut the fuck *up?*

50   Kiowa shook his head sadly and glanced over at the hole where Lieutenant Jimmy Cross sat watching the night. The air was thick and wet. A warm dense fog had settled over the paddies and there was the stillness that precedes rain.

After a time Kiowa sighed.

One thing for sure, he said. The lieutenant's in some deep hurt. I mean that crying jag—the way he was carrying on—it wasn't fake or anything, it was real heavy-duty hurt. The man cares.

Sure, Norman Bowker said.

Say what you want, the man does care.

55   We all got problems.

Not Lavender.

No, I guess not, Bowker said. Do me a favor, though.

Shut up?

That's a smart Indian. Shut up.

60   Shrugging, Kiowa pulled off his boots. He wanted to say more, just to lighten up his sleep, but instead he opened his New Testament and arranged it beneath his head as a pillow. The fog made things seem hollow and unattached. He tried not to think about Ted Lavender, but then he was thinking how fast it was, no drama, down and dead, and how it was hard to feel anything except surprise. It seemed unchristian. He wished he could find some great sadness, or even anger, but the emotion wasn't there and he couldn't make it happen. Mostly he felt pleased to be alive. He liked the smell of the New Testament under his cheek, the leather and ink and paper and glue, whatever the chemicals were. He liked hearing the sounds of night. Even his fatigue, it felt fine, the stiff muscles and the prickly awareness of his own body, a floating feeling. He enjoyed not being dead. Lying there, Kiowa admired Lieutenant Jimmy Cross's capacity for grief. He wanted to share the man's pain, he wanted to care as Jimmy Cross cared. And yet when he closed his eyes, all he could think was Boom-down, and all he could feel was the pleasure of having his

boots off and the fog curling in around him and the damp soil and the Bible smells and the plush comfort of night.

After a moment Norman Bowker sat up in the dark.

What the hell, he said. You want to talk, *talk.* Tell it to me.

Forget it.

No, man, go on. One thing I hate, it's a silent Indian.

65 For the most part they carried themselves with poise, a kind of dignity. Now and then, however, there were times of panic, when they squealed or wanted to squeal but couldn't, when they twitched and made moaning sounds and covered their heads and said Dear Jesus and flopped around on the earth and fired their weapons blindly and cringed and sobbed and begged for the noise to stop and went wild and made stupid promises to themselves and to God and to their mothers and fathers, hoping not to die. In different ways, it happened to all of them. Afterward, when the firing ended, they would blink and peek up. They would touch their bodies, feeling shame, then quickly hiding it. They would force themselves to stand. As if in slow motion, frame by frame, the world would take on the old logic—absolute silence, then the wind, then sunlight, then voices. It was the burden of being alive. Awkwardly, the men would reassemble themselves, first in private, then in groups, becoming soldiers again. They would repair the leaks in their eyes. They would check for casualties, call in dustoffs, light cigarettes, try to smile, clear their throats and spit and begin cleaning their weapons. After a time someone would shake his head and say, No lie, I almost shit my pants, and someone else would laugh, which meant it was bad, yes, but the guy had obviously not shit his pants, it wasn't that bad, and in any case nobody would ever do such a thing and then go ahead and talk about it. They would squint into the dense, oppressive sunlight. For a few moments, perhaps, they would fall silent, lighting a joint and tracking its passage from man to man, inhaling, holding in the humiliation. Scary stuff, one of them might say. But then someone else would grin or flick his eyebrows and say, Roger-dodger, almost cut me a new asshole, *almost.*

There were numerous such poses. Some carried themselves with a sort of wistful resignation, others with pride or stiff soldierly discipline or good humor or macho zeal. They were afraid of dying but they were even more afraid to show it.

They found jokes to tell.

They used a hard vocabulary to contain the terrible softness. *Greased* they'd say. *Offed, lit up, zapped while zipping.* It wasn't cruelty, just stage presence. They were actors. When someone died, it wasn't quite dying, because in a curious way it seemed scripted, and because they had their lines mostly memorized, irony mixed with tragedy, and because they called it by other names, as if to encyst and destroy the reality of death itself. They kicked corpses. They cut off thumbs. They talked grunt lingo. They told stories about Ted Lavender's supply of tranquilizers, how the poor guy didn't feel a thing, how incredibly tranquil he was.

There's a moral here, said Mitchell Sanders.

70 They were waiting for Lavender's chopper, smoking the dead man's dope.

The moral's pretty obvious, Sanders said, and winked. Stay away from drugs. No joke, they'll ruin your day every time.

Cute, said Henry Dobbins.

Mind blower, get it? Talk about wiggy. Nothing left, just blood and brains.

They made themselves laugh.

75   There it is, they'd say. Over and over—there it is, my friend, there it is—as if the repetition itself were an act of poise, a balance between crazy and almost crazy, knowing without going, there it is, which meant be cool, let it ride, because Oh yeah, man, you can't change what can't be changed, there it is, there it absolutely and positively and fucking well *is*.

They were tough.

They carried all the emotional baggage of men who might die. Grief, terror, love, longing—these were intangibles, but the intangibles had their own mass and specific gravity, they had tangible weight. They carried shameful memories. They carried the common secret of cowardice barely restrained, the instinct to run or freeze or hide, and in many respects this was the heaviest burden of all, for it could never be put down, it required perfect balance and perfect posture. They carried their reputations. They carried the soldier's greatest fear, which was the fear of blushing. Men killed, and died, because they were embarrassed not to. It was what had brought them to the war in the first place, nothing positive, no dreams of glory or honor, just to avoid the blush of dishonor. They died so as not to die of embarrassment. They crawled into tunnels and walked point and advanced under fire. Each morning, despite the unknowns, they made their legs move. They endured. They kept humping. They did not submit to the obvious alternative, which was simply to close the eyes and fall. So easy, really. Go limp and tumble to the ground and let the muscles unwind and not speak and not budge until your buddies picked you up and lifted you into the chopper that would roar and dip its nose and carry you off to the world. A mere matter of falling, yet no one ever fell. It was not courage, exactly; the object was not valor. Rather, they were too frightened to be cowards.

By and large they carried these things inside, maintaining the masks of composure. They sneered at sick call. They spoke bitterly about guys who had found release by shooting off their own toes or fingers. Pussies, they'd say. Candyasses. It was fierce, mocking talk, with only a trace of envy or awe, but even so the image played itself out behind their eyes.

They imagined the muzzle against flesh. So easy: squeeze the trigger and blow away a toe. They imagined it. They imagined the quick, sweet pain, then the evacuation to Japan, then a hospital with warm beds and cute geisha nurses.

80   And they dreamed of freedom birds.

At night, on guard, staring into the dark, they were carried away by jumbo jets. They felt the rush of takeoff. *Gone!* they yelled. And then velocity—wings and engines—a smiling stewardess—but it was more than a plane, it was a real bird, a big sleek silver bird with feathers and talons and high screeching. They were flying. The weights fell off; there was nothing to bear. They laughed and held on tight, feeling the cold slap of wind and altitude, soaring, thinking *It's over, I'm gone!*—they were naked, they were light and free—it was all lightness, bright and fast and buoyant, light as light, a helium buzz in the brain, a giddy bubbling in the lungs as they were taken up over the clouds and the war, beyond duty, beyond gravity and mortification and global entanglements—*Sin loi!* they yelled, *I'm sorry, mother-fuckers, but I'm out of it, I'm goofed, I'm on a space cruise, I'm gone!*—and it was a restful, unencumbered sensation, just riding the light waves, sailing that big silver freedom bird over the mountains and oceans, over America, over the farms and great sleeping cities and cemeteries and highways and the golden arches of McDonald's, it was flight, a kind of fleeing, a kind of falling, falling higher and higher, spinning off the edge of the earth and beyond the sun and through the vast, silent vacuum where there were no burdens and where everything weighed exactly nothing—*Gone!* they screamed—*I'm sorry but I'm gone!* and so at night, not quite dreaming, they gave themselves over to lightness, they were carried, they were purely borne.

On the morning after Ted Lavender died, First Lieutenant Jimmy Cross crouched at the bottom of his foxhole and burned Martha's letters. Then he burned the two photographs. There was a steady rain falling, which made it difficult, but he used heat tabs and Sterno to build a small fire, screening it with his body, holding the photographs over the tight blue flame with the tips of his fingers.

He realized it was only a gesture. Stupid, he thought. Sentimental, too, but mostly just stupid.

Lavender was dead. You couldn't burn the blame.

85 Besides, the letters were in his head. And even now, without photographs, Lieutenant Cross could see Martha playing volleyball in her white gym shorts and yellow T-shirt. He could see her moving in the rain.

When the fire died out, Lieutenant Cross pulled his poncho over his shoulders and ate breakfast from a can.

There was no great mystery, he decided.

In those burned letters Martha had never mentioned the war, except to say, Jimmy, take care of yourself. She wasn't involved. She signed the letters Love, but it wasn't love, and all the fine lines and technicalities did not matter. Virginity was no longer an issue. He hated her. Yes, he did. He hated her. Love, too, but it was a hard hating kind of love.

The morning came up wet and blurry. Everything seemed part of everything else, the fog and Martha and the deepening rain.

90 He was a soldier, after all.

Half smiling, Lieutenant Jimmy Cross took out his maps. He shook his head hard, as if to clear it, then bent forward and began planning the day's march. In ten minutes, or maybe twenty, he would rouse the men and they would pack up and head west, where the maps showed the country to be green and inviting. They would do what they had always done. The rain might add some weight, but otherwise it would be one more day layered upon all the other days.

He was realistic about it. There was that new hardness in his stomach. He loved her but he hated her.

No more fantasies, he told himself.

Henceforth, when he thought about Martha, it would be only to think that she belonged elsewhere. He would shut down the daydreams. This was not Mount Sebastian, it was another world, where there were no pretty poems or midterm exams, a place where men died because of carelessness and gross stupidity. Kiowa was right. Boom-down, and you were dead, never partly dead.

95   Briefly, in the rain, Lieutenant Cross saw Martha's gray eyes gazing back at him. He understood.

It was very sad, he thought. The things men carried inside. The things men did or felt they had to do.

He almost nodded at her, but didn't.

Instead he went back to his maps. He was now determined to perform his duties firmly and without negligence. It wouldn't help Lavender, he knew that, but from this point on he would comport himself as an officer. He would dispose of his good-luck pebble. Swallow it, maybe, or use Lee Strunk's slingshot, or just drop it along the trail. On the march he would impose strict field discipline. He would be careful to send out flank security, to prevent straggling or bunching up, to keep his troops moving at the proper pace and at the proper interval. He would insist on clean weapons. He would confiscate the remainder of Lavender's dope. Later in the day, perhaps, he would call the men together and speak to them plainly. He would accept the blame for what had happened to Ted Lavender. He would be a man about it. He would look them in the eyes, keeping his chin level, and he would issue the new SOPs in a calm, impersonal tone of voice, a lieutenant's voice, leaving no room for argument or discussion. Commencing immediately, he'd tell them, they would no longer abandon equipment along the route of march. They would police up their acts. They would get their shit together, and keep it together, and maintain it neatly and in good working order.

100   He would not tolerate laxity. He would show strength, distancing himself.

Among the men there would be grumbling, of course, and maybe worse, because their days would seem longer and their loads heavier, but Lieutenant Jimmy Cross reminded himself that his obligation was not to be loved but to lead. He would dispense with love; it was not now a factor. And if anyone quarreled or complained, he would simply tighten his lips and arrange his shoulders in the correct command posture. He might give a curt little nod. Or he might not. He might just shrug and say, Carry on, then they would saddle up and form into a column and move out toward the villages of Than Khe.

➤ QUESTIONS FOR READING AND WRITING

1. Describe Jimmy Cross. What do you know about him? How does he change?
2. How are you affected by the setting? What brings the setting to life?
3. Kiowa believes that Cross is crying over Lavender's death. Do you agree? Is there any other reason he might be crying? Explain.
4. In addition to the physical things they carried, the narrator says, "They carried all the emotional baggage of men who might die." What do you think he means?
5. Why does Cross burn Martha's letters?
6. Why are things repeated so often in the story?

FLANNERY O'CONNOR (1925–1964)

Flannery O'Connor was born in Savannah, Georgia, and at the age of 12, moved with her family to nearby Midgeville. After graduating from the local women's College of Georgia, O'Connor attended the University of Iowa, earning a master of fine arts degree in 1947. Following graduation, she stayed for a short time at Yaddo, a prestigious writer's colony in Saratoga Springs, New York, and then with friends in New York City and Connecticut. In 1950, after she was diagnosed with lupus, an autoimmune disease, she returned to Midgeville, where she spent the rest of her life.
O'Connor was a devout Roman Catholic. A profound faith permeates her work, which, with its blend of grotesque characterizations and religious faith, is often characterized as Southern gothic. About her stories she wrote, "My subject in fiction is the action of grace in a territory held largely by the devil."

EVERYTHING THAT RISES MUST CONVERGE   [1965]

Her doctor had told Julian's mother that she must lose twenty pounds on account of her blood pressure, so on Wednesday nights Julian had to take her downtown on the bus for a reducing class at the Y. The reducing class was designed for working girls over fifty, who weighed from 165 to 200 pounds. His mother was one of the slimmer ones, but she said ladies did not tell their age or weight. She would not ride the buses by herself at night since they had been integrated, and because the reducing class was one of her few pleasures, necessary for her health, and *free,* she said Julian could at least put himself out to take her, considering all she did for him. Julian did not like to consider all she did for him, but every Wednesday night he braced himself and took her.

She was almost ready to go, standing before the hall mirror, putting on her hat, while he, his hands behind him, appeared pinned to the door frame, waiting like Saint Sebastian for the arrows to begin piercing him.[1] The hat was new and had cost her seven dollars and a half. She kept saying, "Maybe I shouldn't have paid that for it. No, I shouldn't have. I'll take it off and return it tomorrow. I shouldn't have bought it."

Julian raised his eyes to heaven. "Yes, you should have bought it," he said. "Put it on and let's go." It was a hideous hat. A purple velvet flap came down on one side of it and stood up on the other; the rest of it was green and looked like a cushion with the stuffing out. He decided it was less comical than jaunty and pathetic. Everything that gave her pleasure was small and depressed him.

[1] **Sebastian** a Christian martyr, who was tied to a tree and shot with arrows

She lifted the hat one more time and set it down slowly on top of her head. Two wings of gray hair protruded on either side of her florid face, but her eyes, sky-blue, were as innocent and untouched by experience as they must have been when she was ten. Were it not that she was a widow who had struggled fiercely to feed and clothe and put him through school and who was supporting him still, "until he got on his feet," she might have been a little girl that he had to take to town.

5   "It's all right, it's all right," he said. "Let's go." He opened the door himself and started down the walk to get her going. The sky was a dying violet and the houses stood out darkly against it, bulbous liver-colored monstrosities of a uniform ugliness though no two were alike. Since this had been a fashionable neighborhood forty years ago, his mother persisted in thinking they did well to have an apartment in it. Each house had a narrow collar of dirt around it in which sat, usually, a grubby child. Julian walked with his hands in his pockets, his head down and thrust forward and his eyes glazed with the determination to make himself completely numb during the time he would be sacrificed to her pleasure.

The door closed and he turned to find the dumpy figure, surmounted by the atrocious hat, coming toward him. "Well," she said, "you only live once and paying a little more for it, I at least won't meet myself coming and going."

"Some day I'll start making money," Julian said gloomily—he knew he never would—"and you can have one of those jokes whenever you take the fit." But first they would move. He visualized a place where the nearest neighbors would be three miles away on either side.

"I think you're doing fine," she said, drawing on her gloves. "You've only been out of school a year. Rome wasn't built in a day."

She was one of the few members of the Y reducing class who arrived in hat and gloves and who had a son who had been to college. "It takes time," she said, "and the world is in such a mess. This hat looked better on me than any of the others, though when she brought it out I said, 'Take that thing back. I wouldn't have it on my head,' and she said, 'Now wait till you see it on,' and when she put it on me, I said, 'We-ull,' and she said, 'If you ask me, that hat does something for you and you do something for the hat, and besides,' she said, 'with that hat, you won't meet yourself coming and going.'"

10   Julian thought he could have stood his lot better if she had been selfish, if she had been an old hag who drank and screamed at him. He walked along, saturated in depression, as if in the midst of his martyrdom he had lost his faith. Catching sight of his long, hopeless, irritated face, she stopped suddenly with a grief-stricken look, and pulled back on his arm. "Wait on me," she said. "I'm going back to the house and take this thing off and tomorrow I'm going to return it. I was out of my head. I can pay the gas bill with that seven-fifty."

He caught her arm in a vicious grip. "You are not going to take it back," he said. "I like it."

"Well," she said, "I don't think I ought . . ."

"Shut up and enjoy it," he muttered, more depressed than ever.

"With the world in the mess it's in," she said, "it's a wonder we can enjoy anything. I tell you, the bottom rail is on the top."

15   Julian sighed.

"Of course," she said, "if you know who you are, you can go anywhere." She said this every time he took her to the reducing class. "Most of them in it are not our kind of people," she said, "but I can be gracious to anybody. I know who I am."

"They don't give a damn for your graciousness," Julian said savagely. "Knowing who you are is good for one generation only. You haven't the foggiest idea where you stand now or who you are."

She stopped and allowed her eyes to flash at him. "I most certainly do know who I am," she said, "and if you don't know who you are, I'm ashamed of you."

"Oh hell," Julian said.

20   "Your great-grandfather was a former governor of this state," she said. "Your grandfather was a prosperous land-owner. Your grandmother was a Godhigh."

"Will you look around you," he said tensely, "and see where you are now?" and he swept his arm jerkily out to indicate the neighborhood, which the growing darkness at least made less dingy.

"You remain what you are," she said. "Your great-grandfather had a plantation and two hundred slaves."

"There are no more slaves," he said irritably.

"They were better off when they were," she said. He groaned to see that she was off on that topic. She rolled onto it every few days like a train on an open track. He knew every stop, every junction, every swamp along the way, and knew the exact point at which her conclusion would roll majestically into the station: "It's ridiculous. It's simply not realistic. They should rise, yes, but on their own side of the fence."

25   "Let's skip it," Julian said.

"The ones I feel sorry for," she said, "are the ones that are half white. They're tragic."

"Will you skip it?"

"Suppose we were half white. We would certainly have mixed feelings."

"I have mixed feelings now," he groaned.

30   "Well let's talk about something pleasant," she said. "I remember going to Grandpa's when I was a little girl. Then the house had double stairways that went up to what was really the second floor—all the cooking was done on the first. I used to like to stay down in the kitchen on account of the way the walls smelled. I would sit with my nose pressed against the plaster and take deep breaths. Actually the place belonged to the Godhighs but your grandfather Chestny paid the mortgage and saved it for them. They were in reduced circumstances," she said, "but reduced or not, they never forgot who they were."

"Doubtless that decayed mansion reminded them," Julian muttered. He never spoke of it without contempt or thought of it without longing. He had seen it once when he was a child before it had been sold. The double stairways had rotted and been torn down. Negroes were living in it. But it remained in his mind as his mother had known it. It appeared in his dreams regularly. He would stand on the wide porch, listening to the rustle of oak leaves, then wander through the high-ceilinged hall into the parlor that opened onto it and gaze at the worn rugs and faded draperies. It occurred to him that it was he, not she, who could have appreciated it. He preferred its threadbare elegance to anything he could name and it was because of it that all the neighborhoods they had lived in had been a torment to him—whereas she had hardly known the difference. She called her insensitivity "being adjustable."

"And I remember the old darky who was my nurse, Caroline. There was no better person in the world. I've always had a great respect for my colored friends," she said. "I'd do anything in the world for them and they'd . . ."

"Will you for God's sake get off that subject?" Julian said. When he got on a bus by himself, he made it a point to sit down beside a Negro, in reparation as it were for his mother's sins.

"You're mighty touchy tonight," she said. "Do you feel all right?"

35   "Yes I feel all right," he said. "Now lay off."

She pursed her lips. "Well, you certainly are in a vile humor," she observed. "I just won't speak to you at all."

They had reached the bus stop. There was no bus in sight and Julian, his hands still jammed in his pockets and his head thrust forward, scowled down the empty street. The frustration of having to wait on the bus as well as ride on it began to creep up his neck like a hot hand. The presence of his mother was borne in upon him as she gave a pained sigh. He looked at her bleakly. She was holding herself very erect under the preposterous hat, wearing it like a banner of her imaginary dignity. There was in him an evil urge to break her spirit. He suddenly unloosened his tie and pulled it off and put it in his pocket.

She stiffened. "Why must you look like *that* when you take me to town?" she said. "Why must you deliberately embarrass me?"

"If you'll never learn where you are," he said, "you can at least learn where I am."

40   "You look like a—thug," she said.

"Then I must be one," he murmured.

"I'll just go home," she said. "I will not bother you. If you can't do a little thing like that for me . . ."

Rolling his eyes upward, he put his tie back on. "Restored to my class," he muttered. He thrust his face toward her and hissed, "True culture is in the mind, the *mind*," he said, and tapped his head, "the mind."

"It's in the heart," she said, "and in how you do things and how you do things is because of who you *are*."

45   "Nobody in the damn bus cares who you are."

"I care who I am," she said icily.

The lighted bus appeared on top of the next hill and as it approached, they moved out into the street to meet it. He put his hand under her elbow and hoisted her up on the creaking step. She entered with a little smile, as if she were going into a drawing room where everyone had been waiting for her. While he put in the tokens, she sat down on one of the broad front seats for three which faced the aisle. A thin woman with protruding teeth and long yellow hair was sitting on the end of it. His mother moved up beside her and left room for Julian beside herself. He sat down and looked at the floor across the aisle where a pair of thin feet in red and white canvas sandals were planted.

His mother immediately began a general conversation meant to attract anyone who felt like talking. "Can it get any hotter?" she said and removed from her purse a folding fan, black with a Japanese scene on it, which she began to flutter before her.

"I reckon it might could," the woman with the protruding teeth said, "but I know for a fact my apartment couldn't get no hotter."

50 "It must get the afternoon sun," his mother said. She sat forward and looked up and down the bus. It was half filled. Everybody was white. "I see we have the bus to ourselves," she said. Julian cringed.

"For a change," said the woman across the aisle, the owner of the red and white canvas sandals. "I come on one the other day and they were thick as fleas—up front and all through."

"The world is in a mess everywhere," his mother said. "I don't know how we've let it get in this fix."

"What gets my goat is all those boys from good families stealing automobile tires," the woman with the protruding teeth said. "I told my boy, I said you may not be rich but you been raised right and if I ever catch you in any such mess, they can send you on to the reformatory. Be exactly where you belong."

"Training tells," his mother said. "Is your boy in high school?"

55 "Ninth grade," the woman said.

"My son just finished college last year. He wants to write but he's selling typewriters until he gets started," his mother said.

The woman leaned forward and peered at Julian. He threw her such a malevolent look that she subsided against the seat. On the floor across the aisle there was an abandoned newspaper. He got up and got it and opened it out in front of him. His mother discreetly continued the conversation in a lower tone but the woman across the aisle said in a loud voice, "Well that's nice. Selling typewriters is close to writing. He can go right from one to the other."

"I tell him," his mother said, "that Rome wasn't built in a day."

Behind the newspaper Julian was withdrawing into the inner compartment of his mind where he spent most of his time. This was a kind of mental bubble in which he established himself when he could not bear to be a part of what was going on around him. From it he could see out and judge but in it he was safe from any kind of penetration from without. It was the only place where he felt free of the general idiocy of his fellows. His mother had never entered it but from it he could see her with absolute clarity.

60 The old lady was clever enough and he thought that if she had started from any of the right premises, more might have been expected of her. She lived according to the laws of her own fantasy world, outside of which he had never seen her set foot. The law of it was to sacrifice herself for him after she had first created the necessity to do so by making a mess of things. If he had permitted her sacrifices, it was only because her lack of foresight had made them necessary. All of her life had been a struggle to act like a Chestny without the Chestny goods, and to give him everything she thought a Chestny ought to have; but since, said she, it was fun to struggle, why complain? And when you had won, as she had won, what fun to look back on the hard times! He could not forgive her that she had enjoyed the struggle and that she thought *she* had won.

What she meant when she said she had won was that she had brought him up successfully and had sent him to college and that he had turned out so well—good looking (her teeth had gone unfilled so that his could be straightened), intelligent (he realized he was too intelligent to be a success), and with a future ahead of him (there was of course no future ahead of him). She excused his gloominess on the grounds that he was still growing up and his radical ideas on his lack of practical experience. She said he didn't yet know a thing about "life," that he hadn't even entered the real world—when already he was as disenchanted with it as a man of fifty.

The further irony of all this was that in spite of her, he had turned out so well. In spite of going to only a third-rate college, he had, on his own initiative, come out with a first-rate education; in spite of growing up dominated by a small mind, he had ended up with a large one; in spite of all her foolish views, he was free of prejudice and unafraid to face facts. Most miraculous of all, instead of being blinded by love for her as she was for him, he had cut himself emotionally free of her and could see her with complete objectivity. He was not dominated by his mother.

The bus stopped with a sudden jerk and shook him from his meditation. A woman from the back lurched forward with little steps and barely escaped falling in his newspaper as she righted herself. She got off and a large Negro got on. Julian kept his paper lowered to watch. It gave him a certain satisfaction to see injustice in daily operation. It confirmed his view that with a few exceptions there was no one worth knowing within a radius of three hundred miles. The Negro was well dressed and carried a briefcase. He looked around and then sat down on the other end of the seat where the woman with the red and white canvas sandals was sitting. He immediately unfolded a newspaper and obscured himself behind it. Julian's mother's elbow at once prodded insistently into his ribs. "Now you see why I won't ride on these buses by myself," she whispered.

The woman with the red and white canvas sandals had risen at the same time the Negro sat down and had gone further back in the bus and taken the seat of the woman who had got off. His mother leaned forward and cast her an approving look.

65 Julian rose, crossed the aisle, and sat down in the place of the woman with the canvas sandals. From this position, he looked serenely across at his mother. Her face had turned an angry red. He stared at her, making his eyes the eyes of a stranger. He felt his tension suddenly lift as if he had openly declared war on her.

He would have liked to get in conversation with the Negro and to talk with him about art or politics or any subject that would be above the comprehension of those around them, but the man remained entrenched behind his paper. He was either ignoring the change of seating or had never noticed it. There was no way for Julian to convey his sympathy.

His mother kept her eyes fixed reproachfully on his face. The woman with the protruding teeth was looking at him avidly as if he were a type of monster new to her.

"Do you have a light?" he asked the Negro.

Without looking away from his paper, the man reached in his pocket and handed him a packet of matches.

70 "Thanks," Julian said. For a moment he held the matches foolishly. A NO SMOKING sign looked down upon him from over the door. This alone would not have deterred him; he had no cigarettes. He had quit smoking some months before because he could not afford it. "Sorry," he muttered and handed back the matches.

The Negro lowered the paper and gave him an annoyed look. He took the matches and raised the paper again.

His mother continued to gaze at him but she did not take advantage of his momentary discomfort. Her eyes retained their battered look. Her face seemed to be unnaturally red, as if her blood pressure had risen. Julian allowed no glimmer of sympathy to show on his face. Having got the advantage, he wanted desperately to keep it and carry it through. He would have liked to teach her a lesson that would last her a while, but there seemed no way to continue the point. The Negro refused to come out from behind his paper.

Julian folded his arms and looked stolidly before him, facing her but as if he did not see her, as if he had ceased to recognize her existence. He visualized a scene in which, the bus having reached their stop, he would remain in his seat and when she said, "Aren't you going to get off?" he would look at her as at a stranger who had rashly addressed him. The corner they got off on was usually deserted, but it was well lighted and it would not hurt her to walk by herself the four blocks to the Y. He decided to wait until the time came and then decide whether or not he would let her get off by herself. He would have to be at the Y at ten to bring her back, but he could leave her wondering if he was going to show up. There was no reason for her to think she could always depend on him.

He retired again into the high-ceilinged room sparsely settled with large pieces of antique furniture. His soul expanded momentarily but then he became aware of his mother across from him and the vision shriveled. He studied her coldly. Her feet in little pumps dangled like a child's and did not quite reach the floor. She was training on him an exaggerated look of reproach. He felt completely detached from her. At that moment he could with pleasure have slapped her as he would have slapped a particularly obnoxious child in his charge.

He began to imagine various unlikely ways by which he could teach her a lesson. He might make friends with some distinguished Negro professor or lawyer and bring him home to spend the evening. He would be entirely justified but her blood pressure would rise to 300. He could not push her to the extent of making her have a stroke, and moreover, he had never been successful at making any Negro friends. He had tried to strike up an acquaintance on the bus with some of the better types, with ones that looked like professors or ministers or lawyers. One morning he had sat down next to a distinguished-looking dark brown man who had answered his questions with a sonorous solemnity but who had turned out to be an undertaker. Another day he had sat down beside a cigar-smoking Negro with a diamond ring on his finger, but after a few stilted pleasantries, the Negro had rung the buzzer and risen, slipping two lottery tickets into Julian's hand as he climbed over him to leave.

75   He imagined his mother lying desperately ill and his being able to secure only a Negro doctor for her. He toyed with that idea for a few minutes and then dropped it for a momentary vision of himself participating as a sympathizer in a sit-in demonstration. This was possible but he did not linger with it. Instead, he approached the ultimate horror. He brought home a beautiful suspiciously Negroid woman. Prepare yourself, he said. There is nothing you can do about it. This is the woman I've chosen. She's intelligent, dignified, even good, and she's suffered and

she hasn't thought it *fun*. Now persecute us, go ahead and persecute us. Drive her out of here, but remember, you're driving me too. His eyes were narrowed and through the indignation he had generated, he saw his mother across the aisle, purple-faced, shrunken to the dwarf-like proportions of her moral nature, sitting like a mummy beneath the ridiculous banner of her hat.

He was tilted out of his fantasy again as the bus stopped. The door opened with a sucking hiss and out of the dark a large, gaily dressed, sullen-looking colored woman got on with a little boy. The child, who might have been four, had on a short plaid suit and a Tyrolean hat with a blue feather in it. Julian hoped that he would sit down beside him and that the woman would push in beside his mother. He could think of no better arrangement.

As she waited for her tokens, the woman was surveying the seating possibilities —he hoped with the idea of sitting where she was least wanted. There was something familiar-looking about her but Julian could not place what it was. She was a giant of a woman. Her face was set not only to meet opposition but to seek it out. The downward tilt of her large lower lip was like a warning sign: DON'T TAMPER WITH ME. Her bulging figure was encased in a green crepe dress and her feet overflowed in red shoes. She had on a hideous hat. A purple velvet flap came down on one side of it and stood up on the other; the rest of it was green and looked like a cushion with the stuffing out. She carried a mammoth red pocketbook that bulged throughout as if it were stuffed with rocks.

To Julian's disappointment, the little boy climbed up on the empty seat beside his mother. His mother lumped all children, black and white, into the common category, "cute," and she thought little Negroes were on the whole cuter than little white children. She smiled at the little boy as he climbed on the seat.

Meanwhile the woman was bearing down upon the empty seat beside Julian. To his annoyance, she squeezed herself into it. He saw his mother's face change as the woman settled herself next to him and he realized with satisfaction that this was more objectionable to her than it was to him. Her face seemed almost gray and there was a look of dull recognition in her eyes, as if suddenly she had sickened at some awful confrontation. Julian saw that it was because she and the woman had, in a sense, swapped sons. Though his mother would not realize the symbolic significance of this, she would feel it. His amusement showed plainly on his face.

80 The woman next to him muttered something unintelligible to herself. He was conscious of a kind of bristling next to him, a muted growling like that of an angry cat. He could not see anything but the red pocketbook upright on the bulging green thighs. He visualized the woman as she had stood waiting for her tokens—the ponderous figure, rising from the red shoes upward over the solid hips, the mammoth bosom, the haughty face, to the green and purple hat.

His eyes widened.

The vision of the two hats, identical, broke upon him with the radiance of a brilliant sunrise. His face was suddenly lit with joy. He could not believe that Fate had thrust upon his mother such a lesson. He gave a loud chuckle so that she would look at him and see that he saw. She turned her eyes on him slowly. The blue in them seemed to have turned a bruised purple. For a moment he had an uncomfortable sense of her innocence, but it lasted only a second before principle rescued him. Justice entitled him to laugh. His grin hardened until it said to her as plainly as if he were saying aloud: Your punishment exactly fits your pettiness. This should teach you a permanent lesson.

Her eyes shifted to the woman. She seemed unable to bear looking at him and to find the woman preferable. He became conscious again of the bristling presence at his side. The woman was rumbling like a volcano about to become active. His mother's mouth began to twitch slightly at one corner. With a sinking heart, he saw incipient signs of recovery on her face and realized that this was going to strike her suddenly as funny and was going to be no lesson at all. She kept her eyes on the woman and an amused smile came over her face as if the woman were a monkey that had stolen her hat. The little Negro was looking up at her with large fascinated eyes. He had been trying to attract her attention for some time.

"Carver!" the woman said suddenly. "Come heah!"

85   When he saw that the spotlight was on him at last, Carver drew his feet up and turned himself toward Julian's mother and giggled.

"Carver!" the woman said. "You heah me? Come heah!"

Carver slid down from the seat but remained squatting with his back against the base of it, his head turned slyly around toward Julian's mother, who was smiling at him. The woman reached a hand across the aisle and snatched him to her. He righted himself and hung backwards on her knees, grinning at Julian's mother. "Isn't he cute?" Julian's mother said to the woman with the protruding teeth.

"I reckon he is," the woman said without conviction.

The Negress yanked him upright but he eased out of her grip and shot across the aisle and scrambled, giggling wildly, onto the seat beside his love.

90   "I think he likes me," Julian's mother said, and smiled at the woman. It was the smile she used when she was being particularly gracious to an inferior. Julian saw everything lost. The lesson had rolled off her like rain on a roof.

The woman stood up and yanked the little boy off the seat as if she were snatching him from contagion. Julian could feel the rage in her at having no weapon like his mother's smile. She gave the child a sharp slap across his leg. He howled once and then thrust his head into her stomach and kicked his feet against her shins. "Behave," she said vehemently.

The bus stopped and the Negro who had been reading the newspaper got off. The woman moved over and set the little boy down with a thump between herself and Julian. She held him firmly by the knee. In a moment he put his hands in front of his face and peeped at Julian's mother through his fingers.

"I see yoooooooo!" she said and put her hand in front of her face and peeped at him.

The woman slapped his hand down. "Quit yo' foolishness," she said, "before I knock the living Jesus out of you!"

95   Julian was thankful that the next stop was theirs. He reached up and pulled the cord. The woman reached up and pulled it at the same time. Oh my God, he thought. He had the terrible intuition that when they got off the bus together, his mother would open her purse and give the little boy a nickel. The gesture would be as natural to her as breathing. The bus stopped and the woman got up and lunged to the front, dragging the child, who wished to stay on, after her. Julian and his

mother got up and followed. As they neared the door, Julian tried to relieve her of her pocketbook.

"No," she murmured, "I want to give the little boy a nickel."

"No!" Julian hissed. "No!"

She smiled down at the child and opened her bag. The bus door opened and the woman picked him up by the arm and descended with him, hanging at her hip. Once in the street she set him down and shook him.

Julian's mother had to close her purse while she got down the bus step but as soon as her feet were on the ground, she opened it again and began to rummage inside. "I can't find but a penny," she whispered, "but it looks like a new one."

100   "Don't do it!" Julian said fiercely between his teeth. There was a streetlight on the corner and she hurried to get under it so that she could better see into her pocketbook. The woman was heading off rapidly down the street with the child still hanging backward on her hand.

"Oh little boy!" Julian's mother called and took a few quick steps and caught up with them just beyond the lamppost. "Here's a bright new penny for you," and she held out the coin, which shone bronze in the dim light.

The huge woman turned and for a moment stood, her shoulders lifted and her face frozen with frustrated rage, and stared at Julian's mother. Then all at once she seemed to explode like a piece of machinery that had been given one ounce of pressure too much. Julian saw the black fist swing out with the red pocketbook. He shut his eyes and cringed as he heard the woman shout, "He don't take nobody's pennies!" When he opened his eyes, the woman was disappearing down the street with the little boy staring wide-eyed over her shoulder. Julian's mother was sitting on the sidewalk.

"I told you not to do that," Julian said angrily. "I told you not to do that!"

He stood over her for a minute, gritting his teeth. Her legs were stretched out in front of her and her hat was on her lap. He squatted down and looked her in the face. It was totally expressionless. "You got exactly what you deserved," he said. "Now get up."

105   He picked up her pocketbook and put what had fallen out back in it. He picked the hat up off her lap. The penny caught his eye on the sidewalk and he picked that up and let it drop before her eyes into the purse. Then he stood up and leaned over and held his hands out to pull her up. She remained immobile. He sighed. Rising above them on either side were black apartment buildings, marked with irregular rectangles of light. At the end of the block a man came out of a door and walked off in the opposite direction. "All right," he said, "suppose somebody happens by and wants to know why you're sitting on the sidewalk?"

She took the hand and, breathing hard, pulled heavily up on it and then stood for a moment, swaying slightly as if the spots of light in the darkness were circling around her. Her eyes, shadowed and confused, finally settled on his face. He did not try to conceal his irritation. "I hope this teaches you a lesson," he said. She leaned forward and her eyes raked his face. She seemed trying to determine his identity. Then, as if she found nothing familiar about him, she started off with a headlong movement in the wrong direction.

"Aren't you going on to the Y?" he asked.

"Home," she muttered.

"Well, are we walking?"

110   For answer she kept going. Julian followed along, his hands behind him. He saw no reason to let the lesson she had had go without backing it up with an explanation of its meaning. She might as well be made to understand what had happened to her. "Don't think that was just an uppity Negro woman," he said. "That was the whole colored race which will no longer take your condescending pennies. That was your black double. She can wear the same hat as you, and to be sure," he added gratuitously (because he thought it was funny), "it looked better on her than it did on you. What all this means," he said, "is that the old world is gone. The old manners are obsolete and your graciousness is not worth a damn." He thought bitterly of the house that had been lost for him. "You aren't who you think you are," he said.

She continued to plow ahead, paying no attention to him. Her hair had come undone on one side. She dropped her pocketbook and took no notice. He stooped and picked it up and handed it to her but she did not take it.

"You needn't act as if the world had come to an end," he said, "because it hasn't. From now on you've got to live in a new world and face a few realities for a change. Buck up," he said, "it won't kill you."

She was breathing fast.

"Let's wait on the bus," he said.

115   "Home," she said thickly.

"I hate to see you behave like this," he said. "Just like a child. I should be able to expect more of you." He decided to stop where he was and make her stop and wait for a bus. "I'm not going any farther," he said, stopping. "We're going on the bus."

She continued to go on as if she had not heard him. He took a few steps and caught her arm and stopped her. He looked into her face and caught his breath. He was looking into a face he had never seen before. "Tell Grandpa to come get me," she said.

He stared, stricken.

"Tell Caroline to come get me," she said.

120   Stunned, he let her go and she lurched forward again, walking as if one leg were shorter than the other. A tide of darkness seemed to be sweeping her from him. "Mother!" he cried. "Darling, sweetheart, wait!" Crumpling, she fell to the pavement. He dashed forward and fell at her side, crying, "Mamma, Mamma!" He turned her over. Her face was fiercely distorted. One eye, large and staring, moved slightly to the left as if it had become unmoored. The other remained fixed on him, raked his face again, found nothing and closed.

"Wait here, wait here!" he cried and jumped up and began to run for help toward a cluster of lights he saw in the distance ahead of him. "Help, help!" he shouted, but his voice was thin, scarcely a thread of sound. The lights drifted farther away the faster he ran and his feet moved numbly as if they carried him nowhere. The tide of darkness seemed to sweep him back to her, postponing from moment to moment his entry into the world of guilt and sorrow.

➤ *QUESTIONS FOR READING AND WRITING*

1. Whom do you find yourself favoring? Julian or Julian's mother? Why? If this were your own mother, how would you deal with her?
2. Describe Julian's mother. What shapes her as a character?
3. Describe Julian. What shapes him as a character? He claims he is "free of prejudice." Do you think he is? Julian describes his mother as living "in her own fantasy world." Do you think he lives in the "real" world? Explain.
4. Julian tells his mother that "true culture is in the mind." She responds, "It's in the heart and in how you do things." What do you think?
5. What was your response when Julian's mother offered Carver a penny? Did you think it was bigotry?
6. What is Julian's reaction when he discovers that his mother and Carver's mother are wearing the same hat? What is your reaction to the final scene, when Julian's mother collapses?
7. What is the theme of this story? Why do you think it's called "Everything That Rises Must Converge"?

FRANK O'CONNOR (1903–1966)

Frank O'Connor was the adopted pen name of Michael Donovan, who was born in Cork, Ireland. When he was only in the fourth grade, his impoverished parents were forced to take him out of school so he could go to work. Nevertheless, while toiling at numerous odd jobs, he developed a lifelong love of reading and writing. During the "troubles" of 1918–1921, which led to an independent Ireland, O'Connor was a soldier in the Irish Republican Army. He later wrote about his experiences in his 1931 collection of short stories, Guest of the Nation. *Following the war, O'Connor worked first as a librarian, and later as a director of the famous Abbey Theatre in Dublin. He then moved to the United States, where he held teaching positions at Harvard University and Northwestern University, and achieved some celebrity appearing on Sunday morning television telling stories. His work—which includes stories, novels, plays, poetry, and criticism—is noted for its humor, poetic sensibility, and superb craftsmanship.*

MY OEDIPUS COMPLEX   [1950]

Father was in the army all through the war—the first war, I mean—so, up to the age of five, I never saw much of him, and what I saw did not worry me. Sometimes I woke and there was a big figure in khaki peering down at me in the candlelight. Sometimes in the early morning I heard the slamming of the front door and the clatter of nailed boots down the cobbles of the lane. These were Father's entrances and exits. Like Santa Claus he came and went mysteriously.

In fact, I rather liked his visits, though it was an uncomfortable squeeze between Mother and him when I got into the big bed in the early morning. He smoked, which gave him a pleasant musty smell, and shaved, an operation of astounding interest. Each time he left a trail of souvenirs—model tanks and Gurkha knives with handles made of bullet cases, and German helmets and cap badges and button-sticks, and all sorts of military equipment—carefully stowed away in a long box on top of the wardrobe, in case they ever came in handy. There was a bit of the magpie about Father; he expected everything to come in handy. When his back was turned, Mother let me get a chair and rummage through his treasures. She didn't seem to think so highly of them as he did.

The war was the most peaceful period of my life. The window of my attic faced southeast. My mother had curtained it, but that had small effect. I always woke with the first light and, with all the responsibilities of the previous day melted, feeling myself rather like the sun, ready to illumine and rejoice. Life never seemed so simple and clear and full of possibilities as then. I put my feet out from under the clothes—I called them Mrs. Left and Mrs. Right—and invented dramatic situations for them in which they discussed the problems of the day. At least Mrs. Right did; she was very demonstrative, but I hadn't the same control of Mrs. Left, so she mostly contented herself with nodding agreement.

They discussed what Mother and I should do during the day, what Santa Claus should give a fellow for Christmas, and what steps should be taken to brighten the home. There was that little matter of the baby, for instance. Mother and I could never agree about that. Ours was the only house in the terrace without a new baby, and Mother said we couldn't afford one till Father came back from the war because they cost seventeen and six. That showed how simple she was. The Geneys up the road had a baby, and everyone knew they couldn't afford seventeen and six. It was probably a cheap baby, and Mother wanted something really good, but I felt she was too exclusive. The Geneys' baby would have done us fine.

5   Having settled my plans for the day, I got up, put a chair under the attic window, and lifted the frame high enough to stick out my head. The window overlooked the front gardens of the terrace behind ours, and beyond these it looked over a deep valley to the tall, red-brick houses terraced up the opposite hillside, which were all still in shadow, while those at our side of the valley were all lit up, though with long strange shadows that made them seem unfamiliar; rigid and painted.

After that I went into Mother's room and climbed into the big bed. She woke and I began to tell her of my schemes. By this time, though I never seem to have noticed it, I was petrified in my nightshirt, and I thawed as I talked until, the last frost melted, I fell asleep beside her and woke again only when I heard her below in the kitchen, making the breakfast.

After breakfast we went into town; heard Mass at St. Augustine's and said a prayer for Father, and did the shopping. If the afternoon was fine we either went for a walk in the country or a visit to Mother's great friend in the convent, Mother St. Dominic. Mother had them all praying for Father, and every night, going to bed, I asked God to send him back safe from the war to us. Little, indeed, did I know what I was praying for!

One morning, I got into the big bed, and there, sure enough, was Father in his usual Santa Claus manner, but later, instead of uniform, he put on his best blue suit, and Mother was as pleased as anything. I saw nothing to be pleased about, because, out of uniform, Father was altogether less interesting, but she only beamed, and explained that our prayers had been answered, and off we went to Mass to thank God for having brought Father safely home.

The irony of it! That very day when he came in to dinner he took off his boots and put on his slippers, donned the dirty old cap he wore about the house to save him from colds, crossed his legs, and began to talk gravely to Mother, who looked anxious. Naturally, I disliked her looking anxious, because it destroyed her good looks, so I interrupted him.

10   "Just a moment, Larry!" she said gently.

This was only what she said when we had boring visitors, so I attached no importance to it and went on talking.

"Do be quiet, Larry!" she said impatiently. "Don't you hear me talking to Daddy?"

This was the first time I had heard those ominous words, "talking to Daddy," and I couldn't help feeling that if this was how God answered prayers, he couldn't listen to them very attentively.

"Why are you talking to Daddy?" I asked with as great a show of indifference as I could muster.

15   "Because Daddy and I have business to discuss. Now, don't interrupt again!"

In the afternoon, at Mother's request, Father took me for a walk. This time we went into town instead of out to the country, and I thought at first, in my usual optimistic way, that it might be an improvement. It was nothing of the sort. Father and I had quite different notions of a walk in town. He had no proper interest in trams, ships, and horses, and the only thing that seemed to divert him was talking to fellows as old as himself. When I wanted to stop he simply went on, dragging me behind him by the hand; when he wanted to stop I had no alternative but to do the same. I noticed that it seemed to be a sign that he wanted to stop for a long time whenever he leaned against a wall. The second time I saw him do it I got wild. He seemed to be settling himself forever. I pulled him by the coat and trousers, but, unlike Mother who, if you were too persistent, got into a wax and said: "Larry, if you don't behave yourself, I'll give you a good slap," Father had an extraordinary capacity for amiable inattention. I sized him up and wondered would I cry, but he seemed to be too remote to be annoyed even by that. Really, it was like going for a walk with a mountain! He either ignored the wrenching and pummeling entirely, or else glanced down with a grin of amusement from his peak. I had never met anyone so absorbed in himself as he seemed.

At teatime, "talking to Daddy" began again, complicated this time by the fact that he had an evening paper, and every few minutes he put it down and told Mother something new out of it. I felt this was foul play. Man for man, I was prepared to compete with him anytime for Mother's attention, but when he had it all made up for him by other people it left me no chance. Several times I tried to change the subject without success.

"You must be quiet while Daddy is reading, Larry," Mother said impatiently.

It was clear that she either genuinely liked talking to Father better than talking to me, or else that he had some terrible hold on her which made her afraid to admit the truth.

20   "Mummy," I said that night when she was tucking me up, "do you think if I prayed hard God would send Daddy back to the war?"

She seemed to think about that for a moment.

"No, dear," she said with a smile. "I don't think he would."

"Why wouldn't he, Mummy?"

"Because there isn't a war any longer, dear."

25   "But, Mummy, couldn't God make another war, if He liked?"

"He wouldn't like to, dear. It's not God who makes wars, but bad people."

"Oh!" I said.

I was disappointed about that. I began to think that God wasn't quite what he was cracked up to be.

Next morning I woke at my usual hour, feeling like a bottle of champagne. I put out my feet and invented a long conversation in which Mrs. Right talked of the trouble she had with her own father till she put him in the Home. I didn't quite know what the Home was but it sounded the right place for Father. Then I got my chair and stuck my head out of the attic window. Dawn was just breaking, with a guilty air that made me feel I had caught it in the act. My head bursting with stories and schemes, I stumbled in next door, and in the half-darkness scrambled into the big bed. There was no room at Mother's side so I had to get between her and Father. For the time being I had forgotten about him, and for several minutes I sat bolt upright, racking my brains to know what I could do with him. He was taking up more than his fair share of the bed, and I couldn't get comfortable, so I gave him several kicks that made him grunt and stretch. He made room all right, though. Mother waked and felt for me. I settled back comfortably in the warmth of the bed with my thumb in my mouth.

30   "Mummy!" I hummed, loudly and contentedly.

"Sssh! dear," she whispered. "Don't wake Daddy!"

This was a new development, which threatened to be even more serious than "talking to Daddy." Life without my early-morning conferences was unthinkable.

"Why?" I asked severely.

"Because poor Daddy is tired."

35   This seemed to me a quite inadequate reason, and I was sickened by the sentimentality of her "poor Daddy." I never liked that sort of gush; it always struck me as insincere.

"Oh!" I said lightly. Then in my most winning tone: "Do you know where I want to go with you today, Mummy?"

"No, dear," she sighed.

"I want to go down the Glen and fish for thornybacks with my new net, and then I want to go out to the Fox and Hounds, and—"

"Don't-wake-daddy!" she hissed angrily, clapping her hand across my mouth.

40   But it was too late. He was awake, or nearly so. He grunted and reached for the matches. Then he stared incredulously at his watch.

"Like a cup of tea, dear?" asked Mother in a meek, hushed voice I had never heard her use before. It sounded almost as though she were afraid.

"Tea?" he exclaimed indignantly. "Do you know what the time is?"

"And after that I want to go up the Rathcooney Road," I said loudly, afraid I'd forget something in all those interruptions.

"Go to sleep at once, Larry!" she said sharply.

45   I began to snivel. I couldn't concentrate, the way that pair went on, and smothering my early-morning schemes was like burying a family from the cradle.

Father said nothing, but lit his pipe and sucked it, looking out into the shadows without minding Mother or me. I knew he was mad. Every time I made a remark Mother hushed me irritably. I was mortified. I felt it wasn't fair; there was even something sinister in it. Every time I had pointed out to her the waste of making two beds when we could both sleep in one, she had told me it was healthier like that, and now here was this man, this stranger, sleeping with her without the least regard for her health!

He got up early and made tea, but though he brought Mother a cup he brought none for me.

"Mummy," I shouted, "I want a cup of tea, too."

"Yes, dear," she said patiently. "You can drink from Mummy's saucer."

50   That settled it. Either Father or I would have to leave the house. I didn't want to drink from Mother's saucer; I wanted to be treated as an equal in my own home, so, just to spite her, I drank it all and left none for her. She took that quietly, too.

But that night when she was putting me to bed she said gently:

"Larry, I want you to promise me something."

"What is it?" I asked.

"Not to come in and disturb poor Daddy in the morning. Promise?"

55   "Poor Daddy" again! I was becoming suspicious of everything involving that quite impossible man.

"Why?" I asked.

"Because poor Daddy is worried and tired and he doesn't sleep well."

"Why doesn't he, Mummy?"

"Well, you know, don't you, that while he was at the war Mummy got the pennies from the Post Office?"

60   "From Miss MacCarthy?"

"That's right. But now, you see, Miss MacCarthy hasn't any more pennies, so Daddy must go out and find us some. You know what would happen if he couldn't?"

"No," I said, "tell us."

"Well, I think we might have to go out and beg for them like the poor old woman on Fridays. We wouldn't like that, would we?"

"No," I agreed. "We wouldn't."

65   "So you'll promise not to come in and wake him?"

"Promise."

Mind you, I meant that. I knew pennies were a serious matter, and I was all against having to go out and beg like the old woman on Fridays. Mother laid out all my toys in a complete ring round the bed so that, whatever way I got out, I was bound to fall over one of them.

When I woke I remembered my promise all right. I got up and sat on the floor and played—for hours, it seemed to me. Then I got my chair and looked out the attic window for more hours. I wished it was time for Father to wake; I wished someone would make me a cup of tea. I didn't feel in the least like the sun; instead,

I was bored and so very, very cold! I simply longed for the warmth and depth of the big featherbed.

At last I could stand it no longer. I went into the next room. As there was still no room at Mother's side I climbed over her and she woke with a start.

70   "Larry," she whispered, gripping my arm very tightly, "what did you promise?"

"But I did, Mummy," I wailed, caught in the very act. "I was quiet for ever so long."

"Oh, dear, and you're perished!" she said sadly, feeling me all over. "Now, if I let you stay will you promise not to talk?"

"But I want to talk, Mummy," I wailed.

"That has nothing to do with it," she said with a firmness that was new to me. "Daddy wants to sleep. Now, do you understand that?"

75   I understood it only too well. I wanted to talk, he wanted to sleep—whose house was it, anyway?

"Mummy," I said with equal firmness, "I think it would be healthier for Daddy to sleep in his own bed."

That seemed to stagger her, because she said nothing for a while.

"Now, once for all," she went on, "you're to be perfectly quiet or go back to your own bed. Which is it to be?"

The injustice of it got me down. I had convicted her out of her own mouth of inconsistency and unreasonableness, and she hadn't even attempted to reply. Full of spite, I gave Father a kick, which she didn't notice but which made him grunt and open his eyes in alarm.

80   "What time is it?" he asked in a panic-stricken voice, not looking at Mother but at the door, as if he saw someone there.

"It's early yet," she replied soothingly. "It's only the child. Go to sleep again. . . . Now, Larry," she added, getting out of bed, "you've wakened Daddy and you must go back."

This time, for all her quiet air, I knew she meant it, and knew that my principal rights and privileges were as good as lost unless I asserted them at once. As she lifted me, I gave a screech, enough to wake the dead, not to mind Father. He groaned.

"That damn child! Doesn't he ever sleep?"

"It's only a habit, dear," she said quietly, though I could see she was vexed.

85   "Well, it's time he got out of it," shouted Father, beginning to heave in the bed. He suddenly gathered all the bedclothes about him, turned to the wall, and then looked back over his shoulder with nothing showing only two small, spiteful, dark eyes. The man looked very wicked.

To open the bedroom door, Mother had to let me down, and I broke free and dashed for the farthest corner, screeching. Father sat bolt upright in bed.

"Shut up, you little puppy!" he said in a choking voice.

I was so astonished that I stopped screeching. Never, never had anyone spoken to me in that tone before. I looked at him incredulously and saw his face convulsed with rage. It was only then that I fully realized how God had codded me, listening to my prayers for the safe return of this monster.

"Shut up, you!" I bawled, beside myself.

90   "What's that you said?" shouted Father, making a wild leap out of the bed.

"Mick, Mick!" cried Mother. "Don't you see the child isn't used to you?"

"I see he's better fed than taught," snarled Father, waving his arms wildly. "He wants his bottom smacked."

All his previous shouting was as nothing to these obscene words referring to my person. They really made my blood boil.

"Smack your own!" I screamed hysterically. "Smack your own! Shut up! Shut up!"

95   At this he lost his patience and let fly at me. He did it with the lack of conviction you'd expect of a man under Mother's horrified eyes, and it ended up as a mere tap, but the sheer indignity of being struck at all by a stranger, a total stranger who had cajoled his way back from the war into our big bed as a result of my innocent intercession, made me completely dotty. I shrieked and shrieked, and danced in my bare feet, and Father, looking awkward and hairy in nothing but a short gray army shirt, glared down at me like a mountain out for murder. I think it must have been then that I realized he was jealous too. And there stood Mother in her nightdress, looking as if her heart was broken between us. I hoped she felt as she looked. It seemed to me that she deserved it all.

From that morning out my life was a hell. Father and I were enemies, open and avowed. We conducted a series of skirmishes against one another, he trying to steal my time with Mother and I his. When she was sitting on my bed, telling me a story, he took to looking for some pair of old boots which he alleged he had left behind him at the beginning of the war. While he talked to Mother I played loudly with my toys to show my total lack of concern. He created a terrible scene one evening when he came in from work and found me at his box, playing with his regimental badges, Gurkha knives and button-sticks. Mother got up and took the box from me.

"You mustn't play with Daddy's toys unless he lets you, Larry," she said severely. "Daddy doesn't play with yours."

For some reason Father looked at her as if she had struck him and then turned away with a scowl.

"Those are not toys," he growled, taking down the box again to see had I lifted anything. "Some of those curios are very rare and valuable."

100   But as time went on I saw more and more how he managed to alienate Mother and me. What made it worse was that I couldn't grasp his method or see what attraction he had for Mother. In every possible way he was less winning than I. He had a common accent and made noises at his tea. I thought for a while that it might be the newspapers she was interested in, so I made up bits of news of my own to read to her. Then I thought it might be the smoking, which I personally thought attractive, and took his pipes and went round the house dribbling into them till he caught me. I even made noises at my tea, but Mother only told me I was disgusting. It all seemed to hinge round that unhealthy habit of sleeping together, so I made a point of dropping into their bedroom and nosing round, talking to myself, so that they wouldn't know I was watching them, but they were never up to anything that I could see. In the end it beat me. It seemed to depend on being grown-up and giving people rings, and I realized I'd have to wait.

But at the same time I wanted him to see that I was only waiting, not giving up the fight. One evening when he was being particularly obnoxious, chattering away well above my head, I let him have it.

"Mummy," I said, "do you know what I'm going to do when I grow up?"

"No, dear," she replied. "What?"

"I'm going to marry you," I said quietly.

105   Father gave a great guffaw out of him, but he didn't take me in. I knew it must only be pretence. And Mother, in spite of everything, was pleased. I felt she was probably relieved to know that one day Father's hold on her would be broken.

"Won't that be nice?" she said with a smile.

"It'll be very nice," I said confidently. "Because we're going to have lots and lots of babies."

"That's right, dear," she said placidly. "I think we'll have one soon, and then you'll have plenty of company."

I was no end pleased about that because it showed that in spite of the way she gave in to Father she still considered my wishes. Besides, it would put the Geneys in their place.

110   It didn't turn out like that, though. To begin with, she was very preoccupied— I supposed about where she would get the seventeen and six—and though Father took to staying out late in the evenings it did me no particular good. She stopped taking me for walks, became as touchy as blazes, and smacked me for nothing at all. Sometimes I wished I'd never mentioned the confounded baby—I seemed to have a genius for bringing calamity on myself.

And calamity it was! Sonny arrived in the most appalling hullabaloo—even that much he couldn't do without a fuss—and from the first moment I disliked him. He was a difficult child—so far as I was concerned he was always difficult— and demanded far too much attention. Mother was simply silly about him, and couldn't see when he was only showing off. As company he was worse than useless. He slept all day, and I had to go round the house on tiptoe to avoid waking him. It wasn't any longer a question of not waking Father. The slogan now was "Don't-wake-Sonny!" I couldn't understand why the child wouldn't sleep at the proper time, so whenever Mother's back was turned I woke him. Sometimes to keep him awake I pinched him as well. Mother caught me at it one day and gave me a most unmerciful flaking.

One evening, when Father was coming in from work, I was playing trains in the front garden. I let on not to notice him; instead, I pretended to be talking to myself, and said in a loud voice: "If another bloody baby comes into this house, I'm going out."

Father stopped dead and looked at me over his shoulder.

"What's that you said?" he asked sternly.

115   "I was only talking to myself," I replied, trying to conceal my panic. "It's private."

He turned and went in without a word. Mind you, I intended it as a solemn warning, but its effect was quite different. Father started being quite nice to me. I could understand that, of course. Mother was quite sickening about Sonny. Even at mealtimes she'd get up and gawk at him in the cradle with an idiotic smile, and tell Father to do the same. He was always polite about it, but he looked so puzzled you could see he didn't know what she was talking about. He complained of the way Sonny cried at night, but she only got cross and said that Sonny never cried except when there was something up with him—which was a flaming lie, because Sonny never had anything up with him, and only cried for attention. It was really painful to see how simple-minded she was. Father wasn't attractive, but he had a fine intelligence. He saw through Sonny, and now he knew that I saw through him as well.

One night I woke with a start. There was someone beside me in the bed. For one wild moment I felt sure it must be Mother, having come to her senses and left Father for good, but then I heard Sonny in convulsions in the next room, and Mother saying: "There! There! There!" and I knew it wasn't she. It was Father. He was lying beside me, wide awake, breathing hard and apparently as mad as hell.

After a while it came to me what he was mad about. It was his turn now. After turning me out of the big bed, he had been turned out himself. Mother had no consideration now for anyone but that poisonous pup, Sonny. I couldn't help feeling sorry for Father. I had been through it all myself, and even at that age I was magnanimous. I began to stroke him down and say: "There! There!" He wasn't exactly responsive.

"Aren't you asleep either?" he snarled.

120 "Ah, come on and put your arm around us, can't you?" I said, and he did, in a sort of way. Gingerly, I suppose, is how you'd describe it. He was very bony but better than nothing.

At Christmas he went out of his way to buy me a really nice model railway.

➤ QUESTIONS FOR READING AND WRITING

1. What is an Oedipus complex? Do you think "My Oedipus Complex" is an appropriate title for this story? Explain.
2. Who is the narrator in this story? How does the narrator's point of view establish the tone? What makes the story humorous?
3. How does the relationship between the narrator and his father change as the story develops?
4. In what way is the ending, like much of the story, ironic?

TILLIE OLSEN (b. 1913)

Tillie Olsen was born in Omaha, Nebraska. Her parents had emigrated from Russia, fleeing czarist persecution for their socialist views. Forced to quit school after the eleventh grade, she went to work to help support her family. Olsen married in 1936, and she spent the following 20 years raising her four children and working full time in a series of secretarial jobs. She wrote at odd moments at work or late at night after her children had gone to bed. Except for a few poems and a short story published before her marriage, Olsen published nothing until "I Stand Here Ironing" appeared in 1954.

Though her stories have appeared in numerous publications, her only volume of short stories to date, Tell Me a Riddle, *was published in 1961. In 1974, she completed a* novel, Yonnonido, *which she started when she was 19 and had put aside for over 30 years. Olsen has held teaching positions at many institutions including UCLA, Stanford, the Massachusetts Institute of Technology, and Kenyon College.*

I Stand Here Ironing   [1961]

I stand here ironing, and what you asked me moves tormented back and forth with the iron.

"I wish you would manage the time to come in and talk with me about your daughter. I'm sure you can help me understand her. She's a youngster who needs help and whom I'm deeply interested in helping."

"Who needs help." . . . Even if I came, what good would it do? You think because I am her mother I have a key, or that in some way you could use me as a key? She has lived for nineteen years. There is all that life that has happened outside of me, beyond me.

And when is there time to remember, to sift, to weigh, to estimate, to total? I will start and there will be an interruption and I will have to gather it all together again. Or I will become engulfed with all I did or did not do, with what should have been and what cannot be helped.

5   She was a beautiful baby. The first and only one of our five that was beautiful at birth. You do not guess how new and uneasy her tenancy in her now-loveliness. You did not know her all those years she was thought homely, or see her poring over her baby pictures, making me tell her over and over how beautiful she had been—and would be, I would tell her—and was now, to the seeing eye. But the seeing eyes were few or nonexistent. Including mine.

I nursed her. They feel that's important nowadays. I nursed all the children, but with her, with all the fierce rigidity of first motherhood, I did like the books then said. Though her cries battered me to trembling and my breasts ached with swollenness, I waited till the clock decreed.

Why do I put that first? I do not even know if it matters, or if it explains anything.

She was a beautiful baby. She blew shining bubbles of sound. She loved motion, loved light, loved color and music and textures. She would lie on the floor in her blue overalls patting the surface so hard in ecstasy her hands and feet would blur. She was a miracle to me, but when she was eight months old I had to leave her daytimes with the woman downstairs to whom she was no miracle at all, for I worked or looked for work and for Emily's father, who "could no longer endure" (he wrote in his good-bye note) "sharing want with us."

I was nineteen. It was the pre-relief, pre-WPA world of the depression. I would start running as soon as I got off the streetcar, running up the stairs, the place smelling sour, and awake or asleep to startle awake, when she saw me she would break into a clogged weeping that could not be comforted, a weeping I can hear yet.

10   After a while I found a job hashing at night so I could be with her days, and it was better. But it came to where I had to bring her to his family and leave her.

It took a long time to raise the money for her fare back. Then she got chicken pox and I had to wait longer. When she finally came, I hardly knew her, walking quick and nervous like her father, looking like her father, thin, and dressed in a shoddy red that yellowed her skin and glared at the pockmarks. All the baby loveliness gone.

She was two. Old enough for nursery school they said, and I did not know then what I know now—the fatigue of the long day, and the lacerations of group life in the kinds of nurseries that are only parking places for children.

Except that it would have made no difference if I had known. It was the only place there was. It was the only way we could be together, the only way I could hold a job.

And even without knowing, I knew. I knew the teacher that was evil because all these years it has curdled into my memory, the little boy hunched in the corner, her rasp, "why aren't you outside, because Alvin hits you? that's no reason, go out, scaredy." I knew Emily hated it even if she did not clutch and implore "don't go Mommy" like the other children, mornings.

15   She always had a reason why we should stay home. Momma, you look sick. Momma, I feel sick. Momma, the teachers aren't there today, they're sick. Momma, we can't go, there was a fire there last night. Momma, it's a holiday today, no school, they told me.

But never a direct protest, never rebellion. I think of our others in their three-, four-year-oldness—the explosions, the tempers, the denunciations, the demands—and I feel suddenly ill. I put the iron down. What in me demanded that goodness in her? And what was the cost, the cost to her of such goodness?

The old man living in the back once said in his gentle way: "You should smile at Emily more when you look at her." What *was* in my face when I looked at her? I loved her. There were all the acts of love.

It was only with the others I remembered what he said, and it was the face of joy, and not of care or tightness or worry I turned to them—too late for Emily. She does not smile easily, let alone almost always as her brothers and sisters do. Her face is closed and somber, but when she wants, how fluid. You must have seen it in her pantomimes, you spoke of her rare gift for comedy on the stage that rouses laughter out of the audience so dear they applaud and applaud and do not want to let her go.

Where does it come from, that comedy? There was none of it in her when she came back to me that second time, after I had had to send her away again. She had a new daddy now to learn to love, and I think perhaps it was a better time.

20   Except when we left her alone nights, telling ourselves she was old enough. "Can't you go some other time, Mommy, like tomorrow?" she would ask. "Will it be just a little while you'll be gone? Do you promise?"

The time we came back, the front door open, the clock on the floor in the hall. She rigid awake. "It wasn't just a little while. I didn't cry. Three times I called you, just three times, and then I ran downstairs to open the door so you could come faster. The clock talked loud. I threw it away, it scared me what it talked."

She said the clock talked loud again that night I went to the hospital to have Susan. She was delirious with the fever that comes from red measles, but she was fully conscious all the week I was gone and the week after we were home when she could not come near the new baby or me.

She did not get well. She stayed skeleton thin, not wanting to eat, and night after night she had nightmares. She would call for me, and I would rouse from exhaustion to sleepily call back: "You're all right, darling, go to sleep, it's just a dream," and if she still called, in a sterner voice, "now go to sleep, Emily, there's nothing to hurt you." Twice, only twice, when I had to get up for Susan anyhow, I went in to sit with her.

25   Now when it is too late (as if she would let me hold and comfort her like I do the others) I get up and go to her at once at her moan or restless stirring. "Are you awake, Emily? Can I get you something?" And the answer is always the same: "No, I'm all right, go back to sleep, Mother."

They persuaded me at the clinic to send her away to a convalescent home in the country where "she can have the kind of food and care you can't manage for her, and you'll be free to concentrate on the new baby." They still send children to that place. I see pictures on the society page of sleek young women planning affairs to raise money for it, or dancing at the affairs, or decorating Easter eggs or filling Christmas stockings for the children.

They never have a picture of the children so I do not know if the girls still wear those gigantic red bows and the ravaged looks on the every other Sunday when parents can come to visit "unless otherwise notified"—as we were notified the first six weeks.

Oh it is a handsome place, green lawns and tall trees and fluted flower beds. High up on the balconies of each cottage the children stand, the girls in their red bows and white dresses, the boys in white suits and giant red ties. The parents stand below shrieking up to be heard and the children shriek down to be heard, and between them the invisible wall: "Not to Be Contaminated by Parental Germs or Physical Affection."

There was a tiny girl who always stood hand in hand with Emily. Her parents never came. One visit she was gone. "They moved her to Rose Cottage," Emily shouted in explanation. "They don't like you to love anybody here."

30   She wrote once a week, the labored writing of a seven-year-old. "I am fine. How is the baby. If I write my letter nicely I will have a star. Love." There never was a star. We wrote every other day, letters she could never hold or keep but only hear read—once. "We simply do not have room for children to keep any personal possessions," they patiently explained when we pieced one Sunday's shrieking together to plead how much it would mean to Emily, who loved so to keep things, to be allowed to keep her letters and cards.

Each visit she looked frailer. "She isn't eating," they told us.

(They had runny eggs for breakfast or mush with lumps, Emily said later, I'd hold it in my mouth and not swallow. Nothing ever tasted good, just when they had chicken.)

It took us eight months to get her released home, and only the fact that she gained back so little of her seven lost pounds convinced the social worker.

I used to try to hold and love her after she came back, but her body would stay stiff, and after a while she'd push away. She ate little. Food sickened her, and I think much of life too. Oh she had physical lightness and brightness, twinkling by on skates, bouncing like a ball up and down up and down over the jump rope, skimming over the hill: but these were momentary.

35   She fretted about her appearance, thin and dark and foreign-looking at a time when every little girl was supposed to look or thought she should look a chubby

blonde replica of Shirley Temple. The doorbell sometimes rang for her, but no one seemed to come and play in the house or be a best friend. Maybe because we moved so much.

There was a boy she loved painfully through two school semesters. Months later she told me how she had taken pennies from my purse to buy him candy. "Licorice was his favorite and I brought him some every day, but he still liked Jennifer better'n me. Why, Mommy?" The kind of question for which there is no answer.

School was a worry to her. She was not glib or quick in a world where glibness and quickness were easily confused with ability to learn. To her overworked and exasperated teachers she was an overconscientious "slow learner" who kept trying to catch up and was absent entirely too often.

I let her be absent, though sometimes the illness was imaginary. How different from my now-strictness about attendance with the others. I wasn't working. We had a new baby, I was home anyhow. Sometimes, after Susan grew old enough, I would keep her home from school, too, to have them all together.

Mostly Emily had asthma, and her breathing, harsh and labored, would fill the house with a curiously tranquil sound. I would bring the two old dresser mirrors and her boxes of collections to her bed. She would select beads and single earrings, bottle tops and shells, dried flowers and pebbles, old postcards and scraps, all sorts of oddments; then she and Susan would play Kingdom, setting up landscapes and furniture, peopling them with action.

40   Those were the only times of peaceful companionship between her and Susan. I have edged away from it, that poisonous feeling between them, that terrible balancing of hurts and needs I had to do between the two, and did so badly, those earlier years.

Oh there are conflicts between the others too, each one human, needing, demanding, hurting, taking—but only between Emily and Susan, no, Emily toward Susan that corroding resentment. It seems so obvious on the surface, yet it is not obvious. Susan, the second child, Susan, golden- and curly-haired and chubby, quick and articulate and assured, everything in appearance and manner Emily was not; Susan, not able to resist Emily's precious things, losing or sometimes clumsily breaking them; Susan telling jokes and riddles to company for applause while Emily sat silent (to say to me later: that was *my* riddle, Mother, I told it to Susan); Susan, who for all the five years' difference in age was just a year behind Emily in developing physically.

I am glad for that slow physical development that widened the difference between her and her contemporaries, though she suffered over it. She was too vulnerable for that terrible world of youthful competition, of preening and parading, of constant measuring of yourself against every other, of envy, "If I had the copper hair," "If I had that skin . . . ." She tormented herself enough about not looking like the others, there was enough of the unsureness, the having to be conscious of words before you speak, the constant caring—what are they thinking of me? without having it all magnified by the merciless physical drives.

Ronnie is calling. He is wet and I change him. It is rare there is such a cry now. That time of motherhood is almost behind me when the ear is not one's own but must always be racked and listening for the child cry, the child call. We sit for a while and I hold him, looking out over the city spread in charcoal with its soft aisles of light. "*Shoogily,*" he breathes and curls closer. I carry him back to bed, asleep. *Shoogily.* A funny word, a family word, inherited from Emily, invented by her to say: *comfort.*

In this and other ways she leaves her seal, I say aloud. And startle at my saying it. What do I mean? What did I start to gather together, to try and make coherent? I was at the terrible, growing years. War years. I do not remember them well. I was working, there were four smaller ones now, there was not time for her. She had to help be a mother, and housekeeper, and shopper. She had to set her seal. Mornings of crisis and near hysteria trying to get lunches packed, hair combed, coats and shoes found, everyone to school or Child Care on time, the baby ready for trans- portation. And always the paper scribbled on by a smaller one, the book looked at by Susan then mislaid, the homework not done. Running out to that huge school where she was one, she was lost, she was a drop; suffering over the unpreparedness, stammering and unsure in her classes.

45   There was so little time left at night after the kids were bedded down. She would struggle over books, always eating (it was in those years she developed her enormous appetite that is legendary in our family) and I would be ironing, or preparing food for the next day, or writing V-mail to Bill, or tending the baby. Sometimes, to make me laugh, or out of her despair, she would imitate happenings or types at school.

I think I said once: "Why don't you do something like this in the school ama- teur show?" One morning she phoned me at work, hardly understandable through the weeping: "Mother, I did it. I won, I won; they gave me first prize; they clapped and clapped and wouldn't let me go."

Now suddenly she was Somebody, and as imprisoned in her difference as she had been in anonymity.

She began to be asked to perform at other high schools, even in colleges, then at city and statewide affairs. The first one we went to, I only recognized her that first moment when thin, shy, she almost drowned herself into the curtains. Then: Was this Emily? The control, the command, the convulsing and deadly clowning, the spell, then the roaring, stamping audience, unwilling to let this rare and precious laughter out of their lives.

Afterwards: You ought to do something about her with a gift like that—but without money or knowing how, what does one do? We have left it all to her, and the gift has as often eddied inside, clogged and clotted, as been used and growing.

50   She is coming. She runs up the stairs two at a time with her light graceful step, and I know she is happy tonight. Whatever it was that occasioned your call did not happen today.

"Aren't you ever going to finish the ironing, Mother? Whistler painted his mother in a rocker. I'd have to paint mine standing over an ironing board." This is one of her communicative nights and she tells me everything and nothing as she fixes herself a plate of food out of the icebox.

She is so lovely. Why did you want me to come in at all? Why were you con- cerned? She will find her way.

She starts up the stairs to bed. "Don't get me up with the rest in the morning." "But I thought you were having midterms." "Oh, those," she comes back in, kisses me, and says quite lightly, "in a couple of years when we'll all be atom-dead they won't matter a bit."

She has said it before. She *believes* it. But because I have been dredging the past, and all that compounds a human being is so heavy and meaningful in me, I cannot endure it tonight.

55   I will never total it all. I will never come in to say: She was a child seldom smiled at. Her father left me before she was a year old. I had to work her first six years when there was work, or I sent her home and to his relatives. There were years she had care she hated. She was dark and thin and foreign-looking in a world where the prestige went to blondeness and curly hair and dimples, she was slow where glibness was prized. She was a child of anxious, not proud, love. We were poor and could not afford for her the soil of easy growth. I was a young mother, I was a distracted mother. There were other children pushing up, demanding. Her younger sister seemed all that she was not. There were years she did not want me to touch her. She kept too much in herself, her life was such she had to keep too much in herself. My wisdom came too late. She has much to her and probably little will come of it. She is a child of her age, of depression, of war, of fear.

Let her be. So all that is in her will not bloom—but in how many does it? There is still enough left to live by. Only help her to know—help make it so there is cause for her to know—that she is more than this dress on the ironing board, helpless before the iron.

➤ *QUESTIONS FOR READING AND WRITING*

1. The story opens with a reference to "you." Who is this "you" supposed to be?
2. The protagonist is the narrator of the story. How do you feel about her? How do you think her daughter Emily would tell this story?

LUIGI PIRANDELLO (1867–1936)

Luigi Pirandello was born in Sicily to well-to-do parents. He attended the University of Rome and the University of Bonn, where he first began writing poetry and fiction. In 1896, he married the daughter of his father's business partner. The marriage was a happy one, and Pirandello pursued a career as a writer until the collapse of the family business in 1904 left him impoverished. The stress of these events drove his wife insane, and for the next 15 years Pirandello took care of her, until finally committing her to an institution in 1919. Though he accepted a position as a teacher at a girls' school in order to support his family, Pirandello

continued to write and publish novels, stories, and plays. In 1924, he became the director of his own company, the Art Theatre of Rome, which eventually toured throughout the world, influencing a generation of directors, playwrights, and actors. In 1934, he was awarded the Nobel Prize for Literature. Questions about the perception of reality, truth, and the self are at the center of much of his work. Nowhere are his concerns more clearly presented than in his most famous work, the play Six Characters in Search of an Author, *which created a sensation when it appeared in 1922.*

WAR [1939]

The passengers who had left Rome by the night express had had to stop until dawn at the small station of Fabriano in order to continue their journey by the small old-fashioned local joining the main line with Sulmona.

At dawn, in a stuffy and smoky second-class carriage in which five people had already spent the night, a bulky woman in deep mourning was hoisted in—almost like a shapeless bundle. Behind her, puffing and moaning, followed her husband—a tiny man, thin and weakly, his face death-white, his eyes small and bright and looking shy and uneasy.

Having at last taken a seat he politely thanked the passengers who had helped his wife and who had made room for her; then he turned round to the woman trying to pull down the collar of her coat, and politely inquired:

"Are you all right, dear?"

5   The wife, instead of answering, pulled up her collar again to her eyes, so as to hide her face.

"Nasty world," muttered the husband with a sad smile.

And he felt it his duty to explain to his traveling companions that the poor woman was to be pitied, for the war was taking away from her her only son, a boy of twenty to whom both had devoted their entire life, even breaking up their home at Sulmona to follow him to Rome, where he had to go as a student, then allowing him to volunteer for war with an assurance, however, that at least for six months he would not be sent to the front and now, all of a sudden, receiving a wire saying that he was due to leave in three days' time and asking them to go and see him off.

The woman under the big coat was twisting and wriggling, at times growling like a wild animal, feeling certain that all those explanations would not have aroused even a shadow of sympathy from those people who—most likely—were in the same plight as herself. One of them, who had been listening with particular attention, said:

"You should thank God that your son is only leaving now for the front. Mine had been sent there the first day of the war. He has already come back twice wounded and been sent back again to the front."

10   "What about me? I have two sons and three nephews at the front," said another passenger.

"Maybe, but in our case it is our *only* son," ventured the husband.

"What difference can it make? You may spoil your only son with excessive attentions, but you cannot love him more than you would all your other children if you had any. Paternal love is not like bread that can be broken into pieces and split amongst the children in equal shares. A father gives *all* his love to each one of his children without discrimination, whether it be one or ten, and if I am suffering now for my two sons, I am not suffering half for each of them but double . . ."

"True . . . true . . ." sighed the embarrassed husband, "but suppose (of course we all hope it will never be your case) a father has two sons at the front and he loses one of them, there is still one left to console him . . . while . . ."

"Yes," answered the other, getting cross, "a son left to console him but also a son left for whom he must survive, while in the case of the father of an only son if the son dies the father can die too and put an end to his distress. Which of the two positions is the worse? Don't you see how my case would be worse than yours?"

15 "Nonsense," interrupted another traveler, a fat, red-faced man with bloodshot eyes of the palest gray.

He was panting. From his bulging eyes seemed to spurt inner violence of an uncontrolled vitality which his weakened body could hardly contain.

"Nonsense," he repeated, trying to cover his mouth with his hand so as to hide the two missing front teeth. "Nonsense. Do we give life to our children for our own benefit?"

The other travelers stared at him in distress. The one who had had his son at the front since the first day of the war sighed: "You are right. Our children do not belong to us. They belong to the Country . . ."

"Bosh," retorted the fat traveler. "Do we think of the Country when we give life to our children? Our sons are born because . . . well, because they must be born and when they come to life they take our own life with them. This is the truth. We belong to them but they never belong to us. And when they reach twenty they are exactly what we were at their age. We too had a father and mother, but there were so many other things as well . . . girls, cigarettes, illusions, new ties . . . and the Country, of course, whose call we would have answered—when we were twenty— even if father and mother had said no. Now at our age, the love of our Country is still great, of course, but stronger than it is the love for our children. Is there any one of us here who wouldn't gladly take his son's place at the front if the could?"

20 There was a silence all round, everybody nodding as to approve.

"Why then," continued the fat man, "shouldn't we consider the feelings of our children when they are twenty? Isn't it natural that at their age they should consider the love for their Country (I am speaking of decent boys, of course) even greater than the love for us? Isn't it natural that it should be so, as after all they must look upon us as upon old boys who cannot move any more and must stay at home? If Country exists, if Country is a natural necessity, like bread, of which each of us must eat in order not to die of hunger, somebody must go to defend it. And our sons go, when they are twenty, and they don't want tears, because if they die, they die inflamed and happy (I am speaking, of course, of decent boys). Now, if one dies young and happy, without having the ugly sides of life, the boredom of it, the pettiness, the bitterness of disillusion . . . what more can we ask for him? Everyone should stop crying; everyone should laugh, as I do . . . or at least thank God—as I do—because my son, before dying, sent me a message saying that he was dying satisfied at having ended his life in the best way he could have wished.

That is why, as you see, I do not even wear mourning . . . "

He shook his light fawn coat as to show it; his livid lip over his missing teeth was trembling, his eyes were watery and motionless, and soon after he ended with a shrill laugh which might well have been a sob.

"Quite so . . . quite so . . . " agreed the others.

The woman who, bundled in a corner under her coat, had been sitting and listening had—for the last three months—tried to find in the words of her husband and her friends something to console her in her deep sorrow, something that might show her how a mother should resign herself to send her son not even to death but to a probably dangerous life. Yet not a word had she found amongst the many which had been said . . . and her grief had been greater in seeing that nobody—as she thought—could share her feelings.

25   But now the words of the traveler amazed and almost stunned her. She suddenly realized that it wasn't the others who were wrong and could not understand her but herself who could not rise up to the same height of those fathers and mothers willing to resign themselves, without crying, not only to the departure of their sons but even to their death.

She lifted her head, she bent over from her corner trying to listen with great attention to the details which the fat man was giving to his companions about the way his son had fallen as a hero, for his King and his Country, happy and without regrets. It seemed to her that she had stumbled into a world she had never dreamt of, a world so far unknown to her and she was so pleased to hear everyone joining in congratulating that brave father who could so stoically speak of his child's death.

Then suddenly, just as if she had heard nothing of what had been said and almost as if waking up from a dream, she turned to the old man, asking him:

"Then . . . is your son really dead?"

Everybody stared at her. The old man, too, turned to look at her, fixing his great, bulging, horribly watery light gray eyes, deep in her face. For some little time he tried to answer, but words failed him. He looked and looked at her, almost as if only then—at that silly, incongruous question—he had suddenly realized at last that his son was really dead—gone for ever—for ever. His face contracted, became horribly distorted, then he snatched in haste a handkerchief from his pocket and, to the amazement of everyone, broke into harrowing, heart-rending, uncontrollable sobs.

➤ QUESTIONS FOR READING AND WRITING

1. How do you feel about sacrificing a family member or loved one to war?
2. At one point the red-faced man says, "I do not even wear mourning." How does the narrator's description of him bear this out?
3. What is your reaction to the ending of the story? Why do you think the red-faced man begins to sob when the woman asks him, "Then . . . is your son really dead?"
4. Do you think this is a story about war or about parents' love for their children, or something else? Explain.

LESLIE MARMON SILKO (b. 1948)

Of mixed Native American, Mexican, and Caucasian descent, Leslie Marmon Silko was raised on the Laguna Pueblo reservation in New Mexico. After graduating from the University of New Mexico, she studied law for a short time before deciding to pursue writing as a career. Her first novel, Ceremony *(1977), told the story of a young Native American's return to the reservation following World War II. In addition, she has written collections of poems and short stories, as well as* Yellow Woman *and* A Beauty of the Spirit, *a collection of essays about modern Native American life. Her latest novel,* Almanac of the Dead, *was published in 1991. In her work, Silko often draws upon the rich storytelling tradition of her Pueblo Indian heritage to explore the conflict between Native American values and the dominant white culture.*

THE MAN TO SEND RAIN CLOUDS

One

They found him under a big cottonwood tree. His Levi jacket and pants were faded light-blue so that he had been easy to find. The big cottonwood tree stood apart from a small grove of winterbare cottonwoods which grew in the wide, sandy arroyo. He had been dead for a day or more, and the sheep had wandered and scattered up and down the arroyo. Leon and his brother-in-law, Ken, gathered the sheep and left them in the pen at the sheep camp before they returned to the cottonwood tree. Leon waited under the tree while Ken drove the truck through the deep sand to the edge of the arroyo. He squinted up at the sun and unzipped his jacket—it sure was hot for this time of year. But high and northwest the blue mountains were still deep in snow. Ken came sliding down the low, crumbling bank about fifty yards down, and he was bringing the red blanket.

Before they wrapped the old man, Leon took a piece of string out of his pocket and tied a small gray feather in the old man's long white hair. Ken gave him the paint. Across the brown wrinkled forehead he drew a streak of white and along the high cheekbones he drew a strip of blue paint. He paused and watched Ken throw pinches of corn meal and pollen into the wind that fluttered the small gray feather. Then Leon painted with yellow under the old man's broad nose, and finally, when he had painted green across the chin, he smiled.

"Send us rain clouds, Grandfather." They laid the bundle in the back of the pickup and covered it with a heavy tarp before they started back to the pueblo.

They turned off the highway onto the sandy pueblo road. Not long after they passed the store and post office they saw Father Paul's car coming toward them. When he recognized their faces he slowed his car and waved for them to stop. The young priest rolled down the car window.

5   "Did you find old Teofilo?" he asked loudly.

Leon stopped the truck. "Good morning, Father. We were just out to the sheep camp. Everything is O.K. now."

"Thank God for that. Teofilo is a very old man. You really shouldn't allow him to stay at the sheep camp alone."

"No, he won't do that any more now."

"Well, I'm glad you understand. I hope I'll be seeing you at Mass this week— we missed you last Sunday. See if you can get old Teofilo to come with you." The priest smiled and waved at them as they drove away.

Two

10   Louise and Teresa were waiting. The table was set for lunch, and the coffee was boiling on the black iron stove. Leon looked at Louise and then at Teresa.

"We found him under a cottonwood tree in the big arroyo near sheep camp. I guess he sat down to rest in the shade and never got up again." Leon walked toward the old man's bed. The red plaid shawl had been shaken and spread carefully over the bed, and a new brown flannel shirt and pair of stiff new Levis were arranged neatly beside the pillow. Louise held the screen door open while Leon and Ken carried in the red blanket. He looked small and shriveled, and after they dressed him in the new shirt and pants he seemed more shrunken.

It was noontime now because the church bells rang the Angelus. They ate the beans with hot bread, and nobody said anything until after Teresa poured the coffee.

Ken stood up and put on his jacket. "I'll see about the gravediggers. Only the top layer of soil is frozen. I think it can be ready before dark."

Leon nodded his head and finished his coffee. After Ken had been gone for a while, the neighbors and clanspeople came quietly to embrace Teofilo's family and to leave food on the table because the gravediggers would come to eat when they were finished.

Three

15   The sky in the west was full of pale-yellow light. Louise stood outside with her hands in the pockets of Leon's green army jacket that was too big for her. The funeral was over, and the old men had taken their candles and medicine bags and were gone. She waited until the body was laid into the pickup before she said anything to Leon. She touched his arm, and he noticed that her hands were still dusty from the corn meal that she had sprinkled around the old man. When she spoke, Leon could not hear her.

"What did you say? I didn't hear you."

"I said that I had been thinking about something."

"About what?"

"About the priest sprinkling holy water for Grandpa. So he won't be thirsty."

20   Leon stared at the new moccasins that Teofilo had made for the ceremonial dances in the summer. They were nearly hidden by the red blanket. It was getting colder, and the wind pushed gray dust down the narrow pueblo road. The sun was approaching the long mesa where it disappeared during the winter. Louise stood there shivering and watching his face. Then he zipped up his jacket and opened the truck door. "I'll see if he's there."

Four

Ken stopped the pickup at the church, and Leon got out; and then Ken drove down the hill to the graveyard where people were waiting. Leon knocked at the old carved door with its symbols of the Lamb. While he waited he looked up at the twin bells from the king of Spain with the last sunlight pouring around them in their tower.

The priest opened the door and smiled when he saw who it was. "Come in! What brings you here this evening?"

The priest walked toward the kitchen, and Leon stood with his cap in his hand, playing with the earflaps and examining the living room—the brown sofa, the green armchair, and the brass lamp that hung down from the ceiling by links of chain. The priest dragged a chair out of the kitchen and offered it to Leon.

"No thank you, Father. I only came to ask you if you would bring your holy water to the graveyard."

25   The priest turned away from Leon and looked out the window at the patio full of shadows and the dining-room windows of the nuns' cloister across the patio. The curtains were heavy, and the light from within faintly penetrated; it was impossible to see the nuns inside eating supper. "Why didn't you tell me he was dead? I could have brought the Last Rites anyway."

Leon smiled. "It wasn't necessary, Father."

The priest stared down at his scuffed brown loafers and the worn hem of his cassock. "For a Christian burial it was necessary."

His voice was distant, and Leon thought that his blue eyes looked tired.

"It's O.K., Father, we just want him to have plenty of water."

30   The priest sank down in the green chair and picked up a glossy missionary magazine. He turned the colored pages full of lepers and pagans without looking at them.

"You know I can't do that, Leon. There should have been the Last Rites and a funeral Mass at the very least."

Leon put on his green cap and pulled the flaps down over his ears. "It's getting late, Father. I've got to go."

When Leon opened the door Father Paul stood up and said, "Wait." He left the room and came back wearing a long brown overcoat. He followed Leon out the door and across the dim churchyard to the adobe steps in front of the church. They both stooped to fit through the low adobe entrance. And when they started down the hill to the graveyard only half of the sun was visible above the mesa.

The priest approached the grave slowly, wondering how they had managed to dig into the frozen ground; and then he remembered that this was New Mexico, and saw the pile of cold loose sand beside the hole. The people stood close to each other with little clouds of steam puffing from their faces. The priest looked at them and saw a pile of jackets, gloves, and scarves in the yellow, dry tumbleweeds that grew in the graveyard. He looked at the red blanket, not sure that Teofilo was so small, wondering if it wasn't some perverse Indian trick—something they did in March to ensure a good harvest—wondering if maybe old Teofilo was actually at sheep camp corralling the sheep for the night. But there he was, facing into a cold dry wind and squinting at the last sunlight, ready to bury a red wool blanket while the faces of his parishioners were in shadow with the last warmth of the sun on their backs.

35   His fingers were stiff, and it took him a long time to twist the lid off the holy water. Drops of water fell on the red blanket and soaked into dark icy spots. He sprinkled the grave and the water disappeared almost before it touched the dim, cold sand; it reminded him of something—he tried to remember what it was, because he thought if he could remember he might understand this. He sprinkled more water; he shook the container until it was empty, and the water fell through the light from sundown like August rain that fell while the sun was still shining, almost evaporating before it touched the wilted squash flowers.

The wind pulled at the priest's brown Franciscan robe and swirled away the corn meal and pollen that had been sprinkled on the blanket. They lowered the bundle into the ground, and they didn't bother to untie the stiff pieces of new rope that were tied around the ends of the blanket. The sun was gone, and over on the highway the eastbound lane was full of headlights. The priest walked away slowly. Leon watched him climb the hill, and when he had disappeared within the tall, thick walls, Leon turned to look up at the high blue mountains in the deep snow that reflected a faint red light from the west. He felt good because it was finished, and he was happy about the sprinkling of the holy water; now the old man could send them big thunderclouds for sure.

➤ QUESTIONS FOR READING AND WRITING

1. What motivates Leon to paint Teofilo's face and put a feather in his hair?
2. Why don't they tell the priest that Teofilo is dead?
3. Why does the narrator mention that the twin church bells are from the king of Spain?
4. Why do you think the priest changes his mind about sprinkling the holy water on Teofilo's body?
5. What does the narrator mean by "now the old man could send them big thunderclouds for sure"?

JOHN STEINBECK (1902–1968)

John Steinbeck was born and grew up in Salinas, California, where he often witnessed the plight of the oppressed migrant farm workers he would later write about in novels like The Grapes of Wrath, *which won the Pulitzer Prize in 1940. Other of his best-known novels include* Of Mice and Men, Tortilla Flat, In Dubious Battle, East of Eden, *and* The Winter of Our Discontent. *One of America's most acclaimed novelists, Steinbeck received the Nobel Prize for Literature in 1962.*

THE CHRYSANTHEMUMS [1937]

The high grey-flannel fog of winter closed off the Salinas Valley from the sky and from all the rest of the world. On every side it sat like a lid on the mountains and made of the great valley a closed pot. On the broad, level land floor the gang plows bit deep and left the black earth shining like metal where the shares had cut. On the foothill ranches across the Salinas River, the yellow stubble fields seemed to be bathed in pale cold sunshine, but there was no sunshine in the valley now in December. The thick willow scrub along the river flamed with sharp and positive yellow leaves.

It was a time of quiet and of waiting. The air was cold and tender. A light wind blew up from the southwest so that the farmers were mildly hopeful of a good rain before long; but fog and rain do not go together.

Across the river, on Henry Allen's foothill ranch there was little work to be done, for the hay was cut and stored and the orchards were plowed up to receive the rain deeply when it should come. The cattle on the higher slopes were becoming shaggy and rough-coated.

Elisa Allen, working in her flower garden, looked down across the yard and saw Henry, her husband, talking to two men in business suits. The three of them stood by the tractor shed, each man with one foot on the side of the little Fordson. They smoked cigarettes and studied the machine as they talked.

5   Elisa watched them for a moment and then went back to her work. She was thirty-five. Her face was lean and strong and her eyes were as clear as water. Her figure looked blocked and heavy in her gardening costume, a man's black hat pulled down over her eyes, clod-hopper shoes, a figured print dress almost completely covered by a big corduroy apron with four big pockets to hold the snips, the trowel and scratcher, the seeds and the knife she worked with. She wore heavy leather gloves to protect her hands while she worked.

She was cutting down the old year's chrysanthemum stalks with a pair of short and powerful scissors. She looked down toward the men by the tractor shed now and then. Her face was eager and mature and handsome; even her work with the scissors was over-eager, over-powerful. The chrysanthemum stems seemed too small and easy for her energy.

She brushed a cloud of hair out of her eyes with the back of her glove, and left a smudge of earth on her cheek in doing it. Behind her stood the neat white farmhouse with red geraniums close-banked around it as high as the windows. It was a hard-swept looking little house with hard-polished windows, and a clean mud-mat on the front steps.

Elisa cast another glance toward the tractor shed. The strangers were getting into their Ford coupe. She took off a glove and put her strong fingers down into the forest of new green chrysanthemum sprouts that were growing around the old roots. She spread the leaves and looked down among the close-growing stems. No aphids were there, no sow bugs or snails or cutworms. Her terrier fingers destroyed such pests before they could get started.

Elisa started at the sound of her husband's voice. He had come near quietly, and he leaned over the wire fence that protected her flower garden from cattle and dogs and chickens.

10   "At it again," he said. "You've got a strong new crop coming."

Elisa straightened her back and pulled on the gardening glove again. "Yes. They'll be strong this coming year." In her tone and on her face there was a little smugness.

"You've got a gift with things," Henry observed. "Some of those yellow chrysanthemums you had this year were ten inches across. I wish you'd work out in the orchard and raise some apples that big."

Her eyes sharpened. "Maybe I could do it, too. I've a gift with things, all right. My mother had it. She could stick anything in the ground and make it grow. She said it was having planters' hands that knew how to do it."

"Well, it sure works with flowers," he said.

15   "Henry, who were those men you were talking to?"

"Why, sure, that's what I came to tell you. They were from the Western Meat Company. I sold those thirty head of three-year-old steers. Got nearly my own price, too."

"Good," she said. "Good for you."

"And I thought," he continued, "I thought how it's Saturday afternoon, and we might go into Salinas for dinner at a restaurant, and then to a picture show—to celebrate, you see."

"Good," she repeated. "Oh, yes. That will be good."

20   Henry put on his joking tone. "There's fights tonight. How'd you like to go to the fights?"

"Oh, no," she said breathlessly. "No, I wouldn't like fights."

"Just fooling, Elisa. We'll go to a movie. Let's see. It's two now. I'm going to take Scotty and bring down those steers from the hill. It'll take us maybe two hours. We'll go in town about five and have dinner at the Cominos Hotel. Like that?"

"Of course I'll like it. It's good to eat away from home."

"All right, then. I'll go get up a couple of horses."

25   She said, "I'll have plenty of time to transplant some of these sets, I guess."

She heard her husband calling Scotty down by the barn. And a little later she saw the two men ride up the pale yellow hillside in search of the steers.

There was a little square sandy bed kept for rooting the chrysanthemums. With her trowel she turned the soil over and over, and smoothed it and patted it firm. Then she dug ten parallel trenches to receive the sets. Back at the chrysanthemum bed she pulled out the little crisp shoots, trimmed off the leaves of each one with her scissors and laid it on a small orderly pile.

A squeak of wheels and plod of hoofs came from the road. Elisa looked up. The country road ran along the dense bank of willows and cottonwoods that bordered the river, and up this road came a curious vehicle, curiously drawn. It was an old spring-wagon, with a round canvas top on it like the cover of a prairie schooner. It was drawn by an old bay horse and a little grey-and-white burro. A big stubble-bearded man sat between the cover flaps and drove the crawling team. Underneath the wagon, between the hind wheels, a lean and rangy mongrel dog walked sedately. Words were painted on the canvas, in clumsy, crooked letters. "Pots, pans, knives, scissors, lawn mores, Fixed." Two rows of articles, and the triumphantly definitive "Fixed" below. The black paint had run down in little sharp points beneath each letter.

Elisa, squatting on the ground, watched to see the crazy, loose-jointed wagon pass by. But it didn't pass. It turned into the farm road in front of her house, crooked old wheels skirling and squeaking. The rangy dog darted from between the wheels and ran ahead. Instantly the two ranch shepherds flew out at him. Then all three stopped, and with stiff and quivering tails, with taut straight legs, with ambassadorial dignity, they slowly circled, sniffing daintily. The caravan pulled up to Elisa's wire fence and stopped. Now the newcomer dog, feeling out-numbered, lowered his tail and retired under the wagon with raised hackles and bared teeth.

30   The man on the wagon seat called out, "That's a bad dog in a fight when he gets started."

Elisa laughed. "I see he is. How soon does he generally get started?"

The man caught up her laughter and echoed it heartily. "Sometimes not for weeks and weeks," he said. He climbed stiffly down, over the wheel. The horse and the donkey drooped like unwatered flowers.

Elisa saw that he was a very big man. Although his hair and beard were grey-ing, he did not look old. His worn black suit was wrinkled and spotted with grease. The laughter had disappeared from his face and eyes the moment his laughing voice ceased. His eyes were dark, and they were full of the brooding that gets in the eyes of teamsters and of sailors. The calloused hands he rested on the wire fence were cracked, and every crack was a black line. He took off his battered hat.

"I'm off my general road, ma'am," he said. "Does this dirt road cut over across the river to the Los Angeles highway?"

35   Elisa stood up and shoved the thick scissors in her apron pocket. "Well, yes, it does, but it winds around and then fords the river. I don't think your team could pull through the sand."

He replied with some asperity. "It might surprise you what them beasts can pull through."

"When they get started?" she asked.

He smiled for a second. "Yes. When they get started."

"Well," said Elisa, "I think you'll save time if you go back to the Salinas road and pick up the highway there."

40   He drew a big finger down the chicken wire and made it sing. "I ain't in any hurry, ma'am. I go from Seattle to San Diego and back every year. Takes all my time. About six months each way. I aim to follow nice weather."

Elisa took off her gloves and stuffed them in the apron pocket with the scissors. She touched the under edge of her man's hat, searching for fugitive hairs. "That sounds like a nice kind of a way to live," she said.

He leaned confidentially over the fence. "Maybe you noticed the writing on my wagon. I mend pots and sharpen knives and scissors. You got any of them things to do?"

"Oh, no," she said quickly. "Nothing like that." Her eyes hardened with resis-tance.

"Scissors is the worst thing," he explained. "Most people just ruin scissors trying to sharpen 'em, but I know how. I got a special tool. It's a little bobbit kind of thing, and patented. But it sure does the trick."

45 "No. My scissors are all sharp."

"All right, then. Take a pot," he continued earnestly, "a bent pot, or a pot with a hole. I can make it like new so you don't have to buy no new ones. That's a saving for you."

"No," she said shortly. "I tell you I have nothing like that for you to do."

His face fell to an exaggerated sadness. His voice took on a whining undertone. "I ain't had a thing to do today. Maybe I won't have no supper tonight. You see I'm off my regular road. I know folks on the highway clear from Seattle to San Diego. They save their things for me to sharpen up because they know I do it so good and save them money."

"I'm sorry," Elisa said irritably. "I haven't anything for you to do."

50 His eyes left her face and fell to searching the ground. They roamed about until they came to the chrysanthemum bed where she had been working. "What's them plants, ma'am?"

The irritation and resistance melted from Elisa's face. "Oh, those are chrysanthemums, giant whites and yellows. I raise them every year, bigger than anybody around here."

"Kind of a long-stemmed flower? Looks like a quick puff of colored smoke?" he asked.

"That's it. What a nice way to describe them."

"They smell kind of nasty till you get used to them," he said.

55 "It's a good bitter smell," she retorted, "not nasty at all."

He changed his tone quickly. "I like the smell myself."

"I had ten-inch blooms this year," she said.

The man leaned farther over the fence. "Look. I know a lady down the road a piece, has got the nicest garden you ever seen. Got nearly every kind of flower but no chrysanthemums. Last time I was mending a copper-bottom washtub for her (that's a hard job but I do it good), she said to me, 'If you ever run acrost some nice chrysanthemums I wish you'd try to get me a few seeds.' That's what she told me."

Elisa's eyes grew alert and eager. "She couldn't have known much about chrysanthemums. You *can* raise them from seed, but it's much easier to root the little sprouts you see there."

60 "Oh," he said. "I s'pose I can't take none to her, then."

"Why yes you can," Elisa cried. "I can put some in damp sand, and you can carry them right along with you. They'll take root in the pot if you keep them damp. And then she can transplant them."

"She'd sure like to have some, ma'am. You say they're nice ones?"

"Beautiful," she said. "Oh, beautiful." Her eyes shone. She tore off the battered hat and shook out her dark pretty hair. "I'll put them in a flower pot, and you can take them right with you. Come into the yard."

While the man came through the picket gate Elisa ran excitedly along the geranium-bordered path to the back of the house. And she returned carrying a big red flower pot. The gloves were forgotten now. She kneeled on the ground by the starting bed and dug up the sandy soil with her fingers and scooped it into the bright new flower pot. Then she picked up the little pile of shoots she had prepared. With her strong fingers she pressed them into the sand and tamped around them with her knuckles. The man stood over her. "I'll tell you what to do," she said. "You remember so you can tell the lady."

65 "Yes, I'll try to remember."

"Well, look. These will take root in about a month. Then she must set them out, about a foot apart in good rich earth like this, see?" She lifted a handful of dark soil for him to look at. "They'll grow fast and tall. Now remember this: In July tell her to cut them down, about eight inches from the ground."

"Before they bloom?" he asked.

"Yes, before they bloom." Her face was tight with eagerness. "They'll grow right up again. About the last of September the buds will start."

She stopped and seemed perplexed. "It's the budding that takes the most care," she said hesitantly. "I don't know how to tell you." She looked deep into his eyes, searchingly. Her mouth opened a little, and she seemed to be listening. "I'll try to tell you," she said. "Did you ever hear of planting hands?"

70 "Can't say I have, ma'am."

"Well, I can only tell you what it feels like. It's when you're picking off the buds you don't want. Everything goes right down into your fingertips. You watch your fingers work. They do it themselves. You can feel how it is. They pick and pick the buds. They never make a mistake. They're with the plant. Do you see? Your fingers and the plant. You can feel that, right up your arm. They know. They never make a mistake. You can feel it. When you're like that you can't do anything wrong. Do you see that? Can you understand that?"

She was kneeling on the ground looking up at him. Her breast swelled passionately.

The man's eyes narrowed. He looked away self-consciously. "Maybe I know," he said. "Sometimes in the night in the wagon there—"

Elisa's voice grew husky. She broke in on him, "I've never lived as you do, but I know what you mean. When the night is dark—why, the stars are sharp-pointed, and there's quiet. Why, you rise up and up! Every pointed star gets driven into your body. It's like that. Hot and sharp and—lovely."

75 Kneeling there, her hand went out toward his legs in the greasy black trousers. Her hesitant fingers almost touched the cloth. Then her hand dropped to the ground. She crouched low like a fawning dog.

He said, "It's nice, just like you say. Only when you don't have no dinner, it ain't."

She stood up then, very straight, and her face was ashamed. She held the flower pot out to him and placed it gently in his arms. "Here. Put it in your wagon, on the seat, where you can watch it. Maybe I can find something for you to do."

At the back of the house she dug in the can pile and found two old and battered aluminum saucepans. She carried them back and gave them to him. "Here, maybe you can fix these."

His manner changed. He became professional. "Good as new I can fix them." At the back of his wagon he set a little anvil, and out of an oily tool box dug a small machine hammer. Elisa came through the gate to watch him while he pounded out the dents in the kettles. His mouth grew sure and knowing. At a difficult part of the work he sucked his underlip.

80 "You sleep right in the wagon?" Elisa asked.

"Right in the wagon, ma'am. Rain or shine I'm dry as a cow in there."

"It must be nice," she said. "It must be very nice. I wish women could do such things."

"It ain't the right kind of a life for a woman."

Her upper lip raised a little, showing her teeth. "How do you know? How can you tell?" she said.

85 "I don't know, ma'am," he protested. "Of course I don't know. Now here's your kettles, done. You don't have to buy no new ones."

"How much?"

"Oh, fifty cents'll do. I keep my prices down and my work good. That's why I have all them satisfied customers up and down the highway."

Elisa brought him a fifty-cent piece from the house and dropped it in his hand. "You might be surprised to have a rival some time. I can sharpen scissors, too. And I can beat the dents out of little pots. I could show you what a woman might do."

He put his hammer back in the oily box and shoved the little anvil out of sight. "It would be a lonely life for a woman, ma'am, and a scarey life, too, with animals creeping under the wagon all night." He climbed over the singletree, steadying himself with a hand on the burro's white rump. He settled himself in the seat, picked up the lines. "Thank you kindly, ma'am," he said. "I'll do like you told me; I'll go back and catch the Salinas road."

90 "Mind," she called, "if you're long in getting there, keep the sand damp."

"Sand, ma'am? . . . Sand? Oh, sure. You mean around the chrysanthemums. Sure I will." He clucked his tongue. The beasts leaned luxuriously into their collars. The mongrel dog took his place between the back wheels. The wagon turned and crawled out the entrance road and back the way it had come, along the river.

Elisa stood in front of her wire fence watching the slow progress of the caravan. Her shoulders were straight, her head thrown back, her eyes half-closed, so that the scene came vaguely into them. Her lips moved silently, forming the words "Good-bye—good-bye." Then she whispered, "That's a bright direction. There's a glowing there." The sound of her whisper startled her. She shook herself free and looked about to see whether anyone had been listening. Only the dogs had heard. They lifted their heads toward her from their sleeping in the dust, and then stretched out their chins and settled asleep again. Elisa turned and ran hurriedly into the house.

In the kitchen she reached behind the stove and felt the water tank. It was full of hot water from the noonday cooking. In the bathroom she tore off her soiled clothes and flung them into the corner. And then she scrubbed herself with a little block of pumice, legs and thighs, loins and chest and arms, until her skin was scratched and red. When she had dried herself she stood in front of a mirror in her bedroom and looked at her body. She tightened her stomach and threw out her chest. She turned and looked over her shoulder at her back.

After a while she began to dress, slowly. She put on her newest underclothing and her nicest stockings and the dress which was the symbol of her prettiness. She worked carefully on her hair, penciled her eyebrows and rouged her lips.

95 Before she was finished she heard the little thunder of hoofs and the shouts of Henry and his helper as they drove the red steers into the corral. She heard the gate bang shut and set herself for Henry's arrival.

His step sounded on the porch. He entered the house calling, "Elisa, where are you?"

"In my room, dressing. I'm not ready. There's hot water for your bath. Hurry up. It's getting late."

When she heard him splashing in the tub, Elisa laid his dark suit on the bed, and shirt and socks and tie beside it. She stood his polished shoes on the floor beside the bed. Then she went to the porch and sat primly and stiffly down. She looked toward the river road where the willow-line was still yellow with frosted leaves so that under the high grey fog they seemed a thin band of sunshine. This was the only color in the grey afternoon. She sat unmoving for a long time. Her eyes blinked rarely.

Henry came banging out of the door, shoving his tie inside his vest as he came. Elisa stiffened and her face grew tight. Henry stopped short and looked at her. "Why—why, Elisa. You look so nice!"

100   "Nice? You think I look nice? What do you mean by 'nice'?"

Henry blundered on. "I don't know. I mean you look different, strong and happy."

"I am strong? Yes, strong. What do you mean 'strong'?"

He looked bewildered. "You're playing some kind of a game," he said helplessly. "It's a kind of a play. You look strong enough to break a calf over your knee, happy enough to eat it like a watermelon."

For a second she lost her rigidity. "Henry! Don't talk like that. You didn't know what you said." She grew complete again. "I'm strong," she boasted. "I never knew before how strong."

105   Henry looked down toward the tractor shed, and when he brought his eyes back to her, they were his own again. "I'll get out the car. You can put on your coat while I'm starting."

Elisa went into the house. She heard him drive to the gate and idle down his motor, and then she took a long time to put on her hat. She pulled it here and pressed it there. When Henry turned the motor off she slipped into her coat and went out.

The little roadster bounced along on the dirt road by the river, raising the birds and driving the rabbits into the brush. Two cranes flapped heavily over the willow-line and dropped into the riverbed.

Far ahead on the road Elisa saw a dark speck. She knew.

She tried not to look as they passed it, but her eyes would not obey. She whispered to herself sadly, "He might have thrown them off the road. That wouldn't have been much trouble, not very much. But he kept the pot," she explained. "He had to keep the pot. That's why he couldn't get them off the road."

110   The roadster turned a bend and she saw the caravan ahead. She swung full around toward her husband so she could not see the little covered wagon and the mismatched team as the car passed them.

In a moment it was over. The thing was done. She did not look back.

She said loudly, to be heard above the motor, "It will be good, tonight, a good dinner."

"Now you've changed again," Henry complained. He took one hand from the wheel and patted her knee. "I ought to take you in to dinner oftener. It would be good for both of us. We get so heavy out on the ranch."

"Henry," she asked, "could we have wine at dinner?"

115   "Sure we could. Say! That will be fine."

She was silent for a while; then she said, "Henry, at those prize fights, do the men hurt each other very much?"

"Sometimes a little, not often. Why?"

"Well, I've read how they break noses, and blood runs down their chests. I've read how the fighting gloves get heavy and soggy with blood."

He looked around at her. "What's the matter, Elisa? I didn't know you read things like that." He brought the car to a stop, then turned to the right over the Salinas River bridge.

120   "Do any women ever go to the fights?" she asked.

"Oh, sure, some. What's the matter, Elisa? Do you want to go? I don't think you'd like it, but I'll take you if you really want to go."

She relaxed limply in the seat. "Oh, no. No. I don't want to go. I'm sure I don't." Her face was turned away from him. "It will be enough if we can have wine. It will be plenty." She turned up her coat collar so he could not see that she was crying weakly—like an old woman.

➤ QUESTIONS FOR READING AND WRITING

1. Have you ever been frustrated because you were not getting the attention you felt you deserved? If you were placed in Elisa's position, would you feel the same way that she does? Explain.
2. Describe the setting of "The Chrysanthemums." What effect does the setting have on your response to the story? Which passages are most effective in conveying the setting to you?
3. Describe Elisa. Do you learn about her directly or indirectly? Explain.
4. How would you account for Elisa's sadness at the end of the story? Why do you think she is interested in the prize fights? Why does she ask, "do the men hurt each other very much?"
5. What is the primary conflict in the story? Is it external or internal? Explain.
6. What is the theme of this story? Why do you think it is called "The Chrysanthemums"?

AMY TAN (b. 1952)

Amy Tan was born in Oakland, California, several years after her mother and father emigrated from China. Upon the deaths of her brother and father in 1967 and 1968, the family began a haphazard journey through Europe, before settling in Switzerland. For the next seven years, Tan attended five schools before graduating with honors from San Jose State University, where she later earned a master's degree in linguistics. In 1989, The Joy Luck Club *(from which "Two Kinds" is taken) was published and, through word-of-mouth endorsements by independent booksellers,*

became a surprise best-seller. Though Tan wrote the book as a collection of linked short stories, reviewers enthusiastically and erroneously referred to the book as an intricately woven "novel." It was nominated for the National Book Award and the National Book Critics Award and was adapted into a film for Hollywood Pictures in 1994 with Tan as a coscreenwriter. Tan's second novel, The Kitchen God's Wife, *was published in 1991, followed by* The Hundred Secret Senses *in 1995. Her short stories and essays have appeared in* The Atlantic, Harper's, The New Yorker, *and other publications. Her essay "Mother Tongue" was chosen for best American Essays 1991. She was the guest editor for the 1999 Best American Short Stories.*

Two Kinds

My mother believed you could be anything you wanted to be in America. You could open a restaurant. You could work for the government and get good retirement. You could buy a house with almost no money down. You could become rich. You could become instantly famous.

"Of course you can be prodigy, too," my mother told me when I was nine. "You can be best anything. What does Auntie Lindo know? Her daughter, she is only best tricky."

America was where all my mother's hopes lay. She had come here in 1949 after losing everything in China: her mother and father, her family home, her first husband, and two daughters, twin baby girls. But she never looked back with regret. There were so many ways for things to get better.

We didn't immediately pick the right kind of prodigy. At first my mother thought I could be a Chinese Shirley Temple. We'd watch Shirley's old movies on TV as though they were training films. My mother would poke my arm and say, "*Ni kan*"—You watch. And I would see Shirley tapping her feet, or singing a sailor song, or pursing her lips in a very round O while saying, "Oh my goodness."

5   "*Ni kan*," said my mother as Shirley's eyes flooded with tears. "You already know how. Don't need talent for crying!"

Soon after my mother got this idea about Shirley Temple, she took me to a beauty training school in the Mission district and put me in the hands of a student who could barely hold the scissors without shaking. Instead of getting big fat curls, I emerged with an uneven mass of crinkly black fuzz. My mother dragged me off to the bathroom and tried to wet down my hair.

"You look like Negro Chinese," she lamented, as if I had done this on purpose.

The instructor of the beauty training school had to lop off these soggy clumps to make my hair even again. "Peter Pan is very popular these days," the instructor assured my mother. I now had hair the length of a boy's, with straight-across bands that hung at a slant two inches above my eyebrows. I liked the haircut and it made me actually look forward to my future fame.

In fact, in the beginning, I was just as excited as my mother, maybe even more so. I pictured this prodigy part of me as many different images, trying each one on for size. I was a dainty ballerina girl standing by the curtains, waiting to hear the right music that would send me floating on my tiptoes. I was like the Christ child lifted out of the straw manager, crying with holy indignity. I was Cinderella stepping from her pumpkin carriage with sparkly cartoon music filling the air.

10   In all of my imaginings, I was filled with a sense that I would soon become *perfect*. My mother and father would adore me. I would be beyond reproach. I would never feel the need to sulk for anything.

But sometimes the prodigy in me became impatient. "If you don't hurry up and get me out of here, I'm disappearing for good," it warned. "And then you'll always be nothing."

Every night after dinner, my mother and I would sit at the Formica kitchen table. She would present new tests, taking her examples from stories of amazing children she had read in *Ripley's Believe It or Not*, or *Good Housekeeping, Reader's Digest*, and a dozen other magazines she kept in a pile in our bathroom. My mother got these magazines from people whose houses she cleaned. And since she cleaned many houses each week, we had a great assortment. She would look through them all, searching for stories about remarkable children.

The first night she brought out a story about a three-year-old boy who knew the capitals of all the states and even most of the European countries. A teacher was quoted as saying the little boy could also pronounce the names of the foreign cities correctly.

"What's the capital of Finland?" my mother asked me, looking at the magazine story.

15   All I knew was the capital of California, because Sacramento was the name of the street we lived on in Chinatown. "Nairobi!" I guessed, saying the most foreign word I could think of. She checked to see if that was possibly one way to pronounce "Helsinki" before showing me the answer.

The tests got harder—multiplying numbers in my head, finding the queen of hearts in a deck of cards, trying to stand on my head without using my hands, predicting the daily temperatures in Los Angeles, New York, and London.

One night I had to look at a page of the Bible for three minutes and then report everything I could remember. "Now Jehoshaphat had riches and honor in abundance and. . .that's all I remember, Ma," I said.

And after seeing my mother's disappointed face once again, something inside of me began to die. I hated the tests, the raised hopes and failed expectations. Before going to bed that night, I looked in the mirror above the bathroom sink and when I saw only my face staring back—and that it would always be this ordinary face—I began to cry. Such a sad, ugly girl! I made high-pitched noises like a crazed animal, trying to scratch out the face in the mirror.

And then I saw what seemed to be the prodigy side of me—because I had never seen that face before. I looked at my reflection, blinking so I could see more clearly. The girl staring back at me was angry, powerful. This girl and I were the same. I had new thoughts, willful thoughts, or rather thoughts filled with lots of won'ts. I won't let her change me, I promised myself. I won't be what I'm not.

20   So now on nights when my mother presented her tests, I performed listlessly, my head propped on one arm. I pretended to be bored. And I was. I got so bored I started counting the bellows of the foghorns out on the bay while my mother drilled me in other areas. The sound was comforting and reminded me of the cow jumping over the moon. And the next day, I played a game with myself, seeing if my mother would give up on me before eight bellows. After a while I usually counted only one, maybe two bellows at most. At last she was beginning to give up hope.

Two or three months had gone by without any mention of my being a prodigy again. And then one day my mother was watching *The Ed Sullivan Show* on TV. The TV was old and the sound kept shorting out. Every time my mother got halfway up from the sofa to adjust the set, the sound would go back on and Ed would be there talking. As soon as she sat down, Ed would go silent again. She got up, the TV broke into loud piano music. She sat down. Silence. Up and down, back and forth, quiet and loud. It was like a stiff embraceless dance between her and the TV set. Finally she stood by the set with her hand on the sound dial.

She seemed to be entranced by the music, a little frenzied piano piece with this mesmerizing quality, sort of quick passages and then teasing lilting ones before it returned to the quick playful parts.

"*Ni kan,*" my mother said, calling me over with hurried hand gestures, "Look here."

I could see why my mother was fascinated by the music. It was being pounded out by a little Chinese girl, about nine years old, with a Peter Pan haircut. The girl had the sauciness of a Shirley Temple. She was proudly modest like a proper Chinese child. And she also did this fancy sweep of a curtsy, so that the fluffy skirt of her white dress cascaded slowly to the floor like the petals of a large carnation.

25   In spite of these warning signs, I wasn't worried. Our family had no piano and we couldn't afford to buy one, let alone reams of sheet music and piano lessons. So I could be generous in my comments when my mother bad-mouthed the little girl on TV.

"Play note right, but doesn't sound good! No singing sound," complained my mother.

"What are you picking on her for?" I said carelessly. "She's pretty good. Maybe she's not the best, but she's trying hard." I knew almost immediately I would be sorry I said that.

"Just like you," she said. "Not the best. Because you not trying." She gave a little huff as she let go of the sound dial and sat down on the sofa.

The little Chinese girl sat down also to play an encore of "Anitra's Dance" by Grieg. I remember the song, because later on I had to learn how to play it.

30   Three days after watching *The Ed Sullivan Show*, my mother told me what my schedule would be for piano lessons and piano practice. She had talked to Mr.

Chong, who lived on the first floor of our apartment building. Mr. Chong was a retired piano teacher and my mother traded house-cleaning services for weekly lessons and a piano for me to practice on every day, two hours a day, from four until six.

When my mother told me this, I felt as though I had been sent to hell. I whined and then kicked my foot a little when I couldn't stand it anymore.

"Why don't you like me the way I am? I'm *not* a genius! I can't play the piano. And even if I could, I wouldn't go on TV if you paid me a million dollars!" I cried.

My mother slapped me. "Who ask you to be genius?" she shouted. "Only ask you to be your best. For your sake. You think I want you to be genius? Hnnh! What for! Who ask you!"

"So ungrateful," I heard her mutter in Chinese. "If she had as much talent as she has temper, she would be famous now."

35   Mr. Chong, whom I secretly nicknamed Old Chong, was very strange, always tapping his fingers to the silent music of an invisible orchestra. He looked ancient in my eyes. He had lost most of the hair on top of his head and he wore thick glasses and had eyes that always looked tired and sleepy. But he must have been younger than I thought, since he lived with his mother and was not yet married.

I met old lady Chong once and that was enough. She had this peculiar smell like a baby that had done something in its pants. And her fingers felt like a dead person's, like an old peach I once found in the back of the refrigerator, the skin just slid off the meat when I picked it up.

I soon found out why Old Chong had retired from teaching piano. He was deaf. "Like Beethoven!" he shouted to me. "We're both listening only in our head!" And he would start to conduct his frantic silent sonatas.

Our lessons went like this. He would open the book and point to different things, explaining their purpose: "Key! Treble! Bass! No sharps or flats! So this is C major. Listen now and play after me!"

And then he would play the C scale a few times, a simple chord, and then, as if inspired by an old, unreachable itch, he gradually added more notes and running trills and a pounding bass until the music was really something quite grand.

40   I would play after him, the simple scale, the simple chord, and then I just played some nonsense that sounded like a cat running up and down on top of garbage cans. Old Chong smiled and applauded and then said, "Very good! But now you must learn to keep time!"

So that's how I discovered that Old Chong's eyes were too slow to keep up with the wrong notes I was playing. He went through the motions in half-time. To help me keep rhythm, he stood behind me, pushing down on my right shoulder for every beat. He balanced pennies on top of my wrists so I would keep them still as I slowly played scales and arpeggios. He had me curve my hand around an apple to keep that shape when playing chords. He marched stiffly to show me how to make each finger dance up and down, staccato like an obedient little soldier.

He taught me all these things, and that was how I also learned I could be lazy and get away with mistakes, lots of mistakes. If I hit the wrong notes because I hadn't practiced enough, I never corrected myself. I just kept playing in rhythm. And Old Chong kept conducting his own private reverie.

So maybe I never really gave myself a fair chance. I did pick up the basics pretty quickly, and I might have become a good pianist at that young age. But I was so determined not to try, not to be anybody different that I learned to play only the most ear-splitting preludes, the most discordant hymns.

Over the next year, I practiced like this, dutifully in my own way. And then one day I heard my mother and her friend Lindo Jong both talking in a loud bragging tone of voice so others could hear. It was after church, and was leaning against the brick wall wearing a dress with stiff white petticoats. Auntie Lindo's daughter, Waverly, who was about my age, was standing farther down the wall about five feet away. We had grown up together and shared all the closeness of two sisters squabbling over crayons and dolls. In other words, for the most part, we hated each other. I thought she was snotty. Waverly Jong had gained a certain amount of fame as "Chinatown's Littlest Chinese Chess Champion."

45 "She bring home too many trophy," lamented Auntie Lindo that Sunday. "All day she play chess. All day I have no time do nothing but dust off her winnings." She threw a scolding look at Waverly, who pretended not to see her.

"You lucky you don't have this problem," said Auntie Lindo with a sigh to my mother.

And my mother squared her shoulders and bragged: "Our problem worser than yours. If we ask Jing-mei wash dish, she hear nothing but music. It's like you can't stop this natural talent."

And right then, I was determined to put a stop to her foolish pride.

A few weeks later, Old Chong and my mother conspired to have me play in a talent show which would be held in the church hall. By then, my parents had saved up enough to buy me a secondhand piano, a black Wurlitzer spinet with a scarred bench. It was the showpiece of our living room.

50 For the talent show, I was to play a piece called "Pleading Child" from Schumann's *Scenes from Childhood*. It was a simple, moody piece that sounded more difficult than it was. I was supposed to memorize the whole thing, playing the repeat parts twice to make the piece sound longer. But I dawdled over it, playing a few bars and then cheating, looking up to see what notes followed. I never really listened to what I was playing. I daydreamed about being somewhere else, about being someone else.

The part I liked to practice best was the fancy curtsy: right foot out, touch the rose on the carpet with a pointed foot, sweep to the side, left leg bends, look up and smile.

My parents invited all the couples from the Joy Luck Club to witness my debut. Auntie Lindo and Uncle Tin were there. Waverly and her two older bothers had also come. The first two rows were filled with children both younger and older than I was. The littlest ones got to go first. They recited simple nursery rhymes, squawked out tunes on miniature violins, twirled Hula Hoops, pranced in pink ballet tutus, and when they bowed and curtsied, the audience would sign in unison, "Awww," and then clap enthusiastically.

When my turn came, I was very confident. I remember my childish excitement. It was as if I knew, without a doubt, that the prodigy side of me really did exist. I had not fear whatsoever, no nervousness. I remember thinking to myself, This is it! This is it! I looked out over the audience, at my mother's blank face, my father's yawn, Auntie Lindo's stiff-lipped smile, Waverly's sulky expression. I had on a white dress layered with sheets of lace, and a pink bow in my Peter Pan haircut. As I sat down I envisioned people jumping to their feet and Ed Sullivan rushing up to introduce me to everyone on TV.

And I started to play. It was so beautiful. I was so caught up in how lovely I looked that at first I didn't worry how I would sound. So it was a surprise to me when I hit the first wrong note and realized something didn't sound quite right. And then I hit another and another followed that. A chill started at the top of my heard and began to trickle down. Yet I couldn't stop playing, as though my hands were bewitched. I kept thinking my fingers would adjust themselves back, like a train switching to the right track. I played this strange jumble through two repeats, the sour notes staying with me all the way to the end.

55   When I stood up, I discovered my legs were shaking. Maybe I had just been nervous and the audience, like Old Chong, had seen me go through the right motions and had not heard anything wrong at all. I swept my right foot out, went down on my knee, looked up and smiled. The room was quiet, except for Old Chong, who was beaming and shouting "Bravo! Bravo! Well Done!" But then I saw my mother's face, her stricken face. The audience clapped weakly, and as I walked back to my chair, with my whole face quivering as I tried not to cry, I heard a little boy whisper loudly to his mother, "That was awful," and the mother whispered back, "Well, she certainly tried."

And now I realized how many people were in the audience, the whole world it seemed. I was aware of eyes burning into my back. I felt the shame of my mother and father as they sat stiffly throughout the rest of the show.

We could have escaped during the intermission. Pride and some strange sense of honor must have anchored my parents to their chairs. And so we watched it all: the eighteen-year-old boy with a fake mustache who did a magic show and juggled flaming hoops while riding a unicycle. The breasted girl with white makeup who sang from *Madama Butterfly* and got honorable mention. And the eleven-year-old boy who won first prize playing a tricky violin song that sounded like a busy bee.

After the show, the Hsus, the Jongs, and the St. Clairs from the Joy Luck Club came up to my mother and father.

"Lots of talented kids," Auntie Lindo said vaguely, smiling broadly.

60   "That was somethin' else," said my father, and I wondered if he was referring to me in a humorous way, or whether he even remembered what I had done.

Waverly looked at me and shrugged her shoulders. "You aren't a genius like me," she said matter-of-factly. And if I hadn't felt so bad, I would have pulled her braids and punched her stomach.

But my mother's expression was what devastated me: a quiet, blank look that said she had lost everything. I felt the same way, and it seemed as if everybody were now coming up, like gawkers at the scene of an accident, to see what parts were actually missing. When we got on the bus to go home, my father was humming the busy-bee tune and my mother was silent. I kept thinking she wanted to wait until we got home before shouting at me. But when my father unlocked the door to our apartment, my mother walked in and then went to the back, into the bedroom. No accusations. No blame. And in a way, I felt disappointed. I had been waiting for her to start shouting, so I could shout back and cry and blame her for all my misery.

I assumed my talent-show fiasco meant I never had to play the piano again. But two days later, after school, my mother came out of the kitchen and saw me watching TV.

"Four clock," she reminded me as if it were any other day. I was stunned, as though she were asking me to go through the talent-show torture again. I wedged myself more tightly in front of the TV.

65 "Turn off TV," she called from the kitchen five minutes later.

I didn't budge. And then I decided. I didn't have to do what my mother said anymore. I wasn't her slave. This wasn't China. I had listened to her before and look what happened. She was the stupid one.

She came out from the kitchen and stood in the arched entryway of the living room. "Four clock," she said once again, louder.

"I'm not going to play anymore," I said nonchalantly. "Why should I? I'm not a genius."

She walked over and stood in front of the TV. I saw her chest was heaving up and down in an angry way.

70 "No!" I said, and I now felt stronger, as if my true self had finally emerged. So this is what had been inside me all along.

"No! I won't!" I screamed.

She yanked me by the arm, pulled me off the floor, snapped off the TV. She was frighteningly strong, half pulling, half carrying me toward the piano as I kicked the throw rugs under my feet. She lifted me up and onto the hard bench. I was sobbing by now, looking at her bitterly. Her chest was heaving even more and her mouth was open, smiling crazily as if she were pleased I was crying.

"You want me to be someone that I'm not!" I sobbed. "I'll never be the kind of daughter you want me to be!"

"Only two kinds of daughters," she shouted in Chinese. "Those who are obedient and those who follow their own mind! Only one kind of daughter can live in this house! Obedient daughter!"

75 "Then I wish I wasn't your daughter. I wish you weren't my mother," I shouted. As I said these things I got scared. It felt like worms and toads and slimy things crawling out of my chest, but it also felt good, as if this awful side of me had surfaced, at last.

"Too late change this," said my mother shrilly.

And I could sense her anger rising to its breaking point. I wanted to see it spill over. And that's when I remembered the babies she had lost in China, the ones we never talked about. "Then I wish I'd never been born!" I shouted. "I wish I were dead! Like them!"

It was as if I had said the magic words. Alakazam!—and her face went blank, her mouth closed, her arms went slack, and she backed out of the room, stunned, as if she were blowing away like a small brown leaf, thin, brittle, lifeless.

It was not the only disappointment my mother felt in me. In the years that followed, I failed her so many times, each time asserting my own will, my right to fall short of expectations. I didn't get straight As. I didn't become class president. I didn't get into Stanford. I dropped out of college.

80   For unlike my mother, I did not believe I could be anything I wanted to be. I could only be me.

And for all those years, we never talked about the disaster at the recital or my terrible accusations afterward at the piano bench. All that remained unchecked, like a betrayal that was now unspeakable. So I never found a way to ask her why she had hoped for something so large that failure was inevitable.

And even worse, I never asked her what frightened me the most: Why had she given up hope?

For after our struggle at the piano, she never mentioned my playing again. The lessons stopped. The lid to the piano was closed, shutting out the dust, my misery, and her dreams.

So she surprised me. A few years ago, she offered to give me the piano, for my thirtieth birthday. I had not played in all those years. I saw the offer as a sign of forgiveness, a tremendous burden removed.

85   "Are you sure?" I asked shyly. "I mean, won't you and Dad miss it?"

"No, this is your piano," she said firmly. "Always your piano. You only one can play."

"Well, I probably can't play anymore," I said. "It's been years."

"You pick up fast," said my mother, as if she knew this was certain. "You have natural talent. You could been genius if you want to."

"No I couldn't."

90   "You just not trying," said my mother. And she was neither angry nor sad. She said it as if to announce a fact that could never be disproved. "Take it," she said.

But I didn't at first. It was enough that she had offered it to me. And after that, every time I saw it in my parents' living room, standing in front of the bay windows, it made me feel proud, as if it were a shiny trophy I had won back.

Last week I sent a tuner over to my parents' apartment and had the piano reconditioned, for purely sentimental reasons. My mother had died a few months before and I had been getting things in order for my father, a little bit at a time. I put the jewelry in special silk pouches. The sweaters she had knitted in yellow, pink, bright orange—all the colors I hated—I put those in moth-proof boxes. I found some old Chinese silk dresses, the kind with the little slits up the sides. I rubbed the old silk against my skin, then wrapped them in tissue and decided to take them home with me.

After I had the piano tuned, I opened the lid and touched the keys. It sounded even richer than I imagined. Really, it was a very good piano. Inside the bench were the same exercise notes with handwritten scales, the same secondhand books with their covers held together with yellow tape.

I opened up the Schumann book to the dark little piece I had played at the recital. It was on the left-hand side of the page, "Pleading Child." It looked more difficult than I remembered. I played a few bars, surprised at how easily the notes came back to me.

95　　And for the first time, or so it seemed, I noticed the piece on the right-hand side. It was called "Perfectly Contented." I tried to play this one as well. It had a lighter melody but the same flowing rhythm and turned out to be quite easy. "Pleading Child" was shorter but slower; "Perfectly Contented" was longer, but faster. And after I played them both a few times, I realized they were two halves of the same song.

➤ *QUESTIONS FOR READING AND WRITING*

1. The narrator, Jing-Mei, is the protagonist in this story. How does her point of view affect how and what we are told?
2. Describe Jing-Mei. What is the primary conflict she struggles with? Is it external? Internal? Both? Explain. Why is she so resistant to her mother's wishes?
3. To what extent does your background or experience affect your response to the story?
4. Describe her mother. How should she characterize Jing-Mei? What does she want for her daughter? How does her own background influence that?
5. When Jing-Mei shouts at her mother she wishes she was not her daughter, she recalls, "As I said [this] I got scared. I felt like worms and toads and slimy things were crawling out of my chest, but it also felt good, as if this awful side of me had surfaced, at last." What do you think she means?
6. After her mother dies, Jing-Mei is reunited with her piano. What does she realize about herself, her mother, and their relationship?

ALICE WALKER

(See biography on p. 112)

ROSELILY   [1973]

Dearly Beloved,
She dreams; dragging herself across the world. A small girl in her mother's white robe and veil, knee raised waist high through a bowl of quicksand soup. The man

who stands beside her is against this standing on the front porch of her house, being married to the sound of cars whizzing by on highway 61.

we are gathered here

Like cotton to be weighed. Her fingers at the last minute busily removing dry leaves and twigs. Aware it is a superficial sweep. She knows he blames Mississippi for the respectful way the men turn their heads up in the yard, the women stand waiting and knowledgeable, their children held from mischief by teachings from the wrong God. He glares beyond them to the occupants of the cars, white faces glued to promises beyond a country wedding, noses thrust forward like dogs on a track. For him they unsurp the wedding.

in the sight of God

Yes, open house. That is what country black folks like. She dreams she does not already have three children. A squeeze around the flowers in her hands chokes off three and four and five years of breath. Instantly she is ashamed and frightened in her superstition. She looks for the first time at the preacher, forces humility into her eyes, as if she believes he is, in fact, a man of God. She can imagine God, a small black boy, timidly pulling the preacher's coattail.

to join this man and this woman

She thinks of ropes, chains, handcuffs, his religion. His place of worship. Where she will be required to sit apart with covered head. In Chicago, a word she hears when thinking of smoke, from his description of what a cinder was, which they never had in Panther Burn. She sees hovering over the heads of clean neighbors in her front yard black specks falling, clinging, from the sky. But in Chicago. Respect, a chance to build. Her children at last from underneath the detrimental wheel. A chance to be on top. What a relief, she thinks. What a vision, a view, from up so high.

in holy matrimony

5   Her fourth child she gave away to the child's father who had some money. Certainly a good job. Had gone to Harvard. Was a good man but weak because good language meant so much to him he could not live with Roselily. Could not abide TV in the living room, five beds in three rooms, no Bach except from four to six on Sunday afternoons. No chess at all. She does not forget to worry about her son among his father's people. She wonders if the New England climate will agree with him. If he will ever come down to Mississippi, as his father did, to try to right the country's wrong. She wonders if he will be stronger than his father. His father cried off and on throughout her pregnancy. Went to skin and bones. Suffered nightmares, retching and falling out of bed. Tried to kill himself. Later told his wife he found the right baby through friends. Vouched for, the sterling qualities that would make up his character.

   It is not her nature to blame. Still, she is not entirely thankful. She supposes New England, the North, to be quite different from what she knows. It seems right somehow to her that people who move there to live return home completely changed. She thinks of the air, the smoke, the cinders. Imagines cinders as big as hailstones; heavy, weighing on the people. Wonders how this pressure finds it way into the veins, roping the springs of laughter.

If there's anybody here that knows a reason why

But of course they know no reason why beyond what they daily have come to know. She thinks of the man who will be her husband, feels shut away from him because of the stiff severity of his plain black suit. His religion. A lifetime of black and white. Of veils. Covered head. It is as if her children are already gone from her. Not dead, but exalted on a pedestal, a stalk that has no roots. She wonders how to make new roots. It is beyond her. She wonders what one does with memories in a brand-new life. This had seemed easy, until she thought of it. "The reasons why . . . the people who" . . . she thinks, and does not wonder where the thought is from.

these two should not be joined

She thinks of her mother, who is dead. Dead, but still her mother. Joined. This is confusing. Of her father. A gray old man who sold wild mink, rabbit, fox skins to Sears, Roebuck. He stands in the yard, like a man waiting for a train. Her young sisters stand behind her in smooth green dresses, with flowers in their hands and hair. They giggle, she feels, at the absurdity of the wedding. They are ready for something new. She thinks the man beside her should marry one of them. She feels old. Yoked. An arm seems to reach out from behind her and snatch her backward. She thinks of cemeteries and the long sleep of grandparents mingling in the dirt. She believes that she believes in ghosts. In the soil giving back what it takes.

together

In the city. He sees her in a new way. This she knows, and is grateful. But is it new enough? She cannot always be a bride and virgin, wearing robes and veil. Even now her body itches to be free of satin and voile, organdy and lily of the valley. Memories crash against her. Memories of being bare to the sun. She wonders what it will be like. Not to have to go to a job. Not to work in a sewing plant. Not to worry about learning to sew straight seems in workingmen's overalls, jeans, and dress pants. Her place will be in the home, he has said, repeatedly, promising her rest she had prayed for. But now she wonders. When she is rested, what will she do? They will make babies—she thinks practically about her fine brown body, his strong black one. They will be inevitable. Her hands will be full. Full of what? Babies. She is not comforted.

let him speak

10 She wishes she had asked him to explain more of what he meant. But she was impatient. Impatient to be done with sewing. With doing everything for three children, alone. Impatient to leave the girls she had known since childhood, their children growing up, their husbands hanging around her, already old, seedy. Nothing about them that she wanted, or needed. The fathers of her children driving by, waving, not waving; reminders of times she would just as soon forget. Impatient to see the South Side, where they would live and build and be respectable and respected and

free. Her husband would free her. A romantic hush. Proposal. Promises. A new life! Respectable, reclaimed, renewed. Free! In robe and veil.

or forever hold

She does not even know if she loves him. She loves his sobriety. His refusal to sing just because he knows the tune. She loves his pride. His blackness and his gray car. She loves his understanding of her *condition*. She thinks she loves the effort he will make to redo her into what he truly wants. His love of her makes her completely conscious of how unloved she was before. This is something; though it makes her unbearably sad. Melancholy. She blinks her eyes. Remembers she is finally being married, like other girls. Like other girls, women? Something strains upward behind her eyes. She thinks of the something as a rat trapped, concerned, scurrying to and fro in her head, peering through the windows of her eyes. She wants to live for once. But doesn't know quite what that means. Wonders if she has ever done it. If she ever will. The preacher is odious to her. She wants to strike him out of the way, out of her light, with the back of her hand. It seems to her he has always been standing in front of her, barring her way.

his peace.

The rest she does not hear. She feels a kiss, passionate, rousing, within the general pandemonium. Cars drive up blowing their horns. Firecrackers go off. Dogs come from under the house and begin to yelp and bark. Her husband's hand is like the clasp of an iron gate. People congratulate. Her children press against her. They look with awe and distaste mixed with hope at their new father. He stands curiously apart, in spite of the people crowding about to grasp his free hand. He smiles at them all but his eyes are as if turned inward. He knows they cannot understand that he is not a Christian. He will not explain himself. He feels different, he looks it. The old women thought he was like one of their sons except that he had somehow got away from them. Still a son, not a son. Changed.

She thinks how it will be later in the night in the silvery gray car. How they will spin through the darkness of Mississippi and in the morning be in Chicago, Illinois. She thinks of Lincoln, the president. That is all she knows about the place. She feels ignorant, *wrong*, backward. She presses her worried fingers into his palm. He is standing in front of her. In the crush of well-wishing people, he does not look back.

➤ QUESTIONS FOR READING AND WRITING

1. In what way were you affected by having what Roselily is thinking interrupted by the words of the marriage ceremony? What do you know about her from what she is thinking?
2. Who is her husband? How do you think he will treat Roselily? What passages in the story tell you that? Do you think this marriage will last? Explain.
3. Why do you think she thinks about the father of her fourth child? Do you think she regrets having given him her child? Explain.

EUDORA WELTY (1909–2001)

The daughter of an insurance salesman, Eudora Welty graduated from the University of Wisconsin in 1929 and studied advertising at the Columbia University Graduate School of Business. She was born and lived most of her long life in Jackson, Mississippi. Welty has writ-ten many novels, including The Optimist's Daughter, *which won the Pulitzer Prize in 1972, and numerous essays, but she is best known for her short stories. Though the stories are almost invariably set in a specific geo-graphic locale—the small towns of the Mississippi delta—Welty's best stories uncover aspects of the human experience that are universal.*

A WORN PATH [1941]

It was December—a bright frozen day in the early morning. Far out in the coun-try there was an old Negro woman with her head tied in a red rag, coming along a path through the pinewoods. Her name was Phoenix Jackson. She was very old and small and she walked slowly in the dark pine shadows, moving a little from side to side in her steps, with the balanced heaviness and lightness of a pendulum in a grandfather clock. She carried a thin, small cane made from an umbrella, and with this she kept tapping the frozen earth in front of her. This made a grave and persistent noise in the still air, that seemed meditative like the chirping of a soli-tary little bird.

She wore a dark striped dress reaching down to her shoe tops, and an equally long apron of bleached sugar sacks, with a full pocket: all neat and tidy, but every time she took a step she might have fallen over her shoelaces, which dragged from her unlaced shoes. She looked straight ahead. Her eyes were blue with age. Her skin had a pattern all its own of numberless branching wrinkles and as though a whole little tree stood in the middle of her forehead, but a golden color ran underneath, and the two knobs of her cheeks were illumined by a yellow burning under the dark. Under the red rag her hair came down on her neck in the frailest of ringlets, still black, and with an odor like copper.

Now and then there was a quivering in the thicket. Old Phoenix said, "Out of my way, all you foxes, owls, beetles, jack rabbits, coons, and wild animals! . . . Keep out from under these feet, little bob-whites. . . . Keep the big wild hogs out of my path. Don't let none of those come running my direction. I got a long way." Under her small black-freckled hand her cane, limber as a buggy whip, would switch at the brush as if to rouse up any hiding things.

On she went. The woods were deep and still. The sun made the pine needles almost too bright to look at, up where the wind rocked. The cones dropped as light as feathers. Down in the hollow was the mourning dove—it was not too late for him.

5   The path ran up a hill. "Seem like there is chains about my feet, time I get this far," she said, in the voice of argument old people keep to use with themselves. "Something always take a hold of me on this hill—pleads I should stay."

After she got to the top she turned and gave a full, severe look behind her where she had come. "Up through pines," she said at length. "Now down through oaks."

Her eyes opened their widest, and she started down gently. But before she got to the bottom of the hill a bush caught her dress.

Her fingers were busy and intent, but her skirts were full and long, so that before she could pull them free in one place they were caught in another. It was not possible to allow the dress to tear. "I in the thorny bush," she said. "Thorns, you doing your appointed work. Never want to let folks pass, no sir. Old eyes thought you was a pretty little *green* bush."

Finally, trembling all over, she stood free, and after a moment dared to stoop for her cane.

10   "Sun so high!" she cried, leaning back and looking, while the thick tears went over her eyes. "The time getting all gone here."

At the foot of this hill was a place where a log was laid across the creek.

"Now comes the trial," said Phoenix.

Putting her right foot out, she mounted the log and shut her eyes. Lifting her skirt, leveling her cane fiercely before her, like a festival figure in some parade, she began to march across. Then she opened her eyes and she was safe on the other side.

"I wasn't as old as I thought," she said.

15   But she sat down to rest. She spread her skirts on the bank around her and folded her hands over her knees. Up above her was a tree in a pearly cloud of mistletoe. She did not dare to close her eyes, and when a little boy brought her a plate with a slice of marble-cake on it she spoke to him. "That would be acceptable," she said. But when she went to take it there was just her own hand in the air.

So she left that tree, and had to go through a barbed-wire fence. There she had to creep and crawl, spreading her knees and stretching her fingers like a baby trying to climb the steps. But she talked loudly to herself: she could not let her dress be torn now, so late in the day, and she could not pay for having her arm or leg sawed off if she got caught fast where she was.

At last she was safe through the fence and risen up out in the clearing. Big dead trees, like black men with one arm, were standing in the purple stalks of the withered cotton field. There sat a buzzard.

"Who you watching?"

In the furrow she made her way along.

20   "Glad this not the season for bulls," she said, looking sideways, "and the good Lord made his snakes to curl up and sleep in the winter. A pleasure I don't see no two-headed snake coming around that tree, where it come once. It took a while to get by him, back in the summer."

She passed through the old cotton and went into a field of dead corn. It whispered and shook and was taller than her head. "Through the maze now," she said, for there was no path.

Then there was something tall, black, and skinny there, moving before her.

At first she took it for a man. It could have been a man dancing in the field. But she stood still and listened, and it did not make a sound. It was as silent as a ghost.

"Ghost," she said sharply, "who be you the ghost of? For I have heard of nary death close by."

25   But there was no answer—only the ragged dancing in the wind.

She shut her eyes, reached out her hand, and touched a sleeve. She found a coat and inside that an emptiness, cold as ice.

"You scarecrow," she said. Her face lighted. "I ought to be shut up for good," she said with laughter. "My senses is gone. I too old. I the oldest people I ever know. Dance, old scarecrow," she said, "while I dancing with you."

She kicked her foot over the furrow, and with mouth drawn down, shook her head once or twice in a little strutting way. Some husks blew down and whirled in streamers about her skirts.

Then she went on, parting her way from side to side with the cane, through the whispering field. At last she came to the end, to a wagon track where the silver grass blew between the red ruts. The quail were walking around like pullets, seeming all dainty and unseen.

30   "Walk pretty," she said. "This the easy place. This the easy going."

She followed the track, swaying through the quiet bare fields, through the little strings of trees silver in their dead leaves, past cabins silver from weather, with the doors and windows boarded shut, all like old women under a spell sitting there. "I walking in their sleep," she said, nodding her head vigorously.

In a ravine she went where a spring was silently flowing through a hollow log. Old Phoenix bent and drank. "Sweet-gum makes the water sweet," she said, and drank more. "Nobody know who made this well, for it was here when I was born."

The track crossed a swampy part where the moss hung as white as lace from every limb. "Sleep on, alligators, and blow your bubbles." Then the track went into the road.

Deep, deep the road went down between the high green-colored banks. Overhead the live-oaks met, and it was as dark as a cave.

35   A black dog with a lolling tongue came up out of the weeds by the ditch. She was meditating, and not ready, and when he came at her she only hit him a little with her cane. Over she went in the ditch, like a little puff of milkweed.

Down there, her senses drifted away. A dream visited her, and she reached her hand up, but nothing reached down and gave her a pull. So she lay there and presently went to talking. "Old woman," she said to herself, "that black dog come up out of the weeds to stall you off, and now there he sitting on his fine tail, smiling at you."

A white man finally came along and found her—a hunter, a young man, with his dog on a chain.

"Well, Granny!" he laughed. "what are you doing there?"

"Lying on my back like a June-bug waiting to be turned over, mister," she said, reaching up her hand.

40   He lifted her up, gave her a swing in the air, and set her down. "Anything broken, Granny?"

"No sir, them old dead weeds is springy enough," said Phoenix, when she had got her breath. "I thank you for your trouble."

"Where do you live, Granny?" he asked, while the two dogs were growling at each other.

"Away back yonder, sir, behind the ridge. You can't even see it from here."

"On your way home?"

45 "No, sir, I going to town."

"Why, that's too far! That's as far as I walk when I come out myself, and I get something for my trouble." He patted the stuffed bag he carried, and there hung down a little closed claw. It was one of the bob-whites, with its beak hooked bitterly to show it was dead. "Now you go on home, Granny!"

"I bound to go to town, mister," said Phoenix. "The time come around."

He gave another laugh, filling the whole landscape. "I know you old colored people! Wouldn't miss going to town to see Santa Claus!"

But something held old Phoenix very still. The deep lines in her face went into a fierce and different radiation. Without warning, she had seen with her own eyes a flashing nickel fall out of the man's pocket onto the ground.

50 "How old are you, Granny?" he was saying.

"There is no telling, mister," she said, "no telling."

Then she gave a little cry and clapped her hands and said, "Git on away from here, dog! Look! Look at that dog!" She laughed as if in admiration. "He ain't scared of nobody. He a big black dog." She whispered, "Sic him!"

"Watch me get rid of that cur," said the man. "Sic him, Pete! Sic him!"

Phoenix heard the dogs fighting, and heard the man running and throwing sticks. She even heard a gunshot. But she was slowly bending forward by that time, further and further forward, the lids stretched down over her eyes, as if she were doing this in her sleep. Her chin was lowered almost to her knees. The yellow palm of her hand came out from the fold of her apron. Her fingers slid down and along the ground under the piece of money with the grace and care they would have in lifting an egg from under a sitting hen. Then she slowly straightened up, she stood erect, and the nickel was in her apron pocket. A bird flew by. Her lips moved. "God watching me the whole time. I come to stealing."

55 The man came back, and his own dog panted about them. "Well, I scared him off that time," he said, and then he laughed and lifted his gun and pointed it at Phoenix.

She stood straight and faced him.

"Doesn't the gun scare you?" he said, still pointing it.

"No, sir, I seen plenty go off closer by, in my day, and for less than what I done," she said, holding utterly still.

He smiled, and shouldered the gun. "Well, Granny," he said, "you must be a hundred years old, and scared of nothing. I'd give you a dime if I had any money with me. But you take my advice and stay home, and nothing will happen to you."

60 "I bound to go on my way, mister," said Phoenix. She inclined her head in the red rag. Then they went in different directions, but she could hear the gun shooting again and again over the hill.

She walked on. The shadows hung from the oak trees to the road like curtains. Then she smelled wood-smoke, and smelled the river, and she saw a steeple and the cabins on their steep steps. Dozens of little black children whirled around her. There ahead was Natchez shining. Bells were ringing. She walked on.

In the paved city it was Christmas time. There were red and green electric lights strung and crisscrossed everywhere, and all turned on in the daytime. Old Phoenix would have been lost if she had not distrusted her eyesight and depended on her feet to know where to take her.

She paused quietly on the sidewalk where people were passing by. A lady came along in the crowd, carrying an armful of red-, green-, and silver-wrapped presents; she gave off perfume like the red roses in hot summer, and Phoenix stopped her.

"Please, missy, will you lace up my shoe?" She held up her foot.

65   "What do you want, Grandma?"

"See my shoe," said Phoenix. "Do all right for out in the country, but wouldn't look right to go in a big building."

"Stand still then, Grandma," said the lady. She put her packages down on the sidewalk beside her and laced and tied both shoes tightly.

"Can't lace 'em with a cane," said Phoenix. "Thank you, missy, I doesn't mind asking a nice lady to tie up my shoe, when I gets out on the street."

Moving slowly and from side to side, she went into the big building and into a tower of steps, where she walked up and around and around until her feet knew to stop.

70   She entered a door, and there she saw nailed up on the wall the document that had been stamped with the gold seal and framed in the gold frame, which matched the dream that was hung up in her head.

"Here I be," she said. There was a fixed and ceremonial stiffness over her body.

"A charity case, I suppose," said an attendant who sat at the desk before her.

But Phoenix only looked above her head. There was sweat on her face, the wrinkles in her skin shone like a bright net.

"Speak up, Grandma," the woman said. "What's your name? We must have your history, you know. Have you been here before? What seems to be the trouble with you?"

75   Old Phoenix only gave a twitch to her face as if a fly were bothering her.

"Are you deaf?" cried the attendant.

But then the nurse came in.

"Oh, that's just old Aunt Phoenix," she said. "She doesn't come for herself—she has a little grandson. She makes these trips just as regular as clockwork. She lives away back off the old Natchez Trace." She bent down. "Well, Aunt Phoenix, why don't you just take a seat? We won't keep you standing after your long trip." She pointed.

The old woman sat down, bolt upright in the chair.

80   "Now, how is the boy?" asked the nurse.

Old Phoenix did not speak.

"I said, how is the boy?"

But Phoenix only waited and stared straight ahead, her face very solemn and withdrawn into rigidity.

"Is his throat any better?" asked the nurse. "Aunt Phoenix, don't you hear me? Is your grandson's throat any better since the last time you came for the medicine?"

85   With her hands on her knees, the old woman waited, silent, erect and motionless, just as if she were in armor.

"You mustn't take up our time this way, Aunt Phoenix," the nurse said. "Tell us quickly about your grandson, and get it over. He isn't dead, is he?"

At last there came a flicker and then a flame of comprehension across her face, and she spoke.

"My grandson. It was my memory had left me. There I sat and forgot why I made my long trip."

"Forgot?" The nurse frowned. "After you came so far?"

90   Then Phoenix was like an old woman begging a dignified forgiveness for waking up frightened in the night. "I never did go to school, I was too old at the Surrender," she said in a soft voice. "I'm an old woman without an education. It was my memory fail me. My little grandson, he is just the same, and I forgot it in the coming."

"Throat never heals, does it?" said the nurse, speaking in a loud, sure voice to Old Phoenix. By now she had a card with something written on it, a little list. "Yes. Swallowed lye. When was it—January—two—three years ago—"

Phoenix spoke unasked now. "No, missy, he not dead, he just the same. Every little while his throat begin to close up again, and he not able to swallow. He not get his breath. He not able to help himself. So the time come around, and I go on another trip for the soothing medicine."

"All right. The doctor said as long as you came to get it, you could have it," said the nurse. "But it's an obstinate case."

"My little grandson, he sit up there in the house all wrapped up, waiting by himself," Phoenix went on. "We is the only two left in the world. He suffer and it don't seem to put him back at all. He got a sweet look. He going to last. He wear a little patch quilt and peep out holding his mouth open like a little bird. I remembers so plain now. I not going to forget him again, no, the whole enduring time. I could tell him from all the others in creation."

95   "All right." The nurse was trying to hush her now. She brought her a bottle of medicine. "Charity," she said, making a check mark in a book.

Old Phoenix held the bottle close to her eyes and then carefully put it into her pocket.

"I thank you," she said.

"It's Christmas time, Grandma," said the attendant. "Could I give you a few pennies out of my purse?"

"Five pennies is a nickel," said Phoenix stiffly.

100   "Here's a nickel," said the attendant.

Phoenix rose carefully and held out her hand. She received the nickel and then fished the other nickel out of her pocket and laid it beside the new one. She stared at her palm closely, with her head on one side.

Then she gave a tap with her cane on the floor.

"This is what come to me to do," she said. "I going to the store and buy my child a little windmill they sells, made out of paper. He going to find it hard to believe there such a thing in the world. I'll march myself back where he waiting, holding it straight up in this hand."

She lifted her free hand, gave a little nod, turned round, and walked out of the doctor's office. Then her slow step began on the stairs, going down.

▶ QUESTIONS FOR READING AND WRITING

1. The Phoenix is a bird that, according to legend, lived for hundreds of years, burned itself to ashes on a funeral pyre, and then rose from the ashes to live again. Why do you think the protagonist of "A Worn Path" is named Phoenix?
2. Based on what you learn about Phoenix in the story, what is her background?
3. What is your response to the hunter she meets on the path? What is his role in the story?
4. What is the central conflict or struggle in this story? What are the obstacles against Phoenix? How does she overcome them?
5. In what way is "A Worn Path" an appropriate title for this story?

APPENDIX A

Critical Approaches to Literature

Earlier in the text you were briefly introduced to four different perspectives from which to interpret literature: reader-based, text-based, context-based, and author-based approaches. In this section we take a closer look at each of these critical perspectives.

Try to keep in mind that these approaches may easily overlap, and critics will often combine them in their analyses. A reader-based approach, though emphasizing personal response, may call on the text for detailed support or make reference to contextual issues. Text-based approaches, though emphasizing the text, may interpret the elements of the text through contextual knowledge. Context-based approaches may consider the attitudes of the reader and the author, and derive support from the text. Author-based criticism may consider the author's style and structure in the text and the influence of readers and contextual issues on the author.

The difference between one critical approach and another may be more a matter of emphasis than kind, and drawing upon several perspectives can yield a rich interpretation. What distinguishes one approach from another is the answer to a fundamental question: *Where is the meaning?* In the reader? In the text? In the world around the text? In the author? How we answer this question will determine the approach we take.

The explanations below will define each approach. To clarify their differences in practice, let's briefly apply each of them to two works of fiction: James Joyce's "Eveline" (p. 338) and Flannery O'Connor's "Everything That Rises Must Converge" (p. 407). As you read these applications, it will be clear that some works of literature yield better results with some approaches than others.

Reader-Based Criticism

The basic premise of **reader-based** or **reader-response** critical theory is that literature does not exist separate from those who read it. The critical approach reflected in this book is reader-based. Readers are encouraged to respond personally to fiction, to think about the ways their backgrounds influence their responses, and to support their responses with references to the story itself.

Throughout this book, readers have been encouraged to supplement this reader-based approach with other perspectives. Discussions of the elements of fiction and close reading and textual analysis in Chapters 3 and 4 rely on text-, context-, and author-based approaches.

A reader-response approach to "Eveline" might emphasize the reader's identification with the protagonist in the story. The student writer of the essay in the Case Study in Research (p.338), for example, compares his situation with Eveline's. He cites passages that remind him of his own situation and draws support from both his own life and the text of the story to illustrate similarities and differences.

An example of a reader-response approach to "Everything that Rises Must Converge" might include identification with or personal reactions to Julian, his mother, or the woman and her son on the bus. Readers might pass judgments on Julian or his mother or imagine how they would have behaved in Julian's situation. They might address which character is most like them, identify characters that remind them of people they know, and comment on how these personal connections affect their responses.

Further Reading on Reader-Based Criticism

Bleich, David. *Subjective Criticism*. Baltimore, MD: Johns Hopkins University Press, 1978.

Iser, Wolfgang. *The Act of Reading*. Baltimore, MD: Johns Hopkins University Press, 1978.

Rosenblatt, Louise. *The Reader, the Text, the Poem*. Carbondale, IL: Southern Illinois University Press, 1978.

Tompkins, Jane O. *Reader-Response Criticism: From Formalism to Post-Structuralism*. Baltimore, MD: Johns Hopkins University Press, 1980.

Text-Based Criticism

Formalism

Formalism seeks to *objectify* the text—to examine it in isolation from its reader, its context, and its author. **New Criticism**, the most popular type of formalism, is not new. It was given its name more than half a century ago as a reaction to the older biographical and historical approaches that preceded it. Though its popularity has now declined, it was the most dominant form of literary criticism in the twentieth century. As the designation "formalism" suggests, this approach closely examines elements of form/structure and language such as genre, plot, characterization, narration, tone, irony, diction, imagery, metaphor, and symbol. A formalist critic constructs meaning by focusing exclusively on the elements of the text and on the way they work together to form a unified, coherent whole.

Because the background, values, and feelings of the reader and the author cannot be objectively evaluated, formalism sees them as irrelevant or erroneous in the construction of a stable meaning. It classifies reliance on a reader's emotional response as an **affective fallacy** and reliance on knowledge of an author's life or intentions as an **intentional fallacy**.

A formalist response to "Eveline," for example, would stick closely to the text of the story. It might try to establish the meaning of the story through analysis of the language, images, symbols, narrator's tone, and how they work together to build and to support Eveline's decision at the end of the story.

A similar approach to the O'Connor story might consider how well the plot structure sets up the terrible climax of the story. It might examine the elements of the plot and details of characterization and the way these parts form an organic unity—how the structure of the story naturally culminates in the final desperate moment.

Further Reading on Formalist Criticism

Empson, William. *Seven Types of Ambiguity*. New York: Noonday Press, 1958.
Ransom, John Crowe. *The New Criticism*. New York: New Directions, 1941.
Richards, I. A. *Practical Criticism*. New York: Harcourt, 1928.

Deconstruction

Like formalism, **deconstruction** focuses exclusively on the text and requires close reading. Unlike formalism, however, which examines parts and relationships to construct a whole, the intention of deconstruction, as its name suggests, is to break down the whole—to deconstruct its meaning. While formalism emphasizes structure and the stability of interpreting the text in isolation, deconstruction insists on the instability and transitory nature of the text.

An early proponent of deconstruction was Jacques Derrida, who explained it through the French word *différence*, which means both "to differ" and "to defer." First, this view asserts that nothing can be known in isolation. We can know the meaning of something only by how it differs from something else to which it is related. All knowledge is based on difference, and all language is relational. We can know "dark" only in relation to "light," "up" to "down," "good" to "evil." Second, any stable or definitive meaning or interpretation must be deferred or put off perpetually because meaning, like the world, is always changing. What authors intend is different from what they write or what readers read. No text has a definitive meaning. So we cannot say that one interpretation is right and another is wrong.

Rather than attempting to construct an interpretation of its own, a deconstructionist approach to either "Eveline" or "Everything That Rises Must Converge" might try to reveal any number of alternative meanings for the stories. It might question the credibility of the narrators in the stories and attempt to dismantle all other interpretations by demonstrating the instability of their meaning.

Further Reading on Deconstruction Criticism

Culler, Jonathan. *On Deconstruction: Theory and Criticism after Structuralism*. Ithaca, NY: Cornell University Press, 1981.
de Man, Paul. *Allegories of Reading*. New Haven, CT: Yale University Press, 1979.
Derrida, Jacques. *Of Grammatology*. Trans. Gayatri Spivak. Baltimore, MD: Johns Hopkins University Press, 1974.
Hartmann, Geoffrey H., et al. *Deconstruction and Criticism*. New York: Continuum, 1979.

Context-Based Criticism

Historical Criticism

The basic premise of **historical criticism** is that literature benefits from being read in its own historical context. Important to this perspective are the political, economic, and psychological influences of the era that produced the literature and its author. The audience for whom it was written and how its meaning and the connotations of its language may have changed over time are among the factors important to this type of interpretation.

A recent development in historical criticism, **New Historicism**, questions the validity of traditional historical criticism and argues that we can view the past only from the "informed" present. It insists that we see the past through our own values and view the "official" history of the ruling classes with skepticism, that the history of those defeated and oppressed must also be revealed.

A historical critic's view of "Eveline" might identify the period in which the story is set and examine the forces at work in that era. Joyce's story is set during one of the peak periods of Irish migration. Research into the economic conditions prevalent during this time in Ireland might help the reader understand the nature of Eveline's plight and the gravity of her decision.

A similar view of "Everything That Rises Must Converge" might focus on the mother's background and the attitudes that prevailed in the white, southern culture that produced her. And, in turn, it might examine how her expression of these attitudes has turned Julian against her.

Further Reading on Historical Criticism

Auerbach, Erich. *Mimesis: The Representation of Reality in Western Literature.* Princeton, NJ: Princeton University Press, 1953.

Foucault, Michel. *Madness and Civilization.* Trans. Richard Howard. New York: Pantheon, 1965.

Greenblatt, Stephen. *Renaissance Self-fashioning: From More to Shakespeare.* Chicago, IL: University of Chicago Press, 1980.

Patterson, Annabel. "Historical Scholarship." *An Introduction to Scholarship in Modern Languages and Literatures.* 2nd ed. ed. Joseph Gibaldi. New York: MLA, 1992. 183–200.

Gender Criticism

Gender criticism examines how literature reflects sexual identity or orientation. It may address the ways in which an author's gender has influenced his or her work. It may examine the gender-based portrayal of literary characters and their behavior. It may explore the way in which literature supports or rejects societal norms that foster gender stereotypes. It may emphasize gay and lesbian issues.

Its most popular form is **Feminist Criticism**, which has emerged as a powerful literary force during the last 50 years. Among the issues feminist critics address are literary depictions of women, assumptions about women generated by male writers, the recurring pattern in literature of male dominance, female passivity, and sexism in literature as it reflects the societies that fostered it.

A feminist response to "Eveline" might consider the nature of a father-daughter relationship that has required Eveline to give up her life to take care of her father. It might conjecture that if Eveline were male, she would not be pressured to be responsible for her father and would be given the freedom to build her own life independent of the men who demand her attention.

A similar approach to "Everything That Rises Must Converge" might emphasize the mother's reliance on Julian and how her narrow-mindedness results from training by a system that makes women value themselves only as social adornments not thinkers, questioners, or leaders.

Further Reading on Gender Criticism

Abel, Elizabeth, ed. *Writing and Sexual Difference.* Chicago, IL: University of Chicago Press, 1982.

Fetterly, Judith. *The Resisting Reader: A Feminist Approach to American Fiction.* Bloomington, IN: Indiana University Press, 1978.

Ruthven, K. K. *Feminist's Literary Studies: An Introduction.* New York: Cambridge University Press, 1984.

Sedgwick, Eve. *Epistemology of the Closet.* Berkeley, CA: University of California Press, 1991.

Political-Economic Criticism

Political-economic criticism focuses on the influence and the consequences of the economic social order in literature. Its most popular form is **Marxist Criticism**, which argues that literature reflects the class structure and class struggle that produced it. It emphasizes the social content of literature and scrutinizes the economic circumstances of literature for instances of exploitation. It also analyzes the ways in which text, author, and readers reveal class attitudes.

A Marxist view of "Eveline" might emphasize the poor economic situation of Eveline and her father—how their economic plight and its consequence—and his demands and her unending labor to make ends meet—have created circumstances that make it impossible for them to have a reasonable relationship and family life.

A similar view of "Everything That Rises Must Converge" might expose the haughtiness of the mother as typical of the class she comes from—and how her condescending treatment of the mother and child on the bus illustrates this class separation.

Further Reading on Political-Economic Criticism

Eagleton, Terry. *Criticism and Ideology: A Study in Marxist Literary Theory.* London: New Left Books, 1976.

Lentricchia, Frank. *Criticism and Social Change.* Chicago, IL: University of Chicago Press, 1983.

Sartre, Jean-Paul. *What Is Literature?* New York: Philosophical Library, 1949.

Williams, Raymond. *Marxism and Literature.* Oxford: Oxford University Press, 1977.

Psychoanalytic Criticism

Derived from the psychological theory of Sigmund Freud, **psychoanalytic criticism** emphasizes the underlying meaning in the narrative, actions, and dialogue of literature. Sexual symbols, dreams, and repressed feelings are central to a psychological analysis of the characters. The creative process and psychological makeup of the author may also be of special interest.

A psychoanalytic view of "Eveline" for example, might focus on the repressed feelings of the protagonist and the mixed emotions she feels about her father and about herself as a replacement for the dead mother. It might also focus on Frank and what Eveline both loves and fears in what he represents.

Given the love/hate relationship between Julian and his mother in "Everything That Rises Must Converge," a psychoanalytic critic might be overwhelmed with material for exploration. What does Julian's mother represent to him? Despite his objections to what she says and does, he continues to rely on her. What is he repressing in this relationship? Why is he so horrified at the end of the story? What has he lost?

Further Reading on Psychoanalytic Criticism

Crews, Frederick C., ed. *Psychoanalysis and Literary Process*. Cambridge, MA: Winthrop, 1970.

Hartmann, Geoffrey. *Psychoanalysis and the Question of Text*. Baltimore, MD: Johns Hopkins University Press, 1979.

Kurzweil, Edith, and William Phillips, eds. *Literature and Psychoanalysis*. New York: Columbia University Press, 1983.

Trilling, Lionel. *Freud and the Crisis of Our Culture*. Boston, MA: Beacon, 1955.

Archetypal Criticism

Derived from the theories of psychologist Carl Jung, this approach assumes that we share a "collective unconscious" that has been shaped by the repeated experiences of our ancestors. It asserts that through this collective unconscious, we indirectly share a knowledge of **archetypes**: universal images, patterns, and forms like the seasons, the sun, the moon, the wise old man or woman, fire, night, and blood. Of special interest to an archetypal critic are images, descriptive detail, plot patterns, and types of characters that appear frequently in literature and that seem to evoke non-rational but powerful responses from our unconscious memory.

An archetypal critic, for example, might approach "Eveline" by identifying some of the more powerful images and symbols in the story. Both the protagonist's and the reader's responses to the religious artifacts as archetypal images might prompt some rich exploration.

A similar view of "Everything That Rises Must Converge" might explore the many images, symbols, and symbolic actions that seem to drive both mother and son throughout the story.

Further Reading on Archetypal Criticism

Campbell, Joseph. *The Hero with a Thousand Faces*. New York: Pantheon, 1949.
Frye, Northrop. *Anatomy of Criticism*. Princeton, NJ: Princeton University Press, 1957.
Lentricchia, Frank. *After the New Criticism*. Chicago, IL: University of Chicago Press, 1980.

Author-Based Criticism

Author-based, or **biographical**, criticism emphasizes the relationship between authors' lives and their works. Finding out about an author's life, of course, requires reading a **biography** or **autobiography** of the author. An effective literary biography brings the author's work and life together. And literary biographies can be highly controversial. A recent biography of poet Anne Sexton (see below), which published the private notes of her psychiatrist, prompted a strong reaction and raised serious questions about confidentiality.

Of special interest in biographical criticism is the way in which authors' lives have influenced their writing-how details and people in their own lives have entered their work. Exploring these connections may lead to a deeper understanding of a work's meaning.

A biographical critic's response to "Eveline," for example, might include research on James Joyce's own growing up years and his relationship with his father and his sisters—and his reaction to his mother's death.

A similar view of "Everything That Rises Must Converge" might examine Flannery O'Connor's background—and find insights into her characterization of Julian's mother based on her personal knowledge and experience as a native of the South.

Further Reading and Examples of Biographical Criticism

Ackroyd, Peter. *Dickens*. New York: HarperCollins, 1990.
Edel, Leon. *Literary Biography*. New York: Harper and Row, 1957.
Ellmann, Richard. *James Joyce*. Oxford: Oxford University Press, 1983.
Jellinek, Estelle C. *Women's Autobiography*: Essays in Criticism. Boston, MA: Twayne, 1986.

Research and Documentation—Some Basics

What Must Be Documented

1. Information that is not common knowledge-knowledge that you or most others would not have without reference to this or a similar source.
2. Information or ideas from another source (text or interview) that you have paraphrased (rephrased in your own words) or summarized (reduced to its essential points).
3. Direct quotations from another source (text or interview).

Where and How

1. In the text of the essay itself, you must indicate the author and page number(s) of borrowed information or quotations.
2. On a separate page at the end of the essay, you must include an alphabetized list of all the sources you have used in the essay.

Avoid Plagiarism

Plagiarism is taking someone else's ideas or words and passing them off as your own. The most basic rule of all documentation is that direct quotations and summarized or paraphrased information or ideas from another source must be appropriately credited. To use other people's words and ideas and not give them credit is a serious academic offense.

The Physical Layout of the Research Essay

Individual course requirements may vary from this MLA format, so check with your instructor before writing your essay.

Type of Paper Your research essay should be typed on 8 1/2" x 11" unlined paper.

A Directory of MLA Formatting and Documentation

Margins   Top and bottom margins should be 1 inch from the edge of the paper. Left and right margins should be 1 inch from the edge of the paper.

Spacing   The text of your research essay should be double-spaced. Quotations should be double-spaced. Your works cited page should be double-spaced.

Page Numbers   Number all pages in the upper-right-hand corner about 1/2 inch from the top edge of the paper. If possible, type your name before the page number.

Heading and Title   Your research essay does not require a separate title page. At the top and left margin of your first page, include the following:

Your Name
Your Instructor's Name
The Title and Number of the Course
The Date

Center the Title
(Do not underline, place in quotation marks, or capitalize all the letters in your title. Double-space between the title and the first line of your writing.)

The Text

of Your

Essay

Works Cited Page   The works cited page is a separate page at the end of the essay.

1. Works are listed in alphabetical order.
2. Each listing is double-spaced, and there is double-spacing between listings.
3. The first line of each listing begins at the left margin. All other lines are indented.
4. Only works cited in the text should be included.

DOCUMENTATION—MLA STYLE

Because it is the most popular form for those who do literary research, the style we use here for documentation is taken from the *MLA Handbook for Writers of Research Papers*.

Citing Sources in the Text of the Essay

The source from which you have taken the information is cited directly in the essay through parenthetic reference in the following ways:

1. Ideas or information rephrased in your own words.

   The author's last name and the page number in parentheses: (Brown 253)

   Example:

   The conditions in those schools were reported as terrible (Brown 253).

2. Ideas or information put into your own words but with the author's name mentioned in the text.

   Page number in parentheses: (253)

   Example:

   Brown reported that the conditions in the schools he visited were terrible (253).

3. Direct quotation—prose

   Direct prose quotations of *four lines or fewer* are put in quotation marks and integrated into the text of your writing.

   Example:

   "I could not believe the appalling conditions I saw" (Brown 253).

   or

   Brown said, "I could not believe the appalling conditions I saw" (253).

4. Direct prose quotations of *five or more lines* are double-spaced and separated from the text of your writing by starting the quotation on a new line and indenting the left margin an inch.

   Example:

   It was very clear that Dr. Grantly was taking much longer to die than anyone expected:

   > A month since the physicians had named four weeks as the outside period during which breath could be supported within the body of the dying man. At the end of the month the physicians wondered, and named another fortnight. The old man lived on wine alone, but at the

> end of the fortnight he still lived; and the tidings of the ministry
>
> became more frequent. (Trollope 3)

5. Direct quotation—poetry

Direct quotations of *three lines or fewer* may be put in quotation marks and integrated into the text of your writing. Use a slash (/) with a space on each side to separate the lines of verse.

Example:

I sense deep regret in Robert Hayden's last lines: "What did I know, what did I know / of love's austere and lonely offices?" (13-4)

6. Direct quotations of *more than three lines* should be double-spaced and begin on a new line. Indent all quoted lines 1 inch from the left margin and use no quotation marks.

Example:

I was deeply affected by the scene described in William Stafford's poem:

> The car aimed ahead its lowered parking lights;
>
> under the hood purred the steady engine.
>
> I stood in the glare of the warm exhaust turning red;
>
> around our group I could hear the wilderness listen. (13-6)

7. Direct quotation—drama

Quoted dialogue between two or more characters should be separated from the text. Begin each quotation with the character's name indented 1 inch from the left margin, written in all capital letters, and followed by a period. All additional lines below that first line should be indented three additional spaces. Line-numbered verse plays are cited in parentheses by act, scene, and line numbers; prose plays by page numbers.

Example:

In Sophocles's play, Ismene's attempt to talk Antigone out of her defiance is futile:

> ISMENE. But no one must hear of this, you must tell no one! I
>   will keep it a secret, I promise!
> ANTIGONE. Oh, tell it! Tell everyone!
>   Think how they'll hate you when it all comes out
>   If they learn that you knew about it all the time!

ISMENE. So fiery! You should be cold with fear.

ANTIGONE. Perhaps. But I am doing what I must. (Pro. 68-75)

Documenting the Works Cited

The descriptions and examples below account for many of the sources you are likely to use, but this is not an exhaustive list. If the source you are using is not accounted for, the best source of additional information is Joseph Gibaldi's *MLA Handbook for Writers of Research Papers*, Fifth Edition, published by the Modern Language Association of America, 1998.

Books

1. A Book by One Author

   Author's Name (reversed). <u>Title of Book</u> (underlined). City of Publication: Publishing Company, Year of Publication.

   Examples:

   Ellmann, Richard. <u>James Joyce</u>. New York: Oxford UP, 1959.

   Sledge, Linda Ching. <u>A Map of Paradise</u>. New York: Bantam Books, 1997.

2. A Book by Two or Three Authors

   Author's Name (reversed), and Second Author's Name. <u>Title of Book</u> (underlined). City of Publication: Publishing Company, Year of Publication.

   Examples:

   Desmond, Adrian, and James Moore. <u>Darwin</u>. New York: Warner, 1991.

   Gilbert, Sandra, and Susan Gubar. <u>The Madwoman in the Attic: The Woman Writer and the Nineteenth Century Literary Imagination</u>. New Haven, Yale UP, 1979.

3. A Work in an Anthology

   Author's Name (reversed). "Name of the Work" (in quotation marks). <u>Title of the Anthology</u> (underlined). # of edition. Editor's Name. City of Publication: Publishing Company, Year of Publication. Page Range.

   Examples:

   Chopin, Kate. "The Story of an Hour." <u>Literature for Composition</u>. 4th ed. Ed. Sylvan Barnet, Morton Berman, William Burto, and Marcia Stubbs. New York: HarperCollins, 1996. 14-6.

   Valdez, Luis. "Los Vendidos." <u>Exploring Literature</u>. Ed. Frank Madden. New York: Longman, 2001. 1244-52.

4. A Work in a Collection by the Same Author

    Author's Name (reversed). "Title of the Work" (in quotation marks). <u>Title of the Collection</u> (underlined). City of Publication: Publishing Company, Year of Publication. Page Range.

    Examples:

    Cheever, John. "The Enormous Radio." <u>The Stories of John Cheever</u>. New
        York: Knopf, 1978. 33-41.

    Sontag, Susan. "The Aesthetics of Silence." <u>Styles of Radical Will</u>. New York:
        Farrar, 1969. 3-34.

5. An Introduction, Foreword, or Afterword

    Author's Name (reversed). Introduction. <u>Title of Book</u> (underlined). By (author of book's name). City of Publication: Publishing Company, Year of Publication. Page Range.

    Examples:

    Costanzo, William V. Introduction. <u>Reading the Movies</u>. By William Costanzo.
        Urbana, IL: NCTE, 1992.

    Orne, Martin T. Foreword. <u>Anne Sexton</u>. By Dianne Wood Middlebrook.
        Boston: Houghton Mifflin, 1991. xii-xxiii.

6. A Reference Book (Encyclopedia, Dictionary, etc.)

    Title of Entry (if a person, reverse the name). <u>Title of Reference Book</u> (underlined). Number and/or Year of Edition.

    Examples:

    "Symbol." <u>The New Encyclopedia Britannica: Micropaedia</u>. 1974 ed.

    Sheridan, Richard Brinsley. <u>The Oxford Companion to English Literature</u>.
        5th ed. 1985.

7. An Author with Two or More Works

    Author's Name (reversed, in first entry of author only). Remaining Publication Information.

    In subsequent listings, type three hyphens, followed by a period and the title.

Examples:

Costanzo, William V. The Electronic Text. Englewood Cliffs, NJ: Educational
    Technology Pub., 1989.

---. Reading the Movies. Urbana, IL: NCTE, 1992.

8. A Translated Book

Author's Name (reversed). Title of Book (underlined). Translator. City of
    Publication: Publishing Company, Year of Publication.

Example:

Homer. The Odyssey. Trans. Robert Fagles. New York: Penguin, 1996.

Periodicals

9. An Article in a Magazine

Author's Name (reversed). "Title of Article" (in quotation marks). Title of
    Magazine (underlined). Date of Publication (day, month, year): Page
    Range. If monthly or bimonthly, list month(s) as date. If no author's
    name appears, begin with the title of the article (but not "a" or "the").

Examples:

Korda, Michael. "The Third Man." New Yorker 25 Mar. 1996: 44-51.

Updike, John. "The Literary Life." Civilization Dec. 1996: 56-73.

10. An Article in a Scholarly Journal

Author's Name (reversed). "Title of Article" (in quotation marks). Title of
    Journal (underlined) and Volume Number (year of publication, in
    parentheses): Page Range.

Examples:

Kamps, Ivo. "Possible Pasts: Historiography and Legitimation in Henry
    VIII." College English 58 (1996): 192-215.

Wilkinson, James. "A Choice of Fictions: Historians, Memory, and
    Evidence." PMLA 111 (1996): 80-92.

11. An Article in a Newspaper

Author's Name (reversed). "Title of Article" (in quotation marks). Title of
    Newspaper (underlined) and Date. Edition: Section Letter and
    Beginning Page Number.

Examples:

Grimes, William. "A Woman of Words That Win Pulitzers." <u>New York Times</u>
    4 June 1996: C1.

Wu, Jim. "Authors Praise New Forms." <u>New York Times</u> 8 Mar. 1987: Sec.
    2:1.

12. A Review

Reviewer's Name (reversed). "Title of Review" (in quotation marks). Rev.
    of Title of Work Reviewed, by Author of Work Reviewed.
    <u>Publication</u> (underlined). Publication Date: Inclusive Page Numbers.

Examples:

Fraser, Kennedy. "Piper Pipe That Song Again." Rev. of <u>Blake</u>, by Peter
    Ackroyd. <u>New Yorker</u> 27 May 1996: 127-31.

Vendler, Helen. Rev. of <u>Essays on Style</u>, ed. Roger Fowler. <u>Essays in</u>
    <u>Criticism</u> 16 (1966): 457-63.

Electronic Sources

Electronic sources include databases on CD-ROM, diskette, and magnetic tape,
and online sources from the Internet.

13. A Periodical CD-ROM Database

Author's Name (reversed). "Title" (in quotation marks). <u>Name of Source</u>
    (electronic journal, conference, database, etc., underlined). Number
    of Volume or Issue. Year or Date of Publication. Publication Medium
    (CD-ROM, diskette, tape). Vendor. Date of Electronic Publication.

Example:

Barron, James. "After 17 Years, Cicada Emerges for Ritual of Sex and
    Death." <u>New York Times Ondisc</u>. CD-ROM. UMI-Proquest. 4 June 1996.

14. A Nonperiodical CD-ROM Publication

Author's Name (reversed). <u>Title</u> (underlined). Medium of Publication. City
    of Publication. Publisher. Date of Publication.

Example:

Shakespeare, William. <u>All's Well That Ends Well</u>. <u>William Shakespeare: The</u>
    <u>Complete Works on CD-ROM</u>. CD-ROM. Abingdon, Eng.: Andromeda
    Interactive, 1994.

15. Online Sources from the Internet

    (If print source)

    Author's Name (reversed). Title (in quotation marks or underlined as appropriate). Print Source Information (same as print citation). <u>Title of Project, Database, Etc.</u> (underlined). Volume, Issue, or Identifying Number (if available). Date of Electronic Publication. Page, Paragraph, or Section Numbers. Institution or Organization Sponsoring the Site. Date of Access. Electronic Address (within angle brackets).

    Example (online print source):

    Twain, Mark. <u>The Adventures of Tom Sawyer</u>. Internet Wiretap Online Library. Carnegie-Mellon University. 22 Feb. 1999.)

    <http:www.cs.cs.cmu.edu/Web/people/rgs/sawyr-table.html>

    Example (online Web site):

    <u>Voice of the Shuttle English Literature</u>. University of California, Santa Barbara. Rev. 1999. 22 Feb. 1999

    <http://www.humanitas.ucsb.edu/shuttle/english.html>

Other Sources

16. A Personal Interview

    Person's Name (reversed). Type of Interview (telephone, mail, online, personal, etc.). Date.

    Examples:

    Courage, Richard. E-mail to the author. 10 Mar. 2000.

    Timm, Christine. Telephone interview. 3 June 1999.

17. A Lecture

    Speaker's Name (reversed). "Title of the Lecture" (in quotation marks). Nature of the Meeting. Location. Date.

    Examples:

    Haynes, Terry. "The Problematic Essay: Right and Responsibility." Conference on College Composition and Communication. Hyatt Regency, Milwaukee. 28 Mar. 1996.

    Worley, Demetrice A. "Telling Tales in School: An African American Woman's Voice in Composition." MLA Convention. Sheraton Washington, Washington, D.C. 28 Dec. 1996.

18. A TV or Radio Program

> "Title of Episode or Segment" (in quotation marks). <u>Title of Program</u> (underlined). Name of the Network. Call Letters of the Local Station. Date of Broadcast.

Examples:

"The Irish Question." <u>The Story of English</u>. PBS. WNET, New York. 6 Apr. 1985.

<u>Brideshead Revisited</u>, Episode 4. With Anthony Andrews and Jeremy Irons. PBS. WETA, Washington, D.C. 24 July 1984.

19. A Sound Recording

> Name of Person (composer, conductor, performers—whoever should be emphasized). <u>Title of the Recording</u> (underlined). Manufacturer, Year of Issue. Medium (CD, LP, audiocassette, audiotape).

Examples:

Mozart, Wolfgang Amadeus. Symphony no. 40 in G minor. Vienna Philharmonic. Cond. Leonard Bernstein. Deutsche Grammophon, 1984. Audiocassette.

Rea, Stephen. <u>James Joyce's Ulysses</u>. BBC Audio, 1993. Audiocassette.

20. A Film or Video Recording

> <u>Title of Film or Video</u> (underlined). Director. Distributor, Year.

Examples:

<u>Agamemnon</u>. By Aeschylus. Dir. Peter Hall. The National Theatre of Great Britain, 1983.

<u>Rozencrantz and Guildenstern Are Dead</u>. Dir. Tom Stoppard. Perf. Gary Oldman, Tim Roth, and Richard Dreyfuss. Cinecom Entertainment, 1990.

Sample Works Cited Page

Works Cited

<u>Agamemnon</u>. By Aeschylus. Dir. Peter Hall. The National Theatre of Great Britain, 1983.

Barron, James. "After 17 Years, Cicada Emerges for Ritual of Sex and Death." <u>New York Times Ondisc</u>. CD-ROM. UMI-Proquest. 4 June 1996.

Cheever, John. "The Enormous Radio." The Stories of John Cheever. New
York: Knopf, 1978. 33-41.

Costanzo, William V. The Electronic Text. Englewood Cliffs NJ: Educational
Technology Pub., 1989.

---. Reading the Movies. Urbana, IL: NCTE, 1992.

Desmond, Adrian, and James Moore. Darwin. New York: Warner, 1991.

Ellmann, Richard. James Joyce. New York: Oxford UP, 1959.

Fraser, Kennedy. "Piper Pipe That Song Again." Rev. of Blake, by Peter
Ackroyd. New Yorker 27 May 1996: 127-31.

Grimes, William. "A Woman of Words That Win Pulitzers." New York Times 4
June 1996: C1.

Haynes, Terry. "The Problematic Essay: Right and Responsibility."
Conference on College Composition and Communication. Hyatt Regency,
Milwaukee. 28 Mar. 1996.

Homer. The Odyssey. Trans. Robert Fagles. New York: Penguin, 1996.

"The Irish Question." The Story of English. PBS. WNET, New York. 6 Apr.
1985.

Kamps, Ivo. "Possible Pasts: Historiography and Legitimation in Henry VIII."
College English 58 (1996): 192-215.

Korda, Michael. "The Third Man." New Yorker 25 Mar. 1996: 44-51.

Martin, James. Telephone interview. 3 June 1996.

Rea, Stephen. James Joyce's Ulysses. BBC Audio, 1993. Audiocassette.

Sheridan, Richard Brinsley. The Oxford Companion to English Literature. 5th
ed., 1985.

Sledge, Linda Ching. A Map of Paradise. New York: Bantam Books, 1997.

Twain, Mark. The Adventures of Tom Sawyer. Internet Wiretap Online
Library. Carnegie-Mellon University. 22 Feb. 1999.
<http:www.cs.cs.cmu.edu/Web/people/rgs/sawyr-table.html>

Valdez, Luis. "Los Vendidos." Exploring Literature. Ed. Frank Madden. New
York: Longman, 2001. 1244-52.

Voice of the Shuttle English Literature. University of California, Santa
Barbara. Rev. 1999. 22 Feb. 1999.
<http://www.humanitas.ucsb.edu/shuttle/english.html>

GLOSSARY OF
LITERARY TERMS

abstract language words that represent broad qualities or characteristics (e.g., *interesting, good, fine, horrible, lovely*)

allegory an extended metaphor

allusion a reference to another literary / artistic/ historic, work, author, character, or event (frequently biblical or mythological)

anecdote a brief personal story used to illustrate a point

antagonist a character who seems to be the major force in opposition to the protagonist or main character

atmosphere the dominant mood or tone of the setting

autobiography an account of the author's own life

character a person in fiction

characterization the development of characters in fiction

climax the turning point of the plot in fiction

complication the building of the conflict in the plot as part of the rising action

concrete language words that represent specific, particular, graphic qualities and characteristics

conflict the struggle of opposing external or internal forces. **External conflict** may be physical (characters against nature) or social (characters against each other or against society). **Internal conflict** is a struggle of opposing forces within a character.

connotation the personal definition or association triggered by a word

convention an accepted or traditional feature of a work

crisis the turning point of the plot (closely related to "climax," which seems to complete its action)

denotation the literal, dictionary definition of a word

denouement the resolution of the plot in fiction (an "untying" of the complications at the end of the story line)

dialogue conversation of characters in fiction

didactic teaching a lesson or having a moral

documentation accounting for and giving credit to the origin of a source

ellipsis (. . .) indication of an omission of words in a quotation

epiphany a sudden insight or moment of realization when something—a circumstance, a person, an object—is seen in a new light. Originating as a term and feast day in Christian theology, it was popularized as a literary term by James Joyce whose stories often end with such moments of realization, as exemplified by "Araby" (p. 51) and "Eveline" (p. 338). It is a popular feature of modern fiction, and can be found in many other stories in this text.

explication a line-by-line explanation of a literary work

exposition the introduction of essential characters, setting, circumstances of a story

falling action the action that follows the crisis and climax (*see also* denouement, resolution)

figurative language language that expresses more than a literal meaning (e.g., metaphor, simile)

flat character a character not fully developed who seems to represent a "type" more than a real personality (*see also* stock character)

genre a form or type of literature (e.g., fiction, poetry, drama, the essay)

hyperbole an exaggeration in figurative language

image / imagery descriptive language that helps us see, hear, smell, taste, or feel

inductive/deductive reasoning inductive reasoning moves from observation of specific circumstances and makes a general conclusion; **deductive** reasoning takes a general truth and applies it to specific circumstances

interpretation an analysis of a work to determine its meaning

magical realism fiction that blends realistic or ordinary details and events with those that are magical or fantastic. Gabriel Garcia Marquez's "A Very Old Man with Enormous Wings" (p. 368) exemplifies this form.

metafiction fiction that explores the process of its own language and creation as it tells the story. Donald Bartheleme's "At the Tolstoy Museum" (p. 200) and Italo Calvino's "If on a winter's night a traveler" (p. 220) are good examples of this approach.

metaphor an implied comparison of two apparently dissimilar things

microcosm a smaller version or "little world"

monologue a speech by a single character

mood the atmosphere or tone of a work

narrator the voice of the speaker in a story

paraphrase to record someone else's words in the writer's own words

personification giving human qualities to nonhuman things

point of view The perspective from which the narrator speaks to us. Generally, the pronoun that dominates the narration will signal which point of view is represented. The terms most commonly used to identify point of view are **first person**, **third person**, **omniscient**, **objective**, and **shifting**.

plot The structure of the story. It's the pattern of twists and turns the story takes.

primary / secondary sources A **primary source** is the original text or materials. A secondary source is commentary about that original material.

protagonist the main character in a story

Realism A movement in literature to represent life as it really is. It is often characterized by accurate depictions of ordinary people in their natural surroundings.

resolution the final phase of the falling action in the plot when things are returned to normal

rising action that point in the plot when conflict and our emotional involvement intensify

round character a fully developed character with the complexities of a real person

satire ridiculing stupidity, vice, or folly through exaggeration and humor

sentimentality evoking a predictable emotional response with a clichéd prompt

setting the environment in which the work takes place

simile an announced comparison introduced with the words *like* or *as*

speaker the narrator of a story

stock character a character not fully developed who seems to represent a "type" more than a real personality (*see also* flat character)

style the choice of words and sentence structure that makes each author's writing different

summary the material condensed to its main points

symbol an object or action that represents more than itself

syntax the ordering of words in a sentence

theme the overall meaning we derive from a story or essay

thesis the point of an essay

tone the attitude expressed by the writer toward the subject

unreliable narrator a narrator who tells the story from a biased, erroneous perspective

voice the personality or style of the writer or narrator that seems to come to life in the words

LITERARY AND PHOTO CREDITS

LITERARY CREDITS

Achebe, Chinua, "Marriage Is a Private Affair" from *Girls at War and Other Stories* by Chinua Achebe. © 1972, 1973 by Chinua Achebe. Used by permission of Doubleday, a division of Random House, Inc. and Harold Ober Associates, Inc.

Alexie, Sherman, "The Lone Ranger and Tonto Fistfight in Heaven" from *The Lone Ranger and Tonto Fistfight in Heaven* by Sherman Alexie. © 1993 by Sherman Alexie. Used by permission of Grove/Atlantic, Inc.

Alvarez, Julia, From *How the Garcia Girls Lost Their Accents*. © 1991 by Julia Alvarez. Published by Plume, an imprint of Dutton Signet, a division of Penguin Putnam Inc, and originally in hardcover by Algonquin Books of Chapel Hill. Reprinted by permission of Susan Bergholz Literary Services, New York. All rights reserved.

Atwood, Margaret, "Happy Endings," from *Good Bones and Simple Murders* by Margaret Atwood. © 1983, 1992, 1994, by O.W. Toad Ltd. A Nan A. Talese Book. Used by permission of Doubleday, a division of Random House, Inc. and McClelland & Stewart Ltd. *The Canadian Publishers*.

Baldwin, James, "Sonny's Blues" © 1957 by James Baldwin was originally published in *The Partisan Review*. Copyright renewed. Collected in *Going to Meet the Man*, published by Vintage Books. Reprinted by permission of the James Baldwin Estate.

Bambara, Toni Cade, "The Lesson" by Toni Cade Bambara. © 1972 by Toni Cade Bambara, from *Gorilla, My Love* by Toni Cade Bambara. Reprinted by permission of Random House, Inc.

Barthelme, Donald, "The Tolstoy Museum" from *Forty Stories* by Donald Barthelme. © 1987 by Donald Barthelme. Reprinted by permission of The Wylie Agency.

Boyle, T. Corraghessan, "Greasy Lake" by T. Corraghessan Boyle, from *Greasy Lake and Other Stories* by T. Corraghessan Boyle. © 1979, 1981, 1982, 1983, 1984, 1985 by T. Corraghessan Boyle. Used by permission of Viking Penguin, a division of Penguin Putnam Inc.

Butler, Robert Olen, "Snow" from *A Good Scent from a Strange Mountain* by Robert Olen Butler. © 1992 by Robert Olen Butler. Reprinted by permission of Henry Holt and Company, LLC.

Calvino, Italo, "If On a Winter's Night a Traveler" from *If On a Winter's Night a Traveler* by Italo Calvino. © 1979 by Giulio Einaudi editore, s.p.a., Torino, English translation by William Weaver © 1981 by Harcourt, Inc., reprinted by permission of Harcourt, Inc. © 1981 by Italo Calvino. Reprinted by permission of The Wylie Agency.

Carver, Raymond, "What We Talk About When We Talk About Love" from *What We Talk About When We Talk About Love* by Raymond Carver. © 1981 by Raymond Carver. Used by permission of Alfred A. Knopf, a division of Random House, Inc.

Cheever, John, "Reunion" from *The Stories of John Cheever*. © 1978 by John Cheever. Used by permission of Alfred A. Knopf, a division of Random House, Inc.

Chekhov, Anton, "The Lady with the Pet Dog" from *The Portable Chekhov* by Anton Chekhov, edited by Avrahm Yarmolinsky. © 1947, © 1968 by Viking Penguin, Inc. Renewed © 1975 by Avrahm Yarmolinsky. Used by permission of Viking Penguin, a division of Penguin Putnam Inc.

Cisneros, Sandra, "Eleven" from *Woman Hollering Creek*. © 1991 by Sandra Cisneros. Published by Vintage Books, a division of Random House, Inc., and originally in hardcover by Random House, Inc. Reprinted by permission of Susan Bergholz Literary Services, New York. All rights reserved.

DeLillo, Don, "Videotape." Reprinted with the permission of Scribner, a division of Simon & Schuster, Inc., from *Underworld* by Don DeLillo. © 1997 by Don DeLillo.

Ellison, Ralph, "Battle Royal (18.5 pgs.)" by Ralph Ellison, © 1948 by Ralph Ellison, from *Invisible Man* by Ralph Ellison. Used by permission of Random House, Inc.

Erdrich, Louise, "The Red Convertible" from *Love Medicine, New and Expanded Version* by Louise Erdrich. © 1984, 1993 by Louise Erdrich. Reprinted by permission of Henry Holt and Company, LLC.

Faulkner, William, "A Rose for Emily" by William Faulkner, © 1930 and renewed 1958 by William Faulkner, from *Collected Stories of William Faulkner* by William Faulkner. Used by permission of Random House, Inc.

Heker, Liliana, "The Stolen Party" by Liliana Heker. © 1982, which appeared in *Other Fires: Short Fiction by Latin American Women,* edited and translated by Alberto Manguel, © 1985. Used by permission of Clarkson Potter/Publishers, a division of Random House, Inc. and Westwood Creative Artists, Ltd.

Hemingway, Ernest, "Hills Like White Elephants." Reprinted with permission of Scribner, a division of Simon & Schuster, Inc., from *Men Without Women* by Ernest Hemingway. © 1927 by Charles Scribner's Sons. Copyright renewed 1955 by Ernest Hemingway.

Hughes, Langston, "One Friday Morning," from *Short Stories* by Langston Hughes. © 1996 by Ramona Bass and Arnold Rampersad. Introduction copyright © 1996 by Arnold Rampersad. Compilation and editorial contribution copyright © 1996 by Akiba Sullivan Harper. Reprinted by permission of Hill and Wang, a division of Farrar, Straus & Giroux, LLC.

Joyce, James, "Araby" and "Eveline" from *Dubliners* by James Joyce. © 1916 by B. W. Heubsch. Definitive text © 1967 by the Estate of James Joyce. Used by permission of Viking Penguin, a division of Penguin Putnam Inc.

Kafka, Franz, "A Hunger Artist" from *Frank Kafka: The Complete Stories* by Franz Kafka, edited by Nahum N. Glatzer. © 1946, 1947, 1948, 1949, 1954, 1958, 1971 by Schocken Books, a division of Random House, Inc.

Kincaid, Jamaica, "Girl" from *At the Bottom of the River* by Jamaica Kincaid. © 1983 by Jamaica Kincaid. Reprinted by permission of Farrar, Straus and Giroux, LLC.

Marquez, Gabriel Garcia, All pages from "A Very Old Man with Enormous Wings" from *Leaf Storm and Other Stories* by Gabriel Garcia Marquez. © 1971 by Gabriel Garcia Marquez. Reprinted by permission of HarperCollins Publishers, Inc.

Mason, Bobbie Ann, "Shiloh" from *Shiloh and Other Stories* by Bobbie Ann Mason. © 1982 by Bobbie Ann Mason. Reprinted by permission of International Creative Management, Inc.

Maugham, W. Somerset, "An Appointment in Samarra," from *Sheppey* by W. Somerset Maugham. © 1933 by W. Somerset Maugham. Used by permission of Doubleday, a division of Random House, Inc. and Kay Collyer & Boose.

Morales, Rosario, "The Day It Happened." *Callaloo* 15:4 (1992), 970-972, © Charles H. Rowell. Reprinted by permission of the Johns Hopkins University Press.

Moser, Don, "The Pied Piper of Tucson" by Don Moser from *Life* March 4, 1966. © 1966 Time Inc. Reprinted by permission.

Naqvi, Tahira, "Brave We Are" as first published in *Dying in a Strange Country* by Tahira Naqvi. (TSAR Publications, 2001).

Oates, Joyce Carol, "Where Are You Going, Where Have You Been?" from *The Wheel of Love and Other Stories by Joyce Carol Oates.* © 1970 by Ontario Review Press, Inc. Reprinted by permission of John Hawkins & Associates, Inc.

O'Brien, Tim, "The Things They Carried" from *The Things They Carried.* © 1990 by Tim O'Brien. Reprinted by permission of Houghton Mifflin Co./Seymour Lawrence. All rights reserved.

O'Connor, Flannery, "Everything That Rises Must Converge" from *The Complete Stories* by Flannery O'Connor. © 1971 by the Estate of Mary Flannery O'Connor.

O'Connor, Frank, "My Oedipus Complex" from *The Collected Stories of Frank O'Connor* by Frank O'Connor. © 1981 by Harriet O'Donovan Sheehy, Executrix of the Estate of Frank O'Connor. Used by permission of Alfred A. Knopf, a division of Random House, Inc. and Joan Daves Agency.

Olsen, Tillie, "I Stand Here Ironing," © 1956, 1957, 1960, 1961 by Tillie Olsen, from *Tell Me a Riddle* by Tillie Olsen. Introduction by John Leonard. Used by permission of Dell Publishing, a division of Random House, Inc.

Silko, Leslie Marmon, "The Man to Send Rain Clouds" from *Storyteller* by Leslie Marmon Silko. © 1981 by Leslie Marmon Silko. Reprinted with the permission of The Wylie Agency, Inc.

Steinbeck, John, "Chrysanthemums." © 1937, renewed © 1965 by John Steinbeck, from *The Long Valley* by John Steinbeck. Used by permission of Viking Penguin, a division of Penguin Putnam Inc.

Tan, Amy, "Two Kinds" from *The Joy Luck Club* by Amy Tan. © 1989 by Amy Tan. Used by permission of G. P. Putnam's Sons, a division of Penguin Putnam, Inc.

Updike, John, "A & P" from *Pigeon Feathers and Other Stories* by John Updike. © 1962 by John Updike. Used by permission of Alfred A. Knopf, a division of Random House, Inc.

Walker, Alice, "Everyday Use" from *In Love & Trouble: Stories of Black Women.* © 1973 by Alice Walker. Reprinted by permission of Harcourt, Inc. "Roselily" from *In Love & Trouble: Stories of Black Women.* © 1972 by Alice Walker. Reprinted by permission of Harcourt, Inc.

Welty, Eudora, "A Worn Path" from *A Curtain of Green and Other Stories.* © 1941 and renewed 1969 by Eudora Welty. Reprinted by permission of Harcourt, Inc.

PHOTO CREDITS

16: John Camman, *Tucson Daily Citizen, Life Magazine*; 112: AP/Wide World Photos; 125: J. A. Scholten/Missouri Historical Society, St. Louis; 145: CORBIS; 158: AP/Wide World Photos; 163: Marion Ettlinger; 168: Laurance Acland; 171: Bettmann/CORBIS; 194: Annie Valva; 200: Nancy Crampton; 201–207: © 1960 by Donald Barthelme. Reprinted with permission from the Wylie Agency; 206: Nancy Crampton; 213: Philip Gould/CORBIS; 220: Ulf Andersen/The Gamma Liaison Network; 228: Courtesy Scott Foresman and Company; 237: Nebraska State Historical Society, Willa Cather Pioneer Memorial Collection; 252: Bettmann/CORBIS; 264: Courtesy Newark Public Library; 282: Nancy Crampton; 286: Nancy Crampton; 297: Nancy Crampton; 304: Bern Keating/Black Star; 311: Bettmann/CORBIS; 324: Photograph courtesy Peabody Essex Museum; 333: Bettmann/CORBIS; 338: Berenice Abbott/Commerce Graphics, Ltd.; 342: Dublin Street Scene, Bettmann/CORBIS; 349: AP/World Wide Photos; 356: Mur/Bettmann/CORBIS; 368: AP/Wide World Photos; 373: Jerry Bauer: 384: Hulton/Archive; 390: Linda Haas/Courtesy Firebrand Books; 394: Jerry Bauer; 407: AP/Wide World Photos; 418: Elliot Erwitt/Magnum Photos, Inc.; 426: AP/Wide World Photos; 432: AP/Wide World Photos; 436: Nancy Crampton; 439: Courtesy Scott Foresman and Company; 447: Nancy Crampton; 460: AP/Wide World Photos.

INDEX OF
AUTHORS AND TITLES

INDEX OF
TERMS